Discrimination at Work

The law on sex, race and disability discrimination

CAMILLA PALMER is a consultant solicitor with Bindman & Partners working exclusively in the field of discrimination and maternity rights.

GAY MOON is a solicitor at Camden Community Law Centre specialising in employment and discrimination law.

SUSAN COX is a freelance employment law researcher, writer, trainer and consultant.

Discrimination at Work

The law on sex, race and disability discrimination

THIRD EDITION

Camilla Palmer
and
Gay Moon
with
Susan Cox

Legal Action Group
1997

This edition published in Great Britain 1997
by LAG Education and Service Trust Limited
242 Pentonville Road, London N1 9UN

First edition published 1987 as *Sex and Race Discrimination in Employment* by Camilla Palmer and Kate Poulton
Second edition published 1992 as *Discrimination at Work: The law on sex and race discrimination* by Camilla Palmer

British Library Cataloguing in Publication Data
A CIP catalogue record for this book is available from the British Library

ISBN 0 905099 70 2

Typeset by RefineCatch Ltd, Bungay, Suffolk
Printed in Great Britain by Bell & Bain Ltd, Glasgow

Foreword

by LORD LESTER OF HERNE HILL QC

The third edition of this invaluable book has been restructured, and some sections have been substantially changed, such as discrimination in pay and pensions, an extended chapter on the widely misunderstood but crucial concept of indirect discrimination, as well as a new chapter on disability discrimination. It is an excellent practical manual, well-designed, easy to use and tailor-made for trade unions and for lawyers acting for applicants.

The book locates the law within its social, economic and supranational context, and provides a readable and well-informed digest of the vast body of case-law that has developed over the past two decades. It examines the law critically, highlighting areas overdue for reform.

As the authors recognise, the law on sex, race and disability discrimination at work is in a mess. It is more complex and opaque than tax law. The statutory language is unnecessarily technical and restrictive. It has not been sufficiently adapted to the requirements of European Community law. There is a stronger concept of unlawful discrimination for sex and race discrimination than for disability discrimination. The concept of indirect discrimination is interpreted differently for equal pay than for other aspects of sex discrimination in employment. Racial and religious discrimination are unlawful in Northern Ireland, but only racial discrimination is unlawful in Great Britain.

The procedures for bringing equal value claims are tortuous and unworkable. The enforcement agencies – the Commission for Racial Equality and the Equal Opportunities Commission – are deterred from using their investigative powers by fear of becoming enmeshed in a spider's web of legalistic and protracted procedures. Ludicrously, they are prevented by their own codes from sharing information obtained in the course of their investigations. The monitoring and enforcement powers of the CRE and of the EOC are much weaker than are the powers of the Fair Employment Commission in tackling religious discrimination in Northern Ireland. Further, important sources of unfair discrimination, notably on the ground of age, are not yet unlawful.

The authors rightly point out that there is a pressing need for 'much stronger laws to combat sexism, racism and able-bodyism in the workplace and elsewhere, legal aid to assist applicants in discrimination cases as well as a Human Rights Commission to cover all areas of discrimination'. The publication of the third edition is timely, coinciding with the election of a government committed to strengthening anti-discrimination legislation.

Until there is reforming legislation, the authors would like to see a more widespread and vigorous use of existing laws. Like them, I hope that this book will be useful in that endeavour, a spur to more effective action by the statutory agencies, trade unions, discrimination lawyers and public interest groups, so that everyone may enjoy equal and effective protection under the law, in whatever part of the United Kingdom they live and work, against invidious discrimination on whatever ground. That should be our constitutional birthright as a democracy governed by the rule of law.

Preface

Since the first edition of this book was published in 1987 it has trebled in size. This is mainly because of the increasing complexity of discrimination law, equal pay law and the growing impact of European law and the introduction of a new ground of prohibited discrimination, namely disability.

Over the last five years there have been many important developments. For example:

- there is no now limit on the amount of compensation which can be awarded in discrimination cases; compensation can also be awarded for even unintentional indirect sex discrimination;
- the Disability Discrimination Act 1995 came into force in December 1996;
- discrimination against transsexuals is now unlawful;
- the High Court has indicated that discrimination against gays and lesbians is likely to be a breach of European law;
- maternity rights have been greatly extended since the implementation of the Pregnant Workers Directive;
- the interpretation of employer's liability has been broadened, so that employers will be liable for most discrimination in the workplace unless they take adequate steps to prevent it.

Despite these positive advances, the labour market is still deeply divided by sex and race. It is too early to assess the impact of the Disability Discrimination Act. However, there is room for optimism. Since the first draft of this edition, we have had the election of a Labour government. Instead of a government resistant to every progressive anti-discrimination measure coming from Europe, we have promises to implement the Agreement on Part-time Workers, the Parental Leave Directive, the directive on the burden of proof and the Working Time Directive. Let us hope that the present government will also take steps to simplify and strengthen the law as well as to extend protection on grounds of sexuality, age and religion.

This book is intended to provide a simple but detailed account of sex, race and disability discrimination law, maternity rights and equal pay which is useful to lawyers and non-lawyers. It is divided into six sections, some of which deal with the technical and complex aspects of discrimination law, such as indirect discrimination and equal pay, and those which look at the practical aspects of discrimination.

It is hoped that the book will enable lawyers, advice workers and trade unions to advise those who have suffered discrimination. Second, it is hoped that employers will find it useful in formulating and implementing equal opportunities policies in relation to recruitment, terms and conditions of employment, dismissal, redundancy and occupational pensions. Finally, it aims to be of use to academics, students and those providing training on equal opportunities.

The law is stated for England and Wales as at 1 June 1997. Where possible, account has been taken of more recent case-law at proof stage.

Acknowledgments

Firstly, we would like to thank Anthony Lester for his support and encouragement and for writing the foreword. We would also like to record our thanks to some of those who contributed their thoughts, ideas and comments on the text, particularly Susan Cox, Vivienne Gay, Pauline Matthews and Robin Allen. We are also grateful to those who read and commented on particular parts of the book: Virginia Kerridge, Robin Lewis, Julia Sohrab, Pat Ryder, Peter Duffy, Roger Self and Andrew Nicol. We are grateful to Susan Cox for writing the chapter on disability and to the staff at LAG for their patient editing of the text as each new section arrived. Finally we should record our thanks to our children Robert, Jamie, Kit and Luke who lost out while we were preocuppied with 'the book'.

Camilla Palmer
Gay Moon
July 1997

Contents

PART V: DISABILITY DISCRIMINATION

PART VI: ENFORCEMENT

Table of cases

Table of statutes

Table of statutory instruments

Table of European Law

Table of codes of practice

Abbreviations

ACAS	Arbitration and Conciliation Advisory Service
All ER	All England Law Reports
art 119	EC Treaty article 119
CA	Court of Appeal
CAC	Central Arbitration Committee
CMLR	Common Market Law Reports
COIT	Central Office of Industrial Tribunals
CRE	Commission for Racial Equality
CS	Court of Session
DCLD	Discrimination Case Law Digest
DDA	Disability Discrimination Act 1995
DSS	Department of Social Security
EA	Employment Act 1989
EAT	Employment Appeal Tribunal
EC	European Community
ECA	European Communities Act 1972
ECJ	European Court of Justice
ECHR	European Court of Human Rights
EOC	Equal Opportunities Commission
EOR	*Equal Opportunities Review*
EPCA	Employment Protection (Consolidation) Act 1978
EPD	Equal Pay Directive 75/117/EEC
ERA	Employment Rights Act 1996
EqPA	Equal Pay Act 1970
ETD	Equal Treatment Directive 76/207/EEC
EU	European Union
EWC	expected week of confinement
GOQ	genuine occupational qualification
HC	High Court of Justice
HL	House of Lords
ICR	Industrial Cases Reports
IDS Brief	*Income Data Services Brief*
IE	independent expert
IRLR	Industrial Relations Law Reports
IT	industrial tribunal
ITA	Industrial Tribunals Act 1996
IT1	industrial tribunal application form
IT3	industrial tribunal respondent's reply form
IT Rules	Industrial Tribunals (Constitution and Rules of Procedure) Regulations 1993 SI No 2687 Schedules 1 and 2
JES	job evaluation scheme

MLP	maternity leave period
NICA	Northern Ireland Court of Appeal
NIRC	Northern Ireland Relations Court
OPRA	Occupational Pension Regulatory Authority
PWD	Pregnant Workers Directive 92/85/EEC
RRA	Race Relations Act 1976
SDA	Sex Discrimination Act 1975
SERPS	State Earnings Related Pension Scheme
SMP	statutory maternity pay
SMP Regs	Statutory Maternity Pay (General) Regulations 1986 SI No 1960
SSCBA	Social Security Contributions and Benefits Act 1992
SSD	Social Security Directive 79/7/EEC
SSP	statutory sick pay
WLR	Weekly Law Reports

Introduction

All human beings are born free and equal in dignity and rights.
Universal Declaration of Human Rights 1948 art 1

To be treated and judged as a unique individual should be a fundamental human right for each one of us. However, every day people are pre-judged or misjudged according to preconceptions about their race, colour, sex, sexuality, disability or other irrelevant factors. Each time this happens not only does an individual suffer unfair discrimination but an employer risks losing the opportunity of employing or promoting a better employee. Discrimination of this kind not only diminishes the person affected but impoverishes the wider community.

In Britain, as in many other industrial countries, the workforce is divided by sex and race. The features of these divisions in the workforce are well known. Women workers are concentrated in low-paid, unskilled jobs, largely excluded from skilled manual jobs, and under-represented in managerial and many professional occupations. Women's work is concentrated in the service sector of the economy and, in particular, in low-paid service industries that are not organised by trade unions. Domestic and childcare responsibilities mean that most part-time workers are women. Black workers in the UK face disadvantage in the labour market and suffer a much higher unemployment rate than white people. Male black workers on average earn less than male white workers, and black workers, like women workers, are over-represented in many of the low-paying, poorly organised industries. However, there are considerable variations among different ethnic minority groups as well as between the men and women as can be seen from Table 1 below.

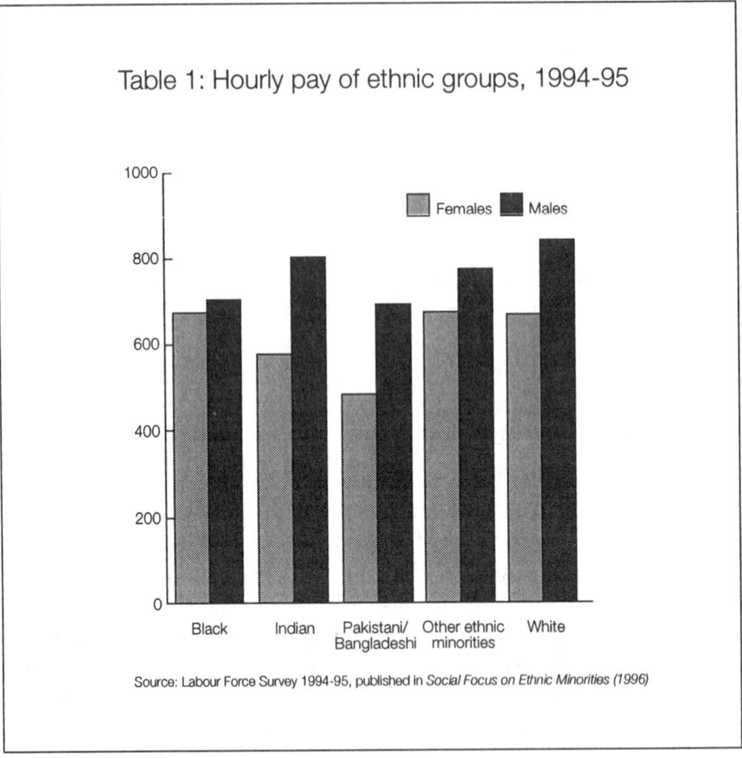

Recent figures also illustrate the degree to which disabled people are excluded from employment. The winter 1995/96 Labour Force Survey confirmed that the unemployment rate for disabled people was 21% compared with 8% for all people of working age, and that the long-term unemployment rate was higher among disabled people than non-disabled people.[1]

Development of race and sex discrimination law

During the last 40 years one of the greatest changes to employment patterns in the UK has been the increase in women's participation in the workforce. More women return to work sooner after having children, though many tend to return to part-time jobs often needing fewer skills and less responsibility. Single parents, the majority of

1 'Disability and the labour market' *Labour Market Trends*, September 1996.

whom are women, are particularly vulnerable. Assumptions are often made that single parents do not have the same commitment to work and will need time off to care for their children. Such assumptions will be discriminatory.

In common with many other industrial countries, the UK has domestic laws which are intended to reduce discrimination in the labour market; these were heralded on their introduction as a comprehensive attack on these divisions and inequalities. Additionally, the domestic laws on sex discrimination are supplemented by the European equality laws which in many ways are more comprehensive than UK laws and with which British courts must comply.

Prior to the Sex Discrimination Act (SDA) 1975, the Equal Pay Act (EqPA) 1970 (which came into force in 1975), and the Race Relations Act (RRA) 1976, employers could lawfully discriminate against women, and discrimination against black workers, while unlawful, was very difficult to challenge, as only the Race Relations Board (established under the Race Relations Act 1965) was empowered to initiate legal proceedings against discriminators.

The legislation of the mid-1970s made unlawful both direct and indirect discrimination on the grounds of sex and race. The Sex Discrimination Bill, which was the model for the subsequent RRA, originally prohibited only direct discrimination, ie, less favourable treatment of someone on the ground of their sex (or race). But during the passage of the Bill through Parliament, evidence given on United States law persuaded the government to extend the Act to include indirect discrimination. Indirect discrimination occurs when practices which seem fair in form in fact have a disparate adverse impact on one sex or one or more racial groups. It arises when conditions are laid down which fewer women than men, or fewer black people than white people, can comply with and which the employer cannot show to be objectively justifiable.

The prohibition on indirect discrimination is of great potential significance for two reasons; first, it is not just concerned with individual actions but addresses the impact on groups of people, so that a favourable judgment for one employee can have implications for many others; and second, it takes account of the relationship between employment practices and general inequalities, past and present, both inside and outside the labour market. That potential is being increasingly explored but remains as yet unfulfilled.

In the 20 odd years since the SDA and RRA, the Acts have been used to challenge labour market practices which, because of social conditions and inequalities have led to job segregation and a denial of equal opportunities. This, and more comprehensive research, means that there is now a better understanding of the causes underlying discrimination as they affect individual cases. A representative or industrial tribunal (IT) with no understanding of the social context of this legislation risks misunderstanding the issues. The picture is of course a dynamic one; so the obstacles that faced women and ethnic minorities when the legislation came into force have changed, though not dramatically. So what are these inequalities that keep women and black workers confined to lower-paid, lower-status jobs?

Inequalities affecting women

The International Labour Organisation says: 'Equality of opportunity and treatment for women in employment has yet to be achieved anywhere in the world'.[2]

Men and women participate in the workforce on very different terms. The differences between men's and women's work are vast. Women are concentrated in a small number of occupations, and often in less advantageous positions within those occupations.[3] Twenty-five per cent of men are employed in manufacturing compared to 12% of women;[4] 40% of the female workforce are employed in public administration, education and health. Although there are four times as many women as men in the health sector and twice as many women as men in education, men still predominate in the higher level jobs: for instance only 30% of secondary headteachers and deputy headteachers are female.[5]

Occupational segregation has been a major cause of continuing inequality in pay particularly in the lower pay sector. The EqPA is ill-designed to meet inequality between occupations and has largely failed to make any impact on occupational pay differences. The segregation of women's jobs is reflected in levels of pay. The pay gap is narrowing very slowly: in 1987 the average hourly earnings of women were 73% of those of men, while in 1996 they were 80%. Differentials are much larger at higher wages: 15% of men earned in excess of

2 *Per* Michael Hanseanne, Director General of the International Labour Organisation (1996) 69 EOR.

3 Segregation by occupation or sector is sometimes called horizontal segregation. Segregation by grade, where women and ethnic minorities reach a 'glass ceiling' beyond which they do not progress, is known as vertical segregation.

4 *Social Trends 1996* (HMSO), at p81.

5 Ibid, p87.

£550 per week compared to 4% of women.[6] However, there are some signs that the proportions of women in management are slowly increasing from a very low level.[7]

For the vast majority of women, having children and other domestic commitments determine the course of their working lives. Most women leave work for a while to look after young children though women are now taking shorter breaks and many return to work between children. Because of childcare responsibilities, many women take part-time work (82% of part-time workers are women).[8] During their working life women spend shorter average periods in any single job than do men, although this gap may now be decreasing.[9] This is closely related to unskilled work and poorer pay and conditions. In 1995 part-time women workers earned 60% of the gross average hourly wage of a full-time male employee. There is a strong association between taking part-time work and downward mobility. Many women who return to work after having children, go back to lower level occupations than the ones they left.

Although women's work patterns are determined by their gender they are also determined by race. Ethnic minority women face double discrimination (see Table 1 above, p2).

Women's work patterns differ between ethnic groups. A very high proportion of West Indian women – 72% – are economically active, compared to 21% of Bangladeshi women.[10] Part-time work is more common for white women than for ethnic minority women.[11] Black women are found in the lower echelons of the workforces where they are employed, for example, as ancillary workers in the NHS, in low-skilled jobs in local government and welfare offices, not in expanding, high technology areas like banking, finance and telecommunications.

6 '1996 New Earnings Survey' (1996) 70 EOR.

7 See 'National Management Salary Survey 1996' by the Institute of Management and Remuneration Economics (1996) 68 EOR and 'Opportunity 2000 4th year Report' (1996) 65 EOR.

8 *Women in the Labour Market: results from the Spring 1996 Labour Force Survey* (Labour Market Trends, March 1997), p99.

9 Elias and White, *Recruitment in Local Labour Markets* (DoE Research Paper no 86, 1991).

10 CRE Factsheet 1997 derived from *Labour Force Survey* Summer 1995, Spring 1996.

11 In 1995 29% of white women worked part time compared to 15% of black African/Caribbean women and 19% of Indian women (*Social Trends 1996* (HMSO), p83).

Women are still in a very vulnerable position in the economy. Although there is increasing employment amongst women, full-time jobs are being lost, while part-time jobs increase and more women work part-time in low-paid jobs. The number of women with second jobs has doubled in the last 12 years, and the number of women working on temporary contracts increased by 27% between 1992 and 1995.

Other trends in the economy encourage the differential pay systems which indirectly discriminate against women; employers continue to operate wage payment systems which allow men to augment their earnings by overtime, shift premia, bonus and other pay components which are far less frequently available to women. More than 20 years after the equality legislation, despite major changes in public attitudes and women's expectations, all the signs are that the economic position of women has barely improved.

Inequalities affecting racial minorities

The reasons why black people are disadvantaged in the labour market are different. Black people were brought to Britain first, many years ago as servants and seamen. More recently black workers from Britain's colonies and ex-colonies have been used as a source of cheap labour in the British imperial economy. In the post-war period, many black people migrated to work in Britain and many were directly recruited by the British government. They were recruited to do jobs which no one else would do in a period of labour shortage – such as unskilled jobs in the transport services and the NHS. So black workers have occupied a particular place in the class and occupational structure, the disadvantages of which are compounded by the effects of racism.

Thus, black workers, particularly Afro-Caribbean workers, are under-represented in top managerial and professional jobs. Black workers are more likely to work in low-paying industries like clothing and textiles and service sector jobs in hospitals, shops and catering. Male black workers earn less than white male workers, although the difference between black and white women workers is less marked. Black workers – women and men – are more likely to work shifts, in particular, nightshifts. A PSI survey found that shiftwork is more likely to be worked by those who are not fluent in English. Fluency in English is an important factor in determining job levels and pay and conditions; Asian men and women who do not speak English well have higher rates of unemployment, lower job levels, and lower wages as well as more often working shifts.[12]

Since the end of the 1960s, restrictive legislation and government policies have effectively put an end to immigration of all but the relatives of those already here. This means that the black workforce will increasingly be composed of people born in the UK. It is therefore likely that some barriers – such as language – will become less significant over time. Other barriers, however, such as educational qualifications will continue to exist, and continuing educational disadvantage will limit opportunities in the job market.

Black people suffer a much higher rate of unemployment than white: 9% of white men were unemployed in 1995 compared with 27% of black African, 22% of Afro-Caribbean, 13% of Indian and 26% of Pakistani/Bangladeshi men.[13] This is partly because of the younger age structure of the black population, partly because of the over-representation of black workers among unskilled and semi-skilled workers (who are the majority of the unemployed) and partly because of continuing direct discrimination in the job market. In the last decade ethnic minority employment in manufacturing has fallen much faster than white employment, conversely ethnic minority employment in the service industries has risen much faster than white employment.[14]

The areas in which ethnic minorities live are concentrated geographically – mainly in the West Midlands and Greater London for Black and Afro-Caribbeans, and the West Midlands, Leicester, West Yorkshire and Greater London for Asians. This reflects the location of the industries in which the immigrant workforce came to work. These areas have seen high rates of unemployment among the immigrant communities reflecting a decline in those industries.

Although it is over 30 years since the first anti-race discrimination law was introduced, there is still evidence of continuing discrimination against black people in the job market. In these circumstances, it is unfortunate that informal methods of recruitment are still the most favoured method – despite being found to be racially discriminatory. Research has shown that 42% of jobs are filled by informal methods.[15] A study of 1993 graduates showed that ethnic minority

12 Colin Brown, *Black and White Britain: the third PSI Survey* (PSI, 1984). See also CRE Factsheet: Employment and Unemployment (1997) and *Ethnic Data from the Labour Force Survey: averages for June 1995–May 1996* (CRE, 1997).

13 CRE Factsheet: Employment and Unemployment (1997).

14 Ibid.

15 See House of Commons Employment Committee report 1990 (HMSO).

graduates took longer to get their first job compared to white graduates and they were likely to have longer periods of unemployment.[16]

Once in work, ethnic minorities find it harder to achieve promotion compared to white candidates. For instance, in the police force although ethnic minorities make up 1.4% of all officers they make up only 0.2% of superintendents and there are no ethnic minority officers in the highest ranks.[17] In the Civil Service ethnic minorities remain under-represented at management level despite an increase in ethnic minority employees overall; an example is given of the Benefits Agency where of 3,000 higher executive officers only 27 are black.[18]

The European Community (EC) has so far taken little action on race discrimination because it has been a controversial issue. However, it has designated 1997 to be the European Year against Racism. The Commission has issued its first Communication on Racism, Xenophobia and Anti-Semitism. This identifies key areas for action as including promoting integration and 'opening pathways for inclusion', promoting equal opportunities and reducing discrimination, raising public awareness, monitoring and combating prejudice and considering European-level legislation. The possibility of an initiative in this field during the Inter Governmental Conference 1996/97 has been suggested. It is to be hoped that this will be the first step towards EC legislation against race discrimination.

The situation for black workers in Britain in the 1990s is not easy. Current trends in the economy exacerbate the racial segmentation of the workforce; the work patterns of black and white have become self-perpetuating and combine with discrimination to make it difficult for black workers to move out of those parts of the labour market to which they have been confined.

Inequalities affecting disabled people

In 1995, after considerable pressure and the threat of a successful backbencher's Bill, the government introduced the Disability Dis-

16 Institute for Employment Studies 'Ethnic minority graduates: differences by degrees' (1996) 70 EOR.

17 The highest ranks are those above the rank of superintendent. See *Developing diversity in the Police Service, Equal Opportunities thematic inspection report 1995* (Home Office, 1996). CRE, 'Race and Equal Opportunities in the Police Service: a programme for action' (1996) 66 EOR.

18 'Equal Opportunities in the Civil Service – a progress report: women race disability 1993–5' and 'Civil Service Data Summary 1996' (Development and Equal Opportunities Division, Office of Public Service) (1997) 71 EOR.

crimination Act (DDA). It outlaws direct discrimination against disabled people. This new Act has now become law and for the first time has provided substantive individual rights for disabled people not to be discriminated against in employment.

Six per cent of the UK labour force have a long-term health problem or disability. However, the vast majority of workplaces are organised for the 'average' person without any disability. This necessarily excludes a substantial number of people from taking up employment opportunities that would otherwise be open to them. Disabled people have a much lower employment rate (32% in 1995/96) than non-disabled people (77% in 1995/96).[19]

The particular problems that face those who are HIV positive also need to be considered. As 86% of those who are HIV positive in the UK are men any discrimination against them may also be indirect sex discrimination.[20]

The EC has recently issued a Communication on Equality of Opportunity for People with Disabilities; it calls on member states to adopt equal opportunities policies to promote the integration of people with disabilities into the mainstream.[21]

Other inequalities that cause discrimination

Many employers have equal opportunities policies which prohibit discrimination on the ground of sexual orientation. At present UK law does not provide any express protection against such discrimination. The European Court of Justice (ECJ) has been slowly extending the scope of the principle of equal treatment in EC law to prohibit discrimination against transsexuals and is likely to prohibit discrimination on the ground of sexuality (see **2.6**).

Discrimination against older people (or in some cases against younger people) used to be very common. The developing awareness of unnecessary age limitations has made this less overt. There are proposals to prohibit discrimination on the ground of age. It may also be indirect sex discrimination.

There are still no express prohibitions on religious or political discrimination in Great Britain, although both are outlawed in Northern

19 'Disability and the labour market' *Labour Market Trends*, September 1996.
20 Communicable Diseases Report of the Public Health Laboratory Service, Volume 6, no 16, April 1996.
21 COM (96) 406.

Ireland.[22] There have been some moves to harmonise the protections afforded in Northern Ireland with those in Great Britain: race discrimination is now outlawed in Northern Ireland.[23] It is to be hoped that the government will prohibit religious discrimination in the UK.

Current labour market trends

The framework of the labour market has changed significantly in the last ten years with factors such as compulsory competitive tendering, permanent secure jobs being replaced by short-term contracts, the erosion of jobs with the introduction of new technologies, the reduction of layers of management and increasing numbers of part-time and temporary jobs. These trends have led to more insecure employment where employees have been reluctant to insist on their rights through fear of jeopardising their jobs. This has eroded the progress of equal opportunities which had been achieved in the 1980s. In 1995 the Equal Opportunities Commission (EOC) published a study of the effect of compulsory competitive tendering in local government on women. It concluded that it affected women worse than men and part-time women workers were particularly badly hit.[24]

What can be done?

Equal opportunities policies

The codes of practice issued by the EOC and the Commission for Racial Equality (CRE), and the code issued by the Secretary of State for Education and Employment under the DDA, encourage the adoption of equal opportunities policies. Their object is to set in place good employment practices which will help to prevent discrimination from occurring and identify where there is not equality of opportunity. The codes aim to help employers ensure that everyone has the same opportunities for a job, for promotion, and for training. A good equal opportunity policy will aim to ensure that at every stage of employment:

22 Fair Employment (Northern Ireland) Acts 1976 and 1989.
23 Race Relations (Northern Ireland) Order 1997.
24 K Escott and D Whitfield, 'The gender impact of CCT in local government' (EOC) (1995) 61 EOR.

- the criteria for decisions are objective and clear to every person who is potentially affected;
- the decisions are actually taken on the agreed criteria; and
- the rationale for all decisions taken is available to all those affected.

Such procedures encourage decisions to be taken only on the relevant criteria and not for any irrelevant reasons. Where decisions are fully 'transparent' in this way the scope for discrimination whether intentional or unintentional is greatly reduced.

Many employers now say that they operate equal opportunities policies. However, the evidence is that once a 'policy' has been adopted it is not always systematically and fully applied at every level. A simple statement that an employer is an equal opportunities employer is not sufficient. ITs are required to take the codes of practice into account (see below, **1.1.7**) and hence an employer who has a good equal opportunities policy which is conscientiously followed is in a much better position to defend a complaint of discrimination. Conversely, the failure to adopt or implement such a policy may well lead to an inference that there has been discrimination.

Legal remedies

Although the main statutory rights under the RRA and the SDA have changed little since they were enacted, progress has been made as tribunals and courts have come to understand better the social context within which the law operates. Additionally, EC law has had a substantial progressive effect on the interpretation of UK sex discrimination legislation. The removal of the upper limit on awards of damages for discrimination has resulted in an overall increase in the size of awards made to reflect the degree of damage inflicted.

Nonetheless, in some respects these laws are not widely understood and pursued. Despite the limitations of the law (such as its complexity and the restricted definition of discrimination in the legislation) the legal provisions, particularly those prohibiting indirect discrimination, constitute powerful tools for change, and EC law is very important in respect of sex discrimination. These laws present unusual opportunities for individuals to take legal action that potentially benefits not just the individual but also groups and classes of people. Successful cases have confronted some of the structural barriers which have been identified as crucial determinants of work opportunities for women and ethnic minority workers. Discrimination against part-timers, maximum age limits, stringent language tests and unnecessary demands for UK qualifications are all examples of employment practices that have been successfully challenged as unlawful.

Legal cases – even those that do not succeed – can be useful in identifying the hurdles that face women, black people and disabled people at work. They can therefore be complementary to collective bargaining strategies. The dispute over equal pay for women sewing machinists at Ford is the most obvious example of this. This group of women workers had been pressing their equal pay demands since the end of the 1960s, and, getting nowhere under the original EqPA, took one of the first cases under the equal value regulations introduced in 1984. Although they lost their case, they continued to campaign through their union, and eventually won their pay award through independent arbitration.

Trade unions

There are signs that unions are beginning to regard the law as more relevant and useful than in the past; many unions have taken cases under the equal value amendment and have integrated these legal actions – or the threat of resorting to legal action – in formulating pay claims and pressing employers to re-open job evaluation discussions.

It is hoped that this book will be used by trade unions because trade union representation on behalf of members in this field can and should be improved. CRE research showed that, of a sample survey of 377 applicants, nearly a quarter regarded their trade union as their first source of assistance in taking a case; but only 18% of applicants actually got any union assistance.[25]

There are good reasons why trade unions should be able to use the law more effectively. The millions of union members who are women and/or black and ethnic minority workers and/or disabled workers have a right to as good a service in this area of law as in any other. There is often nowhere else that those who have suffered discrimination can turn for assistance; employment law does not qualify for legal aid and so does not attract many lawyers – often a worker's chance of getting advice depends on help from the EOC or CRE or a local law centre, and the combined resources of these organisations are not sufficient. Enormous job losses in the manufacturing sector of the economy have meant that the movement has lost many members.

25 V Kumar, *Industrial tribunal applicants under the Race Relations Act 1976: a research report* (CRE, 1986).

This has resulted in some strategic planning in unions to try to attract those who have been poorly organised in the past – low-paid workers in the service industries, part-time and temporary workers, and hence effectively women and black and ethnic minority workers who are over-represented in these jobs. While it is acknowledged that the law is no substitute for organisational strength and collective bargaining, a greater use of anti-discrimination legislation should be encouraged.

After a long period when the legal rights of working people have been undermined, the right not to be discriminated against has been reinforced and extended. Even though other individual rights won in the 1970s have been taken away or reduced in the 1980s, maternity rights have been improved and discrimination laws remain firmly in place, strengthened in some respects by European law and judgments in the ECJ which have forced further legislation in the UK. A most important aspect of them is that, despite their weaknesses, they have acted as a stimulus to the adoption by employers of equal opportunities employment policies, even if they have not in themselves always delivered equal opportunities.

Contract compliance

'Contract compliance' is where public authorities require their contractors to adopt and maintain good employment practices, such as equal opportunities policies, as a condition of the contract. Thus, companies are persuaded to adopt equal opportunities policies for commercial reasons when perhaps they would not otherwise adopt them. However, Tory legislation outlawed such clauses. It is hoped that the new government will eliminate or reduce the constraints on contract compliance and also address some of their limitations. One essential step for the more effective enforcement of contract compliance clauses is to enable the employees of the contractor, as well as the contracting local authority, to take action if the clause is breached.

There is little doubt that in 1997 equal opportunity is an important issue in industrial relations. Originally, in the early 1980s, local authorities were in the forefront of adopting comprehensive policies to combat discrimination. Equal opportunities employment policies appeared to spread quite rapidly from the public to the private sector, though the strength and quality of policies of course varied; at best they can be comprehensive programmes of action, at worst they can be just a formal adoption of an equal opportunities statement which raises expectations which are later confounded.

The even-handedness of the law which prohibits discrimination in favour of women or black people has made it difficult for employers to take positive action. But nonetheless, the operation of the legislation has acted as a framework within which to identify barriers facing women and ethnic minority workers at work.

The future

As this book is published, a Labour government has been elected after 18 years of Conservative rule. Labour has promised to sign the Social Chapter of the Maastricht Treaty which will bring into operation the Parental Leave Directive probably by the end of 1999. It has promised to introduce a minimum wage which is expected to improve the position of women, particularly those from ethnic minorities, who receive the lowest rates of pay.[26]

In the EC a new framework agreement has been reached on part-time work. This is likely to become a directive by the end of 1997 and be effective by the end of 1999. It provides that part-time workers must not be treated less favourably than comparable full-time workers unless the difference is objectively justified. It also provides that employers should give consideration to requests to transfer to full- or part-time work and facilitate access to part-time work at all levels of the enterprise. This is likely to make it easier for workers to transfer between full- and part-time work and to encourage flexible patterns of employment.

Labour's policy document, *Building Prosperity – Flexibility, Efficiency and Fairness at Work*, proposed to outlaw discrimination on grounds of age and sexual orientation as well as sex, race and disability. A national childcare strategy will enable more women to go to work if they so choose, and there is discussion of family-friendly employment policies. It is to be hoped that the government will also rationalise and simplify the equal pay and maternity laws and abolish the lower earnings limit for non-contributory benefits which prevents many women from claiming any statutory maternity pay.

There need to be much stronger laws to combat sexism, racism and able-bodyism in the workplace, and elsewhere, legal aid to assist applicants in discrimination cases as well as a Human Rights Commission to cover all areas of discrimination, for example, on grounds of age, sexuality and religion. Until there is legislation, we would like

26 See 'Minimum wage benefits women and ethnic minorities' (1997) 73 EOR.

to see a more widespread and vigorous use of existing laws and it is hoped that this book will be useful in that endeavour.

Northern Ireland

Northern Ireland has the same sex discrimination laws though different acts as the rest of the UK. It has recently introduced race discrimination provisions parallel to those in the rest of the UK. It does, however, have a religious discrimination law.

Part I

Legal framework of sex and race discrimination

CHAPTER 1

The legal structure

1.1 Discrimination legislation and codes of practice

1.1.1 Sex Discrimination Act 1975 (SDA)

As amended by the Sex Discrimination Act 1986 (SDA 1986) and the Employment Act 1989 (EA 1989)

The SDA prohibits direct and indirect discrimination against women (and men) on the ground of sex. It does not provide for the removal of all discrimination but lays down the circumstances when discrimination is unlawful. This book is concerned only with discrimination in employment but the Act also covers discrimination in education and in the provision of goods, facilities, services and premises.

The Act excludes discrimination in pay and other contractual terms as this is covered by the Equal Pay Act 1970. The two Acts are mutually exclusive (see **5.7.1**). Both are subject to EC law.

1.1.2 Sex Discrimination Act 1986

Apart from amending the SDA 1975, the main substantive provisions of the 1986 Act relate to discriminatory provisions in collective agreements and rules of undertakings.[1]

1.1.3 Equal Pay Act 1970 (EqPA)

The EqPA was passed in 1970 but did not come into force until 1975. The equal value provisions (see (c) below) came into force on

1 The provisions were further amended by the Trade Union and Labour Relations (Consolidation) Act 1992 and the Trade Union Reform and Employment Rights Act 1993.

1 January 1984. The Act, as amended by the equal value provisions,[2] provides that a man and woman working for the same employer should receive the same pay and be subject to the same contractual terms if:

a) they are doing similar work; or
b) there has been a job evaluation scheme (JES) and the man's and woman's work has been rated as equivalent; or
c) they are doing work of equal value,

provided that the material factor defence (see Chapter 21) does not apply. An equality clause is implied into the contract of employment.

The Act, as amended by the SDA 1986, further provides that discriminatory provisions in collective agreements and rules of employers, trade unions, employers' associations, professional organisations and qualifying bodies are void or unenforceable.

1.1.4 Pensions Act 1995

The Pensions Act provides for equal treatment for men and women in occupational pension schemes. The relevant sections (ss62 to 66) came into force on 1 January 1996.[3] It covers terms on which persons become members of a scheme and the way members are treated. An occupational pension scheme is treated as containing an equal treatment rule where a woman is employed on like work, work rated as equivalent or work of equal value. This is enforced in the same way as an equal pay claim.

1.1.5 Race Relations Act 1976 (RRA)

The RRA is very similar to the SDA and prohibits direct and indirect discrimination on racial grounds in specified circumstances. Racial grounds include colour, race, nationality or ethnic or national origins. In addition, the RRA covers discrimination in pay and other contractual terms; there are no separate provisions dealing with race discrimination in pay. This book is concerned only with discrimination in employment but the RRA also covers discrimination in education and in the provision of goods, facilities, services and premises.

2 Equal Pay (Amendment) Regs 1983 SI No 1794.
3 Pensions Act 1995 (Commencement No 2) Order 1995 SI No 3104 (C71).

1.1.6 Disability Discrimination Act 1995 (DDA)

While the stated aim of the DDA is to prohibit discrimination against disabled people, it provides that where such discrimination can be objectively justified it is not unlawful. Unlike the SDA and the RRA, the DDA does not outlaw indirect discrimination, but it does impose an obligation on employers to make reasonable adjustments to their premises and practices in order to accommodate disabled people. Although these parts of the Act are not covered in this book, the DDA also makes it unlawful to discriminate unjustifiably against disabled people in the provision of goods, facilities and services, and in the disposal and management of premises.

1.1.7 Codes of Practice

The Equal Opportunities Commission (EOC), the Commission for Racial Equality (CRE) and the Secretary of State for Education and Employment have produced codes of practice, their purpose being to eliminate discrimination in employment and to promote equality of opportunity in employment.[4] The EOC has also produced a code of practice on equal pay, parts of which are reproduced in Appendix 3 at p595.

The codes provide guidance for employers (and, in the case of the CRE and DDA codes, for trade unions and employment agencies) about practices which they recommend should be adopted to promote equality. The CRE code came into force on 1 April 1984[5] the EOC sex discrimination code on 30 April 1985,[6] the DDA code on 2 December 1996[7] and the equal pay code on 26 March 1997. The codes do not have the same standing as either the legislation or case-law. Failure by an employer to observe any provision of a code is not in itself unlawful but it may be taken into account by a tribunal or court.[8] Thus, failure to observe the code may lead to a presumption of discrimination.

In *Berry v Bethlem & Maudsley NHS Trust* and *Hink v (1) Riva Systems and (2) Lumsden*,[9] the EAT held that tribunals were required to have regard to any breach of a code of practice.

4 SDA s56A; RRA s47; DDA s53.
5 Race Relations Code of Practice Order 1983 SI No 1081.
6 Sex Discrimination Code of Practice Order 1985 SI No 387.
7 Disability Discrimination (Guidance and Code of Practice) (Appointed Day) Order 1996 SI No 1996.
8 SDA s56A(10); RRA s47(10); DDA s53(4) to (6).
9 (1997) 31 DCLD.

1.1.8 EC law

EC law is concerned only with sex discrimination not race discrimination (though it does prohibit, in some circumstances, discrimination between nationals of member states), nor disability discrimination. EC law generally takes precedence over UK law (see **9.6**). If there is a dispute over the interpretation of EC law it can be referred, by a UK court or tribunal, to the European Court of Justice (ECJ). EC legislation comprises the treaties and articles which established the European community and the regulations and directives issued by the Council of Ministers. In many situations, EC law is more far-reaching than UK law and may provide a remedy where there is none in UK law. It should be considered in *any* sex discrimination or equal pay claim. There are five relevant provisions:

- *article 119* of the Treaty of Rome which lays down the principle of equal pay for work of equal value;
- the *Equal Pay Directive* which expands on the principle of equal pay contained in Article 119;[10]
- the *Equal Treatment Directive* which provides for equal treatment between men and women in respect of access to employment, training, promotion, working conditions and dismissal;[11] and
- the *Pregnant Workers Directive* which lays down minimum rights for pregnant women, including paid time off for ante-natal care, 14 weeks' maternity leave, protection from dismissal and health and safety rights.
- the *Occupational Social Security Directive* (as amended).

1.2 Other employment legislation

1.2.1 Employment Rights Act 1996 (ERA)

This Act consolidated provisions of the Employment Protection (Consolidation) Act 1978 and other employment statutes. It came into force on 22 August 1996.

The ERA gives employees some protection against unfair dismissal, redundancy and dismissal on the ground of pregnancy. It also gives women the right to maternity leave and to their job back on return

10 Directive 75/117/EEC.
11 Directive 76/207/EEC.

from maternity leave. There are, however, a number of qualifying conditions, the most important being that, in order to claim protection from unfair dismissal (apart from on pregnancy-related grounds) an employee must have worked for the employer for two years. This is currently under challenge in *R v Secretary of State for Employment ex p Seymour Smith*.[12]

1.3 Adjudication structure

The Industrial Tribunals Act 1996 consolidates statutes relating to industrial tribunals and the Employment Appeal Tribunal. It came into force on 22 August 1996. Regulations cover all procedural aspects.[13]

The structure of tribunals and courts and how to appeal from one to the other is fully explained in Chapter 25.

1.4 Interpretation of discrimination law

The complexity of discrimination and equal pay law has been the subject of much judicial comment. It is always worth bearing in mind the purpose of the legislation. In *Jones v Tower Boot Ltd*[14] the CA had no hesitation in holding that a purposive interpretation should be adopted, saying:

> The legislation now represented by the Race and Sex Discrimination Acts currently in force broke new ground in seeking to work upon the minds of men and women and thus affect their attitude to the social consequences of differences between the sexes or distinction of skin colour. Its general thrust was educative, persuasive, and (where necessary) coercive. The relief accorded to the victims (or potential victims) of discrimination went beyond the ordinary remedies of damages and injunction – introducing, through declaratory powers in the court or tribunal and recommendatory powers in the relevant Commission, provisions with a pro-active function, designed as much to eliminate the occasions for discrimination as to compensate its victims or punish its perpetrators . . . Consistently with the broad front on which it operates, the legislation has traditionally been given a wide interpretation.

12 [1995] IRLR 464, CA.

13 Industrial Tribunals (Constitution and Rules of Procedure) Regulations 1993 SI No 2687.

14 [1995] IRLR 529, EAT.

The CA then quoted approvingly from *Savjani v IRC*:[15]

> . . . the Act was brought in to remedy a very great evil. It is expressed in very wide terms, and I should be slow to find that the effect of something which is humiliatingly discriminatory in racial matters falls outside the ambit of the Act.

The same principles apply to sex discrimination.

In *London Underground v Edwards (No 2)*[16] (a case about the impact of anti-social hours on a female lone parent) the EAT echoed the Court of Appeal's views on the purpose of the Equal Treatment Directive (in *R v Secretary of State for Employment ex p Seymour Smith*), that it was to eliminate all sex discrimination in the employment field: 'Equality of treatment is the paramount consideration.' In *Edwards* the EAT said that:

> [the] more clear it is that the employers unreasonably failed to show flexibility in their employment practices, the more willing the Tribunal should be to make a finding of unlawful discrimination.

The principles applying to equal treatment were aptly summarised by the Advocate General in *P v S*[17] when he expressed his 'profound conviction' that:

> what is at stake is a universal fundamental value, indelibly etched in modern legal traditions and in the constitutions of the more advanced countries: *the irrelevance of a person's sex with regard to the rules regulating relations in society* [his emphasis].

15 [1981] 1 QB 458.
16 [1997] IRLR 157 para 22.
17 [1996] IRLR 347.

CHAPTER 2

Direct discrimination on grounds of sex and race

2.1 Introduction

Direct discrimination requires evidence of less favourable treatment on the ground of a person's race or sex. (Disability discrimination is defined differently – see Chapter 24.) Proving direct discrimination is often difficult, as most employers are aware of the existence of discrimination laws and know that they have to be cautious about admitting discriminatory preferences.

Sometimes, though rarely, employers admit a preference for white male workers; in *Morris and Others v Scott & Knowles*,[1] women were easily able to prove sex discrimination as their employer claimed that the cost of implementing the Agricultural Wages Order 1976 as amended by the EqPA meant that the women's hours would have to be reduced and their employment status casualised. However, it is unlikely that this sort of evidence will be readily available, as generally employers will claim that they were motivated by other non-discriminatory considerations. In *Khanna v Ministry of Defence*[2] it was said:

> evidence of discrimination is seldom going to be available . . . equally, racial discrimination does undoubtedly exist, and it is highly improbable that a person who has discriminated is going to admit the fact, quite possibly even to himself.

2.2 Less favourable treatment

First, it is necessary to show that there has been less favourable treatment. The fact that a complainant feels that s/he has been unfavourably treated does not of itself establish unfavourable treatment. It is for

1 [1976] IRLR 238.
2 [1981] IRLR 331.

the tribunal to decide whether it was reasonable for the complainant to experience it as less favourable treatment.[3] In *R v Birmingham CC ex p Equal Opportunities Commission*,[4] where, as a result of selection policies, more grammar school places were allocated to boys than girls, the HL held that it was not necessary to show that selective education is 'better' than non-selective education. It is enough that, by denying the girls the same opportunity as the boys, the council was depriving them of a choice which was valued by them, or at least by their parents, and which is a choice obviously valued, on reasonable grounds, by many others. The HL approved the CA decision in *Gill v El Vino Co Ltd*,[5] where it was held that the refusal to serve women at the bar (even though they would be served when sitting at tables) was unlawful as it deprived the women of the option of standing at the bar. Words or acts of discouragement can amount to less favourable treatment of the person discouraged,[6] as can harassment.

Segregation on the ground of sex is not unlawful *per se*; the treatment must be less favourable. Under the RRA, segregation on racial grounds is itself treated as less favourable treatment (s1(2)) (see **6.1.2**).

2.3 On the ground of race or sex

The reason for the less favourable treatment must be the complainant's sex, race or marital status. The HL said in the *Birmingham City Council* case, there is discrimination if the relevant girl would have received the same treatment as a boy *'but for'* her sex. *James v Eastleigh BC*[7] reaffirmed the importance of the *but for* test in identifying gender- or race-based criteria.

2.4 Discrimination on the ground of another's race

The definition of direct discrimination is worded slightly differently in the RRA and SDA. Under the RRA, discrimination 'on racial grounds' is unlawful, whereas under the SDA, discrimination against a woman 'on the ground of her sex' is unlawful. This means that, under the RRA, someone can complain that s/he has been dis-

3 *Burrett v West Birmingham Health Authority* [1994] IRLR 307.
4 [1989] IRLR 173.
5 [1983] IRLR 206.
6 *Simon v Brimham* [1987] IRLR 307.
7 [1990] IRLR 288.

criminated against on the ground of someone else's race, eg, a white woman, refused a job because she has a black husband, could bring a claim of discrimination.

In *Zarcynska v Levy*,[8] a barmaid had been dismissed because she refused to comply with her boss's instructions not to serve black customers, and the EAT ruled that this was unlawful discrimination on racial grounds. This decision was followed in *Showboat Entertainment Centre Ltd v Owens*,[9] where a white manager of an amusement centre had been instructed to exclude young blacks from the centre, and had been dismissed for refusing to carry out the instruction.

2.5 Race or sex need not be the only cause

It is not necessary to show that race or sex was the only ground for less favourable treatment, but it is necessary to show that it was a factor in the decision-making process which carried sufficient weight to be a cause of the action. In *Owen & Briggs v James*[10] a firm of solicitors made clear their preferences when one of the partners, rejecting a black job applicant, remarked (to a white candidate): 'I can't understand why an English employer would want to take on a coloured girl when English girls are available.' The firm tried to argue that there were other grounds for rejecting her, but the CA upheld the IT and EAT findings that racial considerations were an important factor and that discrimination had occurred.

Similarly, in *O'Neill v Governors of St Thomas More School*[11] an unmarried teacher of 'religious education and personal relationships' was dismissed when it became clear that she was pregnant as a result of a relationship with a local Roman Catholic priest. The IT rejected her complaint of sex discrimination saying that 'an important motive for the dismissal was not the Applicant's pregnancy per se but the fact that the pregnancy was by a Roman Catholic priest' and that as a result her position as a teacher was untenable. It found that the respondents had mixed motives. The EAT said that their mixed motives were inextricably linked to her pregnancy and hence it was not possible to say that the ground for dismissal was anything other than pregnancy (see **17.6.13.1**).

8 [1978] IRLR 532.
9 [1984] IRLR 7.
10 [1982] IRLR 502; see also *Nagarajan v Agnew* [1994] IRLR 61.
11 [1996] IRLR 372.

If, however, the less favourable treatment (such as dismissal) is found to be for some entirely different reason than discrimination, the IT cannot then make a finding that the treatment was discriminatory. In *Inshon Ltd v Denny*,[12] the IT held that the dismissal was caused wholly by the applicant's conduct but still held that there had been discrimination. The EAT overturned the finding of discrimination.

2.6 Gender re-assignment and sexuality

In *P v S and Cornwall CC*[13] the ECJ construed the principle of equal treatment in the Equal Treatment Directive (ETD) to apply to a person who was dismissed following an operation to undergo gender reassignment(see also **5.1.4**). It is thus clear that transsexuals (and probably transvestites) are protected under EC law. The ETD is directly enforceable only against employers who are an emanation of the state (see **9.6.7**). However, it is well established that the SDA 1975 should also be construed so as to accord with the ETD wherever possible, so in *R v C* the EAT held that the SDA does protect transsexuals from discrimination.[14]

The ECJ did not have to consider the position of gays and lesbians but its decision suggests that the ETD should be construed so as to prohibit discrimination against homosexuals. However, prior to the judgment of the ECJ the CA had rejected the argument that the ETD protected discrimination on grounds of sexuality (in *R v MOD ex p Smith*[15]). This must be of questionable authority now in the light of *P v S*. EC law enables ITs to disregard precedents if they are no longer consistent with ECJ rulings.[16] Accordingly it is arguable that *R v MOD ex p Smith* should not be followed[17] (see also **5.1.5**). This point has now been referred to the ECJ in *R v Secretary of State for Defence ex p Perkins*.[18]

12 EAT 268/88.
13 [1996] IRLR 347.
14 EAT 27 June 1997.
15 [1996] IRLR 100 and see also *Smith v Gardner Merchant Ltd* [1996] IRLR 342.
16 *Case 166/73 Rheinmühlen Dusseldorf v Einfuhr- und Vorratstelle für Getreide* [1974] ECR 33.
17 In *Grant v South West Trains* (1996) 65 EOR 2, IT, the right of a lesbian employee to the same employee benefits as a heterosexual employee (a travel pass for her partner) has been referred to the ECJ.
18 [1997] IRLR 297.

2.7 Motive

It is not necessary to prove that the defendant had the intention or motive to discriminate. Thus, it is not a good defence for employers to show that they discriminated against women not because they intended to do so, but, for example, because of customer preference, or to save money, or even to avoid controversy. In *Din v Carrington Viyella Ltd (Jersey Kapwood Ltd)*,[19] the applicant, a Pakistani, was involved in a row with his foreman which ended in the foreman pushing him. The manager, however, refused to make the foreman apologise, which angered Mr Din's workmates (who were also Pakistani). When Mr Din came back from his holiday the firm refused to re-employ him because it thought that this would defuse the unrest. The IT accepted that the employer's motives were not racial but industrial. The EAT ruled that motive, while relevant, was not the decisive factor, and that the action had nevertheless been discriminatory. If an act of racial discrimination had given rise to industrial unrest, then to seek to banish the unrest by removing the person discriminated against was unlawful. Similarly in *R v Commission for Racial Equality ex p Westminster CC*[20] the withdrawal of an offer of employment to a black road sweeper by a manager who feared a racially motivated strike was held by the CA to be racial discrimination.

It is no defence for employers to say that they are not prejudiced. In *Hafeez v Richmond School*,[21] Mr Hafeez's application to teach English was rejected as the students wanted to be taught by an English person. Even though the school's principal was not prejudiced, he was found to have acted unlawfully. In *Ramsey v John James Hawley (Speciality Works) Ltd*,[22] a West Indian employee was given a number of warnings because of pressure from other racist employees, even though his work did not warrant it. This was found to be unlawful discrimination by his employer.

In *James v Eastleigh BC*,[23] the council allowed those who had reached the state pension age (65 for men and 60 for women) to swim for no charge. Mr James was 62 and was charged the standard fee while his wife, also aged 62, could swim free of charge. The HL held that this was unlawful despite the fact that there was no intention to discriminate. A useful test is to ask whether the applicant would have

19 [1982] IRLR 281.
20 [1984] IRLR 230.
21 1981 COIT 1112/38.
22 1978 COIT 804/139.
23 [1990] IRLR 288.

been treated the same way *but for* the fact that she was a woman or black (see also 2.5) If, however, there is evidence of a discriminatory motive this will clearly be very relevant.

2.8 Stereotyping

Preconceptions that people of a particular sex, marital status or race possess or lack certain characteristics are discriminatory. The CA so held in *Coleman v Skyrail Oceanic Ltd,*[24] where the employer had dismissed the applicant on the assumption that men are more likely to be the primary supporters of a family than women. In *Horsey v Dyfed CC,*[25] the employer had assumed that most women would follow their husbands if they moved jobs and so Mrs Horsey was likely to do this. The EAT relied on the CA ruling in *Coleman* to find this discriminatory. In *Hurley v Mustoe*[26] the EAT held that a policy not to employ women with children was discriminatory and was not justified. In *Cockroft v Restus Ltd,*[27] an IT said it was unlawful discrimination to assume that the work (as a warehouse assistant) was for a 'big strong lad' and was unsuitable for a 'young lady'.

2.9 Same or similar relevant circumstances

Direct discrimination involves a comparison between persons of different racial groups or sex or marital status. The relevant circumstances in the one case must be the same, or 'not materially different', from those in the other.[28] The question to be asked in each case is whether a man or white person would, in the same or similar circumstances, have been treated in the same way as the applicant.

In *Re Equal Opportunities Commission for Northern Ireland's Application,*[29] an education board decided that 27% of boys and 27% of girls would be awarded grammar school places on the basis of exam performance. After this decision had been successfully challenged because the pass rate for boys was lower than that for girls, the papers were re-marked and 305 additional girls became eligible on the

24 [1981] IRLR 398.
25 [1982] IRLR 395.
26 [1981] IRLR 208.
27 12420/89.
28 SDA s5(3); RRA s3(4).
29 [1989] IRLR 64.

same pass mark. They were offered places. The board then decided, on the basis of fairness, not to withdraw the offers from the 422 boys who had already been notified that they had places. Many girls had achieved the same or higher marks than these 422 but were not awarded places. The board argued that the relevant circumstances were materially different as the boys were offered places only because it was unfair to withdraw them. The Northern Ireland High Court held that the difference was caused by sex discrimination so could not be relied upon.

In comparing relevant circumstances, it is the facts of the particular case which are relevant and not hypothetical situations. In *Grieg v Community Industry and Ahern*,[30] the applicant had been refused a job on a painting and decorating team because she would have been the only woman on the team. The employer argued that if a man had applied for a job with an all-woman team, he would have been refused. Refusal to appoint a woman on an all male team is discrimination as is the refusal to appoint a man on an all female team (see also *Smyth v Croft Inns Ltd*[31]).

In *Bain v Bowles*,[32] a male applicant living in Italy complained that he was not allowed to put an advertisement in *The Lady* magazine for a housekeeper. *The Lady* said that it was worried about the danger of sexual harassment of girls who accepted positions outside the UK with male employers. The CA rejected *The Lady's* argument that the relevant circumstances were different and upheld the complaint.

2.9.1 *Relevant circumstances must not be discriminatory*

The HL held, in *James v Eastleigh BC* (see **2.7**), that, as the pensionable age is itself discriminatory, it could not be treated as a relevant circumstance in making the comparison under SDA s5(3). Any comparison which takes a discriminatory base line such as pensionable age was wrong said the HL. In *Dhatt v McDonalds Hamburgers Ltd*,[33] on the other hand, the CA held that a factor which itself discriminates on racial grounds can qualify as a relevant circumstance. *James* was distinguished on the basis that it was the council which adopted the discriminatory criterion whereas in *Dhatt* the discrimination was sanctioned by statute. As argued elsewhere (see **6.4.1.6** at p141), the discrimination in *Dhatt* was not sanctioned by statute and

30 [1979] IRLR 158.
31 [1996] IRLR 84, NICA.
32 [1991] IRLR 356.
33 [1991] IRLR 130.

these two decisions are inconsistent. The HL decision in *James* should prevail.

2.9.2 Dress

Circumstances which have been held to be different include rules on dress applied to men and women. In *Schmidt v Austicks Bookshops*,[34] Ms Schmidt's complaint that women being forbidden to wear trousers was discriminatory did not succeed. This was partly because the EAT found that the circumstances between men and women were different: men would not be asked to wear skirts. It said:

> But it seems to us . . . realistic . . . to say that there were in force rules restricting wearing apparel and governing appearance which applied to men and also applied to women, although obviously, women and men being different, the rules in the two cases were not the same.

This decision is arguably wrong. The relevant circumstances are that men can wear trousers; it is irrelevant that they would not be asked to wear skirts – that is an entirely hypothetical question. If men have the choice of wearing trousers then women should also be able to do so if they wish (see **2.2** to **2.3**).

This case was approved by the Court of Appeal in *Smith v Safeway plc*[35] a case concerning different rules applied to men and women about the length of their hair. The tribunal had found that Safeway had a dress and appearance code which did not make identical provision for men and women, but that the rules for men and women were equally rigorously applied. The CA said that it was necessary for a complainant to show not merely that the sexes were treated differently, but that the treatment of one sex was less favourable than the treatment given to the other. A code providing for a conventional standard of appearance for both sexes was likely to operate equally favourably between the sexes. It concluded that 'looking at the code as a whole, neither case was to be treated less favourably as a result of its application'. However, a deprivation of choice *is* less favourable treatment. Such denial of choice is based on assumptions about the proper appearance of men and women; it is both sex-based and likely to disadvantage ethnic minorities. This case is almost certainly wrong (see also **11.6.3.1**).

In *R v Birmingham CC ex p EOC*[36] the HL said that in order to

34 [1977] IRLR 360.
35 [1996] IRLR 456, CA.
36 [1989] IRLR 173.

show less favourable treatment it was enough to show that girls were deprived of a choice that was valued by them. Clearly in the *Safeway* case Mr Smith considered that he had been deprived of such a choice and been treated less favourably. Additionally, this is contrary to the ETD which provides:

> the principle of equal treatment shall mean that there shall be no discrimination *whatsoever* on grounds of sex . . . (art 2(1))
> and
> the application of the principle of equal treatment with regard to working conditions . . . means that men and women shall be guaranteed the same conditions without discrimination on grounds of sex. (art 5(1))

The Advocate General in *P v S*[37] said:

> . . . sex should be irrelevant to the treatment everyone receives, the Directive should be construed in a broader perspective, including therefore all situations in which sex appears as a discriminatory factor.

It is also inconsistent with the decision of the House of Lords in *James v Eastleigh BC* (see above) where the *but for* test of less favourable treatment was approved. Clearly, but for the fact that Mr Smith was a man the male 'dress code' would not have applied to him. Safeway's requirement of conformity with the male dress code is plainly a gender-based requirement.

2.9.3 Pregnancy

Discrimination on the ground of a woman's pregnancy, or her capacity to bear children, is now accepted to be sex discrimination without the need to compare her situation to that of any man. The ECJ has now clearly established that discrimination against a woman because she is pregnant is a breach of the ETD and hence the SDA must be interpreted in line with this. There is no need, held the ECJ, to show that a man in similar circumstances would have been treated more favourably (see **17.6.13**).

2.10 Proving discrimination

Since employers rarely admit to discriminatory intentions, it is usually necessary for applicants to invite the IT to infer discrimination

37 [1996] IRLR 347.

from the facts of the case. The IT must make findings of the primary facts from which the inference is drawn.[38]

Lord Lowry said in *Wallace v South Eastern Education and Library Board*:[39]

> Only rarely would direct evidence be available of discrimination on the ground of sex; one is more often left to infer discrimination from the circumstances. If this could not be done, the object of the legislation would be largely defeated, so long as the authority alleged to be guilty of discrimination made no expressly discriminatory statements and did not attempt to justify its actions by evidence.

This general approach was subsequently affirmed by the CA in *Baker v Cornwall CC*.[40] Further, in *King v Great Britain-China Centre*,[41] summarised the principles and guidance which could be extracted from case-law as follows:

> (1) It is for the applicant who complains of racial discrimination to make out his or her case. Thus if the applicant does not prove the case on the balance of probabilities he or she will fail.
> (2) It is important to bear in mind that it is unusual to find direct evidence of racial discrimination. Few employers will be prepared to admit such discrimination even to themselves. In some cases the discrimination will not be ill-intentioned but merely based on an assumption that 'he or she would not have fitted in.'
> (3) The outcome of the case will therefore usually depend on what inferences it is proper to draw from the primary facts found by the tribunal. These inferences can include, in appropriate cases, any inferences that it is just and equitable to draw in accordance with section 65(2)(b) of the Act of 1976 from an evasive or equivocal reply to a questionnaire.
> (4) Though there will be some cases where, for example, the non-selection of the applicant for a post or for promotion is clearly not on racial grounds, a finding of discrimination and a finding of a difference in race will often point to the possibility of racial discrimination. In such circumstances the tribunal will look to the employer for an explanation. If no explanation is then put forward or if the tribunal considers the explanation to be inadequate or unsatisfactory it will be legitimate for the tribunal to infer that the discrimination was on racial grounds. This

38 See *Chapman v Simon* [1994] IRLR 124.

39 [1980] IRLR 193. See also *Khanna v MOD* [1981] IRLR 331, EAT; *Chattopadhyay v Headmaster of Holloway School* [1981] IRLR 487, EAT; *Dornan v Belfast CC* [1990] IRLR 179, NI CA; and *Noone v North West Thames Regional Health Authority* [1988] IRLR 195, CA.

40 [1990] IRLR 194.

41 [1991] IRLR 513.

is not a matter of law but, as May L.J. put it in *North West Thames Regional Health Authority v Noone* 'almost common sense.'
(5) It is unnecessary and unhelpful to introduce the concept of a shifting evidential burden of proof. At the conclusion of all the evidence the tribunal should make findings as to the primary facts and draw such inferences as they consider proper from those facts. They should then reach a conclusion on the balance of probabilities, bearing in mind both the difficulties which face a person who complains of unlawful discrimination and the fact that it is for the complainant to prove his or her case.

2.11 Bad management

Poor management can often disguise discrimination. Employers may argue that all employees were treated equally badly so there was no discrimination.[42] In *Qureshi v LB Newham*,[43] the CA stressed that incompetence does not become discrimination merely because the person affected is from an ethnic minority. Mr Qureshi was unsuccessful in his job application and alleged that the employer's failure to comply with the equal opportunities policy was discriminatory, there being an assumption that the policy had been applied to other applicants. The CA refused to accept that inference, saying that it was likely that the policy had not been applied to other applicants either, and this was due to incompetence not discrimination. Similarly, in *Glasgow CC v Zafar*[44] the Court of Session found that the fact that the employer had not acted reasonably did not mean that it had treated the employee less favourably than other employees on the ground of his race.

However, bad management should not excuse discriminatory treatment. Applicants should use the questionnaire procedure to find out how other employees in similar situations were treated.

The RRA and SDA codes were designed to encourage employers to take steps to increase equal opportunities, eliminate discrimination and to establish procedures with this in mind. Thus, in recruitment their aim is to encourage employers to adopt more rational, systematic and justifiable recruitment procedures, and to record them, so as to eliminate the possibility of unconscious discrimination.

42 This might lead to a finding of unfair dismissal (if relevant) but not to discrimination.
43 [1991] IRLR 264.
44 [1997] IRLR 229.

Incompetence may mean that there is a *lack of transparency* in the workplace, for example, if there are no records of how and why decisions on recruitment are made. If statistics suggest discrimination, then the employers may be called on to show an absence of discrimination in a particular sense.

2.12 EC law: the importance of 'transparency'

Although tribunals may be prepared to draw inferences from primary facts, under UK law, the burden of proof still remains with the applicant. The position under EC law may, since the historic *Danfoss*[45] case, be different. The facts of *Danfoss* are set out at **21.3**; in brief the ECJ held that:

> where an undertaking applies a pay system which is characterised by a total lack of transparency, the burden of proof is on the employer to show that his pay practice is not discriminatory where a female worker establishes, by comparison with a relatively large number of employees, that the average pay of female workers is lower than that of male workers . . .

The concept of 'transparency' is an important one as it requires the employer to give a rational explanation for decisions, practices and procedures which appear to be discriminatory. Although *Danfoss* is an equal pay case, arguably the principles can be applied to other discrimination cases. So, for example, where a disproportionate number of men or white people are appointed or promoted where there are equally qualified female and black applicants, the employer may be required to provide an explanation. Failure to do so may then lead to a finding of sex or race discrimination.

2.13 What kind of evidence?

In asking an IT to infer discrimination from the facts, there is wide latitude as to what evidence can be put before it. In *Chattopadhyay v Headmaster of Holloway School*,[46] the applicant complained that he had been discriminated against in being passed over for promotion. He presented evidence relating to acts which occurred after the deci-

45 *Handels-og Kontorfunktionaerernes Forbund i Danmark v Dansk Arbedjsgiverforening (acting for Danfoss)* [1989] IRLR 532.
46 [1981] IRLR 487.

sion not to promote him had been taken by the school governors. The EAT held that evidence of events which occurred both before *and* after the act complained of, were admissible.

In *Eke v Commissioners of Customs and Excise*,[47] Mr Eke claimed that he had been passed over for promotion. His employers tried to argue that evidence relating to events which took place outside the three-month time limit for a tribunal complaint could not be used as evidence. The EAT disagreed, saying that, although no award could be based on them because of the time limit, they were admissible as evidence of the discrimination. See also *West Midlands Passenger Transport v Singh*,[48] below.

Applicants should therefore point to all less favourable treatment when building up a picture of discrimination – they do not have to limit themselves to acts that are overtly racist or sexist, or discrimination which is the subject of the proceedings.

Evidence of a discriminatory motive, while not necessary to prove discrimination, will be crucial evidence. As the EAT said in *Elahi v Bristol and Weston Health Authority*:[49]

> the existence of racial prejudice . . . is highly relevant to an issue as to whether there was disciminatory conduct. It is self-evident that if there is such prejudice, discriminatory conduct is much more likely to have occurred.

In *Saunders v Richmond BC*,[50] Ms Saunders complained about discriminatory questions put to her at an interview. Although the EAT said that the questions were not in themselves discriminatory and unlawful, the fact that they had been asked was evidence in determining whether she had been discriminated against in not being appointed (see **10.14**).

Applicants should use the questionnaire procedure to ask respondents or potential respondents questions relating to the background and circumstances of their case. Questionnaires can be used to ask about their equal opportunities procedure and practice or for relevant statistics on the racial or sexual breakdown of the workforce. These questionnaires must be sent within three months of the discriminatory act concerned or within 21 days of an application to the IT. If the employer fails to reply to this the IT can draw inferences from the refusal (see Chapter 25).

47 [1981] IRLR 344.
48 [1988] IRLR 186.
49 EAT 138/89.
50 [1977] IRLR 362.

Once the employer's reply is received, either party can ask for further and better particulars of their opponent's claim, as well as request 'discovery', ie, the chance to see and copy any relevant documents. Either side can also ask the other relevant questions, called 'written questions'. If either side fails or refuses to respond to any of these enquiries the IT can order that they should be produced (see Chapter 25).

2.13.1 Statistics

Statistical evidence of the numbers of women and black people in a workforce or in a particular part of the workforce may be used to infer discrimination. The Race Relations code of practice recommends that employers should regularly monitor the effects of selection decisions and personnel practices and procedures and suggests that this is best done by providing records which show the ethnic origins of existing employees and job applicants (para 1.34). Hence the absence of such records can be used to infer discrimination (see 1.1.7).

In *Marshall v F Woolworth & Co Ltd*,[51] the applicant suspected that the reason that she was not offered a job was because she was black; the tribunal inferred discrimination from the fact that there was no black person working in the store, even though there was a sizeable black population in the locality and about half the job applicants were black.

In *West Midlands Passenger Transport Executive v Singh*,[52] Mr Singh applied unsuccessfully for promotion as senior inspector and he complained of discrimination. The employer denied this, referring to its equal opportunities policy and a system it had of ethnic monitoring of applications and appointments. While the employer voluntarily produced details of the ethnic origins, qualifications and experience of all applicants for the job of senior inspector, it refused to give details of the ethnic origins of applicants for, and appointees to, posts within a band of grades broadly comparable to senior inspector covering the period since the equal opportunities policy was adopted. The CA ruled that the applicant was entitled to information about the number of white and non-white persons who applied for similar jobs, categorised as to whether or not they had been appointed, covering the two-year period prior to his own unsuccessful application for

51 COIT 1404/80.
52 [1988] IRLR 186.

promotion. The court held that the statistical material ordered was relevant as it was logically probative of whether the employers discriminated against him.

Evidence of national or regional patterns of behaviour may provide additional evidence to support a case of indirect discrimination, for example, national statistics would show that the majority of single parents are women. See **25.1.7.2** for details of sources of national statistics.

The CA made the following general points:

1 Statistical evidence may establish a discernible pattern in the treatment of a particular group; if that pattern demonstrates a regular failure of members of that group to obtain promotion in particular jobs and to under-representation in such jobs, it may give rise to an inference of discrimination. That is why the Race Relations Code of Practice recommends ethnic monitoring.[53]
2 Statistics obtained through monitoring are not conclusive in themselves, but if they show racial or ethnic imbalance or disparities, they may indicate areas of racial discrimination.
3 Any suggestion that it is unreasonable to expect employers to maintain records of the colour or ethnic origins of their employees is inconsistent with the code of practice.
4 If a practice is being operated against a group, then, in the absence of a satisfactory explanation in a particular case, it is reasonable to infer that the complainant as a member of the group has been treated less favourably on the ground of race.
5 Since the suitability of candidates can rarely be measured objectively and often requires subjective judgment, if there is evidence of a high percentage rate of failure to achieve promotion at particular levels by a certain group, this may indicate that the real reason for refusal is a conscious or unconscious racial attitude which involves stereotyped assumptions about members of that group.
6 If evidence of an employer's non-discriminatory attitude is accepted as having probative force, so is evidence of a discriminatory attitude on its part.
7 A tribunal may refuse a request for disclosure of documents if it requires the provision of material not readily to hand or if it means the employer embarking on a course which would add unreasonably to the length and cost of the hearing.

53 See also *King v Great Britain-China Centre* [1991] IRLR 513, CA.

Access to information is not always easy if, for example, large numbers of personnel records are involved. Sometimes, it is possible to build a case by pointing to less favourable treatment of other black or female employees, and they may be willing to be witnesses. Applicants should use the SDA and RRA questionnaires and tribunal discovery and written answers procedures to obtain such information (see Chapter 25). In *Carrington v Helix Lighting*,[54] the EAT said that the applicant could apply on notice to an IT for a second questionnaire to be served if necessary. However, the written answers procedure can also be used to ask additional questions (see Chapter 25).

2.14 Justifying direct discrimination

Although a respondent may rely on the specifically permitted *genuine occupational qualifications* for a job (see **5.4.3** and **6.4.1.15**) and there are certain statutory exceptions set out at **5.4** and **6.4**, neither the SDA nor the RRA makes any general provision for the justification of direct discrimination equivalent to the provision made for indirect discrimination.

Some argue that, under EC law, direct discrimination may be justified. As Professor Hepple says: this is a 'dangerous heresy' which is 'threatening to subvert the developing principle of equality in Community law'.[55] It is also based on a misinterpretation of case law, such as *Roberts v Birds Eye Walls Ltd*.[56]

Roberts is an equal pay case, concerned with a pension-bridging provision (whereby the employer gave employees top-up payments so they received the same pension benefits if they worked until the state pension age). The employer reduced the amount payable to women between the age of 60 and 65 because it was assumed that they would receive an old age pension from the state. The Advocate General considered this was direct discrimination but justifiable because the employer was trying to achieve substantial equality. The ECJ held that there was no discrimination because men and women were in a different position. The ECJ said that 'article 119 cannnot be interpreted in a way as to create unequal treatment, whereby some women gain a two-fold benefit'. This must be correct. The important point is that the same calculation was carried out for men and women; the

54 [1990] IRLR 6.
55 55 EOR 48.
56 [1994] IRLR 29.

state pension was deducted from the top-up payments. Men and women received the same total amount (from the employer and the state), so there was substantial equality.[57] As the ECJ recognised, this was not a question of justifying direct discrimination.

The HL has stated unequivocally, in *Ratcliffe*,[58] that there can be no question of justifying direct discrimination (see **21.4**).

DIRECT DISCRIMINATION: KEY POINTS

- There must be *less favourable* treatment on the ground of race or sex, though a comparison can be made with a hypothetical person. Depriving a person of choice is likely to be less favourable treatment.
- The treatment must be on the ground of sex or race. Would the woman have received the same treatment as the man *but for* the fact that she is a woman?
- It is not necessary to prove that the intention or motive was to discriminate on sexual or racial grounds. It is no defence for an employer to say that it discriminated only because of pressure from others, either customers or workers.
- It is unlawful under the RRA to discriminate on the ground of another's race. The same does not apply to sex discrimination.
- It is not necessary to show that sex or race was the only ground for the less favourable treatment – though it must be more than a factor in the chain of events leading to the less favourable treatment.
- Sexual and racial stereotyping is discriminatory. It is discriminatory to presume that women are likely to be unreliable because of childcare responsibilities.
- When comparing a man and a woman, the relevant circumstances must be the same or 'not materially different'. Any differences caused by discrimination should be ignored and it is the actual circumstances, not hypothetical ones, which are relevant. There is no need, however, to compare a pregnant woman with a man in similar circumstances, as discrimination on the ground of pregnancy is unlawful (see Chapter 17).

57 Under the SDA the 'relevant circumstances' would not be the same.
58 *Ratcliffe and Others v North Yorkshire* CC [1995] IRLR 439, HL.

- Direct discrimination can be proved by inference. This does not alter the fact that the burden of proof, under UK law at least, remains with the applicant.
- Evidence that there is a white, male-dominated workforce may point to discrimination, as may a discriminatory motive or discriminatory comments. Details of the qualifications and experience of other applicants for a job may be crucial.

CHAPTER 3

Indirect discrimination on grounds of sex and race

3.1 Introduction – the concept of indirect discrimination

Indirect discrimination is concerned with practices which have the effect, without necessarily the intention, of discriminating against women and/or racial groups, either because of past direct discrimination or existing social conditions (see Introduction). (There are no indirect discrimination provisions relating to disability – see Chapter 24.) The concept of indirect discrimination is complex, has been little understood by tribunals and courts and has too often been wrongly applied.

The concept of indirect discrimination came from America, in particular from the first decision of the Supreme Court on indirect racial discrimination, *Griggs v Duke Power Co.*[1]

In *Griggs*, job applicants and employees seeking promotion were required either to have attended high school or to pass intelligence tests. It was shown that the standard required was not significantly related to successful job performance, but the requirement disqualified blacks at a much higher rate than whites. The requirement was therefore unlawful.

The American and European definition of indirect discrimination is general and broadly defined and so can be interpreted to suit individual circumstances of the situation under review. By contrast, in UK law the SDA and RRA definition of indirect discrimination is very technical; the Acts define indirect discrimination as existing where a requirement or condition is applied which has unequal impact.

3.2 Definition

The RRA and SDA follow the same formula.

1 401 US 424, (1971) 3 FED 75.

3.2.1 *Sex Discrimination Act*

A person discriminates against another in any circumstances relevant for the purposes of any provision of the SDA if:

(b) he applies to her a requirement or condition which he applies or would apply equally to a man but -
  (i) which is such that the proportion women who can comply with it is considerably smaller than the proportion of men who can comply with it; and
  (ii) which he cannot show to be justifiable irrespective of the sex of the person to whom it is applied; and
  (iii) which is to her detriment because she cannot comply with it.

3.2.2 *Race Relations Act*

A person discriminates against another in any circumstances relevant for the purposes of any provision of the RRA if:

(b) he applies to that other a requirement or condition which he applies or would apply equally to persons not of the same racial group as that other but -
  (i) which is such that the proportion of persons of the same racial group as that other who can comply with it is considerably smaller than the proportion of persons not of that racial group who can comply with it; and
  (ii) which he cannot show to be justifiable irrespective of the colour, race, nationality or ethnic or national origins of the person to whom it is applied; and
  (iii) which is to the detriment of that other because he cannot comply with it.

This definition is concerned with 'requirements' or 'conditions' and so appears to exclude 'practices' or 'preferences' (see **3.6.2.4**). Otherwise the approach of UK law accords generally with European and American law in that it has three stages:

a) the proof by the applicant that a requirement or condition has a disproportionate adverse impact on persons of one sex, or racial group;
b) the proof by the applicant that the requirement or condition is to his/her detriment;
c) the obligation on the respondent to show that the requirement or condition is justified on grounds which are not affected by race, sex or marital status.

However, the way in which UK statute law has been interpreted does not always correspond with the European law approach which is more concerned with the overall effect.

3.3 Direct and indirect discrimination in EC law compared

In European law it is sometimes said that direct discrimination occurs when the same circumstances are treated differently, ie, two equally qualified applicants of different sexes apply for a job. The man is shortlisted, the women is not. Their identical circumstances have been treated differently and if this is on the ground of race or sex this is direct discrimination.

Indirect discrimination occurs when different circumstances are treated in the same way. For example, women have a shorter average height compared to men. A decision not to employ anyone less than 1.75 metres tall treats every group as if they are the same without taking account of their different circumstances. Indirect discrimination is concerned with requirements or conditions which appear to treat all equally but in fact, because the circumstances of the different sexes are not the same, they impact harder on one sex than the other. However, indirect discrimination will not be unlawful if it is justifiable.

In a draft Directive on the Burden of Proof in Cases of Discrimination based on Sex the European Commission have proposed a definition for indirect discrimination based on the case-law of the ECJ:

> . . . indirect discrimination exists where an apparently neutral provision, criterion or practice disproportionately disadvantages the members of one sex, by reference inter alia to marital or family status, unless the aim pursued corresponds to a real need of the undertaking or meets a necessary aim of the social policy of a Member State, in itself is completely unrelated to sex and as such is objectively justified and unless the means of achieving this aim are appropriate and necessary . . .

As with direct discrimination, indirect discrimination can affect a worker on grounds of race or sex either at the recruitment stage[2] or at work[3] or in dismissal.[4] Examples of indirect discrimination are given in Chapters 5, 6 and 8.

2 SDA s6(1); RRA s4(1).
3 SDA s6(2)(a); RRA s4(2)(a).
4 SDA s6(2)(b); RRA s4(2)(c).

3.4 No need to prove an intention to discriminate

There is no need to prove that the discriminator intended to discriminate and often there is no such intention. If the requirement or condition was imposed by an employer because s/he knew it would be to the disadvantage of an employee there may be direct discrimination. For example, it would be direct discrimination for a firm to impose a 'no beard' rule in order to exclude Sikhs. Advisers should always consider both direct and indirect discrimination (see **3.6.2.3**).

3.5 Compensation

In unintentional indirect sex discrimination cases compensation can now be awarded.[5]

Damages cannot be awarded for indirect race discrimination unless the employer can show that it did not intend to discriminate (see **26.1.7**).[6] In *J H Walker v Hussain and Others*[7] the EAT held that if the respondent is aware of the discriminatory effect of the requirement or condition s/he will be liable to pay damages.

3.6 Proving indirect discrimination

A number of specific questions must be answered in order to prove indirect discrimination (whether on the ground of sex or race). In *Raval v DHSS and Civil Service Commission*[8] (a race discrimination case) the EAT adopted the 10 questions posed by the applicant's counsel and this approach has been followed in other cases. The questions are set out below, though some have been subdivided to deal with issues which did not arise in Ms Raval's case.

The way that the EAT answered these questions in *Raval* was sometimes wrong or confused. Moreover, the EAT did not have to consider European law because it was a race discrimination case. However, these questions still provide a useful framework for the consideration of indirect discrimination.

5 Sex Discrimination and Equal Pay (Miscellaneous Amendments) Regulations 1996 SI No 428.
6 See RRA s57(3).
7 [1996] IRLR 11.
8 [1985] IRLR 370.

3.6.1 *Question 1: Does the applicant belong to the racial group(s) or gender that s/he claims?*

The purpose of this question is to define the groups to be compared to assess whether there is disparate impact.

In sex discrimination cases, the comparison is relatively straightforward: it is between men and women in the relevant pool.

In race discrimination cases the comparison is more difficult. 'Racial group' is defined by colour, race, nationality or ethnic or national origins.[9] It will be for the applicant to choose the racial group(s) to which s/he claims s/he belongs. S/he may fall within a number of different racial groups.

Although there are similarities between the types of discrimination experienced by ethnic minorities, there are also many important differences between racial groups. The characteristics and economic and social circumstances of different racial groups vary enormously.

A minimum height requirement may disqualify most Asians but very few West Indians. A requirement to wear skirts may have an adverse impact on Asian Muslim women but would not affect West Indian or other Asian women. In some cases a comparison between whites and non-whites might reveal little disparity. However if the comparison were between Asians and non-Asians a disparity might be quite obvious.

RRA s3(2) states that the fact that a racial group comprises two or more racial groups does not prevent it from constituting a particular racial group. So, for instance, in a particular case, all non-whites, all Asians, or all West Indians, could be described as one racial group. On the other hand, sub-groups of these groups could also comprise a racial group, so that Sikhs could constitute a racial group. Thus a requirement or condition which has a disparate impact on any identifiable racial group(s) may be challengeable.

3.6.1.1 *Choosing the right group for comparison*

It is important to define the racial group carefully; choosing the wrong group, even if the applicant belongs to it, may be fatal to the case, as disparate impact must be proved (see questions 5–7 below).

It is advisable to consider and argue other racial groups to which the applicant may belong bearing in mind the need to show disparate impact. This is often best dealt with by agreement, if possible, before the main hearing.

9 See RRA s3.

In *Orphanos v Queen Mary College*,[10] a Cypriot citizen of Greek nationality alleged that the college's policy of charging higher fees to overseas students (defined as those who had not been resident in the UK or another EU country for the previous three years) was indirectly discriminatory on the ground of race. It was agreed by the parties that Mr Orphanos belonged to three racial groups – Cypriot, non-British and non-EU – and that the proportion of such groups who could comply with a permanent residence requirement or an ordinary residence requirement was considerably smaller than the proportion of persons not of that racial group.

The HL said that, although it could proceed simply on the basis of this admission, without considering whether it had been made correctly, it felt that it should attempt to clarify the position. Its views are therefore obiter, though no doubt will be of persuasive value.

It is interesting that the Lords agreed that Mr Orphanos belonged to three racial groups and that racial groups can be defined negatively as, for instance, non-British and non-EU. They also accepted that fewer non-British than British, and non-EU than EU, people could comply with the requirement in question. They did not accept that fewer Cypriots than non-Cypriots could comply.

The comparison, they said, must be between the case of a person of the same racial group as Mr Orphanos and the case of a person not of that racial group, but it must be such that 'the relevant circumstances in the one case are the same, or not materially different, in the other' (see **3.6.5**). The relevant circumstances were that Mr Orphanos wished to be admitted as a student at the college, so the comparison must be between persons of the same racial group as he who wished to be admitted, and persons not of that racial group who so wished. The Lords thought that no sensible comparison could be made between a group consisting of those of Cypriot nationality and those not of Cypriot nationality, as it would be impracticable to ascertain the numbers of such persons wishing to be admitted to the college.

There is nothing in the decision to indicate whether the Lords even considered comparing Cypriots with British (rather than non-Cypriots); if they had, disparate impact could have been proved. Nor was it clear from the judgment whether the comparison was between Cypriots and non-Cypriots in the UK or in the world. It would not be so difficult to assess the relative numbers in the UK, as the majority of non-Cypriots would be British and it would be possible to show that

10 [1985] IRLR 349.

fewer Cypriots than non-Cypriots could comply with the requirement. If the Lords, as it appears, were not restricting the comparison to the UK then the comparison does indeed become impossible. Not only were the Lords' comments in relation to Cypriots and non-Cypriots obiter but they are so fraught with uncertainties that they cannot and should not be followed in subsequent cases.

The lesson from *Orphanos* is that it is important for applicants who fall into a number of racial groups to argue these in the alternative, taking account of questions 5, 6 and 7 below.

3.6.2 *Question 2: Has the respondent applied any requirement or condition to the applicant?*

3.6.2.1 *What does 'requirement' or 'condition' mean?*

There is a substantial overlap between requirement and condition. The EAT has said that the purpose of the draughtsmen in using both words must have been to extend the ambit of what is covered so as to include anything which fairly falls within the ordinary meaning of either word and should not be given a narrow construction. In *Clarke v Eley Kynoch Ltd*,[11] the employer argued that a procedure whereby part-time workers were dismissed first could not be a requirement, as a requirement meant that the person had to do a certain act. The EAT disagreed, saying that requirement meant a provision which a person has to fulfil to obtain a benefit.

In one case, the employer argued that full-time work was not a requirement but an essential part of the job. The EAT rejected the argument saying that:

> Requirement or condition are plain words of wide import fully capable (for example) of including an obligation of full-time work and there was no basis for giving them a restrictive interpretation in the light of the policy underlying the Act or in the light of public policy.[12]

However, in *Clymo v Wandsworth LBC* [13] the EAT held that the employers had not 'applied' a requirement or condition in refusing to allow a woman who was formerly employed full-time to change her hours. The EAT said that full-time working was a requirement or condition of the terms of employment but was not something which

11 [1982] IRLR 482.
12 *Holmes v Home Office* [1984] IRLR 299 at p301.
13 [1989] IRLR 241.

the employers had positively 'applied' to her other than when they had offered her employment. The EAT drew an extraordinary distinction between different types of jobs, saying that if a cleaner is required to work full-time it would clearly be a requirement or condition, whereas in the case of a managing director it would be in the nature of the appointment and not a requirement or condition.

In *Briggs v North Eastern Education and Library Board*[14] the Northern Ireland Court of Appeal followed the earlier case of *Home Office v Holmes*[15] instead of *Clymo* and held that an obligation to work full-time was indeed a requirement. This is the better authority. Moreover, it has been accepted under EC law that discrimination against part-time workers may be unlawful[16] and, in the case of doubt, UK law should be interpreted so as not to conflict with EC law.

With the exception of *Clymo*, the courts and tribunals have agreed that a wide interpretation should be given to 'requirement' and 'condition'. This, they have said, is in line with the American cases and with the purpose of the legislation, which is to eliminate practices which have a disproportionate impact on women.[17] Recent cases have found that an obligation to work extra hours,[18] or to change shift patterns were requirements or conditions under the Act.[19] See also **14.3.1**.

3.6.2.2 Requirements/conditions with future consequences

A requirement or condition can include one which has not yet taken effect or been implemented. In *Meade-Hill and NUCPS v British Council*[20] there was a mobility clause in a woman's contract of employment. This required any employee above grade G to work in any part of the UK as dictated by her employers. Even though she had not yet been required to move the CA held that this clause could be potentially indirectly discriminatory because a greater proportion of women than men were secondary earners and therefore less able or willing to move.

14 [1990] IRLR 181; see also EAT judgment in *British Telecom plc v Roberts* [1996] IRLR 601.

15 [1984] IRLR 229.

16 See *Bilka-Kaufhaus GmbH v Weber von Hartz* [1986] IRLR 317, ECJ.

17 See *Watches of Switzerland Ltd v Savell* [1983] IRLR 141.

18 See *Robinson v Oddbins Ltd* Case no 4225/95, IT, approved by EAT Case no 188/96.

19 See *Edwards v London Underground Ltd* [1995] IRLR 355 and EAT/16/96 and *Headley and Others v Copygraphic Ltd* (1996) 30 EOR DCLD.

20 [1995] IRLR 478.

3.6.2.3 Is it really direct discrimination?

It is important to note that some conditions or requirements are so linked to gender or race that they are in reality not cases of indirect discrimination at all. For instance, a condition or requirement to be white (in order to be eligible for, say, promotion) would not be indirect but direct discrimination.

Sometimes the link is not quite so obvious. The application of a sex- or race-based requirement or condition will be an act of direct discrimination. For example, in *James v Eastleigh BC*[21] the council gave reduced price admission to persons of pensionable age. The HL reversed the decision of the CA that this was indirect discrimination. It held that because women were pensionable at the age of 60 and men at 65 the criterion was sex-based. It directly discriminated against men in favour of women.

3.6.2.4 Where to find the requirement or condition

Requirements and conditions are often hidden, and may be difficult to define under the statutes. The way in which the requirement or condition is defined is crucial, as a failure to identify correctly a requirement or condition could result in the defeat of what would otherwise be a good claim.

Requirements and conditions may be explicit or implied. They may be found, for example, in:

- a job description;
- a contract of employment;
- a collective agreement;
- notices, letters or memos;
- union rules or procedures;
- employment practices.

It may not always be clear whether the employer is applying a requirement. In *Thorndyke v Bell Fruit (North Central) Ltd*,[22] the IT said that although a requirement not to have young children was 'not made explicit' it was in the employer's mind and this was sufficient. The employer had made a note of this on the successful applicant's form. Similarly, the requirement to work full-time may not be stated but is often implicit; it is nonetheless a job requirement.

In *Weaver v National Association of Teachers in Further and*

21 [1990] IRLR 288.
22 [1979] IRLR 1.

Higher Education[23] a union member argued that it was indirectly discriminatory for the union to refuse to act for her because it had a policy not to support the claim of one member when another member's job was at stake. The union argued that there was no condition, as the policy related to the nature of the complaint. The applicant argued that the condition was that assistance would be provided only on condition that this was not a complaint of race discrimination which threatened another member's job. The EAT rejected the argument that there was no condition but held that the condition was: 'You cannot bring a claim if one of our members' jobs is at risk.' This made it impossible to prove disparate impact as it affected black and white members equally (see **3.6.6**).

It is important to look very carefully at what is required and to extract from practices and procedures requirements that discriminate on the ground of sex or race and consider which requirement is appropriate. The questionnaire procedure may be very useful in teasing out what requirements or conditions have been applied if they are not explicit (see **25.8**).

A typical advertisement might read:

> SCREWETT AND FIXIT LTD
> Require full-time manager for sales department.
> Applicants should be:
> – a graduate from a UK university
> – experienced in dealing with engineering parts
> – able to travel at short notice
> – willing to work overtime when required
> – aged under 28
> – able to communicate well.

In this advertisement there are seven requirements with which applicants must comply to be eligible for the job – the six different aspects of the person specification and the requirement to work full-time.

3.6.2.5 *Is the requirement or condition an absolute bar?*

Under the SDA and RRA the applicant must establish that s/he *has* to comply with a requirement or condition; it has to be a 'must'. It is not enough to show that factors taken into account by the employer merely weigh against the applicant or in favour of other applicants.

In *Perera v Civil Service Commission* (*No 2*),[24] Mr Perera, in a

23 EAT 551/87.
24 [1983] IRLR 166.

complaint of race discrimination, argued that his employer had taken into account various factors, such as experience in the UK, command of English and age, all of which worked to his disadvantage, and that these were, therefore, requirements or conditions. The CA said that none of the factors could be regarded as a requirement or condition in the sense that lack of any of them would be an absolute bar to getting the job; absence of one could be offset by another quality. In other words, unless an employer makes compliance with one or all of the factors a precondition for getting the job it does not amount to a requirement.

The court pointed out that a brilliant man who lacked one of the relevant factors might have been promoted. Yet in this case higher standards were imposed on those who, because of their race or sex, suffered the sort of disadvantage that Mr Perera did.

In *Meer v LB Tower Hamlets*[25] the CA followed *Perera* and held that a preference of Tower Hamlets for employees with local knowledge was not a requirement or condition. This approach has been much criticised. Such a preference certainly disadvantaged some racial groups. It seems clear that the failure to treat it as an act of indirect discrimination is not consistent with the approach taken in *Griggs* and is wrong (see **3.1**). It was recognised in *Meer* that EC law may not require proof that a requirement or condition was an absolute bar. In *Hall v Shorts Missile Systems*[26] the Northern Ireland Court of Appeal approved *Meer*. However, leave to appeal to the House of Lords has been granted in this case.

However, a careful definition of the requirement or condition may avoid this pitfall. The case of *Watches of Switzerland Ltd v Savell*[27] is a good example. Ms Savell argued that a promotion procedure was discriminatory on the ground of sex. She gave a number of reasons, including the fact that impending appointments were not advertised to staff and women were less likely than men to ask to be considered for promotion, that persons under consideration for promotion were not interviewed, and that the criteria for promotion were subjective (see **11.5.3.1**).

The tribunal accepted that there was a 'requirement' or condition that:

> to be promoted to the post of manager in a London branch of the retail business owned by the appellant one must satisfy the criteria of a vague,

25 [1988] IRLR 399.
26 (1997) 72 EOR 39.
27 [1983] IRLR 141.

> subjective, unadvertised promotion procedure which does not provide any or any adequate mechanisms to prevent subconscious bias unrelated to the merits of candidates or prospective candidates for the post of manager.[28]

In *Watches of Switzerland v Savell* compliance with the overall recruitment procedure (which included preferences) was a requirement or condition. This was a clever but apt way around the problems set out above. A similar requirement or condition could be constructed in the context of most practices or procedures which adversely affect women if the 'requirement' or 'condition' is said to be 'compliance with a practice or procedure'.

The approach of the CA in *Meer* is certainly inconsistent with the 'result-orientated' approach of EC law. There is nothing in the Treaty of Rome art 119 or the ETD which requires that there be a 'requirement or condition'. They are concerned with 'hurdles' to equal treatment (see *Enderby v Frenchay Health Authority*[29]).

The difference between the EC and UK approaches was emphasised in the decision of the EAT in *Bhudi v IMI Refiners Ltd.*[30] The IT held that Mrs Bhudi's employers had not indirectly discriminated against her when they dismissed the evening cleaners who were all female in preference to the daytime cleaners who were all male. The IT held that there was no requirement or condition because the employers explained that the reason for the dismissal was that the evening cleaners required disproportionate administration. The EAT refused to interpret the SDA in accordance with *Enderby* (where the ECJ held that there was no need to identify a requirement or condition in indirect discrimination cases) and held that a 'requirement or condition' must be established. However, it allowed the appeal and remitted the case on alternative grounds holding that in effect there may have been a requirement or condition not to work outside normal hours.

This case might also have been argued as a case of direct discrimination as the cleaners were entirely segregated by sex: male cleaners working during the day and females at night. The fact that the evening workers were entirely female may itself raise a presumption of direct discrimination.

Thus, it is important to define the requirement with precision as it may well affect the way in which disproportionate adverse impact is

28 Ibid, at p145.
29 [1993] IRLR 591.
30 [1994] IRLR 204.

proved (see questions below). Where there is some ambiguity, alternative formulations can and should be pleaded.[31]

3.6.3 *Question 3: When was such requirement or condition applied to the applicant? (the 'material time')*

This question is whether the applicant could comply with the requirement or condition at the time when it was applied to him/her. It will not be relevant that at a different time s/he might have been able to comply with the requirement or condition.

In *CRE v Dutton*,[32] where a pub refused to serve 'travellers', the CA held that the moment when ability to comply with a requirement falls to be judged is the date at which the requirement has to be fulfilled. The requirement in *Dutton* was not to be a traveller and it was alleged that fewer gypsies than non-gypsies could comply with this. Ability to comply had to be judged at the time the gypsy was outside the pub wishing to enter rather than at some other date when the gypsy could have acquired housing accommodation and therefore become able to meet the condition for entrance.

This EAT in *Clarke v Eley Kynoch Ltd* followed *Dutton* (above). The *Clarke* case concerned the decision to make part-time workers redundant first. The employers argued that one of the part-time workers could, in the past, have transferred to full-time work, though she could not have done so at the time that the redundancies were being negotiated. The EAT said that the relevant time was when the redundancies were taking place and it was irrelevant that she could have transferred to full-time work in the past.

In *Meade-Hill* (above) the Court of Appeal decided that the impact of a requirement is to be judged at the time it comes to be incorporated into the contract between the parties not at the point when it becomes reasonably foreseeable that the applicant will be unable to comply with it nor when the employer seeks to enforce the requirement. However, it is arguable that when the employer comes to enforce the requirement a further condition/requirement arises which may, in turn, be challengeable. In any event the requirement is likely to be different as it is likely to be a requirement to move to a particular location or locations.

It is often difficult to ascertain when the relevant act was done. In *Cast v Croydon College*[33] Ms Cast informed her employers of her

31 See *Meer v LB Tower Hamlets* [1988] IRLR 399.
32 [1989] IRLR 8.
33 [1997] IRLR 14.

pregnancy and before she went on maternity leave asked to return either on a part-time basis or on a job share. This was refused. On her return to work she renewed her requests for part-time work which were again refused. The EAT found that the requests were not a continuing act of discrimination and that the only challengeable act was the first refusal. So, the material time for judging the detriment was the date the request was first refused, namely, before she went on maternity leave. This decision cannot be right: either there was a continuing act of discrimination or alternatively the refusals of part-time working which occurred after her return to work were further separate acts of discrimination. The later refusals should be viewed as separate acts since by then her position and circumstances had changed. The EAT decision has the absurd effect that a woman is better off giving her employer no prior notice of her wish to return to work on a part-time basis after maternity leave. Alternatively, she will be forced to issue proceedings close to the time of birth and before she returns to work. This decision cannot be to the benefit of employers or employees. It is being appealed to the CA.

3.6.4 *Question 4: Did such requirement or condition apply equally to other persons not of the same sex/racial group as the applicant?*

The applicant must show that the requirement or condition applies or would apply equally to a man or a person not of the same racial group. If the requirement or condition is not applied equally to men and women, or different racial groups, it is not indirect discrimination. Different requirements for men and women or different racial groups is properly characterised as direct discrimination (see *James v Eastleigh BC* discussed above).

3.6.5 *Questions 5 and 6: The 'relevant circumstances' and the pool*

In *Raval*, the EAT stated that questions 5 and 6 were as follows:

> 5 What are the relevant circumstances necessary to ensure that the proportionate comparison to be made under s1(1)(b)(i) complies with the 'like with like' requirement in RRA s3(4); SDA s5(3)?
> 6 Within what section of the community does the proportionate comparison fall to be made?

Questions 5 and 6 are so closely connected that it makes more sense to look at them together. Indirect discrimination involves looking at the comparative effect of requirements and conditions on men and women or different racial groups to ascertain whether they have a disproportionately adverse effect on one sex or racial group.

3.6.5.1 Compare like with like

Both Acts say that the 'relevant circumstances' for the comparison of the impact of the requirement or condition must be the same or not materially different.[34]

In *Price v Civil Service Commission*,[35] for example, the civil service required job applicants to be under the age of 28. The EAT said that the comparison was not between all men and all women, it was between men and women who might wish to apply for the job and who were qualified to obtain the job because they met another requirement which was not challenged, ie, that they had two 'A' levels.

In sex discrimination cases, the pool will be a section of men and women as defined by the relevant circumstances. In race discrimination cases the pool will comprise a section of the racial group into which the applicant falls under question 1 above, as defined by the relevant circumstances. The pool will consist of the people who wish to obtain the benefit on offer who are suitably qualified for it, *and* also those people who would be suitably qualified for it if the challenged requirement were not applied. The requirement or condition in question may be posed in a negative way so that it is concerned with selection for a detriment such as redundancy. In that case the pool will consist of those who avoid the detriment because they do not meet the condition or requirement for selection for the detriment *and* those who would avoid the detriment but for the challenged requirement. The comparison between men and women, or different racial groups will then take place within that pool of people.

It has been suggested that if the challenge is to the only job requirement, eg, one 'A' level, the comparison should be between women and men generally, as everyone would be qualified apart from those who cannot comply with the challenged requirement. If the challenge is to one of two or more requirements, the comparison

34 SDA s5(3); RRA s3(4).
35 [1977] IRLR 291.

should be between men and women qualified in other ways, apart from the requirement in dispute.[36]

The major problem with looking only at qualified applicants, as pointed out by the applicant in *Pearse v City of Bradford*[37] is that it is often difficult to obtain the actual information about the numbers of potentially qualified applicants. If it is not immediately available, there is a limit to the extent that a tribunal will go to order an employer to discover or create documents necessary to compile the evidence (but see **25.9.3**).

3.6.5.2 *What are the relevant circumstances?*

The relevant circumstances will vary from case to case according to who is affected by the condition or requirement. It may be the whole population of the UK or the employees of a particular workplace or those who have a particular qualification (within a particular workforce or generally).

3.6.5.3 *The relevant circumstances must not be discriminatory*

Care must be taken to ensure that the 'relevant circumstances' are not themselves discriminatory.

In *Kidd v DRG (UK) Ltd*,[38] the applicant challenged as discriminatory on marital grounds a redundancy procedure whereby part-time workers were dismissed first (the requirement being to work full-time). The EAT said that the pool was the section of the population living in households needing to provide child care to an extent that would normally be incompatible with acceptance of full-time employment by the person providing it. By defining the relevant circumstances as the need to provide care for children, the EAT restricted the pool to those who largely could not comply with the requirement to be a full-time worker, omitting all those who could comply with it, thus making it very difficult to show disparate impact.

As a matter of law it must be wrong to limit the pool by the very factors (such as child care responsibilities) which gave rise to the applicant's inability to comply with the requirement. The whole point is to compare the effect of a requirement on both the 'advantaged' and 'disadvantaged' group, not between two sections of a 'disadvan-

36 See R Townshend-Smith *Sex Discrimination in Employment Law: law, practice and theory* (Sweet & Maxwell, 1989), p71.

37 [1988] IRLR 379.

38 [1985] IRLR 190.

taged' group. Applicants should therefore take great care in their choice of pool. It is unlikely that the EAT would follow the approach in *Kidd* now that there have been so many ECJ decisions in which the adverse impact of a requirement or condition on female part-time workers has been upheld as indirectly discriminatory.

This was emphasised correctly in *R v Secretary of State for Education ex p Schaffter*[39] where the applicant challenged, as indirectly discriminatory on the ground of sex, a statutory education scheme which restricted hardship grants for lone parents to those parents who had been married. This scheme was outside the SDA because it was made under statutory authority and the applicant relied on the ETD. The evidence was that 80% of lone parents are female, although equal proportions of male and female lone parents had previously been married. The court held that to limit the pool to only unmarried lone parents would build discrimination into the comparison because women were more likely to be unmarried and to have parental responsibility. The court held that the correct pool was that of all lone parents thereby avoiding the discriminatory effect of selecting the smaller pool.

3.6.5.4 *Size of the group or pool*

The result of the comparison may differ according to the size (and identity) of the groups chosen. If, in the case of part-time workers, the pool were all men and women in the labour market (as opposed to a particular workforce), given that 82% of part-time workers in the labour market are women,[40] disparate impact would be proven, whether there were 100 or 500 or no full-time male workers in the workforce. The actual composition of the workforce would be irrelevant. Far fewer women in general can comply with a requirement to work full-time because it tends to be women who are primarily responsible for child care.

3.6.5.5 *Defining the pool by area*

The pool might be limited to a local area, the UK or extend across the world. In cases where the essential issue concerns the requirements or conditions for application for a particular job and there is no geographical restriction on the area from which persons may apply, the pool may be the 'travel to work' area for the job. But if the job is a mobile one or a fairly senior one, a wider area would be more

39 [1987] IRLR 53, HC.
40 *Labour Market Trends* (March 1997), p99.

appropriate. In many cases jobs are advertised nationally, in which case the national pool of potential applicants for the job will be relevant.

3.6.5.6 Internal pools

Where the challenge is to a practice which only affects the workforce (such as a redundancy procedure or promotion) the pool may be existing employees, but see *Edwards (No 2)* below.

In *Fulton and Others v Strathclyde RC*,[41] the applicants complained that their employer's failure to make full-time job vacancies open to part-timers on a job-share basis was indirectly discriminatory. The applicants were part-time social workers, who worked under temporary contracts but had been promised permanent part-time posts in the future. When vacancies for full-time social workers arose, four women applied for two posts on a job-sharing basis, but the council refused to consider their application. They argued that this was indirect discrimination. The IT said that the 'pool' was qualified social workers employed by the council (the jobs were advertised only internally), and the number of women who could comply with the requirement was only 10% smaller than the pool of men. The appellants challenged this on appeal saying that, since the council employed fewer part-timers than any other Scottish Region, it was likely to employ fewer women and therefore the calculations should have been weighted to reflect this. The EAT, upholding the IT decision, said that the SDA made no provision for 'built-in' discrimination in calculating the pool and in any case it was a finding of fact which could not be overturned. However, this is arguably wrong and inconsistent with *Edwards (No 2)* (see below).

In *Pearse v City of Bradford MC*,[42] the applicant challenged an employer's requirement that only full-time employees could apply for a post. She chose as the pool all the staff at the college. The IT held that the pool should be restricted to those qualified for the post. As the applicant had produced statistical evidence relating only to the entire staff, as opposed to the qualified staff, her claim was dismissed. The EAT said that the selection of an appropriate section of the population for comparison is a matter for the good sense of the tribunal.

The choice of pool is crucial. The same claim of discrimination

41 EAT 949/83.
42 [1988] IRLR 379.

(say, against part-time workers) could succeed in one workforce but fail in another, just because of the composition of the workforce. In *Kidd*, for example (**3.6.5.3** above), there was an all-female workforce, comprising part-time and full-time workers. If the pool had been the workforce and the complaint one of sex discrimination (as opposed to marital discrimination) no disparity could have been proved. If there had been one man working full-time (and no men working part-time) disparity on the basis of sex discrimination could have been proved, as 100% of the men in the workforce could comply with the requirement (the one man), but a much smaller percentage of women could comply. The EAT has said that SDA s1(1)(b) applies to men and women generally and not to the accidental fact that, at any particular time, within a limited pool of equally qualified persons, there happen to be considerably more men than women.[43]

Where the pool is too small and hence statistically unreliable(according to the presence or absence of a few people) it is appropriate for the court to take account of national statistics or patterns. In *London Underground Ltd v Edwards (No 2)*[44] where all the 2,000 men could comply with the requirement and only 1 of the 21 women could not comply, the EAT held that:

> in assessing the extent of the disproportionate effect, the tribunal is entitled to take account of a wider perspective. It is for this reason that statistics showing the percentage of women in employment who have primary care responsibility for a child, in contrast to the percentage of men in that position are relevant.

This argument could have been used in the *Fulton* case (above).

3.6.5.7 National pools

The EAT has held that a pool for comparison does not have to be shown to be a statistically perfect match of the persons who would be capable of and interested in filling the post offered. In *Greater Manchester Police Authority v Lea*[45] (see **3.6.7.3**), the EAT held that the IT could decide that the economically active population was an appropriate pool of persons for the purpose of determining the proportion of men and women who could comply with a condition of not being in receipt of an occupational pension, notwithstanding that the statistical base was wider than perfection would have dictated.

43 *Turnbull and Another v Record Production Chapel and Others* (1984) EAT 955/83.
44 [1997] IRLR 157.
45 [1990] IRLR 372.

In *University of Manchester v Jones*,[46] Ms Jones was a mature graduate of 46 years who applied for a job as a careers adviser. The employers expressed a preference for candidates between 27 and 35 years old. She challenged the age restriction. The CA held that the appropriate pool for comparison was all those who had the required qualifications excluding the requirement that was the subject of the complaint. The requirement cannot be sub-divided so as to fit an individual case. In this case the CA held that the correct pool was that of graduates and not merely mature graduates, since the potential job applicants were not limited to mature graduates, only to graduates.

If the practice relates to job applicants, the pool should include at least all those who may have wished to apply for the job. If it does not do so, all those who were deterred from applying because of the impugned requirement will be excluded (see *Orphanos* at **3.6.1.1** and *Fulton* at **3.6.5.6**). It may be impossible to get these statistics, in which case applicants should try to produce the relevant national statistics to support their point.

3.6.5.8 Geographical distortions

In some cases local factors may produce a geographical distortion. Although this may happen in sex discrimination cases (there could be a particular workforce where the vast majority of part-timers are men) it is fairly rare, as men and women are distributed evenly all over the country. In race discrimination cases, however, the number of non-whites in the labour market is relatively small and often concentrated in certain parts of the country, particularly inner-city areas. A person complaining of a discriminatory requirement in an area where s/he is the only person in his/her racial group, may find it hard to prove reliable statistical disparity as s/he would be the only person of his/her racial group in the pool. Although strictly speaking s/he may be able to show that 0% of people in his/her racial group could comply with the requirement (ie, him/herself) the courts may be unwilling to accept such statistical data as being representative. If this is the case, the pool must be increased to comprise a representative sample but see *Edwards (No 2)* (above).

3.6.5.9 Ascertaining the pool

Ideally the parties should agree on the relevant pool. If this is not possible, the safest way of proceeding is to put forward alternative

46 [1993] IRLR 218.

pools and provide statistical evidence in relation to each one. The questionnaire procedure can be used (see 25.8).

If there is doubt about the identity of the pool it can be decided by the IT as a preliminary point. If this is not done, then the statistical evidence adduced (sometimes at some cost) may prove to be irrelevant.

3.6.6 Question 7: Statistical disparity

> 7 Does the application of the proportionate comparison within such community section result in a finding that the proportion of women who could comply with the condition or requirement at the material time is considerably smaller than the proportion of men?

Question 7 is concerned with proof of unequal treatment as shown by the disparity between the effect of the requirement or condition on women and men or between one racial group and those not of that racial group. In most cases, detailed statistical evidence will be required. While some courts and tribunals are prepared to take judicial notice of 'ordinary' behaviour, others are reluctant to do so. It is never safe to assume that tribunals will make any assumptions about 'normal practice'.

3.6.6.1 A proportionate comparison

The SDA and RRA pose the question as whether a *considerably smaller proportion* of the relevant group *can comply* with the requirement.

ETD art 2, however, provides:

> . . . the application of the principle of equal treatment means that there shall be no discrimination **whatsoever** on grounds of sex either directly or indirectly . . .

The ETD makes no mention of 'considerably smaller' or of 'proportions' nor does it limit its consideration to those who 'can comply'. This should influence the interpretation of the SDA as it must be interpreted in line with the ETD. So in *R v Secretary of State for Employment ex p Seymour Smith*[47] the CA held:

> . . . the underlying principle is equal treatment. It will be remembered that by article 2.1 of the ET Directive the principle of equal treatment means that 'there shall be no discrimination whatsoever on grounds of sex'. Accordingly, the weight to be attached to the word 'considerable' must not be exaggerated.

47 [1995] IRLR 464.

Applicants need to show that within the appropriate 'pool' there is a considerably smaller proportion of his/her race or sex who can comply with the requirement.

For example, in the case of a job requiring people over 1.75 metres tall, women or Asian men might claim that they were disadvantaged. If a woman wished to challenge this she would need to make the following comparison:

Women	*Men*
1. Find the number of women in the relevant pool (call this 'W in pool').	4. Find the number of men in the relevant pool ('M in pool').
2. Ascertain the number of women in the pool who can comply with the requirement, ie, are over 1.75 metres tall ('W can comply').	5. Ascertain the number of men in the pool who can comply with the requirement, ie, are over 1.75 metres tall ('M can comply').
3. Divide the number of women who can comply, ie, are over 1.75 metres tall, by the number of women in the pool.	6. Divide the number of men who can comply, ie, are over 1.75 metres tall, by the total number of men.

The two proportions found at steps 3 and 6 above can then be compared, by asking whether 3 (the left-hand side of the next box) is considerably smaller than 6 (the right-hand side of the next box).

It can be seen that the key question in a sex discrimination case can be stated:

$$\text{Is } \frac{\text{W can comply}}{\text{W in pool}} \text{ considerably smaller than } \frac{\text{M can comply}}{\text{M in pool}} ?$$

Similarly, if an Asian thought that s/he had suffered indirect discrimination the steps would be:

Asians	*Non-Asians*
1. Find the number of Asians in the relevant pool (call this 'A in pool').	4. Find the number of non-Asians in the relevant pool ('N-A in pool').
2. Ascertain the number of Asians in the pool who can comply with the requirement, ie, are over 1.75 metres tall ('A can comply').	5. Ascertain the number of non-Asians in the pool who can comply with the requirement, ie, are over 1.75 metres tall ('N-A can comply').
3. Divide the number of Asians who can comply, ie, are over 1.75 metres tall, by the number of Asians in the pool.	6. Divide the number of non-Asians who can comply, ie, are over 1.75 metres tall, by the total number of non-Asians.

Again the two proportions found at steps 3 and 6 above are then compared, by asking whether 3 (the left-hand side of the next box) is considerably smaller than 6 (the right-hand side of the next box).

The key question in a race discrimination case in which the racial group in question is Asians can be stated as:

$$\text{Is } \frac{\text{A can comply}}{\text{A in pool}} \text{ considerably smaller than } \frac{\text{N-A can comply}}{\text{N-A in pool}} \text{ ?}$$

If there was a different racial group appropriate changes to the question would have to be made.

3.6.6.2 *What is considerably smaller?*

'Considerably smaller' does not mean that there has to be a large difference. What is being considered is equal treatment which means no discrimination whatsoever. If the pool is large enough then a small difference in the two percentages may be important, because it may show that a large *number* of people are actually disadvantaged.

In *R v Secretary of State for Employment ex p Seymour Smith*[48] two women challenged the two-year qualification period for unfair dismissal protection as being indirectly discriminatory against women. They were able to show that between 1985 and 1991 the percentage of the female working population disadvantaged by the requirement was 8% larger than the percentage of the male population who were so disadvantaged. A key reason for this was that women have, on average, shorter periods of continuous employment, mainly because of breaks to have and care for children. The CA held:

> before a presumption of indirect discrimination on the ground of sex arises there must be a considerable difference in the *number* or *percentage* of one sex in the *advantaged* or *disadvantaged* group as against the other sex and not simply a difference which is more than de minimis.

The CA found that in 1985, for example, there were 370,000 more women disadvantaged by the qualification than would have been expected had there been no discrimination. They went on to point out that this represented 5% of the total female working population and concluded that this did raise the presumption of indirect discrimination.

3.6.6.3 The Jones prediction test

The CA in *Jones v Chief Adjudication Officer*[49] and *R v Secretary of State ex p Seymour Smith* (above) formulated a test for indirect discrimination which started by considering what the outcome should be if there were equal treatment and then considering what the difference was between that predicted and the actual outcome. This approach starts with the assumption that the same proportion of men and women should be able to comply with the requirement as the proportion of men and women in the workforce. Finally, one looks at how many fewer women than men can comply.

In *Jones* the CA said:

> What we must consider is whether, if one looks not at individuals but at the population of claimants as a whole, it can be seen that there is indirect discrimination. The parties agree that for this purpose it is the effect, not the intent, of the legislation which counts. They also agree

48 [1995] IRLR 464.

49 [1990] IRLR 533 (a social security case).

that what was called the 'demographic' argument represents one way in which indirect discrimination can be established. As I understand it, the process for establishing discrimination on this basis takes the following shape. (For ease of illustration, I will assume that the complaint stems from the failure of a woman to satisfy a relevant positive qualification for selection, and that only one such qualification is in issue.)
1. Identify the criterion for selection;
2. Identify the relevant population, comprising all those who satisfy all the other criteria for selection . . . ;
3. Divide the relevant population into groups representing those who satisfy the criterion and those who do not;
4. Predict statistically what proportion of each group should consist of women;
5. Ascertain what are the actual male/female balances in the two groups;
6. Compare the actual with the predicted balances;
7. If women are found to be under-represented in the first group and over-represented in the second, it is proved that the criterion is discriminatory.

This test for 'considerably smaller' assumes that the requirement or condition has no adverse effect and then looks to see how closely the statistics meet that prediction. Following the *Jones* test helps produce the clearest picture of whether and to what extent discrimination is operating.

Example of the application of the Jones test

Suppose a local authority that employs 6,750 people, 3,500 of whom are male and 3,250 of whom are female. It decides to give an extra day's holiday every year to the 160 staff who have over 20 years' service with them. It turns out that 100 of these are male and 60 female. A female employee complains that this requirement for the extra day's holiday is discriminatory.

The *Jones* test has the following steps:

Step 1: *Identify the criterion for selection.* The criterion for selection is service for over 20 years.
Step 2: *Identify the relevant pool, comprising all those who satisfy all the other criteria for selection.* The relevant pool is 6,750 people, ie, 3,500 men and 3,250 women.[50]
Step 3: *Divide the relevant pool into groups representing those who satisfy the criterion and those who do not.* The relevant pool who

50 As the whole workforce is potentially affected by the provision, the pool consists of the entire workforce; there is no need to break it down into those otherwise qualified.

satisfy the criteria is 160 people, the remaining 6,590 people do not satisfy the criteria.

Step 4: *Predict statistically what proportion of each group should consist of women and what of men.* The assumption if there is no discrimination is that the requirement has an equal effect on women and men. On this assumption the ratio between the total number of persons who (irrespective of gender) can comply with the requirement to the total workforce should be the same as the two other ratios, ie:

a) the ratio of women who can comply to the total female workforce; and also
b) the ratio of men who can comply to the total male workforce.

This will be true only if the impact of the requirement does not differ according to the sex of the persons to whom it is applied. Assuming this ratio is constant (ie, assuming equal treatment), it is possible to predict how many men and women should meet the requirement by using the following formula.

Females	*Males*
$\frac{\text{(Total number can comply)} \times \text{total women}}{\text{Total number in workforce}}$	$\frac{\text{(Total number can comply)} \times \text{total men}}{\text{Total number in workforce}}$
$\frac{160 \times 3{,}250}{6{,}750} = 77$	$\frac{160 \times 3{,}500}{6{,}750} = 83$

Another way of reaching the same result is as follows.

Calculate the percentage of men and women in the workforce, ie (3,500/6,750) × 100% = 51.85% men: (3,250/6,750) × 100% = 48.15% women.
Assuming that the number who can comply (160) is divided as between males and females on the same basis as the whole workforce, calculate what that number should be. This calculation requires that these percentages be applied to the total number who can comply, ie, 160 × 51.85% and 160 × 48.15%
It can be seen that 160 who can comply should be divided as 83 men and 77 women.

Step 5: *Ascertain the actual male/female balances in the group.* The actual numbers who can comply are 100 men and 60 women,
Step 6: *Compare actual and predicted balances.* The predicted numbers who can comply are 83 males and 77 females. This means that there are (100 – 83) too many men, ie, 17 men, and (77 – 60) too few women, ie, 17 women, than would be expected if the requirement had equal impact.
Step 7: *If the women are found to be under-represented in the first group and over-represented in the second it is proved that the criterion is discriminatory.* The calculations show that women are under-represented in the group of persons who can comply with the requirement and over-represented in the group who cannot comply with it. Prima facie indirect discrimination is therefore proved.

Using this example it can be seen that the difference in impact can be expressed in three different ways.

	Females	*Males*
PROPORTIONS Proportions who can comply using the formulae	$\frac{\text{W can comply}}{\text{W in pool}}$ $\frac{60}{3{,}250} = \frac{6}{325}$	$\frac{\text{M can comply}}{\text{M in pool}}$ $\frac{100}{3{,}500} = \frac{10}{350}$
PERCENTAGES If the proportions above are converted to percentages who can comply the result is:	$\frac{\text{W can comply} \times 100\%}{\text{W in pool}}$ $\frac{60 \times 100}{3{,}250} = 1.86\%$	$\frac{\text{M can comply} \times 100\%}{\text{M in pool}}$ $\frac{100 \times 100}{3{,}500} = 2.86\%$
JONES TEST Numbers who can comply compared with the predicted number (see above) if there were equal treatment, ie, *Jones* test.	60 – 77 = 17 too few	100 – 83 = 17 too many

This comparison helps to show up the advantages and disadvantages of each approach.

The proportions show that there is a large number of persons in each part of the pool. However, it is very difficult to make sense of how $\frac{6}{325}$ compares to $\frac{10}{350}$ because there is no common denominator, ie, there are different numbers of men and women. It therefore makes sense to translate the proportion into a percentage.

The percentages show the relative size of these two proportions. Although it appears that a one percentage point (ie, 2.86 – 1.85) difference between the two percentages is insignificant, in fact 2.86% is more than one-and-a-half times as large as 1.85%. Once the figures are expressed as percentages the actual numbers are obscured. So a large percentage difference where there is a small pool can appear more significant than it is; correspondingly a small percentage difference in a large pool can appear much less significant than it is. The larger the pool of persons the less likely is it that the percentages are fortuitous: one or two persons joining the workforce will not eradicate the difference.

The *Jones* test highlights the difference between the expected outcome and the actual outcome. It most clearly describes the actual discriminatory effect of the requirement or condition and the significance of the disparate impact. Where the disparity is not clear, it is always sensible to carry out the *Jones* test, and to show the actual numbers, proportions or percentages as well.

3.6.6.4 *Are the figures fortuitous or do they really show an unequal impact?*

The apparent adverse impact could be the result of purely fortuitous or random events. The court or tribunal when testing for 'considerably smaller' needs to consider the significance of the results.[51] This is a particular problem when percentages alone are compared, because in a small workforce they may differ significantly if one or more persons leave or join the pool.

The following example shows how the consideration of percentages alone and not the actual numbers could be misleading.

> Suppose a firm has 20 shop floor employees of whom half are male and half female. The boss wants to promote a shop floor employee to be a supervisor. He says that to be considered for promotion an employee must have five years' service with the firm. The figures show that 60% of the men are eligible but only 40% of the women. The difference between

51 *Enderby v Frenchay Health Authority* [1993] IRLR 591.

> 40% and 60% looks 'considerable'. But when the percentages are converted back into proportions they do not look so considerably different: they mean that 6 out of the 10 men have worked for more than five years while 4 out of the 10 women have worked for that period. Only two events could eliminate this difference. If one eligible man left and was replaced by a new man and one more woman passed her fifth anniversary there would actually be no percentage difference.
>
> By contrast, if instead of having 20 employees the firm had 200,000, there would have to be 20,000 changes for the disparity to be eliminated. 10,000 eligible men would have to leave and 10,000 women would have to pass the five-year mark. 40% of 100,000 women is obviously considerably smaller than 60% of 100,000 men.

So without careful consideration of what the figures are behind the percentages it would be easy for the court or tribunal to go wrong in deciding what is 'considerable'.

Where there is a small workforce it will help to show that they are consistent with a national pattern.

The existence of a long-term pattern can be important. Thus, in *ex p Seymour Smith* the CA was impressed by the 'persistency and consistency' of the figures over a period of seven years. In *R v Secretary for State for Employment ex p Unison*[52] the High Court looked again at the figures in *Seymour Smith* but did not take account of the continuing consistent and persistent pattern where arguably it should have done. The HL in *R v Secretary of State for Employment ex p Seymour Smith*[53] has now referred to the ECJ questions as to the right approach to be taken in determining whether statistics show adverse impact.

3.6.6.5 *The ease or difficulty of the requirement or condition is irrelevant*

The proportion of men and women or of one racial group who can meet a particular requirement may be large in one case and tiny in another. A requirement to have a PhD would clearly be met only by a very small number of people. A requirement to have an English GCSE would be met by a large number. Even though there may be only small numbers involved, the difference between the proportions able to comply may be substantial. Thus if only 2% of men and only 0.5% of women have a PhD the difference is obviously substantial. On these figures four times as many men as women can meet the requirement.

52 [1996] IRLR 438.
53 [1997] IRLR 315, HL.

3.6.6.6 *The disadvantaged group is important*

There is of course a straightforward mathematical relationship between the proportion advantaged and the proportion disadvantaged. So, for example:

> Suppose 96% of women can comply with the requirement, accordingly 4% cannot comply. Suppose 98% of men can comply, and thus 2% cannot comply. 96% and 98% are relatively similar percentages. However, the percentages of women and men who cannot comply is 4% and 2%. This means that twice as many women as men cannot comply with the requirement.

It must be remembered that the purpose of the test is to see whether the requirement or condition needs to be justified in relation to the person disadvantaged. Thus, the impact on the disadvantaged group is also relevant.

3.6.6.7 *Relevance of national statistics and evidence of social customs*

Elaborate statistics will not always be available. However, the court or tribunal will often take into account its own experience, or commonly known facts (see *Edwards (No 2)*[54]).

In *Home Office v Holmes*[55] (see **3.6.7.4**), the IT said, when finding that few women could work full-time, 'it is still a fact that the raising of children tends to place a greater burden on women than it does on men'. In contrast, in *Kidd*,[56] the tribunal, rather surprisingly, said that there was no evidence that more women than men, or married women than unmarried women, gave up full-time work to look after children. The EAT upheld the IT's decision, saying that it was up to the IT to decide what could be taken for granted and what needed proper statistical evidence.

It seems unlikely that an IT would take the same approach now. First, the tribunal took into account the wrong 'relevant circumstances' (see **3.6.5.2** and **3.6.5.3**). Second, it was apparently not given any evidence at all about the fact that women carry the burden of child care. The EAT stressed this point saying, in future cases, it will

54 [1997] IRLR 157. See also *Meade Hill* (above) and *Briggs v North Eastern Education and Library Board* [1990] IRLR 181, NI CA.

55 [1984] IRLR 299.

56 *Kidd v DRG* [1985] IRLR 190, EAT.

be essential to produce such evidence.[57] Third, *Kidd* was decided before *Bilka*[58] (see **3.6.7.1**). The view taken by the EAT in Ms Kidd's case is startling; it is not true that men take an equal role in child care and there is ample evidence to support this.[59]

In *Perera v CSC*[60] (see **3.6.2.5**), Mr Perera showed that out of the 47 executive officers where he worked, 22 were under the age of 32 but none of the black workers was under the age of 32. The proportion of blacks who could comply with the age requirement was 0%. It may have been a mere coincidence that none of the black workers was under 32 and many of the white applicants were, but it is unlikely that this would have been sufficient to prove discrimination. The tribunal relied on the fact that a substantial number of black people are adult immigrants and also that the Civil Service had not put in any evidence to rebut Mr Perera's. The EAT said that it was most undesirable that in all cases elaborate statistical evidence should be required.

Statistical evidence of the proportion of men and women or of racial groups who cannot comply with the requirement nationally will always provide an important insight into the causes why a particular requirement is disadvantageous. Evidence of the reasons why a particular group or sex have difficulty complying with the requirement will also be relevant. In *CRE v Dutton* (see **3.6.3**), the HL said that clearly the proportion of gypsies who will satisfy the 'no travellers' condition at a pub is considerably smaller than the proportion of non-gypsies. Although between one-half and one-third live in houses, it was apparent that a far higher proportion of gypsies are leading a nomadic way of life than the rest of the population or, more narrowly, than the rest of the population who might wish to resort to the pub which had banned travellers. Thus, the pool could either have been all gypsies or those living close to the pub. If these figures are unavailable it may be necessary to refer to national statistics to establish the claim.

57 Despite the comments of the EAT in *Holmes* (see above) that it could be assumed that more women and married women regularly undertook a child-caring role. See also *Briggs* (above) and *Perera* (below), where the court said that it was most undesirable to require elaborate statistical evidence.

58 *Bilka-Kaufhaus GmbH v Karin Weber von Hartz (No 170/84)* [1986] IRLR 317, ECJ.

59 *Part-time employment and attitudes to part-time work* (*Employment Gazette*, May 1993); *Women in the labour market: results from the Labour Force Survey* (*Labour Market Trends*, March 1997).

60 [1983] IRLR 166, CA.

In *London Underground Ltd v Edwards* (above), where there was only one woman who could not comply, the IT calculated that this meant that 100% of the men could comply with the requirement compared to 95.2% of the women.

The IT said:

> Equality of treatment is the paramount consideration . . . The IT is entitled to have regard to the possibility that, where the number of women as against the number of men is, in percentage terms, very slight, some kind of generalised assumption may exist at the workplace that the particular type of work concerned is 'men's' and not 'women's' work. . . . in assessing the extent of the disproportionate effect, the tribunal is entitled to take account of a wider perspective. It is for this reason that statistics showing the percentage of women in employment who have primary care responsibility for a child, in contrast to the percentage of men in that position, are relevant.

3.6.6.8 There is no four-fifths rule

In the past, in America a four-fifths rule has been used in some situations. The American Equal Employment Opportunities Commission said that if the proportion of one advantaged group was within four-fifths of the other then there was insufficient adverse impact. However, this approach is an over-simplification and gives rise to many statistical problems, particularly where the figures are very large or very small. It has been rejected by the Northern Ireland Court of Appeal in *McCausland v Dungannon DC*.[61]

Different tribunals have held differing opinions as to what constitutes a 'considerably smaller' proportion. Whether the differential is sufficient to impose a burden of proof on the respondent to justify the requirement is ultimately a question of fact for the tribunal and the EAT may be reluctant to intervene.

3.6.6.9 Nil as a proportion of the whole

If it is impossible for any member of a racial group to comply with a requirement or condition it cannot be a case of indirect discrimination. In *Wong v GLC*,[62] the EAT said that:

> a 'condition' has to be one which is such that the proportion of persons of the same racial group as Mr Wong who can comply with it is considerably smaller than the proportion of persons not of that racial group who can comply with it. It is obvious that somebody who is brown

61 [1993] IRLR 583.
62 (1980) EAT 524/79.

> cannot comply at all with the condition that the candidate has to be white. Therefore it is really quite impossible to look for a smaller proportion of people who are unable to satisfy the condition.

It is different if there happen to be no women or members of particular racial group who can comply. In *Greencroft Social Club and Institute v Mullen*,[63] the employer argued that if no women could comply with a requirement, 'how could it be said, for the purpose of the statutory comparison required by s1(1)(b), that a smaller proportion of women can comply than the proportion of men who can?' An employee of a working men's club was suspended but was denied the right to a disciplinary hearing which was given to members. The 'requirement' was that in order to have a disciplinary hearing you had to be a member. Women could not be members. The EAT categorically rejected the employer's argument, saying that such an interpretation would run counter to the spirit and purpose of the SDA if a requirement which otherwise fell within s1(1)(b) fell outside the Act because no women could comply with it. In reality this is a case of direct discrimination because the requirement itself was a sex-based criterion.

Wong can be distinguished from *Greencroft*. A condition to be white or a woman is the same as a rule which says 'no blacks' or 'no women' and this is less favourable treatment on the ground of sex or race, ie, direct discrimination. A requirement that a person has to be a member of a club in order to have the right to a hearing is not necessarily one which is inextricably linked to the sex of the applicant so is unlikely to be direct discrimination – however, in this case it was.

On the other hand if it really is fortuitous that in a workforce no women could work full-time this would not be direct discrimination. The fact that no women could comply with the requirement should not be a bar to a claim of indirect discrimination.

3.6.6.10 Relationship between justification and adverse impact

It has been argued that an applicant does not have to show as much adverse impact if the employers can show no justification for the requirement. In *London Underground v Edwards (No 2)*[64] the EAT said that: '. . . Although there is no direct correlation between the two we would anticipate that in accordance with the purpose of the ETD of eliminating discrimination between the sexes in the employment field, the less justification London Underground had for the way they

63 (1985) 290 IRLIB 13, EAT.
64 [1997] IRLR 157.

treated Ms Edwards, the less likely it is that a tribunal will conclude that she has failed to show that the disproportionate effect of the condition was considerable.'

3.6.6.11 *When is adverse impact to be tested?*

The House of Lords in *R v Secretary of State for Employment ex p Seymour Smith*[65] decided to ask the ECJ to rule on when the adverse impact of the two-year qualification period for unfair dismissal should be assessed statistically. It was not clear whether it should be assessed when the legislation came into force or when it had an impact on the applicants or at some other time.

Where the challenge is not to a statutory provision the relevant statistics will be at or as near as possible to the time at which the applicant suffered a detriment.

3.6.7 *Question 8: Can the requirement or condition be shown by the respondent to be justifiable, irrespective of any sex or race factors?*

Once the complainant has proved that the requirement or condition is more disadvantageous to him/her and s/he cannot comply with it, then the burden of proof shifts to the employer to prove that it is justifiable. The employer must give reasons for any difference of treatment. A mere assertion is insufficient. In *Schaffter* (see **3.6.5.3**), the Secretary of State said that the regulations were aimed at a particular and limited category of students. The court said this did not amount to a justification, as no reasons were given for the distinction between single lone parents and married lone parents.

3.6.7.1 *Main principles/meaning of justifiable*

'Justifiable' means capable of being justified; irrespective of means, without regard to race or sex.

The accepted interpretation of 'justifiable' was set out by the ECJ in *Bilka-Kaufhaus*[66] and it has been adopted in discrimination cases. The questions are:

- is the condition objectively justified on grounds other than sex?
- do the means chosen correspond to a real need?
- are they appropriate to achieve that aim?
- are they necessary in order to achieve that end?

65 [1997] IRLR 315, HL.
66 *Bilka-Kaufhaus GmbH v Weber von Hartz Case 170/84* [1986] IRLR 317.

These principles were re-affirmed in the later ECJ case of *Rinner-Kuhn*[67] and now form the basis of any defence of justification.

In *Hampson v DES*,[68] a race discrimination case, the CA applied the *Bilka* test and said that it was obviously desirable that the tests of justifiability, applied in all the closely related fields, should be consistent with each other. The HL has re-affirmed the approach taken by the CA in *Hampson* and in *Webb v EMO Air Cargo*[69] (see also *Briggs v North Eastern Education and Library Board*[70]).

The test of justifiability is the same as the test for 'material difference' in equal pay cases. In *Rainey*,[71] an equal pay case, the HL said that:

> there would not appear to be any material distinction in principle between the need to demonstrate objectively justified grounds of difference for purposes of s1(3) material factor defence in equal pay cases and the need to justify a requirement or condition under s1(1)(b)(ii) of the Act of 1975.

3.6.7.2 Evidence required to support a defence of justification

In cases of indirect discrimination it is not sufficient to assert that there is a non-discriminatory justification for the action, respondents must provide evidence to support this. In *Rinner-Kuhn*, the German government argued that it was justified in excluding part-time workers from a sick pay scheme because workers who work less than 10 hours a week are not integrated in and connected with the undertaking in a way comparable to that of other workers. The ECJ said that this was a generalised statement which could not be regarded as an objective criterion unrelated to any sex discrimination.

A similar decision was reached in *Nimz v Freie und Hansestadt Hamburg*,[72] where part-timers were required to have more years of service than full-timers before being moved to a higher grade. The ECJ held that, in order to justify such a practice, the employer must show that there is a relationship between the nature of the duties performed and the experience afforded by the performance of those

67 *Rinner-Kühn v FWW Spezial-Gebaudereinigung GmbH Case 171/88* [1989] IRLR 493.
68 [1990] IRLR 302.
69 [1993] IRLR 27, HL.
70 [1990] IRLR 181. See also *Board of Governors of St Matthias School v Crizzle* [1993] IRLR 472.
71 [1987] IRLR 26. See Chapter 21 for further analysis of this case.
72 [1991] IRLR 222.

duties after a certain number of hours had been worked. The argument that full-time workers acquire necessary skills more quickly and have greater experience, insofar as they were generalisations, could not amount to objective criteria.

In *R v Secretary of State for Employment ex p EOC*,[73] the Secretary of State for Employment claimed that longer qualification periods for part-time workers were justified as they would increase the availability of part-time work. The HL found that an increase in part-time work is a beneficial social policy aim, however, it did not accept that these qualification periods were necessary in order to achieve this aim as the Secretary of State was unable to produce any evidence that the length of the qualification period for redundancy payments had any effect on job creation.[74] A similar decision was reached in the case of *R v Secretary of State for Employment ex p Seymour Smith* when the Secretary of State said that he was justified in imposing a two-year qualification period for unfair dismissal protection because it would promote job creation. The Court of Appeal held that:

> We have found nothing in the evidence, either factual or opinion, which obliges or enables us to draw the inference that the increase in the threshold period has lead to an increase in employment opportunities.

In both cases a number of research studies on influences on labour market behaviour covering the last 20 years influenced the courts. The correct way to approach the question of justification has now been referred to the ECJ by the HL.[75]

3.6.7.3 Proportionality

Bilka[76] was also considered in detail by the EAT in 1989,[77] when it held that tribunals must carry out a balancing exercise, taking into account all the surrounding circumstances and giving due emphasis to the degree of discrimination caused, against the object or aim to be achieved – the principle of proportionality. Employers are entitled to take a broad and rational view, provided that it is based on logic, and is a tenable view. It has been argued that employers are under no

73 [1994] IRLR 176.

74 TUC Report, *Eating their words* (1996) shows that the number of part-time jobs has increased, not decreased, since the extra qualification period for part-time workers was removed.

75 [1997] IRLR 315.

76 [1986] IRLR 317 (see n66).

77 See *Cobb & Others v Secretary of State for Employment and MSC* [1989] IRLR 464.

obligation to prove that there was no other way of achieving their object. If an alternative is proposed, and the employer ought reasonably to have considered and adopted it, the IT might find that the discriminatory requirement was not justifiable.

In *Greater Manchester Police Authority v Lea*,[78] the EAT said that there has to be 'a nexus established between the function of the employer . . . and the imposition of the condition, otherwise it is impossible to carry out the objective balance'. The EAT held that, although the tribunal may have erred on the side of strictness in looking for something which was necessary, that was not a significant difference from the law as laid down in *Hampson* (above). In *Lea*, the police tried to justify a policy of not employing those in receipt of an occupational pension, by saying that there were about three million people unemployed; that persons with a pension were likely to be less distressed by unemployment than those who did not have one; that the burden on the state of maintaining the persons who had no employment is reduced by employing those who had no other means of income; and that the policy created additional but undefined employment opportunities for the unemployed.

The applicants pointed out that the police did not exclude people who had jobs elsewhere. The tribunal said that there was no need to impose such a condition and the condition was extraneous to the police authority's function. Furthermore, the condition was not appropriate in relation to attaining the object in question as it did not single out the unemployed to be offered positions, but merely those with occupational pensions.

By analogy, the same test, as set out in *Bilka* and *Rainey* (see above) and subsequent decisions, should be applied to cases under the RRA.

The following are some examples of factors which have been taken into account when determining whether a condition is justifiable.

3.6.7.4 Economic considerations

In *Home Office v Holmes*,[79] the employers, in attempting to justify refusing a woman part-time work, said that accommodation and national insurance costs would rise. The EAT preferred Ms Holmes' evidence which showed that the civil service was losing valuable trained personnel when they left to start families (the Kemp-Jones report) and that in some departments efficiency increased when part-timers were introduced. A higher executive officer gave evidence that

78 [1990] IRLR 372.
79 [1984] IRLR 299, EAT.

part-timers in his section were more efficient, better time-keepers and did not need so much supervision.

In *London Underground Ltd v Edwards*[80] London Underground tried to justify its new shift patterns for train drivers on the grounds that they were being introduced to cut running costs. However, the EAT concluded that:

> London Underground could and, we would add, should, have accommodated Ms Edward's personal requirements . . . (they) could have made arrangements which would not have been damaging to their business plans but which would have accommodated the reasonable demands of their employees.

It is clear that the courts expect employers to consider alternative non-discriminatory methods to achieve economies. In *Orphanos* (see **3.6.1.1**), the HL pointed out that other methods of curtailing expenditure were possible, such as cutting all student grants, increasing all fees or restricting grants by other means.

The existence of a separate non-discriminatory pay bargaining system for female-dominated and male-dominated professions does not amount to objective justification. In *Enderby v Frenchay Health Authority*[81] the ECJ considered the effect of separate Whitley Council agreements for the rates of pay for speech therapists, clinical psychologists and senior pharmacists. The health authority claimed that the pay differentials were due to market forces, namely, that the male-dominated professions had to increase the rates of pay in order to attract candidates. The ECJ concluded that market forces could constitute an objective justification but this was a matter for the national courts to resolve.

However, it should be remembered that the market itself is often tainted with sex as well as race discrimination as can be seen from the sexual and racial breakdown of the national average weekly wage, and this was recognised by the HL in *Ratcliffe* (see **21.4**).

3.6.7.5 Trade union practices

The fact that a practice is long-established and supported by trade unionists should not be taken into account. In *Clarke v Eley Kynoch*[82] the EAT held that a policy making part-timers redundant before full-timers was 'grossly discriminatory' and not justifiable despite the fact that it was widely accepted by the workforce and commonly applied.

80 [1995] IRLR 355, EAT. See also *Kidd v DRG* [1985] IRLR 190, EAT.
81 [1993] IRLR 591.
82 [1982] IRLR 482, EAT. See also *Hall v Shorts Missiles* (1997) 72 EOR 39.

In *London Underground Ltd v Edwards* (see note above) the employer had suggested a scheme called the 'Single Parent Link' to accommodate the needs of single parents, however, this was rejected by the unions. Had such a scheme been implemented Ms Edwards would not have been forced to bring her case.

3.6.7.6 Health and safety requirements

In *Panesar v The Nestlé Co Ltd*,[83] a rule prohibiting beards in a chocolate factory was held by the EAT to be justifiable in the interests of hygiene. In the light of *Bilka* (see above), the employer would have to prove a real hygiene threat caused by beards and if there were other means of achieving the object, such as covering up beards, that should be sufficient. This was well illustrated in the case of *Blakerd v Elizabeth Shaw Ltd*[84] where the IT ruled that the employer's requirement that all employees wear a head-covering supplied by them was indirectly discriminatory against a Sikh. This case was settled with an order that the employer obtain and maintain a supply of white turbans for the use of Sikh employees.

In *Singh v British Rail Engineering Ltd*,[85] the EAT held that a requirement for railway repair workers to wear protective headgear was justifiable, notwithstanding that Sikhs were obliged by their religion to wear turbans so could not wear the headgear. The EAT took account of the fact that the majority of workers would resent an exception being made, though said that this alone would not be sufficient justification for the rule. It also took account of the fact that the employer could be liable for damages if it had knowingly exposed an employee, whom it believed to be inadequately protected, to a real risk. Since the Employment Act 1989 came into force, Sikhs are exempt from wearing safety helmets on construction sites; it is discriminatory to require them to do so and the employer will not be liable for any injury sustained as a direct result of the failure to wear a helmet. Note that the exemption applies only to construction sites.

3.6.7.7 Government justification on grounds of social policy

In *Nolte*[86] and *Megner*[87] the ECJ ruled that in legislating in the field of social policy governments have a wide discretion. The case concerned

83 [1980] IRLR 64.

84 COIT case no 27486/83.

85 [1986] ICR 22.

86 *Nolte v Landesversicherungsanstalt Hannover C-317/93* [1996] IRLR 225.

87 *Megner & Scheffel v Innungskrankenkasse Vorderpfalz C-444/93* [1996] IRLR 236.

the social security entitlements of employees in 'minor employment' (less than 15 hours a week). The court found that the exclusion of such employees was a 'structural principle' of the German social security scheme and that it fulfilled a legitimate social policy aim that was appropriate to achieve that aim and necessary in order to do so. The real problem in these cases was that there was a demand for such minor employment but if employees working these short hours were brought within the social security system it would encourage employers to employ persons outside the system and within the black economy. The rulings in these cases run contrary to the principles set out in *Rinner-Kuhn*[88] (although that case was cited in the ECJ) where the ECJ said that generalised statements are insufficient to establish justification. Since both these cases concern contributory social security benefits they can be distinguished from statutory employment provisions. Since *Nolte* and *Megner* the ECJ has interpreted justification in *Lewark*,[89] an employment case concerned with legislative provisions, in a way which is consistent with the *Rinner-Kuhn* criteria, rather than *Nolte* and *Megner*.

In *R v Secretary of State for Employment ex p Seymour Smith*[90] the HL asked the ECJ to rule on the right approach to justification in respect of statutory provisions requiring a two-year qualification period for unfair dismissal.

3.6.7.8 A question of fact and law

Justification is a question of mixed fact and law because the correct legal test must be applied to the facts found by the tribunal. The facts should be interpreted according to the *Bilka* test. The appeal courts have been increasingly unwilling to overturn IT decisions unless the tribunal applied the wrong test, failed to give an adequate statement of its reasons or the decision was perverse.

3.6.8 Question 9: Could the applicant, at the material time, comply with the requirement?

The question is whether the applicant is capable in practice of complying; theoretical but impractical possibilities are disregarded. Thus maximum age limits may discriminate against women who, because

88 *Rinner-Kuhn v FWW Spezial-Gebaudereinigung GmbH* [1989] IRLR 493, ECJ.
89 Case C-457/93 Judgment 6 February 1996.
90 [1997] IRLR 315, HL.

of child bearing, enter or re-enter the job market at an older age. In *Price v Civil Service Commission* (see **3.6.5.1**), the EAT said:

> it is relevant in determining whether women can comply with the condition to take into account the current usual behaviour of women in this respect as observed in practice, putting aside behaviour and responses which are unusual.

In *Mandla v Lee*[91] a headmaster of a private school had refused to accept a Sikh boy unless he removed his turban and cut his hair. The HL said that 'can' means 'can in practice' or 'can consistently with the customs and cultural conditions of the racial group' rather than 'can physically'. *Mandla* was followed by the HL in *CRE v Dutton*[92] where the HL held that the expression 'can comply' means 'can comply without giving up the distinctive customs and cultural rules of gypsies' and that it could not be said that gypsies could comply with the 'no travellers' condition without giving up their customs and culture.

In *Raval* (see above), a requirement to have an English language 'O' level was challenged as being discriminatory on the ground of race. Ms Raval was denied a job with the civil service because she could not comply with this condition. The IT found that the same proportion of Asian and English people could take and pass 'O' level English language. The EAT disagreed, saying that 'can comply' denoted an ability to produce proof that the relevant qualification had been obtained. It was not correct to suggest that Ms Raval should go and take an 'O' level. Furthermore, the EAT thought that fewer Asians could pass an English 'O' level as they were bound to be at a disadvantage if English were their second language. (The EAT went on to say that the requirement was justified and Ms Raval had not suffered a detriment.)

In *Meade-Hill & NUCPS v British Council* (see **3.6.2.2**) the mobility requirement had not been enforced by the employers. The CA took the view that the impact of a requirement must be judged at the moment when the term in question becomes incorporated into a contract, not when it is reasonably foreseeable that the applicant will be unable to comply with it nor when the employer seeks to enforce it (but see **3.6.3**).

In *Clymo v Wandsworth LBC*[93] the IT took the view that there was 'no firm evidence' that the proportion of qualified women librarians

91 [1983] IRLR 209.
92 [1989] IRLR 8.
93 [1989] IRLR 241, EAT.

who could work full-time was considerably smaller than the proportion of qualified male librarians. The tribunal said, and the EAT did not criticise the decision, that:

> at this level of income, and most particularly in the London area, with child minding facilities readily available, people of these qualifications and this combined income and with a professional career both behind and ahead of them could certainly conduct their family arrangements on less old-fashioned bases than the less qualified and more lowly paid.

This ignores all the factors which make it difficult for women to combine full-time work and child care, it takes no account of the fact that parents may choose to spend some of their time with their children, and it is contrary to several HL decisions.[94] It is not for the courts to engage in re-constructing applicants' domestic arrangements ignoring current usual behaviour as observed in practice. This was accepted in *London Underground Ltd v Edwards* (above) where Ms Edwards was unable to comply with the new rotas because of her child care needs.

3.6.9 Question 10: Was it to her detriment that she could not comply with the requirement or condition?

A woman cannot complain of a requirement being indirectly discriminatory unless she cannot comply with it at the time that the requirement is imposed. The Northern Ireland CA has pointed out that the verb 'can' in 'cannot comply with' must be given the same interpretation as the verb 'can' in the term 'can comply with' and that the two subparagraphs are reverse sides of the same test, in so far as they refer to being able to comply.

In *Clymo*,[95] the EAT refused to accept that a requirement to work full-time was to the applicant's detriment because she could not comply with it. The EAT continued by saying that 'in trying to fit society into the framework of the statute and the statute into our society, in every employment ladder there will come a stage at which a woman who has family responsibilities must make a choice'. This is an extraordinary comment, as the purpose of the Acts is to enable women and black people to combine work with customary and cultural practices, which in the case of women include caring for children. It is very difficult to reconcile *Clymo* with the HL decisions in *Mandla* and

94 See *Mandla v Lee* and *CRE v Dutton* (above).

95 [1989] IRLR 241, EAT.

Dutton and it was doubted by the Northern Ireland CA in *Briggs*.[96] *Clymo* should not be followed on this point.

It should be irrelevant if at some time in the past or future she might have been able or would be able to comply with it. In *Dutton*,[97] for example, it was not disputed that a nomadic gypsy had suffered a detriment by being excluded from a pub.

In *Raval*,[98] the EAT concluded that the applicant suffered no detriment because she could have in the past, and could in the future, obtain the qualification. This must be wrong and is inconsistent with *Dutton*.

In *Watches of Switzerland v Savell*,[99] the EAT said that, although the promotion procedures were biased against women, Ms Savell failed to show that she had suffered a detriment because she was unable to prove that she could not achieve promotion.

In both *Savell* and *Raval* the tribunal confused the question of whether the applicant 'can comply' with whether she had suffered a detriment. 'Can comply' means whether the woman is able to meet the requirement at the time it was imposed, not whether steps could have been taken, or could be taken, to comply with the requirement.

In *Orphanos*, the HL did not say that Mr Orphanos could in the past have spent or could in the future spend three years in the EU thus entitling him to lower fees; the very fact that he had not spent three years in the EU was sufficient to show detriment. Detriment under SDA s6(2)(b) and RRA s4(2)(c) means that the applicant had him/herself suffered a disadvantage.[100] The EAT has said that detriment in RRA s1 has the same meaning as in SDA s6(2)(b).[101]

Although the contrary was suggested by the EAT in *Enderby* (an equal pay case), it should not be necessary for the applicant to prove that the reason she could not comply with a requirement was because she suffered a disadvantage associated with her sex. Thus, there would not appear to be anything preventing a woman worker complaining of being denied access to a benefit (such as access to training) because she worked part-time, even if there was no reason, such as child care responsibilities, for her working part-time. Such a woman apparently passes the statutory test; a requirement (to work full-time)

96 *Briggs v North Eastern Education and Library Board* [1990] IRLR 181, NI CA.
97 [1989] IRLR 8.
98 *Raval v DHSS* [1985] IRLR 370, EAT.
99 [1983] IRLR 141, EAT.
100 See *Jeremiah v Ministry of Defence* [1979] IRLR 436.
101 See *Home Office v Holmes* [1984] IRLR 299.

has been imposed; she could not comply with it at the material time (the time when the requirement was imposed) because full-time work was not offered; it is to her detriment because she cannot comply with it; and the requirement is probably not justifiable. Yet if the same woman complained of a requirement to work part-time in order to get a job, she would fail, as she could, in practice, comply with it.

There is nothing in the SDA which prevents *all* women taking advantage of provisions aimed at removing requirements which discriminate against *some* women. It is irrelevant that, for example, more women than men are appointed to the job in question nor does it have to be shown that the woman, but for the requirement, would have been successful. What is relevant is whether the specific requirement is more disadvantageous to women than men (see *Price v CSC*).

3.6.10 Subsequent direct discrimination claim

Where employers change a requirement as a result of a successful indirect discrimination claim by a woman it might lead to a direct discrimination claim by a man if the change does not benefit men as well. If an employer has a policy which is indirectly discriminatory it should be changed so there is no direct or indirect discrimination against women or men or different racial groups.

3.7 Conclusion

The definition of indirect discrimination is so complex and has been so misunderstood by tribunals and courts that it is useful to return to the underlying principle behind the concept; that is the prohibition of practices which adversely affect women and certain racial groups. Thus, the CA in *R v Secretary of State for Employment ex p Seymour Smith* (see above) ruled:

> But the underlying principle is equal treatment. It will be remembered that by article 2.1 of the ET Directive the principle of equal treatment means that 'there shall be no discrimination whatsoever on grounds of sex'.

This led it to conclude:

> It follows therefore that any proposed legislation, particularly in the social field, which may have a disparate impact between the sexes, will have to be examined before it is introduced to see whether any consequential disparity can be objectively justified.

Although these principles were applied to a sex discrimination case they apply equally to race discrimination.

INDIRECT DISCRIMINATION: KEY POINTS

- The definition of indirect discrimination under EC law – as set out in *Bilka*, *Danfoss*, *Kowalska*, etc – should always be considered.

  There are then 10 questions which must be addressed:

  1. In race discrimination cases, it is important to choose with care the racial groups between which comparisons are to be made – the effect of a requirement or condition may differ greatly as between one racial group and another; in cases of doubt, alternative comparisons should be put forward.
  2. The requirements or conditions must be carefully identified. They should be broadly defined. They may be explicit or implicit and may be found in the contract, in employment practices, in collective agreements, etc. The courts have held that the requirement or condition must be an absolute bar rather than a preference. This interpretation may be contrary to EC law. More than one formulation of the requirement or condition may be considered.
  3. The material time: could the applicant comply with the requirement or condition at the time that it was applied to him/her?
  4. The applicant must show that the requirement or condition applies or would apply equally to a man or persons of a different racial group.
  5. The relevant circumstances must be the same or similar, thus the comparison is not between *all* men and women (or all of one racial group and all of another racial group) but between relevant men and women in the pool.
  6. Care must be taken to ensure that there is no discrimination in the 'relevant circumstances' or choice of pool; the pool may be restricted to men and women (or the identified racial groups) in the area or in the particular workforce. Where there is doubt about the identity of the pool, the case should be argued on the basis of

different pools; failure to identify the correct pool may be fatal to the case.

7 The applicant must show that the proportion of women (or those of one racial group) who can comply with the condition or requirement is 'considerably smaller' than the proportion of men (or those of the other racial group). Usually, detailed statistical evidence will be required but the courts may take judicial notice of 'ordinary behaviour'.

8 The comparison is proportionate. The principle in the test is equal treatment. It is important to compare what might be expected if there were equal treatment with the actual outcome.

9 Once disparate impact has been proved, the employer will have a defence if s/he can prove that the requirement/condition is justifiable. The objective that the requirement is intended to achieve must be identified. The requirement must be shown to be necessary and appropriate to achieve that end before it can be justified. The justification must not itself be sex- or race-based. If the end can be achieved in another non-discriminatory way then the requirement will not be justifiable.

10 Could the applicant comply with the requirement? Theoretical but impractical possibilities should be disregarded; current usual behaviour must be taken into account.

11 The applicant must show that she suffered a disadvantage or 'detriment' because of his/her inability to comply with the requirement at the time it was imposed.

CHAPTER 4

Victimisation

Victimisation occurs when a person (the victim) is treated less favourably (by the discriminator) than another person and the reason is because the victim has complained of discrimination, has supported someone who has complained or has done anything else under the Acts.[1] Thus, for example, if a woman is dismissed or demoted because she has complained of harassment this will be unlawful victimisation. Although there have not yet been any cases under the DDA, the same principles are likely to be applied because the definition of victimisation under the DDA is similar to that under the earlier discrimination legislation (see **24.9.1**).

The victimisation may be carried out by someone other than the person who discriminated in the first place. Thus, if an employer does not appoint a person because in the past s/he has brought proceedings against a former employer, this will be victimisation.

The Acts that deal with victimisation include the RRA 1976, SDA 1975, EqPA 1970, DDA 1995 and the Pensions Act 1995.

4.1 Victimisation by itself not unlawful

In order to complain of victimisation there must have also been a prohibited act of discrimination (see **5.4.1** and **6.4**). Thus, the victim must, for example, have been refused employment or dismissed or

1 The SDA s4 and RRA s2 state that: 'A person ("the discriminator") discriminates against another person ("the person victimised") in any circumstances relevant for the purposes of any provision of this Act if he treats the person victimised less favourably than in those circumstances he treats or would treat other persons, and does so by reason that the person victimised has . . .' done a protected act. The DDA s55 is the corresponding provision for victimisation on the ground of disability.

subjected to some other detriment. In *Nagarajan v Agnew and Others*[2] the applicant settled various race complaints against his employer and was unemployed for a while. He then applied to work for his former employer and his previous manager said he should not be considered. The tribunal found this was partly because he had made complaints of racial discrimination. The applicant complained that this was victimisation.

The EAT held that the victimisation provisions must be read with the prohibited acts set out in RRA Part II; victimisation in itself was not unlawful. Thus, the applicant could not complain that he had been subjected to a detriment under RRA s4(2) as this section only applied to existing employees. However, if instead he had complained that the prohibited act was a refusal to employ him under RRA s4(1) it is likely that he would have succeeded in proving victimisation.

In order to prove victimisation the worker must show that s/he:

a) has done a protected act;
b) was treated less favourably under the Acts;
c) was treated less favourably *because* s/he had done a protected act;
d) s/he acted in good faith and the allegation was not false.

4.2 Definition of protected acts

The definition is very wide. Thus it is unlawful to treat less favourably a person because s/he has:

a) brought proceedings against the discriminator or any other person under the Acts; or
b) given evidence or information in connection with proceedings brought by any person against the discriminator or any other person under the Acts; thus, those who are witnesses in proceedings are protected;
c) done anything else under or by reference to the SDA, EqPA or RRA in relation to the discriminator or any other person; or
d) made allegations against the discriminator that s/he has discriminated in a way that would be a breach of the Acts (whether or not the allegation specifically states this).

In relation to both (a) and (b) proceedings must have been brought, though in (b) the proceedings need not have been brought at the time of the victimisation.

2 [1994] IRLR 61.

If the discriminator treats a person (the victim) less favourably because s/he knows or suspects that the victim intends to do any of the above or has done any of them this will also be victimisation.[3]

In *Cornelius v University College of Swansea*,[4] the CA said that the purpose of SDA s4 was to protect those who sought to rely on the SDA. Discrimination under s4 was not discrimination on the ground of sex but discrimination on the ground of conduct of the type described in that section (ie, falling within (a) to (d) above). Thus, in all the relevant substantive employment sections, 'discrimination' bears both its SDA s1 and s4 meanings (and parallel provisions under the RRA).

In order to be protected, the applicant (victim) must have made the allegation in good faith, but it does not need to be proven. Even if an applicant loses a discrimination or equal pay case, if s/he is subsequently dismissed because of bringing proceedings, s/he can claim s/he has been victimised.

Victimisation on the ground of race is unlawful even if the victim is employed in a private household (see **6.4.1.1**).

4.3 Has the victim done a 'protected act'?

The meaning of (a) is quite clear; it covers those who have brought discrimination proceedings; the proceedings do not have to have been brought against the person who is alleged to have carried out the victimisation.

The meaning of (b), (c) and (d) is not so clear. In *Kirby v MSC*,[5] the applicant was transferred to a less desirable post after he had reported several incidents of racial discrimination. Proceedings were taken after one such complaint but only after Mr Kirby had been transferred. He claimed compensation for victimisation, arguing that he had done a protected act under (b), (c) and (d).

In relation to (b), the EAT held that, although proceedings under the RRA had been brought in one case, and the applicant had given evidence, this happened long after he had been transferred. Although giving information prior to proceedings could fall within para (b), the victimisation must have occurred after proceedings had been brought.

3 SDA s4; RRA s2. The two sections are identical.

4 [1987] IRLR 141, CA.

5 [1980] IRLR 229, EAT.

The EAT further held, in *Kirby*, that the applicant had not done something 'under' the Act (see para (c)) as that required something to be done under a specific provision of the RRA. However, he had done the act 'by reference' to the RRA which is also covered by (c).

Finally, the EAT held that the applicant had not done a protected act under (d) as the allegations made did not amount to allegations of a contravention of the RRA. He only suggested that there may have been a breach. This is a very narrow interpretation of the Act.

In *Aziz v Trinity St Taxis*,[6] the applicant was a member of TST, a company which operated a radio system for its members. Mr Aziz thought he was being unfairly treated by being charged £1,000 to enable a third taxi of his to be admitted to the system. In order to prove his complaint he secretly made tape-recordings of his conversations with seven other members. Mr Aziz's allegations of discrimination were dismissed by an IT. Subsequently he was expelled from TST and he alleged he had been victimised. The CA held that the making of secret tape-recordings was a protected act under RRA s2(1)(c) as it was necessary only to prove that the act was done by reference to the race relations legislation in the broad sense, even though the victim does not focus his/her mind specifically on any provision of the Act.

In *Waters v Commissioner of Police of the Metropolis*[7] a woman who had been sexually assaulted while off duty complained that her employer had subsequently victimised her by removing her name from a list of specially trained police officers. She claimed that she had been treated less favourably because she had alleged there had been a contravention of the Act (ie, under (d) above). The EAT held that, because the employer was not vicariously liable for the sexual assault (as it was not done 'in the course of employment'), the employer had not contravened the Act. As there had been no 'protected act' there was no victimisation.

In *Waters* the applicant partly relied on ETD art 7 which provides that:

> Member States shall take the necessary measures to protect employees against dismissal by the employer as a reaction to a complaint within the undertaking or to any legal proceedings aimed at enforcing compliance with the principle of equal treatment.

The applicant argued that 'within the undertaking' was wider than

6 [1986] IRLR 435, EAT; [1988] IRLR 204, CA.
7 [1995] IRLR 531.

'in the course of employment'. The EAT rejected this interpretation because of the requirement for there to have been a 'contravention of this Act' and there was only a contravention if the original act was done in the course of employment.

At the IT, in *Waters*, the applicant did not argue that the protected act was doing 'anything under or by reference to' the Act 'in relation to the discriminator or any other person'. This is much wider, does not require proof of an actual contravention and might have led to a different result. The CA has granted leave to appeal in *Waters* on the ground that the statutory defence to a claim of victimisation requires both that the protected act was false and not done bona fide (see **4.6**). The CA thought, at the stage of leave, that this may mean that bona fide complaints which in fact cannot be brought within the Act are protected. The CA has upheld the EAT decision.

These cases show the importance of identifying carefully the 'protected act'. It is advisable to argue in the alternative.

Because of the ambiguity of what is a protected act, a worker should make it clear to the employer that s/he is complaining of discrimination and preferably put this in writing. A generalised complaint that there has been some unspecified discrimination may not be sufficient.[8] If a worker fears that s/he may then be victimised it is worth advising the employer that the worker should not be prejudiced in any way as a result of making the allegation.

4.4 Was the victim treated less favourably?

In *Aziz*[9] the CA held that, in order to show less favourable treatment, the comparison is between the complainant and a person who has not done the protected act. In *Aziz* the comparison was with members who had not made and would not make secret recordings; applying this test it was clear that by expelling Mr Aziz from membership the respondents had treated him less favourably than other persons.

4.5 Was the less favourable treatment a direct result of the protected act?

The CA said in *Aziz* (above) that it must be shown that the very fact that the protected act was done by the complainant 'under or by

8 In *Benn v LB Hackney* the IT held that allegations of a racist or sexist 'culture' did not amount to an allegation that the Acts had been contravened (6 May 1993; Case No: 22956/91 DCLD 19).

9 [1986] IRLR 435, EAT; [1988] IRLR 204, CA.

reference to' the RRA influenced the discriminator in his unfavourable treatment of the complainant. The IT found that Mr Aziz was expelled because the making of the secret recordings had been an underhand action and a breach of trust and not because they had been made by reference to the RRA. As the respondents' decision would have been the same, even if Mr Aziz's purpose in making the recordings had had nothing to do with the RRA, his claim failed.[10]

In *Re York Truck Equipment Ltd*[11] the EAT said that the applicant was dismissed because of her conduct, not her allegations of discrimination. However, her conduct consisted of making allegations, described as 'bothering the company with her private life problems'; these problems being a rape by a man for whom she was employed to clean. The decision is arguably wrong (see below).

4.6 Complaint must be bona fide

A person victimised will not be protected if the allegation was false and not made in good faith.[12] Thus, if a person knowingly makes a false claim that there has been discrimination, s/he will not be protected if subsequently s/he is victimised, ie, treated less favourably because of the false allegation.

4.7 Interpretation of the victimisation provisions

In both *Kirby* and *Aziz*, the victimisation provisions were interpreted very narrowly. In both, it was accepted that the reason for dismissal was an act committed while attempting to prove discrimination as opposed to the allegation of discrimination itself. Yet the two should not be separated. There is a difference between an employee breaching trust or disclosing confidential information in order to prove discriminatory treatment, and disclosing it for some other reason. The aim of the provisions is to protect those who complain of discrimination (see *Cornelius v University College of Swansea*[13]); if the discriminator can argue that it was the means or method of making such a complaint which led to the dismissal and not the complaint itself, little protection is left for the victim.

10 See also *Kirby v MSC* [1980] IRLR 229, EAT.
11 EAT 109/88.
12 SDA s4(2); RRA s2(2).
13 [1987] IRLR 141, CA.

4.8 Examples of victimisation

Examples include:

a) A secretary in a solicitors' firm who was dismissed after she alleged she had been sexually harassed.[14]
b) A trade union official who was dismissed by his union because he alleged that his boss and the union had racially discriminated against him.[15]
c) An applicant, who had taken out a grievance after not being shortlisted for an appointment, was then treated differently by his head of department who became more formal and hostile.[16]
d) A lecturer brought race discrimination proceedings in 1991 which were settled. His applications for two subsequent posts failed and he claimed victimisation. He claimed he had been further victimised when he failed to get promotion and later when his head of department placed him last in a list of 18 recommended candidates for performance-related pay, giving him little chance of receiving such a payment; this was despite positive reports about him. He was awarded £15,000 for hurt feelings.[17]
e) An employee who had complained that he had been discriminated against at interview was not given the feedback which was given to two other unsuccessful candidates who were white. Although the tribunal found the rejection had not been due to race discrimination, so the complaint was false, it had been made in good faith. Thus, he had suffered victimisation.[18]
f) A black employee was barred from a bonus scheme and given a written warning after accusing his managing director of being a racist.[19]
g) A black lecturer was required to commence a teacher training course after he had commenced proceedings alleging racial abuse.

14 *Tuohy v Stoneham Langton & Passmore* 30 June 1995; Case No: 58319/93; DCLD 28.

15 *McFadden v Union of Shop, Distributive and Allied Workers* 8 December 1995; Case No: 14873/94.

16 *Bryans v Northumberland College of Arts & Technology and Others* 4 May 1995; Case No: 36674/94; DCLD 26. In this case the applicant was awarded £5,000 for aggravated damages, partly as a result of the victimisation.

17 *Majid v London Guildhall University* 2 May 1995; Case Nos: 49165/92 and 60612/93; DCLD 25.

18 *Shah v Rochdale MBC* 6 June 1995; Case Nos: 50157/93 and 32094/94.

19 *Leacock v Zeller & Sons plc* 28 September 1994; Case Nos: 30339/93 and 3593/94; DCLD 23.

He refused to do the training, was disciplined, given a written warning and then threatened with a final warning.[20]

h) A woman was made to feel like 'a leper' after she complained of sexual harassment.[21]

i) A woman was reduced to a 'gibbering idiot' after she refused to support her employer in defending a discrimination claim.[22]

4.9 Victimisation by former employer

In *Coote v Granada Hospitality Ltd*[23] the applicant claimed that failure by her previous employer to provide her with a reference was victimisation because she had earlier taken a sex discrimination case against the employer. The EAT referred to the ECJ the question of whether a claim for victimisation could be made under the ETD when the applicant was no longer in the respondent's employment. Such a claim cannot be made under the SDA.

4.10 EC law

ETD art 7 and EPD art 5 provide protection from victimisation (see **9.4.5.1** and **9.4.5.2**). It is strongly arguable that the very restrictive approach adopted by the UK tribunals and courts contravenes the broad principle laid down by the Directive, ie, that employees must be protected from dismissal when they make a complaint of sex discrimination. However, protection under the Directive may be limited to protection from dismissal as opposed to protection from other less favourable treatment.

VICTIMISATION: KEY POINTS

- It is unlawful to treat a person less favourably for:
  a) bringing proceedings under the Acts; or
  b) giving evidence in connection with such proceedings; or
  c) doing anything else by reference to the Acts; or
  d) alleging that the discriminator has acted unlawfully under the Acts.

20 *Jenkins v Governing Body of Thanet Technical College* 23 February 1994; Case No: 44852/92; DCLD 20.

21 *Pedelty v Rotherham MBC* 21 Sepember 1993; Case No: 62051/92.

22 *Bell v Tocher Neal & Co* 7 August 1996; Case No: 72964/95; DCLD 32.

23 EAT/1332/95.

- A claim must be genuine and in good faith.
- The applicant must show that:
  - the act comes within (a) to (d) above; and
  - there was less favourable treatment; and
  - the applicant was treated less favourably because s/he had done a protected act.
- To show less favourable treatment, the comparison is between the complainant and a person who has not done the protected act.
- The less favourable treatment must be as a direct result of the protected act and not for some other reason.
- Applicants should always consider EC law when arguing victimisation on the basis of sex discrimination.

CHAPTER 5

Sex and marital discrimination

Statutory references throughout this chapter are to the SDA 1975 unless otherwise stated. This chapter expalins what forms of sex discrimination are unlawful and in what circumstances, sets out the exceptions and summarises the difference between the SDA and EqPA.

5.1 Types of discrimination

Direct discrimination is where a woman is or would be treated less favourably than a man on the ground of her sex (see Chapter 2).[1]

Indirect discrimination is concerned with practices which have the effect, without necessarily the intention, of discriminating against women, either because of past direct discrimination or existing social conditions (see Chapter 3).

The SDA provides protection from direct and indirect discrimination on the basis of sex (s1), being married (s3) and victimisation (s4).[2] Both women and men are protected (s2), so that discrimination in favour of women (ie, against men) is unlawful except under the positive discrimination provisions. 'Woman' includes females of any age and 'man' males of any age.[3]

Section 3 applies only if the couple is married at the time of the discriminatory act.[4] The SDA does not protect single people even if engaged to be married,[5] nor unmarried people who are living

1 SDA s1(1)(a).

2 In *Cornelius v University College of Swansea* [1987] IRLR 141, the CA held that the word 'discriminate' included victimisation. In the SDA 'discrimination' covers all types of discrimination (s5(1)(a)) but 'sex discrimination' covers only discrimination against a man or a woman (s5(1)(b)).

3 SDA s5(2).

4 *McLean v Paris Travel Service Ltd* [1976] IRLR 202, IT.

5 *Bick v Royal West of England Residential School for the Deaf* [1976] IRLR 326, IT.

together. The comparison must be with someone of the same sex who is unmarried. A married woman could not compare herself with an unmarried man but, if treated less favourably than him, it might be direct or indirect sex discrimination.

There is no minimum requirement as to length of service or hours of work.

5.1.1 Single people and lone parents

Under the SDA, the prohibited discrimination is on the basis of being married, not marital status, so that discrimination against single people is not prohibited unless it is *sex* discrimination.

Lone parents may be protected through the indirect discrimination provisions of the SDA,[6] or on the basis that single parenthood constitutes 'family status' under EC law (see below). Provisions allow for special treatment of lone parents in relation to training so, although these discriminate against married people, they are not unlawful (see **8.4.1**).

5.1.2 EC law

The ETD art 2(1) provides that 'there shall be no discrimination whatsoever on grounds of sex either directly or indirectly by reference in particular to marital or family status'. It is not clear whether the discrimination on grounds of marital or family status must also be sex discrimination in order to be unlawful;[7] if so, discrimination against single people would not be unlawful unless it were also sex discrimination.[8] However, in *Byrne v Gloucestershire Paper Products*[9] the tribunal noted that the prohibition in the ETD of discrimination on grounds of 'marital status' is intended to protect unmarried as well as married persons, unlike the SDA. The tribunal found no discrimination in the circumstances as married and unmarried people (who had 'illicit' relationships outside marriage) were treated the same way.[10]

6 See *R v Secretary of State for Education ex p Schaffter* [1987] IRLR 53, HC.

7 See, eg, *London Underground Ltd v Edwards* [1995] IRLR 355, EAT; *(No 2)* [1997] IRLR 157.

8 This was the view taken by the EAT in *Berrisford v Woodward Schools (Midland Division) Ltd* [1991] IRLR 247, EAT.

9 29 July 1996; Case No: 25442/96; DCLD 30.

10 Note, however, that the ETD is enforceable only against public sector employers (see **9.6.7**).

In *Hyland v Minister for Social Welfare and the Attorney-General*[11] the court said, obiter, that under the parallel provisions of the Social Security Directive (7/79) it was lawful to discriminate between married and unmarried people if there were no sex discrimination. The Directive was aimed at sex discrimination which could often be disguised as discrimination based on marital status. Thus, where married men and married women were treated equally but in both cases worse than single men or single women the Directive was irrelevant. In *Aer Lingus Teoranta v The Labour Court*[12] the Irish High Court held that less favourable treatment of married women than single women was unlawful. Women, not men (who married before a certain date), were forced to resign on marriage, were refused permanent employment and did not get recognition for past service. The court held that it made no difference that other married women as well as single women would be treated differently, since it was the particular marital status of the complainants which was significant.

5.1.3 Discrimination on the ground of pregnancy

This will usually be unlawful in itself (see Chapters 15 to 17).

5.1.4 Discrimination against transsexuals

In *P v S and Another*[13] the applicant (who was born a man) was dismissed because of her proposal to undergo gender reassignment – which involved a period of dressing and behaving as a woman followed by surgery. The IT held that the situation was not covered by the SDA and referred the question to the ECJ. The ECJ held that the Directive did apply to discrimination arising from gender reassignment of the applicant, stating that: 'the scope of the directive cannot be confined simply to discrimination based on the fact that a person is of one or other sex . . .' Discrimination arising from gender reassignment 'is based essentially if not exclusively on the sex of the person concerned'. In *R v C* the EAT held that discrimination against transsexuals is unlawful under the SDA.[14]

11 [1989] 2 CMLR 44, Irish HC.
12 [1989] 1 CMLR 857.
13 Case C-13/94 [1996] IRLR 347, ECJ.
14 EAT 27 June 1997; Case no: 1063/96.

5.1.5 Discrimination against lesbians and gays

Discrimination against lesbians and gays is not unlawful under the SDA. In *R v Ministry of Defence ex p Smith and Grady*[15] the MOD policy of not allowing gay men and lesbians to serve in the armed forces was challenged as being a breach of the ETD. The CA held that the ETD did not cover sexual orientation but was solely directed to gender discrimination.[16]

However, the ECJ decision in *P v S* is likely to have implications for discrimination on the ground of sexuality. In law, there is little difference between issues in relation to gender reassignment and sexuality. The treatment is based on the sex of the person concerned. As the ECJ said, the ETD is not confined to discrimination based on the fact that a person is of one or other sex.

In *R v Secretary for State for Defence ex p Perkins*,[17] Mr Perkins was dismissed from the armed forces for being a homosexual. There is a long-standing policy of the armed forces to discharge any employee who is a homosexual. A homosexual is defined as a 'person who is sexually attracted to a member of the same sex'. The High Court said that:

> [it was] scarcely possible to limit the application of the Directive to gender discrimination, as was held in the Smith case, and there must be a real prospect that the European Court will take the further courageous step to extend protection to those of homosexual orientation, if a courageous step is necessary to do so.

The court said that all that is needed is to apply in a constructive manner the implication of the judgment in the *P v S* case. The High Court has referred to the ECJ in *Perkins* the question of whether the prohibition on discrimination under the ETD covers discrimination based on a person's sexual orientation.[18] It concluded by saying that the prospects of the ECJ upholding Mr Perkins' argument 'must be significant'.

Such discrimination on grounds of sexuality may also be a breach of the European Convention on Human Rights and the *Smith and*

15 [1996] IRLR 100, CA; and see *R v Admiralty Board of the Defence Council ex p Lustig-Prean and Beckett* [1996] IRLR 101.

16 The CA also held that the MOD policy was not irrational; it did not fall outside the significant margin of appreciation vested in the Secretary of State.

17 [1997] IRLR 297.

18 Further questions as to whether the discrimination is direct or indirect, and if so whether it can be objectively justified, were also referred to the ECJ.

Grady case (above) is likely to be referred to the European Court of Human Rights.[19]

5.2 Which workers?

Discrimination, in prescribed circumstances, is prohibited against different groups of workers. Job applicants are protected (s6(1)) (see Chapter 10) and also employees (s6(2)) (see Chapter 11). 'Employees' includes women working under a contract of service or of apprenticeship or a contract personally to execute any work or labour.[20] This definition is wider than that in the Employment Rights Act 1996 (ERA) which covers only people working under a contract of employment.[21]

A contract personally to execute work covers the self-employed and independent contractors. It included, for example, a research fellow who had a contract to study and do research,[22] a self-employed driving instructor where it was clear that the British School of Motoring had power to nominate the franchisee[23] and a special constable.[24]

The EAT has said that:

> the concept of a contract for the engagement of personal work or labour lying outside the scope of a master-servant relationship is a wide and flexible one, intended by Parliament to be interpreted as such . . . Those who engage, even cursorily, the talents, skill or labour of the self-employed are wise to ensure that the terms are equal as between men and women.[25]

If the contract relates primarily to training, the trainee is protected under s14 which makes it unlawful, in certain circumstances, for those

19 In *Perkins* the High Court also referred to: (a) the Resolution of the European Parliament of 8 February 1993 on equal rights for homosexuals and lesbians in the European Community (OJC 61/40–43); (b) the European Commission's proposals (approved by the European Parliament on 20 February 1997) prohibiting discrimination on the ground of sexual orientation in respect of EC officials; and (c) the International Covenant on Civil and Political Rights which recognises the right not to be discriminated against on the ground of sexual orientation.

20 SDA s82(1).

21 ERA s223.

22 *Hugh-Jones v St John's College, Cambridge* [1979] ICR 848.

23 *Mankoo v British School of Motoring Ltd* 657/82, EAT.

24 *Sheikh v Chief Constable of Greater Manchester Police* [1989] 2 All ER 684, CA.

25 *Quinnen v Hovells* [1984] IRLR 227 and *Tanna v The Post Office* [1981] ICR 374, EAT.

providing vocational training to discriminate against trainees (see **8.4** below).

The relevant contract is that between the person doing the work and the person for whom the work is done. A contract worker does not have an employment contract with the principal (only with her agency). Such a worker is protected under s9[26] (see **8.6**).

There must be a contract. A doctor, who applied to join a district health authority's medical list and was rejected, was barred from bringing a claim under the RRA because he was not in employment as defined above.[27] The EAT said that the doctor worked under a statutory scheme which conferred rights and obligations but there was no contract with any particular body. Nor was the Secretary of State vicariously liable under RRA s32(2) because the National Health Service Act 1977[28] said that proceedings could not be brought against the Secretary of State.[29] EC law might have filled the gap if the case had been one of sex discrimination.

In *Mirror Group Newspapers Ltd v Gunning*,[30] the CA said that a contract personally to execute any work or labour means a contract where the dominant purpose is an obligation by one contracting party personally to execute any work or labour. In this case the dominant purpose was found to be the regular and efficient distribution of newspapers and not that the distributor should himself personally carry out the work. It does not appear that EC law was argued, and again this might have provided the protection lacking under the SDA.

In *Armitage v (1) Relate (2) Heller (3) National Relate*[31] an IT held that a volunteer counsellor with Relate was in employment and so protected under the RRA. The IT found that there was a legally binding contract whereby the applicant would receive training and in return had to carry out a minimum amount of work.

26 *BP Chemicals Ltd v Gillick* [1995] IRLR 128, EAT.

27 RRA s78(1).

28 Sch 5 para 15.

29 *Wadi v Cornwall and Isles of Scilly Family Practitioners Committee and Medical Practices Committee* [1985] ICR 492. However, this may not be followed now in the light of the HL decision in *Roy v Kensington & Chelsea and Westminster Practitioner Committee* [1992] 2 WLR 239, HL. In *Roy* the HL held that a GP is entitled to enforce his private-law right by bringing an action against his family practitioner committee for withholding part of his practice allowance, even though proceedings would involve a challenge to a public law decision.

30 [1986] IRLR 27, CA.

31 8 December 1994; Case No: 43538/94 (DCLD 26).

Where an employee has been summarily dismissed, so that his/her contract immediately comes to an end, s/he will no longer be an employee, so will be unable to make a claim under the Act in relation to a subsequent appeal hearing. In *Adekeye v Post Office (No 2)*[32] the applicant was summarily dismissed on 8 June 1991 and was informed on 17 August that her appeal was unsuccessful. She complained of race discrimination in the conduct of the appeal. The CA held that she was not a 'person employed' or an employee at the date of her appeal hearing and the Act (RRA) did not cover a former employee. Nor could she argue that she was an 'applicant' seeking reinstatement on appeal. She therefore had no remedy. If the case had been one of sex discrimination she may have had a remedy under the ETD (see *Coote v Granada Hospitality Ltd*) (see **4.9**).

5.2.1 *Special categories of workers*

5.2.1.1 *Crown employees (s85)*

The SDA applies to Crown employees except Ministers of the Crown and holders of statutory posts (eg, magistrates and rent officers[33]). SDA s86 provides that the Crown or government department must not discriminate in making the appointment or in making the arrangements for determining who should be offered a statutory post. The remedy would be by way of judicial review.[34]

5.2.1.2 *The police (s17)*

The Act applies to the police. Section 17 provides that regulations under the Police Act 1964 shall not treat men and women differently except as to:

a) requirements relating to height, uniform or equipment or allowances in lieu of uniform or equipment – this is likely to be contrary to EC law (see **5.6**);[35]
b) special treatment afforded to women in connection with pregnancy or childbirth;[36] and

32 [1997] IRLR 105, CA.
33 *Knight v Attorney-General* [1979] ICR 194, EAT, and *DoE v Fox* [1980] 1 All ER 58, EAT.
34 See, eg, *R v Army Board of Defence Council ex p Anderson* [1991] IRLR 425, DC; see **6.2.2**.
35 SDA s17(2)(a).
36 SDA s17(2)(b).

c) pensions for special constables or police cadets.[37]

Special constables are also protected.[38]

Proceedings should be brought against the chief constable and/or the police authority.[39]

5.2.1.3 Prison officers (s18)

The Act applies to prison officers except that discrimination in relation to height is lawful. This is likely to be contrary to EC law (see **5.6**).

5.2.1.4 Armed forces

The army, navy and air forces are no longer excluded from the SDA except to ensure 'the combat effectiveness of the naval, military or air forces of the Crown'.[40] It is difficult to envisage any situations which would fall within this exception (particularly as men and women have to pass physical tests). It is likely that this broad exception is in breach of the ETD.

When the Armed Forces Act 1996 comes into force (probably in 1997) applicants will first have to use the internal procedure. The time limit for bringing a claim will be extended from three to six months. This extra requirement may breach EC law.

5.2.1.5 Barristers and advocates

It is unlawful for a barrister or barrister's clerk to discriminate on the ground of sex in recruiting pupils or tenants, in the terms offered or given to them, in training and access to benefits, facilities and services and in dismissal or any other detriment.[41] The provisions relating to barristers and their clerks are slightly different to those for other employed and self-employed persons and claims can only be brought in the county court. Contractual terms, including pay, are covered by the SDA and not the EqPA. It is also unlawful for a person to discriminate on the ground of sex in the giving or withholding of instructions to a barrister.[42] Similar provisions apply to advocates.[43]

37 SDA s17(2)(c).
38 *Sheikh v Chief Constable of Greater Manchester Police* [1989] 2 All ER 684, CA.
39 SDA s17(1).
40 SDA s85(4); Sex Discrimination Act 1975 (Application to Armed Forces etc) Regulations 1994 SI No 3276 as from 1 February 1995.
41 SDA s35A.
42 SDA s35A(3).
43 SDA s35B.

5.2.1.6 Illegal contracts

A person working under an illegal contract can bring a claim under the SDA, at least where the discrimination is in the course of employment but probably not under the ERA. In *Leighton v (1) Michael and (2) Charalambous*[44] the EAT held that a sex discrimination claim is not dependent upon the existence of an enforceable contract of employment as it does not seek to enforce contractual obligations. There was therefore nothing to disqualify a person, who is employed, from protection under the SDA by reason of illegality in the contract. It is not clear if the same principles would apply to a dismissal.

5.3 Discrimination by whom?

The Act prohibits discrimination by employers (s6), those employing contract workers (s9), partners (s11), trade unions and organisations of employers (s12), qualifying bodies (s13), persons concerned with provision of vocational training (s14) and employment agencies (s15). Individuals working for or as agents for such bodies may also be liable (see 7.10). Different provisions apply to each and they are set out later.

5.4 Sex and marital discrimination by employers

5.4.1 Prohibited sex discrimination by employers

Discrimination in the following circumstances is prohibited:

a) in the arrangements made by an employer for determining who should be offered employment (eg, selection procedures, advertising) (s6(1)(a)) (see Chapter 10);
b) in the terms and conditions on which a person is offered a job (eg, if a woman is offered shorter holidays, fewer perks, lower pay;
c) by refusing or deliberately omitting to offer a woman a job (s6(1)(c)) (see Chapter 10);
d) by refusing or not giving a woman the same opportunities for transfer, training or promotion (s6(2)(a)) (see Chapter 11);
e) by giving women fewer or less favourable benefits, facilities or services (eg, if free travel were provided for the families of men but not women) (s6(2)(a)) (see Chapter 11); this includes benefits,

44 [1996] IRLR 67.

facilities or services provided by another person (other than the employer) provided the employer facilitates access to them. The actual provider may also be liable under s40;

f) by dismissing a woman (s6(2)(b)) (see Chapter 14);
g) by subjecting a woman to any other detriment (ie, by treating a woman less favourably in any other way – provided such treatment is not excluded by the Act (s6(2)(b)) (see Chapters 11 and 13).

The first three situations apply only to job applicants and the last four apply to women already employed. Dismissal under (f) includes the expiry of a fixed-term contract which is not renewed and constructive dismissal.[45]

5.4.2 What is excluded by the SDA?

There are many situations where workers have no or only limited protection. In some of these cases, workers who are excluded by the UK legislation may have a remedy under EC law. The ETD prohibits discrimination in access to employment, training, working conditions, promotion and dismissal but there are far fewer exceptions (see **5.5**). Note, however, that only employees of emanations of the sate (see **9.6.7**) can rely on the directive though, where possible, UK law should be interpreted in accordance with EC law. Private sector employees can try and enforce EC law by other means (see **9.7** and **9.8**).

The following lists the situations where workers are now not protected under the SDA.

5.4.2.1 Death and retirement

The SDA,[46] as amended by the SDA 1986, exempts provisions in relation to death and retirement except, in respect of retirement, in relation to:

a) terms on which employment is offered which provide access to opportunities for promotion, transfer or training or which provide for the woman's dismissal or demotion; or
b) the way the woman is given (or refused) access to opportunities for promotion, transfer or training; or
c) dismissal or any detriment which results in her dismissal or demotion[47] (see **14.3**).

45 SDA s82(1A).
46 SDA s6(4).
47 SDA 1986 s2.

Although most discrimination by employers in relation to retirement is unlawful, the SDA does not cover access to benefits, facilities or services or subjecting a woman to any other detriment. Thus, occupational pension schemes are still outside the SDA, though covered by the EqPA and EC law (see **23.3.1**). There are separate statutory provisions covering pensions and these are set out in Chapter 23.

An employer cannot have a different retirement age for men and women (see **14.5.1**) nor a different age at which men and women become entitled to a redundancy payment (see **14.5.1.3**).

5.4.2.2 Cases where the EqPA applies

Cases where the EqPA applies are not covered by the SDA.[48] This exception is designed to avoid any overlap between the two Acts. For details of which Act applies in what circumstances see **5.7.1**.

5.4.2.3 Employment for purposes of religion

Employment for the purposes of an organised religion where employment is limited to one sex so as to comply with the doctrines of the religion or to avoid the religious susceptibilities of members of the religion.[49]

5.4.2.4 Pregnancy and maternity leave

The provision of special treatment for women relating to pregnancy, childbirth and maternity leave.[50] Men cannot, for example, claim that failure to give them paternity leave is unlawful.

There is a case before the European Court of Human Rights where a father is claiming that the refusal to allow him to claim parental leave payments (so that he could care for his child while his wife continued to work) is a breach of art 8 (guaranteeing the right to respect for family life) in conjunction with art 14 (prohibiting discrimination). The Commission, in declaring the application admissible, found that the refusal to pay him parental leave payments as a father amounted to discrimination in relation to his right to respect for family life.[51]

48 SDA ss6 and 8.

49 SDA s19.

50 SDA s2(2).

51 *AP v Austria (Application No 20458/92)* [1996] EHRLR 76; EHRLR 201.

5.4.2.5 Protective legislation

There are no longer restrictions on women working in the mines, though there are still some limited restrictions on work which can be done by both men and women and young people.[52]

5.4.2.6 Statutory authority

The EA 1989 s1 removed the blanket exclusion which used to exist for acts done under statutory authority.[53] The provisions of statutes which pre-exist the SDA (including those subsequently re-enacted), which impose a requirement which would be unlawful under the SDA, are overridden by the SDA. In the case of requirements which are indirectly discriminatory, the employer will be treated as having imposed the requirement and must justify it[54] (see **3.6.7**). If the employer cannot justify the requirement it will be unlawful. Note that this applies only to *statutory* requirements as opposed to *contractual* requirements. The Secretary of State has power both to preserve and exempt particular acts of discrimination from the SDA.[55]

In addition, discriminatory acts for the protection of women, relating to employment and vocational training, contained in legislation passed before the SDA, are exempt from the SDA where the act is *necessary* either:

a) to comply with a requirement of an existing statutory provision concerning the protection of women;[56] or
b) to comply with a provision under the Health and Safety at Work Act 1974 Pt I and it was done for the protection of women;[57] and

in either case the protection of women means their protection as regards pregnancy or maternity or other circumstances giving rise to risks specifically affecting women.

The EA 1989 lists a number of statutory provisions concerned with the protection of women, which are exempt from the Act. These include the prohibition on women working in a factory within four weeks of childbirth, or at sea or on aircraft during pregnancy.[58] Women will be entitled to suitable alternative available work or to be

52 EA 1989 s9.
53 It used to be the case that where statutes which pre-existed the SDA allowed discrimination, that discrimination was not unlawful.
54 EA 1989 s1(3).
55 EA 1989 s2.
56 SDA s51(1)(c)(i).
57 SDA s51(1)(c)(ii).
58 EA 1989 s4 and Sch 1.

suspended on full pay where, because of pregnancy or childbirth, they cannot work because of such a statutory prohibition (see **15.4**).

It is not clear whether these provisions comply with EC law. One of the exceptions to the principle of equal treatment is provisions concerning the protection of women, particularly as regards pregnancy and maternity. It is interesting to note that in a US Supreme Court case,[59] it was held that it was unlawful to prohibit women of child-bearing age from working in jobs involving lead exposure. The court held that discrimination against a woman because she was of child-bearing age was unlawful. It is unclear whether the exception in the ETD would apply where the risk is *only* greater to women (than men) because they *might* have children, as opposed to a risk for women who are, or intend to become, pregnant.

5.4.2.7 Statutory right of appeal

An IT has no jurisdiction to hear a complaint where there is a statutory right of appeal.[60] However, the substantive provisions of the SDA still apply and the appellate body must follow certain procedures.[61] This exclusion may well be in breach of EC law as it deprives the applicant of a judicial hearing.

5.4.2.8 Positive action

Positive action training by certain bodies including employers is excluded.[62] This covers special training for women, aimed at giving them opportunities that they have lacked in the past (see **12.1.2** and **12.2**). This includes encouraging women to do particular types of jobs where they are under-represented. There are also special provisions relating to lone parents[63] (see **8.4.1**).

5.4.2.9 National security

Acts safeguarding national security are excluded.[64] A certificate signed by a minister used to be conclusive evidence that the act was done to safeguard national security but this is no longer the case (see **5.6**). It is difficult to envisage a situation where this exception might apply.

59 *International Union, United Auto Workers v Johnson Controls Inc* 37 EOR 26.
60 SDA s63(2); see *Khan v General Medical Council* [1994] IRLR 646 where the CA held that the right to a review of a decision of the General Medical Council was the equivalent of an appeal so as to preclude a complaint under the RRA.
61 See *R v Department of Health ex p Gandhi* [1991] IRLR 431, DC.
62 SDA ss47–49.
63 EA 1989 s9.
64 SDA s52.

5.4.2.10 Working abroad

Women working, wholly or mainly, at an establishment outside GB are excluded.[65] If work is not done at an establishment it shall still be treated as being done at the one with which it has the closest connection.[66] Great Britain includes UK territorial waters which are adjacent to GB (not Northern Ireland which has parallel provisions) and any area designated under the Continental Shelf Act 1964 or the Oil and Gas (Enterprise) Act 1982, ie, offshore industries.[67]

In the case of women either (a) employed on a ship registered in GB, or (b) employed on aircraft or hovercraft registered in the UK and operated by someone whose main place of business or ordinary residence is in GB, the employment will be treated as in GB unless the employee works wholly or mainly outside GB.[68]

If the complaint of discrimination relates to a refusal to offer the applicant a job, the place of employment is that which the parties would have contemplated had the employment been offered.[69]

Women working in an EU country will be protected by EC law.

5.4.2.11 Public service providers

Where the employer is concerned with the provision of benefits, facilities or services to the public (such as a shop, leisure centre), discrimination in relation to those provided for the employee is not unlawful unless:

a) the provision is different for the employee;
b) the provision is contained in the contract of employment; or
c) the benefits, facilities or services relate to training.[70]

Such discrimination may be unlawful under the section of the Act which deals with discrimination in the provision of goods, facilities or services to the public.[71]

65 SDA ss6 and 10; see *Wood v Cunard Line Ltd* [1990] IRLR 281, CA.
66 SDA s10(4).
67 SDA s10(5) (s82); see Sex Discrimination and Equal Pay (Offshore Employment) Order 1987 SI No 930.
68 SDA s10(2). In *Haughton v Olau (UK) Ltd* [1986] IRLR 465, the CA held that a person employed on a ship which is not British-registered and whose work is done mainly outside British waters was outside the Act.
69 *Deria and Others v General Council of British Shipping* [1986] IRLR 108, CA.
70 SDA s6(7).
71 SDA s29.

5.4.2.12 *Competitive sport*

Competitive sport where the physical strength, stamina or physique of the average woman puts her at a disadvantage to the average man is excluded.[72] This only applies to *competitive* sport, not to referees.[73]

5.4.2.13 *Provisions in charitable instruments*

Any provision contained in a charitable instrument where benefits are conferred on persons of one sex is excluded.[74] This does not include employment by a charity.[75] This exception would almost certainly contravene EC law if the benefit comes within the scope of EC law.

5.4.2.14 *Certain educational appointments*[76]

The following educational appointments are exempt:

a) recruitment of a head teacher or principal of an educational establishment if it is necessary to comply with an instrument, relating to the establishment, which provides that its head should be the member of a particular religious order;
b) recruitment of a canon professor for a university;
c) recruitment of a woman to an academic position in a university college where this is currently required.

5.4.2.15 *Communal accommodation*

There is an exclusion where the employer provides communal accommodation (which includes shared sleeping accommodation or communal washrooms or sanitary facilities) which, for reasons of privacy or decency, should be used by one sex only.[77] If there are separate facilities no problem arises. If facilities are provided for one sex only, factors relevant to deciding whether the exception applies are:

- whether it would be reasonable to alter or extend the accommodation;
- the frequency with which the accommodation is demanded by members of the excluded sex.

72 SDA s44.
73 See *British Judo Association v Petty* [1981] IRLR 484.
74 SDA s43.
75 See *Hugh-Jones v St John's College, Cambridge* [1979] ICR 848 where discriminatory provisions in college statutes were held to be lawful.
76 EA 1989 s5.
77 SDA s46.

Thus, if it would be reasonable to partition the accommodation and/or there is a regular demand by the excluded sex, the employer may be obliged to provide separate facilities. For example, if a nurses' home or prison has accommodation for men only but women rarely require accommodation, the employer will probably not be obliged to provide it. If there is a demand and/or it would be reasonable to extend the accommodation there will be an obligation to do so. However, if an employer relies on this section, s/he must make appropriate arrangements to compensate the employee, by, for example, paying for other accommodation.[78] If an employee is prevented from working because of the lack of facilities the employer can argue that there is a genuine occupational qualification (GOQ) (see below).

5.4.3 Genuine occupational qualification (GOQ)

There is an exclusion where sex (not marital status) is a GOQ (s7). The statutory list is exhaustive. It is sufficient if only some of the duties of the job are a GOQ. Note that this may apply to both men and women, though the following examples only refer to the need for a man to do the job.

There is a GOQ in the following circumstances:

1 Where the essential nature of the job calls for a man for reasons of physiology (excluding physical strength or stamina) (s7(2)(a)). Modelling is one example. Similarly, if a dramatic performance or other entertainment requires a man to do a job for reasons of authenticity it would be lawful to recruit a man. It is not sufficient for an employer to show that a job would be more effectively done by a man; only if the essential nature of the job would be different if done by a woman does this exception apply.

2 Where the job needs to be held by a man to preserve decency or privacy because:

a) it is likely to involve physical contact with men in circumstances where they might reasonably object to its being carried out by a woman; or
b) the holder of the job is likely to do his work in circumstances where men might reasonably object to the presence of a woman

78 SDA s46(3).

because they are in a state of undress or are using sanitary facilities (s7(2)(b)), for example, toilet attendants where the cleaning takes place at a time when the toilets are in use.[79]

Sex was held to be a GOQ for the position of nurse at a home for the elderly where all the residents were women. The nurse's duties involved intimate physical contact with patients so came within 2(a) above.[80] The same principle may be applied to other medical jobs, such as doctors, though in *Drummond v Hillingdon Health Authority*,[81] the IT said that it was not necessary to have a female doctor in the post of airport medical officer as only a brief examination was required and a woman would be present in any event.[82]

In *Rowson v Contessa (Ladieswear) Ltd*,[83] an IT held that the post of manager with a specialist ladies' lingerie retailer needed to be held by a woman. The job involved physical contact with women where they might reasonably object to its being carried out by a man and when women are in a state of undress.[84]

The exception is not limited to job duties but also covers matters which are incidental to the job, such as the need to undress during a rest period. In *Sisley v Britannia Security Systems Ltd*[85] the employees, all of whom were women, worked long shifts and were provided with a bed for up to five hours at a time. They slept in their underwear. The EAT found that it was necessary to have such rest periods and that sex was a GOQ. In *Sisley* the EAT also said (obiter) that 2(b) above did not cover the situation where someone other than the holder of the job might object to the presence of a member of the opposite sex (eg,

79 *Carlton v Personnel Hygiene Services Ltd* 16327/85 and *Bank v Viroy Cleaning Services Ltd* COIT 1588/239.

80 *Stubbs v Hughesdon* (1980) (32662/79). See also *Salisbury v Philip and Judy Calvert t/a Aster House Nursing Home* 27 May 1992; Case No: 53/92 (DCLD 14) and *Hamer v Roberts* COIT 1704/89.

81 COIT 1479/4.

82 See also *Holman v Malvern Girls College Ltd* 1862/127.

83 21 September 1994; Case No: 06899/94 (DCLD 23).

84 In *Wylie v Dee & Co (Menswear) Ltd* [1978] IRLR 103, IT, the applicant had applied for a job as a sales assistant in a men's clothing store. She was rejected by the employer because, it said, the job involved taking men's inside leg measurements, and so had to be done by a man to preserve decency and privacy. However, the tribunal found that there was not much evidence to show that this was often required, as most men know their measurements, and in any case the shop employed seven other assistants who were male, any of whom could take measurements (see also s7(4)).

85 [1983] IRLR 404, EAT.

where women customers might object to a male employee in a dress shop because the women were in a state of undress). This may however, be covered by 2(a).

3 Where the job involves working or living in a private house and it needs to be done by a man (or woman) because objection might reasonably be taken to allowing a woman (or man) to have:

a) the degree of physical or social contact with a person living in the home; or
b) the knowledge of intimate details of the person's private life.

This covers jobs involving nursing care, companionship or personal attendance on a member of the family. An IT held, in one case, that being a woman was a GOQ for the job of nanny because the mother liked to bath with the baby and the nanny would be expected to come into the bathroom.[86]

In *Phillips v Cox t/a the Chaseley Rest Home*[87] the tribunal held that the job of cleaner in a rest home for high-dependence elderly, who were mainly women, did not need to be held by a woman as precautions could be taken to avoid the cleaner entering rooms where the resident is using the sanitary facilities or is in a state of undress.

4 Where the nature or location of the establishment where the employee works necessitates the employee living on the premises and:

a) the only available premises are usually lived in by men doing a particular job and are not equipped with separate sleeping and sanitary facilities for use by women in privacy from men; and
b) it is not reasonable for the employer to provide such separate facilities (s7(2)(c)).

This section is aimed at jobs in remote places, such as lighthouses and ships. It does not cover cases where employees might rest on the premises but only where they reside, either temporarily or permanently.[88] A substantial burden is placed on employers to provide separate facilities.[89]

5 The nature of the establishment where the work is done requires the job to be held by a man because:

86 *Neal v Watts* 9324/89.
87 16 April 1996; Case No: 68443/95.
88 See *Sisley v Britannia Security Systems Ltd* [1983] IRLR 404, EAT.
89 *Hermollee v Government Communications HQ* (1979) COIT 963/107.

a) it is, or is part of, a hospital, prison or other establishment for persons requiring special care, supervision or attention; and
b) those persons are all men (disregarding any woman whose presence is exceptional); and
c) *it is reasonable*, having regard to the essential character of the establishment, that the job should not be held by a woman (s7(2)(d)).

In *Henley v Secretary of State for Scotland*,[90] a policy of not employing women as assistant governors in men's prisons was held to be unlawful because women had been appointed to similar posts on an 'experimental' basis.[91]

6 Where the holder of a job provides individuals with personal services promoting their welfare or education, or similar services, and those services can most effectively be provided by a man (s7(2)(e)). This could cover social workers, probation officers, welfare workers. It probably does not allow discrimination in order to maintain a balanced team of men and women.[92] It does not cover teachers for single sex schools,[93] nor, for example, a teaching post on women-only courses run by an all-women organisation.[94]

The EAT held an IT was wrong to state that the GOQ exception did not apply because a man with the right personality and qualifications could do the work as effectively as a woman.[95] The correct comparison was between a woman and a man, both with the right personality and qualifications. Otherwise the GOQ exception would apply only if a woman would *necessarily* be better than a man.

Customer or client preference may be taken into account in some circumstances so that, for example, being a woman would be a GOQ for the post of teaching Muslim women, as they might otherwise not attend the lessons. It has been suggested that customer preference should provide a defence only where the essence of the services would be undermined if a woman were to be selected.[96]

90 (1982) unreported.
91 See also *Fanders v St Mary's Convent Preparatory School* 19043/89.
92 *Roadburg v Lothian RC* [1976] IRLR 283, IT.
93 *Fanders* (n91 above).
94 *Moult v Nottinghamshire* CC 17 June 1994; Case No: 5961/94.
95 *Greenwich Homeworkers Project v Mavrou* EAT 161/89; 37 EOR 35, EAT.
96 In *Roadburg v Lothian RC* [1976] IRLR 283 the IT held that being a man was not a GOQ where most clients were male and might resort to drunken, disorderly or threatening conduct.

7 Where the job has to be held by a man because it is likely to involve the performance of duties outside the UK in a country whose laws or customs are such that the duties could not effectively be performed by a woman (s7(2)(g)).

8 Where the job is one of two to be held by a married couple (s7(2)(h)).

5.4.3.1 Applicability of the GOQ

The GOQ exception applies only to arrangements made for recruitment, refusal to appoint a woman and to access to training, promotion or transfers. It does not allow employers to discriminate in the terms offered to an employee, in the provision of benefits, in subjecting a woman to any other detriment or in relation to dismissal. Where there is a redundancy situation the GOQ may apply to the alternative employment offered (see *Timex Corporation v Hodgson*[97]). It is not a defence to a claim of victimisation nor does it apply to discrimination on the ground of marital status.

Apart from 8 above, the exception does not apply in relation to the filling of a vacancy if the employer already has male employees:

a) who are capable of carrying out the work which can only effectively be done by a man; and
b) it would be reasonable to employ those male employees to do that work; and
c) whose numbers are sufficient to meet the employer's likely requirements without due inconvenience (s7(4)).

In *Etam plc v Rowan*, the EAT held that a man could have done most of the job, and the fitting of women's clothes could be done by a female employee.[98]

If only a small part of the job is covered by the GOQ exception it will be more difficult for the employer to argue that there is no male (or female) employee who could cover it. It is up to the employer to prove that the work falls within this exception[99] and the GOQ must relate to the specific job in question.

The EOC Code of Practice states that there are few instances of jobs where a GOQ applies and recommends that jobs for which one was used in the past should be re-examined if the post falls vacant (EOC Code of Practice Pt 1 para 14).

97 [1981] IRLR 522, EAT.
98 [1989] IRLR 150, EAT.
99 *Timex Corporation v Hodgson* [1981] IRLR 530, EAT.

5.5 Exceptions under EC law

EC law lays down general principles prohibiting sex discrimination in employment and, like UK law, it has its exceptions. These must be interpreted strictly. Many of the exceptions contained in the SDA have been repealed or amended to bring them in line with EC law, but there are still situations where applicants who fall within the SDA exceptions will have to rely on EC law. The following are excepted from the ETD.

5.5.1 Occupational activities: art 2(2)

Occupational activities for which, by reason of their nature or the context in which they are carried out, the sex of the worker constitutes a determining factor are excepted. This is similar to the GOQ exception under the SDA, but unlike the SDA, the Directive does not give examples of what activities are covered. Each GOQ must be justified. In *Commission of the European Communities v UK*,[100] the ECJ said that the principle of equality of treatment had to be reconciled with the principle of respect for private life.

In *Johnston v Chief Constable of the Royal Ulster Constabulary*[101] the ECJ considered whether the RUC could justify refusing to renew Ms Johnson's contract relying on art 2(2). Ms Johnston was a member of the Royal Ulster Constabulary Reserve. It was RUC policy not to issue female members with firearms nor to give them training in firearms because it was thought that, if women were armed, it would increase the risk of their being targets for assassination and that armed women would be less effective in areas where women were better suited, such as welfare work. In 1980, women's contracts were not renewed on the ground that a substantial part of police duties involved the use of firearms. The court held that a member state may take into consideration requirements of public safety in order to restrict general policing duties to men equipped with firearms in an internal situation characterised by frequent assassinations. However, art 2(2) had to be interpreted strictly, observing the principle of proportionality (see above). In this case, the principle of equal treatment had to be reconciled as far as possible with the requirements of public safety. The court said that it was for the national court to decide the question.

100 [1984] IRLR 29, ECJ. The ECJ held that the exclusion from the SDA of private households was not within the art 2(2) exception and was therefore a breach of the ETD.

101 [1986] IRLR 263, ECJ.

5.5.2 Protection of women: art 2(3)

Provisions concerning the protection of women, particularly as regards pregnancy and maternity are excepted. The parallel provisions under the SDA are those which allow for the special treatment of women in relation to pregnancy, childbirth and maternity leave[102] and the legislation which protects women against risks arising out of pregnancy or maternity or other circumstances giving rise to risks specifically affecting women.

This exception was also relied upon in *Johnston* (above). The ECJ said that it was clear from the express reference to pregnancy and maternity that the Directive is intended to protect a woman's biological condition and the special relationship which exists between a woman and her child. It does not allow women to be excluded from a certain type of employment on the ground that public opinion demands that women be given greater protection than men against risks which affect men and women in the same way. In the present case, it did not appear that the risks and dangers to which women are exposed when performing their duties in the police force are different from those of men. A total exclusion of women from such an occupational activity was not one that art 2(3) allows out of a concern to protect women.

The extent of art 2(3) was also raised in a French case.[103] French law allows employers to provide certain privileges for women, including extended maternity leave, time off for caring for sick children, payment of allowances for costs of a nursery or child-minder, grant of bonuses from the birth of the second child for pension calculation, some hours off on Mother's Day and a day off on the first day of school term. The ECJ held that the continuing privileges for women workers were much wider than those permissible under ETD art 2(3): they were not justified by the objective in art 2(4) which is to eliminate *de facto* inequalities (see also **5.4.2.5**).[104]

5.5.3 Promotion of equal opportunity: art 2(4)

Measures to promote equal opportunity for men and women and to remove existing inequalities which affect women's opportunities in working conditions and in access to employment, promotion and

102 SDA s2(2); see *Hofmann v Barmer Ersatzkasse* [1984] 3 CMLR 169.
103 *In Protection of Women re: EC Commission v France* [1989] 1 CMLR 408, ECJ.
104 See also the US case of *International Union* (n59 above).

training are excepted. They are similar to the provisions in the SDA which enable employers and other bodies to provide special training for women and encourage them to take advantage of opportunities for doing that work.[105]

This exception has been construed narrowly by the ECJ. In *Kalanke v Freie Hansestadt Bremen*[106] the ECJ held that national rules which guarantee women absolute and unconditional priority for appointment or promotion go beyond promoting equal opportunities and overstep the limits of the exception. Thus, a rule which stated that where two shortlisted candidates were equally qualified preference had to be given to the woman, in sectors where women were under-represented, was a breach of the ETD (see **12.5**).

5.6 The effect of EC law on the exclusions contained in the SDA

In 1984 the ECJ found that the exclusion of private households, small employers and provisions relating to retirement contained in the SDA infringed the ETD. As a result, the government was forced to pass the SDA 1986.

In *Johnston v the Chief Constable of the RUC*[107] the Northern Ireland Order[108] provided that a certificate signed by the Secretary of State, certifying that an act was done for the purpose of national security or of protecting public safety or public order, shall be conclusive. The Secretary of State had issued such a certificate. Ms Johnston conceded that she was thus barred from making a claim under the order and relied instead on the ETD.

ETD art 6 provides that member states shall introduce into their national legal systems such measures as are necessary to enable everyone who considers that they have been discriminated against under the Directive to pursue their claims by judicial process. This principle, the ECJ said, did not allow a national authority to issue a certificate – stating that the conditions for derogating from the principle of equal treatment for the purpose of protecting public safety were satisfied – so as to exclude review by the courts. The court said that acts of sex discrimination done to protect the public safety must be examined in

105 SDA ss47–49.
106 [1995] IRLR 660, ECJ.
107 [1986] IRLR 263, ECJ.
108 Sex Discrimination (Northern Ireland) Order 1976 SI No 1042.

the light of the exceptions to the principle of equal treatment. Only certain articles in the treaty allowed derogations relating to the public interest and it could not be inferred from them that there was a general proviso covering all measures taken for reasons of public safety.

Thus, the Northern Ireland order, with its blanket exclusion, infringed the directive. As a result of *Johnston*, the SDA was amended to remove the provision that a certificate signed by a minister certifying that an act was done to safeguard national security was conclusive. In future, therefore, any act purportedly done to protect public safety must fall within one of the specified exceptions.

The decision has important implications. The court said that in the light of art 6, it is for member states to ensure that there is effective judicial control. If a certificate by the Secretary of State can deprive an individual of the possibility of asserting her rights under the Directive and by so doing infringes EC law, so too do the exceptions laid down in the Act. Thus, by analogy, the decision calls into question the validity of excluding, or giving special treatment to, other categories of workers such as religious workers, the police, prison officers and the armed forces. It may be that, in specific circumstances, some individuals in these categories would be found to be carrying out an occupational activity where sex was a determining factor but this would be a question of fact in each case. Blanket exclusions for categories of workers arguably infringe the Directive. Women in such exempted categories should always consider if they would be protected by EC law.

5.7 Equal Pay Act 1970

The theory behind the EqPA is that men and women who are doing like work, work rated as equivalent under a job evaluation scheme (JES) or work of equal value should be paid the same and have the same terms and conditions of employment. For provisions relating to collective agreements see Chapter 22. The EqPA is not restricted to pay but also covers other contractual terms.

The problem with the EqPA is that, since many women whose pay and conditions are poor, are part of an exclusively female workforce, they have no male colleagues with whom to compare their pay and conditions. If there is no man with whom a woman can compare herself she cannot make a claim under the EqPA (see Chapter 18).

5.7.1 Which Act – EqPA or SDA?

The EqPA and SDA are mutually exclusive. The CA has said that:

> [both Acts] should be construed and applied as a harmonious whole and in such a way that the broad principles which underlie the whole scheme of legislation are not frustrated by a narrow interpretation or restrictive application of particular provisions.[109]

In *Rainey*,[110] the Lords, said too that EqPA s1(3) should be read as one with SDA 1975 s1(1)(b). Both Acts should also be interpreted in the light of EC law.

The EqPA deals only with matters contained in the contract of employment. A contract does not have to be in writing; it may be oral or arise out of the day-to-day practices at work. A contract usually covers pay, holidays, sick pay and other benefits.

There is an obligation on employers to provide every employee with a written statement of the terms and conditions of their employment within two months of starting employment[111] but this is often ignored. It can be enforced by the employee at an IT and should be negotiated through the union (if there is one). An employee who demands a written statement and is dismissed as a result will be treated as automatically unfairly dismissed under the ERA.[112] In practice, having a written statement does not make a great deal of difference, because, in the absence of one, the courts will construct a contract on the basis of what happens in practice.

The EqPA applies only if there is a 'comparable man' (meaning a man doing like work, work rated as equivalent under a JES or work of equal value). If the matter complained of is not in the contract or if there is no 'comparable man', only the SDA applies. Discrimination which falls outside the EqPA (such as recruitment, training and promotion) may be covered by the SDA.

The EqPA operates through the 'equality clause'. If the Act applies (see below), the woman's contract is deemed to include an equality clause. This modifies the less favourable term in the woman's contract to make it as favourable as the relevant term in the comparable man's contract.[113]

109 *Shields v E Coomes (Holdings) Ltd* [1978] ICR 1159 at p1178.
110 [1987] IRLR 26, HL.
111 ERA s1.
112 ERA s104. There is no qualifying period and there is no need to show that the right exists or has been infringed. It is enough if the claim is made in good faith.
113 EqPA s1.

The SDA covers discrimination on the grounds of sex and marital status and situations where a woman would have been treated more favourably had she been a man; it is not restricted to matters covered by the contract of employment. The EqPA covers sex discrimination only, is restricted to contractual conditions and a woman must compare herself to an actual man who is doing like work, work rated as equivalent or work of equal value. In *McKenzie-Wynn v Rowan Dartington & Co Ltd* [114] the IT held that payment of a lower *discretionary* bonus to a woman came under the SDA because there was no contractual entitlement to the bonus.

There are circumstances where neither Act applies, for example, if a woman is subject to a contractual term consisting of the payment of money by an employer who employs no men so that the equality clause could not operate (but see *Macarthys v Smith* at **18.9.4**).

The difficulties involved in deciding under which Act a case should be brought was highlighted by *Barclays Bank plc v James*.[115] Mrs James was employed by the bank in 1969 when the bank had a policy of retiring women at the age of 60 and men at 65. This was changed in 1973 so that there was a common retiring age of 60 for those who joined the bank after 1973. In 1987 a policy was introduced whereby employees in certain higher grades were allowed to work until they were aged 65. This did not include Mrs James and when she applied to work until she was 65 the bank refused and she had to retire. The EAT held that she could not make a complaint under the SDA as she could have brought a case under the EqPA by comparing herself with a Mr Barry who, said the bank, was doing equivalent work. As SDA s8(5) provides that a claim cannot be brought under the SDA where there is breach of an equality clause, the EAT said that she was precluded from complaining under the SDA. The EAT said that with a claim under the EqPA the employer can set up a defence under EqPA s1(3) by arguing that the genuine material factor defence applied. This extraordinary decision can be criticised for the following reasons:

a) If a woman were precluded from bringing a claim under the SDA because there was a comparator under the EqPA, this would effectively introduce a complex defence to a direct discrimination claim. The clear intention of SDA s8(5) was to prohibit a claim being brought under the SDA when the comparator was doing equal work, not where there existed another employee doing equal work.

114 8 November 1996; Case no: 29293/96.

115 [1990] IRLR 90, EAT.

b) In no other discrimination case has a claim been dismissed on these grounds. In *Pickstone v Freemans plc*,[116] a similar point of statutory interpretation arose. Under the EqPA s1(2)(c) an equal value claim cannot be made if there is a like or equivalent work claim. The HL said this applied only where the *comparator* was doing like work and not where there was another man doing like work. The same construction should be put on SDA s8(5).
c) *James* was concerned with a dismissal which is clearly covered by the SDA.
d) The EAT's interpretation is clearly contrary to EC law where there is no demarcation between contractual and non-contractual terms.

James highlights the need for applicants to complain under both the SDA and EqPA, as well as EC law. Note, however, that both sides in this case agreed that there were errors of law in the EAT decision and a reference to the CA was withdrawn. Barclays Bank settled the case in favour of the applicants.

Where there is less favourable treatment of a woman, the table opposite sets out which Act will provide the woman with a remedy.

116 [1988] IRLR 357, HL.

Sex Discrimination Act	Equal Pay Act
1. Non-contractual provision *offered* to a woman (SDA s6(1)(b)), eg, less favourable discretionary bonus.	
2. Contractual term *offered* to a woman which is not payment of money where the equality clause would not apply because, eg, no men are employed (SDA ss6(1)(b) and 8(3)). If the term relates to money, neither Act applies.[117]	
3. Contractual term *offered* to a woman even though, if employed, the equality clause could apply (SDA ss6(1), (5), (6) and 8(3)).	Contractual term relating to provision of benefits other than money where the equality clause could apply (SDA ss6(2)(a) and 8(5); EqPA s1).
4. Non-contractual provision relating to benefits whether or not consisting of payment of money (SDA s6(2)(a)).	Contractual terms relating to the provision of benefits consisting of the payment of money, where the equality clause could apply (SDA ss6(2)(a) and 8(5); EqPA s1).
5. Contractual term relating to benefits, other than money, but where the equality clause does not apply (SDA s6(2) and (5)).	
6. Other less favourable treatment.	

Contractual terms relating to the provision of benefits consisting of the payment of money where the equality clause does not apply are not covered by either Act, but EC law may apply.

117 But EC law is likely to fill the gap.

The SDA never applies to wages (except the *offer* of lower wages). The EqPA never applies to non-contractual matters (such as promotion) and applies only if there is a 'comparable man'.

It is not always easy to work out whether the discrimination complained of is part of a woman's contract. If in doubt *always* make a complaint of discrimination under both Acts in the alternative and EC law. The EqPA is covered in detail in Chapter 18.

SEX AND MARITAL DISCRIMINATION: KEY POINTS

- The SDA prohibits both direct and indirect discrimination.
- Both men and women are protected. Single people (even if engaged to be married) are not protected.
- EC law provides very broad protection against discrimination.
- Discrimination arising from gender reassignment (ie, against transexuals) is unlawful under EC law (*P v S*).
- It is likely that discrimination against gays and lesbians is now also unlawful after *P v S* and *Perkins*.
- Protected workers are:
  - job applicants;
  - employees;
  - the self-employed;
  - apprentices;
  - independent contractors;
  - trainees;
  - barristers, trainee barristers, advocates.

  There are no maximum or minimum age limits. Most Crown employees are protected.
- Discrimination is unlawful whether by:
  - employers;
  - partners;
  - trade unions;
  - employers' organisations;
  - persons concerned with the provision of vocational training.
- Discrimination in the following areas is prohibited:
  - in the arrangements made for deciding who should be offered employment;
  - in the terms and conditions on which a person is offered a job;

  - by refusing or omitting to offer a woman a job;
  - by not giving a woman the same opportunities for transfer, training or promotion;
  - by giving women fewer benefits, facilities or services;
  - by dismissing a woman;
  - by subjecting a woman to any other detriment.
- There are a number of exclusions, such as certain provisions relating to retirement, some existing statutory provisions (particularly for the protection of women as regards pregnancy), positive action and where sex is a genuine occupational qualification.
- The exceptions under EC law are:
  - occupational activities where sex is a determining factor;
  - provisions relating to the protection of women, particularly as regards pregnancy and maternity;
  - measures to promote equal opportunity for men and women and to remove existing inequalities.
- Some of the exclusions contained in the SDA may be in breach of EC law.
- The EqPA covers pay and other contractual terms where there are men and women who are doing like work, work rated as equivalent under a JES or work of equal value. Both direct and indirect discrimination are prohibited.
- The SDA and EqPA are mutually exclusive though should be construed as a 'harmonious whole'. If in doubt both should be pleaded as well as EC law.

CHAPTER 6

Race discrimination

Statutory references throughout this chapter are to the RRA 76 unless otherwise stated.

6.1 Race Relations Act 1976: definition of discrimination

The RRA is modelled on the SDA and the definitions of direct and indirect discrimination and victimisation are very similar.

A person directly discriminates against another if 'on racial grounds he treats that other person less favourably than he treats or would treat other persons'.[1] This includes discrimination against someone because of another person's race, for example, where a white person is dismissed for refusing to follow instructions from an employer to discriminate against a black person[2] (see also **2.4**).

Indirect discrimination is concerned with practices which have the effect, without necessarily the intention, of discriminating against a racial group or racial groups, either because of past direct discrimination, religious beliefs, cultural norms or existing social conditions (see Introduction).

6.1.1 Victimisation

Victimisation is a form of discrimination. The EAT has held that a claim for 'discrimination' in an IT1 is sufficient to cover a claim for victimisation[3] (see **25.3**).

1 RRA s1(1)(a).

2 *Zarcynska v Levy* [1978] IRLR 532; *Showboat Entertainment Centre Ltd v Owens* [1984] IRLR 7, EAT.

3 *Quarcoopome v Sock Shop Holdings Ltd* [1995] IRLR 353, EAT.

6.1.2 *Segregation*

Segregation on racial grounds is automatically treated as less favourable treatment.[4] Thus, an employer cannot, for example, stipulate that black and white workers use different facilities, even if they are equal.

Where an employer had recruited only Asian workers who had been recommended by friends, the other workers complained. The EAT said that failure to recruit non-Asian workers was not a breach of the RRA as there was no intention to segregate.[5] However, an unsuccessful applicant could have complained of direct or indirect discrimination under RRA s1(1) (see Chapters 2 and 3).

6.1.3 *Racial grounds/group*

'Racial grounds' covers colour, race, nationality or ethnic or national origins: 'racial group' means a group of persons defined by reference to the same.[6] It is important that a person's racial group is chosen properly[7] though alternative choices can be made (see **3.6.1**). A racial group may consist of two or more racial groups.[8]

Discrimination on the ground of religion or culture alone is not forbidden unless it falls within the definition of 'ethnic origins' (see below). Thus, it has been held that rastafarians are a religious (and political) group not an ethnic group as there is not enough to distinguish them from the rest of the Afro-Caribbean community.[9] Religious or cultural characteristics may, however, coincide with racial characteristics, as for example, those possessed by Muslims, and so be indirectly discriminatory. A distinction should be made between racial and religious characteristics (see **6.1.3.3**).

6.1.3.1 *Colour*

In *LB Lambeth v CRE*[10] the CA held that racial group can be defined by colour so the group could consist of more than one ethnic origin. Thus, different treatment of a group comprising Afro-Caribbeans and Asian applicants may be discrimination on the ground of colour.

4 RRA s1(2).

5 *PEL Ltd v Modgill* [1980] IRLR 142, EAT.

6 RRA s3(1).

7 This is particularly true for indirect discrimination, see *Tower Hamlets LBC v Quayyum* [1987] ICR 729 and *Orphanos v Queen Mary's College* [1985] IRLR 349, HL.

8 RRA s3(2).

9 *Dawkins v Department of the Environment* [1993] IRLR 284, CA.

10 [1990] IRLR 230, CA.

6.1.3.2 *Nationality*

Nationality covers nationality or citizenship of a state, whether acquired at birth or subsequently.[11]

In *Dhatt v McDonald's Hamburgers Ltd*[12] the CA held that it was not discriminatory to distinguish between British citizens and EC nationals on the one hand and other applicants who were not British citizens or EC nationals on the other. This was because citizens and EC nationals did not require a permit to work so the relevant circumstances were not the same. This is arguably wrong as it incorporates the very discrimination complained of into the comparative test (see **3.6.5.3**). The question of 'relevant circumstances' should not restrict the applicant's choice of racial group; it is the individuals *within* those groups who must be in a comparable situation.

6.1.3.3 *Ethnic or national origins*

This is wider than racial origins as it takes account of religious and cultural differences. The HL said in *Mandla v Lee*[13] that 'ethnic' should be construed relatively widely in a broad cultural and historic sense.[14] The question was whether Sikhs were an ethnic group. The Lords said that for a group to form an 'ethnic group', it had to regard itself as a distinct community by virtue of certain characteristics, two of which were essential. These were:

a) a long shared history, of which the group was conscious as distinguishing it from other groups; and
b) a cultural tradition of its own, including family and social customs and manners – often, but not necessarily, associated with religious observance.

In addition, the Lords said that the following characteristics could be relevant:

- either a common geographical origin or descent from a small number of common ancestors;
- a common language, which did not necessarily have to be peculiar to the group;
- a common literature peculiar to the group;

11 RRA s78.
12 [1991] IRLR 130.
13 [1983] 2 AC 548, HL.
14 In *Mandla* a boy was refused a place at a school because he insisted on wearing a turban. This was a case of indirect discrimination; there were other Sikhs at the school who did not wear a turban.

- a common religion different from that of neighbouring groups;
- the characteristic of being a minority or being an oppressed or a dominant group within a larger community.

The HL also said that a person could fall into a particular racial group either by birth or by adopting and following the customs of the group; provided a person feels a member and is accepted as such, that is sufficient.

The HL found that Sikhs were a distinct ethnic group and therefore protected by the Act. In the same case one judge said that Jews were also protected by the Act (see also *Seide v Gillette Industries*).[15] It is important to distinguish Jews as a racial group (in which case any less favourable treatment will be direct discrimination) and their religious characteristics, when the discrimination is likely to be indirect.

Muslims are probably not a racial group. In *Tariq v Young and Others*[16] an IT held that Muslims were not a racial group, as Muslims were identified by their religion and not by their race or nationality or as being an ethnic group. The tribunal distinguished *Mandla* (above) by saying that Sikhs are found in a particular part of India and are bound by culture as well as religion.[17]

Tribunals have held that Mirpuries from Kashmir are not a racial group,[18] nor are Pushtuns from Pakistan.[19] A different IT may take a different view.

Following *Mandla*, the CA has held that gypsies constitute a racial group.[20] It said that whether there is an identifiable group of persons who are defined by reference to ethnic origins is essentially a question of fact. Gypsies are a minority, with a long-shared history and a common geographical origin. They have certain, albeit limited, customs of their own, a language, and a repertoire of folk tales passed from one generation to the next. They have a language or dialect which consists of up to one-fifth Romany words in place of English words. Although they are no longer derived from a common racial stock in biological terms, that in itself did not prevent them from

15 [1980] IRLR 427, EAT; see also *Wetstein v Misprestige Management Services Ltd* EAT/523/9, 19 March 1993.

16 24773/88.

17 See also *Nyazi v Rymans* (1988) EAT 6/88 and *Kesar v (1) British Red Cross (2) Refugee Council* 8 September 1994; Case no: 4714/94; DCLD 23, p2.

18 *Bhatti v Sandwell Muslim Organisation and Others* 29 July 1993; Case no: 48589/92; DCLD 20, p3.

19 *Kabir v Bangladesh Women's Association* 10 March 1993; Case no: 10026/92; DCLD 18, p2.

20 *CRE v Dutton* [1989] IRLR 8, CA.

being a racial group. The fact that a substantial number have abandoned the nomadic way of life or have become assimilated into the general population was not decisive as there was still a discernible minority which retained its own discrete identity, separateness, and a self-awareness of being gypsies.

It has been held that 'Irish' is a national origin, comprising people from both the north and the south.[21] The Act, said the IT, should deal with the perceptions of ordinary people who would regard someone as Irish even if s/he were from Northern Ireland and, therefore, a British citizen. The Welsh are a separate ethnic group as may be Scottish people.[22]

Language alone does not determine a racial group. Thus, it could not be said that Welsh people who could not speak Welsh constituted one racial group and Welsh-speaking Welsh people formed another.[23]

In *Tejani v Superintendent Registrar for the District of Peterborough*[24] the CA held that less favourable treatment of persons born outside GB (than those born in GB) was not 'on the ground of national origins' so was not unlawful discrimination. Mr Tejani, a British citizen, complained that the registrar required him, as all others who were born abroad, to produce his passport in order to prove his residence for the purposes of his marriage. The court said that 'national' had to be identified with a particular country of origin rather than citizenship and could not cover those who came from anywhere abroad. Thus, held the CA, there was no discrimination on grounds of racial or national origins.

This is arguably wrong as it means that discrimination against those who come from 'abroad' is lawful unless a particular country is identified. It ignores the wording of the RRA, which provides that 'The fact that a racial group comprises two or more distinct racial groups does not prevent it from constituting a particular racial group' (s3(2)), and the HL decision in *Orphanos* (see **3.6.1.1**) where the Lords held that the fact that a racial group comprises two or more distinct racial groups does not prevent it from constituting a particu-

21 *Bogdeniec v Sauer-Sundstrand Ltd* (1988) 383 *IDS Brief* 15, EAT.

22 *Cameron v Argon BC* (1987) COIT 1713/71. In *Power v Northern Joint Police Board* 18 February 1997; Case no: S/101410/96; DCLD 32, an IT accepted that the Scots and English have different national origins. However, in *Boyce v British Airways plc* 25 March 1997; Case no: S/400597/96; DCLD 32, a different decision was reached.

23 *Gwynedd CC v Jones* (1986) 336 *IDS Brief* 15, EAT.

24 [1986] IRLR 502, CA.

lar racial group. Although this was not an employment case, if followed by tribunals it would allow employers to exclude from jobs 'anyone who comes from abroad', disclosing a gaping loophole in the Act. Note that in some circumstances, discrimination against those 'born abroad' might be indirect discrimination. The requirement in *Tejani* to produce a passport was not, however, one with which fewer black people than white people could comply.

6.1.3.4 Racial group

Most cases of direct discrimination are on grounds of colour, so the problem of defining the racial group for the purposes of comparison does not arise. With cases of indirect discrimination, where careful and precise comparisons have to be made between groups, or sections of groups, the definition of racial group can be crucial (see **3.6.1.1**).

6.1.4 Relevant circumstances

When making a comparison between a person of a particular racial group with that of a person not of that group, the circumstances in each case must 'not be materially different'[25] (see **2.9** for direct discrimination and **3.6.5** for indirect discrimination).

6.2 Which workers?

The same categories of workers are protected under the RRA as under the SDA (see Chapter 5). Thus employees, job applicants, the self-employed, contract workers and agency workers are covered by the Act.

There are no maximum age limits or minimum length of service requirements.

6.2.1 Crown employees (s75)

Crown employees are, in the main, protected by the Act (as they are by the SDA) except that there are rules restricting recruitment of Crown employees on grounds of birth, nationality, descent or residence, but not race or colour.[26] Crown employees who are not protected by the Act are:

25 RRA s3(4).
26 RRA s75(5).

a) those holding an office created by statute, such as justices of the peace[27] and CRE commissioners;
b) Ministers of the Crown.[28]

The Act applies to House of Commons and House of Lords staff.

6.2.2 *Armed forces (s75(2)(c))*

The RRA applies to service in the armed forces though complaints can only be made under the internal procedure. When the Armed Forces Act 1996 comes into force complaints may be made subsequently to an IT.[29] The time limit will be extended to six months in such cases. Job applicants can complain direct to an IT

In *R v Army Board of Defence Council ex p Anderson*,[30] the High Court quashed the Army Board's decision to deny the applicant compensation or other redress, saying that the board should have made a finding on whether the complaint was proved and considered whether compensation ought to be paid. The High Court pointed out that the board must achieve a high standard of fairness; there should be a proper hearing, the complainant should have access to all material seen by the board and the board should meet.

6.2.3 *Police officers (s16)*

Applicants for and members of the police force are protected.[31] Complainants must sue the chief officer of police or the police authority. A special constable comes within this section.[32]

6.2.4 *Prescribed bodies (s75(5))*

Certain prescribed bodies, such as the Bank of England, the British Council and the National Gallery,[33] are permitted to restrict employment to persons of particular birth, nationality, descent or residence.

27 *Knight v Attorney General* [1979] ICR 194, EAT.
28 RRA s75(10)(c).
29 Armed Forces Act 1996 s23.
30 [1991] IRLR 425, DC.
31 *Singh v Chief Constable of Nottinghamshire Constabulary* Case no: 08807/88.
32 *Sheikh v Chief Constable of Greater Manchester Police* [1989] 2 All ER 684, CA.
33 Race Relations (Prescribed Public Bodies) (No 2) Regulations 1994 SI No 1986.

6.2.5 *Barristers and advocates*

Barristers (pupils and tenants) and advocates are protected against discrimination by barristers, advocates and barristers' clerks and also by those instructing them (ie, solicitors).[34] The provisions are very similar to those under the SDA (see **5.2.1.5**). Complaints[35] may only be brought in the county court.

6.3 Discrimination by whom?

As with the SDA, discrimination (in the defined circumstances) is prohibited whether by employers (s4), by firms with more than six partners (s10), those employing contract workers (s7), trade unions and employers' organisations (s11), qualifying bodies (s12), vocational training bodies (s13) and employment agencies (s14).

6.4 Prohibited race discrimination by employers (s4)

Race discrimination in employment is covered by identical statutory provisions as sex discrimination (see Chapter 5), except that the RRA covers all terms of employment. There is no distinction in the RRA between pay and other contractual terms,[36] so both direct and indirect discrimination in relation to pay are unlawful (see **18.2**).

Thus, discrimination in recruitment, transfer, training, promotion, dismissal or subjecting a person to a detriment is unlawful. These issues are covered in Chapters 10 to 13.

6.4.1 *Exclusions under the RRA*

There are far fewer exceptions under the RRA than under the SDA. They apply to discrimination against job applicants and employees.

6.4.1.1 *Private households*

Employment for the purposes of a private household in relation to job applicants is exempt.[37] If, however, the job is really for a company,

34 RRA ss26A and 26B as amended by Courts and Legal Services Act 1990 ss64 and 65.

35 Under ss26A and 26B.

36 There is no separate statute dealing with pay.

37 RRA s4(3).

then the employee may be protected. In one case, a man applied to be a private chauffeur to a company chair.[38] His job was mainly connected with the company. The tribunal said that as the employment was primarily for business purposes it did not fall within the exception.

The exemption does not cover discrimination by victimisation so that if the employee makes a complaint of discrimination and is sacked s/he will be protected. Nor does the exemption apply to contract workers. Note that there is no protection against racial discrimination under EC law.

6.4.1.2 Employment abroad

Employment outside GB is excepted. Employees working wholly or mainly at an establishment outside GB are not covered by the RRA.[39] This exception is similar to SDA s10 (see **5.4.2.10**). The difference is that in the case of a person either:

a) employed on a ship registered in GB; or
b) employed on an aircraft or hovercraft registered in the UK and operated by a person whose principal place of business or ordinary residence is in GB;

s/he will be protected unless s/he works **wholly** outside GB.[40]

This does not apply if there is a contract with a person whose main place of business or residence is outside the UK in which case the employee will not be protected.

6.4.1.3 Seamen

Seamen recruited abroad are not covered unless the employment is concerned with the exploration of the continental shelf. It is not unlawful for an employer (under s4) to discriminate against a seaman who applies for a job or was engaged for a job outside GB. This exception also applies to a person brought to GB with a view to his/her entering into an agreement in GB to be employed on a ship.[41] There is no parallel exception under the SDA.

38 *Heron Corporation v Commis* [1980] ICR 713, EAT.
39 RRA ss4, 8 and 78.
40 RRA s8(2).
41 RRA s9(4).

6.4.1.4 Statutory authority

Acts which are authorised by a statute (whether passed before or after the RRA) are exempt.[42] Discrimination under the RRA is lawful if done:

a) 'in pursuance of' an Act of Parliament, an Order in Council or an instrument made under an enactment by a government minister (whether passed before or after the RRA);
b) in order to comply with any condition or requirement imposed by a Minister by virtue of any enactment.[43]

The HL adopted a narrow construction of the words 'in pursuance of any instrument' in *Hampson v Department of Education and Science*.[44] A Hong Kong trained teacher was refused qualified teacher status in England because she only had two years' training. The Secretary of State did not consider this to be comparable to the three years required in England. As the regulations[45] did not require a minimum number of years' training (but only comparable training), the Secretary of State had exercised his discretion in not treating the training as comparable. The HL said that these words were confined to 'acts done in necessary performance of an express obligation contained in the instrument and do not also include acts done in exercise of a power or discretion conferred by the instrument'.

Thus the action must be specified in the enactment, order or instrument to be protected by this exemption. The exemption does not protect administratively chosen requirements or conditions which represent one of a variety of possible modes of doing those actions. As pointed out by the HL, almost every discretionary decision taken by a statutory body is taken against a statutory background which imposes some duty and a wide interpetation would lead to an unacceptably wide exemption.

Similarly, in *General Medical Council v Goba*,[46] the EAT said that s41 did not provide an 'umbrella protection' against all discriminatory acts carried out by a statutory body. Under the Medical Act 1983 the GMC can determine the registration of persons qualifying overseas. To do this, the GMC requires applicants to take a six-part English qualification test. There are limits on the number of times a

42 RRA s41.
43 RRA s41(1).
44 [1990] IRLR 302, HL.
45 Education (Teachers) Regulations 1982 SI No 106.
46 [1988] IRLR 425.

doctor may take the test and Dr Goba failed the test seven times so was prohibited from taking the test again for a period. The EAT said that the phrase 'in pursuance of' means that the act must have been one which was 'reasonably necessary in order to comply with any condition or requirement of the statute or order'. It did not provide a blanket defence to Dr Goba's claim that he had been discriminated against in his claim for registration as a doctor in the UK.

Also exempt is discrimination (on the basis of nationality, place of residence or length of residence in or outside the UK) if the act is done:

a) in pursuance of any arrangements made by a government minister; or
b) in order to comply with a condition imposed by a government minister under any enactment.

'In pursuance' has the same meaning as set out above. This means that discrimination under the Immigration Act or Rules will not generally be unlawful, unless it is covered by EC law relating to EU nationals. A certificate signed by a Minister confirming this is conclusive.[47]

6.4.1.5 Immigration Rules

The Immigration Rules and the Immigration Act 1971 discriminate on the grounds of both race and sex. However, they cannot generally be challenged under the RRA because of the above exclusion. It is worth checking the source of any potentially discriminatory rules or practices to see if they arise from a statutory obligation. Only those actions reasonably necessary to comply with any requirement or condition are excluded from the Act; if there is no specific condition or requirement they may be unlawful.

6.4.1.6 Asylum and Immigration Act 1996

Section 8 of the 1996 Act creates a new offence of employing a person who is subject to immigration control. This is a person who requires leave to enter or remain in the UK under the Immigration Act 1971. It applies only to employees, not the self-employed. The Labour Party said it would not enforce these provisions, however, the Labour government has not yet repealed them.

47 RRA s69(2)).

The employer commits the offence where s/he employs a person aged 16 or over, who is subject to immigration control under the Immigration Act 1971, unless:

a) that person has current and valid permission to be in the UK and that permission does not prevent him/her from taking the job in question; or
b) the person comes into a category where such employment is otherwise allowed.

The employer has a defence if s/he proves the following:

a) before the employment began, the employee produced to the employer a document, which the employer *believed* to be an original, to relate to the employee and be of a specified description.[48] Thus, if the employer makes a mistake about the nature of the document s/he still has a defence. The test is subjective. A summary of the list of specified documents can be found in Appendix 6.[49]
and
b) the employer retains either the document, or a copy or other record of it (such as scanning it on to a computer database).

However, the defence does not apply where the employer *knew* that the employee has not been granted leave to enter or remain or that the leave is not valid and subsisting or is subject to a condition precluding him/her taking employment.

Implementation. This applies only to employees who started work on or after 27 January 1996. The offence cannot be committed in respect of any employee who started work prior to this date.

Home Office guidance. The Home Office has produced guidance for employers. Employers are advised to carry out checks which, the Home Office suggests, could be built into their normal recruitment procedures. Such checks are not compulsory but if the employer employs a person with no right to work, s/he will not have the

48 The guidance states that the employer needs to be satisfied that the document *appears* to be: an original; and related to the person in question; and one of the specified documents.
49 A full description of the relevant documents is contained in Appendix A to the Home Office guidance.

statutory defence. The guidance states that if an employer tries to 'avoid prosecution by refusing to consider for a job anyone who looks or sounds foreign, [they] are likely to contravene the Race Relations Act 1976'. The guidance also states that checks must be made in a non-discriminatory manner.

The assumption is that employers will normally rely on documented National Insurance numbers where they are available. The guidance states that this should cover the vast majority of potential new employees. There is no need to ask for more than one document. Employers are not expected to investigate the validity or authenticity of documents they have seen.

The guidance points out that 'most people from ethnic minorities are British citizens.' It makes it clear that the best way to ensure that the employer does not discriminate is to '*treat all applicants in the same way at each stage of the recruitment process*'.

Examples of unlawful discrimination would be

- if checks are carried out on only some employees; the guidance states that if checks are carried out on potential employees who by their appearance or accent seem to be other than British, this might constitute unlawful racial discrimination;
- if an employer asks only some applicants for proof of their right to work; the guidance states that if an employer asks for a document from one applicant, the employer should ask for a document from all applicants under consideration at that stage;
- if different requirements (to produce documents) are imposed because of a person's race, colour, nationality, ethnic or national origins. The guidance gives the example of asking a person who looks or sounds foreign for their passport whereas a person who looks and sounds British is asked only for a document which includes their National Insurance number;
- if an employer accepts only employees with a British passport and will not accept other documents which show that the individual has a right to work;
- if, in order to avoid the need to carry out a check, the employer adopts a method of recruitment which is discriminatory, such as 'word of mouth recruitment' (see **10.2.2**).

The guidance also gives advice on verifying, recording and retaining relevant documents, categories of workers and their ability to work (such as working holiday-makers, au pairs, asylum seekers), liability and other common questions.

Penalty. The maximum penalty, in relation to each charge, is a level 5 fine, currently £5,000. The magistrates' court will take account of the seriousness of the offence and the financial circumstances of the employer.

Helpline. There is a helpline for employers which will give guidance to employers. If an employer has doubts about an applicant's immigration status, the employer should be encouraged to ring the helpline.[50]

The guidance also refers to the CRE Race Relations Code of Practice and the CRE guidance entitled 'The Asylum and Immigration Act 1996: Implications for Racial Equality' (see Appendix 6).

Conclusion. It is likely that the Act will lead to employers increasingly recruiting only those who they are sure are not subject to immigration control. This is illustrated by the CA decision in *Dhatt v McDonalds Hamburgers Ltd.*[51] The applicant, who was born in India but was given indefinite leave to enter the UK, had no restrictions with regard to employment. His passport showed that he had leave to enter for an indefinite period and this indicated that he did not need a work permit. However, he was dismissed because, the employer did not accept his passport as proof of his right to work. He argued that a requirement to produce a work permit (when not required to do so by law) was directly discriminatory on the ground of nationality as the employers did not make a similar request of British and EU citizens.

The CA held that an employer had a general duty to ensure that its employees complied with immigration law and that to distinguish between British and EU nationals on the one hand and other nationals on the other did not constitute unlawful discrimination.

This is a bad decision and arguably wrong. Less favourable treatment of a person because of his/her nationality is unlawful under the RRA unless it falls within one of the exceptions. Refusal to employ a person who, because of their nationality, is *not* legally allowed to work will come within the exception, but Mr Dhatt *was* allowed to work. The CA held that Mr Dhatt could not compare himself with UK and EU nationals because they do not need permission to work so the circumstances are different. However, this incorporates discrimination into the comparison and, in the light of *James v Eastleigh BC*,[52] is arguably wrong (see **2.9.1**).

50 Telephone number: 0181 649 7878; open Monday to Friday, 9am to 5pm.

51 [1991] IRLR 130, CA.

52 [1990] IRLR 288, HL.

At the time of the decision there was no obligation on employers to check an employee's immigration status. Even now, the employer's decision to dismiss Mr Dhatt would arguably be unlawful. The Home Office guidance makes it clear that if employers 'refuse to consider anyone who looks or sounds "foreign", this is likely to be unlawful discrimination'. Similarly if employers 'carry out checks only on potential employees who by their appearance or accent seem . . . to be other than British this . . . may constitute unlawful racial discrimination'. The crucial point is that all applicants must be treated in the same way at each stage of the recruitment process. Now that it is clear that employers may carry out specified checks, there is no need for the court to imply to employers a 'general responsibility to ensure that those who work in his business comply with the law' as it did in *Dhatt*.

There are special rules for EU nationals. The basic principle is that EU workers should be able to work freely in all EU countries. In practice, this freedom is not all that it seems, but discussion of these rules and immigration law is beyond the scope of this book.

6.4.1.7 Statutory right of appeal

An IT has no jurisdiction to hear a race discrimination complaint where there is a statutory right of appeal in respect of the complaint (s54(2)). In *Khan v GMC*[53] the CA held that there was no jurisdiction to hear a discrimination claim by a doctor who had been refused full registration because he had qualified in Pakistan. The CA held that because the applicant had a right of review of the GMC's decision (under Medical Act 1983 s25) this was 'a proceeding in the nature of an appeal' within the meaning of the s54(2), so he was barred from making a complaint to an IT. In order to fall within this exception the review must have the characteristics of fairness enabling the decision to be changed.

The High Court has held that, where there is an appeal, the substantive provisions of the RRA apply. The procedures followed in such an appeal must be fair and an oral hearing should be held where the issues cannot be fairly resolved otherwise. Appellants are entitled to disclosure of all the material necessary to enable them to present their appeal and they should generally have access to relevant documents, provided that they are not covered by public interest immunity or considerations of confidentiality.[54]

53 [1994] IRLR 646, CA.

54 See *R v Department of Health ex p Gandhi* [1991] 431, DC.

6.4.1.8 National security

Acts safeguarding national security are excepted.[55] A certificate to this effect, signed by a Minister, is conclusive.[56] This is similar to the exception in the SDA (see above).

6.4.1.9 Sports selection

Discrimination in relation to selection for sports to represent an area or country on the basis of nationality, place of birth or length of residence are exempted.[57] There is no parallel exemption under the SDA.

6.4.1.10 Training for work abroad

There is an exception for provision by employers of training for skills to be exercised outside GB by a person not normally resident in GB.[58] There is no parallel exception under the SDA.

6.4.1.11 Special training

Special training provisions for certain racial groups are exempt.[59] Thus, training providers and employers can provide special training in certain circumstances. These provisions are set out in detail in Chapter 12.

6.4.1.12 Public service providers

Where the employer is concerned with the provision of benefits, facilities or services to the public, discrimination in relation to those provided for the employee is not unlawful unless:

a) the provision is different for the employee;
b) the provision is contained in the contract of employment; or
c) the benefits, facilities or services relate to training.[60]

This is identical to SDA s6(7). However, such discrimination may be unlawful under RRA s20 which deals with discrimination in the provision of goods, facilities or services to the public.

55 RRA s42.
56 RRA s69(2)(b).
57 RRA s39.
58 RRA s36.
59 RRA ss37 and 38.
60 RRA s4(4).

6.4.1.13 *Special needs*

Measures taken to give persons of a particular racial group access to facilities or services or to meet the special needs of persons of that group with regard to their education, training, welfare or ancillary benefits are excepted.[61] This is a very broad exception but it is not clear if it covers the employment of a person of a particular racial group in order to work to provide for the special needs of that group.

6.4.1.14 *Safety helmets on construction sites*

The EA 1989 s11 exempts Sikhs who wear turbans from any statutory requirement to wear safety helmets on building sites. The Act also states that an employer will not be liable for any injury sustained by a Sikh which he would not have suffered had he been wearing a helmet. An employer who insists that a Sikh wear a helmet will be deemed to have discriminated indirectly as s12 provides that such a requirement will not be 'justifiable'.

Where the exception does not apply, for example, if a Sikh is required to wear a safety helmet in another job, there may be indirect discrimination unless it can be justified.[62]

6.4.1.15 *Genuine occupational qualifications*

There is exemption where the race of the person is a GOQ (s5). The Act does not specify where the burden of proof lies though it is likely that the employer must prove there is a GOQ defence.

There will be a GOQ if:

a) the job involves participation in some dramatic performance or entertainment where a person of a particular racial group is required for authenticity (s5(2)(a)); this is similar to SDA s7(2); or
b) the job involves participation as an artist's or photographic model in the production of a work of art or visual image and the race of the model is required for reasons of authenticity (s5(2)(b)); or
c) the job is in a place where food or drink is served to the public (or a section of it) and waitresses or waiters of a particular race are required to make the atmosphere authentic (s5(2)(c)); this would apply, for example, to the employment of Chinese waiters in a Chinese restaurant; or

61 RRA s35.
62 *Dhanjal v British Steel plc* (1994) unreported, 24 June.

d) the job holder provides persons of the worker's racial group with personal services promoting their welfare and those services can most effectively be provided by a person of a certain racial group (s5(2)(d)); this is the same as SDA s7(2)(e).

The GOQ exemption applies where some or all of the duties fall within any of (a) to (d) above.

In *Tottenham Green Under Fives Centre v Marshall*,[63] a day care centre wanted to replace an Afro-Caribbean nursery nurse who had left with another person of Afro-Caribbean origin.[64] The centre had a policy of maintaining a balance between ethnic backgrounds, both among the children and the staff. Thus, children were taken from the waiting list, not in order but by ethnic background in order to try to balance between age, sex and ethnic background. The EAT said that a delicate balancing exercise had to be carried out 'bearing in mind the need to guard against discrimination and the desirability of promoting racial integration . . . where genuine attempts are being made to integrate ethnic groups into society, too narrow a construction might stifle such initiatives'. It held that:

a) the particular racial group will need to be clearly defined because it will have to be that of the holder of the post and also that of the recipient of the personal services;[65]
b) the holder of the post must be directly involved in the provision of the services, although this need not necessarily be on a one-to-one basis. If the post-holder provides several personal services to the recipient, the defence is established provided that one falls within the GOQ;
c) the phrase 'promoting their welfare' is very wide and it would be undesirable to seek to narrow it;
d) the question of whether the services can most effectively be provided by a person of a particular racial group is a question of fact. If a tribunal accepts that the conscious decision of a responsible employer to rely on the GOQ is founded on a genuinely held and reasonably based opinion that a GOQ requirement will best promote the welfare of the recipient, considerable weight should be given to that decision. It would not, however, be enough to use the GOQ to achieve a racial balance amongst the staff.

63 [1989] IRLR 147, EAT.

64 As some children used Afro-Caribbean dialect at home, the worker should be able to read to the children in that dialect. There were also special areas of concern in health.

65 *Tottenham Green Under Fives Centre v Marshall* [1989] IRLR 147, EAT.

In the same case, on a second appeal from the IT, the EAT held that no duty should be ignored, even if relatively minor, unless it were *de minimis* or a sham.[66]

In a subsequent case,[67] a more restrictive interpretation was adopted. A council advertised two managerial jobs in the housing benefit section. Over half of the tenants dealt with by the section were Afro-Caribbean or Asian so the council decided that the jobs should be held by Afro-Caribbean or Asian applicants. The EAT held that the holders of the posts would not be providing 'personal services'. The phrase, said the EAT, envisages circumstances where there is direct contact – mainly face-to-face or where there could be susceptibility in personal, physical contact – and where language or a knowledge and understanding of cultural and religious background are of material importance. This was confirmed by the CA, which also said that the exception did not provide for positive action.

The GOQs under the RRA are very much narrower than those under the SDA. The exception applies only to arrangements made for recruitment, failure to recruit, and access to promotion and transfer, not to the terms on which a job is offered or provided, nor to other benefits, facilities or services provided. It does not allow employers to discriminate in dismissal or in subjecting employees to any other detriment, nor does it provide a defence to a claim of victimisation. The exception applies where only some of the duties fall within the GOQ categories as well as where all of them do (RRA s5(3)).

The exception does not apply in relation to the filling of a vacancy if the employer already has employees of the racial group in question:

a) capable of carrying out the duties falling within the exception; and
b) whom it would be reasonable to employ on those duties; and
c) whose numbers are sufficient to meet the employer's likely requirements in respect of those duties without due inconvenience (s5(4)); this is identical to SDA s7(4) (see **5.4.3.1**).

Note that an individual cannot make a complaint about the placing of a discriminatory advertisement unless s/he applied for the position. Only the CRE or EOC can take action where there is simply an 'intention' to discriminate.[68]

66 *Tottenham Green Under Fives Centre v Marshall (No 2)* [1991] ICR 320, EAT.
67 *LB Lambeth v CRE* [1989] IRLR 379, EAT; [1990] IRLR 231, CA.
68 *Cardiff Women's Aid v Hartup* [1994] IRLR 390, EAT.

RACE DISCRIMINATION: KEY POINTS

- Direct and indirect discrimination and victimisation are unlawful under the RRA.
- Discrimination against someone because of *another* person's race is unlawful under the RRA, unlike the SDA.
- Segregation on racial grounds is less favourable treatment under the RRA.
- 'Racial grounds' covers colour, race, nationality and ethnic or national origins; 'racial group' means a group defined by reference to racial grounds and may comprise two or more racial groups. 'Ethnic' should be construed relatively widely (*Mandla*).
- Religious discrimination is not prohibited unless it is indirect race discrimination.
- The same categories of workers are protected as under the SDA, ie, employees, job applicants, the self-employed, contract workers, agency workers.
- There are no minimum age limits or minimum length of service requirements.
- Discrimination is prohibited whether by:
  - employers;
  - firms with more than six partners;
  - trade unions;
  - employers' organisations;
  - qualifying bodies;
  - vocational training bodies;
  - employment agencies.
- Special categories:
  - most Crown employees are protected, except statutory post-holders and those employed by certain prescribed bodies;
  - although the Act applies to the armed forces, complainants must normally follow an internal procedure;
  - police officers are protected.
- The RRA covers *all* terms of employment, including contractual ones. There is no separate statute dealing with pay.
- There are fewer exclusions than under the SDA.
- The Asylum and Immigration Act 1996 creates a new criminal offence of employing a person who has no right to work; employers are advised to carry out checks to ensure their employees have a right to work, but these must be carried out in a non-discriminatory way.

CHAPTER 7

Liability for discrimination

7.1 Employers' liability

An employer is liable for discrimination carried out by a worker (whether an employee or self-employed)[1] in the course of his or her employment.[2] This is the case whether or not the discrimination was done with the employer's knowledge or approval. The employer has a defence if it can prove that it took such steps as were reasonably practicable to prevent the discrimination.[3]

7.2 Employees' liability

An employee who carries out discrimination 'in the course of his employment' will also be personally liable under the SDA, RRA and DDA. This applies even where the employer has a defence (see below). Thus, the applicant should consider bringing an action against both employee and employer.[4] If the discrimination does not occur in the course of employment the employee is not liable under the SDA, RRA or DDA.[5]

7.3 Liability of others aiding discrimination

A person who knowingly aids (or helps) another person to discriminate unlawfully is also treated as having discriminated. This does not

1 Defined by SDA s82; RRA s78; DDA s68(1) (see **5.2**).

2 SDA s41; RRA s32; DDA s58.

3 SDA s41(1) and (3); RRA s32(1) and (3); DDA s58(5).

4 In *ARG Armitage, N Marsden and HM Prison Service v Johnson* [1997] IRLR 162 £500 was awarded against each of the individual respondents as well as £27,500 against the Prison Service. The low amount against each of the individual respondents, according to the IT, was because they were employees.

5 There may be other liability for harassment (see **13.8**).

apply if the person has relied on a statement by the discriminator that the act was not unlawful. For example, if a number of employees were involved in an attempt to harass or get rid of an employee because of his/her race, sex or disability, each employee would be liable. Only if the employee relied on a statement by the perpetrator that the reason for the action was for some other non-discriminatory reason would s/he escape liability.

7.4 Liability of employers for acts of third parties

In *Burton and Rhule v De Vere Hotels*[6] the EAT held that an employer had subjected its employees to racial harassment where a third party (an entertainer at the employer's hotel)[7] racially and sexually harassed the employer's employees. The test was whether the event in question was something which was sufficiently under the control of the employer that it could, by the application of good employment practice, have prevented or reduced the harassment (see **13.5**). This case shows the extent to which employers may be liable for discrimination where it is within their control. It may apply, for example, to hospitals in a situation where a patient racially or sexually abuses or harasses an employee or where an outside contractor (working for the employer) harasses an employee. Employers must therefore take all practicable steps to ensure that the working environment is free from discrimination; otherwise they may be liable for the acts of discrimination against their employees by third parties.

7.5 In the course of employment

In determining whether an employer is liable for the acts of a worker, the initial question is whether the worker was acting 'in the course of his employment'.

The test as to whether the discrimination is 'in the course of employment' has now been clarified by the CA decision in *Jones v Tower Boot Co Ltd* which supersedes previous decisions that interpreted this phrase restrictively.[8] The CA decided that employers are liable for all acts of racial and sexual harassment committed by the

6 [1996] IRLR 596.
7 For whose actions the employer would not be vicariously liable under the Acts.
8 [1997] IRLR 168; [1997] ICR 254, CA. *Irving v The Post Office* [1981] IRLR 289, CA, must now be wrong.

employees, which take place during their employment, unless employers can show they have done everything practicably possible to prevent the discrimination. Although this was a case under the RRA, the CA stated that the same principles would apply under the SDA and there seems no reason to doubt that the same principles would also apply under the DDA.

In *Jones v Tower Boot Co Ltd* the applicant, a 16-year-old boy, was subjected to horrific physical and verbal racial abuse. This included employees burning his arm with a hot screwdriver, whipping him on the legs with a welt, throwing bolts at him and trying to put his arm in a lasting machine. The EAT adopted the test of vicarious liability which applies in relation to acts of negligence by employees for which the employer may be liable. This involves proof that the employee acted in a way which was authorised by the employer or in a way which was a mode, although an improper mode, of acting in an authorised way. Thus, the EAT held that the employer was not liable because the acts could not be described, by any stretch of the imagination, as an improper mode of performing authorised tasks. The CA robustly rejected this test together with the implicit assumption that the more heinous the acts of harassment the less likely the employer will be liable under the discrimination legislation.

The CA held that the test to determine whether an employer is liable for discrimination by a worker was not the same as the test for vicarious liability for tortious (negligent) acts of employees at common law. The purpose of the sections[9] is, said the CA:

> to deter racial and sexual harassment in the workplace through a widening of the net of responsibility beyond the guilty employees themselves, by making all employers additionally liable for such harassment, and then supplying them with the reasonable steps defence under s32(3) which will exonerate the conscientious employer who has used his best endeavour to prevent such harassment, and will encourage all employers who have not yet undertaken such endeavour to take the steps necessary to make the same defence available in their own workplace.

Thus, the RRA, SDA and DDA impose a duty on employers to prevent discrimination by their employees. Accordingly, employers are made responsible for a much wider range of acts of their employees than under common law. Harassment of all kinds (and other forms of discrimination) carried out at work is likely to be 'in the course of employment'.

9 RRA s32; SDA s41.

In conclusion, the CA said that to allow such racial harassment to slip through the net of employer responsibility would 'seriously undermine the statutory scheme of the discrimination Acts and flout the purposes which they were passed to achieve'.

7.5.1 Liability extends to acts of all employees

Employers are potentially liable for the acts of all employees, not just managers. This was confirmed in *De Souza v Automobile Association*, where the CA said that it was quite clear that an employer was liable for any employee 'acting in the course of his employment'.

Where racial harassment took place by a sales representative while the applicant was on a sales and marketing training course,[10] the IT found that the incidents took place within working hours and on the company's premises and were committed in the course of the sales representative's employment.

7.5.2 Express prohibition by employer does not remove liability

The fact that the employer expressly prohibited the employee from carrying out the act does not take it outside the 'course of employment', though it may provide a defence if accompanied by other measures.[11]

7.5.3 Discrimination outside working hours

In *Jones v Tower Boot Co Ltd* (above) the CA recognised that there may be situations where there is discrimination by one employee against another but it is done outside the workplace. It may occur in a rest break, just before going home or outside the workplace. There are, as the CA said, an infinite variety of circumstances and it will be a question of fact for each tribunal to resolve.

In *Waters v Commissioner of Police of the Metropolis*[12] the applicant was allegedly assaulted by a fellow officer while she was in a section house when she and the perpetrator were off duty. It was assumed this did not fall within the common law test of vicarious liability. However, the statutory test under the discrimination Acts was not considered.

10 *Robinson v Inter Office Products Ltd* 4039/89.
11 *Canadian Pacific Railway Co v Lockhart* [1942] 2 All ER 464.
12 [1995] IRLR 531.

In another case[13] the applicant was subject to racist remarks in the mess room just before he went home. The IT held that the remarks were not made in the course of employment, though they would have been if the employees had been working at the time. However, this is now probably wrong as the IT relied on *Irving*[14] which was overruled in *Tower Boot.* Arguably, the cut-off point should be when the employees actually leave the workplace. However, there may be exceptions to this, such as work-related social occasions like the Christmas party.[15] Preparation to start and leave work and breaks during the working day should be treated as being 'in the course of employment'. It is clear from the *Tower Boot* decision that a wide interpretation must be given to the scope of liability otherwise it would be all too easy to undermine the purpose of the Acts – which is to protect victims and punish perpetrators.

7.6 The employer's defence

The employer has a defence if it proves that it took 'such steps as were reasonably practicable to prevent the employee from doing that act, or from doing in the course of his employment acts of that description'.[16] An IT has held that this means that the employer must take steps *before* any act occurs.[17]

Failure to adopt an equal opportunities policy, as recommended by the code of practice and lack of explanation as to why there is not one, may lead to a finding that there is no defence.[18] In *A v Civil Aviations Authority*[19] an IT held that a large employer must ensure that an adequate policy is 'understood, implemented and observed throughout the workplace'.

In *Balgobin and Francis v LB Tower Hamlets*,[20] two women were sexually harassed by a co-worker and when they complained to man-

13 *Lawal v Regional Railways North Eastern Ltd* DCLD 28, 15 April 1996; Case No: 70807/95.

14 *Irving v The Post Office* [1981] IRLR 289, CA.

15 In *Cumberbatch v Hickson and Department of Social Security* 20 October 1994; Case No: 3221/94, an IT chair said it could 'see little logical difference between a racially insulting remark made by a manager to colleagues whether in the course of employment at work or at a work-related social occasion', though in this case the abuse was held to be not in the course of employment.

16 SDA s41(3); RRA s32(3); DDA s58(5).

17 *Carter v Westcliff & Hall (Sidmouth) Ltd* 31165/90.

18 *Johnson v ABC Employment Agency and Whitworths Ltd* 19643/89.

19 6 July 1995; Case No: 25987/94; DCLD 27.

20 [1987] IRLR 401, EAT.

agement, the harasser was suspended pending the outcome of an inquiry. The inquiry was inconclusive and the harasser returned to work. The majority of the EAT held that the employers were not liable for the sexual harassment as there was proper and adequate staff supervision and the employer had made known its policy of equal opportunities; it had therefore established a defence. The EAT found that 'it was very difficult to see what steps in practical terms the employers could reasonably have taken to prevent that which had occurred from occurring'.

If all that an employer has to do to establish a defence is to show that there is a system for supervising staff and an equal opportunities policy, then it would be all too easy to avoid liability. There are many other steps that could be taken, as pointed out by the applicant in *Balgobin* (above), such as the provision of training for all staff, clear guidelines for dealing with harassment and categorisation of harassment as gross misconduct.

It is highly arguable that, in the light of the strong policy statements made by the CA in *Tower Boot* about the prevention of discrimination, the decision in *Balgobin* is wrong. It was also decided before the European code on sexual harassment which should now be taken into account (see **13.2.1**).

In other IT cases, employers have not been allowed to avoid liability so easily and tribunals have said that equal opportunities policies must be translated into reality and may require employers to provide training and supervision. In *Earlam v (1) VMP Ltd and (2) Andrews*[21] the tribunal said that, bearing in mind the European Code of Practice, a large company should take the following steps:

- issue a policy statement about harassment, defining it and stating that it will not be permitted or condoned;
- establish a complaints procedure, specifying to whom complaints should be made and setting out the consequences for perpetrators;
- provide training;
- ensure managers and supervisors are aware of the factors which contribute to a working environment free of sexual harassment.

In one case,[22] an employer was held liable for recurring sexual harassment because it failed to take adequate precautions to prevent it

21 29 November 1994; Case No: 19199/94; see also *Hurtley v Halfords & Leach* 7 December 1994; Case No: 19199/94; *Wilson v J. Sainsbury plc* 1 May 1995; Case No: 7957/94 and *Dias v Avon* CC 11 May 1995; Case No: 9660/94. All reported in DCLD 25, p8.

22 *Coyle v Cahill Motor Engineering (Northern Ireland) Ltd* (1989) COIT 1808/87.

happening and failed to tell the victim that she should complain to the manager if she were harassed. In another case,[23] the tribunal held that the fact that the employer organised a six-hour training session on the RRA and SDA, a refresher course and gave the manager a copy of the company's race relations policy was sufficient to avoid liability. Similarly, in *Taylor v Asda Stores Ltd*[24] the employer reacted to a racist comment by investigating the complaint, after which the perpetrator apologised, and instituting the first stage of the disciplinary procedure against the perpetrator. The perpetrator had received thorough equal opportunities training. However, another employer's one-hour induction course on discrimination, as well as instructions on the company's policy of non-discrimination were held insufficient.[25] The larger the employer the more it will be expected to do.[26]

7.7 Does the victim need to make a formal complaint?

In harassment cases, once the behaviour has been revealed, it should not be necessary for the victim to make a formal complaint, though preferably the matter should be raised with someone in authority.[27] In *Bracebridge Engineering v Darby*,[28] the applicant reported sexual harassment to her manager. The EAT found that the manager's investigation of the complaint was not an in-depth inquiry and that she was too easily persuaded that there was insufficient evidence to substantiate the claims. The manager should have known that the allegation could have led to the harassers' suspension and in any event she should have carried out a full investigation. The applicant was therefore entitled to take the view that her allegations were being brushed aside and was justified in terminating her contract of employment. The EAT said that it must be asked whether the 'term whereby the mutual obligation, trust, confidence and support and the obligation not to undermine the confidence of the female staff had been breached. In a case of this nature where sexual discrimination and investigation are concerned it is an extremely important one for the female staff'.[29]

23 *Carney v Bass Mitchells & Butler Ltd* 19708/88.
24 13 January 1994; Case No: 41315/93.
25 *Edwards Batters v Bolivar Stamping Ltd* 3966/89.
26 Ibid.
27 See *Robinson v Inter Office Products Ltd* 4039/89.
28 [1990] IRLR 3.
29 Ibid, at p6.

In an IT decision[30] the applicant, when asked whether he wanted to make a complaint, declined. The existence of a 'comprehensive' sexual harassment complaints procedure established the defence.

7.8 Failure to deal adequately with complaints

In another case,[31] the employer was held liable not only for the sexual harassment but also for the failure to deal with the complaints adequately (see Chapter 13). Note also that in harassment cases, employers may be liable for assault or battery carried out by their employees (see **13.8**).

7.9 Codes of practice

In order to avoid liability for discrimination, employers should follow and adopt the CRE and EOC Codes of Practice, the Code of Practice issued under the DDA, the Code of Practice issued by the European Commission and the CRE guidance.[32]

7.10 Liability of principals

The relationship of principal and agent arises when one person, the principal, consents to another person, the agent, acting on his/her behalf. The agent has authority (either express or implied, and whether given before or after the event) to act for the principal. If the agent is acting within his/her authority at the time of the discriminatory act, then both will be liable.[33]

Employees and agents will not be liable if they reasonably rely on a statement by their employer or principal that the act is not discriminatory.[34]

In *Nagarajan v Agnew and Others*[35] the EAT held that an employee was only liable for the discrimination of a fellow employee if there was a relationship of principal and agent. In *Nagarajan* the applicant's former manager (against whom the applicant had made

30 *Davies v Secretary of State for Social Security* 11 July 1994; Case No: 43819/93.
31 *Whittington v Morris and Greenwich Health Authority* 17846/89.
32 *Racial Harassment at Work: what employers can do about it* (CRE, 1995).
33 SDA s41(2); RRA s32(2); DDA s58(2); SDA s42; RRA s33; DDA s57.
34 SDA s42(3); RRA s33(3); DDA s57(3).
35 [1994] IRLR 61.

allegations of discrimination) told personnel that he should not be re-engaged because of his attitude to management. The IT held that the employer and personnel officer, who then refused to re-engage the applicant, were liable for the acts of the applicant's former manager. The EAT overruled this, saying that there was no relationship of principal and agent between two employees. The position would be different if one employee was the manager of the other.

LIABILITY FOR DISCRIMINATION: KEY POINTS

- An employer is generally liable for discrimination carried out by all its employees during their employment, ie, where it is in working hours or at work-related social events.
- The employee will also be personally liable, as will any other person who knowingly aids a person to discriminate unlawfully.
- The test of liability under the SDA, RRA (and by extension the DDA) is much wider than under the common law (for negligence).
- An employer may also be liable for the acts of third parties, such as an entertainer contracted for one night's entertainment.
- Employers are potentially liable for the acts of all employees, not just managers' actions.
- An express prohibition by an employer on the doing of the act does not in itself exonerate the employer though may provide a defence.
- An employer may be liable for an act about which it is ignorant.
- The employer has a defence if it took such steps as were reasonably practicable to prevent the employee doing the act, or from doing it in the course of his/her employment;
- The employer may be liable not only for the discrimination carried out by an employee but for any subsequent failure to deal with complaints of discrimination.
- Principals may be liable for acts of their agents where the agent is acting within his/her authority.
- Employees and agents committing acts of discrimination are also liable.

CHAPTER 8

Discrimination by bodies other than employers

Most discrimination cases involve employers but it is also unlawful for partners, trade unions and professional organisations, qualifying bodies, vocational training bodies and employment agencies to discriminate. Contract workers (employed by agencies but working for a third party) are also protected. This chapter looks at sex and race discrimination in these situations. Disability discrimination is covered in Chapter 24. These bodies may also discriminate against their employees, in which case the employment provisions apply (see Chapters 5 and 6). The provisions relating to victimisation and instructions and pressure to discriminate may also be relevant.

8.1 Partners

It is unlawful for a firm of partners (which, for the purposes of race discrimination cases, consists of six or more partners[1]) to discriminate on the ground of race or sex in the following ways:

a) in the arrangements made to decide who should be offered a partnership; partnerships which are exclusively or mainly white and male may raise a rebuttable presumption that there has been discrimination (see **2.13.1**);
b) in the terms on which a partnership is offered; or
c) by refusing to offer a partnership; or
d) where the person is already a partner:
   - in the way the partner is given access to or refused benefits, facilities or services;
   - by expelling a partner or subjecting him/her to any other detriment.[2]

1 RRA s10(1).
2 RRA s10; SDA s11.

'Expulsion' under the SDA specifically includes the expiry of a fixed-term contract and constructive dismissal.[3] The provisions are similar under the SDA and RRA (but see below).

These provisions apply to persons proposing to form a partnership as well as to existing firms.[4]

It is not unlawful to discriminate in (a) and (c) above where the sex or race of the partner would be a GOQ.[5]

In the case of sex discrimination, there is an exception for provisions relating to death and retirement. The exception does not, however, allow different retirement ages for men and women. It would be unlawful to provide that men had to retire at the age of 65 and women at 60.[6] The retirement exception does apply to the provision of benefits, facilities or services and any other detriment (apart from expulsion).[7] EC law may provide protection where the exception does apply.

Marital discrimination (see **5.1**) and victimisation (see Chapter 4) is also unlawful.

8.2 Trade unions and professional and employers' organisations

It is unlawful for a trade union, organisation of employers or organisation whose members carry on a particular profession or trade to discriminate on the ground of sex or race in the following ways:

a) in the terms on which it is prepared to admit an applicant to membership; or
b) by refusing, or deliberately omitting to accept, an application for membership; or
c) in the case of an existing member, to discriminate:
   - in the way s/he is given access to any benefits, facilities or services, or by refusing or deliberately omitting to afford him/her access to them; or

3 SDA s82(1A); the SDA 1975 was amended by the Sex Discrimination Act 1986. The RRA was not so amended. There is no parallel definition under the RRA though it could be argued that expulsion should also include the expiry of a fixed-term contract and constructive dismissal.

4 SDA s11(2); RRA s10(2).

5 SDA s11(3); RRA s10(3); see **5.4.3** and **6.4.1.15**.

6 SDA s11(4).

7 SDA s11(4).

- by depriving him/her of membership, or varying the terms on which s/he is a member; or
- by subjecting him/her to any other detriment.[8]

In *National Federation of Self-employed and Small Businesses Ltd*[9] *v Philpott* the EAT held that the Federation came within these provisions notwithstanding that not all of its members are employers. The expression 'organisation of employers' should not be given a narrow meaning.

The provisions are identical, except that the death and retirement exemption applies only to the SDA not the RRA.

In the case of sex discrimination, the above do not apply to provisions made in relation to the death or retirement of a member.[10] This exclusion is not affected by the SDA 1986, so that *all* provisions relating to death and retirement are excluded, though women may be able to rely on the ETD. Article 4 of the Directive states that:

> any provisions contrary to the principle of equal treatment which are included in collective agreements, individual contracts of employment, internal rules of undertakings or in rules governing the independent occupations and professions shall be, or may be declared, null and void or may be amended.

8.2.1 Discrimination by unions

In one case, it was held that a union chapel unlawfully discriminated against women cleaners by excluding them from the chapel and thereby depriving them of the chance of transferring to another job as transfer depended on membership of the chapel[11] (see also **10.2.5**).

A dispute could arise where a union supports one worker (say a black worker) as against other workers. This can lead to threatened industrial action by another union which supports the white workers in an attempt to force the other union to withdraw support from the black worker. It is a breach of the RRA and SDA to put pressure on a person to do an unlawful act and the CRE and/or EOC may take action (see **27.2.1**).[12]

If a union negotiates discriminatory provisions in a collective agreement it may also be liable for pressure to discriminate and/or

8 SDA s12; RRA s11.
9 [1997] IRLR 341.
10 SDA s12(4).
11 *Turnbull v The Record Production Chapel and Others* 955/83.
12 RRA s31; SDA s40.

aiding an unlawful act (see **7.3**). Collective agreements are covered in Chapter 22.

In *FTATU v Modgill*[13] the EAT held that a complaint that a union did not give sufficient support to Asian members, or dealt with them inefficiently, was not evidence of less favourable treatment or racial discrimination. Thus, it would be necessary to show that they had been treated less favourably than other persons and the reason was their race. The questionnaire procedure may be useful in obtaining evidence about different treatment (see **25.8**).

Difficult issues arise when one union member makes a complaint of discrimination against another and the union has to decide whether it will act for either party. In one case,[14] a woman complained that NATFHE had indirectly discriminated against her because it refused to support her claim before her employer. The IT and EAT upheld the definition of requirement proposed by the union, namely, 'you cannot bring a claim if one of our member's job is at risk'. The IT agreed that in racial complaints the union's policy would have a greater impact on black members than on white. However, no member would be able to comply with the condition where another member's job was threatened. Therefore, the applicant had failed to show that a smaller proportion of her racial group could comply with the condition. The IT also found that the condition was justifiable, as the union had to strike a balance between its legitimate duty to protect the tenure of its members and the avoidance of representational conflicts. The EAT upheld the IT's decision. However, this may no longer be followed. The CRE has been increasingly concerned with trade unions which do not take up discrimination cases.

In another case,[15] a union and its shop steward pressurised a member to withdraw discrimination proceedings against another member and were found liable for unlawful victimisation.

A union is liable for the discriminatory acts of not only its appointed officers but also the shop stewards[16] if they are acting within the authority of the union. In addition, the officer or shop steward will be personally liable as s/he will be treated as aiding the principal unless s/he relied on a statement that the act was not unlawful. Making a false statement is an offence.[17]

13 [1980] IRLR 142, EAT.
14 *Weaver v NATFHE* EAT 551/87.
15 *Vahramian v ACTSS* 302244/90.
16 SDA s41; RRA s32.
17 SDA s42; RRA s33.

8.3 Qualifying bodies

Qualifying bodies include the Law Society, British Medical Association, and other similar organisations. It is unlawful for a body which can confer an authorisation or qualification which is needed for or facilitates engagement in a particular profession or trade to discriminate on the ground of sex or race in the following ways:

- in the terms on which it is prepared to confer an authorisation or qualification;
- by refusing to grant an application for the authorisation or qualification;
- by withdrawing the authorisation or qualification or varying the terms on which it is held.[18]

The provisions under both Acts are identical except that, under the SDA, there is an exception for authorisations or qualifications limited to one sex in order to comply with religious doctrine. In addition, the SDA imposes a duty on a body which is required to show its good character, to have regard to any evidence that the person has discriminated in the carrying on of any profession or trade.[19] Discrimination by educational bodies is dealt with separately.[20]

The EAT has held that this section covers all cases where the qualification in fact facilitates the person's employment, whether or not it is intended so to do.[21] It is not necessary to prove that the discriminatory term (as opposed to the qualification) has adversely affected the applicant's employment prospects, only that the qualification helps his/her job prospects.

It may be unlawful for a professional body, for example, the General Medical Council or the Law Society, to refuse to recognise qualifications obtained abroad if they are similar to English qualifications that are considered acceptable.[22] The CRE code provides that overseas degrees, diplomas and other qualifications which are comparable with UK qualifications should be accepted as equivalents. The rules, whether contractual or non-contractual, of qualifying

18 SDA s13; RRA s12.
19 SDA s13(2).
20 SDA ss22 and 23; RRA ss17 and 18.
21 *British Judo Association v Petty* [1981] IRLR 484.
22 See *Hampson v Department of Education and Science* [1989] IRLR 69, CA. In *General Medical Council v Goba* [1988] IRLR 425, EAT, the applicant argued that a requirement to take a six-part English qualification test, with restrictions on the number of times it could be taken, was indirectly discriminatory (see **6.4.1.4**).

bodies which are unlawful under the SDA are also void (see **22.1**).[23]

In *Jepson and Dyas-Elliott v Labour Party*[24] Mr Jepson was not considered for selection as a Labour Party candidate in two constituencies because those constituencies were required to have all-women shortlists. The tribunal held that the adoption of a prospective parliamentary candidate is an 'authorisation' which 'facilitates engagement in a particular profession' and the requirement to have all-women shortlists was unlawful. The tribunal said that the section was widely drafted to cover all kinds of professions, vocations, occupations and trades in which persons may engage, whether paid or unpaid, and whether or not they be 'employment' (as defined by SDA s82) (eg, doctors, lawyers and judges) including thereby persons who hold public offices. What, one might ask, would a tribunal say about hereditary peerages in the House of Lords which, of course, go to the eldest son, ignoring older daughters!

The tribunal, in *Jepson*, did not accept that the ETD allowed for such positive discrimination, particularly in the light of *Kalanke*[25] (see **12.4** or **12.5**).

Where there is a statutory procedure for appealing or proceedings in the nature of an appeal, such as for complaints against the Law Society or General Medical Council, this must be pursued before making an application to an IT.[26] In *Khan v General Medical Council*[27] the CA held that the right, under Medical Act 1983 s29 (as the provision then was), to apply to a Review Board for a review of the General Medical Council's decision, was a proceeding 'in the nature of an appeal' within the meaning of RRA s54(2). This phrase meant that the decision could be reversed by a differently constituted set of persons. The possibility that some of the same people, who made the original decision, may be on the appeal did not make it any less an appeal.[28]

8.4 Vocational training bodies

It is unlawful for a person who provides, arranges or facilitates vocational training which would fit the trainee for any employment to discriminate:

23 SDA s77(2).
24 [1996] IRLR 116.
25 *Kalanke v Freie Hansestadt Bremen (C-450/93)* [1995] IRLR 660, ECJ (see **12.5**.).
26 SDA s63(2); RRA s54(2) (see Chapters 5 and 6).
27 [1994] IRLR 646, CA.
28 Though it might be in breach of natural justice.

- in the terms on which a person is given access to training courses or other facilities concerned with such training; or
- by refusing or deliberately omitting to offer a person training or other facilities; or
- by terminating his/her training; or
- by subjecting him/her to any detriment during the course of the training.[29]

These provisions, which are almost identical in both Acts, were amended by the EA 1989[30] to extend their scope to all vocational training, whoever provides it, and to discrimination during training. Note that it does not apply to the arrangements made for the purpose of deciding who should be offered training.[31] This gap was highlighted in *Ilyas v Manpower Services Commission*,[32] where a tribunal held that a black applicant who had been refused an interview for a training course could not complain of race discrimination. The IT held that RRA s4 did not protect trainees, nor did s13(1) prohibit a vocational training body from discriminating in the arrangements made to determine who should be offered training. This was a very narrow interpretation of the RRA as the tribunal could have held that there had been a refusal to give the applicant access to training (by denying him an interview).

A remedy may, however, lie, in sex discrimination cases, under the ETD which applies to vocational training[33] and it is unlawful to refuse or deliberately omit to afford a person access to training and this would include a refusal to interview.[34]

Discrimination by educational bodies is covered by SDA ss22 and 23; RRA ss17 and 18. See also the provisions relating to positive action (see Chapter 12).

8.4.1 Exclusion for lone parents

The EA 1989 s8 gives the Secretary of State power to exempt from the SDA, discrimination in favour of lone parents in relation to vocational training. Regulations have now been passed allowing special treatment of lone parents by:

29 SDA s14; RRA s12.
30 EA 1989 s30.
31 Cf, SDA s6(1)(a); RRA s4(1)(a).
32 2149/87.
33 ETD art 4.
34 RRA s13.

- the making of any payment in connection with the participation of a lone parent in employment training; or
- the fixing of any special condition for the participation of lone parents in employment training.[35]

8.4.2 Discrimination by the Secretary of State in the provision of training

SDA s16 and RRA s15 provide that it is unlawful for the Secretary of State to discriminate in the provision of facilities or services under Employment and Training Act 1973 s2, unless SDA s14 or RRA s13 applies or the Secretary of State is acting as an employment agency. Under the Employment and Training Act 1973 s2, there is a duty to assist persons to select, train for, obtain and retain employment suitable for their ages and capacities and to obtain suitable employees.[36]

Discrimination by educational establishments and local education authorities is dealt with separately.[37]

8.5 Employment agencies

It is unlawful for an employment agency to discriminate on the ground of sex or race:

- in the terms on which the agency offers its services; or
- by refusing to provide its services; or
- in the way it provides its services.[38]

'Services' include guidance on careers and other services related to employment. The provisions are identical under the SDA and RRA.

It is also unlawful for a local education authority to discriminate when exercising its functions under Employment and Training Act 1973 s8.

An 'employment agency' is defined as a person who, for profit or not, provides services for the purpose of finding employment for

35 Sex Discrimination Act 1975 (Exemption of Special Treatment for Lone Parents) Order 1989 SI No 2140 and Sex Discrimination Act 1975 (Exemption of Special Treatment for Lone Parents) Order 1991 SI No 2813.

36 See *Chandler v Secretary of State for Employment and MSC* (1985) 1759/85; (1986) EAT 611/85; *Cobb and Others v Secretary of State for Employment and MSC* [1989] IRLR 464, EAT and *Training Commission v Jackson* [1990] ICR 222, EAT.

37 See SDA ss22 and 23; RRA ss17 and 18.

38 SDA s15; RRA s14.

workers or supplying employers with workers.[39] Included are private agencies, job centres and agencies for the self-employed.[40] A trade union chapel (branch) has also been held to be an employment agency when it had control over filling vacancies,[41] as has a school sending candidates for a job vacancy.[42]

Discrimination by employment agencies and local education authorities is not unlawful where the employer could refuse to offer the woman employment.

An employment agency or local education authority will not be liable for a discriminatory act if it was relying (and it was reasonable to rely) on a statement by an employer that the discrimination was lawful.[43] Making a false or misleading statement is an offence.[44]

In *Mavudzi v Employment Service for Scotland and Others*[45] the applicant, a black student from Botswana, was offered a job by Pizza Hut. She was refused permission to undertake the work by officials at her local job centre because local labour could easily be recruited. However, a few weeks before, a white American had been given permission by the job centre to work part-time in a local bar. The complaint was upheld, the tribunal taking account of the way the job centre officer had treated the application from the white American (who had been given permission) and a Thai schoolgirl who had been refused permission.

8.6 Discrimination against contract workers

Contract workers are individuals working for a person (the principal) who are not employed by the principal but by a third party who supplies them under a contract with the principal. There must be an undertaking by the general employer to provide the particular labour to the principal.[46] Temporary secretaries, supplied by agencies, are contract workers.[47]

39 SDA s82(1); RRA s78(1).
40 *Bramble v Clibbens Car Hire* (1978) COIT 809/192.
41 *Turnbull* (n11 above).
42 *CRE v Imperial Society of Teachers of Dancing* [1983] IRLR 315.
43 SDA s15(5); RRA s14(5).
44 SDA s15(6); RRA s14(6).
45 31 May 1996; Case No: S/3793/95.
46 *Rice v Fon-a-Car* [1980] ICR 133.
47 See *Young v (1) McLeod and (2) John McLeod & Co* 20 June 1995; Case No: 5271/95, where an agency temporary secretary was abused by a partner in a firm of solicitors.

It is unlawful for the principal to discriminate against a contract worker:

a) in the terms on which it allows him/her to work; or
b) by not allowing him/her to continue to work (unless the GOQ exception applies); or
c) in the way it affords him/her access to any benefits, facilities or services or by refusing such access; or
d) by subjecting him/her to any other detriment.[48]

In cases of race discrimination the above does not apply if:

- the contract worker is not ordinarily resident in GB, where the purpose of the work is to provide training in skills which the worker intends to exercise wholly outside GB; or
- the contract worker is a seaman recruited outside the UK.

In both race and sex cases, the GOQ exception applies (see **5.4.3** and **6.4.1.15**) and (c) does not apply to benefits, facilities or services if the principal provides the same to the public (see **5.4.2.11** and **6.4.1.12** where the exception is set out).[49]

8.6.1 Wide interpretation to be given to provisions

In *Harrods Ltd v Remick and Others*[50] three women worked for concessionaires operating in Harrods. The concessionaires had a contract with Harrods to have a sales counter in the store. One of the conditions was that employees of concessionaires were required to have 'store approval' from Harrods in order to work there; this included adhering to a dress code. Three women were refused store approval for failing to comply with the dress code (one, for example, wore a nose stud). They brought complaints of race discrimination against Harrods.

The EAT pointed out that for the section to apply there must be three persons or class of person:

a) the principal, in this case Harrods;
b) individuals (contract workers) employed by a person other than the principal;

48 SDA s9; RRA s7.
49 SDA s9(4); RRA s7(5).
50 [1997] IRLR 9.

c) the employer of the contract workers (ie, the concessionaires).

In addition there must be two types of contract:

a) a contract of employment between the individual workers and their employers (the concessionaires);
b) a contract between the employer of the individual contract workers and the principal, under which the employer supplies the contract workers. There must be a contractual obligation to supply individuals to work.[51]

Employment has an extended meaning so covers employees and the self-employed (see **5.2**). The EAT held that 'work' must be *for*, ie, for the benefit of, the principal and must be work 'which is available for doing by individual contract workers who are not employed by the principal himself'. In these cases the work was done in Harrods store for the benefit of Harrods and ultimately under Harrods' control, it was therefore work 'for' Harrods under s7. Thus, the applicants were entitled to bring claims against Harrods.[52]

8.6.2 Job applicants and workers protected

The provisions cover not only a contract worker who is actually working but the selection of contract workers by the principal from workers supplied by the agency. In *BP Chemicals Ltd v Gillick*[53] an employment agency had a contract to provide personnel for consideration by BP. Staff were paid by the agency who then invoiced BP. The applicant worked under this arrangement from 1988 to 1991 when she stopped work due to pregnancy. She then approached BP with a view to returning to work. She was not given her old job but offered a less favourable job. She claimed discrimination against the principal, BP. The EAT held that she could bring a complaint against the principal, BP, saying that it had a duty not to discriminate when selecting contract workers.

In *Sodah v Bookwise Extra Ltd*[54] a contract worker was told to leave by his principal after he complained of racial abuse. The IT found this to be unlawful discrimination.

51 *Rice v Fon-a-Car* [1980] ICR 133 at p136 D-H.
52 Leave to appeal to the CA was granted.
53 [1995] IRLR 128, EAT.
54 4 October 1989; Case No: 4163/89; DCLD 3.

8.7 Exceptions

In relation to discrimination by all the above bodies the following general exceptions apply:

To race and sex cases

a) acts safeguarding national security;[55]
b) special training provisions;[56]
c) employment abroad;[57]
d) provisions contained in charitable instruments;

In relation to race only

e) acts done under statutory authority;[58]
f) acts done to provide persons of a particular racial group with access to facilities or services to meet the special needs of persons of that group in relation to their education, training or welfare, or other ancillary benefits;[59]

In relation to sex discrimination

g) acts done under statutory authority where they are necessary to protect women in relation to maternity or pregnancy or other risks specifically affecting women;
h) special provisions for women relating to pregnancy and childbirth;[60]
i) competitive sport where the physical strength, stamina or physique of the average woman puts her at a disadvantage.[61]

In sex discrimination cases some of these exceptions may be contrary to EC law (see **5.6**).

DISCRIMINATION BY OTHER BODIES: KEY POINTS

- It is unlawful for partners (except in race cases where there are fewer than six partners) to discriminate in:
  - recruitment;
  - the terms on which a partnership is offered;

55 SDA s52; RRA s42.
56 SDA ss47 and 48; RRA ss37 and 38.
57 SDA s10; RRA s8.
58 RRA s41.
59 RRA s35.
60 SDA s2(2).
61 SDA s44.

- the provision of benefits, facilities or services;
- expelling a partner;
- subjecting a partner to any other disadvantage.

There is a broad exception relating to death and retirement in sex discrimination cases and the GOQ exceptions apply.

- It is unlawful for a trade union, employers' organisation or trade/professional organisation to discriminate in similar ways. All provisions relating to death and retirement are excluded under the SDA though EC law may provide protection. A union may be liable for the discriminatory acts of its officers and shop stewards, who will also be individually liable.
- Bodies which can confer an authorisation or qualification needed for a particular profession or trade must not discriminate in the terms on which an authorisation or qualification is conferred, refused or withdrawn. There are some minor exceptions.
- It is unlawful for a provider of vocational training to discriminate in the terms of access to courses and facilities for training or by refusing or terminating training or other facilities. There are special provisions for the training of lone parents.
- It is unlawful for the Secretary of State to discriminate in the provision of facilities or services under the Employment and Training Act 1973.
- It is unlawful for an employment agency (which is widely defined) to discriminate:
  - in the terms on which the agency offers its services;
  - by refusing to provide its services;
  - in the way it provides its services.
- It is unlawful for a principal to discriminate against a contract worker:
  - in the terms on which s/he allows him/her to work;
  - by not allowing him/her to continue to work;
  - in the access to benefits, facilities or services;
  - by subjecting him/her to any other detriment.

  There are some exceptions including GOQs.
- In relation to discrimination by all the above bodies there are some general exceptions which are set out at **8.7**.

CHAPTER 9

European Community law

> The tide of Community law is coming in fast. It has not stopped at high-water mark. It has broken the dykes and the banks. It has submerged the surrounding land so much so that we have to learn to become amphibious if we wish to keep our heads above water.[1]

EC law is important because it has long recognised the fundamental principle of equal treatment and it gives specific rights to protection from sex discrimination. The commitment of EC law to equal treatment and human rights has influenced UK legislation, and the interpretation of all legislation by the UK courts. EC law also gives rise to substantive rights which are in some cases more extensive than comparable UK law rights. EC law should always be considered in sex discrimination cases.

The original aim of the EC anti-discrimination provisions in relation to women was to ensure that free competition was not distorted by the employment of women at lower pay rates than men doing the same work. If employers were able to pay women less than men, they could charge lower prices for their goods and services and this would be against the EC spirit of fair competition. It is now also acknowledged that the improvement of living and working conditions is also part of the function of the EC.

This chapter considers the different ways in which EC law affects UK discrimination law as well the specific rights that EC law gives over and above UK law.

1 Per Lord Denning in *HP Bulmer Ltd v J Bollinger SA* [1974] Ch 401.

9.1 European Communities Act 1972

The UK joined the EC in 1973, when it signed the Treaty of Rome; it has subsequently signed the Single European Act in 1987 and the Maastricht Treaty in 1992. These international treaties do not by themselves confer rights or duties on individuals. Parliament passed the European Communities Act 1972 (ECA) specifically to give effect to the EC Treaties in the UK.[2]

The HL has held that the effect of the ECA is to imply a section in all UK legislation whereby the provisions of the particular statute are to be subject to any directly enforceable Community rights.[3] Generally, therefore EC law can be relied on by nationals of member states.

However, it is important to distinguish between which rights are:

- directly effective, ie, enforceable without further implementation; and
- directly applicable, ie, enforceable against private individuals.

9.1.1 Directly effective

In order to be enforceable in the UK, EC rights must be unconditional and sufficiently precise. In other words they must be clear enough to be applied in a member state.

9.1.2 Directly applicable

An EC provision is directly applicable where it can be enforced against a private individual (as well as the state). Employees can rely only on rights set out in directives where the employer is a state body (see **9.6.7**).

9.1.3 Directly enforceable

This is where an EC right is both directly effective and directly applicable.

2 ECA s2(1) provides that 'all rights, powers, liabilities, obligations and restrictions' arising by or under community law which, under EC law 'are without further enactment to be given legal effect or used in the UK shall be recognised and available in law, to be enforced, allowed and followed accordingly'. Section 2(4) provides that '... any enactment passed or to be passed ... shall be construed and have effect subject to the foregoing'.

3 Per Lord Bridge in *Factortame Ltd v Secretary of State for Transport* [1989] 2 WLR 997 at p1011.

9.1.4 UK law to be interpreted in line with EC law

In all cases domestic legislation must be interpreted as far as possible to comply with EC law (see **9.6.1**).

Although European Communities Act 1972 s2(4) would suggest that EC law should, in all cases, take precedence over UK law, in practice the implementation of this seemingly straightforward principle has not been so simple.

9.2 The different kinds of EC legislation

The EU Treaty can be divided into three parts or (as they are commonly called) 'pillars'. The first pillar contains those parts of the treaty which are under the jurisdiction of the ECJ, these include all the articles to which reference is made in this chapter.[4]

There are three main types of EC legislation with which advisers should be familiar: Treaty articles, regulations and directives.

9.2.1 Treaty articles

These are the articles of the Treaty of Rome as amended by the Single European Act 1987 and the Treaty of European Union (the proper name for the 'Maastricht' Treaty). The Treaty of Rome as amended is now called the EC Treaty (though it is still called the Treaty of Rome in the reports of old cases).

The articles of the Treaty do not all have the same effect in law. Some articles are intended to set out general principles and as an aid to interpretation and some articles are directly effective and applicable, eg, art 119, which provides for equal pay.

9.2.2 Regulations

Regulations are binding in their entirety and directly applicable in all member states.[5] This means that anyone can rely on European regulations in litigation whether they are suing the state or a private individual. Regulations are equivalent to primary UK legislation. There is only one relevant regulation (see **9.4.4**).

4 The second and third pillars relate to justice and home affairs and foreign policy. These two pillars do not ordinarily fall within the jurisdiction of the ECJ, and will not usually be directly relevant in a discrimination claim.

5 EC Treaty art 189.

9.2.3 Directives

Directives are only 'binding, as to the result to be achieved', on each member state to which they are addressed. This means that they leave to the national authorities of the member states the choice of form and methods for their implementation.[6] Usually the member states are given a time limit within which to implement a directive.

Where the due date for implementation has passed but the directive has not been implemented by the member state:

- an employee of a state body (see **9.6.7**) can rely directly on the provisions of a directive if its provisions are sufficiently clear and precise;
- an employee of a private employer cannot rely directly on a directive.

However, the ECJ has held that a failure by the state to implement a directive which was intended to confer rights on individuals may give rise to a right to damages against the State. These are often called 'Francovich' claims after the case in which these kinds of claims were first developed. These points are discussed below.

There are also three other kinds of provision which may be relevant:

- recommendations;
- opinions; and
- codes of practice.

Recommendations and *opinions* have no binding force. They cannot be relied upon in themselves to found discrimination claims. However, recommendations and opinions often precede the making of directives and the ECJ will take them into account when interpreting a directive.[7] The ECJ has also ruled that recommendations should be taken into account by national courts.[8] *Codes of practice* can sometimes be attached to recommendations; these will have the same weight as the recommendations.

6 Ibid.

7 The ECJ operates a 'teleological' system of interpretation, to give effect to what it conceives to be the spirit rather than the letter of the legislation: *R v Henn* [1981] AC 850. This means that it will be very aware of the context in which a directive is made including any recommendations and opinions that may have led to it.

8 *Grimaldi v Fonds des Maladies Professionnelles: Case 322/88* [1990] IRLR 400.

9.3 The EC institutions

The Council of Ministers is the main decision-making body in the EC. Directives, recommendations and codes are usually made by the Council. The European Commission's role is to enforce community law and propose policies to promote 'improved working conditions and an improved standard of living for workers'. The European Parliament has powers to suggest legislation but only the Council of Ministers can finalise legislation. The relationship between these three bodies is complicated and differs according to different types of legislation. The most important institution is the European Court of Justice to which points of law can be referred by courts and tribunals of member states.

9.3.1 Reference to the European Court of Justice

The ECJ plays a central role in making the EU Treaty work. Under EU Treaty art 177 the ECJ has power to give preliminary rulings on the proper interpretation of EC law. It states that a national court may refer a question of interpretation, if necessary, to the ECJ. The national court *must* make a reference if there is no remedy under national law, unless the question:

- is irrelevant;
- has already been interpreted by the ECJ; or
- the answer is clear.[9]

Any tribunal or court may, either if requested by a party to proceedings or of its own volition, refer a question of interpretation of EC law to the ECJ.

The power given to courts and tribunals to make a reference to the ECJ on any question may be exercised even if there seems to be a binding decision of a superior domestic court of a member state on the same point.[10] So, for example, an IT could make a reference even if there were a CA decision which appeared to provide a precedent.

9.3.1.1 Procedure on referral by court

The procedure is as follows:

9 This is sometimes described as 'acte clair'. See *R v Secretary of State for Defence ex p Perkins* [1997] IRLR 297 at paras 17 and 18 and *R v Stock Exchange ex p Else Ltd* [1993] QB 545 at p545E.

10 *Rheinmühlen-Dusseldorf v Einführ- und Vorratsstelle für Getreide Case no 166/73* [1974] ECR 33 (paras 3 and 4).

a) Both parties can submit to the national court or tribunal draft questions for reference, but the court or tribunal will make the final decision on the form of the questions.
b) The national court or tribunal sends its Order of Reference to the ECJ. This is likely to contain an interim judgment setting out the facts, identifying the issues of law which arise and explaining why a reference is appropriate. Attached to this will be the questions to be answered.
c) These documents are then translated and notified to the parties, the Community institutions and all the member states. Other documents in the case may also be sent to the ECJ but they will not be translated and will be held at the Court.
d) The parties, the Community institutions and the member states have two months from the time that the ECJ notifies them of the registration of the case in which to supply their written submissions to the court.
e) There is then an oral hearing, at which the parties have 30 minutes each for making submissions.
f) The Advocate General gives his/her opinion and suggests answers to the questions.
g) The ECJ will then produce its judgment.

Although the Advocate General's opinion is not binding, it is often followed by the ECJ and is frequently referred to by UK courts. The ECJ is not bound to follow its previous decisions but usually does so. The national court must then implement the decision in the light of the facts of the case.[11] For example, in the case of *Webb* (see **17.6.13**) the ECJ ruled that the dismissal of a pregnant worker was contrary to the ETD and the HL held that the SDA had to be interpreted in line with this.

9.3.1.2 Costs and legal aid

Legal aid can be extended to cover a reference to the ECJ for a preliminary ruling. This is not available if the reference is by an IT as legal aid is not available for IT proceedings. It can therefore be important that the reference is made by the EAT or higher court, however, this will result in further delay. Legal aid may also be available from the ECJ. The ECJ will decide whether to grant legal aid on an application which should be made to the registrar. There is no

11 See EC Treaty art 5.

form for such an application; parties should write direct setting out their financial circumstances.

The ECJ can make an order for costs but normally leaves this to the referring court. Hence if the referral has come from an IT, costs are not likely to be awarded.

9.4 EC legislation

This book is mainly concerned with Treaty of Rome art 119 and some of the directives. However, other provisions of the EC Treaty also prohibit discrimination against workers who are nationals of other member states.

9.4.1 Article 119

Article 119 lays down the principle that men and women should receive equal pay for equal work (see **9.6.4**).

9.4.2 Article 6

This Article says that any discrimination on grounds of nationality between citizens of member states shall be prohibited. It does not prohibit discrimination in itself but requires that any other EC law right must be applied without discrimination against nationals of member states.

9.4.3 Article 48

This concerns freedom of movement of community nationals who are workers. It says:

> Freedom of movement shall entail the abolition of any discrimination based on nationality between workers of the member states as regards employment, remuneration and other conditions of work and employment. It shall entail the right subject to limitations justified on grounds of public policy, public security, or public health.

In most cases discrimination against EC nationals will be contrary to the RRA, however, it is possible that art 48 could be applied to extend the scope of the RRA where otherwise an act of discrimination might not be covered, eg, in the case of a UK worker recruited in the UK to work in Italy.

9.4.4 Regulation 1612/68 on the Free Movement of Workers

Regulation 1612/68 amplifies the scope of the protection under Article 48. The Regulation outlaws discrimination against community nationals in job offers as well as in treatment at work. It also covers the right of a community national to bring his/her family to live with him/her.

9.4.5 The directives

There are four directives relevant to sex discrimination:

- the Equal Pay Directive (EPD);[12]
- the Equal Treatment Directive (ETD);[13]
- the Social Security Directive;[14]
- the Pregnant Workers Directive (PWD);[15] and
- the Occupational Social Security Directive (as amended) (OSSD).

The third being outside the scope of this book. The directives are subdivided into articles. These should not be confused with the articles in the EC Treaty, such as art 119.

There is a directive on parental and family leave but this is not likely to be implemented in the UK until the end of 1999. A new directive on shifting the burden of proof in equal pay cases has been drafted but not yet implemented, and a framework agreement has been reached on a new directive on part-time workers.

9.4.5.1 Equal Pay Directive

The EPD states that all discrimination on the ground of sex in respect of all aspects of pay should be eliminated. In *Jenkins v Kingsgate*,[16] the ECJ said that this Directive was principally designed to facilitate the practical application of the principle of equal pay outlined in art 119 and does not alter the content or scope of that principle as defined in the Treaty. The Directive provides for:

a) the 'principle of equal pay', meaning equal pay for the same work or for work to which equal value is attributed and for the elimination of all discrimination on the ground of sex with regard to all aspects and conditions of remuneration, including job

12 75/117/EEC.
13 76/207/EEC.
14 79/7/EEC.
15 92/85/EEC.
16 [1981] 2 CMLR 24; [1981] IRLR 228, ECJ.

classification systems. Job classification schemes are to be based on the same criteria for men and women and so drawn up as to exclude any sex discrimination;

b) the abolition of discriminatory provisions in collective agreements, wage scales, wage agreements or individual contracts of employment;
c) the abolition of all discrimination arising from laws, regulations or administrative provisions which is contrary to the principle of equal pay;
d) member states to introduce into their legal systems measures to enable those who believe that they are wronged by failure to apply the principle of equal treatment to pursue their claims by judicial process. They shall introduce measures to protect employees against dismissal by the employer as a reaction to a complaint or any legal proceedings aimed at enforcing compliance with the principle of equal pay;
e) member states to bring the provisions of the directive to employees' notice.

There are no exceptions to the principles laid down in art 119 and the EPD.

9.4.5.2 The Equal Treatment Directive

The ETD states that there should be no discrimination *whatsoever* on the ground of sex, either directly or indirectly, by reference in particular to marital or family status. It prohibits discrimination in:

- access to employment;
- access to training and vocational guidance;
- working conditions;
- promotion;
- dismissal.

This applies to collective agreements, individual contracts of employment, internal rules or rules governing the independent occupations and professions.

Member states are required to introduce into their legal systems measures to enable victims of discrimination to pursue their claims by judicial process. Member states are also required to introduce measures to protect employees against dismissal by their employer as a reaction to a complaint.

The exceptions to the Directive are set out at **5.5**.

9.4.5.3 The Pregnant Workers Directive

The PWD is intended to encourage improvements in the safety and health at work of pregnant workers, workers who have recently given birth or are breastfeeding.

It provides that employers of pregnant workers shall undertake a risk assessment of the workplace. If they conclude that the working conditions or working hours pose a risk to the pregnant worker her working conditions should be temporarily adjusted or she should be moved to another job or given paid leave (see **15.4**).

Pregnant workers:

- shall not be obliged to do night work;
- shall be entitled to a minimum period of 14 weeks' maternity leave;
- shall be entitled to time off with pay for ante-natal examinations;
- shall not be dismissed without a good reason which is unconnected with their pregnancy;
- shall be entitled to an 'adequate allowance' during the minimum period of maternity leave;
- shall have a legal remedy if these requirements are not complied with.

9.4.5.4 The Occupational Social Security Directive

This has been amended with effect from 1 July 1997 in order to comply with ECJ pensions decisions, such as *Barber*, *Vroege*, *Fisscher*, *Ten Oever*, *Neath* and *Coloroll* (see Chapter 23). The aim of the Directive is to make the provisions relating to occupational pensions consistent with the equal pay provisions of art 119.

9.5 EC principles

9.5.1 Equal treatment

Equal treatment (sometimes described as non-discrimination) is a fundamental principle within the EC,[17] in the EC treaty itself, in regulations and directives, and rulings of the ECJ. The principle of equal treatment also applies in other areas of community law, the

17 The first ECJ case dealing with indirect discrimination was in 1957! – *Case 2/56 Geitling Selling Agency v ECSC* [1957] ECR 3. The ECJ began the development of the definition of the non-discrimination principle in *Case 14/59 Societes des Fonderies de Pont-a-Mousson* [1959] ECR 215.

idea being that each member state should be treated equally. Thus, commercial cases involving the principles of equal treatment may be relevant in employment cases.

The general principle of equal treatment is referred to in many different cases. It can be formulated in different ways but a typical statement is:

> comparable situations are not to be treated differently and different situations are not to be treated alike unless such treatment is objectively justified.[18]

In other words a similarly qualified man and woman should be treated in the same way and it will be discrimination to appoint a man because he is a man. However, there may be circumstances where a woman with childcare responsibilities should not be treated in the same way as a man without childcare responsibilities unless there is objective justification for the difference in treatment. So it may be indirect discrimination to refuse to allow the woman to work part-time but not discrimination to refuse to allow the man to work part-time. However, once indirect discrimination has been established and a woman is allowed to work part-time the man may have a direct discrimination claim if he has childcare responsibilities and is not allowed to work part-time (see **3.6.10**).

9.5.2 Respect for fundamental human rights

EC law specifically recognises the importance of human rights laws. In *ERT*[19] the ECJ ruled that fundamental rights form an integral part of the general principles of EC law. The ECJ has ruled specifically that the European Convention on Human Rights has special significance[20] and 'the Community cannot accept measures which are incompatible with observance of the human rights thus recognized and guaranteed'.[21]

18 For example, *Case 203/86 Kingdom of Spain v Council of the European Communities* [1988] ECR 4563 para 25; *Gillespie and Others v Northern Health and Social Services Board* [1996] IRLR 214 and *Secretary of State for Trade & Industry v Cook* [1997] IRLR 150. See **3.3** for fuller discussion of this principle.

19 *Elliniki Radiophonia Tileorassi Anonimi Etairia and Panellinia Omospondia Syllogon Prossopikou ERT v Dimotiki Etairia Pliroforissis and Others Case 260/89* [1991] I-2925 at para 41.

20 *Case C-222/84 Johnston v Chief Constable of the Royal Ulster Constabulary* [1987] ICR 83 para 18.

21 *Case C-5/88 Wachauf v Federal Republic of Germany* [1989] ECR 2609.

Neither the principle of equal treatment nor the European Convention on Human Rights by themselves create rights which can be relied upon in a situation which is not otherwise governed by EC law. However, these principles will be used to help define and interpret EC rights in any case in which there may be discrimination.

For example, in *Johnston v Royal Ulster Constabulary*[22] the ECJ ruled that a ministerial certificate which purported to prevent an IT from hearing a complaint of sex discrimination was incompatible with the principles of the European Convention and therefore contrary to EC law.

The government intends to incorporate the European Convention into UK law so it will become more important.

9.6 How EC law changes UK law

9.6.1 Interpreting UK law to comply with EC law

The European Communities Act 1972, and EC law have resulted in a new principle of statutory interpretation: UK law must be interpreted so as to conform with EC law. This is particularly important where the parallel EC provisions are not directly effective so do not automatically take precedence over UK law. Obviously where EC law is paramount, an individual can rely on those directly effective EC law rights without requiring that the interpretation of the UK law be constrained in any way (see below).

If UK law is ambiguous, the ambiguity should be resolved in a manner consistent with EC law.[23] The ECJ has also said:

> in applying the national law and in particular the provisions of national law specifically introduced in order to implement Directive 76/207 [the ETD], national courts are required to interpret their national law in the light of the wording and the purpose of the Directive.[24]

In *Marleasing SA v La Comercial Internacional de Alimentacion SA*,[25] the ECJ held that member states must fulfil their obligations

22 *Case C-222/84* [1987] ICR 83.

23 See Lord Diplock's speech in *Garland v British Railway Engineering Ltd* [1982] 2 All ER 402, HL.

24 *Von Colson and Kamann v Land Nordrhein-Westfalen Case 14/83* (1984) *Times*, 25 April, ECJ.

25 *Case C-106/89* [1993] BCC 421, ECJ.

under a Directive to achieve its objective. This duty binds all authorities of member states, including their national courts. In applying national law, whether the provisions concerned pre-date or post-date the Directive, the national court is bound to interpret national law in such a way as to achieve the results envisaged by the Directive. The UK courts must now adopt this approach.

This ruling was followed by the HL in *Litster v Forth Dry Dock Co Ltd*[26] which implied into the English statute words necessary to conform to EC law. The Lords said that, if the legislation can reasonably be construed so as to conform with EC obligations under the directives and case-law, such a purposive construction will be applied even though, perhaps, it may involve some departure from the strict and literal application of the words of the legislation.

Webb v EMO[27] is a very good example of just how far the UK courts will go to construe domestic legislation with EC law (see 17.6.13).

9.6.2 Relying on EC law rights in the UK

It is important to understand when and how rights created by EC law are available in UK tribunals and courts. This depends on whether the particular provision is *directly effective* and *directly applicable* (see 9.1 above).

9.6.3 Article 48

Article 48 is directly applicable and can be relied upon in member states not just against the state but also against individuals (see *Van Duyn v Home Office*[28] and *Bosman*[29]).

9.6.4 Article 119

Article 119 is directly applicable and directly effective where its terms are sufficiently precise. In *Barber v GRE Assurance Group*,[30] the ECJ held that art 119 may be relied on in national courts and it is for those courts to safeguard the rights which art 119 confers on individuals. This view is supported by the UK courts.

26 [1989] IRLR 161, HL.
27 [1993] IRLR 27, HL; [1994] IRLR 482, ECJ.
28 [1975] 3 All ER 190.
29 *Union Royale Belge des Sociétés de Football Association ASBL v Bosman* [1996] All ER (EC) 97.
30 [1990] IRLR 240, ECJ.

In *Pickstone v Freemans plc*,[31] the CA held that where art 119 applies directly to the facts of the case, the article is binding on the English court and the individual has the right to apply to the English court for relief. The court followed *Defrenne v Sabena (No 2)*,[32] where the ECJ distinguished between 'direct and overt discrimination which may be identified solely with the aid of criteria based on equal work and equal pay' and 'indirect and disguised' discrimination which means discrimination which cannot be identified without reference to more explicit implementing legislation. The ECJ said that the complete implementation of the aim of art 119 (ie, universal equal pay) in relation to entire branches of industry and even of the economic system as a whole may require the taking of appropriate measures at community and national level. The removal of such discrimination, which would include comparing women's and men's wages across industry, could not be carried out without further legislation.

It is important to distinguish between disguised discrimination as defined above, and disparate impact discrimination as defined in *Bilka*:[33] both are sometimes called indirect discrimination, but it is only disparate impact discrimination which is prohibited by art 119 and is directly effective (see **9.1.1**). There are no rulings of the ECJ which have amplified on what the ECJ had in mind in relation to the passage from *Defrenne v Sabena (No 2)*. The passage is thought to refer to the kind of structural discrimination or segregation that can occur as a result of certain sectors of industry being more attractive to one gender.

If the EqPA can be interpreted consistently with EC law then this should be done. If, however, the words of the EqPA are unambiguous and conflict with art 119, as in *Pickstone*, then if the position under EC law is sufficiently clear it can be dealt with by the UK court without reference to the ECJ. The UK tribunal or court must set aside the conflicting provision. Note that the HL in *Pickstone* decided the case on the basis of UK law alone, so found it unnecessary to consider whether art 119 was directly enforceable.

Article 119 can, therefore, be treated as being part of UK law (subject to matters of interpretation being referred to the ECJ) and is enforceable against private as well as state employers, even if there is a conflict between EC and UK law.

31 [1988] IRLR 357, HL.
32 *Case 149/77* [1978] ECR 1365.
33 *Bilka-Kaufhaus GmbH v Weber von Hartz* [1986] IRLR 165, CA.

The word 'pay' in art 119 has been given a very wide interpretation by the ECJ. In *Garland v British Rail Engineering Ltd*[34] it ruled that it included any consideration, whether in cash or in kind, whether immediate or future, that a worker receives, albeit indirectly, in respect of his/her employment from his/her employer. This has been held to include redundancy payments,[35] pension contributions and payments,[36] piece work payments,[37] overtime payments,[38] payment of wages to a worker when s/he is sick,[39] notice payments,[40] cheap travel facilities for staff and former staff and their families[41] and payments for time spent on training courses or trade union duties.[42] It is still not clear whether it covers compensation for unfair dismissal and this question has been referred to the ECJ (see **18.8.4**).

9.6.5 Direct effect of art 119 may not be retrospective

In *Defrenne v Sabena (No 1)*[43] in 1981 the ECJ ruled for the first time that individuals could rely on art 119. This was a surprise as for 18 years member states and most lawyers had thought that this was not possible. To deal with this revolutionary interpretation the ECJ held that their decision was to have effect only in respect of the future. Likewise in *Barber* (see **23.4.1.2**), the ECJ held that its decision was not retrospective. In *Barber* the ECJ said that member states were reasonably entitled to consider that art 119 did not apply to contracted-out pensions and that overriding considerations of legal certainty precluded the questioning of past discrimination where it would upset the financial balance of many contracted-out pension schemes. It is only the ECJ (and not the courts of member states) that can rule that interpretations of EC law have effect for the future only.

34 [1982] 2 All ER 402, HL.
35 *Barber v Guardian Royal Exchange Assurance Group* [1990] IRLR 240.
36 Ibid, and see *Coloroll Pension Trustees Ltd v Russell* [1994] IRLR 586; *Bilka-Kaufhaus GmbH v Weber von Hartz* [1986] IRLR 317; *Vroege v NCIV Instituut voor Volkhuisvesting BV* [1994] IRLR 651.
37 *Specialarbejderforbundet i Danmark v Dansk Industri* [1995] IRLR 648.
38 *Stadt Lengerich v Helmig* [1995] IRLR 216.
39 *Rinner-Kuhn v FWW Spezial-Gebaudereinigung GmbH* [1989] IRLR 493.
40 *Clark v Secretary of State for Employment* [1995] IRLR 421.
41 *Garland v British Rail Engineering Ltd* [1982] IRLR 111.
42 *Arbeiterwohlfahrt der Stadt Berlin eV v Botel* [1992] IRLR 423.
43 [1981] 1 All ER 122, ECJ.

9.6.6 *Directives*

As seen above, UK law should be interpreted so as not to conflict with EC law, particularly (but not only) if the national measure was passed subsequent to the EC directive. If there is a conflict between UK and EC law, the question arises as to which law UK courts should follow.

Even if the national legislation cannot be interpreted consistently with the directive, where the provisions of a directive are unconditional and sufficiently precise, they may be relied on by an individual against a state employer where that state fails to implement the directive correctly.[44] The state is not limited to the government but includes other state bodies or 'emanations of the state' (see **9.6.7**).

It had been suggested that an individual ought to be able to rely on directives against individuals other than the state. However, in *Marshall v Southampton and South-West Hampshire Area Health Authority*[45] the ECJ held that it is only the member state and its emanations who are bound by a directive. This ruling was reaffirmed in *Faccini Dori.*[46]

9.6.7 *What is an 'emanation of the state'?*

The term 'emanation of the state' should be widely interpreted and 'must be taken broadly as including all the organs of the State'.[47] In *Johnston* (see above), the ECJ said that the chief constable was charged by the state with the maintenance of public order and safety; he was therefore not acting as a private individual but as a state authority.

In *Foster and Others v British Gas plc*[48], the ECJ made a number of important points:

a) the ECJ does have power to determine the categories of persons against whom the provisions of a directive may be relied on, though ultimately it is for the national court to rule on whether the specific undertaking was a 'state body';
b) where a person is able to rely on a directive as against the state s/he may do so regardless of the capacity in which the latter is acting,

44 *Marshall v Southampton Area Health Authority (No 1)* [1986] IRLR 140.
45 Ibid.
46 *Paolo Faccini Dori v Recreb SRL Case C-91/92* [1995] All ER (EC) 1.
47 See *Marshall (No 1)* (n44 above).
48 [1990] IRLR 353.

whether as employer or as public authority. The ECJ has held that it is important to prevent the state from taking advantage of its own failure to comply with community law;

c) individuals may rely on an unconditional and sufficiently precise provision of a directive against a public sector body.

An *emanation of the state* is defined as a body, whatever its legal form, which has been made responsible by the state for:

- providing a *public service*;
- which is under the *control of the state*; and
- where that body has *special powers* beyond those which result from the normal rules applicable in relations between individuals.

When *Foster* came before the HL again,[49] it held that the principle laid down by the ECJ was that the state must not be allowed, in whatever capacity it was acting, to take advantage of its own failure to comply with EC law. There was no justification, it said, for a narrow or strained construction of the ECJ ruling which was couched in terms of 'broad principle and purposive language'. As the British Gas Corporation (as it was then) was created to provide a public service, was under the control of the state and had a special monopoly power created by legislation, it was a public body and so bound by the ETD.

In *Rolls-Royce plc v Doughty*,[50] the EAT said that the test was whether the body can be said to be an organ or agent of the state carrying out a state function. Where the body is a commercial trading company, a useful test is whether 'on the established facts, a company is so utterly subservient or subordinate to the will or wishes of some other person . . . that compliance with that other person's demands can be regarded as assured'. Despite the state's 100% shareholding in the company and the latter's trading connection with the state being significant to the defence of the realm, it could not be said that Rolls-Royce was an organ or agent of the state or that it was carrying out a state function. The CA distinguished *Foster*, saying that the control test was not conclusive. The crucial point was that Rolls-Royce, unlike British Gas, did not provide a public service; it was a commercial undertaking. Nor did it have the special powers which had been given to British Gas. This case has been criticised and may be too restrictive.

49 [1991] IRLR 268, HL.

50 [1987] IRLR 447, EAT. See also *Griffin v South West Water Services* [1995] IRLR 15.

The current trends towards privatisation of public services has meant that it is more difficult to see which bodies will be treated as emanations of the state and which will not. However, the CA in *NUT and Others v St Mary's Church of England (Aided) Junior School*[51] held that the criteria in *Foster* should be treated merely as indicators not as a rigid definition. It held that a voluntary aided school was an emanation of the state. The school was providing a public service which had to run subject to state regulation, although it could not be said to have any 'special powers.' The CA noted that the effect of finding that the school was not an emanation of the state would be that the local education authority and the state would benefit from the state's failure to implement the directive properly, and this was contrary to the purpose set out in *Foster*. This reasoning should therefore apply to all state-funded education services and health services.

9.6.8 Remedies and procedure are to be determined according to the law of the member state

It is a fundamental principle of EC law that a member state's domestic laws govern the procedural rules for a claim brought under community law. However, that rule is subject to two very important limitations. First, the rules must be *no less favourable* than those relating to other domestic actions, and second, they must not make it virtually *impossible in practice* to enforce the rights conferred by community law. This principle was first set out by the ECJ in *Rewe v Landwirtschaftskammer Saarland*.[52]

This means that normally the relevant domestic time limits will apply to such claims.This principle was modified by *Emmott v Minister for Social Welfare*[53] when the ECJ held that while a directive has not been properly implemented by a member state, time cannot start to run.

As art 119 is directly effective and directly enforceable in the UK the principles in *Emmott* will not apply to art 119 claims and these are subject to the relevant domestic time rules.

These principles were considered in the case of *Biggs v Somerset CC*.[54] In *Biggs*, a part-time teacher, who worked for 14 hours a week

51 [1997] IRLR 242, CA.
52 [1976] 2 ECR 1989.
53 [1991] IRLR 387.
54 [1996] IRLR 203.

and was dismissed in 1976, was unable to bring a claim for unfair dismissal because she had not worked for sufficient hours per week. After *R v Secretary of State for Employment ex parte EOC*,[55] when the HL held that the time qualification periods for part-time workers were indirectly discriminatory against women, Ms Biggs tried to bring an unfair dismissal claim against her former employers. She brought her claim under art 119. The CA held that it was 'reasonably practicable' for her in 1976 to have brought a case similar to that taken by the EOC (14 years later). This was so even though the fact that UK laws might have been subject to EC law was appreciated only by a comparatively small number of people. The CA also held that her complaint was not presented within a reasonable period after the expiry of the time limit. It seems quite unreasonable to suggest that an ordinary worker in 1976 should have been able to envisage challenging the qualification period for part-time workers as indirectly discriminatory at a time when the possibility of challenging UK law in the ECJ was virtually unknown. This decision is inconsistent with *Rewe* when the ECJ held that 'the conditions and time limits made it impossible *in practice* to exercise the rights'.[56] In *BCC v Keeble*[57] (a sex discrimination case) the EAT distinguished *Biggs*, holding that where it was out of time through a 'wholly understandable misapprehension of the law', it was 'just and equitable' to extend time (see 25.2.4).

The principle in *Rewe* also applies to remedies. In *Foster*, the Advocate General said that, although member states are free to choose between different solutions for achieving the objectives of the directive, if a member state makes provision for compensation, then in order to ensure that it is effective and that it has a deterrent effect, the compensation must be adequate in relation to the damage sustained.

This was re-affirmed in *Marshall (No 1)* (above) and was developed in *Marshall (No 2)*.[58] In *Marshall (No 2)* the ECJ held that financial compensation for discrimination must be adequate to enable the applicant to recover her full loss and damage. The ECJ held that the upper limit on the amount of compensation payable was contrary to

55 [1994] IRLR 176.

56 It may be arguable that her claim was not presented within a reasonable time bearing in mind the difficulty of producing evidence of events that occured 20 years ago.

57 [1997] IRLR 337.

58 [1993] IRLR 445.

the ETD. It also held that interest must be payable on all awards in respect of discrimination so that an applicant is not disadvantaged by the time taken to enforce her rights. The EqPA limits claims for back pay to two years. This is less favourable than either a claim under the SDA or the RRA. The question of whether this is compatible with EC law has been referred to the ECJ for a ruling.[59]

9.6.9 Bypassing UK law

In *Blaik v Post Office*,[60] the applicant brought a claim relying – not on the SDA – but only on EC law. The EAT held that this was not possible as there were no free-standing rights under EC law. An EC claim is made through national legislation such as the SDA and EqPA. This was re-affirmed in the case of *Biggs v Somerset CC*.[61] Thus, even where there appears to be no remedy under UK law, applicants should always bring proceedings under the SDA, EqPA and EC law.

9.6.10 Enforcement of directives through legal proceedings against the government

ETD art 6 provides that:

> Member States shall introduce into their national legal systems such measures as are necessary to enable all persons who consider themselves wronged by failure to apply to them the principle of equal treatment . . . to pursue their claims by judicial process.[62]

An action in the High Court for judicial review of domestic legislation can be brought requesting a declaration that the government was in breach of its obligations to implement EC law.

In *R v Secretary of State for Employment ex p EOC*,[63] the EOC, together with Mrs Day, brought judicial review proceedings against the Secretary of State for Employment. They alleged that the conditions which excluded part-time workers from claiming a redundancy payment under the Employment Protection (Consolidation) Act 1978 (now the ERA) were discriminatory and in breach of EC law. This was because there were substantially more women part-time workers compared to men. The HL held that the EOC could bring judicial

59 *Levez v TH Jennings (Harlow Pools) Ltd* [1996] IRLR 499 (see also **23.4.6**).
60 [1994] IRLR 280.
61 [1996] IRLR 203.
62 There are parallel provisions in the EPD art 2 and the PWD art 12.
63 [1994] IRLR 176, HL.

review proceedings to seek such a declaration. However, Mrs Day herself should bring her claim in the IT as she had directly enforceable rights under art 119.

An individual who is directly affected by the non-implementation of a directive can also seek a declaration from the High Court (by way of judicial review) that the UK law is incompatible with EC law.[64] Such an individual who has suffered financial loss as a result of the non-implementation of a directive can sue the government for damages (see below). However, s/he cannot enforce a directive against an individual employer who is not an emanation of the state.

9.7 Claims for damages against the state for breach of EC law

In some circumstances a member state may be required to compensate an individual who has suffered as a result of a failure to implement EC law. This was first established in *Francovich and Bonifaci v Italian Republic*[65] where the ECJ ruled that there was 'a right founded directly on community law' for individuals to obtain reparation. Claims for damages are often called 'Francovich' claims after this case. Such claims will usually be brought for a failure to transpose a directive into domestic law.

In *Paola Faccini Dori v Recreb SRL*[66] the ECJ reaffirmed the right to claim such damages. The ECJ pointed out that there were three conditions which had to be satisfied in order to bring a Francovich claim. These were:

a) the purpose of the Directive must be to grant rights to individuals;
b) it must be possible to identify the content of those rights on the basis of the provisions of the Directive;
c) there must be a causal link between the breach of the state's obligation and the damage suffered.

In *Brasserie du Pecheur SA v Germany* and *R v Secretary of State for Transport ex p Factortame Limited (No 4)*[67] the ECJ again considered the conditions for establishing liability against the state. In this case the ECJ emphasised that the conditions for claims against the state

64 See *R v Secretary of State for Employment ex p Seymour Smith* [1997] IRLR 315, HL.
65 *Cases C-6/90* and *9/90* [1995] ICR 722.
66 *Case C-91/92* [1995] All ER (EC) 1.
67 [1996] 2 WLR 506.

should not unreasonably inhibit the state from legislating. Accordingly it contrasted the situations where the state had a wide discretion and where the discretion was narrow. Where the ECJ had already ruled on an issue then the state would have little discretion. The ECJ emphasised that it was not every breach that would give rise to liability but that the breach had to be sufficiently serious. It ruled that in deciding whether the breach was sufficiently serious the court had to consider:

a) the clarity and precision of the rule breached;
b) the measure of discretion left by that rule to the national or community authorities;
c) whether the infringement and the damage caused was intentional or involuntary;
d) whether any error of law was excusable or inexcusable;
e) the fact that the position taken by a community institution may have contributed towards the omission; and
f) the adoption or retention of national measures or practices contrary to community law.[68]

In *R v Ministry of Agriculture, Fisheries and Food ex p Hedley Lomas (Ireland) Ltd*[69] the ECJ also had to review the conditions for a successful claim for damages for failing to implement a directive. The court ruled that if a directive gives a member state no choice and that member state fails to take any action then it is in sufficiently serious breach of the directive to merit an award of damages.

More recently, in *Dillenkoffer and Others v Federal Republic of Germany*[70] the ECJ ruled that where a member state, within the time period laid down by the directive, fails to take any of the steps required by the directive then it will be treated as manifestly and gravely disregarding the limits on its discretion.

The ECJ also ruled that a serious breach of community law did not require the existence of intentional thought or negligence on the part of the organ of the State to which the infringement of the duty to implement the Directive was attributable.

In *Potter v Secretary of State for Employment*[71] the CA ruled that such claims against the Government for damages should be brought

68 Ibid, paras 54 and 55.
69 [1996] All ER (EC) 493.
70 Joined cases *C-178/94, C-179/94, C-188/94, C-189/94 and C-190/94* [1996] All ER (EC) 917.
71 [1997] IRLR 21.

in the county court or High Court but not in ITs. Cases should be brought against the Attorney-General in England and Wales, the Lord Advocate in Scotland and the Attorney-General for Northern Ireland.

9.8 Challenging UK law through the European Commission

The Commission can take action against the UK government if it considers that the UK has not fulfilled its obligations under EC law. If a directive cannot be relied on in UK courts, an individual can request the European Commission to take proceedings against the government for failing to implement it. Such complaints can be started by letter to the Commissioner for Social Affairs. If the Commission considers the complaint to be valid it will then ask the member state to submit its observations. Initially the Commission will attempt to reach a settlement. If there is a dispute, the Commission will send an opinion to the state asking that the infringement cease. If the state fails to comply, the Commission may bring an action in the ECJ.

This has lead to some very important changes to UK legislation such as the amendment of the EqPA to allow for equal pay for equal value claims following the decision of the *Commission of the European Communities v UK*.[72] The process is very political and can be lengthy. The TUC and the EOC made a complaint when Wages Councils were abolished in 1993. No response has been received to date.

9.8.1 How useful is EC law?

The status of EC law is complex and the above is only a brief summary. It is, however, always important to understand the relevant EC law and to rely on it in the UK tribunals and courts. The tribunal or court may apply EC law itself or alternatively refer specific questions to the ECJ for a ruling. The ECJ will not decide the case at issue, only answer the questions of law put to it and refer it back to the national court to apply the law to the facts of the case.

Article 119 and the directives are considerably wider than the SDA and EqPA. There have been a number of cases which were lost under UK law but won under EC law. EC law establishes broad principles which apply to a wide range of discriminatory acts and which may go

72 [1982] ICR 578.

beyond the tight definitions of discrimination contained in the SDA and EqPA. There are far fewer exceptions under EC law (see 5.5). Although the breadth of EC law often makes it difficult to apply to specific situations, it is an important legal tool.

EC LAW: KEY POINTS

- EC law applies only to sex discrimination and discrimination on the basis of nationality.
- Relevant EC legislation is:
  - art 119 which provides that men and women should receive equal pay for work of equal value;
  - the EPD which expands art 119, stating that discrimination in all aspects of pay must be eliminated;
  - the ETD which provides that there shall be no discrimination in access to employment, training, working conditions, promotion and dismissal. It has three main exceptions: occupational qualifications, provisions for protecting women as regards pregnancy and maternity and measures to promote equality of opportunity.
  - art 48 which prohibits discrimination in the free movement of EU nationals between member states.
- EC law prohibits direct and indirect discrimination.
- Applicants should always consider bringing an action under EC law though should not rely on EC law alone. EC law is generally of much wider application than UK law.
- The effect of EC law in UK courts:
  - ITs have the same jurisdiction to apply EC law as the courts;
  - UK courts and tribunals must set aside any national legislation which prevents a person from relying on directly effective EC law;
  - where possible, national tribunals and courts should interpret all UK legislation, whenever passed, so as to comply with EC law;
  - if there is a clear and direct conflict between UK and EC law, the latter's effect depends on whether it is directly effective, ie, unconditional and sufficiently precise, and directly applicable, ie, enforceable against private as well as state employers;
  - art 119 is directly applicable *and* directly effective where its terms are sufficiently precise;

- where their provisions are sufficiently clear and precise, both the directives are directly effective but not directly applicable.

- An individual can request the European Commission to take enforcement action against his/her government for failing to implement a directive.
- An interested body or an individual may commence judicial review proceedings against the Secretary of State if the UK is in breach of its obligations under EC law.
- An individual can sue the Attorney-General (or the Lord Advocate in Scotland) for damages if the government is in breach of one of the directives and s/he has suffered loss as a result.
- An IT or court can refer a question of interpretation to the ECJ and must do so in certain circumstances.
- There are no procedural rules under EC law but the parallel domestic procedures probably apply in most cases.
- Legal aid can be extended to cover a reference to the ECJ by the EAT or higher court. Alternatively, legal aid may available from the ECJ.

Part II

Sex and race discrimination in practice

CHAPTER 10

Getting work

10.1 Introduction

Recent surveys paint a depressing picture for black and female workers. In 1995/96 of the population of working age 5.9% are from ethnic minority groups. Of these 18% are unemployed, compared to 8% of white people.[1] This cannot be accounted for by a difference in qualifications. In a formal investigation carried out by the CRE into the Cardiff workforce, there was evidence that ethnic minorities were significantly under-represented and discriminatory recruitment practices were still common (such as 'word of mouth' recruitment). A report by the Employment Institute found that one-third of private employers refused to interview Asian and Afro-Caribbean applicants, yet interviewed equally experienced white applicants.

Women receive less training than men, are under-represented in management and are concentrated in a narrow range of low-status, low-paid jobs. For example, although 50% of medical graduates are women, only 15% of consultants are women.[2] Women are also under-represented in trade unions, both in the membership and the hierarchy.[3]

This situation persists despite the fact that the SDA and the RRA make it unlawful for an employer to discriminate on grounds of sex and race in the arrangements made for the purposes of determining who should be offered that employment.[4] It is irrelevant whether or not the employer intended to discriminate.

In *Brennan v Dewhurst Ltd*,[5] the applicant claimed that the shop

1 See *The Wages of Discrimination: black workers and low pay in 1995* (TUC) and 'The hidden truth of black unemployment' (1996) 73 EOR 9.
2 *Women doctors and their careers* (Department of Health, 1991).
3 *Women in trade unions* (Labour Research Department, 1991); see also 'Women in the unions' (1996) 70 EOR.
4 SDA s6(1)(a); RRA s4(1)(a).
5 [1983] IRLR 357.

manager who interviewed her for a job made it obvious by his manner that he did not want a woman. The EAT held that even though the employer may not have **intended** to discriminate, the interviewing process was discriminatory. Even though there was no discrimination in the making of the arrangements, their effect was to discriminate and so they were unlawful. The EAT went on to say that in all stages in applying for and obtaining employment a woman should be on an equal footing with a man.

'Arrangements made' can include the advertisement for the job. Although only the CRE and EOC can take legal action against the publication of unlawful advertisements, if a woman is claiming that she did not get a job because of the arrangements made for determining who should get the job, then the advertisement counts as one of the 'arrangements'.

It is unlawful to discriminate in the terms on which an employer offers employment. It would be unlawful, for example, to offer a woman or a black worker shorter holidays, fewer perks or lower pay.[6] It is also unlawful to discriminate by refusing or deliberately omitting to offer him/her employment.[7]

Both the CRE and EOC codes of practice cover the recruitment and selection of staff. The codes recommend the establishment of consistent criteria for selecting staff which are related to the job and free of bias of sex and race. There are specific recommendations on advertising, the use of selection tests, the treatment of applicants, shortlisting and interviewing. These are covered in the relevant sections below.

The ETD also prohibits discrimination against women on the ground of sex (not race). Article 3 states:

> Application of the principle of equal treatment means that there shall be *no discrimination whatsoever* on grounds of sex in the conditions, including selection criteria, for access to all jobs and posts, whatever the sector or branch of activity, and to all levels of the occupational hierarchy.

Most tribunal complaints are of direct discrimination. Applicants feel that, from the employer's attitude or remarks, it is obvious that it does not want a woman or a black person to do the job. Chapter 2 deals with proving direct discrimination, and gives examples of cases where there is no direct evidence of discrimination but it has been inferred from the circumstances, such as the employer's attitude or

6 SDA s6(1)(b); RRA s4(1)(b).
7 SDA s6(1)(c); RRA s4(1)(c).

the way that the interview was conducted. But in a divided labour market there are also many structural barriers to women and black workers getting jobs which have traditionally been done by white men; some of these barriers may be indirectly discriminatory (see Chapter 3).

10.2 Recruitment

Recruitment procedures vary enormously between industry, occupation, and size of establishment. Examination of these procedures has shown that many discriminate indirectly against women and black workers.

10.2.1 Informal recruitment

Procedures for recruitment are often informal, for example, 'word of mouth' recruitment. Such methods are likely to be used more widely by small employers because they are cheap. They are also widespread in industries where the demand for labour fluctuates and the workforce needs to be flexible, eg, in the building industry. Unskilled manual workers are more likely to be recruited in this way than skilled manual or white-collar workers.

There is evidence that young West Indian and white women rely on state employment agencies much more than white, male job applicants who depend on contacts and information from family and friends. According to other research this is apparently true of other minority school leavers. A Department of Employment research report in 1990 showed that 42% of job vacancies are filled by informal methods.[8]

Some informal recruitment methods have been found to be unlawful. There have been several successful CRE investigations of large and profitable firms which have highlighted discriminatory informal recruitment practices.

10.2.2 'Word of mouth' recruitment

In the past 'word of mouth' recruitment has been very common. This tends to favour members of the dominant community in the workplace so it is likely to be indirectly or even directly discriminatory. This practice has gone on for many years; in 1978, the CRE began an

8 *House of Commons Employment Committee Report* (HMSO, 1990).

investigation into F Broomfield Ltd.[9] The transport manager recruited most of his drivers on the recommendations of existing drivers. All of his 45 drivers were white; only one non-white driver had ever been recruited – the brother-in-law of one of the drivers. The commission concluded that Broomfields was applying a condition or requirement that in order to be considered first for recruitment an applicant had to be recommended by a driver already employed. The company tried to argue that the practice was justifiable because it produced more reliable staff, but failed to produce any evidence that this was so. The commission decided that these recruitment procedures constituted unlawful racial discrimination. It has been suggested that male social networks and sports clubs may be important in recruitment and these are networks from which women, in practice, are excluded.

The CRE code states that recruitment should not be through the recommendation of existing employees where the workforce is mainly white and the labour market is predominantly multi-racial (para 1.10(a)). Similarly, the EOC code recommends that 'word of mouth' recruitment should be avoided in a workforce predominantly of one sex, if in practice it prevents members of the opposite sex from applying (para 19(c)).

10.2.3 Selective recruitment

In recruiting for professional or managerial jobs, employers may confine their search to places where they will find a disproportionate number of white, male candidates, for example, recruiting staff from public schools only, or from certain universities (such as Oxford or Cambridge). Such practices may be unlawful if they cannot be justified. The Policy Studies Institute discovered that many law firms were discriminating against ethnic minority applicants for training posts because they recruited from higher education institutes which were mainly white. The chance of an average or below average candidate achieving a training post was 40% less for an ethnic minority candidate when compared with a white counterpart with similar academic qualifications.[10]

10.2.4 'Head-hunting'

The practice of 'head-hunting' for top managerial and professional jobs is quite common. Firms who use this approach – targeting indi-

9 *F Broomfield Ltd: Report of a formal investigation* (CRE).
10 *Entry into the legal professions: the law student cohort study (year 3)* (PSI, 1995).

viduals for the firm's top jobs – are confining their search to those already in such jobs – overwhelmingly white men. Whether this is justifiable will be a question of fact in each case, but the employer must fulfil the four *Bilka* requirements (see **3.6.7.1**). There seems to be no reason why employers should not advertise all jobs, and only if they cannot fill them in this way, subsequently invite suitable people to apply.

The CRE code states that job vacancies should be made known to all eligible employees and in particular employers should not confine recruitment unjustifiably to those agencies, job centres, careers offices and schools which, because of their particular source of applicants, provide only or mainly applicants of a particular racial group (para 1.9).

10.2.5 Recruitment through unions

For some jobs, applicants are supplied wholly or mainly through unions, particularly where there is a union membership agreement. This practice is likely to reproduce the character of the existing work-force, which may be predominantly white and male.

In *Turnbull and Another v Record Production Chapel and Others*,[11] Ms Turnbull complained that direct and indirect sex discrimination had prevented her from obtaining a job in the production department of the newspaper for which she worked. The chapel was found to have directly discriminated, as there was evidence from minutes of union meetings and remarks of members and officers that showed they had acted in a sexually discriminatory way. The tribunal also held that there was indirect discrimination. The condition for transfer to the job Ms Turnbull wanted (membership of the production chapel) was one with which a considerably smaller proportion of women than men could comply. SOGAT appealed to the EAT, who upheld the findings of discrimination. The tribunal, in addition to awarding Ms Turnbull compensation, recommended that within three months, the chapel should be reorganised to allow her the right to transfer.

Other women in the same position benefited because the EOC took preliminary action under SDA s73 with a view to seeking an injunction to stop the discrimination (see **27.1.8**). The tribunal made an order that arrangements for filling vacancies should be reorganised within the same three-month period so that all cleaners would have transfer rights.

11 Case no 955/83.

The CRE code recommends that recruitment should not be through procedures whereby applicants are mainly supplied through trade unions where this means that only members of a particular racial group come forward (para 1.10(b)). The EOC recommends that where applicants are supplied through trade unions and members of one sex only come forward, this should be discussed with the unions and an alternative approach adopted (para 19(d)).

10.2.6 Internal recruitment

Some employers limit recruitment for certain posts to internal candidates alone, either on the ground that this is a cheaper method of recruitment, or to give their own employees a career structure within their workplace. Many unions have defended this practice, since it gives obvious advantages to their existing members. Nevertheless, it may have a discriminatory effect where the composition of the existing workforce is racially or sexually biased, as internal recruitment reinforces the status quo. In order to open up opportunities for women and black workers the employers would have to recruit externally. (See **11.5.3** for promotion practices which are indirectly discriminatory.)

Sometimes posts are not advertised at all and the employer decides who to promote from the existing workforce. This means that potential candidates have no opportunity to put forward their aptitude for the post in question. In *Watches of Switzerland v Savell*[12] such an unadvertised internal promotion procedure was found to be indirectly discriminatory (see **11.5.3.1**).

In *Henry v Rover Group Ltd*[13] a black worker applied to move from the production line into the 'bone shop'. He was the second most senior on the list. The job was given to a white man who was first on the list but he left after a short period. Normally the second most senior person would then have been given the job, ie, Mr Henry. However, after a discussion between junior management and the union the job was deleted. The IT found that this particular shift had become a 'white man's club', Mr Henry had been discriminated against and this was 'racial prejudice of the naked sort'.

On the other hand, internal recruitment could, potentially, offer opportunities for those stuck in low-paid, low-status jobs. It is, after all, much easier to get promoted within the same organisation than to

12 [1983] IRLR 141.
13 (1996) 29 EOR DCLD.

find better work with a new employer. Employers who are genuinely committed to equal opportunities, and who are prepared to train up their own staff could therefore use internal recruitment to provide opportunities for those trapped in the worst jobs within their organisations. This would of course depend on there not being a predominantly white, male workforce throughout the organisation, and would undoubtedly be assisted by the use of positive action on training (see Chapter 12).

10.2.7 Refusal to recruit on the ground of pregnancy

In *Dekker v Stichting Vormingscentrum Voor Jonge Volwassen (VJV-Centrum) Plus*[14] the ECJ held that it was a breach of the ETD for an employer to refuse to employ a suitable female applicant because she is pregnant. The employer had refused to employ Mrs Dekker as a trainer because it would not be reimbursed the benefits which it would have to pay her during her maternity leave. As a result it would lose some of its training places.

The ECJ held that a refusal to employ because of the financial consequences of absence connected with pregnancy was based principally on the fact of the pregnancy and was discriminatory. It was irrelevant that there was no male applicant. The ECJ stressed that no account could be taken of justification provided under national law.

10.3 Advertising

Under the SDA and RRA, it is unlawful to publish or cause to be published an advertisement which indicates that the employer intends to discriminate, either directly or indirectly.[15] The RRA exempts from these provisions advertisements for persons of any class defined other than by colour, race or by ethnic or national origins, who are required for employment outside GB.[16] Both the publisher and employer may be liable for a discriminatory advertisement unless the publisher reasonably relied on a statement that the advertisement was lawful (see *Bain v Bowles* at **2.9** above).

An advertisement includes every form of advertisement or notice, whether to the public or not, and whether in a newspaper or other

14 [1991] IRLR 27.
15 SDA s38; RRA s29.
16 RRA s29(3).

publication, by television or radio, by display of notices, signs, labels, showcards or goods, by distribution of samples, circulars, catalogues, price lists or other material, by exhibition of pictures, models or films, or in any other way.[17] Only the CRE or EOC can bring complaints about a discriminatory advertisement unless an applicant can show that the advertisement constituted part of 'the arrangements made' for determining who should be offered employment[18] (see **10.1**). In such a case, an IT has held that the potential job applicant must show that she has been treated less favourably. If she applied and was rejected in favour of a better candidate, there is not any less favourable treatment on the ground of sex or race.

An advertisement specifying that candidates should be over six feet tall would be unlawful (provided that the height requirement could not be justified), as would an advertisement stating that candidates should be male.

10.3.1 The wording of advertisements

Use of a job description with a sexual connotation (such as 'waiter', 'salesgirl', 'postman' or 'stewardess') shall be taken to indicate an intention to discriminate, unless that advertisement contains an indication to the contrary.[19]

The EOC code suggests that all advertising material and attached literature should be reviewed to ensure that it avoids presenting men and women in stereotyped roles as this tends to perpetuate sex segregation in jobs and can also lead people of the opposite sex to believe that they would be unsuccessful in applying for particular jobs (para 19(a)). In *EOC v Rodney Day Associates Ltd*,[20] an IT held that an advertisement headed 'Genuine career opportunities for rugby players', with a picture of a male rugby player, could indicate an intention to discriminate.

The CRE code recommends avoiding requirements, such as length of residence or experience in the UK, and where a particular qualification is required it should be made clear that a comparable qualification obtained overseas is as acceptable as a UK qualification (para 1.6(b)).

17 SDA s82; RRA s78.
18 See *Cardiff Women's Aid v Hartup* [1994] IRLR 390.
19 SDA s38(3).
20 (1989) 379 IRLIB 11.

10.3.2 Where to advertise

Placing advertisements in publications read mainly by white people or men may be indirectly discriminatory. Trade journals, which are available to, or only read by, existing members of that trade may be indirectly discriminatory against non-members and people out of work, thus excluding more women and black applicants amongst whom there is a higher unemployment rate. The question for the tribunal will be whether such restrictive advertising is justifiable. Apart from the cost, there is no good reason why advertisements should not be placed in more accessible places. The CRE code recommends that employers should try not to confine advertisements to publications which would exclude or disproportionately reduce the numbers of applicants of a particular racial group (para 1.6(a)).

The EOC code recommends that job advertising should be carried out in such a way as to encourage applications from suitable candidates of both sexes. This can be achieved both by the wording of the advertisements and, for example, by placing advertisements in publications likely to reach both sexes (para 19(a)).

Employers who want to encourage applicants from under-represented groups often use the ethnic minority press and magazines read mainly by women to get more black and female candidates (see Chapter 12).

10.3.3 What if the discrimination is lawful?

Under the SDA some discrimination is lawful (for a list of exceptions see 5.4.2) and in these circumstances it is not unlawful to publish an advertisement which indicates that there will be discrimination (SDA s38(2)). Under the RRA, it may be unlawful to publish a discriminatory advertisement even if the discrimination is lawful. For example, if the employer is a private household s/he cannot lawfully advertise for a white person. However, if race is a genuine occupational qualification or the statutory authority exception or positive action provision apply, then the advertisement may lawfully specify this (RRA s29(2)).

10.4 Employment agencies

Many employers do not recruit staff directly, but through other agencies – employment agencies, job centres, careers offices, and schools.

Under both the SDA and RRA it is unlawful for an employment agency to discriminate against a person on the ground of race or sex (see **8.5**).

It is also unlawful to request an employment agency to discriminate in the candidates that it sends for job interviews.[21]

In order to avoid indirect discrimination, the CRE code recommends that employers should not confine themselves to agencies, schools, etc, where candidates from racial minorities are not represented and suggests that employers should use employment agencies and careers offices in areas where under-represented racial groups are concentrated (para 1.45).

The EOC code states that, when notifying vacancies to the careers service, employers should specify that these are open to both boys and girls. If dealing with single-sex schools, they should ensure, where possible, that both boys' and girls' schools are approached: mixed schools should be reminded that jobs are open to both boys and girls (para 20).

10.5 Requirements of the job

10.5.1 Qualifications

Candidates for most jobs are required to have specific qualifications or experience. Fewer women have certain types of qualifications such as scientific, technical or apprenticeship training.

Although fewer women can comply with such requirements they are not necessarily unlawful. They may be justified by the nature of the job, particularly in skilled trades, engineering, technology and the professions. What is justifiable is a question of fact. It is not justifiable for employers to say that a qualification is a 'useful' tool in their selection procedure – it must be necessary and an appropriate means of achieving the desired objective (see **3.6.7.1**). This is reinforced by the CRE code which says that care should be taken to ensure that a higher standard of educational qualifications than strictly necessary should not be required (para 1.13(a)).

10.5.2 UK qualifications

A requirement that a candidate has a UK qualification may indirectly discriminate against ethnic minority applicants who have not always

21 For example, see *CRE v NUCO Investments Ltd t/a Cost Cutter & Nutter & NUCO Enterprises Ltd* (1996) 29 EOR DCLD.

lived in the UK and who may have comparable overseas qualifications. The Council of Legal Education, for example, was held to have unlawfully discriminated by requiring graduates from overseas to complete a two-year course of study before becoming barristers, whereas graduates with a UK degree had to do only one year's study.[22]

In *Sunderalingam v Ealing Health Authority,*[23] the applicant applied for a state registered nurse secondment scheme but was told he had to take a special test because he did not meet the minimum entry requirement of five 'O' levels. He had eight 'O' levels but these were not recognised because he had taken them in Sri Lanka. A white nurse with equivalent qualifications was admitted on the course without taking a test. The health authority admitted that Mr Sunderlingham's qualifications were sufficient, and the tribunal made a finding of discrimination.[24]

The CRE code recommends that overseas degrees, diplomas and other qualifications which are comparable with UK qualifications should be accepted as equivalents (para 1.13(c)). The Department of Education and Science, the National Equivalents Unit of the British Council or the education department of the appropriate foreign embassy should be able to give advice on whether an overseas qualification is comparable.

10.5.3 Experience

Experience is a common job requirement. The industrial and occupational job segregation in the labour market means that the majority of women and black workers in the workforce is confined to a relatively small range of occupations – many of which are the low-paid, unskilled industries, particularly the service industries, and are found in a relatively small range of occupations. Some jobs, such as clerical, secretarial, catering and cleaning jobs are nearly always 'women's jobs', whereas others – mainly skilled manual jobs – are done almost exclusively by men.[25]

22 *Bohon-Mitchell v Common Professional Examination Board and Council of Legal Education* [1978] IRLR 525.

23 Case no 34674/83.

24 See also *Raval v DHSS* [1985] IRLR 370; *Khan v General Medical Council* [1994] IRLR 646; and *R v General Medical Council ex p Virik* [1996] ICR 433.

25 See *Women in the labour market: results from the spring 1996 Labour Force Survey* (Labour Market Trends, March 1997).

In *Azhashemi v Engineering ITB*[26] an Iranian was refused a place on an engineering course because he lacked experience in the UK although he had experience abroad. This was held to be indirectly discriminatory.

In *Meer v LB Tower Hamlets*,[27] the applicant complained of the criteria used for short-listing. They included experience of local government, of senior management and of Tower Hamlets and length in present post. Although the case was dismissed because no one factor was essential, so there was no 'requirement', such considerations are likely to exclude black applicants and it is hoped that in due course the HL will overturn this restrictive interpretation of requirement (see **3.6.2.5**).

In *McCausland v Dungannon DC*[28] the NI CA found that a requirement to be a local government employee was indirectly discriminatory because a considerably smaller proportion of Roman Catholics than Protestants could comply with it. (The Fair Employment (Northern Ireland) Act outlaws discrimination on the ground of religious belief.)

Because of the restricted opportunities for women and black workers in the labour market they may be denied the experience necessary to get many jobs. The legal issue is likely to turn on justifiability; how much experience is necessary for the job and can the employer justify selecting candidates on this basis?

10.6 Tests and application forms

At first sight, it may seem that tests and application forms are useful, objective means of assessing the suitability of applicants, but often they are neither objective nor necessary and may be indirectly discriminatory on the ground of race.

Employers are also increasingly using psychometric tests to select staff; these tests are of varied quality, and can be indirectly discriminatory.[29]

Employers need to be sure that any tests used address their real needs for staff. For example, in 1988 19 Asians and six Whites applied to become train drivers. They all had to sit new aptitude and 'safety' tests. Four of the white candidates and none of the Asians were

26 (1984) COIT 27486/83.
27 [1988] IRLR 399.
28 [1993] IRLR 583.
29 See 'Psychometrics should make assessment fairer' (1996) 67 EOR 27.

successful. In 1989 eight of the Asian applicants brought a case against British Rail alleging that the tests had indirectly discriminated against them. The case was settled in 1991 when British Rail agreed to introduce an improved driver selection procedure, review its equal opportunities policy and consider positive action training.[30] The CRE consultants who examined the tests and their results found that the Asians worked more slowly and accurately than their white counterparts, this put them at a disadvantage as higher scores were available for attempting as many questions as possible. They found that the Asians were inadequately prepared for these 'test strategies', however, 'test strategies' did not relate to their abilities to drive a train. British Rail set up an Occupational Psychology Centre which improved the fairness of the tests and introduced practice tests to enable candidates to learn test taking strategies. These practice tests were found to have a higher impact on the ethnic minority pass rate than that of white candidates.

10.6.1 Language and literacy tests

For many menial jobs, fluency in English, literacy and familiarity with the prevailing culture are irrelevant and should not, therefore, be used (see CRE code para 1.13(a), (b), (d) and (e)). British Leyland at one time required applicants for unskilled manual jobs to complete application forms unassisted in their own handwriting. Two Pakistani applicants complained that this was indirectly discriminatory. BL conceded that fewer Pakistani applicants could comply with the requirement and agreed it was not necessary for employees to be able to complete the forms in order to be able to do the work.[31]

The use of literacy tests by British Steel Corporation was challenged in *Ullah and Others v BSC* (see n31). The applicants used to work for short periods, then leave to go to Bangladesh and later return to work. In 1977 they were faced with a barrage of language and literacy tests before British Steel would re-employ them. Only 29.5% of the blacks passed, but 95.2% of the whites did. It was clearly a requirement that was on the face of it discriminatory. British Steel argued that these written tests were justifiable because training and warning signs were in English and oral English was necessary to

30 See *A fair test? Selecting train drivers at British Rail* (CRE).

31 See *Isa and Rashid v BL Cars Ltd* (1981) COIT 1103/125; *Laparta and Others v Henry Telfer Ltd* and *Ullah and Others v British Steel Corporation*, cited in *CRE Annual Report 1982*.

ease communication and enable it to comply with its duties under the Health and Safety at Work Act 1974. However, no practical evidence of this was presented. The applicants showed that in over 7,000 accidents in the corporation in 1975 not one had been caused by language problems. All the applicants had worked for BSC before and all had good safety records. The case was settled before the tribunal hearing. BSC compensated the applicants and undertook to review its appointment methods.

The standard of English required depends on the type of job. An employer will be able to justify a higher standard of English for more technical jobs.[32]

10.6.2 Codes of practice

The CRE code recommends that selection tests should not use irrelevant questions which may be unfamiliar to racial minority applicants (para 1.13), and both the CRE and EOC recommend that selection tests should be reviewed to ensure that they are relevant to the job requirements.

10.7 Age limits

According to a Gallup survey of 250 personnel directors, almost 90% of employers give preference to job applicants under 35 and a third recruited people of under 25 to the majority of their vacancies. Many employers specify that applicants for a job should be under a certain age, and almost all trade apprenticeships are offered exclusively to those under 25. These maximum age limits may well discriminate against female and black applicants. Two civil servants have successfully challenged age bars.

In *Price v Civil Service Commission (No 2)*,[33] Ms Price made a claim of indirect sex discrimination against the CSC because the executive officer's post for which she had applied was open only to candidates under 28 years of age. Ms Price was 36. She argued that a considerably smaller proportion of women than men could comply with the age limit because women took time out of the labour market in their twenties to have children. The tribunal upheld her complaint. What was important, it said, was whether or not a person could comply in practice – not what was theoretically possible. So, it was

32 *Chiu v British Airways plc* [1982] IRLR 56.
33 [1978] IRLR 3.

relevant in determining whether a woman can comply with such an age limit to take into account the current usual behaviour of women in this respect. Considerable numbers of women in their twenties and thirties are looking after young children and therefore cannot seek employment, so the age bar discriminates against women. The IT (to which the case was remitted from the EAT) found that the practice was not justifiable, adopting the test laid down in *Steel v The Post Office*,[34] 'that the requirement or condition must be necessary . . . and consideration should be given to whether there is some other non-discriminatory way of achieving the object'. The tribunal accepted that there was a need for the respondent to ensure that a proportion of direct entrants to the executive officer grade was drawn from the lower age groups in order to maintain a balanced career structure, but said that there were, at the relevant time, ways other than the imposition of a rigid age bar by which this balance could be maintained. The age bar was a convenient tool and its abandonment and the adoption of other methods would be difficult but possible. The tribunal's approach was similar to that taken in *Bilka* (see **3.6.7.1**).

In *Leavers v CSC*[35] the tribunal held that an age limit of 'under 32' for appointment to the diplomatic service was justifiable because if a person were to enter above the age limit s/he would not have sufficient service to have a reasonable number of years as an ambassador before retirement. This was an exceptional case dealing with very high level appointments, and age considerations should only be relevant, if at all, in such restricted cases. It is also arguable that if the case had been decided after *Bilka* the tribunal would have had to adopt a different approach and look at evidence as to whether the age limit did achieve the required object, whether special consideration could be given to women such as Ms Leavers and whether the age limit was necessary.

Another employee challenged the age bar in the civil service on the ground that it was racially discriminatory. In *Perera v Civil Service Commission (No 2)*,[36] the applicant complained that the requirement for all applicants to the post of executive officer in the VAT office to be under 32 was one that fewer black people than white people could meet, because of adult immigration. The EAT upheld the complaint. However, in future tribunals may be reluctant to do this, as primary adult immigration into this country is now at negligible levels, and the proportion of black workers who are UK-born is therefore rising.

34 [1978] IRLR 198.
35 (1985) 8 EOR 38.
36 [1983] ICR 428; [1983] IRLR 166, CA.

10.8 Children

Some employers are reluctant to employ women with dependent children, although this feeling is not often openly articulated. Lone parents can be particularly vunerable to discrimination on these grounds (see **5.1.1**). Refusal to employ a woman because she has children could be direct or indirect discrimination, or it could be marital discrimination depending on the circumstances.

In *Hurley v Mustoe,*[37] the applicant's employer dismissed her on the ground that she had small children. The IT held that there had been direct discrimination, as there was no evidence to support the employer's contention that he applied this policy equally to men and women. It was also held to be indirect marital discrimination, as the employer's policy had an adverse impact on married people as more married, than unmarried, people have children. However, the tribunal decided that this discrimination was justifiable for the needs of a small business and therefore not unlawful. On appeal, the EAT ruled that there was no evidence that such a condition was justifiable, and pointed out that if the employer was concerned about a particular employee's reliability this can be tested by other means such as references.

10.9 Hours of work

'Full-time', 'must be prepared to work overtime', 'evening work sometimes necessary', 'must be available at weekends', 'shift work': these requirements are ones with which fewer women than men, fewer married people than unmarried, are able to comply. They are all potentially indirectly discriminatory. Where part-timers are paid a lower hourly rate than full-timers or are given fewer pro rata benefits, this may also be indirect discrimination (see Chapter 3).

In *Oddbins Ltd v Robinson*[38] a branch manager's contract required her to work 'such hours as may be necessary' over and above her full-time hours. This was held to be indirectly discriminatory and the EAT said that the employer should have given proper consideration to her request to job share.

The extent to which hours of work prevent women from getting or applying for jobs is considerable. In 1996 82% of part-time workers

37 [1981] ICR 490; [1981] IRLR 208.
38 EAT Case no 188/96.

were women, and of these 79% worked part-time by choice.[39] The reasons for women working part-time are overwhelmingly family responsibilities. In 1996 63% of employed women with children worked part-time compared to 33% of women without dependent children.[40] A survey carried out by the European Commission highlighted the difficulties faced by women who want to work part-time, such as school hours and holidays, the need to care for a dependent relative, a dependant's illness, etc.[41] So the ability to job share, work part-time and do flexible hours is crucial to women's participation in the workforce and a refusal to facilitate such arrangements may be indirectly discriminatory.

In *Home Office v Holmes*,[42] Ms Holmes claimed that the Home Office was indirectly discriminating against her by the requirement to work full-time, which considerably fewer women than men could comply with because of the large numbers of women looking after children. She presented evidence that the advantages to the employer of part-timers outweighed the disadvantages (see **3.6.7.4**). The Home Office failed to show that the requirement was justifiable.

This ruling has far-reaching implications for women workers. Although Ms Holmes was already in the job – she was seeking a return from maternity leave on a part-time basis – a woman applying for a job who could not work the required hours could also complain that the requirement to work full-time was discriminatory. Instead of turning down jobs, or not even looking for jobs, because of having young children, women can argue for the right to work part-time or to job share.

There will, however, be occasions when the employer will be able to justify laying down rigid working hours. If an employee is only occasionally required to work inconvenient hours and the employer can show there is no other time the work can reasonably be done, it will be difficult to challenge.

A refusal to allow women to work flexible hours may also be indirectly discriminatory. In *Wright v Rugby Council*,[43] the applicant, a single parent, had asked her employer if she could come into work

39 See *Women in the Labour Market: results from the spring 1996 Labour Force Survey* (Labour Market Trends, March 1997) and the *Labour Force Survey Historical Supplement 1996*, table 11.

40 Ibid.

41 'Employment in Europe', a survey carried out by the European Commission, 1990.

42 [1984] 3 All ER 549; [1984] IRLR 299.

43 (1984) 23528/84.

half an hour late and take only half an hour for lunch, to allow her to deliver and collect her child for whom she had made childcare arrangements. The council refused and she complained to a tribunal. The tribunal held it indirectly discriminatory to require Ms Wright to work the rigid hours laid down by the council, particularly since many other council employees worked flexible hours.

10.9.1 Race discrimination

Rigid working hours will generally discriminate against women but may also discriminate indirectly on the ground of race because of prayer times and religious holidays.

In *Ahmad v Inner London Education Authority,*[44] a Muslim was employed as a full-time teacher. In order to attend the mosque for prayers on a Friday he was 45 minutes late back after the lunch break. Mr Ahmad was told that if he wanted to continue attending the mosque he would have to take a part-time contract covering four and a half days with a reduction in salary. Mr Ahmad resigned and applied for compensation and reinstatement.

The case revolved around the Education Act 1944 and the Trade Union and Labour Relations Act 1974 and no claim was made under the RRA. The Education Act 1944 s30 provides that 'no person shall be disqualified by reason of his religious opinions, or of his attending or omitting to attend religious worship, from being a teacher in a county school or in any voluntary school . . . ; and no teacher in any such school shall . . . receive any less emolument or be deprived of, or disqualified for, any promotion or other advantage . . . by reason of his religious opinions or of his attending or omitting to attend religious worship . . .' The CA said that this could not be construed as authorising a breach of contract by a teacher who missed school to attend religious worship.

Lord Scarman dissented from the majority CA decision, saying that s30 would override provisions in Mr Ahmad's contract although it would be necessary to imply a limitation that the period of absence be 'no longer than is reasonably necessary, nor so frequent or for such duration as to make it impossible for the teacher to offer full-time service'. Scarman considered that 45 minutes off once a week was short enough time to be consistent with full-time work, especially since the contract expressly provided for whole days to be taken off on full pay on religious holidays. Scarman also considered that the

44 [1978] 1 All ER 574; [1977] ICR 490.

education authority should make suitable administrative arrangements to ensure that the children were taught, that Muslim teachers attended their mosques and that their colleagues were not unfairly burdened. He said: 'it may mean employing a few more teachers either part-time or full-time; but when that cost is compared with the heavy expenditure already committed to the cause of non-discrimination in our society, expense would not in this context appear to be a sound reason for requiring a narrow meaning to be given to the words of the statute'.

If Mr Ahmad had argued that the requirement to work such hours was indirectly discriminatory under the RRA he may well have succeeded. However, he would have to show that Muslims are a racial, as opposed to a religious, group or that he fell within a racial group which would find it more difficult to comply with the requirement compared to those not of that racial group (see **3.6.1**). The Metropolitan police force changed its policy on duty rosters in order to accommodate a police constable who complained that his shift-working patterns were incompatible with the requirements of his Jewish faith.

The CRE code recommends that if cultural and religious needs conflict with existing work requirements, employers should consider whether they can adapt the requirements to fit in with such needs (para 1.24). For example, Jews would find it harder to comply with the requirement for weekend and evening work because of their Friday evening/Saturday Sabbath (see **11.6.2**). There are proposals to prohibit discrimination on religious grounds, however, at the moment only discrimination on the ground of race is prohibited.

10.10 Other legislation

10.10.1 Protective legislation for women

Until 1986, there were legal restrictions on the hours that women could work, particularly in factories and mines. Most protective legislation has been repealed by the SDA 1986 and EA 1989.

10.10.2 Health and Safety at Work Act 1974

Health and Safety at Work Act 1974 s2 places on the employer a general obligation to look after the health, safety and welfare of his/her employees. An employer has a duty to protect the health and safety of pregnant women (see **15.4**).

Health and safety considerations have also been used as grounds for justifying indirect race discrimination (see **11.6.3.2**).

10.11 Residence

If an employer confines recruitment of staff to particular geographical areas, this may have an adverse impact on certain racial groups. Residence patterns and discrimination in the housing market mean that some areas, particularly inner-city areas, have a high proportion of black residents, while some areas are mainly white.

An employer's refusal to employ someone because of where s/he lives may be indirectly discriminatory under the RRA. In *Hussein v Saints Complete House Furnishers*,[45] Mr Hussein was recommended by a local employment agency for a job with a firm in the centre of Liverpool. He was turned down because he lived in the city centre and the employer said it was likely, in view of the high unemployment in the area, that his unemployed friends would start hanging around the shop. Mr Hussein argued that this was indirect discrimination; over 50% of the population in the centre of Liverpool were black compared to 2% in the rest of Merseyside. The requirement not to live in the city centre was therefore one with which fewer black people could comply. A recommendation was made under RRA s56 that the company refrain from imposing such residential requirements in future.

10.12 Mobility

Many advertisements specify that the successful candidates must be mobile; they may have to travel in the course of the job, or be prepared to move as and when the company specifies. Such a mobility requirement is likely to discriminate against women, particularly married women and women with children. Although women may have careers of their own, it is still a widely-held assumption that the man's job is the most important, and that it is legitimate to expect a family to move when the man has a new job. The man is less likely to follow his wife to a new place because her career requires it. Additionally, as men in general earn more than women, it is quite likely that it would not be economically feasible for the couple to follow the woman's job. Even though many men would expect their wives to

45 [1979] IRLR 337.

move, to follow the man's job – and many couples may still operate on this basis – it is unlawful for an employer to assume this.[46]

Mobility requirements may be indirectly discriminatory. In *Meade Hill v British Council*[47] there was a clause requiring members of middle management to 'serve in such parts of the UK . . . as the Council may in its discretion require . . .' The CA held that such a clause had a disproportionate impact on women. Judicial notice could be taken of the fact that a higher proportion of women than men are secondary earners so would find it impossible in practice to comply with a mobility clause.

The EOC conducted a formal investigation into the Leeds Permanent Building Society, studying the recruitment of management trainees in 1978/79. It found that the mobility requirement in the contractual form applied by the Society was not justifiable and amounted to unlawful discrimination.

10.13 Attitudes

Employers usually have their own prejudices about the kind of person they think is best for the job. Quite often these feelings can be racially or sexually biased. Employers may have quite fixed ideas about which jobs should be done by men and which jobs by women, while levels of racism can be so deep that some employers do not want black people to work for them at all, in any job. In *Baker v Cornwall CC*,[48] the CA acknowledged that 'discrimination can often result from a wish to preserve an existing pattern of employment . . . An excuse such as "we wanted someone who would fit in" is often a danger signal that the choice was influenced not by the qualifications of the successful candidate but by the sex or race of that candidate.'

In *Singh v LB Ealing*[49] an Asian job applicant for a job-share vacancy was rejected despite being 'an outstanding candidate' because it was felt that he would not fit in with the other part of the job-share who was a white woman. He was awarded £10,000 for injury to his feelings.

46 *Horsey v Dyfed* CC [1982] IRLR 395.

47 [1995] IRLR 478.

48 [1990] IRLR 194.

49 (1995) 24 EOR DCLD. See also *Marrington v University of Sunderland* (1995) 25 EOR DCLD, where a woman lecturer was refused promotion because she would not 'fit in'; *Abraham v Fenland DC* (1995) 23 EOR DCLD, where it was felt that a Sri Lankan-born job applicant would not 'fit in'; and *Bishop v Cooper Group plc* (1994) 21 EOR DCLD, where it was felt that only boys would 'fit in'.

In a CRE inquiry into the National Bus Company, it emerged that while the company employed many Asian bus conductors, they were not promoted or getting the more popular jobs of drivers and inspectors. The CRE found evidence that Asian applicants were being stereotyped as too 'weak' or 'passive' for inspector jobs.[50]

Black or female job candidates often suspect that an employer is making discriminatory assumptions and they are likely to be rejected on the ground of sex or race, but if the employer or his/her agent does not make any overtly sexist or racist remark, the applicant may have no more than a hunch that this is why s/he has been rejected. In view of the difficulty of getting evidence on employers' attitudes, rejected candidates may have to rely on inference from the facts surrounding the appointment (see Chapter 2 on proving direct discrimination). For example, it is common for a black applicant to be told that the vacancy no longer exists, as the post has been filled. Proof that this was not true was often obtained by telephoning the employer later to find out that the vacancy is still open. Some applicants have got white friends to go and enquire about the job. In *Matan v Famous Names Ltd*,[51] a black man, twice rejected for the job of packer, proved that all white people were appointed on the first occasion, he had been rejected twice yet the firm still had vacancies.

Proving direct discrimination is difficult and the questionnaire procedure can be crucial in such cases to elicit more information (see Chapter 25). It will be important to get access to candidates' application forms, internal memos and the interviewers' notes as these may reveal the prejudices of the interviewers.

10.14 Recruitment procedure

10.14.1 Interviews

Many interviewers are not trained to interview candidates in an unbiased, unprejudiced way. In *Best v Rotherham MBC*,[52] an IT recommended that all members of an interview panel should attend the council's discrimination courses. Sometimes the line of questioning in interviews will provide evidence of discrimination if the applicant does not get the job. Biased questions will not in themselves be

50 *National Bus Company* (CRE, 1985).
51 (1983) COIT 1399/1450.
52 Case no 1553/89.

unlawful but they can affect the candidate's ability to perform well, in which case s/he will have suffered a detriment, that of being unable to perform to his/her best abilities because of the biased questions.

In *Saunders v Richmond upon Thames BC*,[53] Ms Saunders claimed that the council had discriminated against her when it did not appoint her to the job of golf professional. During the course of her interview, she had been asked questions such as, 'Do you think men respond as well to a woman golf professional as a man?', and, 'Are there any women golf professionals in clubs?' Ms Saunders argued that these questions were in themselves discriminatory. The EAT said that although the questions were not unlawful, they may be relevant evidence in determining whether there had been discrimination in making the appointment. In *Smith v North Western Regional Health Authority*[54] the applicant was asked detailed questions about her childcare arrangements when a man with a family was asked no such questions. The tribunal held that the applicant had suffered direct discrimination. However, in *Woodhead v Chief Constable of West Yorkshire Police*,[55] the EAT said that questioning a female applicant on the details of her childcare and domestic arrangements was simply to find out how the children were to be cared for and this was not a breach of the Act. This must be wrong because it was irrelevant to the job and is almost certainly a breach of EC law.

In *Brice v J Sainsbury plc*,[56] all single applicants for the post of management trainee were asked the question, 'Do you plan to get married?', but only single women were asked the question, 'Do you plan to have a family?' A tribunal found that the employer had discriminated in the arrangements made for the purposes of determining who should be offered employment. Where a candidate was asked if he had worked with white technicians before and whether he had any trouble supervising them, the tribunal found that the question showed that his race was considered and this, taken together with the employer's failure to complete an RRA s65 questionnaire, led the tribunal to infer that there had been unlawful discrimination.[57] In another case, the applicant, who was Irish, was asked if he had a drink problem. The tribunal held that the question implied that there

53 [1978] ICR 75; [1977] IRLR 362.
54 COIT 1842/176.
55 (1990) 430 IRLIB 14, EAT.
56 (1985) COIT 1709/180.
57 *Virdee v ECC Quarries* [1978] IRLR 295.

was racial stereotyping and this could have led the applicant to perform less well than others who were not asked such a question.[58]

In *Nwoke v Government Legal Service and Civil Service Commissioners*[59] the IT inferred indirect discrimination from the fact (among others) that every white candidate with local government experience was marked 'C' or above, whereas no ethnic minority candidate with local government experience was graded 'C' or above. The interviewers had included comments like 'will fit in' on their assessment sheets. The IT held that subjectivity played a large part in the assessments and that the applicant had been discriminated against both on grounds of race and sex.

Equal opportunities procedures do not necessarily ensure that discrimination has been removed from the interviewing process. In *Umerji v Blackburn BC*[60] an Asian candidate scored the highest number of points at his interview and it was agreed to offer him the job. A few days later the panel reconvened and reversed their decision and offered the job to the next highest candidate who was a white man. The IT concluded that this was 'a blatant and bad case of discrimination'.

In an extraordinary decision, the CA, in *Simon v Brimham Associates*,[61] held that asking a Jewish applicant about his religion, with the explanation that if he were Jewish he might be precluded from getting the job, was not discriminatory as the same question was asked of all candidates. This must be wrong.

If some members of an interviewing panel take account of discriminatory factors, this will not be sufficient to prove discrimination unless the final decision was influenced by such factors.[62]

10.14.2 *Reasons for decisions must be clear*

Unsuccessful job applicants are given many different reasons for their rejection, some of which are untrue (such as that the post has already been filled when a subsequent enquiry shows that it has not), some are ambigious, such as 'the successful candidate would fit in better' or 'he was more suitable', and some more specific but still not strictly related to the job specification (for example, where attributes are

58 *O'Driscoll v Post Office* Case no: 25671/89.
59 (1996) 28 EOR DCLD.
60 (1995) 24 EOR DCLD.
61 [1987] IRLR 307.
62 See *Bowskill v Secretary of State for Scotland* (1987) 17 EOR.

taken into account which were not mentioned in the job description). In *Danfoss*, the ECJ stressed the importance of transparency, particularly where there is evidence of a system apparently working to the disadvantage of women. Although *Danfoss* was a decision about pay (see **21.3**) it is relevant to other areas such as recruitment, training and promotion. If the workforce is largely white and male, and the rationale for decisions about appointments is not clear, then arguably the burden should shift to the employer to justify the racial and sexual imbalance, in the same way that the ECJ says it should shift where a pay system results in the average pay of female workers being lower than that of male workers.

10.14.3 CRE and EOC codes of practice

Both the CRE and EOC codes make recommendations on the treatment of applicants and on shortlisting and interviewing processes.

The CRE code recommends that:

a) Gate, reception and personnel staff should be instructed not to treat casual or formal applicants from particular racial groups less favourably than others. These instructions should be confirmed in writing.
b) Staff responsible for shortlisting, interviewing and selecting candidates should be:
   - clearly informed of selection criteria and of the need for their consistent application;
   - given guidance or training on the effects which generalised assumptions and prejudices about race can have on selection decisions;
   - made aware of the possible misunderstandings that can occur in interviews between persons of different cultural backgrounds.
c) Wherever possible, shortlisting and interviewing should not be done by one person alone but should at least be checked at a more senior level (para 1.14(a)(b)(c)).

The EOC code recommends that:

a) Employers should ensure that personnel staff, line managers and all other employees, who may come into contact with job applicants, should be trained in the provisions of the SDA, including the fact that it is unlawful to instruct or put pressure on others to discriminate.

b) Applications from men and women should be processed in exactly the same way. There should not be separate lists of male and female or married and single applicants. All those handling applications and conducting interviews should be trained in the avoidance of unlawful discrimination and records of interviews kept, where practicable, showing why applicants were or were not appointed.
c) Questions should relate to the requirements of the job. Where it is necessary to assess whether personal circumstances will affect performance of the job (for example, where it involves unsocial hours or extensive travel) this should be discussed objectively without detailed questions based on assumptions about marital status, children and domestic obligations. Questions about marriage plans or family intentions should not be asked, as they could be construed as showing bias against women. Information necessary for personal records can be collected after a job offer has been made (para 23(a)(b)(c)).

GETTING WORK: KEY POINTS

- The CRE and EOC codes of practice offer guidance on how to avoid discrimination, and failure to follow them may be taken into account by an IT or court.
- Examples of discriminatory recruitment procedures are:
  - informal procedures, such as 'word of mouth' recruitment, recruitment by unsolicited letters of application;
  - selective recruitment, whereby employers confine their search to places dominated by white men (such as public schools);
  - head-hunting;
  - recruitment through unions where union membership is largely white and/or male;
  - internal recruitment where the workforce is largely white and/or male.
- It is unlawful to publish an advertisement which indicates that the employer intends to discriminate, either directly or indirectly. Only the CRE or EOC can bring complaints unless the advertisement is part of the arrangements made for determining who should be offered employment.
- It is unlawful for an employment agency to discriminate against a person on the ground of race or sex.

- Trainees are protected.
- A requirement to have UK qualifications or qualifications or experience over and above those necessary for the job may be discriminatory on the grounds of race and/or sex.
- Language and literacy tests and application forms may discriminate on the ground of race.
- Maximum age limits may discriminate against women.
- A requirement not to have children, whether overt or covert, is discriminatory on the ground of sex and/or marital status.
- There are some statutory provisions restricting the work that women can do, but these are few and apply only to protect women from risks associated with pregnancy and childbearing.
- Confining recruitment of staff to particular geographical areas may discriminate on the ground of race.
- A requirement to work full-time, evenings, weekends, or shifts may be discriminatory on the ground of sex and race.
- A requirement to be mobile may discriminate against women.
- Discriminatory attitudes are often revealed in interviews and may be useful evidence in a discrimination claim.

CHAPTER 11

At work

11.1 Introduction

Low-paid jobs are generally jobs with little training, no promotion prospects and few perks. Job segregation between men and women, between white workers and black workers is extensive (see Introduction). Many women are in part-time jobs, which are of a particularly low status and badly paid. This chapter looks at situations at work where discrimination might arise (apart from harassment which is explained in Chapter 13). Discrimination in pay systems is covered in Chapter 23. Disability discrimination is covered in Chapter 24.

The EqPA covers discrimination in pay and other terms of the contract if there is a comparable man in the same employment (see Chapter 18). The SDA covers discrimination outside the contract of employment (such as training, transfers, promotion, discretionary benefits) and where there is no man doing like work, work rated as equivalent or work of equal value (see **5.7.1** for which Act is relevant).

The RRA prohibits discrimination in the terms and conditions of employment, both contractual and non-contractual. There is no separate statute dealing with contractual terms.

Both the SDA and RRA provide that it is unlawful for an employer (and other bodies) to discriminate in access to opportunities for promotion, transfer or training, or to any other benefits, facilities or services, or by refusing or deliberately omitting to give access.[1]

EC law (art 119 and the EPD) prohibits discrimination in pay (widely defined to include any benefit which can be quantified in money terms). The ETD provides that the principle of equal treatment applies to 'promotion and to vocational training and . . . working conditions'.

1 SDA s6(2)(b); RRA s4(2)(b).

The CRE and EOC codes of practice will also be relevant (see 1.1.7).

11.2 European Council Recommendation on Childcare

This is a statement of policy which, though not binding, should be taken into account by ITs when deciding disputes. It is an aid to interpretation.[2] Thus, a person who has suffered sex discrimination related to childcare responsibilities (whether direct or indirect) should ask the IT to take the Recommendation into account.

The Recommendation recommends four areas for action:

a) the provision of childcare services while parents are working, training or seeking a job;
b) special leave for employed parents with responsibility for the care and upbringing of children;
c) initiatives which create a workplace which takes into account the needs of all working parents with responsibility for the care of children;
d) the sharing of occupational, family and upbringing responsibilities arising from the care of children between women and men.

It will be relevant, for example:

- where a woman, with childcare responsibilities, is not allowed to work part-time or flexible hours;
- where a part-time woman worker is treated less favourably than a full-time worker;
- where a man is denied a place in a workplace creche because they are reserved for women;
- where a woman, who failed to return to work after maternity leave because her baby was sick, is dismissed;
- where a woman is refused time off to look after a sick child; men should also be allowed time off but in practice it is usually women who are the primary carers;
- to ensure that training is arranged so it is accessible to women who work part-time.[3]

2 See *Grimaldi v Fonds des Maladies Professionelles* [1990] IRLR 400.

3 The EOC has produced a guidance note on the European Council Recommendation on Childcare.

11.3 Parental Leave Directive (96/34/EC)

The Labour government has said that it will sign the Social Chapter of the Maastricht Treaty. This will include adopting the provisions of the Parental Leave Directive. The date by which the Directive must be brought into force is 3 June 1998 and it is likely the provisions will be implemented by the end of 1998.

The aim of the Directive is to enable men and women to reconcile obligations. General considerations include:

- encouragement of the introduction of new flexible ways of organising work and time;
- the promotion of women's participation in the labour force;
- encouragement of men to assume an equal share of family responsibilities including the taking of parental leave.

The specific measures apply to all workers who have an employment contract or employment relationship and provide for the following.

11.3.1 Three months' parental leave

All workers have an individual right to take parental leave of up to three months after the birth or adoption of a child; the period of leave can be taken from birth up until the child is eight years old.[4] This means that both parents can take three months' leave each, but the leave cannot be transferred to enable one party to take six months' leave.

The conditions of access to leave will be decided by each member state, so that it might be granted on a full-time or part-time basis, in a piecemeal way or in the form of a time-credit system. Conditions may be imposed, including:

- a maximum one-year length of service condition;
- notice periods to be given by the worker;
- special provisions allowing leave to be postponed for justifiable reasons related to the operation of the business, eg, where work is of a seasonal nature;
- special arrangements to meet the operational and organisational requirements of small undertakings.

4 Clause 2(1).

Workers taking such leave must be given protection from dismissal and there is a right to return to the same job at the end of the leave or, if that is not possible, to an equivalent or similar job.

The leave is additional to maternity leave.

11.3.2 Time off work for urgent family reasons

Workers are entitled to time off work for urgent family reasons where sickness or accident make the immediate presence of the worker indispensable. Conditions of access to such time off is to be decided by member states and it may be limited to a certain amount of time per year.

11.4 Training

Training is crucial to getting a good job. Discrimination in access to apprenticeships and training is prohibited by the SDA not the EqPA (as it is unlikely to be a term of the contract). It is also unlawful under the RRA.[5] For provisions relating to positive action in training see Chapter 12.

Few jobs offer training. Where training opportunities exist employers often want to train employees whom they think will fit in and are likely to be a good investment. Preference may be given to employees who work long hours, whom they consider are likely to stay long term and employees with long service. This can discriminate against women because they often interrupt their working lives to have children, and even if they do not, employers tend to assume that they will, even though such assumptions are directly discriminatory. Some examples are set out below.

11.4.1 Stereotyping

In *Jackson v North Western Road Car Company Ltd*[6] the tribunal upheld a discrimination claim by a woman apprentice fitter working for a bus company. She was the only woman among 47 fitters and was denied access to training which would have enabled her to get a fitter's job. The tribunal found that a man with the applicant's characteristics and determination would have been given the training.

5 SDA s6(2)(a); RRA s4(2)(b).
6 27 April 1995; Case No: 55185/94.

11.4.2 *Service requirement*

A long service requirement may be indirectly discriminatory, in the same way that the two-year qualifying period for claiming unfair dismissal may be discriminatory (see *R v Secretary of State for Employment ex p Seymour Smith* at **14.1.1.1**). Refusal to provide training to a woman because she is about to go on maternity leave will be discriminatory (see **2.9.3**).

11.4.3 *Part-time workers*

Denying a woman training because she works part-time may be indirectly discriminatory. Training arrangements often favour employees who are prepared to work extra hours, be flexible and mobile, and attend training courses which are residential. For women with childcare and domestic commitments, all these criteria are more difficult to meet, and may be indirectly discriminatory (see **11.9**). Note that where a woman attends a training course for more hours than she usually works, she should be paid for all those hours – not just her normal part-time wage.[7] The European framework agreement on part-time work provides that part-time workers should have pro rate rights as full-time workers, althouth different treatment may be justified on objective grounds.[8] A directive will implement these provisions.

11.4.4 *Training limited to high grade jobs*

Access to training may be confined to certain grades and sections. For example, it is rare for typists to be offered training, apart from word-processing. If there is job segregation in the workforce then this may indirectly discriminate against women who may not be in the relevant grades, though capable of doing the training. The key question will be whether the denial of training is justified. The situation is similar to that where promotion is confined to certain grades – see below.

7 *Arbeiterwohlfahrt der Stadt Berlin eV v Botel* [1992] IRLR 423 ECJ and *Kuratorium Fur Dialyse und Nierentransplantation eV v Lewark* [1996] IRLR 637 (see **22.3.2.7**).

8 See 74 EOR 37 and also **22.3.3**.

11.4.5 Is there an obligation to provide training?

Failure to provide training could in some circumstances be discriminatory. In *Bayoomi v British Railways Board*[9] an IT held that it was unreasonable to expect Mr Bayoomi, an Arab born in Aden, to be able to work a telex machine within a six-month probationary period without being given training. It was agreed by the parties that it would be more difficult for someone from abroad to grasp the operating procedures and the lack of training was held to be indirectly discriminatory.[10]

11.4.6 Language training

Language training may be crucial for employees whose first language is not English. Employers can take positive action to provide this under RRA s35 (see Chapter 12), and there are industrial language training units all over Great Britain.

The CRE code states that although there is no legal requirement to provide language training, difficulties in communication can endanger equal opportunity in the workforce. The code recommends that:

> where the workforce includes current employees whose English is limited it is recommended that steps are taken to ensure that communications are as effective as possible. These should include, where reasonably practicable:
>
> a) provision of interpretation and translation facilities, for example in the communication of grievance and other procedures, and of terms of employment;
> b) training in English language and in communication skills;
> c) training for managers and supervisors in the background and culture of racial minority groups;
> d) the use of alternative or additional methods of communication, where employees find it difficult to understand health and safety requirements, for example
>   - safety signs; translation of safety notices;
>   - instructions through interpreters;
>   - instruction combined with industrial language training.

9 *Bayoomi v British Railways Board*; *Malik v Lex Mead* [1981] IRLR 431, IT.
10 See also *Chatprachong v Mecca Leisure Group* 9482/90 and *Malik v Lex Mead* 9463/90.

11.4.7 Age limits for training

Training is a benefit which is often only offered to the young. Many young women leaving school do not think about an apprenticeship, but at a later stage decide they would like to do one and find themselves barred by maximum age limits for entry, eg, 18 or occasionally 24. Career structures operate age barriers too; a Banking, Insurance and Finance Union report on one bank noted that 'the closed career structure is age-related and so all training is geared to age and there are difficulties in escaping the system'. For example, eligibility for study leave exists only within the first few years after entry to the bank, and women who have not made career choices at this stage are locked into the lower ranks of banking with no possibility of advancing. Similarly, day release is often offered only to those who have recently left school. Age barriers may amount to unlawful discrimination; the legality of them is discussed in Chapter 10.

11.4.8 Providers of vocational training

The SDA and RRA make it unlawful for anyone providing vocational training to discriminate against trainees (see **8.4**).

11.4.9 The codes of practice

The CRE code recommends that staff responsible for selecting employees for training, whether induction, promotion or skill training, should be instructed not to discriminate on racial grounds. Selection criteria for training opportunities should be examined to ensure that they are not indirectly discriminatory. It also says that job and training vacancies and the application procedure should be made known to all eligible employees, and not in such a way as to exclude or disproportionately reduce the numbers of applicants from a particular racial group (para 1.16).

The EOC code suggests that policies and practices regarding selection for training, day release and personal development should be examined for unlawful direct and indirect discrimination. Where there is found to be an imbalance in training as between sexes, the cause should be identified to ensure that it is not discriminatory. This guidance was reinforced by the ECJ in *Danfoss* (see **2.12**). Additionally, age limits for access to training (and promotion) should be questioned (para 25(f) and (g)).

11.5 Promotion and transfers

For those in manual and unskilled jobs promotion is often out of the question. In jobs with promotion prospects white workers and men are more likely to be promoted.[11]

11.5.1 Direct discrimination

There may be overt direct discrimination occurring – 'I don't think we could have a woman as the boss', 'I don't think the white workers would take orders from a black supervisor'. More often there are covert discriminatory assumptions which maintain the glass ceiling beyond which women and ethnic minority workers are less often found.

In order to prove direct discrimination in relation to promotion decision it will generally be necessary to draw inferences from the facts (see **2.10**). Account may be taken of:

- the lack of safeguards, such as interviews or marking;
- the lack of any formal procedures;
- failure to follow existing procedures;
- the use of subjective criteria;
- expectations which are biased in favour of white and male workers; this would include behaviour at an interview;
- suggestions that the person would not 'fit in';
- assumptions that men are often considered to be more aggressive, competitive and ambitious than women, and such characteristics are considered necessary qualities for management;
- racist stereotypes, eg, that Asians are passive;
- the fact that promotion often depends to an extent on friendship networks, and because of the social segregation between races in British society, this discriminates against black employees.

The following are examples of some tribunal decisions.

In *Silva v British Airways plc and Others*[12] the applicant, an Asian woman, applied for promotion along with nine other employees. The procedures required all applicants to submit a CV or application form and for managers to draw up a shortlist for interview. Instead of following this procedure, a white woman was appointed on the basis

11 Where a claim relates to promotion it comes under SDA s6(2) and RRA s4(2), not s6(1) or s4(1) which relates to job applicants; see *Clymo v Wandsworth LBC* [1989] IRLR 241.

12 16 July 1996; Case No: 66783/94. See also *D'Silva v Hambleton & Nurdin & Peacock plc* [1997] 1 CL 254.

that she was suitable for the job. The tribunal, distinguishing *Quereshi v LB Newham* (see **2.11**), found that the managers deliberately decided to bypass the procedures to enable them to select the white woman; this was race discrimination.[13]

In *Deb-Gupta v Board of Governors Beech Hill Infant School and Bedfordshire* CC[14] an Asian teacher failed to get promotion, despite having greater experience than the successful white candidate. Apart from 'grave defects' in the procedure and the dangers of subjectivity, the tribunal said that great store was placed on the manner in which the answers to questions were given by the interviewees. This might put a person with an 'ethnic minority background' at a 'subjective disadvantage' as 'he or she might not react to a question the same way a white person would'.

In *Marrington v University of Sunderland*[15] a female lecturer who was refused promotion because it was believed she would not fit into the male-dominated culture of the university won her sex discrimination claim. The tribunal took account of the male climate and culture of the university, the statistical evidence of a glass ceiling (beyond which women were not appointed) and the failure to follow a proper objective set of principles when interviewing and marking.[16]

There must, however, be evidence of discrimination on the ground of race or sex. An unsatisfactory system for promotion or failure to follow procedure might lead to an inference of discrimination (and is often treated suspiciously by a tribunal[17]) but this in itself is not enough.[18]

13 See also *Henry v Rover Group Ltd* (29 May 1996; Case No: 23289/95), where a black worker successfully claimed race discrimination after he was excluded by junior management and the 'grass roots' union from promotion to a part of the production line which had become a sort of 'white man's club'. The IT underlined the importance of an equal opportunities policy.

14 5 April 1994; Case No: 48188/92; DCLD 22.

15 5 August 1994; Case No. 52606/93; DCLD 25.

16 See also *Charles v Nottinghamshire* CC (5 July 1994 and 6 October 1994; Case No: 11221/93; DCLD 23) where it was held that failure to shortlist a black candidate for interview for a senior social worker post was unlawful race discrimination.

17 See *Williams v Milton Keynes BC* (5 January 1994; Case No: 27129/91; DCLD 22) where the tribunal said that where there is no formal procedure but a large element of subjective managerial assessment 'coloured people and women are often particularly vulnerable to being overlooked completely or bypassed in favour of their white colleagues or men'. See also *Patterson v Kwik Save Group plc* (25 March 1994; Case No: 49642/93; DCLD 22).

18 See *Kwik Save Group plc v Patterson* 19 May 1995; EAT No: 424/94; DCLD 25.

11.5.2 Pregnancy discrimination

In *Pearson v Swindells and British Telecommunications Ltd*[19] the applicant attended an interview while eight months pregnant and no account had been taken of the possibility that her poor performance at interview might have been affected by her being pregnant and on leave. The IT held that she failed to obtain promotion because of her absence on leave and this was discrimination.

In *McLacklan v Central Scotland Health Care NHS Trust*[20] the tribunal held that a decision to transfer the applicant because she was female, part-time and due to go on maternity leave was direct discrimination (because it was related to the applicant's maternity leave) and indirect discrimination (in that she was selected because she worked part-time).

11.5.3 Indirect discrimination

There are also structural barriers which prevent women and black workers from moving up in an organisation's hierarchy. Most of these barriers also prevent women and black workers from getting jobs and some of these have been identified in Chapter 10 above. Promotion may depend on factors such as qualifications, experience, length of service and age, all of which can be discriminatory. Career structures should be examined to identify these kinds of barriers. Discrimination at the recruitment stage may have a long-term effect, as higher level jobs are often offered to existing employees. Thus access to the appropriate job at an early stage may be crucial to career prospects.

11.5.3.1 Ladders

In most workplaces there are different points of entry. A woman might start work in a typing pool, then work as a secretary, then become a personal assistant. She will rarely be able to break out of the secretarial mould. A man may start as a postboy, move on to being a filing clerk, then a senior clerk and finally a manager. It would be unusual for a secretary to jump across the ladders and become a manager. Job segregation creates barriers to promotion.

19 14 November 1994; Case No 48222/93.
20 14 June 1995; Case No S/4932/94; Glasgow IT.

In one case,[21] an IT held that two men, who had been sent to jobs where they had a good chance of promotion, had been given a discriminatory advantage over a woman applicant who had been moved to a lower grade job.

In *Bath v British Airways Engineering Overhaul Ltd*,[22] the applicant was an aircraft component worker in grade 6. She had been refused a job as a production assistant – a grade 3 job – on the ground that such jobs were open only to certain workers in grades 1, 2 and 4. Ms Bath argued that the requirement for promotion – to be in one of these grades – indirectly discriminated against women who were not represented in them. The tribunal accepted this, and decided that the restriction was not justifiable. Tribunals in other cases,[23] have held that lack of promotion opportunities in the lower grades could form the basis for a claim, the requirement being that to be considered for promotion one had to be in one of the higher grades. In *Bilka*,[24] the ECJ accepted that restricting benefits and opportunities to higher grades may be discriminatory.

In *Hay v Lothian RC*,[25] a lecturer who taught secretarial studies was turned down for a senior post in the business studies department because she lacked business experience. Although she showed the tribunal how it was almost impossible for women to break out of secretarial studies and into the business side, the tribunal found the requirement justifiable.

In *Savell v Watches of Switzerland*,[26] it was held that there had been indirect discrimination in the promotion procedures used (see **3.6.2.5**). Ms Savell argued that the vagueness of her employer's promotion procedures amounted to indirect discrimination. She criticised its promotion procedures on the following grounds:

a) impending appointments were not advertised to staff, and women were less likely than men to ask to be considered for promotion (because they lacked the confidence);
b) persons under consideration for promotion were not interviewed;
c) there were no clear guidelines to branch managers about the criteria to be applied in the regular assessments and appraisals

21 *Sloane v Strathclyde RC* S/1676/78.
22 (1981) 33607/79.
23 *Francis and Others v British Airways Engineering Overhaul* [1982] IRLR 10, EAT, and *Wheeler v London Ambulance Service* 23911/89.
24 [1986] IRLR 317, ECJ.
25 (1984) S/913/83.
26 [1983] IRLR 141, EAT.

and some appraisals, including those of Ms Savell, were out of date;

d) the criteria for promotion were not written; they were subjective and were not made known to persons in line for promotion;
e) the individual managers made a point of promoting their own staff and paid particular attention to training when searching for potential managers, but Ms Savell was unaware of the importance attached to training for which she could have volunteered;
f) the failure to consult a candidate's branch manager resulted in higher management being unaware that Ms Savell no longer required to stay at the branch where she then worked and was willing to undertake Saturday work.

Managers often want to see evidence from candidates for promotion that they are ambitious, and frequently assume that women are not. For example, in *Bridge v Tayside RC*,[27] the applicant had taught music for seven years and then applied for a job as head of department. She was acting head already when the selection board passed her over in choosing a less experienced man for the post. The Board told her that it preferred someone who wanted to move higher up the ladder, and that two of the interviewers thought that men were more ambitious than women, as evidenced by the fact that many more men than women were in senior posts. The IT held that this was indirectly discriminatory as fewer women wanted to be in the grades above head of department and a requirement to do another job of a different nature could not be justified.

11.5.3.2 Past discrimination

Indirect discrimination may occur as a result of past practices which were directly discriminatory. Although the overt discrimination may have been removed, its effect often lasts for years afterwards. This is illustrated in *Steel v The Post Office (No 2)*.[28] In Ms Steel's workplace there were three kinds of postmen and women: temporary part-time, temporary full-time and permanent full-time. Prior to 1975 women could not attain permanent status. This changed in 1975 but women's seniority, which, like the men's, was based on length of service as permanent employees, dated only from 1975. In 1977 Ms Steel applied to be transferred to a more popular walk but was refused because the most senior postmen were given the first choice and although Ms Steel

27 S/1789/83,
28 [1978] IRLR 198, IT.

had worked for the Post Office for 16 years she had only two years' seniority. The EAT said that although the SDA did not operate retrospectively, some acts of discrimination were of a continuing nature and should, as far as possible, be removed.

It was a condition that the successful applicant must be the most senior, fewer women could comply with this condition and, the EAT held, this was not justifiable.

11.5.4 Codes of practice

The EOC code recommends that where an appraisal system is in operation, the assessment criteria should be examined to ensure that they are not unlawfully discriminatory, and the scheme monitored to assess how it is working in practice. It continues by saying that when a group of workers predominantly of one sex is excluded from an appraisal scheme, access to promotion, transfer and training and to other benefits, the situation should be reviewed to ensure that there is no unlawful indirect discrimination (para 25(a), (b)). This is now supported by *Danfoss* (see **2.12**). The code also recommends that promotion and career development patterns are reviewed to ensure that the traditional qualifications are justifiable. Length of service is an example of criteria which may be unlawful. The code suggests that when general ability and personal qualities are the main requirements for promotion to a post, care should be taken to consider favourably candidates of both sexes with differing career patterns and general experience (para 25(c) and (d)).

The CRE code has fewer but similar provisions specifically on promotion, though the recommendations on selection for recruitment are intended to apply to promotion, transfer and training as well (para 1.18).

A discriminatory promotion procedure may justify an employee resigning and claiming constructive dismissal.[29] However, it is important first to write to the employer and give him/her a chance to rectify the situation. Additionally, the letter of resignation should set out the reasons for the resignation (see **14.2.7**).

11.6 Terms and conditions

As a rule, manual jobs and lower-paid jobs offer terms and conditions which are worse than those of white-collar and better-paid work.

29 *Pearce v Somersvale Ltd* COIT 1501/140.

Some of the conditions of employment are contractual, eg, holidays and sick pay, and are therefore covered by the EqPA and RRA, while non-contractual matters (eg, 'perks' or one-off benefits) are covered by the SDA and RRA. Article 119 and the ETD should also be considered.

11.6.1 Sick leave

It may be indirect discrimination to deny a part-time female worker sick leave (see **11.9**). A common problem is time off to care for sick children. It is generally women who care for children and it is arguable that refusing to allow a woman to take sick leave when her child is sick is indirectly discriminatory. The requirement would be either 'not to take time off when a dependent child is sick' or a requirement 'to work when a dependent child is sick'. The main question is whether such a requirement is justifiable. If an employee is allowed time off when she is sick, should not a child's sickness entitle her to time off – at least taken as part of her sick leave entitlement. The Parental Leave Directive (when implemented) will give a right to time off.

11.6.2 Holidays

Holiday entitlement is normally determined by the contract of employment. A new EC Working Time Directive came into effect in November 1996. This provides that all workers shall have a minimum of four weeks' paid holiday per year. This is not in force in the UK but the Labour government has said that it will be implemented (see **11.8**).

Discrimination in holiday entitlement is covered by the EqPA or SDA, depending on whether there is a 'comparable man' (see **5.7.1**) and the RRA and ETD (see **6.4** and **9.4.5.2**). Part-time workers should get the same pro rata holiday entitlement as full-time workers (see **11.9**).

In *J H Walker Ltd v Hussain*[30] 17 Muslims from the Indian sub-continent requested a day off to celebrate Eid – one of the most important religious occasions in the Muslim calendar. The EAT upheld the IT's decision that refusal to allow a day off was indirect discrimination. The employers had imposed a requirement that no holiday could be taken during the May-July period. The tribunal

30 [1996] IRLR 11.

accepted that the company had acted for what it genuinely believed was a good business reason. However, balancing the discriminatory impact of the requirement on the Asian workers with the reasonable needs of the company, the requirement was not justifiable, especially bearing in mind that the applicants were willing to work additional hours to make up any backlog.

The CRE code points out that employees might request extended leave from time to time in order to visit relatives in their countries of origin or who have emigrated to other countries. Many employers have policies which allow annual leave entitlement to be accumulated, or extra unpaid leave to be taken to meet these circumstances. Employers should take care to apply such policies consistently and without unlawful discrimination (para 1.21).

11.6.3 Dress and appearance

There are dress requirements in many jobs. Employees may be required to wear uniform or other company clothing or merely to look smart. Women may be asked to wear skirts, men told they cannot wear earrings or keep their hair long. Assumptions about appropriate dress and smart appearance will inevitably include assumptions based on sex, and also attitudes that are culturally specific and may be directly or indirectly discriminatory on the ground of sex and/or race. Employers often argue that rules about dress are imposed to create a 'smart image', or for hygiene or health and safety reasons.

11.6.3.1 Sex discrimination

In *Schmidt v Austicks Bookshops Ltd*,[31] the EAT said that it was lawful to require women to wear skirts because men were subject to similar restrictions – they were not allowed to wear T-shirts. The EAT said that clothing rules had to be considered generally, and not on a garment-by-garment basis (see **2.9.2**).

In *Smith v Safeway plc*[32] a male delicatessen assistant was dismissed because the length of his hair contravened the employer's rules that men (not women) should have 'tidy hair not below shirt-collar length . . . ' Women, on the other hand, could have hair down to their waist if they wished. However, the CA held that there is no sex discrimin-

31 [1977] IRLR 360, EAT.
32 [1996] IRLR 456.

ation where conventional standards are applied, provided there is an even-handed approach between men and women.

The application of different appearance rules for men and women is such obvious discrimination on the grounds of sex, using the 'but for' test in *James*, that the decision must be wrong (see **2.9.2**).

If an employer moves a woman to a different job because she is pregnant and 'would not look good' dealing with customers, this will be discrimination.[33] In *Martin v McConkey*[34] the applicant was told she would have to leave when her pregnancy showed because the employer did not want people talking. This was unlawful sex discrimination.

11.6.3.2 Race discrimination

The assumption that to look smart, a woman must wear a skirt, may have arisen in white English culture, but is not shared by all other cultures. In *Malik v British Home Stores*,[35] a Muslim successfully challenged the company's rule that female employees had to wear a skirt; the tribunal accepted that this discriminated against Muslim women who are obliged to wear clothes that cover their legs, and that this outweighed the justification put forward by the employer, who claimed that it was in the interest of the company's image. In *Kingston and Richmond Area Health Authority v Kaur*,[36] the applicant claimed that the NHS uniform rules, which demand that nurses wear skirts, discriminated against Sikh women who, like Muslims, are required to wear trousers. Although the EAT found that the requirement was justifiable because a variation would have been contrary to statutory regulations, the rules were changed as a result of this case.[37] Note that, under the SDA, provisions in statutory regulations are no longer a defence unless they are for the protection of women in certain circumstances related to pregnancy and child-bearing (see **5.4.2.6**).

If employers try to justify different clothing rules, they should act consistently. Thus, if it is argued that the rules are necessary in the interest of health and safety, the same rules must be applied to men and women and different racial groups.

Cases concerning clothing rules have been taken by Sikh men where

33 *O'Neill v Walthamstow Building Society* Case No 27886/89; DCLD 6.
34 Case No 1577/89, Northern Ireland IT; DCLD 5.
35 (1980) COIT 987/12.
36 [1981] IRLR 337, EAT.
37 See also *Mandla* (**3.6.8**).

they have been denied jobs on the ground that company rules would not allow the wearing of beards or turbans. While tribunals have accepted that these rules discriminate against Sikh men, in some cases discriminatory rules have been successfully justified by employers on the grounds of hygiene and/or health and safety (see **3.6.7.6**).

In *Singh v Rowntree Mackintosh Ltd*,[38] the applicant had applied for a job at a confectionery factory. He was told that he would be offered the job if he shaved off his beard, as there was a company rule prohibiting the wearing of beards by employees who came into contact with the company's products. The IT recognised that it was in the public interest, on the ground of hygiene, to have such a rule but also recognised that it was in the public interest that employers should not discriminate against Sikhs. Weighing the two, in what they described as the balance of convenience, they favoured the public interest in hygiene. The tribunal equated 'justifiable' with that which is generally equitable and reasonable in an objective sense.

The EAT did not disagree that the test was one of necessity but said that unless the word 'necessity' is to be rigidly construed, the tribunal could not be said to have reached a wrong conclusion. The EAT added that consideration had to be given to what is reasonable. The EAT seems to have adopted two tests, necessity and reasonableness, and to have based its decision on the latter. The test must, since *Bilka* (see above), be one of necessity and it is difficult to understand how, on the facts of the case, the tribunal could legitimately hold that the requirement not to have a beard was necessary, particularly as the majority of the respondent's factories did not apply the rule and so did not consider it to be necessary.

Note that it is now unlawful indirect discrimination to require Sikhs to wear helmets on construction sites (see **3.6.7.6**).

The CRE code of practice says that employers should not refuse employment to a turbaned Sikh because he could not comply with unjustifiable uniform requirements.

11.7 Failure to investigate complaints of discrimination

Failure to deal with a grievance or investigate a complaint of discrimination may be unlawful if the reason is due to the race or sex of the complainant. For example, in *Usman v Watford BC*[39] it was held that a local authority which took nine months to publish the findings

38 [1979] IRLR 199, EAT. See also *Blakerd v Elizabeth Shaw Ltd* (**3.6.7.6**).
39 6 June 1996; Case No: 30379/95; DCLD 29.

of an investigation into allegations made by a Pakistani employee under its harassment policy, rather than the 21 days stated in the policy, unlawfully discriminated. The tribunal said the delay was 'inordinate, inexcusable and unprecedented'.

11.8 Working Time Directive

The aim of this Directive is to lay down minimum health and safety requirements relating to working hours. There are a number of exceptions which are outside the scope of this book.[40] The main provisions are for:

- minimum daily rest periods;
- a minimum period of paid annual leave (see **11.6.2**);
- a maximum normal working period of 8 hours in 24 for night workers;
- a maximum average working week of 48 hours calculated over a period of up to four months.

The provision for a maximum average working week of 48 hours and a minimum period of paid holiday are the most important provisions. Employees expected to work over 48 hours per week may be able to rely on the Directive as well as the indirect sex discrimination provisions of the SDA (see Chapter 3).

11.9 Part-time workers

Entitlement to work part-time is covered at **17.5**. Discrimination in pay is covered at **22.3.3**. Similar issues arise when part-time workers are denied benefits to which full-timers are entitled.

There are many ways that part-time workers lose out. Not only do they work in low-paid jobs and suffer discrimination under various pay systems, but they also are often excluded from other employment-related benefits and conditions enjoyed by full-timers.

Holiday entitlement is often disproportionately lower for part-timers. Part-timers who do not work on Mondays do not get the benefit of bank holidays; rarely are there provisions entitling them to another day off instead.

The arrangement of hours of work often means that part-timers

40 See E Deards, 'The Working Time Directive and its effect in the UK' March 1997 *Legal Action* 18.

lose out on meal and tea breaks. For example, in the retail industry it is common practice for employers to have two part-time workers to cover a day's work, so that shops can be generously staffed at the busiest period at lunch time.

Less favourable treatment of part-time workers is likely to be unlawful indirect discrimination under either UK or EC law. The four-pronged test laid down in *Bilka* (see **3.6.7.1**) was adopted by the HL in *Rainey*[41] and applies equally under the SDA and RRA.

It will not be sufficient for employers to say that it would be too expensive to provide pension schemes (or other benefits) for part-timers. If part-time workers are paid the same rate as full-timers (on a proportionate basis) they should be entitled to the same benefits (see **22.3.3**).

Employers may be able to justify refusing to employ part-timers if they can show that the requirement for a full-time worker is justifiable but will now find it more difficult to justify distinguishing between existing full-time and part-time workers. There is to be a new EC Directive giving part-time workers pro rata rights with full-time workers unless different treatment is justified on objective grounds (see **22.3.3**).

A refusal to allow workers to vary their hours of work or less favourable treatment of part-timers may be indirectly discriminatory on grounds of sex and race (see **17.5** and **22.3.3**).

11.10 Benefits, facilities and services

Discrimination in access to benefits, facilities and services is unlawful, whether provided directly by the employer or indirectly by a third party.[42]

Refusal of a mortgage subsidy to a woman, when a man in similar circumstances would have received one, was held to be discriminatory in *Calder v James Finlay Corporation Ltd*.[43] Other benefits include company cars and free parking. In *Burnett and Tyler v Electric Actuator Co Ltd*,[44] an IT held that it was unlawful to exclude women from meetings where pay was discussed. If employees are entitled to benefits, facilities or services which are offered on the same basis to

41 *Rainey v Greater Glasgow Health Board* [1987] IRLR 26, HL.
42 SDA ss6(2)(a) and 50(1); RRA ss4(2)(b) and 40(1).
43 [1989] IRLR 55, EAT.
44 COIT 810/99.

the public, a discrimination claim can be made only under SDA s29 or RRA s20.

The EOC code recommends that employers should regularly review their benefits, facilities and services to avoid discrimination. Part-time work, domestic leave, company cars and benefits for dependants should be available to male and female employees in similar circumstances. Part-timers should be entitled to pro rata benefits.

11.11 Any other detriment

Both the SDA and RRA contain a broad, catch-all provision which prohibits employers from subjecting their employees to 'any other detriment'.[45]

11.11.1 What is 'detriment'?

'Detriment' is not defined in the statute. In *Barclays Bank plc v Kapur and Others*,[46] the CA said that detriment was to be given its 'broad, ordinary meaning' and almost any discriminatory conduct by an employer against an employee in relation to the latter's employment is unlawful as constituting a detriment.

In *De Souza v Automobile Association*,[47] the CA said that to establish a detriment it must be found that the reasonable worker had been disadvantaged in the circumstances in which s/he had to work, as a result of the acts being complained about. The court held that racial insults were not a detriment unless they were meant to be overheard by the applicant or it could reasonably have been anticipated that s/he would overhear or become aware of them. The court confirmed that there did not have to be a breach of contract – such as an enforced transfer or demotion – for there to be a detriment.

Words or acts of discouragement can amount to a detriment under the Acts:[48] eg, in *Ahmed v Derby Pride Ltd*[49] an Asian manager was excluded from the interview panel for the appointment of a member of her staff; in *Asante v Reject Shop and Rich*[50] the applicant was told, 'I don't trust you . . . you're black and all black people are criminals'. These cases resulted in a finding of discrimination.

45 SDA s6(2)(b); RRA s2(2)(c).
46 [1989] IRLR 387.
47 [1986] IRLR 103.
48 See *Simon v Brimham Associates* [1987] IRLR 307.
49 (1997) 31 EOR DCLD.
50 (1996) 28 EOR DCLD.

'Detriment' has been defined by the CA as 'putting under a disadvantage' in *Jeremiah v Ministry of Defence*.[51] The applicant worked as an examiner in a Royal Ordnance factory, supervising production in a group of shops. In one of the shops, the 'colour-bursting' shop, conditions were dusty and dirty; only men were required to work there. Mr Jeremiah claimed that he had suffered a detriment because when he volunteered for overtime he was often asked to work in the colour-bursting shop while women were not. The CA held that this was a detriment, even though the men were compensated for working in the dirty conditions by additional payment – employers cannot buy a right to discriminate said the court.

11.11.2 Harassment and bullying

Sexual or racial harassment is clearly a detriment; see Chapter 13. Bullying will also be a detriment if directed at a person because of his/her race or sex. Thus, if a woman is bullied when a man in a similar situation would not be, that is discrimination. However, if the bullying is applied equally to men and women, or to all races, it will not be a detriment for the purposes of a discrimination action although if it leads to a dismissal it is likely to be an unfair one. In *Francis v Bentham & Co Ltd*[52] the IT found that the applicant's manager had made personal and insulting remarks about her work and attitude, often in public. It found that he bullied all staff but female staff in particular and this was a detriment. In contrast, in *Orpe v Kent CC and Cawthra*[53] the IT found that the applicant's manager bullied both male and female staff. It therefore concluded that this did not amount to discrimination under the SDA.

An employee is entitled to be protected from discrimination not only from his/her managers and co-workers but also from clients. In *Burton and Rhule v De Vere Hotels*[54] it was held that an employer subjects an employee to a detriment if it causes or permits a discriminatory act to occur in circumstances in which it can control whether the discrimination happens or not. The EAT held that the question to be considered was whether the employer could, by the application of good employment practice, have prevented the

51 [1979] IRLR 436.
52 (1996) 30 EOR DCLD.
53 (1996) 28 EOR DCLD.
54 [1996] IRLR 596; this was re-affirmed in *Jones v Tower Boot* [1997] IRLR 168. See also *Jeffers v N Wales Probation Committee* (1997) 31 EOR DCLD.

harassment or reduced the extent of it. This case concerned two Afro-Caribbean waitresses who were employed as casual waitresses at a dinner where the guest speaker was making racially and sexually offensive remarks. This created an atmosphere whereby other guests also made sexist and racist remarks in the same vein. The EAT held that the manager should have warned the assistant managers to keep a look out for what this particular guest speaker said and withdraw the waitresses if the atmosphere became unpleasant. Thus, employers have a duty to anticipate when discrimination might occur, take such steps as are within their power to notify their clients or users that discriminatory acts will not be accepted, and take action to protect possible victims.

11.11.3 Denial of choice

The denial of a choice that is valued by the worker concerned could be a detriment.[55] In *Gill v El Vino Co*[56] the CA found that a wine bar rule depriving women of the choice of buying drinks at the bar, as opposed to ordering at tables, was a deprivation of choice and so unlawful.

11.11.4 Instructions to discriminate

The issuing of instructions to discriminate may amount to a detriment – even if those instructions are not implemented. In *BL Cars Ltd and Another v Brown and Others*,[57] the chief security officer at a BL plant had issued instructions to gate staff to check the identity of every black employee entering. Even though these instructions were not implemented it was held that they were unlawful.

11.11.5 Demotion and transfers

Employees who are demoted or transferred against their will can claim that they have suffered a detriment. In sexual and racial harassment cases it is often the victims who are moved by management. If this happens it is likely to be discrimination (see Chapter 13). There is no need to prove that an enforced transfer involves loss of status or

55 See *R v Birmingham CC ex p EOC* [1989] IRLR 173.
56 [1983] 2 WLR 155. See also *R v Birmingham CC ex p EOC* (see 2.2).
57 [1983] IRLR 193.

pay; being moved to a less attractive and less interesting job has been held by the EAT to constitute a detriment.[58]

'Detriment' also covers being issued with formal warnings,[59] failure to investigate complaints of unfair treatment[60] or to put a grievance procedure into operation.[61]

11.11.6 Codes of practice

The CRE code sets out that responsibility for providing equal opportunities for employees rests with employers. It is therefore recommended that they adopt, implement and monitor an equal opportunities policy to ensure that there is no unlawful discrimination and that equal opportunity is genuinely available.

It states that since it is unlawful to discriminate on racial grounds in affording terms of employment and providing benefits, facilities and services for employees, it recommends that:

- all staff concerned with these aspects of employment should be instructed accordingly; and
- the criteria governing eligibility should be examined to ensure that they are not unlawfully discriminatory (para 1.20 (a) and (b)).

The EOC code recommends that all terms of employment, benefits, facilities and services are reviewed to ensure that there is no unlawful discrimination on the ground of sex or marriage. It also says that, in an establishment where part-timers are solely or mainly women, less favourable treatment of them may be unlawful discrimination. It is therefore recommended that where part-timers do not enjoy pro rata pay or benefits with full-time workers, the arrangements should be reviewed to ensure that they are justified without regard to sex (paras 28(a) and 29(b)).

In EOC code Pt 2, which deals with equal opportunities policies, there are a number of other suggestions about working arrangements. The aim of these is to help women remain in employment when they have young children, and they include childcare facilities, improvements in maternity leave and other leave, residential training and the right to part-time work (para 43(a)–(e)).

58 *Deson v B L Cars Ltd* (1981) EAT 173/80.
59 *Bourne v London Transport Executive* (1978) EAT 123/78.
60 *Eke v Commissioners of Customs and Excise* [1981] IRLR 334.
61 *Sheik v Focus Cinemas* (1978) COIT 839/36.

AT WORK: KEY POINTS

- Female and ethnic minority workers are often treated less favourably in relation to:
  - training;
  - transfers;
  - promotion;
  - other benefits.
- The European Council Recommendation on Childcare should be taken into account in sex discrimination cases where childcare responsibilities are an issue.
- The Labour government has said it will implement the Parental Leave Directive.
- Discrimination in training may arise where:
  - there has been stereotyping as to what is traditionally a male or female job;
  - there are service requirements, which impact adversely on women;
  - part-timers are treated less favourably;
  - training is limited to high grade jobs, where there are fewer female and black workers;
  - there are age limits which impact particularly on women.

  The CRE and EOC codes should be taken into account.
- Discrimination in promotion may occur where:
  - there is sexual or racial stereotyping;
  - there is a lack of formal procedures or failure to follow them where this adversely affects female and black workers;
  - promotion depends on the subjective judgment of individuals as opposed to an open interview process;
  - a woman who is pregnant or on maternity leave is not considered for promotion;
  - there are structural barriers to female and black workers from gaining promotion;
  - there has been past discrimination.
- Other terms and conditions may be discriminatory, such as:
  - denying a part-time female worker sick leave;
  - refusing to allow a woman to take time off if her child is sick;
  - failure to provide holidays for part-time workers;

- failure to allow a worker to take time off for a religious holiday;
- dress and appearance rules – both on grounds of sex and race;
- failure to investigate complaints of discrimination;
- any less favourable treatment of female part-time workers may indirectly discriminate against women.

• Discrimination in the provision of benefits, facilities and services will also be unlawful, such as refusing a mortgage to a woman.

• It is unlawful to subject, on the ground of race or sex, a worker to 'any other detriment'; this includes:

- putting a worker under a disadvantage;
- racial or sexual abuse, or bullying;
- denial of choice;
- instructions to discriminate;
- demotion or transfer.

The Codes of Practice should always be taken into account.

CHAPTER 12

Positive action

The UK sex and race legislation aims to remove discrimination rather than to discriminate positively in favour of women or racially disadvantaged groups. There are limited provisions for positive action. The SDA and RRA allow employers and other bodies to provide training for under-represented racial groups and sexes and to allow employers to 'encourage' them to apply for jobs. However, recruitment on the basis of sex or race is unlawful discrimination. By contrast, there is no prohibition on positive discrimination in favour of people with disabilities.

12.1 Positive action under the RRA: training and 'encouragement'

12.1.1 Employers

Employers can provide access to training for employees of a particular racial group or encouragement for persons of that racial group (whether employees or job applicants) to do particular work in their establishments provided that one or more of the following conditions applied within the last 12 months:

a) there are no persons of that racial group doing that work at that establishment; or
b) the proportion of persons of that group doing that work at that establishment is small in comparison with the proportion of persons of that group:
   (i) among all those employed by that employer there; or
   (ii) among the popultion of the area from which that employer

normally recruits persons for work in its employment at that establishment.[1]

12.1.2 Training providers

Any training provider can provide such opportunities (as set out in **12.1.1**) where at any time in the previous 12 months there were no persons of that racial group doing that work, or the proportion doing that work in GB (or an area of GB) was small in comparison with the proportion of that group among the population of GB (or an area of GB). This means that local authorities, employers and other training providers can provide such training themselves where there is either under-representation in GB or an area of GB.[2]

12.1.3 Special training, education and welfare needs

RRA s35 allows the provision of facilities or services to meet the special needs of persons of a particular racial group with regard to their education, training or welfare or any ancillary benefits. This could cover language training facilities or training to assist with the setting up or running of a business (but would not cover providing funds to enable someone from a particular racial group to set up in business). In *Hughes and Others v LB Hackney*[3] (see **12.4**), the IT said that 'access to facilities and services' was not wide enough to encompass the provision of job opportunities.

12.1.4 Training for overseas employees

It is also lawful to provide special education and training and ancillary benefits for those who normally live outside the UK where the trainees do not intend to live in GB after their education or training.[4]

12.1.5 Code of practice

The CRE Code of Practice recommends that employers should regularly monitor their workforce to see if employees of a particular racial group are concentrated in particular areas of work. Employers can then provide training for members of particular racial groups which have been under-represented in particular work.

1 RRA s38.
2 RRA s37.
3 COIT unreported; 6 February 1986.
4 RRA s36.

It recommends that where members of particular racial groups are under-represented in particular areas of work employers should adopt the following measures:

- job advertisements designed to reach members of those groups and to encourage their applications, such as use of the ethnic minority press;
- use of employment agencies and careers' offices in areas where those groups are concentrated;
- recruitment and training schemes for school-leavers designed to reach members of those groups;
- encouragement of employees from those groups to apply for promotion or transfer opportunities;
- training for promotion or skill training for members of those groups who lack particular expertise but who show potential (see CRE Code para 1.45).

12.2 Positive action under the SDA: training and 'encouragement'

12.2.1 Employers

Employers can provide both access to training for women only, or men only, to take advantage of opportunities for doing particular work in its establishment and encouragement for them to take advantage of opportunities for doing that work provided that one or more of the following conditions apply:

a) where at any time during the last 12 months there were no persons of that sex among those doing that work; or
b) the number of persons of that sex among those doing that work was comparatively small.[5]

12.2.2 Training providers

Any provider of training, including employers, may discriminate in favour of women only, or men only, by giving them special access to training to enable them to do work which no or few women (or men) have done in the past 12 months (whether in GB or within a particular area of GB). This means that local authorities, employers and other training providers can provide special training themselves.[6]

5 SDA s48.
6 SDA s47.

12.2.3 *Special needs of women because of family responsibilities*

Training may also be provided for women who have special needs, having been out of the job market because of family responsibilities, including bringing up children or looking after a sick relative.[7]

These provisions do not apply to training which is treated as 'employment' under SDA s6, such as apprenticeship.

12.2.4 *Code of practice*

The EOC Code of Practice suggests that employers should train their employees for work which is traditionally the preserve of the other sex, eg, training women in skilled manual or technical work, and also that there may be a need for positive encouragement of women to apply for management posts – including the provision of special courses.

The EOC Code also says that where one sex is under-represented, employers may wish to consider measures such as advertisements which encourage applications from the under-represented sex, although it must be made clear that selection will be on merit. They can, for example, notify job agencies that they wish to encourage members of one sex to apply, and ask the agency to inform members of that sex that applications from them are particularly welcome and include such statements in job advertisements.

12.3 Trade unions, employers' organisations and professional bodies

Similar provisions apply to allow trade unions, employers' organisations and professional bodies to give women or members of under-represented racial groups access to training to help them take up posts in the organisation or to encourage them to apply where there are no or few women or a small proportion of black people in those posts.

Such bodies can also encourage women and people from under-represented racial groups to become members.[8] Under the SDA, unions may reserve seats in the organisation or make extra seats available for women.[9] There is no equivalent power to reserve seats for black representatives.

7 SDA s47(3).
8 RRA s38(3)–(5); SDA s48(2) and (3).
9 SDA s49.

12.4 Positive action in practice

It is important to distinguish between, on the one hand, encouraging women and black applicants to apply for jobs by, for example, stating that applications from women and ethnic minorities are welcome and, on the other hand, the recruitment of under-represented groups. It is unlawful to discriminate at the point of recruitment – against both men and women, white and black applicants – unless one of the exceptions applies.

In *Hughes and Others v LB Hackney*,[10] Hackney advertised for gardeners saying it warmly welcomed applications from ethnic minorities. The advertisement was lawful but three white applicants were informed that the posts were open *only* to ethnic minority members. The employer argued that it fell within RRA ss35 (see below) and 38. The tribunal held that 'encouraging' did not extend to providing job opportunities, so s38 did not apply.

In addition, the applicants argued that Hackney had failed to prove that the proportion of ethnic minority workers doing relevant work at the establishment was small in comparison with the proportion of persons of that group among the population from which the council normally recruited. Although there was a smaller proportion of black gardeners compared to the proportion of black people in Hackney, the tribunal said that as only 58% of recruits came from within the borough, the 'area' should not be restricted to Hackney. As there was no evidence of where outside the borough the remaining recruits came from or what proportion of ethnic minority members were within that population, Hackney had not satisfied the conditions set out in s38.

In *Jepson and Dyas-Elliott v Labour Party*[11] the applicants were excluded from selection as a Labour Party candidate because the constituencies were required to have women-only shortlists. The Labour Party's aim was to increase the number of women MPs. The IT held that this was unlawful sex discrimination contrary to the SDA s13 and the ETD.

12.5 Positive action on grounds of sex under EC law

The question has recently arisen as to whether positive action is permitted under the ETD. Article 2(4) provides that the principle of equal treatment shall be 'without prejudice to measures to promote

10 (1986) unreported, 6 February, IT.
11 [1996] IRLR 116.

equal opportunity for men and women . . .' The meaning of this was clarified by the ECJ in a German case. Some German states provide that in recruitment in the public sector a female candidate will be offered the job where:

- there are fewer women than men in the relevant employment catagory; and
- the best male and female candidates are equally well qualified;

unless this would cause unbearable hardship for the man. However, the ECJ ruled in *Kalanke v Freie Hansestadt Bremen*[12] that it is unlawful discrimination for automatic and unconditional priority to be given to the woman.[13] It did not come within the art 2(4) exception. There is a proposal for a new directive to deal with the issues raised by this case, but no agreement has been reached. The European Commission has issued a Communication interpreting the *Kalanke* decision which makes it clear that positive action is permitted provided that it does not give women an 'absolute and unconditional right' to appointment or promotion in preference to a man.

12.6 Removing barriers to employment

Employers can and should review their employment practices in order to remove any barriers on women's employment. For example, employers can introduce less rigid work patterns, job-sharing or more part-time jobs to enable those with childcare responsibilities to work.

POSITIVE ACTION: KEY POINTS

- Employers, and other bodies which provide training, can provide special training for women and black employees to do work where they have been under-represented in the past.
- Employers may encourage under-represented groups to apply for jobs, but they cannot restrict jobs to one race or sex unless there is a genuine occupational qualification for the job (see **5.4.3** and **6.4.1.15**).
- Employers can remove barriers to employment opportunities for ethnic minorities and women.

12 C-450/93 [1995] IRLR 660.

13 For a further discussion of this case see Case note 'Positive Action in Community Law' (1996) ILS 239.

CHAPTER 13

Harassment

13.1 Introduction

Harassment at work is alarmingly common. A survey carried out by the Industrial Society found that 54% of all female employees had experienced some form of sexual harassment in the workplace. However, only 5% of these used their organisation's grievance procedure to complain and many had little confidence in the employer's ability to deal with the harassment effectively.[1] The European Commission has also found that sexual harassment is a serious problem for many working women and is not an isolated phenomenon.[2]

Sexual harassment can take many forms, such as leering, ridicule, embarrassing remarks or jokes, unwelcome comments about dress or appearance, deliberate abuse, repeated and/or unwanted physical contact, demands for sexual favours or physical assaults on workers.[3] Harassment is usually carried out by men towards women but it may come from either sex or from members of the same sex.

For many black workers, it can be a feature of their working lives that they are subjected to racial abuse by their white colleagues; racial harassment can also occur between different ethnic minority groups. Examples of racial harassment include the open expression of

1 *No offence? Sexual harassment: how it happens and how to beat it.* (Industrial Society, 1993). See also *Sexual harassment in the office; a quantitative report on client attitudes and experiences* and *Sexual harassment in the office; a quantitative report on employee attitudes and experiences 1990/91*, available from Alfred Marks.

2 European Commission report on sexual harassment 97B 'The protection of the dignity of women and men at work' *Official Journal of the European Communities* (HMSO, 1992). See also J Gregory, 'Sexual Harassment: Making the best use of European law' (1995) 2 *European Journal of Women's Studies* 421 to 440.

3 *Sexual harassment at work: TUC guidelines.*

racialist views and racially derogatory statements, the use of racial abuse, both verbal and written (eg, graffiti), the repetition of racist jokes and offensive remarks and the open display of hostility to workers, creating a threatening and stressful working environment and adversely affecting their job performance. Harassment can amount to vicious assaults.

Black women may suffer both racial and sexual harassment. The European Commission report found that certain groups were particularly vulnerable to sexual harassment, including women from racial minorities. Harassment can come from fellow employees, from the employer's agents, from employers or from users of the employer's service. An example of the latter can be seen in a recent study by the Policy Studies Institute which found that racial harassment of ethnic minority nurses by patients is widespread.[4]

Harassment may be on grounds of sex, race, disability, sexuality or sexual status.[5] However, as the provisions on harassment on grounds of disability have not yet been developed in practice this form of harassment has not been covered in this chapter, although many of the same principles will apply. Local surveys have shown that such harassment is prevalent, so this area of law is likely to develop.[6]

Workers who have been dismissed or forced to leave because of harassment may also have a claim under the ERA which provides protection against unfair dismissal (see **13.3.4.8**). In addition, the law of tort and the criminal law can also provide a remedy in some circumstances (see **13.8**).

Bringing a complaint of harassment is not easy. Women are understandably reluctant to complain of sexual harassment, men tend to treat it as a joke and harassment almost always occurs where there are no witnesses. Moreover the legal process itself can add to the humiliation. There are far fewer reported cases of racial harassment than sexual harassment but they are equally difficult to prove. However, increasingly, tribunals are taking a very serious view of harassment and damages are often higher than in other areas of discrimination.[7] These higher awards provide some compensation for the injury to feelings inherent in such treatment. Restrictive reporting orders may provide some additional protection (see **13.7**).

4 S Beishon, S Virdee and A Hagell *Nursing in a multi-ethnic NHS* (PSI).
5 *R v C* COIT no 60989/94 (a case involving allegations of serious harassment of a transsexual).
6 *Industrial Society Report on the London Borough of Camden* (1997).
7 See ARG *Armitage, Marsden and H M Prison Service v Johnson* [1997] IRLR 162.

13.1.1 What is harassment in law?

Harassment, whether by management or co-workers takes many forms. The SDA, RRA and DDA do not define 'harassment', so it is important to identify the form of harassment and how it fits in the SDA or RRA framework.[8] Harassment is one type of discrimination so the applicant must show that the harassment is less favourable treatment on the ground of his/her sex or marital status or on the ground of his/her race or for a reason relating to his/her disability (see Chapter 2).

It is then necessary to show that the harassment amounts to a 'detriment' to the victim.[9] The consequences of harassment may also result in an act which is specifically prohibited, eg, dismissal, transfer. However, in practice any less favourable treatment will amount to a detriment. The concepts of less favourable treatment and detriment are almost the same in a harassment case.

The way in which sexual and racial harassment is proved under the SDA, RRA and DDA is similar. There are, however, some crucial differences. For example, in sexual harassment cases (though not usually in racial harassment cases) issues of 'consent' and 'provocation' can arise; some women find that accepting sexual harassment is a condition of promotion or avoiding dismissal, so feel forced to accept such behaviour. It is nonetheless harassment.

13.1.2 Claims on the ground of sexuality or sexual orientation

The EAT in *Smith v Gardner Merchant*[10] held that harassment of a homosexual on the ground of his sexual orientation is not sexual discrimination because the discrimination he suffered was not because he was a man but because he was a homosexual. However, the EC code of practice says that harassment on the ground of sexual orientation undermines the dignity at work of those affected. This decision is not in line with EC law and it is being appealed.

In *P v S and Cornwall CC*[11] the ECJ ruled that discrimination on the ground of gender reassignment is contrary to the ETD. As the employers in this case were in the public sector, P was able to rely on the ETD (see **9.2.3**). Whether employees of private employers can rely

8 See V Gay, 'Sexual Harassment: Legal issues, past and future developments' in M J Davidson and J Earnshaw (eds), *Vulnerable Workers: Psychosocial and Legal Issues* (John Wiley & Sons, 1991), Chapter 7.2.

9 See SDA s6(2)(c); RRA s4(2)(c).

10 [1996] IRLR 342.

11 [1996] IRLR 347.

on this case depends on whether the SDA can be interpreted so as to be consistent with EC law. In *R v C*[12] (a case of serious harassment of a transsexual) the EAT held that the SDA had to be interpreted 'so as to confer the protection of its provisions to a transsexual' (see **5.1.4** and **5.1.5**).

13.2 Codes of practice as a guide to harassment

There are codes of practice from the CRE, the EOC, the DfEE and the EC which are very important and will be taken into account by ITs (see **1.1.7**).

13.2.1 EC code of practice

The EC code of practice is the most comprehensive guide to harassment. It is a good starting point for looking at the effect and impact of sexual harassment, and arguably its analysis should be adapted for use in other harassment cases.

The EC has introduced a set of guidelines which tribunals are using as a guide to interpreting the law on sexual harassment. The European Commission adopted a Code of Practice Protecting the Dignity of Women and Men at Work annexed to the Recommendation on the Protection of Women and Men at Work in November 1991.[13]

In *Wadman v Carpenter Ferrer Partnership*[14] the EAT held specifically that the code provided useful guidance to ITs hearing sexual harassment cases.[15]

The EC code of practice defines sexual harassment as 'unwanted conduct of a sexual nature, or other conduct based on sex affecting the dignity of women and men at work'. This can include unwelcome physical, verbal or non-verbal conduct. The code continues by saying that it is unacceptable if:

12 COIT no 60989/94.

13 Although council recommendations have no binding effect, national tribunals and courts should use them as an aid to construction. This approach was adopted in relation to a commission recommendation in *Grimaldi v Fonds des Maladies Professionelles* [1990] IRLR 400 where the ECJ said that recommendations could not be considered as 'lacking in legal effect'. It held that domestic courts are bound to take those recommendations into consideration in order to decide disputes submitted to them, in particular where they are capable of clarifying the interpretation of other provisions of national or EC law.

14 [1993] IRLR 374.

15 See also *EC Guide to implementing the Code of Practice – How to combat sexual harassment at work* (ISBN 92 826 5225 4).

- such conduct is unwanted, unreasonable and offensive to the recipient;
- rejection or submission to it is used as a basis for a decision which affects that person's access to vocational training or to employment, promotion, salary or any other employment decisions; and/or
- such conduct creates an intimidating, hostile or humiliating working environment for the recipient. (See Appendix 3.)

13.2.2 Statutory codes of practice

The EOC code of practice[16] recommends that:

a) particular care is taken to deal effectively with all complaints of discrimination, victimisation or harassment. It should not be assumed that complaints are made only by those who are over-sensitive (para 31(c));
b) all reasonably practical steps should be taken to ensure that a standard of conduct or behaviour is observed which prevents members of either sex from being intimidated, harassed or otherwise subjected to unfavourable treatment on the ground of their sex (para 32(e)).

The CRE code of practice deals with racial harassment and related issues.[17] In the section on grievances, disputes and disciplinary procedures, it recommends, among other things, that:

a) in applying disciplinary procedures, consideration should be given to the possible effect on an employee's behaviour of racial abuse or other racial provocation (para 1.23);
b) employers should not ignore or treat lightly grievances from members of particular racial groups on the assumption that they are over-sensitive about discrimination (para 1.22);
c) in dealing with the responsibilities of individual employees, the code says that individual employees should refrain from harassment or intimidation of other employees on racial grounds, eg, by

16 *Code of Practice: For the elimination of discrimination on the grounds of sex and marriage and the promotion of equality of opportunity in employment* (EOC, 1985). See also *Consider the cost . . . Sexual harassment at work* (EOC).

17 *Code of Practice: For the elimination of racial discrimination and the promotion of equal opportunity in employment* (CRE, 1984). The CRE has also issued guidance on racial harassment: *Racial harassment at work: what employers can do about it* (CRE, 1995).

encouraging them to leave, and points out that such action may be unlawful if it is taken by employees against those subject to their authority (para 2.3(d));

d) racial harassment is defined as 'unwanted conduct of a racial nature, or other conduct based on race affecting the dignity of women and men at work';

The TUC has also set out guidelines on dealing with sexual harassment at work and racial harassment at work.[18]

The code of practice issued under the DDA recommends that: 'as a minimum first step harassment because of disability should be made a disciplinary matter and staff should be made aware that it will be taken seriously'.[19]

13.3 Main principles

In *Porcelli v Strathclyde RC*[20] the Court of Session said that sexual harassment is a 'particularly degrading and unacceptable form of treatment which it must be taken to be the intention of Parliament to restrain'. The same must be true of racial harassment.

In *Porcelli* two men had harassed, by way of sexual innuendoes, a female colleague whom they disliked, hoping that she would leave. The court asked, 'was the applicant less favourably treated on the ground of her sex than a man would have been treated?'; if the answer was 'yes', there was discrimination.

In harassment cases the applicant must show:

a) *less favourable treatment on the ground of* his/her sex, marital status or race; and
b) that the less favourable treatment was prohibited: generally proof of '*any other detriment*' will be sufficient.

13.3.1 Less favourable treatment on the ground of sex or race

Less favourable treatment is 'on the ground of' sex or race or marital status if it is either:

18 *Racial harassment at work: a TUC guide and workplace programme for trade unionists* (TUC, 1990).

19 *Code of Practice for the elimination of discrimination in the field of employment against disabled persons or persons who have had a disability* (DfEE, 1996).

20 [1986] IRLR 177; [1986] ICR 134.

- obviously specific to the applicant's sex or racial group; or
- of a kind which would not be afforded to a person of a different sex or racial group in a comparable situation.

These points are not mutually exclusive but help to distinguish between two typical but different problems.

13.3.1.1 Treatment which is itself sex- or race-specific

Where the harassment is sex- or race-specific, it should not be necessary to show that the applicant was treated less favourably than a person of a different race or sex. The harassment is in itself on grounds of sex or race and it is not relevant that the employer would also treat a man or person of a different racial group equally unpleasantly.[21]

Offensive and insulting words may have a specific sexual or racial connotation, so will be discriminatory, even if the perpetrator swears at other employees.[22] Thus 'dumb bastard' does not have a sexual connotation because it could be equally applied to a man, but 'goddamn Yank' and 'thick Paddy' do have a specific racial connotation (see **13.3.3.1**).

The harasser's main purpose need not be sex-related. In *Porcelli*,[23] the Court of Session held that unfavourable treatment which includes a significant element of a sexual character to which a man would not be vulnerable is nevertheless sexual harassment even if the harassment was carried out in order to pressurise the woman to leave and an equally disliked man would have been treated in an equally unpleasant way.[24]

13.3.1.2 Treatment which is comparatively less favourable

Usually in cases of direct discrimination a comparison must be made between how the applicant who suffered the discrimination was treated and how a person of a different sex or racial group was or would have been treated. In making the comparison the circumstances of those compared must be the same or not materially different (see **2.9**). The only relevant comparison in a case of

21 See also *Smyth v Croft Inns* [1996] IRLR 84 at p89, and *Wade v West Yorkshire* 1997 EAT no 900/96.

22 See also *Straker v McDonalds Hamburgers Ltd* Case no 18273/98 and *Eribenne v Grand Metropolitan Retailing Ltd and Others* Case no 2537/90.

23 See *Porcelli v Strathclyde RC* [1986] ICR 564 at p568 C-D.

24 See also *Fall v Lothian Community Relations Council* S/107/86 and *Murphy v The Gold Post* S/2647/87.

explicitly sexual or racial harassment is with a man who has been sexually harassed, or a person of a different racial group who has been racially harassed, and s/he too would have suffered discrimination.

Where behaviour is deemed to be 'neutral' as to its effect on men and women (or different racial groups), there may not be less favourable treatment. In *Stewart v Cleveland Guest Engineering Ltd*[25] the EAT refused to overturn as perverse an IT finding that posters of naked women were 'neutral' and that a man could have found them as offensive as did the applicant. The EAT said that there was room for disagreement as to what was less favourable treatment. This is arguably wrong and contrary to the EC Code of Practice (see Appendix 3). Account should be taken of the effect that such posters will have on a woman's self-esteem and dignity; and that they tend to create an intimidating and humiliating environment. Men would clearly not be affected in the same way. However, the IT did find that the applicant had been constructively dismissed because of the employer's inadequate response to her complaints which was in breach of its implied duty of mutual trust and confidence. In *Stewart* the EAT said that its judgment did not mean that such posters would never amount to harassment. Thus, every case should be decided on its own facts.

Bullying may not be explicitly sex- or race-specific. If a person of the opposite sex or a different racial group would not be treated in the same way, it is likely to be discrimination. An IT may infer from the surrounding facts that the applicant was treated less favourably on grounds of sex or race (see **2.10**). Where, as is common, there are a number of incidents of harassment the allegations must be considered as part of a course of conduct. If inferences can be drawn from such conduct it will be easier to prove each specific allegation.[26]

13.3.2 Detriment

In *Porcelli* (above), the Lord President said that 'detriment' as defined in *Jeremiah v MoD*[27] simply means being put at a disadvantage. In *Wileman v Minilec Engineering*,[28] the EAT said that 'sexual harassment' is legal shorthand for activity which is easily recognisable as 'subjecting her to any other detriment'.

25 [1994] IRLR 440.
26 See *Qureshi v Victoria University of Manchester* [1996] EAT no 484/95.
27 [1979] 3 All ER 833.
28 [1988] IRLR 144.

Behaviour which might constitute sexual or racial harassment must be considered in relation to the particular victim. ITs will look at the impact of the behaviour on the recipient not at the intention of the harasser. In *Wileman*, the EAT pointed out that a person may be quite happy to accept the remarks of A or B in a sexual context, and wholly upset by similar remarks made by C. The EAT continued by saying that 'each individual then has the right, if the remarks were regarded as offensive, to treat them as an offence under the Sex Discrimination Act.'[29] This interpretation is supported by the European Commission's Code, which states that it is for individuals to determine what behaviour is acceptable to them and what they regard as offensive.

The IT must look at whether the reasonable woman or black worker would take the view that s/he had been disadvantaged in the circumstances in which s/he had to work. It is not what a mythical reasonable person of indeterminate sex, marital status or colour would think. This is important because it recognises that women and black workers are more likely to be offended by incidents of harassment.

Thus in *De Souza v Automobile Association*,[30] the CA ruled that an overheard racial insult is not enough, by itself, to be a 'detriment', even if the insult caused the employee distress. It said that, before an employee can be said to have suffered a detriment, it must be found that because of the acts complained of a reasonable worker would or might take the view that s/he had been thereby disadvantaged in the circumstances in which s/he had to work. The court said that the applicant could not be said to have been treated less favourably unless the discriminator intended her to overhear the conversation or knew or ought reasonably to have anticipated that the insult would be passed on or that the applicant would become aware of it in some other way. As there was insufficient evidence of this before the tribunal, the applicant could not show that she had suffered a detriment.

Physical contact is not necessary. In *Porcelli v Strathclyde RC*,[31] the EAT said that harassment includes not only unwelcome acts which involve physical contact of a sexual nature, but also conduct falling short of such physical acts. This would include making suggestive remarks, telling offensive jokes, making an employee watch an offensive video, deliberately staring at a woman or behaviour with a sexual

29 See also *Hodgson v McCormick and Petch* Case no 19549/90.

30 [1986] ICR 514; [1986] IRLR 103.

31 [1986] ICR 177; [1986] IRLR 134.

innuendo. In *Insitu Cleaning Co Ltd v Heads*[32] the EAT ruled that 'Hiya Big Tits' was a sexually related remark and one likely to create a hostile working environment. This is in line with the European Commission's Code which covers conduct which creates an intimidating, hostile or humiliating working environment for the recipient.[33]

One act can constitute harassment. In *Bracebridge Engineering Ltd v Darby*,[34] the employer argued that harassment was a 'continuing course of conduct', not a single act. The EAT firmly rejected this intepretation, stating that 'a single incident of sexual harassment, provided it is sufficiently serious ... is an act of discrimination against a woman because she is a woman'. In sexual harassment cases the woman's mode of dress and personal life may lead an IT to conclude that she would not have suffered a detriment and/or it may affect her compensation (see **13.4.2**).

13.3.3 Examples of detriment

In *Johnstone v Fenton Barns (Scotland) Ltd*,[35] the IT held that lewd behaviour can amount to sexual harassment. It said that, 'If a man, working alongside a woman, converses or behaves lewdly with other people in the vicinity, within earshot of the woman, and if the woman has made it clear that she finds such conduct to be offensive, then any future similar occurrences must be regarded as having taken place against her wishes, and thereby directed against her.'

In *ARG Armitage, Marsden & H M Prison Service v Johnson*[36] the applicant complained of a campaign of racial harassment lasting nearly two years following his complaint about fellow officers' handling of a black prisoner. He was refused overtime, warned about sickness absences when a white worker with a poorer record was not warned, ostracised by other officers, and given a warning for leaving early when it was customary to do so. He complained to his employer about the harassment but his complaints were dismissed without proper investigation. He was awarded £20,000 for injury to his feelings and £7,500 aggravated damages for the failure to respond to his complaints.

32 [1995] IRLR 4.
33 See Appendix 3.
34 [1990] IRLR 3.
35 Case no S/1688/89.
36 [1997] IRLR 162.

13.3.3.1 Workplace banter/racist and other insults

Workplace banter may amount to harassment, although many employers try to belittle the seriousness of name-calling. However, in order to constitute sexual or racial harassment the words used must have some sexual or racial connotation. A waitress who was called 'a dumb bastard' was not found to have been sexually harassed because the same words could have been used of a man.[37] However, 'goddamn Yank', 'thick Paddy', 'typical Irish' and 'black cunt' were all said to amount to harassment.[38]

13.3.3.2 Posters

Offensive posters may constitute sexual harassment if it can be shown that there is less favourable treatment and the applicant has suffered a detriment (see **13.3.1.2**).

13.3.3.3 Enforced transfer

A common solution to harassment is to move one of the parties to another office or part of the shop floor. This may be at the request of the victim or at the instigation of the employer.

The transfer may involve a loss of pay or material benefits.[39] However, in order to be a 'detriment', the employee need not have suffered any loss of pay or status or any worsened terms of employment. The transfer itself can be a detriment. As the EAT said in *Deson v BL Cars Ltd*,[40] 'to give someone a less attractive and less interesting job which no one wants is capable of being a detriment'.

If an employer refuses to move an employee who has been harassed and who has requested a move this may also amount to a detriment.

13.3.3.4 Continued working with the harasser

Being required to continue to work with the harasser can aggravate the original discrimination. In *Wagstaff v Elida Gibbs Ltd and Laverick*,[41] the IT made a recommendation under SDA s65(1)(c) that

37 *Smith v Bowater Labels Ltd* (1995) 23 EOR DCLD.

38 *Ruizo v Tesco Stores & Lea* (1995) 24 EOR DCLD; *McCauley v Auto Alloys Foundry Ltd & Taylor* (1994) 21 EOR DCLD and *Bellifantie v British Rail* (1994) 21 EOR DCLD.

39 *Seide v Gillette Industries Ltd* [1980] IRLR 427.

40 EAT case no 173/80.

41 Case no 12085/90.

the perpetrator be moved to a different site to ensure that he would not come into contact with the complainant and that he should be suspended until it was possible to effect the move.[42]

13.3.3.5 Loss of promotion

In many workplaces, promotion procedures are very informal, and often promotion depends on 'getting on well with the boss'. A woman or black person may find that s/he has to put up with sexual or racial harassment from the boss to benefit from promotion or training opportunities.[43] If promotion, performance-related pay or other benefits, depend on a person accepting harassment, this will be a breach of the SDA, RRA or DDA.

13.3.3.6 Policing/security

A racist idea prevalent in British society is the belief that there are more untrustworthy black people than white people. In the same way that black people suffer over-policing of the neighbourhoods where they live, so in the workplace they may find that security measures are directed specifically towards them.[44] In *Sheiky v Argos Distributors Ltd and Stone*[45] the IT said that informing the police that an African-born employee might be an illegal immigrant, which resulted in his wrongful arrest was a detriment contrary to the RRA. The Asylum Act 1996 means that employers have to make specified enquiries as to a prospective employee's status (see **6.4.1.6**), however, this does not allow employers to harass their staff or treat them less favourably in any way.

13.3.3.7 Discrimination by 'cold-shouldering'

In some cases, where, for example, a female employee has made it plain that she will not participate in or tolerate the sexual conduct of her boss, or her colleagues, towards her, the harasser responds by ceasing that conduct and adopting a cold or excluding approach. He may give work to other secretaries, take over the running of his diary, fail to notify the woman of meetings or decisions she needs to know about and generally puts her in a position where she feels undermined

42 See also *Whittington v Morris and Greenwich Health Authority* Case no 17846/89 and *Mullan v DoE* Case no 20113/90.
43 *McDonald v Fife Health Board* Case no S/1423/84.
44 See *BL Cars Ltd v Brown* [1983] ICR 143; [1983] IRLR 193.
45 (1995) 26 EOR DCLD.

and insecure. The 'cold shouldering' should also be regarded as a form of less favourable treatment on the grounds of sex and a detriment.[46]

13.3.3.8 Discrimination in dismissal or forced resignation

Complaints by women about sexual harassment frequently lead to either dismissal or the woman resigning because she finds conditions intolerable. The same applies to racial harassment or harassment on the ground of a disability. It has for some time been accepted that persons forced out of their jobs through harassment may be able to claim constructive unfair dismissal[47] as well as claim for discrimination.

Harassment of an employee by an employer amounts to a fundamental breach of contract because it is a breach of the implied term of mutual trust in the employer/employee relationship. In *Western Excavating v Sharp*,[48] Lawton LJ said that, 'if the employer is guilty of conduct which is a significant breach going to the root of the contract of employment, or which shows that the employer no longer intends to be bound by one or more of the essential terms of the contract, then the employee is entitled to treat himself as discharged from any further performance' and 'persistent and unwanted amorous advances by an employer to a female employee would be conduct leading to breach of contract'.[49]

Women, or racial minorities who have not completed the two-year qualifying period must rely on the SDA or RRA to make a claim under the civil law (see **13.8**). Under the SDA and RRA, an applicant must show that:

- s/he has been subjected to treatment of a sexual/racial nature;
- s/he has been treated less favourably than a man/white worker would have been on grounds of his/her sex or colour;
- s/he has suffered a deriment;
- s/he has been dismissed or forced to resign.

46 See *Whittington v Morris & Greenwich Health Authority* COIT Case no 17846/89/LS.

47 If they satisfy the qualifying conditions in ERA ss108 and 109. It should be remembered that these qualifying conditions may themselves be discriminatory (see **3.6.6.2**).

48 [1978] 1 All ER 713.

49 See *Hyatt v Smithko of Salop Ltd* (1984) COIT 1126/91 and *Wood v Freeloader* [1977] IRLR 455.

13.4 Proving harassment

If an employee complains that she has been harassed, there may be no witnesses to substantiate her claim but the victim's own evidence may be sufficient proof (see **2.10**). In one case,[50] an employee was dismissed for indecently exposing himself to female colleagues. He claimed at the tribunal that the women's evidence was not corroborated, and so could not be relied on by the employer. The tribunal held that his dismissal was lawful, pointing out that the nature of the offence meant that almost inevitably there would be no witnesses to it.

Evidence of other harassment by a perpetrator may be relevant. In *Wileman* (above), the EAT said that the IT was right in refusing to allow evidence of how the director has harassed other women, because sexual remarks made to different people have to be looked at in relation to each person. This is correct, but if it is clear that a person has forced unwanted sexual behaviour on other staff, who are willing to testify to this, this is relevant and should be admissible.[51] In one case,[52] an IT ordered a rehearing after the applicant produced evidence that the perpetrator had subsequently harassed another woman. It is important that a woman who has been sexually harassed, keeps a record or a diary of all incidents of harassment and when they happened and informs at least one colleague or friend. It will then be easier to prove these incidents or rely on them at a later stage if she does not want to take immediate action (but see **13.4.3** with respect to delay).

13.4.1 Proving the harassment caused injury to feelings

The extent to which an applicant suffered a detriment depends on the effect the harassment had on him/her personally. It is a subjective test and the applicant should expect to give evidence about how upsetting the harassment was and its impact on his/her life. Additionally, a friend could be called to give evidence of the distress caused by the harassment as they observed it in the applicant. Medical or psychiatric evidence may also be helpful.

50 *Mellor v Courtaulds Northern Spinning Ltd* COIT Case no 1537/242.

51 In *Fergus v Lawson Fisher Ltd* Case no S/1160/89, evidence that the man had harassed three other women was admitted by the IT. See also *Goundrill v Townhill and Pinefleet Ltd* Case no 21269/90.

52 *Larpiniere v Young and Others* Case no 191/90.

13.4.2 Provocation

In *Wileman* (above) the EAT held that the IT was entitled to take into account the fact that the applicant wore provocative clothes and flaunted herself, when deciding whether she had suffered a detriment. The EAT also stressed, however, that each individual has the right, if the remarks are regarded as offensive, to treat them as in breach of the SDA (or RRA or DDA). This makes clear the important distinction between consensual behaviour and that which is forced on an unwilling victim. Although there had been discrimination, the applicant received damages of only £50.[53] The clear implication of this decision is that the more upset a woman is by harassment the more serious the detriment and the higher the compensation. If she is not at all upset, there may be no detriment at all. The danger of this approach is that it allows the respondent to question the complainant about her personal life, and to imply that a style of life, including mode of dress, detracts from the seriousness of unwanted sexual advances in much the same way as happens in rape trials.

The EC code stresses that the essential feature of sexual harassment is that it is unwanted. It becomes harassment if the behaviour is persisted in once it has been made clear that it is regarded by the recipient as offensive. It is, says the code, the unwanted nature of the conduct which distinguishes sexual harassment from friendly behaviour which is welcome and mutual.

13.4.3 Effect of delay in complaining

The victim should complain to his/her employer or take up a grievance against the harasser without undue delay. People suffering harassment frequently wait for weeks, months or even years before making a complaint. The reasons for this are many and complex, including:

- unwillingness to divulge the humiliating details;
- anxiety that s/he may not be believed;
- knowledge that the perpetrator has friends and supporters in management;
- rebuff of an early attempt to complain;

53 See also *Snowball v Gardner Merchant*, where evidence of the applicant's sexual behaviour was admitted to assess the degree of detriment and the credibility of the applicant, who denied the allegations that she talked freely to fellow employees about her attitude to sexual matters.

- fear of hostility or intimidation (particularly if the perpetrator is well-liked);
- an absence of any clear grievance or harassment procedure (or lack of knowledge about it);
- the apparent complicity of other workers; and perhaps most importantly
- fear of losing his/her job.

Some of these have been recognised by ITs, so in cases of delay it is important to highlight the reasons for this. In *Bracebridge Engineering v Darby*[54] the IT and EAT said that it was reasonable 'that the applicant should be allowed a week in which to decide' about whether to leave and claim constructive dismissal. In *Bennett v Sergio Gambi and Others*[55] the IT doubted that there was harassment because the woman had continued in the job for six weeks, the EAT overturned this decision and remitted the case for re-hearing.

Delay may lead to the complaint being out of time. It will be necessary to prove that the discrimination was part of a continuing course of conduct or that the last act of discrimination was within three months of the complaint to the IT (see **25.2.1**). In cases of sexual harassment if it is intended to prove that the resignation was a constructive dismissal, it will be enough to prove that resignation occurred in circumstances such that s/he is entitled to terminate the contract of employment without notice by reason of the conduct of the employer in order to establish that there was a dismissal.[56] This means that the resignation must not be unduly delayed as the employer may seek to argue that the employee was no longer able to claim to be entitled to resign.[57]

13.5 Who is liable?

The harasser is always liable for acts done in the course of his/her employment and in most cases the employer is liable as well. SDA s41, RRA s32 and DDA s58 provide that anything done by a person in the course of his/her employment shall be treated as done by his/her employer as well as by him/her, whether or not it was done with the

54 [1990] IRLR 3.
55 EAT/34/95.
56 See SDA s82(1A)(b). There are no equivalent provisions in the RRA or DDA.
57 See *Western Excavating v Sharp* [1978] 1 All ER 713.

employer's knowledge or approval (see Chapter 7). Both the EC code of guidance and the CRE guidance emphasise that employers cannot assume that because they have received no complaints of harassment there is no problem.

Employers are liable for *all* acts of racial, sexual or disability harassment of their employees committed during their employment unless the employer can show that it took such steps that were reasonably practicable to prevent the occurrence of such acts. In *Tower Boot Co Ltd v Jones*[58] the CA held that racist name-calling, deliberate branding with a hot screwdriver and whipping were all actions done in the course of employment and hence the employer was liable subject to the defence.

An employer is also liable for the acts of its customers, clients or agents if they harass its employees and the employer fails to take reasonable steps to prevent the harassment occurring or continuing. This will include the situation where an employer takes no action to protect the victim when it is aware of the harassment.

In *Burton and Rhule v De Vere Hotels*[59] two black waitresses were serving at a dinner where the after-dinner speaker addressed a number of obscene racist comments at them; this encouraged other guests to do so too. The waitresses claimed direct discrimination against their employer. The EAT held that the question was whether the event was sufficiently under the employer's control that it could, by the application of good employment practice, have prevented the harassment or reduced the extent of it. The women had complained to a manager during the evening and the EAT said that one of the managers should have removed the waitresses from the dining room as soon as it was clear that they were being harassed.[60]

13.5.1 Employers' defences

The RRA s32, SDA s41 and DDA s58 provide an employer with a specific defence in these cases. An employer will not be liable for an employee's act of harassment if it can show that it took all reasonable steps to prevent the occurrence of harassment.

The EC code sets out a number of recommendations for employers, including:

58 [1997] IRLR 168.
59 [1996] IRLR 596.
60 See also similar decision in *Go Kidz Go Ltd v Bourdouane* EAT Case no 1110/95.

- drawing up and publicising a policy statement on sexual harassment;
- giving managers responsibility for the policy, both in explaining and carrying it out;
- the provision of training;
- the development of clear and precise procedures;
- the designation of a person to provide advice and assistance to employees subjected to sexual harassment;
- the establishment of a complaints procedure;
- the setting up of a sensitive and prompt investigation procedure;
- making sexual harassment a disciplinary offence;
- making provision for the perpetrator to be relocated rather than the victim.

Employers who both set up and implement a harassment policy which has all these elements would not be liable for their employees' acts of harassment. In *Graham v Royal Mail and Nicolson*[61] a black postwoman alleged that she had been racially harassed by a fellow employee. The IT noted the employer's statement of harassment and held that it was satisfied that 'the policy is not only detailed, careful, reasonable and in our view, exemplary, but was acted upon'. It concluded that the employer had 'taken all reasonable steps to avoid discrimination of this nature'. Hence the employer established the defence under RRA s32(3). The fact that the employer is unaware of the harassment does not provide it with a defence.

By way of contrast in *Dillon v Outline Engraving*[62] an artist resigned after having been subjected to sexual harassment and sexist remarks over a prolonged period. Her employer argued that it had been unaware of the allegations until after she had left. The IT quoted the EC code of practice, which says: 'It should be emphasised that a distinguishing characteristic of sexual harassment is that employees subjected to it often will be reluctant to complain.' It found that the employer had no policy or procedure for dealing with complaints of sexual harassment so 'it was not at all surprising' that the employee had failed formally to complain. It therefore found the employer liable.

61 (1994) 26 EOR DCLD, 11 May 1993; Case no 28681/92. See also *Taylor v Asda Stores* (1994) 21 EOR DCLD, 13 January 1994; Case no 41315/93; *Pereira v Post Office* and *Cooley v BRS Ltd* (1995) 23 EOR DCLD 9, 18 July 94; Case no 18088/94 and 1 August 1994; Case no 4890/94.

62 (1994) 22 EOR DCLD, 7 April 1994; Case no 18526/93.

13.5.2 Employers' duty to take action against harassment

The employer has a duty to provide a safe place of work which is free from sexual or racial harassment and a system whereby an employee can complain of behaviour that is unwanted, offensive and humiliating. An effective disciplinary procedure is essential. An employee ought to be able to feel confident that s/he can invoke the grievance procedure to remedy an allegation of harassment without fear of victimisation. The employer's equal opportunity policy should encourage use of the procedure.

In order to avoid liability, an employer must take appropriate action to deal with the harassment and this may well involve disciplining, transferring or dismissing the harasser (see *Wagstaff* above).

The EAT has said that merely warning employees about harassment, without further disciplinary action when harassment continues, is not enough to absolve the employer from liability.[63] In *Mullan v DoE*,[64] an IT heavily criticised an employer for not treating a serious incident of harassment as gross misconduct, not suspending the perpetrator pending enquiries and failing to dismiss him.

In *McGuiness v Finchale Training College*[65] a trainee complained of sexual harassment and no investigation was carried out. This failure to investigate the complaint was considered to be a 'detriment' under the Act.

13.5.3 Dismissal of a harasser

An employer who dismisses a person for harassment must demonstrate to a tribunal that s/he had reasonable grounds for dismissal, and that s/he carried out a proper investigation, after which dismissal was within the range of reasonable responses. The test of reasonableness as set out in *British Home Stores v Burchell*[66] applies. There are three parts to it:

- that the employer genuinely believes that the misconduct has been committed;
- that it had reasonable grounds to hold that belief; and
- that it carried out as much investigation into the matter as was reasonable in the circumstances.

63 *Enterprise Glass Co Ltd v Miles* EAT 538/89, 26 July 1990.
64 Case 20113/90.
65 (1995) 23 EOR DLCD.
66 [1978] IRLR 379.

If the employer passes this test, then it has acted reasonably; it does not matter that someone else, looking at the facts might have concluded that the employee was not guilty of misconduct.

13.6 Compensation for harassment

The main principles relating to compensation are set out in Chapter 26. The Court of Appeal in *Alexander v Home Office*[67] said that in assessing damages for discrimination 'the conduct and character of the complainant and of the discriminator, and the circumstances in which the discrimination occurred, may affect the measure of damages'. In *Snowball v Gardner Merchant*,[68] the EAT followed this, saying that 'compensation for sexual harassment must relate to the degree of detriment and, in that context, there has to be an assessment of the injury to the woman's feelings, which must be looked at both objectively with reference to what any ordinary reasonable female employee would feel and subjectively with reference to her as an individual'.

In *Snowball*, the IT and EAT concluded that evidence about the applicant's sexual attitudes was relevant to show that she was not likely to be very upset by a degree of familiarity with a sexual connotation. A similar view was taken in *Wileman*, where the applicant wore scanty and provocative clothes and posed in a flimsy costume for a newspaper.[69]

Awards in harassment complaints tend to be higher than in other discrimination cases. Now that there are no limits on the amounts of compensation that can be awarded in discrimination cases the amounts of awards particularly for injury to feelings have increased.[70]

A college lecturer who was referred to as an 'Irish prat' and whose complaint of racial harassment was not properly dealt with by the college was awarded £28,000 in total including £15,000 for injury to

67 [1988] IRLR 190.

68 [1987] IRLR 397.

69 In *Wagstaff v Elida Gibbs Ltd and Laverick* an IT awarded the (then) maximum £8,925 compensation for injury to feelings.

70 *Marshall v Southampton and South West Hampshire Area Health Authority (No 2)* [1993] IRLR 445 declared that the upper limit on compensation in sex discrimination cases was contrary to the ETD. Consequently the Sex Discrimination and Equal Pay (Remedies) Regulations 1993 SI No 2798 were passed. These abolished the upper limit on awards of compensation in sex discrimination cases made after 22 November 1993. The Race Relations (Remedies) Act 1994 removed the upper limit on compensation for race discrimination cases.

feelings and £5,000 aggravated damages.[71] A temporary secretary was awarded £8,000 for injury to feelings when she was assaulted and called a 'slag'.[72] A mixed race couple who were each subjected to racial and sexual harassment when she became pregnant were awarded £7,000 each for injury to feelings and total compensation of £38,000.[73] Two students who were working as waitresses were awarded £10,000 each for injury to feelings when they were sexually harassed and assaulted.[74] A trainee pilot was awarded £15,000 for a 'particularly outrageous act of sexual harassment'.[75] A female firefighter was awarded £200,000 in settlement of her sex discrimination case after she had suffered five years of sexual abuse.[76]

13.6.1 Aggravated damages

In *Alexander v Home Office* (above) the Court of Appeal said that compensation should include an element for aggravated damages 'where, for example, the Defendant may have behaved in a high handed, malicious, insulting or oppressive manner in committing the act of discrimination'. Such aggravated damages have been awarded by ITs for an employer's lack of contrition and continuing failure to address or alleviate the problem of racial abuse,[77] for an employer who treated racially abusive notices as a joke during tribunal proceedings and did not offer an apology to the complainants[78] and for an employer who put a young applicant through the distress of being examined and cross-examined on her experience of sexual harassment before admitting it.[79]

71 *Bryans v Northumberland College of Arts and Technology* (1995) 26 EOR DCLD, 4 May 1995; Case no 36674/94.

72 *Young v McLeod and John McLeod & Co* (1995) 25 EOR DCLD, 20 June 1995; Case no 5271/95.

73 *Green and Jones v In Car Insurance Replacement Services Ltd* (1994) 19 EOR DCLD, 23 September 1993; Case nos 7046/93 and 7062/93.

74 *Miss A and Miss B v R1 and R2* (1994) 21 EOR DCLD, 23 March 1994; Case nos 55253/93 and 55254/93.

75 *Hillen v Tuke and Ardsair Ltd* (1996) 30 EOR DCLD.

76 *J Clayton v Hereford & Worcester CC* EAT/692-3/95. She was awarded her costs in addition: (1997) 73 EOR 2.

77 *Ruizo v Tesco Stores and Lea* (1995) 24 EOR DCLD, 17 March 1995; Case no 53435/93.

78 *Patel and Harewood v T & K Home Improvements Ltd and Johnson* (1994) 22 EOR DCLD, 24 March 1994; Case nos 57783/92 and 57778/92.

79 *Knox v Lurgan Community Workshop and McConville* (1994) 19 EOR DCLD, 7 September 1993; Case no 452/93.

13.6.2 Exemplary damages

The courts have decided that exemplary damages cannot be recovered in discrimination cases under the RRA or SDA,[80] or in sex discrimination cases under the ETD (see **26.1.6**).[81] However, this may not be right (see **26.1.6**).

13.6.3 Recommendations

The tribunal can also make recommendations to employers that they introduce formal harassment procedures and train their staff to operate the new procedures (see **26.1.2**).[82] It can recommend that the harasser be moved or that the company work with the EOC or CRE (see **26.1.2**). If the recommendations are not complied with the tribunal can increase the compensation payable to the employee. Such terms could also be included as part of any settlement.

13.7 Publicity in IT cases

The publicity resulting from sexual harassment cases can often be distressing to both parties, however, the Divisional Court has ruled that an IT is not entitled to exclude members of the public (including the press) from the hearing of a harassment case.[83] An IT can make an order, on the application of any of the parties or of its own motion, that there be a restricted reporting order (see **25.9.12**).[84] A similar order can be made in disability cases where evidence of a personal nature is likely to be heard (see **24.9**). The order will specify which parties are not to be identified and it will remain in force until the IT's decision is sent to the parties. Once the decision has been published the media are free to disclose any details from the hearing, but they are usually rather less full in their coverage of what is likely to be a report of a hearing several months earlier (but see **25.9.12**). Tribunals sometimes allow an applicant to use a back door to escape the press!

80 *AB v South West Water Services* [1993] 1 All ER 609, CA.

81 *Ministry of Defence v Meredith* [1995] IRLR 539.

82 *Campbell v Datum Engineering Co Ltd* (1995) 24 EOR DCLD, 20 March 1995; Case no 43749/94.

83 *R v Southampton Industrial Tribunal ex p INS News Group* [1995] IRLR 247.

84 Industrial Tribunals (Constitution and Rules of Procedure) Regulations 1993 SI No 2687 Sch 1 r14; Employment Appeal Tribunal Rules 1993 SI No 2854 r23 as amended by the Employment Appeal Tribunal (Amendment) Rules 1996 SI No 3216.

13.8 Other forms of legal action

As pointed out by the EAT in *Porcelli* (above), unwelcome acts which involve physical contact are offences at common law such as assault and indecent assault. The only remedy is damages, or, if the employee is still employed, an injunction to prevent further harassment. In one claim for assault, battery and false imprisonment against the London Fire Brigade, brought in the High Court, damages of £25,000 were agreed for very serious harassment (including repeated advances, attempts to kiss and fondle) and victimisation.[85] A claim for assault and battery can be made at the same time as a complaint to an IT. In practice, one will be stayed, pending the outcome of the other. If there is a finding of fact in one set of proceedings it may not be possible to re-open the finding in subsequent proceedings; this is known as 'issue estoppel'.

The liability of the employer for acts of assault and battery carried out by an employee is generally restricted to employees (not independent contractors), the definition of 'in the course of employment' is narrower and the employer cannot escape liability by showing that it took reasonable steps to prevent the employee acting unlawfully.

13.8.1 Criminal proceedings

Criminal Justice and Public Order Act 1994 s4A makes intentional racial, sexual or other forms of harassment in a public or private place (other than a dwelling) a criminal offence. It remains to be seen whether any prosecutions will be brought under this section.

13.8.2 The Protection from Harassment Act 1997

A claim for harassment can be brought against the harasser (not the employer) in the county court or High Court.[86] 'Harassment' is defined as being a course of conduct which 'amounts to harassment of another', and which the perpetrator 'knows or ought to know amounts to harassment'.[87] It can include verbal harassment. There must have been at least two incidents of harassment. Such behaviour can also be a criminal offence.[88]

85 See (1990) IRLIB 398, 3 April, p8.

86 See Protection from Harassment Act 1997 s3 and (1997) 72 EOR 32.

87 Protection from Harassment Act 1997 s1.

88 Ibid, s2.

Damages can be awarded for financial loss and any anxiety caused by the harassment. The court can also grant an injunction to restrain future harassment. Breach of the injunction is a criminal offence punishable by up to five years' imprisonment and/or an unlimited fine.

The time limit for bringing such a claim is six years, though, of course, the time limit in the IT is still three months.

13.8.3 Negligence

The EC code states that since sexual harassment is a risk to health and safety, employers have a responsibility to take steps to minimise the risk as they do with other hazards. In the fire brigade case (above), the applicant also alleged that her employer had been negligent in not taking precautions to prevent the foreseeable harassment, she being one of the first female recruits to the brigade. There is a general duty on employers to provide a safe place of work. There is enough public awareness of harassment for employers to anticipate that it is a foreseeable hazard and therefore to take reasonable precautions. The only remedy is damages, but in the High Court these are not subject to any limit and in the county court the ceiling is £50,000 which may be raised by consent. Cases of this kind are becoming more common, sometimes linked to a claim for injury caused by stress.[89]

13.8.4 Breach of contract

An employer has an implied duty of mutual trust and confidence and an implied duty of care towards his/her employees, which obliges it to provide a safe working environment and support for employees. In *Muehring v EMAP and Ibbett*,[90] the applicant sued her employer for breach of contract (as well as in tort and for discrimination under the SDA), alleging that she had been sexually harassed by a director which forced her to leave. She sued her employer, as well as the director, and the case was settled for £25,000.

13.8.5 Mitigation

With claims for negligence, dismissal and breach of contract there is a duty to mitigate the loss (see **26.1.3.1**). Thus, complainants who

89 Such injury was first formally recognised in *Walker v Northumberland* [1995] IRLR 35.

90 Case no 10824/88.

have lost their job should seek alternative employment and provide evidence of this (see Chapter 26).

13.8.6 Legal aid

One of the advantages of bringing an action for assault, battery, negligence or breach of contract is that legal aid may be available, whereas it is not in cases under the SDA, RRA, DDA or ERA.

13.9 Victimisation

Sometimes people take up harassment through the grievance procedure. This may be important to show that the employer knows of the harassment. If as a result of complaining the applicant is dismissed or forced to resign or otherwise treated less favourably than other employees are or would be treated s/he will also have a claim for victimisation (see Chapter 4). In *Longmore v Lee*,[91] an IT said that the test of victimisation was 'whether the complaints of (sexual) harassment . . . were the reason for dismissal'.[92] Only if allegations are untrue **and not made in good faith** will the employer have a defence under SDA s4(2); RRA s2(2); and DDA s55(4).

HARASSMENT: KEY POINTS

- Harassment creates a threatening and stressful working environment.
- Claimants in racial and/or sexual harassment cases must establish that the acts were:
  - less favourable treatment on the ground of race or sex; and
  - a detriment.
- Behaviour that is sex- or race-specific is assumed to be on 'grounds of his/her race or sex'.
- The following points should be noted:
  - there is no need to show that there has been physical contact;

91 Case no 21745/88.

92 See also *Jenkins v Burnley and Others* (1994) 20 EOR DCLD, 23 February 1994; Case nos 4979/91 and 44852/92; *Pedelty v Rotherham MBC* and *Sohall v Walsall MBC* (1994) 20 EOR DCLD, 21 September 1993; Case no 62051/92 and 20 August 1993; Case no 20907/90.

  - one act can constitute harassment provided that it is sufficiently serious;
  - it is for each individual to decide what behaviour is acceptable and what s/he regards as offensive;
  - the test is whether the reasonable woman or reasonable black worker or reasonable disabled worker would be offended (not affected) by the harassment;
  - a claim can also be made by a man or a gay or a lesbian or a transsexual.
- A claim may be made:
  - under the ERA, if harassment leads to dismissal, including constructive dismissal, or if a co-worker is guilty of harassment, the employer fails to deal with it adequately and it leads to dismissal;
  - under the SDA, RRA or DDA, where harassment is treated as a 'detriment' in itself. A person penalised for making a claim of harassment, may have a claim for victimisation;
  - under EC law;
  - in tort or contract, for assault, battery, negligence or for breach of contract.
- If a woman is deemed to have 'provoked' the harassment, she may receive reduced compensation. Injury to feelings constitutes a large element in most compensation awards for harassment, which are generally higher than for other forms of discrimination.
- Racially motivated treatment is harassment; it does not have to be overtly racial. Overhearing racial or sexual abuse is not harassment unless it was intended to be overheard.
- Other detriments include:
  - enforced transfer;
  - continued working with the harasser;
  - loss of promotion;
  - extra policing.
- Both the employer and the harasser may be liable. The employer has a duty to take reasonable steps to prevent harassment and to deal with it if it occurs.
- A lack of witnesses in a harassment case should not be fatal to a claim, although it will make it more difficult. Evidence of similar behaviour should be admissible.

CHAPTER 14

Leaving work

14.1 Overview

An employee who has been dismissed is likely first to consider a claim for unfair dismissal under the ERA. The right not to be unfairly dismissed is better known and in some ways broader in scope than discrimination laws. The detailed provisions of the employment protection legislation are outside the scope of this book. However, a dismissal may also be unlawfully discriminatory contrary to the RRA, SDA and/or DDA.

A discriminatory dismissal is made unlawful in domestic law by SDA s6(2)(b), RRA s4(2)(c) and DDA s4(2)(d). One of the main features of discrimination is that the amount of compensation that can be awarded is unlimited and it will normally include a sum for injury to the complainant's feelings and the questionnaire procedure is available. The ERA allows employees to claim compensation if the dismissal was unfair (ERA ss118 to 127). A major disadvantage of the employment rights legislation is that it protects only employees (not the self-employed or contract workers) who are below retiring age and who have worked for the employer for at least two years (see below). These restrictions do not apply to the SDA, DDA and RRA.

Although there will usually be an overlap with employment rights legislation, as discriminatory dismissals are likely to be unfair, there are occasions when a person will not qualify for protection under the employment rights legislation but only under the SDA, RRA or DDA (eg, if self-employed). On the other hand there will be instances where workers may have more rights under the employment rights legislation; they can, for example, claim reinstatement or re-engagement. It is therefore important to consider both types of protection in dismissal cases.

The ETD provides that the:

> Application of the principle of equal treatment with regard to . . . conditions governing dismissal means that men and women shall be guaranteed the same conditions without discrimination on the ground of sex (art 5(1)).

This means that discriminatory dismissals will also be in breach of the ETD. Pregnancy-related dismissals will also be unlawful under the Pregnant Workers Directive. (For the effect of directives, see **9.2.3**.)

14.1.1 Statutory protection

14.1.1.1 Under the ERA

In order to make a claim under the ERA the applicant must:

- be an employee (the self-employed are not protected; the two categories are often difficult to distinguish and the courts are not bound by the description that has been given to the relationship but will look at the way the relationship works in order to decide the worker's status);[1]
- be under the place of work's normal retirement age or, if there is no normal age, 65 (see **14.5.1**);
- not be working under an illegal contract;[2]
- be ordinarily working in GB; and
- have worked continuously for two years.

The last requirement, to have worked continuously for two years, has been referred to the ECJ as indirectly discriminatory against women and contrary to the ETD and art 119[3] due to the fact that fewer women than men have worked for a continuous period of two years for their current employer (see **3.6.6.2**).

There are some people who are totally excluded from the employment protection laws, such as the police, share fishermen, and those

1 See T Kibling and T Lewis, *Employment Law: an advisers' handbook* (LAG, 3rd edn, 1996) for a fuller discusion of this problem. The relevant cases are: *O'Kelly v Trust House Forte plc* [1983] ICR 728; [1983] IRLR 369; *Nethermere (St Neots) Ltd v Taverna and Gardiner* [1984] ICR 612; [1984] IRLR 240; *McMeechan v Secretary of State for Employment* [1995] IRLR 461; *Lane v Shire Roofing Co (Oxford) Ltd* [1995] IRLR 493 and *Buchan v Secretary of State for Employment* [1997] IRLR 80.

2 *Tomlinson v Dick Evans 'U' Drive Ltd* [1978] ICR 639; [1978] IRLR 77; *Davidson v Pillay* [1979] IRLR 275; *Newland v Simons & Weller (Hairdressers) Ltd* [1981] ICR 521; [1981] IRLR 359; *Broaders v Kilkare Property Maintenance* [1990] IRLR 421 and *Hewcastle Catering Ltd v Ahmed and Others* [1990] IRLR 473.

3 *R v Secretary of State for Employment ex p Seymour Smith* [1995] IRLR 315, HL.

on fixed-term contracts of over one year where the right to claim unfair dismissal has been expressly excluded.[4]

14.1.1.2 Under the SDA, RRA and DDA

Under these Acts workers employed under a contract of service or apprenticeship or a contract personally to execute any work are protected from the first day of employment irrespective of their age and the number of hours they work, provided that they do not fall within the exceptions set out at **5.4** and **5.5**. Thus homeworkers, who are often not categorised as employees and so cannot make a claim of unfair dismissal under the ERA,[5] can claim under the SDA, RRA or DDA if dismissed because of discrimination; so can nurses or secretaries working for agencies (see **8.5**). An illegal contract of employment will not prevent an employee bringing a discrimination case. In *Leighton v Michael and Charalambous*[6] the EAT held that a complaint of sex discrimination did not depend on the existence of an enforceable contract of employment (see **5.2.1.6**), although this is unlikely to apply to an unfair dismissal claim.

Some employees who are not protected by the SDA or RRA may be able to bring a claim under the employment protection legislation, eg, those claiming race discrimination who are employed in a private household.[7] Similar exceptions existed under the SDA 1975 but these were repealed by the SDA 1986.

Applicants who are protected by the ERA, SDA, RRA and DDA should always make a claim under the ERA as well as the discrimination Acts.

14.2 The grounds for dismissal under the ERA

The ERA defines a dismissal as either:

- termination of the contract by the employer;
- expiry of a fixed-term contract or a failure to renew it on the same terms;
- constructive dismissal, whereby a worker resigns after a serious breach of an important term of the contract by the employer (eg, harassment); or

4 ERA ss197 to 200.

5 But see *Nethermere (St Neots) Ltd v Taverna and Gardiner* (n1 above) where the CA held that a group of homeworkers were employees.

6 [1996] IRLR 67.

7 RRA ss4(3) and 10.

– a refusal to allow a woman to return after maternity absence.

It is for the worker to show that s/he has been dismissed.

Under the ERA, there are some grounds for dismissing an employee which are potentially fair and lawful.[8] It is sufficient for the employer to show a genuine and reasonably held belief that one of the grounds apply. Some of these reasons may, however, be discriminatory. The IT must then decide if it was reasonable to dismiss the worker. The grounds are as follows.

14.2.1 Capability or qualifications

'Capability' covers skill, aptitude, health or any other physical or mental quality. An employer setting standards of capability should ensure that they are not discriminatory. In *Birdi v Waites & Waites Architecture*[9] an Asian architect who was the first ethnic minority employee to have a position of authority and seniority within the firm was unjustifiably criticised and dismissed on the ground of capability. The IT found that he had been discriminated against and unfairly dismissed.

Failure to pass an aptitude test can be a fair reason for dismissal, but this may well be discriminatory if the test has a disparate impact on one sex or race and is not justifiable because, for instance, it does not relate directly to the ability of the applicant to do the job in question (see **10.6**).

'Qualifications' means any degree, diploma or other academic, technical or professional qualification relevant to the job.

14.2.2 Conduct

Common examples of dismissal for misconduct are disobedience of disciplinary rules, absenteeism, criminal offences, and bad time-keeping. Employers must operate a consistent standard between different races and sexes. In *Hume v Compass Services (UK) Ltd*[10] a woman was dismissed and a man demoted for the same misconduct. The IT found that the woman had been unlawfully discriminated against.

8 ERA ss98 and 100.
9 (1996) 30 EOR DCLD.
10 (1995) 24 EOR DCLD.

Sometimes women with primary responsibility for young children have problems over time-keeping and absenteeism, for example when their children are ill. It may be possible in some jobs to argue for the right to work flexible hours or to job share.[11] Alternatively, if a woman is dismissed for reasons connected with her child's health and time she has had to take off to care for him/her it may be possible to argue that her dismissal is indirectly discriminatory.

It is quite common for employees to be dismissed for taking extended leave to visit relatives abroad, or for being late back from these holidays. This may be indirect race discrimination.

14.2.3 Redundancy

An employer may lawfully dismiss an employee on the ground of redundancy, however, it cannot select an employee for redundancy on the ground of his/her race or sex (see **14.3.2**).

14.2.4 Statutory requirements

Where the employer could not continue to employ a worker without breaking the law, s/he is entitled to dismiss him/her, for example, if a driver loses his/her licence. The employer must also show that there was no alternative employment available.

14.2.5 Some other substantial reason justifying dismissal

This must relate to something as serious as the other categories. It is a wide, 'catch-all' category whereby the employer must show that it had a fair reason in mind when it decided to dismiss the employee.[12] One of the most common reasons under this head is reorganisation of the business. This may mean ending the employee's existing contract of employment and offering him/her a new one.[13] An employer may re-organise its business to improve efficiency or for other sound business reasons; this is different from a redundancy which occurs when the employer's requirement for employees to carry out work of a particular kind has ceased or diminished.

11 *Home Office v Holmes* [1984] IRLR 299; *Wright v Rugby Council, Given v Scottish Power plc* (1995) 24 EOR DCLD and *British Telecommunications plc v Roberts and Longstaffe* [1996] IRLR 601.

12 *Harper v National Coal Board* [1980] IRLR 260.

13 *Hollister v National Farmers Union* [1979] IRLR 238.

14.2.6 *Reasonableness*

In addition to proving a 'fair' reason for dismissal, the employer must have acted reasonably in the circumstances, taking into account the employer's size and administrative resources, the merits of the case and procedural fairness.[14] This includes giving an employee fair warning, a chance to respond to allegations and a chance to improve.

The EOC code states that care should be taken that members of one sex are not disciplined or dismissed for performance or behaviour which would be overlooked or condoned in the other sex (para 32(a)).

In *Atanasova v Fraiklin*[15] the IT held that the applicant had been the subject of sex discrimination because the fundamental reason behind her dismissal was that the manager was 'simply unable to cope with a woman (as opposed to a man) having the assertive attitude and enthusiasm to succeed demonstrated by the applicant'.

14.2.7 *Constructive dismissal*

Unfair dismissal also includes the situation where an employee terminates his/her contract in circumstances where s/he is entitled to do so because of the employer's conduct.[16] It will be necessary for the employee to prove that there has been a serious breach of an important term of his/her contract of employment (such as a breach of the obligation not to discriminate).[17] This could cover the situation where an employer sexually harasses a woman forcing her to leave (see **13.3.3.7**), where an employer refuses to allow a woman to return to work after maternity leave (see Chapter 17) or where her hours of work are changed so that she can no longer continue working.[18] A discriminatory promotion procedure may found a successful claim for unfair constructive dismissal. Employees who have been constructively dismissed, or fear that they may be, should write to their employers immediately to notify it of the situation and that s/he considers that it is a substantial breach of his/her employment agreement. However, it is very difficult to predict whether the resignation will lead to a successful claim for constructive dismissal.

14 *Polkey v A E Dayton Services Ltd* [1987] IRLR 503.
15 (1996) 28 EOR DCLD.
16 ERA s95.
17 See *Western Excavating v Sharp* [1978] 1 All ER 713; [1978] ICR 221.
18 See *London Underground Ltd v Edwards* [1995] IRLR 355.

14.2.8 Automatically unfair reasons for dismissal

The following are automatically unfair reasons for dismissal:

- pregnancy (see Chapter 17);
- dismissal of a designated health and safety representative for carrying out his/her duties;
- dismissal of an employee for seeking to protect him/herself or others against health and safety risks;
- dismissal of a shop worker or betting worker for refusal to work on a Sunday;
- dismissal of an employee representative for performing or proposing to perform his/her union duties;
- dismissal for acting as a trustee of an occupational pension scheme;
- dismissal for asserting a statutory right, such as the right to antenatal care (see **15.3**);
- certain redundancy dismissals (see **17.6.2.5** and **17.6.2.6**);
- dismissal because of the transfer of an undertaking unless this is for an economic, technical or organisational reason entailing changes to the workplace.

For a good, clear summary of the details of unfair dismissal law see Kibling and Lewis *Employment law: an advisers' handbook* (LAG, 3rd edn, 1996).

14.3 Discriminatory dismissals

A discriminatory dismissal is almost always an unfair dismissal. In *Clarke v Eley (IMI) Kynoch Ltd*[19] (see **3.6.3**), the EAT stated that it did not follow, as a matter of law, that an indirectly discriminatory dismissal was an unfair one, but that it would need very special circumstances to find such a dismissal fair. Where possible, a claim for unfair dismissal and discrimination should be linked, so that the maximum amount of compensation can be claimed, as well as reinstatement or re-engagement (see Chapter 26).

Some of the reasons for dismissal may be indirectly discriminatory. For example, a contractual mobility clause can be indirectly discriminatory against women because a higher proportion of women than men are secondary earners.[20] Thus a dismissal for refusal to move could be indirectly sexually discriminatory. The question would be whether the mobility requirement was justifiable (see **3.6.7**).

19 [1982] IRLR 482.
20 *Meade-Hill v British Council* [1995] IRLR 478.

14.3.1 *Hours of work*

Often business reorganisation will involve changes in hours of work. If an employer alters hours of work without the agreement of the employee, it may be possible for him/her to claim constructive dismissal if the variation is sufficient to constitute a fundamental breach of contract (see below). It can be argued that a discriminatory dismissal has occurred if the new arrangements adversely affect a woman, whose ability to work flexible hours is more restricted than men's because of childcare commitments. In *London Underground v Edwards*[21] the EAT held that if a considerably smaller proportion of women train operators than men train drivers could comply with the new rostering arrangements and the applicant could not comply then these would be indirectly discriminatory (see **3.6.6.7**). The question is whether the requirement is justifiable (see **3.6.7**). It is also possible that a change in hours or a refusal of a holiday leave request would discriminate against racial groups with religious needs[22] (see **6.4.1.13**).

14.3.2 *Redundancy*

An employee may be fairly dismissed under the ERA on the ground of redundancy. The employer must show that a redundancy situation exists (eg, that the business is closing down or the workforce is being reduced because there is less or no need for such workers) and that the selection procedure was fair.[23] Whether a redundancy situation really exists can be challenged.

Employees chosen for redundancy because of their sex or race or for a reason relating to their disability can claim unlawful discrimination under the SDA, RRA or DDA irrespective of their length of service.

14.3.2.1 Selection for redundancy

The employer must show on what basis the selection was made and must show that s/he acted reasonably.[24]

Certain selection criteria may be indirectly discriminatory, such as one whereby part-time workers are made redundant before full-

21 [1995] IRLR 355.
22 *Azam v J H Walker Ltd* (1995) 26 EOR DCLD.
23 ERA s105.
24 ERA s98.

timers. In *Clarke v Eley*[25] the EAT held that to select part-timers first for redundancy was unlawful discrimination. It took into account the fact that the employers were not in complete ignorance of the possibility that they might be infringing the SDA. It is therefore important that employers are made aware of the discriminatory nature of redundancy practices before employees are made redundant.

A common custom is to select on the basis of 'last in first out' (LIFO) which may also be indirectly discriminatory on the ground of sex or race (or in Northern Ireland, religion), as women tend to have shorter service than men. This was raised in *R v LB Hammersmith and Fulham ex p NALGO*[26] and *Hall and Others v Shorts Missile Systems Ltd.*[27] In *Clarke*, the EAT considered, obiter, that LIFO was probably not discriminatory because it has for many years been the most commonly agreed criterion. This is surely no justification if the criterion has an adverse impact on women and this decision is arguably wrong.

LIFO is becoming less common as a means for deciding who should be dismissed. It is more usual for employers to use several criteria which are more directly related to the needs of the business such as aptitude, skill and attendance record. The LIFO practice may also be contrary to the ETD which states that conditions governing dismissal shall be without discrimination on the ground of sex. In *Hall and Others v Shorts Missile Systems* (above) the NICA held that to select for redundancy partly on the basis of points attributed to length of service was not indirectly discriminatory. This case is on appeal to the House of Lords.

Note that it may be possible to challenge a local authority's redundancy policy, if discriminatory, by way of judicial review (see the *NALGO* case above) (see **25.11**).

14.3.2.2 Consultation

The employer is legally obliged to consult with recognised trade unions within specified time limits. This consultation process should be an opportunity to consider if the redundancy procedure is discriminatory. However, the under-representation of women, black workers and disabled workers among elected union officers and full-time officials means that insufficient importance may be attached to this aspect of the arrangements. In *Clarke* and *Kidd v DRG (UK)*

25 [1982] IRLR 482.
26 [1991] IRLR 249.
27 (1997) 72 EOR 39.

Ltd,[28] the employers' defence of justifiability rested on the fact that the agreement had been negotiated with the trade union. In the same way that 'market forces' cannot be relied on as an automatic defence to inequalities in pay so agreements with trade unions cannot be relied on as a defence if those agreements are, in effect, discriminatory. The LIFO principle should be challenged both within trade unions, which are responsible for negotiating redundancy agreements, and in the courts. In each case the employer will have to show that such selection criteria are justifiable but it should now be more difficult for them to justify procedures which are indirectly discriminatory even if they have been negotiated with the union; it is unlikely that such reasons would be acceptable under the *Bilka* test (see **3.6.7**).

If there is no trade union the employer should consult with the employees affected, and this will include any women on maternity leave.

14.3.2.3 Offer of alternative employment

An employer should offer, where it exists, suitable alternative employment and allow the employee a trial period in the new job of at least four weeks. Unreasonable refusal to accept such employment will result in a loss of redundancy pay.

14.3.2.4 Redundancy and maternity rights

A woman selected for redundancy because she is pregnant will be able to claim automatically unfair dismissal under the ERA and discrimination. If she is made redundant while on maternity leave or absence she must be offered suitable alternative employment, if it exists, otherwise she will be treated as having been automatically unfairly dismissed.[29] Under the statutory maternity leave provisions a woman on maternity leave or absence is entitled to be offered any suitable alternative employment;[30] there is no test of reasonableness, unlike the general s98 provisions. She has priority over other redundant employees (see **17.6.2.5** to **17.6.2.6**).

14.3.2.5 Redundancies linked to retirement

Under the SDA, as amended by the SDA 1986, it is unlawful to dismiss a woman on the ground of age when a man of the same age in

28 [1985] IRLR 190.
29 *Community Task Force v Rimmer* [1986] ICR 491; [1986] IRLR 203.
30 ERA ss77 and 99.

comparable circumstances would not be dismissed. If redundancies are linked to differential retirement ages, therefore, they may be challenged as unlawful (see **14.5**).

14.3.2.6 Redundancy pay

An employee dismissed because of redundancy is entitled to redundancy pay provided that s/he meets the qualifying conditions and does not unreasonably refuse an offer of suitable alternative work. If the dismissal is also unfair, s/he is entitled, in addition, to compensation for unfair dismissal (see **26.2**). In discrimination cases compensation is unlimited. For discussion of discrimination and redundancy pay, see **14.5.1.3**, and for redundancy terms in collective agreements, see **22.1.6**.

14.3.2.7 Codes of practice relating to redundancy

The EOC code recommends that:

- redundancy procedures affecting a group of employees predominantly of one sex should be reviewed, so as to remove any effects which could be disproportionate and unjustifiable;
- conditions of access to voluntary redundancy benefit should be made available on equal terms to male and female employees in the same or not materially different circumstances;
- where there is a down-grading or short-time working, the arrangements should not unlawfully discriminate on the ground of sex.

The CRE code recommends that:

- staff responsible for selecting employees for dismissal, including redundancy, should be instructed not to discriminate on racial grounds;
- selection criteria for redundancies should be examined to ensure that they are not indirectly discriminatory.

The DDA code points out that if a redundancy selection criterion would apply to a disabled person for a reason relating to his/her disability, that criterion would have to be 'material' and 'substantial', and that the employer would have to consider whether a reasonable adjustment would prevent the criterion applying to the disabled person after all. (To see how this recommendation links in with the definition of disability discrimination, see Chapter 24.)

14.3.3 Health and safety

A pregnant or breast-feeding woman whose work poses a risk to expectant or new mothers should be offered alternative work or suspended on full pay (see **15.4**). It will be automatically unfair and discriminatory to dismiss her.

14.3.4 Marital status

Dismissal on the ground of marital status may well be unfair dismissal as well as discrimination. If a married woman is bringing a claim of direct discrimination, the relevant comparison is between her and a married man.

In *North East Midlands Co-operative Society Ltd v Allen*,[31] the applicant was dismissed following her marriage. The employer operated a rule whereby female employees who got married were deemed to have terminated their original contract and a fresh contract would be negotiated. When it offered the newly-married Ms Allen alternative employment, she declined, and was subsequently dismissed on the ground of redundancy. The EAT held that this dismissal was discriminatory as the rules under which Ms Allen had been dismissed meant that she had been dismissed because she married and because she was a woman.

Indirect discrimination on the ground of marital status will often overlap with indirect sex discrimination. In *Hurley v Mustoe*[32], it was successfully claimed that not to employ married women with children was directly discriminatory against women, and that the requirement not to have children indirectly discriminated against married people. (For the purposes of indirect discrimination on the ground of marital status, married women cannot be compared with unmarried men, nor married men with unmarried women.)

Complaints of discrimination on the ground of marital status can be made only by persons who are married. Women *intending* to marry are not protected. In *Bick v Royal West of England School for the Deaf*,[33] the applicant had told her employer that she was going to get married and she was informed that she would be dismissed as from her wedding day. She lost her discrimination claim because she was not actually married when she received her letter of dismissal.

31 [1977] IRLR 212.
32 [1981] IRLR 208.
33 [1976] IRLR 326.

The ETD may protect women in Ms Bick's position. It is broader in scope, stating that there shall be no discrimination by reference to marital or family status (see **5.1.2**). For discussion about discrimination against lone parents, see **5.1.1**.

14.3.5 Extended leave

Dismissals following an employee's extended leave may be indirect race discrimination as it is mainly ethnic minority workers who have extended leave. It has not yet been argued that the requirement (not to take extended leave or holidays) is indirectly discriminatory on the ground of race, so making dismissal on the ground of taking such leave unfair. The key question is whether such a requirement would be unfairly justifiable (see **3.6.7**).

Many employers ask employees taking extended leave to sign a contract stating that they will return on a given date, and that if they do not return, they will be deemed to have terminated their employment. In *Igbo v Johnson Matthey Chemicals Ltd*,[34] the CA held that contractual terms which provide for automatic termination of employment if the employee fails to return on a specified date are void because they limit the operation of the statutory right not to be unfairly dismissed.

14.4 Transfer of undertakings

When a business is transferred from one person or body to another and the employees have their employment transferred to the new employer they will have continuity of employment and can enforce any rights accrued under the former employer against the new employer. If the former employer has discriminated against an employee s/he can bring a discrimination claim against the new employer because the new employer is deemed to have stepped into the shoes of the former employer[35] (see **25.3.2**). Any individual from the former employer can still be sued if s/he was responsible for 'aiding' an act of discrimination.

Any dismissal as a result of the transfer will be automatically unfair unless the employer can show that the dismissal was for an

34 [1986] IRLR 215.

35 *DJM International Ltd v Nicholas* [1996] ICR 214; [1996] IRLR 76.

'economic, technical or organisational reason entailing changes to the workforce'. If this applies, the dismissal will be fair if it is for a substantial reason justifying dismissal and in all the circumstances the employer acted reasonably. For further details see Kibling and Lewis *Employment Law* (LAG, 3rd edn, 1996).

DISCRIMINATORY DISMISSALS: KEY POINTS

- A discriminatory dismissal is unlawful under the SDA, RRA, DDA and ERA (provided that the qualifying conditions are satisfied) and, in the case of sex discrimination, the ETD.
- Unfair dismissals under the ERA apply to employees, under the normal retiring age, working in GB for a continuous period of two years with the same employer. The IT will decide if it was reasonable to dismiss for one of the statutory grounds.
- To obtain maximum compensation, claims should be made for both unfair dismissal and discrimination.
- Redundancy:
  - selection criteria, such as LIFO or part-timers out first, may be indirectly discriminatory;
  - selection of a woman because she is pregnant is discriminatory;
  - redundancies linked to retirement, where the retirement age differs for men and women, are unlawful;
  - redundancy pay should be equal for men and women.
- A pregnant or breast-feeding woman whose work poses a risk should be offered alternative work or suspended on full pay.
- Dismissal on the ground of marital status is likely to be unlawful discrimination.
- Dismissal of a woman because she has children is unlawful.
- Dismissal of a worker who takes extended leave to visit family abroad may be indirectly discriminatory on the ground of race.
- Harassment may justify resignation (unfair constructive dismissal) – see Chapter 13.
- Forcing a woman to retire at a different age from male employees is unlawful – see below.

14.5 Retirement

Originally, the SDA excluded all provisions relating to death, retirement and pensions but this exclusion was held to contravene EC law.[36]

The SDA was therefore amended (by the SDA 1986) so that it is now unlawful for an employer to discriminate by making men and women retire at different ages or by relating other work opportunities (such as training and promotion) to differing retirement ages. Pensions are covered separately in Chapter 23.

14.5.1 Retirement age

The UK state pensionable age, when entitlement to a state pension arises, is 65 for men and 60 for women. Such a distinction is lawful under both the SDA and EC law, as provisions relating to state pensions are exempt (see **23.5.3.1**). Other discriminatory provisions linked to the retirement age are likely to be unlawful.

14.5.1.1 Dismissal linked to retirement age

The SDA now prohibits discriminatory retirement-related provisions in respect of promotion, transfer, training, dismissal, demotion or any other detriment which results in dismissal or demotion (see **5.4.2.1**).

Generally, once an employee has reached the normal retiring age, s/he cannot make a claim for unfair dismissal under the ERA, irrespective of how unfair the dismissal was (though a claim can be made under the SDA for discriminatory dismissal).

The ERA[37] prohibits employers having different retirement age limits for men and women. If different ages are stipulated they are replaced by a common retirement age of 65. It is irrelevant what ages the employer sets; even if the retiring age was 55 for men and 54 for women, the substituted age is still 65. Normal retiring age is 'what would be the reasonable expectation or understanding of the employees' and not necessarily the contractual retiring age.[38] It is therefore now unlawful for an employer to dismiss women at 60 and men at 65; where there are different retiring ages, a woman is able to claim unfair dismissal up to the age of 65. Dismissal includes constructive dismissal and the expiry of a fixed-term contract.

36 *Marshall v Southampton and South-West Hampshire Area Health Authority* [1986] IRLR 140, ECJ.

37 Section 189.

38 *Brooks and Others v British Telecommunications Ltd* [1992] IRLR 66, CA.

The position may be different if there are different retiring ages for different groups. In *Bullock v Alice Ottley School*,[39] the school had one retiring age for domestic staff (60) (who were mainly women) and another for gardeners and maintenance staff (65) (who were mainly men). The rationale was that it was difficult to recruit gardeners and maintenance staff and the school argued that the relevant circumstances were different (see **2.9**). The CA held that there was nothing to prevent an employer having a variety of retirement ages for different jobs, provided there was no direct or indirect discrimination. The CA held there was no indirect discrimination as the tribunal was entitled to accept evidence that a later retirement age for gardeners and maintenance staff was necessary because of the problems in recruiting such staff. Thus, the practice was justifiable.

In equal pay cases, such as *Enderby*[40] and *Ratcliffe*,[41] the ECJ and HL accepted that a prima facie case of discrimination was made out if a group of predominantly women were paid less. The same principle applies to other benefits. In *Bullock* the CA emphasised that an IT must look 'very carefully at the circumstances relied on by the employer to explain or justify any discrimination between the treatment of a woman and the treatment of a man who is or appears to be in a similar job'. This is tantamount to implying a defence of justification to direct discrimination, which must be wrong, as stated clearly by the HL in *Ratcliffe*.

In *Mason v Cheesbrough & Sons Grocers Ltd*[42] the applicant was told that she had to retire at 60. All employees were women and the employer said that the normal retirement age for female employees was 60. The tribunal held that there was an inference that men could stay until they were 65 so the applicant could claim unfair dismissal.

Transitional arrangements, whereby existing male employees are allowed to continue to retire at 65, while women have to retire at 60, are also unlawful.[43]

There may be a normal retiring age with limited exceptions. In *Barclays Bank plc v O'Brien and Others*[44] the employer changed

39 [1992] IRLR 564, CA.

40 *Enderby v Frenchay Health Authority and Secretary of State for Health* [1993] IRLR 591, ECJ.

41 *Ratcliffe v North Yorkshire* CC [1995] IRLR 439, HL.

42 (1988) COIT 2044/203.

43 *Nicol v Ben Line Group Ltd* S/182/88; *Benson v Scottish Development Agency* S/0164/88.

44 [1994] IRLR 580, CA.

the retirement age to 60 for all employees. However, after pressure from staff, an exception was made for a relatively small category of employees within particular age limits for a limited period in time. The CA held that there was no reason to doubt the employer's policy of having a normal retiring age of 60 and the limited exception did not destroy that. The limited exception is less likely to apply now that there has been a common retiring age for over ten years.

Where there is a contractual condition stipulating that the contract will come to an end automatically and this is linked to different retirement ages for men and women, this will also be unlawful. In *Beets-Proper v F Van Lanschot Bankiers NV*[45] the contract came to an end automatically without a dismissal actually taking place.

It is unlawful to stipulate that eligibility for training, promotion and other benefits is linked to a retirement age which is different for men and women.

14.5.1.2 Retirement and redundancy

A redundancy policy which provides that women aged 60 and men aged 65 are the first to be selected for redundancy would be unlawful. In these circumstances, women made redundant between 60 and 65 could claim unfair dismissal.

14.5.1.3 Entitlement to redundancy pay

Until 1990, the legislation did not prohibit discriminatory redundancy payments. Thus, although it was unlawful to make men and women redundant at different ages, it was still lawful, under the EPCA (now the ERA), to cease making redundancy payments to women at 60 whereas men could receive payments up to the age of 65.

This was successfully challenged as being contrary to EC law. In *Hammersmith and Queen Charlotte's Special Health Authority v Cato*,[46] the EAT held that a contractual redundancy scheme which reduced payments for women over the age of 59 and men over the age of 64, contravened art 119. In *Cato*, the redundancy payment was made under a collective agreement and was, said the EAT, consideration which the worker received 'in respect of his employment' from his employer. It was therefore 'pay' as defined by art 119.

In *Barber v GRE Assurance Group*,[47] the ECJ held that *statutory*

45 Case 262/84 [1986] ICR 706, ECJ.
46 [1987] IRLR 483, EAT.
47 [1990] IRLR 240, ECJ.

redundancy payments were pay within the meaning of art 119.[48] The EAT, in *McKechnie v UBM Building Supplies (Southern) Ltd*[49] held that the *Barber* decision removed any doubt that a statutory redundancy payment and an ex-gratia payment based on the statutory payment provided by a collective agreement were 'pay' within art 119.

Any payments made in addition to jobseekers' allowance to men who are made redundant between ages 60 and 65 also constitute 'pay' within art 119, rather than a social security benefit. In *Commission of the European Communities v Kingdom of Belgium*[50] the ECJ held that as the payment was the responsibility of the employer and was due to the employment relationship, it was pay.

ERA s156 provides that where there is a normal retiring age of less than 65 which applies equally to men and women, entitlement to redundancy payments (whether contractual or statutory) continues up until that age. If there is no normal retiring age it shall be deemed to be 65. The Act has also changed the tapering provisions whereby those approaching retirement age have their redundancy pay reduced. The position now is that payment may be reduced by one-twelfth for every month after the employee's 64th birthday.

A redundancy, or severance, scheme which is indirectly discriminatory will similarly be in breach of art 119. In *Kowalska v Freie und Hansestadt Hamburg*,[51] the applicant was employed part-time. The collective agreement provided for a severance payment but it was available only to full-time workers. The ECJ held that this was a breach of EC law, as art 119 prohibits employers excluding part-timers from such a scheme where a considerably smaller percentage of women than men work full-time, unless the employer could show that the provision was justified by objective factors unrelated to any discrimination on the ground of sex.[52]

In *R v Secretary of State for Employment ex p EOC*,[53] the Court of Appeal held that the method of calculating redundancy pay, which

48 Thereby superseding the EAT decision in *Secretary of State for Employment v Levy* [1989] IRLR 469. See also *McKechnie v UBM Building Supplies (Southern) Ltd* [1991] IRLR 283, where the EAT held that it was a breach of art 119 to refuse to make a statutory redundancy payment to a woman of 61, where a man of 61 would have been entitled to one.

49 [1991] IRLR 283, EAT.

50 [1993] IRLR 404, ECJ.

51 [1990] IRLR 447, ECJ.

52 See also the section on benefits linked to retirement age at **18.7.2.1** and Chapter 23.

53 [1993] IRLR 10, CA.

penalised those who changed from full-time work to part-time work, was justified even though it had a disparate impact on women. The CA upheld the HC decision which accepted the Secretary of State's argument that to change the system would involve administrative problems which would be complex and costly for employers. The CA also said that redundancy payments were not only reward for length of service, but also the facilitation of the employee's adjustment to the new circumstances resulting from the loss of employment.[54]

This decision was followed by the EAT in *Barry v Midland Bank plc*.[55] The EAT held that the scheme as a whole does not treat a woman less favourably because if Mrs Barry had been either a full-time or part-time worker throughout, she would have no claim. However, this ignores the reality of women's working lives whereby they commonly move from full-time to part-time work when they have children. It is questionable whether the ECJ would have reached the same conclusion.

RETIREMENT: KEY POINTS

- It is unlawful to differentiate between men and women as to when they retire or are made redundant (SDA 1986; *Marshall*).
- It is unlawful to stipulate that access to contractual or statutory redundancy payments arises at different ages for men and women (*Barber*). The terms of access must not discriminate indirectly.
- Redundancy payments, whether statutory or contractual, must be paid on the same basis to men and women and must not be indirectly discriminatory.

54 This part of the decision was not appealed, even though the other issues about part-time work were later decided by the HL.

55 (1995) unreported EAT/817/95.

Part III

Maternity rights

CHAPTER 15

Ante-natal care, health and safety protection and rights to maternity leave and absence

15.1 Introduction

Pregnancy and the arrival of a child forces many women to withdraw from the labour market. However, this trend is declining; between 1984 and 1994 there was a substantial increase in the percentage of working mothers.[1] In addition, an increasing number of women return to work within a year of having a baby, though many return to a lower grade part-time job.

In October 1994 the Government implemented the Pregnant Workers Directive (PWD). The Directive sets minimum standards of health and safety protection, maternity leave and pay and prohibits dismissal on the ground of pregnancy. The present scheme comprises these European rights superimposed on the pre-existing UK scheme. In addition, the UK and EC discrimination legislation provides some protection. The statutory framework is therefore a hotchpotch of European and UK employment, discrimination and social security legislation providing a patchwork of rights which are subject to different qualifying conditions and notification requirements.

Although only women, not men, are entitled to maternity leave and absence and maternity pay, a father denied parental leave payments has challenged this as being a breach of the European Convention on Human Rights (see **5.4.2.4**). The government has also said that it will implement the Parental Leave Directive (see **11.3**). This chapter covers the rights to paid time off for ante-natal care, health and safety protection, maternity leave and absence.

1 In 1984 55% of mothers with children under the age of 16 were economically active; in 1994, 64% were active (*Employment Committee First Report on Mothers in Employment* HC 227-I Session 1994–95).

15.2 The main statutory provisions

When advising on maternity rights it is necessary to consider:

a) the maternity provisions of the Employment Rights Act 1996 (ERA) and the Pregnant Workers Directive (PWD);
b) the ordinary unfair dismissal provisions of the Employment Rights Act 1996;
c) the discrimination and equal pay provisions of UK and EC law, ie:
   - the Sex Discrimination Act 1975 (SDA);
   - the Equal Pay Act 1970 (EqPA);
   - EC Treaty art 119 and the Equal Pay Directive (EPD);
   - the Equal Treatment Directive (ETD);
d) the social security provisions which provide for statutory maternity pay and maternity allowance;
e) the employee's contract of employment which may provide more favourable contractual rights (see **17.4**).

15.2.1 Qualifying conditions for maternity rights under ERA

The following are not protected:

- *Those who are not employees*: the ERA protects only 'employees', ie, an individual who works under a contract of employment (see **14.1.1.1**).[2] Thus, trainees will be protected only if they are also employees.
- *Women who ordinarily work outside GB.*[3]
- *Share fisherwomen.*[4]
- *Women employed in the police service.*[5]

Members of the armed forces are protected but complaints must first be made under the internal service procedures.[6]

15.2.2 Meaning of 'childbirth'

The rights apply to women who give birth to a living child (however premature) or to a child, living or dead, after 24 weeks of pregnancy.[7]

2 ERA s230.
3 ERA s196.
4 ERA s199.
5 ERA s200, though they have similar protection under the Police Regulations 1995 SI No 215.
6 ERA s192.
7 ERA s235.

Thus, women who miscarry after 24 weeks are entitled to the same rights, including maternity leave and absence.

15.3 Right to paid time off for ante-natal care

All pregnant employees, irrespective of the hours they work and length of service, whether permanent or temporary, are entitled to paid time off for ante-natal care.[8] Ante-natal care includes non-medical care such as relaxation classes.[9]

The woman must have an appointment given on the advice of a registered doctor, midwife or health visitor. For the second and subsequent appointments the employer can require the woman to provide a certificate from a doctor, midwife or health visitor stating that she is pregnant and written proof of the appointment.[10]

An employer cannot unreasonably refuse time off for ante-natal care and this includes travelling time.[11] There is no obligation on the woman to arrange ante-natal care outside working hours or to make up the time.[12]

A woman who takes time off for ante-natal care is entitled to be paid as though she were still at work.[13]

If an employer refuses to give paid time off for ante-natal care a

8 ERA s55 and 56. The PWD contains a similar right to time off, without loss of pay, in order to attend ante-natal examinations (art 9).

9 *Satchwell Sunvic Ltd v Secretary of State for Employment* [1979] IRLR 455, EAT. See also *Gregory v Tudsbury Ltd* [1982] IRLR 267. The Secretary of State for Employment said in the parliamentary debates that ante-natal care would include relaxation classes (*Hansard* (HC), Standing Committee F, 12 January 1993, cols 291–292; *Hansard* (HL) 25 March 1993, cols 531–532). See also the DTI guide, *Maternity Rights*.

10 ERA s55(2) and (3).

11 See *Dhamrait v United Biscuits Ltd* COIT 1430/192 where the appointment lasted longer than expected and the woman missed the works bus. She was entitled to be paid for the whole shift. See also *Edgar v Giorgione Inns Ltd* COIT 1803/13.

12 *Edgar v Giorgione Inns Ltd* COIT 1803/13; *Bland v Laws (Confectioners) Ltd* COIT 1613/4 and *Sajil v Carraro t/a Foubert's Bar* COIT 1890/34; but see also *Gregory v Tudsbury Ltd* [1982] IRLR 267 where the tribunal suggested that an employer could reasonably refuse time off if a woman worked part-time and could arrange ante-natal care outside work.

13 If a week's pay is always the same, the hourly rate is calculated by dividing the week's pay by the hours worked. If the pay varies, it should be averaged over a 12-week period, ending with the last complete week before the day on which the time off is taken: ERA s56.

woman can complain (within three months) to an IT, which can make a declaration and order compensation.[14] Dismissal of a woman who alleges that the employer has failed to give paid time off or who complains to a tribunal is automatically unfair.[15]

15.4 Health and safety protection

Apart from their general common law and statutory duties to protect the health and safety of workers[16] employers are required to take particular account of risks to all pregnant women, women who have given birth within the previous six months and women who are breastfeeding (irrespective of the age of the baby).[17] The following is a very brief summary of the provisions (for further details see Palmer, *Maternity Rights* (LAG, 1996)).

15.4.1 Risk assessment

Where the workforce includes women of child-bearing age, the employer must carry out a risk assessment of any risk to the health and safety of a new or expectant mother, or to that of her baby.[18] In particular, the assessment must consider the risks set out in the Annexes to the PWD. These include handling of loads, noise, extremes of cold or heat, movements and postures, travelling and other physical burdens. There are some risks where there is an absolute prohibition on women working (eg, with zinc, lead, radiotherapy x-rays).

Employers must provide their employees with comprehensible and relevant information on the risks to their health and safety as identified by the assessment.

14 ERA s57.

15 For asserting a statutory right under ERA s104 or for a reason related to the woman's pregnancy under s99.

16 Under the Health and Safety at Work Act 1974 and the common law duty of care.

17 The Management of Health and Safety at Work (Amendment) Regulations 1994 SI No 2865 amended the Management of Health and Safety at Work Regulations (MHSWR) 1992 SI No 2051. The regulations do not apply to seafarers, including master and crew. This exception is likely to be in breach of the PWD though a private sector employee cannot rely on the Directive: see *Iske v P & O European Ferries (Dover) Ltd* [1997] IRLR 401. Evidently, steps are being taken to remove this exclusion.

18 MHSWR 1992 reg 3(1). This duty applies to employees and 'persons not in his employment arising out of or in connection with the conduct by him of his undertaking'.

15.4.2 *Preventive or protective action*

If the assessment reveals a risk the employer must consider whether it is possible to take preventive or protective action to avoid the risk. The relevant statutory provisions must be considered.

15.4.3 *Variation of a woman's working conditions*

If preventive action would not avoid the risk, the employer must consider temporarily varying the woman's working conditions if this is reasonable and would avoid the risk.

15.4.4 *Available suitable alternative work*

Where the employer cannot vary the working conditions it must offer the woman available suitable alternative work.[19] Failure to do so will be a breach of the ERA. It is also likely to be discriminatory if such work exists. In *Iske v P & O European Ferries (Dover) Ltd*[20] the EAT held that the failure to offer women seafarers shore-based work after the 28th week of pregnancy was discrimination.

15.4.5 *Suspension on full pay*

If no suitable alternative work is available, an employee must be suspended from work, on full pay, for as long as is necessary in order to avoid the risk. Pay is calculated in accordance with ERA s220 ff. If the woman refuses suitable alternative work she will forfeit her right to be paid while she is suspended.[21]

15.4.6 *Duty to notify employer of pregnancy*

The duties in **15.4.3** to **15.4.5** apply only where the woman has notified the employer of her condition.[22] If requested, in writing, by the employer, the woman must provide the employer with a doctor's or midwife's certificate confirming that she is pregnant.[23]

19 ERA ss66 and 67. The work must be of a kind which is both suitable in relation to her and appropriate for her to do in the circumstances and the terms and conditions must not be substantially less favourable than her existing terms and conditions.

20 See n17.

21 ERA s68.

22 MHSWR 1992 regs 13A(2) and (3) and 13C(1).

23 MHSWR 1992 reg 2.

15.4.7 Nightwork

If a pregnant woman or new mother doing nightwork obtains a certificate from her doctor or midwife stating that it is necessary for her health and safety to avoid such work, the employer must offer her available suitable alternative work. If this is not possible she must be suspended on full pay.[24]

15.4.8 Dismissal

Where a woman is dismissed for refusing to work because of a health and safety risk, this may be automatically unfair (see **17.6.2.1**).

15.4.9 Remedies

Where the employer has either failed to offer the woman available suitable alternative work or failed to give her full pay while suspended, the woman can complain to an IT within three months from the first day the employer failed to pay her or within three months of the first day of suspension.[25] The IT can award compensation. Where there has been a breach of the Management of Health and Safety at Work Regulations 1992 the woman can complain to the Health and Safety Executive. The HSE has issued useful guidance on the operation of the Regulations.[26] A woman injured as a result of a breach of the regulations can sue her employer in the county court.

15.5 Right to general maternity leave and extended maternity absence

There is a two-tier system of leave which depends on the woman's length of service with the employer:

a) *all* pregnant employees, irrespective of length of service or hours of work, are entitled to 14 weeks' *general maternity leave*; and
b) women who have been employed by the same employer for two years at the beginning of the 11th week before the expected week of childbirth (EWC)[27] are entitled to *extended maternity absence*

24 MHSWR 1992 reg 13B.
25 ERA s70.
26 *New and expectant mothers at work – a guide for employers* (1994).
27 'Childbirth' is defined as the birth of a living child or a child (whether living or dead) after 24 weeks of pregnancy. Expected week of childbirth is the week the baby is due; ERA s235.

of up to 29 weeks after the beginning of the week in which the baby was born.[28]

The distinction between 'leave' and 'absence' is important; not all women are entitled to maternity absence and women's rights during the two periods are different. The term 'absence' is also used to refer to the maternity absence to which women were entitled before 1994, when there was no right to maternity leave for all employees.

There is no longer any requirement to have worked a minimum number of hours per week.[29]

Women may also be entitled, under their contract of employment, to more favourable terms, such as longer leave or to extended leave irrespective of length of service. Where a woman has a contractual and statutory right to maternity leave she can take advantage of whichever right is, in any particular respect, more favourable.[30]

15.5.1 General maternity leave

15.5.1.1 Notice provisions

There are strict notice requirements and failure to comply with them may lead to the woman losing her *statutory* right to maternity leave and her rights during leave:[31]

a) the woman must notify her employer *in writing* at least 21 days before her maternity leave starts[32] or, if that is not reasonably practicable, as soon as is reasonably practicable, of:
   - the fact that she is pregnant;
   - the expected week of childbirth; or
   - the date of the birth (if it has occurred);[33] and
   - the fact that she wishes to be paid statutory maternity pay (see **16.5**).

   A woman entitled to extended maternity absence must at the same time give written notice that she intends to return to work (see **15.5.7.2**). If the baby is born before the woman has had a chance

28 The exclusions set out at **15.2.1** apply.

29 Employment Protection (Part-Time Employees) Regulations 1995 SI No 31.

30 ERA ss78 and 85.

31 ERA ss74–76 and 79. See *McPherson v Drumpark House* [1997] IRLR 277, but see also **17.6** for unfair dismissal provisions.

32 Which must not be earlier than the beginning of the 11th week before the expected week of childbirth.

33 ERA s75.

to give notice, she should give written notice of the birth as soon as possible.

b) the woman must inform her employer at least 21 days before her maternity leave starts, or, if that is not reasonably practicable, as soon as is reasonably practicable of the date she intends to start her maternity leave.[34]

The 21-day time limit under (b) does not apply if:

– a woman is absent because of her pregnancy in the six weeks before the EWC and the employer requires her to start her leave (see below); or
– she gives birth before she has notified the employer; or
– she gives birth before the notice expires.[35]

In these circumstances the woman's maternity leave will automatically start and notice must be given to the employer (either of the birth or that the absence is due to pregnancy), as soon as practically possible.[36]

Notice under (b) need be in writing only if requested by the employer.[37] However, in order to avoid any argument about whether notice has been given it is preferable to put it in writing (at the same time that notice under (a) above is given) and to keep a copy.

21 days' clear notice. Twenty-one clear days' notice should be given, excluding the day of notification and the day when maternity leave begins.[38]

Notice required for contractual rights to return. Where the woman claims the benefit of more favourable contractual terms but there is no provision in the contract (or by agreement with the employer) for notice, then the statutory provisions regarding notice will apply.[39]

Not reasonably practicable. It will be a question of fact as to whether it was reasonably practicable to give the 21 days' notice. Absence from work because of pregnancy complications may constitute a good reason particularly if the woman was unaware of her rights.[40] However, notice should always be given on time.

34 ERA s74(1).
35 In which case she will not be able to give appropriate notice.
36 ERA s74(4) and (5).
37 ERA s74(6).
38 *Rightside Properties Ltd v Gray* [1974] 2 All ER 1169.
39 *Kolfor Plant Ltd v Wright* [1982] IRLR 311, EAT.
40 *Simpson v Microponent Development Ltd* COIT 1327/85.

15.5.1.2 Employer's obligation to advise about rights

Employers have an obligation to advise employees of their contractual rights where these are not agreed with the employer but incorporated into the contract through a collective agreement. In *Scally v Southern Health and Social Services Board*[41] the House of Lords held that there was a contractual obligation on employers to take reasonable steps to bring the existence of a right to enhanced pension entitlement to the attention of employees. The same principle should apply to contractual maternity rights.

In *Gray v Smith*[42] an IT held that an employer which failed to provide an employee with any guidance about her statutory maternity rights had waived its right to strict compliance with the statutory notice procedure. There was no written maternity policy nor was any advice given about the applicant's right to maternity leave and/or pay. When Ms Gray asked for a date when she could go back to work, she was told there was no longer a job for her. The IT accepted that she had failed to comply with the notice provisions. The tribunal said that 'as the respondent had demonstrated a reckless disregard for his duties in relation to his employee's employment rights by failing to provide the applicant with a contract of employment and since he had not given her any guidance concerning her maternity rights either in respect of leave or pay, he had in the circumstances waived his rights relating to compliance with the strict provisions' of the law.

15.5.1.3 Provision of certificate giving EWC

If the employer requests the woman to provide a doctor's or midwife's certificate giving the EWC, she must do so within a reasonable time, or she may lose her right to maternity leave.[43] The employer's request must clearly require a certificate.[44]

15.5.2 Commencement of general maternity leave

General maternity leave cannot start earlier than the 11th week before the expected week of childbirth (unless the baby is born before the 11th week) or later than the birth.[45] Otherwise it is up to the woman to decide when her maternity leave starts. It will be the date she

41 [1991] IRLR 522, HL.
42 Case no: 03216/95; DCLD 30; 2 July 1996.
43 ERA s75(2).
44 *Eagles v Cadman t/a Baby Days* COIT 1334/181.
45 ERA s74(2).

notifies to her employer (as above), unless she is forced to commence her leave because of pregnancy-related sickness during the six weeks before the EWC (see below).

To calculate the earliest that maternity leave can start:

a) start with the EWC – the week begins on a Sunday;
b) count back 11 weeks (to the 11th Sunday – a week ends on a Saturday[46]);
c) the earliest leave can start is the 11th Sunday.[47]

Even if there is a provision in the contract stating that the woman must start her maternity leave at a specified time, this is overridden by the ERA which allows women to choose the date.[48]

Return from maternity leave is covered in Chapter 17.

15.5.3 *Illness due to pregnancy during the six weeks before EWC*

A woman who, in the six weeks before the expected week of childbirth, is absent wholly or partly because of her pregnancy will have to commence her leave from this date, unless her employer agrees otherwise.[49] She must notify the employer that the sickness is pregnancy-related (see **15.5.1.1**). This means that a woman who is off work for as little as a couple of hours because of pregnancy-related sickness may have her leave triggered and cannot take sick leave or pay.

Guidance on pregnancy-related illness is provided by the Benefits Agency Medical Service.[50] Absence at an ante-natal class should not count as pregnancy-related absence as there is a separate right to time off for ante-natal care; the DfEE and DSS guide confirms this.[51]

Refusal to allow a woman to take sick leave/pay because her sickness is pregnancy-related may itself be discrimination; any less favourable treatment of a pregnant woman is unlawful under EC law (see **17.7**). In addition, if a man who is on long-term sick pay would

46 See *Secretary of State for Employment v A Ford & Son (Sacks) Ltd* [1986] ICR 882, EAT.

47 Thus, if the baby is due on Wednesday 27 June 1996, the EWC begins on Sunday 23 June and 11 Sundays before this date will be 7 April 1996.

48 *Inner London Education Authority v Nash* [1979] ICR 229, EAT.

49 ERA s72(1). The statutory maternity pay period commences from the first date of pregnancy-related sickness and this cannot be overridden.

50 *Pregnancy related illness* (leaflet NI200) available free from Benefits Agency offices.

51 See *Maternity Rights* (leaflet PL958).

not be disqualified from sick pay/leave for any period of his sickness, then the woman is being treated less favourably, if she is denied sick pay/leave because of her pregnancy. This may be a breach art 119, which covers sick *pay*, or the ETD, which applies to sick *leave*. It may also be a breach of the PWD which has no parallel triggering provision. This question has been referred to the ECJ in *Boyle and Others v EOC*.[52]

15.5.4 *Stillbirths*

Women who have a stillbirth after the 24th week are still entitled to maternity leave and absence.

15.5.5 *Premature births*

The maternity leave period will automatically start from the day the baby is born.[53]

15.5.6 *Dismissal or resignation before the 11th week*

A woman who is dismissed or resigns before she reaches the 11th week will not be employed and will not have the automatic right to maternity leave. If her dismissal is related to her pregnancy it will automatically be unfair (see **17.6.2.1**).

15.5.7 *Extended maternity absence*

A woman who has been employed continuously for two years at the beginning of the 11th week before the expected week of childbirth is entitled to return to the same job on not less favourable terms up to 29 weeks after the beginning of the week in which the baby was born.[54] Maternity absence begins at the end of the maternity leave period. Note that the actual week of childbirth may well be different from the expected week of confinement.

15.5.7.1 *Continuous employment*

The woman must be employed at the beginning of the 11th week before the expected week of childbirth (or have already given birth). Continuous employment includes any week in which the employee

52 Case C-411/96; 97/C 54/23.
53 ERA s72(2).
54 ERA s79.

has a contract of employment with her employer. Thus an employee may be off on sick leave, on holiday, or on unpaid leave and still have a contract of employment.

15.5.7.2 Notice provisions

The notice provisions are the same as for general maternity leave (see **15.5.1.1**) with the following additional requirements:

a) The employee must inform her employer, *in writing*, at least 21 days before her maternity leave begins, or, if that is not reasonably practicable (see **15.5.1.1**), as soon as is reasonably practicable that she intends to return to work.

   An employee is generally well-advised to give notice of intention to return, even if she does not plan to or is unsure of her future plans. An employee who gives notice to return but who is unable or unwilling to return can change her mind later at no loss to herself. A conditional notice to return is not sufficient.

b) The woman must give written notice to the employer, at least 21 days before the day on which she proposes to return, of her proposal to return on that day.[55]

c) Where, not earlier than 21 days before the end of her maternity leave period (ie, after 22 weeks of maternity leave) the employer makes a request for *written* confirmation that she intends to return, the woman must provide written confirmation (of her intention to return) within 14 days of receiving the request (or, if that is not reasonably practicable, as soon as is reasonably practicable).[56] The woman need not give a date for her return until 21 days before she is due to return. The employer's request must be in writing and must explain the effect of this provision.[57]

As with general maternity leave, it is crucial that the notice requirements are followed; failure to do so may result in the right to return being lost. The woman must also provide a doctor's or midwife's certificate giving the EWC, if requested by the employer.

15.5.7.3 Duration of absence

Maternity absence begins at the end of maternity leave. The woman has a right to return to work up to 29 weeks after the beginning of the week of the birth. Postponement of return is covered in Chapter 17.

55 ERA s82(1).
56 ERA s80(2).
57 ERA s80(3).

KEY POINTS

- All pregnant women are entitled to paid time off for ante-natal care, which includes relaxation classes;
- Employers have specific health and safety duties towards pregnant women and new and breastfeeding mothers; this includes:

  a duty to carry out a risk assessment (and inform employees of any risks); and if there is a risk, to consider:
  - first, preventive or protective action;
  - second, varying the woman's working conditions to avoid the risk, and if this is not possible;
  - third, offering the woman suitable alternative work; and if this is not possible;
  - suspending the woman on full pay for as long as is necessary to avoid the risk;
  - where there is a medical certificate stating that there is risk for a woman who is doing nightwork, the employer must offer suitable alternative work or suspend on full pay.
- All pregnant employees are entitled to 14 weeks' maternity *leave.*
- Employers are obliged to advise women of their rights.
- A woman can choose when her leave starts, provided it is not earlier than 11 weeks before the expected week of childbirth, nor later than the birth; the only exception is where she is absent because of her pregnancy in the six weeks before the EWC in which case she may be triggered on to the leave.
- A woman who has been employed for two years at the beginning of the 11th week before the EWC is entitled to return to the same job up to 29 weeks after the beginning of the week of the birth. She must also comply with strict notice provisions.
- Maternity absence begins at the expiry of maternity leave.

CHAPTER 16

Rights during maternity leave and absence

This chapter explains rights during maternity leave and absence, including entitlement to statutory maternity pay.

16.1 Introduction

There is no right to receive full pay during maternity leave or absence unless the contract of employment makes provision for it.[1] In *Gillespie* the ECJ held that although maternity pay was 'pay' within art 119 (see **18.8.4**), there was no right to full pay during maternity leave or absence. This was because it was not possible to compare a woman on maternity leave (or absence) with a person at work. However, the ECJ did find that a pay rise (awarded after the calculation period for assessing maternity pay) should be reflected in a woman's maternity pay. The judgment makes it difficult to distinguish between benefits which are akin to pay (and therefore not payable) and those comparable to a pay rise (from which women should benefit).

Different principles apply to the 14-week maternity leave period and extended maternity absence.

16.2 Rights during maternity leave

During the 14 weeks' maternity leave employees are entitled, under ERA s71, to the same terms and conditions, *other than remuneration*, as they would have received if they had been at work. Remuneration is not defined. The government's view during the passage of the Bill

1 *Gillespie and Others v Northern Health and Social Services Board and Others* [1996] IRLR 214, ECJ.

was that it was narrower than 'pay'.[2] It does not include a company car or mobile phone, subsidised loans, mortgage, health and other insurance, holidays, pensions nor luncheon vouchers.[3] Arguably, remuneration should only include money, such as basic pay which would have been earned by the woman during the 14-week period if she had been at work.

The following is a summary of how different benefits should be treated.

16.2.1 Bonuses and commission

A woman denied a bonus or commission while on leave may have a claim under the ERA, EqPA, PWD or art 119. There may also be an unlawful deduction of wages under ERA Part II.

Whether bonuses and commission count as 'remuneration' under the ERA depends on the type of bonus (or commission) and the terms of the scheme. The test is, arguably, whether the payment is made in relation to work actually done. A contractual bonus or commission payable in respect of work which would have been done by the woman if she had not been on leave may count as remuneration and therefore not be payable. This would apply to productivity pay based on individual performance. A bonus or commission which is payable in respect of work done by the whole workforce should arguably be paid to a woman on leave; it is not dependant on her being at work. In *Iverson v P & O European Ferries (Dover) Ltd* [4] the tribunal held that profit-related pay *was* payable (under the EqPA and art 119) as it was paid whether or not an employee had earned profit.

16.2.2 Company cars and mobile phones

Where a company car or mobile phone is for business and personal use (as opposed to just business use), the woman should be entitled to use it during maternity leave.[5]

2 See *Hansard*, Standing Committee F, 12 January 1993, cols 310, 316 and 317. See also 14 January 1993, col 396, where the government spokesperson said that all the terms and conditions of the contract, with the sole exception of those relating to wages and salary, will continue.

3 Viscount Ullswater considered these should not count as remuneration (*Hansard* (HL), 25 March 1993, col 548).

4 57265/95/C, Ashford IT.

5 See *Hansard*, Standing Committee F, 12 January 1993, col 314.

16.2.3 *Other benefits in kind and 'perks'*

These include subsidised loans and mortgages, participation in share schemes, private health insurance, free travel, club membership. These should continue to be paid during maternity leave.

16.2.4 *Holidays*

Although holiday entitlement accrues during maternity leave, there is no right to carry leave over into the next holiday year or to be paid in lieu; entitlement to this will depend on the contract.

16.2.5 *Pensions*

During maternity leave the employer must continue to pay pension contributions as though the woman were working normally and irrespective of whether she returns to work at the end of her leave. In addition, Social Security Act 1989 Sch 5 provides that a woman on paid maternity leave or absence must be treated as though she were at work and receiving full pay. The employer must pay full contributions but the employee need pay only contributions based on her actual pay (which may merely be SMP). She will continue to accrue rights and benefits during her paid leave.

16.2.6 *Continuity of service is preserved during maternity leave*

During the 14-week maternity leave period the contract of employment continues, irrespective of pay, length of service or hours of work.[6]

16.2.7 *Statutory sick pay*

There is no entitlement to statutory sick pay during the 18-week maternity pay period.[7] This applies even if the woman returns to work before the end of the period and then falls sick.

16.2.8 *Occupational or contractual sick pay*

'Sick pay' is likely to be treated as 'remuneration' so will not be payable under the ERA. In *Todd v Eastern Health and Social Services*

6 ERA s71.
7 Social Security Contributions and Benefits Act 1992 s153 and Sch 11 para 2(h).

Board and DHSS[8] the NICA held that pregnancy could not be compared with sickness. The employer was not, therefore, required to fix maternity pay at the same level as contractual sickness benefit.

16.3 Rights during extended maternity absence

It is unclear whether women are entitled to contractual rights during extended maternity absence and it will mainly depend on the contractual terms and how other employees in a similar situation are treated. There are four possible claims:

a) under the contract;
b) under the SDA and ETD;
c) under the EqPA and art 119;
d) under the PWD.

16.3.1 Under the contract

The status of a woman's contract during maternity absence is unclear and it is important to consider the terms of the contract and any agreement (written or verbal) between employer and employee. It is a question of fact in each case as to whether the contract continues. If the contract does not continue during the absence there will clearly be no entitlement to contractual rights.

In *Institute of the Motor Industry v Harvey*[9] and *Hilton International Hotels (UK) Ltd v Kaissi*[10] the EAT held that the contract continued during the absence if neither party brought it to an end. In *Harvey* the EAT held that if a woman gives notice of intention to take maternity leave, her contract of employment is likely to continue when she goes on maternity leave unless it is terminated by agreement, resignation or dismissal.[11]

8 [1997] IRLR 410.
9 [1992] IRLR 343.
10 [1994] IRLR 273; [1994] ICR 578, EAT.
11 In *Lewis Woolf Griptight Ltd v Corfield* EAT/1073/96 the EAT upheld the IT finding that the contract continued during maternity absence because the employer recognised that C's absence (after the end of the maternity absence) was because of illness. On the other hand, in *Crees v Royal London Insurance* [1997] IRLR 85 the contract of employment specifically provided that the employee forfeited her right to return if she failed to comply with the statutory notice provisions. In *McPherson v Drumpark House* [1997] IRLR 277 the EAT said the payment of maternity pay is neutral as to whether the contract continues. See also *Kwik Save Stores v Greaves* [1997] IRLR 268.

In *Crouch v Kidsons Impey*[12] the EAT held that where there was no right to return to work, and no express agreement or proper inference, the concept of a 'ghost' contract was fanciful. *Crouch* is arguably wrong. Either the employer terminates the contract before or during maternity leave or the contract continues until such later time as it is terminated. In either case the employer risks a claim by the employee for unfair dismissal. An employer can only assume that the employee has resigned if she gives proper notice.[13]

Even if the contract subsists, it is not clear whether all contractual rights (apart from the employer's obligation to pay and the employee's obligation to work) are suspended during the absence (as suggested in *Institute of the Motor Industry v Harvey*[14]). It will be necessary to consider carefully the terms of the contract in each case.

Where, as is common, there is no agreement or termination by employer or employee, the contract should be treated as continuing along with the terms and conditions (apart from remuneration). However, the position is far from clear and will hopefully be resolved by the CA in *Crees* and *Greaves*.

16.3.2 The SDA and ETD

A woman who does not receive a non-contractual benefit while she is on maternity absence may be able to claim discrimination if an employee on other leave would be entitled to the benefit. There are no binding decisions.[15]

16.3.3 EqPA and art 119

There are two arguments:

12 [1996] IRLR 79, EAT. Note the facts arose prior to entitlement to 14 weeks' leave.

13 This is consistent with *Hughes v Gwynedd Area Health Authority* [1977] IRLR 436, EAT, in which it was held that notice to terminate a contract must be specific and a statement of general intention was not proper notice. The courts have also been reluctant to uphold contractual agreements which purport to treat the contract as automatically terminated if the employee commits, or fails to perform, a certain act, particularly if this would deprive an employee of protection: see *Igbo v Johnson Matthey Chemicals Ltd* [1986] IRLR 215.

14 [1992] IRLR 343.

15 But see *Pridden v Warrington Community Health Care (NHS) Trust* (1995) Case no 66232/93, 6 June, Liverpool IT, in which it was held that a woman on maternity absence should be given credit for bank holidays where an employee on sick leave received credit.

a) Any payment or benefit which is payable irrespective of whether the woman is at work should continue to be paid during absence. In *Gillespie* (see above) the ECJ said, in relation to the pay rise, that to deny her an increase while she was on leave (or absence) 'would discriminate against her purely in her capacity as a worker since, had she not been pregnant, she would have received the pay rise'. Arguably, all the ECJ was saying in *Gillespie* was that for the purposes of maternity pay (and other payments received for work actually done) a woman cannot be compared to an employee at work. Any other benefits (which do not depend on her being 'at work') should be paid.

b) A woman on maternity absence should not be treated any worse than any other employee on leave for another reason. Although, following *Gillespie*, a woman may not be able to compare herself with an employee *at work*, she can arguably compare herself with an employee *not at work* (see *Iverson* at **16.2.1**).

16.3.4 Pregnant Workers Directive

The PWD provides that contractual rights must be maintained during maternity leave, which must be a minimum of 14 weeks. It is not clear whether the obligation to maintain contractual rights applies to all periods of maternity leave (including absence) or only the minimum period. Arguably it does, because art 8 sets only a *minimum* period for maternity leave. Note, however, that only public sector employees can rely directly on the Directive (see **16.3.5**).

16.3.5 Reference to ECJ

Many of these issues will be resolved in *Boyle.*[16] The ECJ has been asked to decide if the following are a breach of EC law:

- a condition limiting the time during which annual leave accrues to the statutory minimum period of 14 weeks' maternity leave;
- a condition limiting the time in which pensionable service accrues during maternity leave to when the woman is in receipt of contractual or statutory maternity pay and accordingly excluding any period of unpaid maternity absence.

16 *Boyle & Others v EOC* Case C-411/96; 97/C 54/23.

16.3.6 Continuity of service during extended maternity absence

Even where there is no contract, continuity for the purposes of statutory rights is maintained if the woman returns to work.[17] For the purposes of contractual rights (eg, the woman's seniority) the woman's service after maternity absence is treated as continuous with the period of employment before the end of the leave. The period of absence (ie, from the end of maternity leave until the date she returns) is not counted.[18] When the contract continues the period of maternity absence will count for the purposes of statutory rights.[19]

16.3.7 Remedies

Enforcement of these contractual rights will either be in the IT where the claim is under the SDA, the EqPA or for a deduction of wages under ERA Part II or in the county court for breach of contract.

16.4 Sickness during and at the end of maternity absence

It is unlikely that a woman will be able to claim sick pay while on maternity leave or absence unless the contract provides for this (see **16.2.8**). However, the ECJ has been asked to decide if it is a breach of EC law to prohibit a woman who is unfit for work for any reason while on maternity leave, from taking paid sick leave, unless she elects to return to work and terminate her maternity leave (see *Boyle* above).

Where a woman is sick during her maternity absence she can choose to return to work (by giving 21 days' notice) and should then be able to claim sick pay or SSP (where she qualifies). She will not then be able to go back on to maternity absence.

In order to exercise her return to work, two EAT decisions suggest that the woman must return to work physically.[20] However, in a more recent decision[21] the EAT upheld the IT's finding that the applicant, who was dismissed because sickness prevented her returning to work after her absence, had suffered discrimination. The employer had

17 ERA s212(2).
18 ERA s79(2).
19 ERA s212(2).
20 See *Crees v The Royal London Mutual Insurance Society Ltd* [1997] IRLR 85; see also *Kwik Save Stores Ltd v Greaves* [1997] IRLR 268. This in on appeal.
21 *Lewis Woolf Griptight Ltd v Corfield* EAT/1073/96.

used the statutory provisions designed to protect the employee as an excuse for dismissing her. As such an excuse could not have applied to a man, it was discrimination (see also **16.3.1** and **17.2.5**).

16.5 Statutory maternity pay (SMP)

The provisions are contained in the Social Security Contributions and Benefits Act 1992 (SSCBA) and the Statutory Maternity Pay (General) Regulations 1986 (SMP Regs).[22] SMP is paid only to employees earning more than the lower earnings limit (in the relevant period) but it is not a contributory benefit. A woman who does not normally pay national insurance contributions will still be entitled to SMP, which is paid by the employer.

The main qualifying conditions are that the woman must:

a) be an employee or hold an elective office;
b) have been earning at least the lower earnings limit for national insurance for the eight weeks or two months immediately before and including the qualifying week. The qualifying week is the 15th week before the expected week of childbirth. The lower earnings limit is £62 per week for 1997/98;
c) not fall within one of the limited exceptions (eg, prisoners);
d) have 26 weeks' continuous service at the qualifying week; the woman must have worked for one day of the qualifying week;
e) be pregnant and have reached the 11th week before the EWC; SMP is not payable before the 11th week before the EWC, unless the baby is born before;
f) produce medical evidence, ie, a maternity certificate (form MATB1) showing the EWC. This must be given to the employer by the end of the third week of the maternity pay period;
g) give the employer 21 *clear* days' notice of the date that she intends to stop work because she is pregnant. The notice need be in writing only if the employer so requests;
h) have stopped working.

Note that:

- SMP is payable by the employer even if the woman does not intend to return to work and irrespective of whether the contract subsists during the SMP period;
- if the woman resigns, she does not have to repay her SMP;

22 SI No 1960 (as amended).

- if a woman has more than one employer, each must pay her SMP if she qualified;
- there is no requirement for the woman to be working for a minimum number of hours per week, but the lower earnings limit excludes many part-time women;
- no employers are exempt from paying SMP;
- a week begins on a Sunday.

SMP is paid by the employer for up to 18 weeks, at 90% of full pay for the first six weeks and £55.70 for the remaining 12 weeks. Employers are reimbursed through deductions from their national insurance bill.

SMP is payable from the time the woman stops work and this is usually her decision. However, the SMP payment period will start immediately where a woman has a pregnancy-related absence during the six weeks before the EWC. The detailed provisions are set out in Palmer, *Maternity Rights* (LAG, 1996).

16.6 Contractual maternity pay

A woman may be entitled to contractual maternity pay which is more than the SMP. Some employers impose a condition that this is payable only if the woman states that she intends to return to work and agrees to be liable to repay such maternity pay if she does not return to work for a minimum period. The question of whether this is a breach of EC law has been referred to the ECJ in *Boyle* (see above).

16.7 Maternity allowance

Where there is no entitlement to SMP the woman may be entitled to maternity allowance from the Benefits Agency where:

a) she has been working (either employed or self-employed) for at least 26 weeks in the 66 weeks immediately before the week the baby is due; and
b) she has paid 26 weeks of Class 1 national insurance contributions in the 66-week period; and
c) she is pregnant and has reached the 11th week before the expected week of childbirth (or has given birth).

Finally, pregnant women and women on maternity leave may be entitled to other welfare benefits, such as free prescriptions and dental treatment.

KEY POINTS

- There is no right to full pay during maternity leave (or absence) unless the contract provides for it.

Rights during maternity leave

- The contract continues during the maternity leave period.
- The woman is entitled to the same terms and conditions *except remuneration.*
- Remuneration is narrower than pay and probably includes only basic pay which the woman would have earned had she been at work.
- Contractual benefits which should continue to be paid include:
  - certain bonuses and commission;
  - company car, mobile phone (where not only for business use);
  - other benefits or perks, such as subsidised loans, insurance, club membership;
  - holiday entitlement;
  - occupational pensions.
- Women are not entitled to SSP during the maternity pay period.
- Full pension payments must be maintained during maternity leave and paid absence; the woman will only pay contributions based on her actual income.
- Continuity of service continues during the maternity leave period.
- Where a woman on maternity leave is treated less favourably than an employee on other leave, this may be a breach of the SDA or EqPA.
- A claim will usually be made in the county court (for breach of contract) or in the tribunal if there is discrimination or unlawful deduction from wages.

Rights during maternity absence

- Rights depend on:
  - whether the contract continues during the absence; if it does, which terms and conditions still apply;
  - whether, under the EqPA and art 119, it is discrimination to deny a woman on maternity absence all benefits apart from pay;

  - whether a woman can claim the benefits of any terms and conditions which would be given to an employee on some other form of leave;
  - whether the PWD provides more favourable rights.
- Continuity of service, for the purposes of statutory rights, continues during absence. For contractual rights the absence does not count; the woman's service after the absence is treated as continuous with the period before the end of the leave.
- Statutory maternity pay is payable to employees:
  - who have earned at least the lower earnings limit for national insurance in the eight-week or two-month period immediately before the qualifying week;
  - who have 26 weeks' continuous service with the employer;
  - comply with the notice provisions and provide medical evidence;
  - who have stopped working.
- Women not entitled to SMP may be entitled to maternity allowance.

CHAPTER 17

Returning to work and unfair dismissal

This chapter covers the right to return to work after maternity leave and absence, returning part-time or on a flexible working arrangement and unfair dismissal.

17.1 Right to return to work after maternity leave

The maternity leave usually ends 14 weeks after it began[1] (though there may be an agreement to extend it). If the woman intends to return to work at the end of the 14-week period, there is no requirement to notify the employer; she can just turn up at work. If she wishes to return earlier she must give at least seven days' notice.[2] If she does not give seven days' notice the employer can postpone the woman's return to the day when the notice would have expired, provided it is not later than the end of the 14 weeks. The employer is entitled to refuse to pay the woman until she has given the required notice.[3]

17.1.1 Prohibition on working within two weeks of childbirth

A woman is not allowed to work during the two weeks which begin with the day the baby was born.[4] This applies even if the woman has used up her 14 weeks' maternity leave. Her maternity leave will be extended until two weeks after the birth.

1 ERA s73(1).
2 ERA s76(1).
3 ERA s76(2).
4 ERA s73 and PWD art 8(2) implemented by Maternity (Compulsory Leave) Regulations 1994 SI No 2479 reg 2.

17.1.2 Women working in a factory

Health and safety regulations provide that a woman working in a factory must not return to work within four weeks of childbirth.[5]

17.1.3 Protection from dismissal at end of maternity leave in case of illness

A woman who is unable, because of sickness, to return to work at the end of her leave is protected from dismissal for upto four weeks, provided a medical certificate is given to the employer before the end of the maternity leave period (see **17.6.2.3**).[6] She is not on maternity leave during this period, so is not entitled to the benefit of her contractual terms (see **16.2**). She should be entitled to receive SMP and also occupational sick pay like any other sick employee.

17.1.4 Failure to return at end of maternity leave period

A woman who does not return after her leave should be treated like any other employee who does not return after authorised leave. If the employer dismisses her (and a refusal to allow her to return would amount to a dismissal) for a reason connected to her pregnancy or maternity leave this will be automatically unfair (see **17.6.2**).

Thus, for example, if the woman is dismissed for unauthorised absence or sickness in circumstances where another employee would not be dismissed, there may be an inference that the reason was connected with her absence on maternity leave. The fact that the woman has taken maternity leave should be ignored.

17.1.5 Right to return to the same job after general maternity leave

Women who return to work after 14 weeks' maternity leave have a right to return to *exactly the same job on the same terms and conditions* as if they had never been absent.

17.2 Right to return after extended maternity absence

Whether or not the woman's contract subsists during maternity absence (see **16.3.1**), she has a *statutory* right to return provided she

5 Public Health Act 1936 s205.
6 ERA s99(3).

has complied with the notice provisions. In order to exercise her *statutory* right to return the woman must *physically* return to work.[7] Where she does not have a *statutory* right (for example, because she could not physically return to work due to sickness), the woman may still be protected from unfair dismissal and discrimination provided her contract subsists (see **16.3.1** and **16.4**).

17.2.1 Postponement of return by employer

The employer may postpone the woman's date of return by up to four weeks after the notified date of return if it notifies her, before the notified date of return, that for specified reasons it is postponing her return.[8]

17.2.2 Postponement of return by employee due to sickness

The woman may postpone her return for up to four weeks where, either before the end of the 29 weeks or before the notified date of return, she gives her employer a doctor's certificate saying she will be incapable of work.[9] She can postpone her return only once, even if she has had only a week's extension because of sickness.[10] If a woman is still sick at the end of the extended period, she should be treated like any other employee who is sick at the end of a period of authorised leave (see **16.4**).[11]

17.2.3 Industrial action preventing a return to work

The woman's return may be postponed until after the industrial action.[12] She must still give 21 days' notice of her return.

17.2.4 Right to return to previous job

The right to return is to the job in which the woman was employed when she went on maternity leave:

7 *Crees v Royal London Mutual Insurance Society* [1997] IRLR 85.
8 ERA s82(2).
9 ERA s82(3) and (4).
10 See *Dowuona v John Lewis plc* [1987] IRLR 310, CA.
11 Note, however, that she will only be able to claim unfair dismissal if her contract subsists. In *Kelly v Liverpool Maritime Terminals Ltd* [1988] IRLR 310, CA, it was held that a woman who sent in a sick note could not be said to be exercising her right to return and claiming sick leave. She must physically return to work (see **16.4**).
12 ERA s82(6) and (7).

a) on no less favourable terms and conditions as to remuneration;
b) with preserved seniority, pension rights and other rights;
c) on no other less favourable terms and conditions.[13]

Failure to allow a woman to return at all or to return to the same or equivalent job will be a deemed dismissal (see **17.6.4**).

17.2.5 Exceptions to right to return

There are two exceptions:

a) where it is not reasonably practicable for a small employer[14] to allow the woman to return to her original job and there is no suitable alternative work with the employer or successor;[15]
b) where it is not reasonably practicable for a reason *other than redundancy* for the employer (or successor) to permit the woman to return to her old job and the employer or associated employer has offered her suitable alternative work which she has either accepted or unreasonably refused;[16]

The employer must show that the exception applies. In either case, the failure to allow a woman to return may still be unfair or discriminatory (see **17.6.10** and **17.6.13**).

17.2.6 What is the 'same job'?

'Job' means the nature of the work which the employee is employed to do under her contract and the capacity and place in which she is employed.[17] If a woman is offered a lower grade job or one with less responsibility or different hours or in a different location, it will not be the same job. It will be a question of fact in each case and the tribunal will look at what she is required to do under the contract and in practice and her terms and conditions of employment. For example, in *McFadden v Greater Glasgow Passenger Transport*

13 ERA s79(2). Terms and conditions must be the same as they were at the end of maternity leave (see **16.3.6**).
14 Where the total number of employees (including those of an associated employer) does not exceed five.
15 ERA s96(2) to (4); see *Stewart and Gower t/a Gowers v Male* (1994) 19 MAy, EAT 813/93.
16 ERA s96(2) to (4).
17 ERA s235(1).

Executive[18] the applicant was replaced by another clerk while she was on maternity leave. When she returned she was placed in another section as an unestablished clerk. Although her hours of work and pay were the same the IT held that the new terms and conditions were less favourable as she no longer had her own desk and was not sure of getting a full day's work. She had therefore been unfairly dismissed (see also **17.6**). A change in hours or working time may also be indirectly discriminatory (see **10.9**).

The woman can continue working under protest and make a claim for reinstatement into her old job. Alternatively, she can resign and claim constructive dismissal and possibly discrimination (see **14.2.7**).

17.3 Transfer of undertakings

Where there is a transfer the contract and all rights and obligations are transferred to the transferee. Thus, if there is a transfer when the woman is on leave or absence, she has the same rights against the new employer and her service will be treated as continuous.

17.4 Contractual right to return – composite right

Where an employee has a statutory *and* contractual right (whether written or oral) to maternity leave and/or absence, the employee can take advantage of whichever right is, in any particular respect, the more favourable.[20] If the contractual right is less favourable than the statutory right, the latter will apply.

17.5 Right to return part-time or on flexible hours

A woman returning from either general maternity leave or extended maternity absence can ask to return part-time or as a job-sharer. Refusal to allow a woman to work part-time or to job share *may* be indirectly discriminatory (see Chapter 3). Women may also want to consider other forms of flexible working, such as working partly from home, taking time off in the school holidays. The same principles apply.

18 [1977] IRLR 327.
19 Transfer of Undertakings (Protection of Employment) Regulations 1981 SI No 1794.
20 ERA ss78 and 85.

The main issue will be whether the employer can justify the refusal to allow part-time or flexible working. The following are examples.

17.5.1 *Blanket policy likely to be unlawful*

A blanket policy against flexible working, where no account is taken of individual circumstances, was held to be unlawful discrimination in *Barrett v Newport BC*.[21]

17.5.2 *Job-sharing at managerial/supervisory level*

In *Given v Scottish Power plc*[22] the applicant (who managed 10 to 12 team members) was told that it was a policy that at the applicant's grade she could not job share because of 'operational' matters. The IT held that the employer had not properly assessed the applicant's duties. She was awarded £5,000 for injury to feelings and £30,000 loss of earnings.

17.5.3 *Long hours are part of the job*

In *Robinson v Oddbins Ltd*[23] the EAT held that a term in a branch manager's contract requiring her to work 'such hours as may be necessary' over and above her standard working week was indirectly discriminatory (see **10.9**).

17.5.4 *Part-timers are more expensive*

In *Home Office v Holmes*[24] the EAT rejected the Home Office's argument that two part-timers cost more than one full-timer (see **3.6.7.4**).

17.5.5 *The clients require continuity*

In *Todd v Rushcliffe BC*[25] a housing officer was not allowed to return to work on a job-share because of the alleged need for continuity in dealing with individual members of the public. However, a recently introduced team system meant that any officer could deal with the

21 Case no: 34096/91, IT.
22 (1995) Case no S/3172/94, 20 January, Glasgow IT.
23 (1996) Case no 4224/95, DCLD 27, 5 January.
24 [1984] IRLR 299, EAT.
25 Case no 11339/90, IT.

public and even full-timers were regularly absent because of holidays, sickness, etc. Thus, the refusal was not justified.

17.5.6 Offer of alternative part-time job not sufficient

In *Clay v The Governors, English Martyrs School*[26] a teacher was offered an alternative part-time job. The tribunal held that although the introduction of a job-sharing scheme causes considerable logistical problems, there was no evidence that it could be detrimental to the school. The applicant was entitled to return to the same job on a part-time basis.

Note that the time limit for bringing a claim runs from the date the woman was *first* refused her request to work part-time (see **3.6.3**).[27]

17.5.7 European Council Recommendation on Childcare

This was adopted by the UK government in 1992. Although not legally binding, the ECJ has ruled that domestic courts are bound to take Recommendations into account. The Recommendation takes a broad approach to reconciling employment with the 'upbringing responsibilities arising from the care of children' (see **11.2**).

17.5.8 The European framework agreement on part-time work

The agreement provides that, as far as possible, employers should give consideration to:

a) requests by workers to transfer from full-time to part-time work that becomes available[
b) requests by workers to transfer from part-time to full-time work;
c) the provision of information on the availability of part-time and full-time work.

A directive will be introduced to implement these provisions but this is unlikely to come into force before the end of 1999.

17.6 Unfair dismissal

A dismissal may be automatically unfair, ordinarily unfair or discriminatory. There is no qualifying period for automatically unfair

26 (1993) Case no 52319/91, 8 January, Leicester IT.
27 *Cast v Croydon College* [1997] IRLR 14.

dismissal or for discrimination. Failure to renew a fixed-term contract on the same terms is a dismissal and similar principles apply.[28]

17.6.1 Need to show subsistence of contract if dismissal after maternity leave period

There can only be a dismissal if there is a contract in existence. The contract subsists during maternity leave. If not terminated by either employer or employee it should continue during maternity absence (see **16.3.1**).

If the contract subsists the woman will be able to make a claim for dismissal (ordinary, automatic or discriminatory) even if she has no contractual or statutory right to return.[29]

There are some exceptions (women working outside GB, share fisherwomen, the police and armed forces) which are set out at **15.2.1**.

17.6.2 Automatically unfair dismissal under ERA s99

It is automatically unfair to dismiss a woman where the reason, or main reason for the dismissal is one of the following:

17.6.2.1 Pregnancy-related dismissal

Where a woman is dismissed because she is pregnant or for any other reason connected with her pregnancy this will be automatically unfair and discriminatory[30] (eg, pregnancy-related sickness). This is not limited in time and could apply, for example, to dismissal for a pregnancy-related illness arising after the woman has returned to work.

If the reason for dismissal has anything to do with pregnancy, such as a miscarriage, pregnancy-related sickness, lateness due to morning sickness, inability to do the work because of pregnancy-related tiredness or a health and safety risk, the dismissal is likely to be automatically unfair. Thus, if a woman would not have been dismissed 'but for' the pregnancy-related sickness absence, the dismissal will be unfair.[31] It may also be discriminatory (see **17.6.13**).

28 ERA s95(1)(b); SDA s82(1A). Note that there is an exception where there is a fixed-term contract of one year or more and the employee has agreed in writing to exclude any claim for unfair dismissal. This is likely to be a breach of EC law.

29 *Hilton International Hotels (UK) Ltd v Kaissi* [1994] IRLR 273; [1994] ICR 578, EAT, and other similar cases set out at **16.3.1**.

30 ERA s99(1)(a).

31 See *George v Beecham Group* [1977] IRLR 43; see *James v Eastleigh BC* [1990] IRLR 288..

In order to claim that the dismissal was for a pregnancy-related reason the employer must be aware that the woman is pregnant.[32] It may therefore be advisable to inform the employer, preferably in writing, of pregnancy at an early stage. However, some employeres may fear this could lead to early dismissal and the consequent loss of SMP (see **16.5**).

17.6.2.2 Dismissal during maternity leave period for reason connected to childbirth

Where the woman's maternity leave period (MLP) is ended by dismissal (including the failure to renew a fixed-term contract)[33] and the reason for the dismissal is that she has had a baby or for any reason connected with the childbirth or leave, this will be automatically unfair.[34] The MLP ends at the same time.[35] Thus, she is not entitled to return to work at the end of the 14 weeks but she will have a claim for unfair dismissal.

17.6.2.3 Dismissal during the four weeks after maternity leave period because of sickness

It will be automatically unfair to dismiss a woman where:

- the woman told her employer she would be unable to return to work at the end of her MLP; and
- before the end of her MLP she provided the employer with a doctor's certificate stating she was unable to work for health reasons; and
- she was dismissed during the four weeks after the end of her leave while incapable of working and where she has a doctor's certificate for the period; and
- the reason was that she had given birth or for a reason connected to the birth.[36]

The illness need not be related to the pregnancy or childbirth though the dismissal must be for a reason connected with the woman having given birth. The protection from dismissal only lasts as long as the woman continues to be incapable of work and has a current medical certificate.

32 *Del Monte Foods Ltd v Mundon* [1980] IRLR 224.
33 See *Caruana v Manchester Airport plc* [1996] IRLR 378, EAT.
34 ERA s99(1)(b).
35 ERA s73(3).
36 ERA s99(3).

17.6.2.4 *Dismissal after end of maternity leave period*

Where a woman is dismissed after the end of the MLP and the reason for the dismissal is that the woman has taken maternity leave or the benefits of maternity leave this will be automatically unfair.[37]

17.6.2.5 *Redundancy during maternity leave period and failure to offer suitable alternative work*

Where the woman's MLP is ended by dismissal and the reason for the dismissal is that she is redundant and has not been offered suitable available employment, this will be automatically unfair (see **14.3.2.4**).[38]

17.6.2.6 *Redundancy during maternity absence and failure to offer suitable available work*

Where a woman with a right to extended maternity absence, is denied her right to return because of redundancy and is not offered a suitable alternative vacancy, this will be automatically unfair.[39]

Where there is a suitable alternative job, a woman on maternity leave or absence must be offered it, in preference to other redundant employees.[40] This applies if the job becomes available at any time during the leave or absence period, provided the woman has (in the case of maternity absence) given notice of her intention to return.[41]

The alternative employment (which may be with her employer or its successor or an associated employer) must, in the case of redundancy during maternity leave, take effect immediately on the ending of her previous contract. Where the redundancy takes place during or at the end of maternity absence the terms and conditions must be not substantially less favourable than if she had exercised her right to return to her old job.

The work must be suitable and appropriate for the woman, and the capacity and place in which she is employed and the terms and conditions must be not substantially less favourable.

Note that it is automatically unfair (and discriminatory) to make a woman redundant for a reason related to her pregnancy, childbirth or maternity leave.[42]

37 ERA s99(1)(c).
38 ERA s99(1)(e).
39 ERA s99(4).
40 ERA ss77 and 81.
41 *Philip Hodges & Co v Kell* [1994] IRLR 568, EAT.
42 See *Brown v Stockton-on-Tees BC* [1988] IRLR 263, HL.

17.6.2.7 Dismissal because of requirement to suspend

Where the reason for the dismissal is a requirement or recommendation to suspend on health and safety grounds, this will be automatically unfair.[43] Any dismissal resulting from an employer's attempt to avoid health and safety duties (see **15.4**) is likely to be automatically unfair.[44] In *Habermann Beltermann*,[45] where the employer dismissed a woman night worker because German law prohibited pregnant women working at night, the ECJ held that to allow an employer to dismiss a woman because of the temporary inability of the pregnant employee to perform night-time work would be contrary to the objective of protecting women.

17.6.3 Dismissal does not destroy the right to return

An employer cannot avoid a woman exercising her right to return by dismissing her during her MLP or maternity absence. Despite the dismissal she will be entitled to return to the same job and if the employer does not allow her to return it will be a deemed dismissal. If she does return, she may have to repay any compensation paid as a result of the earlier dismissal if requested to do so.[46]

17.6.4 Dismissal while exercising right to return

An employer who does not allow a woman to return to her job will be deemed to have dismissed her for the reason she is not allowed to return.[47] It is irrelevant whether the contract subsists. If the reason for the dismissal comes within ERA s99 (see above) it will be automatically unfair. It may also be an ordinary dismissal or discriminatory.

17.6.5 Effect of failure to exercise rights to return

Under the old Employment Protection (Consolidation) Act 1978 there were complex provisions which the courts interpreted as preventing a woman claiming unfair dismissal where she had a statutory *and* contractual right to return and failed to give the appropriate notice.[48] In

43 ERA s99(1)(d).

44 ERA ss 99, 100 and 104.

45 *Habermann Beltermann v Arbeiterwohlfahrt, Bezirksverband Ndb/Opf eV (Case C-421/92)* [1994] IRLR 364, ECJ.

46 ERA s84.

47 ERA s96(1), provided one of the exceptions does not apply.

48 See *Lavery v Plessey Telecommunications Ltd* [1983] IRLR 202, CA.

Crouch v Kidsons Impey (see **16.3.1**) and *Greaves* (see **16.3.1**) the EAT considered that these statutory provisions had been wrongly interpreted. As these provisions have not been reproduced in the ERA, the problem should not arise. A woman who has failed to give proper notice, and so has lost her statutory right to return, should be able to claim ordinary unfair dismissal provided her contract subsists (see **16.3.1**). There is an argument that where an employer uses the statutory scheme as an excuse to dismiss a woman who is ill at the end of her absence (so cannot return to work) this is likely to be discriminatory (see **16.4**). Where a woman's contract does not continue during her maternity absence and she has no separate contractual right to return, she will have only her statutory right to return.

17.6.6 *Written reasons for dismissal*

If the woman is dismissed while she is pregnant or where her general maternity leave ends by dismissal the employer must give written reasons for her dismissal.[49] This applies irrespective of the woman's length of service and regardless of whether she requests a statement. The statement is admissible in evidence.[50]

17.6.7 *Burden of proof*

The woman must first prove that she has been dismissed. Where the woman has two years' service, the employer must show the reason for the dismissal. In other cases the woman must establish that the reason for the dismissal is related to her pregnancy or maternity leave. If it is, the dismissal is automatically unfair. The principles are similar to those for establishing discrimination (see Chapter 2). The employer has no defence so cannot justify the dismissal.[51]

17.6.8 *Notice pay*

Where either the employer or employee gives notice to terminate the contract at a time when the woman is absent from work because of

49 ERA s92(4); see also PWD art 10(2).

50 A woman can complain to a tribunal if the employer unreasonably fails to provide written reasons or the particulars are inadequate or untrue. The tribunal may, if it upholds the complaint, make a declaration about the employer's reasons for the dismissal and make an award of two weeks' pay.

51 Even if the dismissal is not automatically unfair, it may be an ordinary unfair dismissal (see **17.6.10**).

pregnancy or childbirth, she is entitled to the minimum remuneration during the statutory notice period, provided she has been employed for at least one month. This does not apply where the contract requires the employer to give a period of notice which is at least one week longer than the statutory minimum, in which case the woman will have to rely on her contractual rights.[52] If maternity pay is paid for the period, this can be offset against the notice pay.[53]

17.6.9 Pregnant Workers Directive

The PWD requires member states to take 'the necessary measures to prohibit the dismissal of workers . . . during the period *from the beginning of their pregnancy to the end of the maternity leave save in exceptional cases not connected with their condition* which are permitted under national legislation'. The ERA should be read with this very wide prohibition on dismissal contained in the Directive.[54]

17.6.10 Unfair dismissal

The dismissal may also be an ordinary unfair dismissal if the employer cannot show a 'potentially fair reason' and it was reasonable to dismiss the woman for this reason (see **14.2**). The burden of proof is on the employer to show the reason for the dismissal.

In *F W Woolworths plc v Smith*[55] the EAT upheld the IT finding that the dismissal was unfair because of the employer's inflexibility. It had not allowed the applicant to return to her original job because she had not complied with the notice provisions. She was then dismissed because she could not attend evening sessions because she was breastfeeding.

17.6.11 Dismissal for assertion of statutory right

It is automatically unfair to dismiss an employee either for bringing proceedings to enforce a statutory right or alleging that the employer has infringed a statutory right. It is irrelevant whether the right has in fact been breached, provided the claim is made in good faith.

52 ERA ss86 to 89.

53 ERA ss88(2) and 89(4).

54 See *Ozkan-Quaynor v Optika (Ltd) Optician* (1995) Case no: 25564/94/LN/C, 11 December, London (North) IT.

55 [1990] ICR 45.

Statutory rights include time off for ante-natal care, maternity leave and health and safety rights.[56]

17.6.12 *Dismissal in health and safety cases*

Where a woman leaves work because of the employer's refusal to take appropriate steps to deal with health and safety risks, and is dismissed as a result, she may be protected under ERA s100.

17.6.13 *Discriminatory dismissal*

Almost all dismissals which are automatically unfair will be discriminatory. A useful starting point is the HL decision in *Brown v Stockton-on-Tees BC*[57] when the HL said that:

> An employer faced with deciding which of several employees to make redundant must disregard the inconvenience that inevitably will result from the fact that one of them is pregnant and will require maternity leave ... Although it is often a considerably inconvenience to an employer to have to make the necessary arrangements to keep a woman's job open for her whilst she is absent from work in order to have a baby, that is a price that has to be paid as a part of the social and legal recognition of the equal status of women in the workplace.

Similarly, the ECJ, in *Habermann-Beltermann*,[58] held that the 'termination of an employment contract on account of the employee's pregnancy . . . concerns women alone and constitutes, therefore, direct discrimination on grounds of sex'.

The importance of claiming discrimination, in addition to unfair dismissal, is that the questionnaire procedure is available and compensation is not subject to any limit and will usually include an amount for injury to feelings.

In *Webb v EMO Air Cargo Ltd*,[59] Mrs Webb was employed to cover for a pregnant employee, though she had a permanent contract and was expected to stay on after the maternity period. Mrs Webb then became pregnant and she was dismissed. The ECJ held that the dismissal of a pregnant woman recruited for an indefinite period cannot be justified because she is unable to work for a temporary period because of her pregnancy.

56 ERA s104(1).
57 [1988] IRLR 263, HL, at p264.
58 *Habermann-Beltermann v Arbeiterwohlfahrt, Bezirksverband Ndb/Opf eV* [1994] IRLR 364, ECJ.
59 [1994] IRLR 482, ECJ.

The HL, following the ECJ ruling, held that there is no need for a comparison to be made with a man in a similar situation; less favourable treatment of a woman for a pregnancy-related reason is itself discrimination.[60]

The HL distinguished permanent and short fixed-term contracts. It was suggested (obiter) that if a woman were employed on a fixed-term contract and would, because of her pregnancy, be absent for the whole of the contract, then it would not be unlawful to dismiss her. Nor, said the HL, would it be unlawful to fail to appoint a pregnant woman in these circumstances. These comments are not binding and were restrictively interpreted in *Caruana v Mancester Airport plc*[61] where the applicant had been employed (as an independent sub-contractor) on a series of fixed-term contracts. Soon after she told her employer that she was pregnant, she was told that her contract would not be renewed. The EAT upheld the IT's decision that the failure to renew the fixed-term contract was because of the applicant's pregnancy and was, therefore, discriminatory.

Although in *Brown v Rentokil Ltd*[62] the Court of Session held that a woman, dismissed because of pregnancy-related illness, had not suffered discrimination, this has been referred to the ECJ. *Brown* has not generally been followed. In *Stephenson v F A Wellworth & Co Ltd*[63] the NICA held that an illness arising out of and occurring during pregnancy is to be treated in the same way as pregnancy. Dismissal of a woman for pregnancy-related sickness is discrimination and there was no need to compare her treatment with that of a man.

In *Rees v Appollo Watch Repairs plc*[64] the applicant was dismissed while on maternity leave because the employer found that her replacement was more efficient. The EAT held that the applicant would not have been dismissed had she not been on maternity leave. Following *Webb* (see above), that meant the dismissal was discriminatory. The EAT said that the protection afforded to women on maternity leave would be drastically curtailed if an employer were able to defeat a complaint of direct discrimination by saying that it preferred her replacement; a state of affairs which had arisen solely as a result of her pregnancy and therefore of her sex.

60 [1993] IRLR 27, HL.
61 [1996] IRLR 378, EAT.
62 [1995] IRLR 211, CS.
63 (1997) 73 EOR; DCLD 32; 21 March 1997.
64 (1996) *Times*, 26 February.

17.6.13.1 Dismissal because pregnant and unmarried

In *O'Neill v (1) The Governors of St Thomas More RCVA Upper School and (2) Bedfordshire CC*[65] the applicant was an unmarried pregnant teacher, working in a Catholic school, who was dismissed when the school discovered that the father was a Catholic priest. The EAT held that the critical question is whether the dismissal was on the ground of pregnancy, motive being irrelevant. The EAT acknowledged that there may have been other grounds for the dismissal (such as the paternity of the child) – but as these were pregnancy-related and it was the applicant's pregnancy which precipitated the decision to dismiss her, the dismissal was unlawful sex discrimination.[66]

17.6.13.2 Dismissal after return to work

In *Hertz*[67] the applicant returned to work after maternity leave and after six months she was absent for a long period suffering from an illness arising out of her pregnancy. She was dismissed. The ECJ held that there was no distinction between an illness which appears after leave or absence and any other illness. If the absence would lead to dismissal of a male worker under the same conditions, there is no sex discrimination. However, no account should be taken of the time off during maternity leave in calculating the period of absence. It is possible, however, that a claim could be made under the automatically unfair dismissal provisions of the ERA (see **17.6.2.1**).

17.7 Other less favourable treatment on grounds of pregnancy, childbirth or maternity leave

The question is whether 'but for' the woman's pregnancy, childbirth or maternity leave, she would have been treated more favourably. There is no need to compare her position with that of a man.

65 [1996] IRLR 372, EAT.

66 The EAT decision in *Berrisford v Woodward Schools (Midland Division) Ltd* [1991] IRLR 247 was distinguished on the basis that in *Berrisford* the applicant was dismissed not because of her pregnancy but because she did not intend to marry and this manifested extra-marital sex, which was unacceptable in a religious school.

67 *Handels-og Kontorfunktionaerernes Forbund i Danmark (acting for Hertz) v Dansk Arbejdsgiverforening (acting for Aldi Marked K/S)* [1991] IRLR 31, ECJ.

68 *Larsson v Dansk Handel og Service Case C-400/95 (96/C-46/15)* 74 EOR 40, ECJ.

However, an employee can only be dismissed for a reason connected with her pregnancy if the employer is aware of her pregnancy.

17.8 Recruitment, promotion and training

Where an employer refused to employ a suitable female applicant because she is pregnant this will be discriminatory and a breach of the SDA and ETD (see **2.9.3**).[70] Less favourable treatment in relation to promotion, transfer and training will also be discrimination (see Chapter 11).

KEY POINTS

Return from maternity leave

- A woman returning from maternity leave can simply turn up to work at the end of her 14 weeks' leave; if she wants to return earlier she must give seven days' notice.
- There is a prohibition on a woman working within two weeks of giving birth. A woman working in a factory must not work for four weeks. Leave will be extended in these circumstances.
- Women who are ill at the end of their leave are protected from dismissal for a further four weeks.
- Women returning from leave are entitled to return to the same job.

Return from maternity absence

- The notice provisions must be followed.
- The employer may delay the woman's return for up to four weeks.
- Where a woman is sick she may delay her return (once only) by up to four weeks, provided she gives proper notice. She must then physically return to work in order to exercise her statutory rights.
- There is a right to return to the same job on *no less favourable* terms and conditions; this is subject to two exceptions.
- If there is a transfer of the undertaking, the woman's rights transfer to the new employer.

69 *Dentons Directories v Hobbs* EAT 821/96 (1997) 589 *IDS Brief*, 18 March 1997.
70 *Dekker v Stichting Vormingscentrum Voor Jonge Volwassen (VJV-Centrum) Plus* [1991] IRLR 27.

- Women who have a statutory and contractual right to leave or absence can take advantage of whichever right is, in any particular respect, the more favourable.
- There may be a 'right' to return part-time or on a flexible working arrangement.

Unfair dismissal

- A dismissal may be automatically unfair, ordinarily unfair or discriminatory.
- In order to claim unfair dismissal there must be a subsisting contract.
- It is automatically unfair to dismiss a woman because of her pregnancy, childbirth or maternity leave. The dismissal may take place during the woman's pregnancy, during maternity leave, or soon afterwards, or during her maternity absence.
- A woman who is made redundant during maternity leave or absence is entitled to any available suitable alternative work; failure to give her such work (in preference to other employees) will make the dismissal automatically unfair.
- A dismissal which is prompted by the employer's health and safety duties is likely to be automatically unfair.
- Dismissal does not destroy the right to return.
- An employer must provide written reasons where a woman is dismissed while pregnant or on maternity leave.
- The PWD provides very broad protection against dismissal.
- It is automatically unfair to dismiss a woman for asserting a statutory right, such as to maternity leave.
- Most dismissals which are automatically unfair will be discriminatory. A dismissal on the grounds of pregnancy, childbirth or maternity leave will be discriminatory without the need to show that the woman has been treated less favourably than a man.
- It is unlawful discrimination for an employer not to appoint a woman because she is pregnant or about to go on maternity leave.

Tabular summary of maternity rights

	Length of service (with same employer)	Employment Status	Earnings	Notice requirements Written notice is often essential and usually advisable	Medical evidence	Other conditions and points to note
A. 14 weeks' *general maternity leave* can start from 11th week before EWC	None. All women irrespective of length of service are entitled to general maternity leave	Employee including employees on fixed-term contracts	Not relevant	– Written notice at least 21 days before start of leave of pregnancy and EWC and – at least 21 days' notice of start of maternity leave. If not reasonably practicable to give 21 days' notice, it must be given as soon as possible	If requested by employer, doctor or midwife's certificate giving EWC	If employee cannot give 21 days' notice because, eg, the baby is born early, she must give notice of the birth as soon as possible. Notice of pregnancy-related absence in the 6 weeks before EWC must be given
B. *Extended maternity absence* – of up to 29 weeks after beginning of week baby was born	2 years' continuous service at the beginning of the 11th week before the EWC	Employee as above	Not relevant	As above and in addition – inform employer in writing, 21 days before leave begins, of intention to return – written notice at least 21 days before date of return, of proposal to return on that day	As above	Where not earlier than 21 days before end of MLP, the employer makes a written request for written confirmation that she intends to return the woman must provide such written confirmation within 14 days
C. *Right to return* to same job after 14 weeks' general maternity leave	None	Employee as above	Not relevant	– Notice is required before taking leave – No notice is required for return at end of 14 weeks – 7 days' notice must be given if return is before end of 14 weeks	N/A	If employee cannot return at the end of the 14 weeks because she is sick she is protected from unfair dismissal for 4 weeks if she gives her employer a medical certificate before the end of her leave
D. *Right to return* after extended maternity absence to substantially the same job	2 years' service (as B above)	Employee as above	Not relevant	– 21 days' written notice of date of return (as B above) – confirmation of intention to return if requested by employer (11 weeks after start of maternity leave)	N/A	There are two situations when return may be postponed – the employer can postpone your return for 4 weeks – employee can postpone her return for 4 weeks if she is sick or there is a strike

	Length of service (with same employer)	Employment Status	Earnings	Notice requirements Written notice is often essential and usually advisable	Medical evidence	Other conditions and points to note
E. *Statutory maternity pay* 6 weeks on 90% of pay subsequent 12 weeks (max) on £55.70 payable from start of MPP	26 weeks up to and into qualifying week (ie 15th week before EWC)	Employee as above Holder of elective office	Average earnings of at least £62 pw for 8 weeks or 2 months before end of qualifying week (ie 15th week before EWC)	21 clear days' notice of the date maternity leave is to start – or if not practicable as much notice as possible	Medical evidence (usually a MAT B1) showing EWC must be given to the employer before the end of the 3rd week of the maternity pay period	– SMP is not repayable if woman does not return to work – woman can claim SMP from 2 or more employers (if you qualify) – SMP is payable during MPP even if there is no contract
F. *Maternity allowance* Higher rate of £54.55 for 18 weeks	Employed in the 15th week before the EWC	The woman must have been working (employed or self-employed) for at least 26 weeks in the 66 weeks immediately before the EWC	Paid 26 Class 1 National Insurance contributions in the previous 66-week period	A claim from the Benefits Agency should be made as soon as possible after the 14th week before the EWC	MAT B1 showing week baby is due	If woman is working for an employer she must send form SMP1 on which employer states why SMP is not payable
G. *Maternity allowance* Lower rate of £47.55 for 18 weeks	None	Self-employed or not working in 15th week	As above	As above	As above	
H. Paid time off for ante-natal care during working hours	None	Employee	Not relevant	Written proof of 2nd and subsequent appointments if requested by employer	Medical certificate showing woman is pregnant, if requested	
I. Protection from automatically unfair dismissal on grounds of pregnancy, childbirth or maternity leave	None	Employee including employees on fixed-term contracts	Not relevant	Not relevant	Not relevant	In case of pregnancy dismissal employer must be aware of pregnancy
J. Protection from ordinary unfair dismissal	2 years	Employee as above	Not relevant	Not relevant	Not relevant	

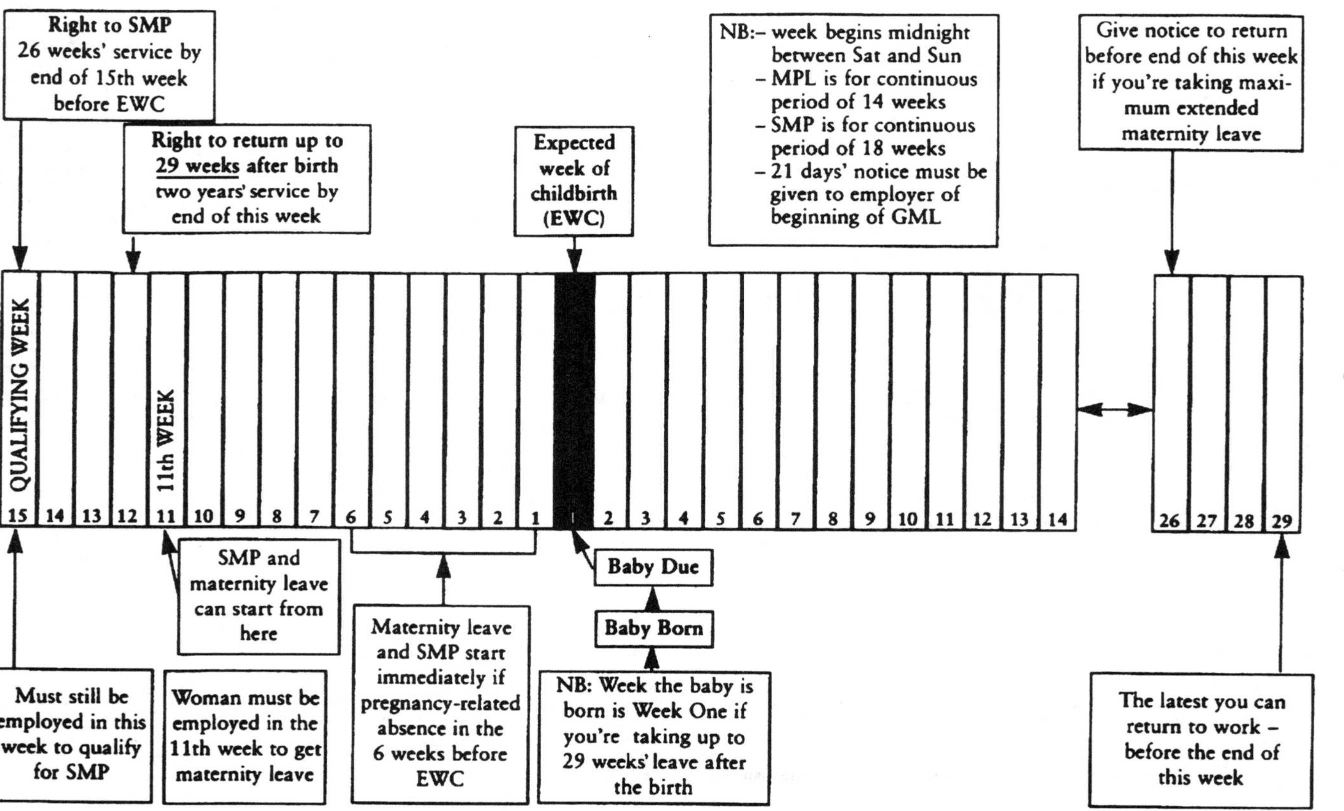
Right to SMP 26 weeks' service by end of 15th week before EWC
Right to return up to 29 weeks after birth two years' service by end of this week
Expected week of childbirth (EWC)
NB:– week begins midnight between Sat and Sun
– MPL is for continuous period of 14 weeks
– SMP is for continuous period of 18 weeks
– 21 days' notice must be given to employer of beginning of GML
Give notice to return before end of this week if you're taking maximum extended maternity leave
QUALIFYING WEEK
11th WEEK
15
14
13
12
11
10
9
8
7
6
5
4
3
2
1
2
3
4
5
6
7
8
9
10
11
12
13
14
26
27
28
29
SMP and maternity leave can start from here
Baby Due
Baby Born
Must still be employed in this week to qualify for SMP
Woman must be employed in the 11th week to get maternity leave
Maternity leave and SMP start immediately if pregnancy-related absence in the 6 weeks before EWC
NB: Week the baby is born is Week One if you're taking up to 29 weeks' leave after the birth
The latest you can return to work – before the end of this week

Part IV

Pay and pensions

CHAPTER 18

Overview of equal pay

This chapter is mainly concerned with the Equal Pay Act 1970 (EqPA) which covers equal pay between men and women. It explains the ambit of the EqPA, the effect of EC law, who is protected, the definition of pay and identification of the comparator. Although both women and men can claim equal pay, it is assumed in this chapter that it is women who make the claim as they are generally paid less than men.

There are no specific legal provisions dealing with race discrimination in pay; a claim must be made under the RRA. Disability discrimination in pay is covered by the DDA (see Chapter 24 and, in particular, **24.4.1.1**).

18.1 Introduction

Although it is over 20 years since the implementation of the EqPA[1] the hourly average pay of women is still one-fifth less than that of men.[2] According to research done by the EOC, as women grow older the discrepancy between their pay and men's pay increases. Thus, a woman in her early twenties earns on average 91% of a man's hourly pay; this falls to 87% for women in their thirties, 75% in their forties and 72% in their fifties.[3]

The European Commission[4] says that the overall pay gap between men and women is still wide and in some cases increasing due to economic difficulties which have tended to affect women more

1 The EqPA did not come into force until 1975 at the same time as the SDA.

2 The New Earnings Survey 1996 shows that full-time women received 72.3% of men's gross weekly earnings and 79.9% of men's gross hourly earnings.

3 70 EOR 2 and 34.

4 *Memorandum on equal pay for work of equal value* COM(94)6, Brussels, 23 June 1994.

severely than men. It points out that horizontal and vertical segregation remain a dominant feature of the structure of female employment. Research from the EOC also suggests that women from ethnic minorities may be particularly disadvantaged in their terms and conditions of employment.[5]

The equal pay legislation was substantially amended in 1983 to include equal value claims.[6] The law and procedure for equal value claims is particularly complex and lengthy and is constantly changing.[7] In addition, in equal pay cases, art 119 and the EPD should always be considered (see **18.3**).

18.2 Race discrimination in pay

Pay inequalities have centred on sex discrimination. Yet studies have shown that there are big pay discrepancies between different racial groups; these are particularly pronounced between black women and white men, where there is sex and race discrimination (see **18.1**).

A worker claiming that s/he is paid less or receives less favourable terms and conditions on the ground of his/her race, will have to prove (under the RRA) that there has been either direct race discrimination (ie, that s/he would have been paid the same but for his/her race or indirect discrimination on the ground of race. This will generally be more difficult than proving that the work is similar or equal, as required under the EqPA.

There have been some challenges to racially discriminatory pay practices. In *Campbell v Datum Engineering Co Ltd*[8] the applicant, who was of Afro-Caribbean origin, was the only ethnic minority employee out of 60. He found out that he was paid 16p an hour less than at least one other person who was doing the same work. He complained about this and the fact that his shift allowance had been deducted from his pay. In the absence of a satisfactory explanation from the employer, the IT found that the discrimination was on racial grounds and he was awarded compensation including an amount for injury to feelings.

5 *A code of practice on equal pay* (EOC, January 1997), in force 26 March 1997 (Code of Practice on Equal Pay (Appointed Day) Order 1997 SI No 131 (C6)).
6 Equal Pay (Amendment) Regulations 1983 SI No 1794.
7 The equal value procedure was amended with effect from 31 July 1996 (see Chapter 20).
8 DCLD 24 (1995) 20 March; Case no: 43749/94.

In *Sougrin v Haringey Health Authority*,[9] three nurses, two black (Ms Sougrin and Mrs Macdonald) and one white, appealed against a grading decision. The white nurse's appeal succeeded on the basis that she was acting up into a higher grade for more than 15% of her time. The appeals by the black nurses failed. The tribunal upheld Mrs Macdonald's claim, finding that the grading system, which involved automatic regrading if a nurse were doing more than 15% acting up to the next grade, indirectly discriminated against her. Mrs Macdonald secured a financial settlement of her claim. Ms Sougrin's case failed because her claim was out of time (see **25.2.1.1**).[10]

The difficulty with bringing such challenges is getting evidence of other employees' pay and proving that the differences are due to race discrimination. The principles of transparency, set out in *Danfoss* (see **21.3**) should also apply in race discrimination cases. This means that where different groups made up predominantly of one racial group are doing similar or equal value work but one group is consistently paid more, this should raise an inference that the reason is race discrimination.

The questionnaire procedure can be used to discover levels of pay and breakdown by grade, race (and sex). Although the employer is not obliged to reply to a questionnaire, failure to do so may lead to the IT making an inference (see **25.8.2**). Where there is a recognised trade union, it has a right to certain information (see **18.9.6**).

18.3 EqPA and art 119

The EqPA covers pay and other contractual terms, provided that there is a 'comparable man'. For the distinction between the operation of the EqPA and SDA see **5.7.1**. References to sections in this chapter are to the EqPA unless otherwise stated. The EOC has issued a Code of Practice which came into force on 26 March 1997 (see **1.1.7** for the effect of the Code).

These rigid distinctions do not apply under EC law. Treaty of Rome art 119 and the EPD lay down the principle of equal pay for work of equal value. They cover pay (widely defined) in contractual and non-contractual matters, unlike the EqPA (which covers only contractual terms). EC law may provide a remedy where there is none under the EqPA and it is advisable to cite art 119 and the EPD as well as

9 [1991] IRLR 447, EAT.
10 This decision was upheld by the CA: [1992] IRLR 416.

the EqPA. Article 119 can be relied on in tribunals as well as courts (see **9.6.4**). The European Commission has adopted a *Memorandum on Equal Pay for Work of Equal Value*[11] and a Code of Practice on the implementation of equal pay for work of equal value for women and men.[12] For the effect of the Memorandum and Code of Practice see **9.2.3**.

18.4 The equality clause

The EqPA provides that where a woman is employed on:

a) like work;
b) work rated as equivalent under a job evaluation scheme (JES); or
c) work of equal value;

with a comparable man in the same employment, her contract shall contain an equality clause. The equality clause has the effect that if any term of her contract is less favourable (whether concerned with pay or not) than a term of a similar kind in the man's contract, the woman's shall be changed so it is the same as the man's.[13] In addition, if a woman's contract does not include a term corresponding to a term benefiting a man, the woman's contract shall be amended to include such a term.

The equality clause also applies where the contract is determined by reference to a collective agreement (see **22.1.7**). Both men and women can make a claim for equal pay.

Parties cannot contract out of the EqPA and any agreement by an employee not to bring a claim is void unless it is part of a settlement made with the assistance of ACAS or a compromise agreement (see **25.7**).[14]

18.5 'Material factor' defence

The equality clause does not operate if the employer proves that the difference in pay between the applicant and her comparator is genuinely due to a material factor which is not the difference of sex (see Chapter 21).

11 COM(94)6 final.
12 COM(96)336.
13 EqPA s1(2) as amended.
14 SDA s77(3).

18.6 Indirect discrimination in pay

Discrimination in pay may be direct or indirect. Thus, it has been held that less favourable treatment of part-time workers in their contractual terms is unlawful sex discrimination where part-time workers are predominantly women. In *Stadt Lengerich v Helmig*[15] the ECJ held that:

> The principle of equal pay excludes not only the application of provisions leading to direct sex discrimination, but also the application of provisions which maintain different treatment between men and women at work as a result of criteria not based on sex where those differences of treatment are not attributable to objective factors unrelated to sex discrimination.

For examples of indirect discrimination in pay see **22.3**.

18.7 Scope of EqPA

The EqPA requires equal treatment for women (and men) in pay and other contractual terms. The provisions relating to victimisation also apply (see Chapter 4).

There is no burden on the applicant in an equal pay claim to show that the reason for the less favourable contractual term is sex. She only has to show that she is doing like, equivalent or equal value work to a man. If so, the employer must give the woman equal pay unless the employer can show a material factor defence.

18.7.1 Which workers are protected?

The EqPA protects those working under a contract of service (ie, employees) or of apprenticeship or a contract personally to execute any work or labour (which includes at least some freelancers).[16] This is the same as the definition of 'employed' under the SDA (see **5.2**) and wider than the definition of employee in the ERA. The EqPA applies to full-time and part-time workers, whether permanent or temporary and irrespective of the age or length of service of the worker.

18.7.1.1 Crown and government employees

With the exception of the armed forces (see **18.7.2.4**) and those holding

15 [1995] IRLR 216, ECJ.
16 EqPA s1(6)(a).

statutory office[17], the EqPA applies to Crown and government department employees.

18.7.1.2 Trainees

Most trainees are likely to be within the extended definition of 'employment' under the EqPA (read with art 119 and the EPD). This will mean that allegations of discrimination in trainees' pay (or other contractual terms) will be dealt with in the same way as discrimination in pay to other employees. If in any particular case the trainee's contract was not within this extended definition, there would, in any case, be a prohibition against discrimination in the terms on which the person was offered training and against subjecting him/her to a detriment under the SDA or RRA. The practical consequence would be that such trainees would have to show that their pay differences were due to sex or race (whether direct or indirect).

18.7.2 Exclusions from the EqPA

18.7.2.1 Retirement and pensions

Until the SDA 1986 came into force (on 7 November 1987), the EqPA, like the SDA, excluded *all* terms and provisions relating to death, retirement and pensions. Now there is an exception to the exclusion for terms or provisions which, in relation to retirement, afford access to opportunities for promotion, transfer or training, or provide for a woman's dismissal or demotion.[18] Thus, to deny men and women promotion or training where they are within, say, five years from the state retirement age would be unlawful, as women aged 56 would be treated less favourably than men aged 56.

Occupational pension schemes are covered in Chapter 23.

For provisions relating to women on maternity leave and absence see **16.2.5**. The position relating to retirement is covered in Chapter 14.

18.7.2.2 Laws regulating the employment of women (s6(1)(a))

Most protective legislation was repealed by SDA 1986 s7 and the Employment Act 1989 and it is difficult to envisage when this would apply. Note that statutes passed prior to the SDA, which impose a requirement to do a discriminatory act, are of no effect (see **5.4.2.6**).

17 EqPA s1(8)(a); see also **5.2.1**.
18 EqPA s6(1A)(b) as amended by SDA 1986 s2(4).

18.7.2.3 Special treatment for women in connection with pregnancy or childbirth (s6(1)(b))

The EqPA, like the SDA, does not require men to be given paternity rights equivalent to the maternity rights which are provided for women (see **5.4.2.4**). Thus, there is no breach if a woman is given extra benefits while on maternity leave. EC law has a similar exception (see **5.5.2**), although there is agreement for parental leave.

18.7.2.4 Armed forces

Women in the armed forces are not yet protected.[19] However, as the ETD applies to the armed forces so will art 119 and the EPD.

The EqPA states that the Secretary of State shall not make a distinction between men and women as regards pay, allowances or leave unless they are attributable to differences between the obligations undertaken by men and women.[20] If the Secretary of State breaches this duty the only remedy would be by way of judicial review.[21]

18.7.2.5 Working wholly or mainly outside GB[22]

This exception is the same as SDA s10 (see **5.4.2.10**). Women working wholly or mainly outside GB are excluded. The EC provisions cover employees working in an EC country, at least where they are EC nationals.

18.7.2.6 Illegal contracts

The position should be the same as under the SDA (see **5.2.1.6**).

18.7.3 Victimisation

Women who are victimised for involvement in an equal pay claim can make a complaint under the SDA (see Chapter 4).

19 EqPA s1(9). Armed Forces Act 1996 s24 (when in force which is likely to be in 1997) will allow a woman to make a claim under the EqPA provided she has first used the internal redress procedures which involve a complaint to the Defence Council. The time limit for bringing a claim is extended to nine months from the end of the employment.

20 EqPA s7.

21 See *R v Army Board of Defence Council ex p Anderson* [1991] IRLR 425, DC.

22 EqPA s1(1), (6) and (12); SDA s10.

18.8 What is 'pay'?

18.8.1 EqPA

Most contracts cover not only wages but bonuses, shift payments, overtime, service pay, sick pay, holiday pay and other money paid (see **22.3** for how pay systems discriminate against women). The EqPA also covers other contractual benefits such as holiday entitlement and free travel (see **5.7.1**). For definition of 'pay' see **18.8.4**.

18.8.2 'Discretionary' pay

In *Benveniste v University of Southampton*,[23] Dr Benveniste was appointed as a lecturer at a lower salary than other lecturers because of financial restraints. When these came to an end she was given extra increments but still received a lower salary than a man of the same age and qualifications. She brought a claim for equal pay and the employer argued that there was no term in Dr Benveniste's contract which was less favourable than in the contracts of her comparators, as the level at which she was appointed was not the subject of any contractual term but was at the discretion of the university. The CA held that there was indeed a term in her contract, namely the term as to her salary, which was less favourable to her than the similar terms in the contracts of the comparators. She won her equal pay claim.

An IT has held that a bonus paid at the discretion of the employer comes within the SDA (see **5.7.1**).

18.8.3 Principle of equal pay applies to each identifiable term

The definition of 'pay' can be important in circumstances where, for example, a woman is paid a lower basic wage but is given better sick pay, holidays, benefits in kind or other allowances. Thus, one term may be less favourable and other terms more favourable. In *Hayward v Cammell Laird Shipbuilders Ltd*,[24] the HL, overruling the EAT and CA, held that each term should be considered separately and that a term of a contract denoted a distinct part which could be compared with a similar provision in another contract. If, for example, the man's contract contains a term that he is to be provided with the use of a car, and the woman's contract does not, then her contract is to be

23 [1989] IRLR 122, CA.
24 [1988] IRLR 257, HL.

treated as including such a term. It was wrong, said the HL, to consider the contract as a whole and determine if the woman's contract was less favourable, taking account of all the different terms.

Thus if, as in *Hayward*, a woman is paid a lower basic rate than her comparator but receives more generous sick pay and meal breaks, she would be entitled to an increase in her basic rate and the comparator could make his own claim arguing that he was entitled to the same sick pay and meal breaks as the woman. This interpretation is supported by the decision in *Barber v GRE Assurance Group*[25] where the ECJ held that equal pay must be ensured in respect of 'each element of remuneration and not only on the basis of a comprehensive assessment of the consideration paid to workers'.

18.8.4 Article 119 and definition of 'pay'

Article 119 defines pay as 'the ordinary basic or minimum wage or salary or any other consideration, whether in cash or in kind, which the worker receives, directly or indirectly, in respect of his employment from his employer'. The key is whether the benefit is received because of the employment relationship.[26] Pay includes 'all emoluments in cash or kind paid or payable, on condition they are paid, even indirectly, by the employer, as a result of the worker's employment'.[27] This is a very wide definition and has been interpreted broadly.

The following have been held to constitute pay:

a) pay supplements[28] and increments based on seniority;[29] shift premia, merit and performance pay would also be covered;
b) payments made by an employer towards an occupational pension scheme;[30] this is a complex area which is covered in more detail in Chapter 23;
c) severance payments made on the termination of employment, whether part of an individual's contract or a collective agreement;[31]

25 [1990] IRLR 240, ECJ.
26 *EC Commission v Belgium* [1993] IRLR 404.
27 *Defrenne v Belgian State (Case no 80/70)* [1974] CMLR 494, at para 6.
28 *Handels-og Kontorfunktionaerernes Forbund i Danmark v Dansk Arbejdsgiverforening (acting for Danfoss)* [1989] IRLR 532, ECJ.
29 *Nimz v Freie und Hansestadt Hamburg* [1991] IRLR 222, ECJ.
30 *Barber v GRE Assurance* [1990] IRLR 240, ECJ.
31 *Kowalska v Freie und Hansestadt Hamburg* [1990] IRLR 447; see also *Barber* (n30).

d) payment of a survivor's pension by an employer;[32]
e) contractual and statutory redundancy payments;[33]
f) contractual and statutory sick pay;[34] by analogy, other statutory benefits, such as guarantee payments, medical suspension pay, payments for time off for union duties, compensation for unfair dismissal,[35] should count as pay;
g) maternity pay, whether contractual or statutory;[36]
h) travel concessions (or other benefits) given, whether during employment or on retirement of an employee and whether for the employee or a person connected with the employee.[37] Thus, all gratuities paid at the discretion of the employer are covered;
i) any rule of a collective agreement which governs the passage to a higher salary grade;[38]
j) overtime pay;[39]
k) paid leave or overtime pay for participation in training courses;[40]

32 *Razzouk and Beydoun v Commission of the European Communities* [1984] 3 CMLR 470, ECJ.

33 *Hammersmith and Queen Charlotte's Special Health Authority v Cato* [1987] IRLR 483, EAT, and *Secretary of State for Scotland and Greater Glasgow Health Board v Wright and Hannah* [1991] IRLR 187, EAT.

34 *Rinner-Kuhn v FWW Spezial-Gebaudereinigung GmbH* [1989] IRLR 493.

35 It is not clear whether unfair dismissal compensation constitutes pay; in *Mediguard Services Ltd v Thame* [1994] IRLR 504 the EAT thought it was, but the CA in *R v Secretary for State ex p Seymour Smith* [1995] IRLR 464 said this was not entirely clear.

36 *Gillespie and Others v Northern Health and Social Services Board and Others* [1996] IRLR 214 (see **16.1**).

37 *Garland v British Rail Engineering Ltd* [1982] IRLR 111.

38 *Nimz v Freie und Hansestadt Hamburg* [1991] IRLR 222, ECJ.

39 *Stadt Lengerich v Helmig* [1995] IRLR 216, ECJ. Note, however, that the ECJ held that there was no discrimination in an agreement which excluded part-time workers from overtime supplements until they had worked the same number of hours as full-time workers (see **22.3.2.1**).

40 *Arbeiterwohlfahrt der Stadt Berline eV v Botel* [1992] IRLR 423, ECJ. See also *Freers and Speckmann v Deutsche Dundespost Case C-278/93*. However, the EAT held, in *Manor Bakeries Ltd v Nazir* [1996] IRLR 604 that art 119 did not cover paid time off to attend a trade union annual conference as a delegate because attendance at such a conference was not 'work' and it was 'fanciful' to suggest that it was. The EAT distinguished *Botel*, saying that work on a staff committee was a species of 'work'. The EAT decision must be wrong and flies in the face of all the ECJ decisions on pay; the test is whether it is a benefit paid by the employer by reason of the employment relationship.

l) notice pay, whether contractual or statutory;[41]
m) piecework pay schemes;[42]
n) concessionary goods.

Note that where a woman is claiming the benefit of a gratuity (or other discretionary and non-contractual benefits) she cannot put her claim under the EqPA which covers only contractual terms. She can claim under the SDA and European law.

Excluded are payments made as part of the state social security system, not as part of the employment relationship;[43] schemes governed by legislation without any element of agreement between employer and employee which are compulsorily applicable to general categories of workers do not come within art 119. They are likely to come within the Equal Treatment Social Security Directive (SSD).[44]

It is not always easy to distinguish between benefits which fall within art 119 and those which are covered by the SSD. The distinction is important because under the SSD the courts are more likely to uphold a defence to a potential claim for indirect discrimination on the ground that it can be objectively justified. There is a greater reluctance to interfere with social security schemes because of the perceived need to maintain equivalence between the contributions paid into the scheme and benefits paid out.[45] Pensions are covered separately in Chapter 23.

There are three factors to be taken into account:

a) whether the payment is *made by the employer as a result (either directly or indirectly) of the employment relationship*; if so, it is likely to be pay under art 119.[46] It is the single most important factor. This would cover, for example, statutory (and contractual) sick pay and statutory (and contractual) maternity pay;
b) whether tax and national insurance are paid in respect of the

41 *Clark v Secretary of State for Employment* [1996] IRLR 578, CA. This was the view of one judge but is not binding as the CA held that the exclusion of women on maternity leave from the right to payment during statutory minimum notice was not unlawful discrimination. Note that the provisions for notice pay in the ERA now include women on maternity leave or absence.

42 *Specialarbejderforbundet i Danmark v Dansk Industri, acting for Royal Copenhagen A/S* [1996] IRLR 648.

43 *Nolte v Landesversicherungsanstalt Hannover* [1996] IRLR 225.

44 Directive 79/7.

45 See *Nolte v Landesversicherungsanstalt Hannover C-317/93* [1996] IRLR 214, ECJ.

46 *Gillespie* (n36 above).

payment; if so, it is likely to be treated as pay under art 119, provided it is paid as a result of the employment relationship;

c) whether the payment is made by the Department of Social Security; if so, it is likely to come within the SSD.

The question of whether the benefit is 'pay' does not depend on whether the payment or benefit derives from legislation or regulations or from a collective agreement[47] or the individual's contract of employment. In *Meyers v Adjudication Officer*[48] the ECJ held that a benefit such as family credit, which is necessarily linked to the working relationship, constitutes a working condition within the ETD.

18.9 The comparable man

The EqPA requires there to be an actual comparator of the opposite sex working in the same employment at the same time.[49] Article 119 is wider in two respects. First, the comparison can be made with a predecessor or successor (see **18.9.4** and **18.9.5**). Secondly, the definition of 'associated employer' is wider (see **18.9.2**).

A comparison cannot be made with a person of the same sex even where the person is a transsexual (but see **5.1.4**).[50]

18.9.1 Working in the same employment

The EqPA provides that the comparator must be working for the *same* employer or an *associated* employer. Employers are treated as associated if either:

a) is a company of which the other has direct or indirect control; or
b) both are companies of which a third person has control.[51]

Whether the woman is working for the same or associated employer, the man must be working either:

a) at the same establishment; or
b) at establishments in Great Britain which include that one, where there are common terms and conditions of employment.[52]

47 *Bestuur van het Algemeen Burgerlijk Pensioenfonds v Beune* [1995] IRLR 103, ECJ.
48 [1995] IRLR 498, ECJ.
49 EqPA s1(2) and (6).
50 *Collins v Wilkins Chapman* DCLD 23; (1994) 14 March, EAT 945/93.
51 EqPA s1(6)(c).
52 EqPA s1(6).

If the employees are working at the same establishment, that is sufficient; the question of whether there are common terms and conditions does not arise.[53]

18.9.2 Definition of 'associated employer'

In *Scullard v Knowles and Southern Regional Council for Education and Training*[54] the applicant was employed as a further education unit manager by an independent voluntary association of local education authorities which was attached to a regional advisory council. The unit was supported and funded by the Department for Education and Employment. The applicant argued that she could compare herself with men working for other regional advisory councils. Her claim was dismissed by the IT because the 'councils' were not 'companies' so did not fall within the definition of associated employers. The EAT held that the test under art 119 was whether the applicant and her comparators are employed 'in the same establishment or service'; no distinction was drawn by the ECJ, in *Defrenne (No 2)*,[55] between work carried out 'in the same establishment or service' of limited companies and of other employers. The EAT suggested that relevant factors were:

- whether the regional advisory councils were directly or indirectly controlled by a third party, eg, the DfEE;
- the extent and nature of control;
- whether common terms and conditions of employment were observed in the regional advisory councils for the relevant class of employees.[56]

53 *Lawson and Others v Britfish Ltd* [1988] IRLR 53, EAT.

54 [1996] IRLR 344.

55 *Defrenne v Sabena (No 2) (Case no 43/75)* [1976] ICR 547, ECJ.

56 In *Hasley v Fair Employment Agency (FEA)* [1989] IRLR 106, NICA, the applicant, who worked for the FEA, compared herself with an employee in the EOC for Northern Ireland, arguing that both bodies were controlled by the same government department. The Northern Ireland CA held that the FEA and EOC were 'statutory bodies' and not 'companies' within the meaning of the Act so the appellant was not employed in the same employment. The NICA observed that neither *Defrenne* nor *Macarthys* (below) treated art 119 as being confined to work carried out in the same establishment or service. The NICA pointed out that the employees were 'in public service of the same kind, holding posts which are graded by the same officers and on the same principles of job evaluation and that the fact that the statutory corporations which employ them are not emanations of the Crown is due solely to the political desirability of making the FEA and the EOC appear to be independent of the State'. The NICA concluded that arguably, art 119 applied.

In *Hayes and Quinn v Mancunian Community Health Trust and South Manchester Health Authority*[57] two dental surgery assistants employed by the Mancunian Community Health Trust compared their work with that done by a senior dental technician working for a different trust. The applicants and their comparators had formerly worked for the South Manchester Health Authority. The IT held that the applicants were employed in the same service as their comparator. The health authority and trusts were all under the control of the Secretary of State for Health. This reasoning could apply to other public sector employees, such as teachers working for the same local authority.

18.9.3 Common terms and conditions

Where the woman and her comparator are not working at the same establishment, there must be common terms and conditions, either generally or for employees of the relevant classes in the two establishments.

In *Leverton v Clywd CC*,[58] a nursery nurse compared herself to a clerical worker working at a different site. The employees were covered by the same collective agreement. The EAT and CA had held that, because the comparator worked different hours and had different holidays to the applicant, they were not in the same employment. The HL disagreed, holding that the comparison was between the terms and conditions of employment observed at the establishment at which the woman is employed and the establishment at which the men are employed, and applicable either generally or to a particular class or classes of employees to which both the woman and the men belong. The Lords pointed out that it was inevitable that individual terms would vary greatly, despite there being common terms and conditions observed generally in the establishments. If terms and conditions were covered by the same collective agreement this was sufficient.

In *British Coal Corporation v Smith*[59] over a thousand canteen workers and cleaners working for British Coal (at 47 different establishments) claimed equal pay with 150 comparators (at 14 different establishments). The HL held that 'common terms and conditions'

57 (1996) 30 July; DCLD 29; Case no: 16977/93.
58 [1989] IRLR 28, HL.
59 [1996] IRLR 404, HL.

means terms and conditions which are substantially comparable on a broad basis, rather than the same terms and conditions subject only to minor differences. In this case the terms and conditions were governed by national agreements, even though there were local variations relating to an incentive bonus and to concessionary coal. There may still be common terms and conditions even though there are local variations of a national scheme.[60]

18.9.3.1 Direct service organisations

In *Ratcliffe and Others v North Yorkshire CC*[61] women employed by a direct services organisation which was set up to submit an in-house tender for council catering services were able to compare themselves with other council employees provided there were common terms and conditions at their different establishments.

18.9.4 Comparison with predecessor or hypothetical man

In *Macarthys Ltd v Smith*,[62] the ECJ said for the purposes of art 119 a woman could compare herself with her male predecessor. Ms Smith also argued that even if there had never been a man doing like work with her she could still claim to be paid the rate which a man would have been paid. The court said that in order to prove this, Ms Smith would have to show that if she had been a man she would have been paid more and this might involve a comparison with men doing similar work or work of equal value for other employers.[63]

Although there is no decision directly on the point, it is doubtful whether, under EC law, a woman, who can identify higher paid men doing work of equal value for other (non-associated) employers,

60 In *Thomas v National Coal Board* [1987] IRLR 451 the EAT found that, notwithstanding that locally negotiated and varying bonus payments and concessionary entitlements formed a substantial part of remuneration, there were 'common terms and conditions of employment' applying to all workers because the entitlement to bonuses and concessions was negotiated nationally. It was only the amount which varied locally, and this did not affect the basic similarity of terms and conditions.

61 [1995] IRLR 439, HL.

62 [1980] IRLR 210, ECJ

63 The ECJ, by way of dicta, said that differences in pay between men and women working for different employers was a form of disguised discrimination which was not prohibited by art 119. The court did not define what it meant by disguised or indirect discrimination, but this should not be confused with disparate impact discrimination as outlawed by *Bilka* (see 22.3.3).

would be entitled to the same pay as the men. It is more likely that she would have a claim if she could show that 'but for' the fact that she was a woman she would receive higher pay. This may be difficult to prove and may involve identifying a man who had, in the past, worked for the employer at a higher grade. Under the SDA, direct discrimination often involves making a comparison with a hypothetical man and the two Acts are meant to be interpreted as a 'harmonious whole'. It is certainly worth arguing that such a comparison can be made both under the EqPA and EC law.

18.9.5 Comparison with successor

In *Diocese of Hallam Trustees v Connaughton*[64] the applicant's successor (a man) was appointed at a considerably higher salary. The EAT held that the applicant was entitled to rely upon art 119 to claim equal pay with her male successor. The EAT said that the scope of art 119 includes complaints based upon the use of an immediate successor as a notional contemporaneous comparator.[65]

18.9.6 Identification of the comparator

It is for the woman, not the tribunal, to choose her male comparator.[66] In some workforces, particularly large or non-unionised ones, it may be difficult for a woman to find a man with whom to compare herself, because of lack of information about other employees' pay and terms and conditions. In *Leverton* (above), a nurse was unable to find a male comparator in her workplace. She produced evidence, from the council and union, that the pay of nursery assistants compared unfavourably with that of clerical staff in local government. She asked the tribunal for discovery of the job descriptions of the men in clerical jobs. The IT granted the application, recognising the difficulty of obtaining information in large organisations. The employer appealed but the EAT upheld the tribunal decision saying that as the nurse had produced evidence of a prima facie case she was entitled to the information (see also **25.9.3** for provisions relating to discovery).

Arguably, the questionnaire procedure can be used (see **25.8**). SDA

64 [1996] IRLR 505.

65 See also *Dennehy v Sealink UK* [1987] IRLR 120, where a comparison was made with a male successor.

66 *Ainsworth v Glass Tubes and Components Ltd* [1977] IRLR 74; [1977] ICR 347, EAT, and see *Pickstone v Freemans* [1987] IRLR 218, CA; [1988] IRLR 357, HL.

s74 and the statutory instrument refer to the Sex Discrimination Act. As the EqPA is a schedule to the SDA, it should be treated as part of the SDA.[67]

There is also a duty on an employer to disclose to a recognised trade union:

> information (a) without which the trade union representatives would be to a material extent impeded in carrying on ... collective bargaining with him, and (b) which it would be in accordance with good industrial relations practice that he should disclose to them for the purposes of collective bargaining'.[68]

The Disclosure of Information Code of Practice covers disclosure of information such as earnings and hours, analysed according to sex, giving – where appropriate – distributions and make up of pay, showing any additions to basic rate of salary and to the numbers analysed according to sex. Employers are exempt from disclosure where the compiling of information would involve a disproportionate amount of work or expenditure compared to the value of the information in the conduct of collective bargaining. A reference may be made to the Central Arbitration Committee if the employer refuses to comply with this obligation and the Committee may order disclosure.[69]

The EPD provides that member states shall take measures necessary to ensure that the principle of equal pay is applied and shall see that effective means are available to ensure that this principle is observed (art 6). Failure to provide adequate means of discovery to enable women to gain access to information about possible comparators is arguably in breach of this duty.

18.9.7 A representative man?

In *Thomas* (above), the EAT rejected the employer's argument that the male comparator should be representative of the men performing like work and that he should not be an anomalous man. As the EAT pointed out, the statute refers to 'a man' not 'a representative

67 In *A-G v Lamplough* (1878) 3 Ex D 214 at p229 the CA held that a schedule in an Act is as much a part of the statute, and is as much an enactment, as any other part (see *Bennion on Statutory Interpretation* (Butterworths, 2nd edn, 1992), p491).

68 Trade Union and Labour Relations (Consolidation) Act 1992 s181.

69 Ibid, s183.

man'.[70] However, if the man is not typical because, for example, he has protected pay, the employer may have a material factor defence (see **21.2.1.2**).

18.9.8 Where there has been a JES

Even if there is a man on the same pay who is doing like work or work rated as equivalent under a JES, the woman can theoretically compare herself with another higher paid man.[71] However, it will generally not be possible for such a claim to succeed if there has been an analytical and non-discriminatory JES which has rated her work at a level lower than the man's work (see **19.2.1**).

18.9.9 Comparison with more than one man

There is no reason why a woman should not compare herself with more than one man. In *Hayward v Cammell Laird Shipbuilders Ltd*,[72] a canteen cook claimed equal value with three male employees, a painter, a joiner and a thermal insulation engineer.[73]

It will generally be in the woman's interest to compare herself with several employees as this will increase her chance of being awarded equal pay with at least one of them. However, some caution should be exercised; in *Leverton* (above), Lord Bridge warned applicants against casting their net over too wide a range of comparators.

18.10 Burden of proof

The burden is on the applicant to show that she is doing like work, equivalent work or work of equal value with her comparator. The burden is on the employer to prove that there is a material factor defence if this is relied upon (see **21.2**).

70 But see *McPherson v Rathgael Centre for Children and Young People and Northern Ireland Office* [1991] IRLR 206, where the NICA doubted, obiter, whether an applicant could choose an anomalous male comparator.

71 *Pickstone and Others v Freemans* [1988] IRLR 357, HL.

72 [1987] IRLR 186, CA; [1988] IRLR 257, HL.

73 In *Langley and Others v Beecham Proprietaries* (1985) COIT 1683/206 the IT allowed a comparison between one woman and two men. The tribunal relied on Interpretation Act 1978 s6 which says that, unless the contrary is indicated, the singular includes the plural and vice versa.

EQUAL PAY: KEY POINTS

- The EqPA and art 119 cover sex discrimination in pay but there are no special provisions dealing with race discrimination in pay.
- A race discrimination pay claim must be made under the RRA; there have been few cases.
- A claim of disability discrimination in pay must be made under the DDA.
- The EqPA covers pay and other contractual terms.
- A woman, under the EqPA, can claim the same pay and contractual terms as a comparable man if she is doing:
  - like work;
  - work rated as equivalent under a job evaluation scheme; or
  - work of equal value.
- Both direct and indirect discrimination in pay is covered.
- Women and men are protected, irrespective of age or length of service.
- Employees, trainees and the self-employed are protected.
- There are certain exclusions, such as armed forces personnel, employees working outside GB and special treatment for women in connection with pregnancy or childbirth.
- Each term of the contract must be considered separately.
- A complaint can be made in relation to a particular term of the contract; it is not necessary to show overall inequality.
- EC law lays down the principle of equal pay for work of equal value; EC law often provides greater protection than the EqPA and covers contractual and non-contractual benefits.
- The definition of pay under the EqPA is very wide and covers wages, bonuses, shift payments, overtime, service pay, mortgages, etc. Under art 119, pay includes contributions by an employer to an occupational pension scheme, redundancy, sick pay, maternity pay and other statutory benefits, travel concessions and other fringe benefits.
- The comparator of the opposite sex must be working in the same employment, ie, for the same or an associated employer, or possibly in the same service.
- The comparator must be working at either the same establishment or at an establishment where there are common terms and conditions of employment.

- A comparison can be made with a predecessor or successor (of sufficiently close time to make the comparison meaningful).
- It is for the applicant to choose her comparator(s) and he need not be a 'representative' man. However, where a male comparator is atypical the employer may have a material factor.
- It may be possible to find out about comparative pay by using the questionnaire procedure or the provisions which entitle recognised trade union representatives to information.

CHAPTER 19

Like work and work rated as equivalent

This chapter looks at like work claims and claims where the work has been rated as equivalent under a job evaluation scheme.[1] A claim may be brought by either a woman or a man but, because women's pay is commonly less than men's, most applicants are women as is assumed in this chapter. This chapter does not apply to race discrimination. There have been relatively few developments in the substantive law in this area over the past ten years: most have concerned the equal value provisions which are set out in Chapter 20.

19.1 Like work

It is for the applicant to show that she is doing like work.

A woman is to be regarded as employed on like work with a man if:

a) the work they do is the same or of a broadly similar nature; and
b) there is no difference or no significant and relevant difference in the tasks they perform.

These stages must be considered separately, though it is often difficult to distinguish them in practice.[2]

19.1.1 Broadly similar work

It is a question of fact whether the work is broadly similar. The type of work and skill and knowledge required to do it must be considered in broad terms. It is the nature of the work which is important and trivial differences must be ignored.

If the work is broadly similar, differences which are not of practical

1 EqPA s1(5).
2 *Capper Pass Ltd v J B Lawton* [1976] IRLR 366, EAT.

importance in relation to the terms and conditions of employment should be disregarded.

In *Capper Pass Ltd v JB Lawton*,[3] the EAT held that differences not likely to be reflected in the terms and conditions of employment ought to be disregarded. The woman cooked between 10 and 20 lunches for managers and directors and worked a 40-hour week: the man cooked 350 meals a day and worked a 45-hour week. Their work was held to be broadly similar.

19.1.2 *Time at which work done not relevant*

The time at which work is done is irrelevant and does not justify a difference in the basic rate of pay. In *Dugdale and Others v Kraft Foods Ltd*,[4] the EAT held that the men (who did the same work as the women, but at night) could be compensated by the payment of a night shift premium. The same principle applies to overtime and Sunday work.[5] If, however, there are other differences of practical importance, such as added responsibility (eg, if the man works alone and unsupervised at night), this will defeat a 'like work' claim.[6]

19.1.3 *Frequency of tasks is important*

The CA has said that ITs should take into account the things done and the frequency with which they are done rather than paying too great attention to contractual obligations.[7] In one case, a woman worked in a betting shop and was paid less per hour than a man doing the same work. The employer argued that the man had an additional security role which justified the higher pay. There had never been any trouble in the shop since the company had taken it over. The applicant was awarded equal pay.[8]

3 Ibid.

4 [1976] IRLR 368, EAT.

5 See *Electrolux Ltd v Hutchinson* [1976] IRLR 410, EAT, and *National Coal Board v Sherwin* [1978] IRLR 122, EAT (see 22.3.2.2).

6 *Thomas v National Coal Board* [1987] IRLR 451, EAT.

7 *E Coomes (Holdings) Ltd v Shields* [1978] IRLR 263, CA.

8 See also *Electrolux Ltd v Hutchinson* [1976] IRLR 410, EAT, where it was held that for a difference to be of practical importance, it must be shown that, as well as being contractually obliged to do additional different duties, the duties are performed to some significant extent.

19.1.4 Responsibility

The EAT held, in *Eaton Ltd v Nuttall*,[9] that a factor such as responsibility may be decisive where it puts one employee into a different grade. This would include supervisory duties (see *Waddington v Leicester Council for Voluntary Services*[10]) or the additional responsibility of working permanently at night without supervision (see *Thomas v NCB*[11]).

19.1.5 Work done in practice cannot be ignored

The EAT has held[12] that, despite the fact that a large part of the man's and woman's job was the same, it was not possible to ignore part of the man's work; if the man had some duties that were significantly different then he was not doing like work. The woman's work mainly involved packing duties and she did some clerical work. The man similarly worked mainly as a packer but also did storeman's duties. The EAT found that they were not employed on like work and so it was irrelevant that the discrepancy in remuneration between them was not commensurate with the difference in the work that each did (see **20.16**).[13]

19.1.6 Would the differences result in different grading?

In *British Leyland v Powell*[14] the EAT held that a practical guide is whether the differences are such as to put the two employments into different categories or grades in an evaluation study. The lay members of the IT (the 'industrial jury') are presumed to have knowledge and experience which will help the IT make this decision. Evidence as to the extent of other differences in duties within the comparator's grade may assist.

9 [1977] IRLR 71.
10 [1977] IRLR 32, EAT.
11 [1987] IRLR 451, EAT.
12 *Maidment v Cooper & Co (Birmingham) Ltd* [1978] IRLR 462, EAT.
13 The UK courts have consistently taken this view in equal pay cases, but it is arguable that this constitutes a breach of art 119 and the EPD which require the elimination of all sex discrimination in pay. So if a woman's work is, say, 80% like work she should not receive only 60% of the man's pay.
14 [1978] IRLR 57, EAT.

19.1.7 Extra responsibilities and lower pay

In *Waddington v Leicester Council for Voluntary Service*,[15] a woman who was supervising a man, yet receiving less pay, was held to be not entitled to equal pay because they were not doing like work. This decision is wrong. The ECJ, in *Murphy v Bord Telecom Eirann*,[16] held that art 119 must be interpreted as covering the case where the applicant is doing work of higher value than that of the comparator: to find otherwise would render the principle of equal pay ineffective, since an employer could circumvent it by assigning additional duties to women, who could then be paid a lower wage.

19.1.8 Conclusion

It is often difficult to judge whether a man and woman are doing like work and it will depend on the facts in each case. Detailed evidence of the work actually done will need to be given. It is important to remember that the applicant may need to call evidence which establishes precisely what the male comparator does.

Women who fail to establish that they were doing like work or broadly similar work may now be able to claim that their work is of equal value (see Chapter 20).

19.2 Equivalent work under a job evaluation scheme (JES)

19.2.1 Introduction

Where an employer has carried out an analytical JES, this will be conclusive; if the woman's and man's work has been rated as equivalent, the pay and other contractual terms must be the same.[17] If the work of the woman and her comparator has not been rated as equivalent and the JES is analytical and non-discriminatory a woman will not succeed in a claim for either like work or equal value (see **20.5** and **20.6**) and cannot claim under the JES. However, if a JES has been carried out but is either not analytical or is discriminatory, the woman may make an equal value claim. The burden is on the employer to prove that the JES is not discriminatory (see **20.6**).

15 [1977] IRLR 32, EAT.
16 [1988] IRLR 267, ECJ.
17 EqPA s1(5).

19.2.2 Work rated as equivalent

A woman is to be regarded as employed on work rated as equivalent with that of a man if her job and his:

a) have been given an equal value, in terms of the demand made on a worker under various headings (for instance, effort, skill, decision) by a job evaluation study. The study must have been undertaken with a view to evaluating the jobs to be done by all or any of the employees; or
b) would have been given equal value but for the evaluation being made under a system setting different values for men and women on the same demands under any heading.[18]

Job evaluation is concerned with assessing the value of different jobs and putting the jobs in order of importance and worth. It is only the job content which is measured, not the person doing it. Length of service and productivity are irrelevant; the assumption is that the job is being done properly. Experience and qualifications are relevant only insofar as they are required for the job. Once the jobs have been rated, a further stage of the process involves setting grade and pay bands, with boundaries usually being fixed between groups of jobs which have scored similarly. If two jobs are likely to be graded the same, they should be rated as equivalent (see **19.2.6**).

There is no obligation on an employer to carry out a JES. However, job evaluation is an essential tool; without it, the effects of gender segregation in the workforce cannot be neutralised. But the method of evaluation is crucial. As one job evaluation expert has pointed out:

> the whole process of job evaluation is inherently judgmental and, insofar as the judgments are made predominantly by men on the basis of existing relativities, inevitably extremely suspect.[19]

19.2.3 Methods of carrying out a JES

There are different types of job evaluation scheme (which are set out below) but the main distinction is between:

- an analytical scheme, which evaluates jobs objectively and analyses the demands of the job, such as responsibility, working conditions, etc; and

18 Ibid.

19 Wainwright 'Why equal value is dynamite for pay structures' (1983) *Personnel Management* October. The same is true today.

– a non-analytical scheme, which compares jobs as a whole without considering the different elements.

A JES must be 'analytical' in order to comply with the provisions of EqPA s1(5). This means that the jobs of each worker covered by the study must have been valued in terms of the demand made on the worker under various headings. It is not sufficient for benchmark jobs to be evaluated on a 'factor demand' basis if the jobs of the applicant and comparator were not evaluated.[20]

Job evaluation is usually carried out by a panel with representatives from unions and management. It involves a comparison of a large number of jobs – unlike the process carried out under the EqPA whereby usually only a limited number of jobs are compared (ie, the applicant and her comparator(s)). The different types were set out in an Appendix to the EAT decision in *Eaton Ltd v Nuttall*.[21]

19.2.3.1 Non-analytical schemes

Job ranking. Each job is considered as a whole and is then given a ranking in relation to all other jobs. A ranking table is then drawn up and the ranked jobs grouped into grades. Pay levels can then be fixed for each grade.

This method involves putting jobs in an order which is felt to be fair. 'Fair' often means maintaining the status quo, so women's jobs are given low value. The job ranking method makes no attempt to analyse why one order of jobs is thought to be fairer than another.

Paired comparison. Each job is compared as a whole with each other job in turn and points (0, 1 or 2) awarded according to whether its overall importance is judged to be less than, equal to or more than the other. Points awarded for each job are then totalled and a ranking order produced.

Like job ranking, there is no analysis of why one job is felt to be more important. Again, this system tends to reinforce the traditional view of men's and women's work and their relative worth. If, as is often the case, women are doing jobs where there are no men working they will be paired with each other and will not benefit from comparison with the higher paid men's jobs.

Job classification. This is similar to ranking except that it starts from the opposite end; a broad grading structure is established first

20 *Bromley v H & J Quick Ltd* [1988] IRLR 249, CA.
21 [1977] IRLR 71.

and individual jobs fitted into it. Individual jobs considered typical of each grade are selected as 'benchmarks'. The other jobs are then compared with these benchmarks and the general description and placed in their appropriate grade.

This may well be discriminatory too, as work done by men and skills mainly held by men are likely to find a place near the top of the grading structure while women's work will be downgraded to the bottom.

19.2.3.2 Analytical schemes

Points assessment. This is the most common system in use. It is an analytical method, which, instead of comparing whole jobs, breaks down each job into a number of factors, eg, skills, responsibility, physical and mental requirements and working conditions. Each of these factors may be analysed further. Points are awarded for each factor according to a predetermined scale and the total points decide a job's place in the ranking order. Usually, the factors are weighted so that, eg, more or less weight may be given to hard physical conditions or to a high degree of skill.

This method provides scope for a complete re-evaluation of the worth of different jobs. It is likely to be effective only if the factors taken into account and the weightings given are not discriminatory (see **19.2.5** and **19.2.6**).

Factor comparison. This method employs the same principles as points assessment but uses only a limited number of factors, such as skill, responsibility and working conditions. A number of 'key' jobs are selected because their wage rates are generally agreed to be 'fair'. The proportion of the total wage attributable to each factor is then decided and a scale produced showing the rate for each factor of each key job. The other jobs are then compared with this scale, factor by factor, so that a rate is finally obtained for each factor of each job. The total pay for each job is reached by adding together the rates for its individual factors.

19.2.4 Example of discriminatory job factors

The following is an example of a discriminatory JES.[22]

22 Taken from *Job Evaluation Schemes free of sex bias (revised edition)* (EOC, 1994).

Factors (each factor is scored on a scale from 1 to 10) (for simplicity, no weights have been applied)	*Maintenance fitter*	*Company nurse*
Skill		
Experience in job	10	1
Training	5	7
Responsibility		
For money	0	0
For equipment and machinery	8	3
For safety	3	6
For work done by others	3	0
Effort		
Lifting requirement	4	2
Strength required	7	2
Sustained physical effort	5	1
Conditions		
Physical environment	6	0
Working position	6	0
Hazards	7	0
TOTAL	64	22

This set of factors is discriminatory because it contains many aspects of the male job and very few characteristics which relate to the female job. Also some of the characteristics which relate to the male job overlap, for example 'strength required' duplicates to some extent 'sustained physical effort'; with the result that a high score on one would often be associated with a high score on the other. The same is true of 'lifting requirement' and 'strength required'. Note that the difference in scores on the factor 'experience in job' completely outweighs the more significant difference in the factor 'training'.

Awarding 0 for a nurse in relation to hazards must be inaccurate as she will be working with people with infectious diseases.

19.2.5 Ways of avoiding bias in JES

An analytical JES which is free of sex bias will prevent a woman bringing an equal value claim (see 20.5 and 20.6). Account should be taken of the EOC's Code of Practice on Equal Pay which came into force on 26 March 1997. It is therefore in the interests of all parties for any JES to be non-discriminatory. The EOC has drawn up guidance on how to avoid sex bias in job evaluation schemes and the CA has approved the use of its booklet on the need to avoid bias (see *Bromley*[23]). The following highlights the main points:

a) A commitment to a fair job evaluation may require a change in traditional assumptions about the value attributed to work predominantly carried out by women. For example, it is a commonly held belief that women are 'natural' carers so that caring for others is not seen as a skill and need not be rewarded. Jobs such as nursing and caring for the elderly or disabled require many skills and should be treated as such and not just as women fulfilling their natural role.[24]
b) There should be a fair representation of women in all job evaluation committees and discussions. Lack of participation by women in the carrying out of a JES may mean that the study is incomplete and open to challenge.
c) Everyone involved in the JES, and particularly chairs of committees, should be given training on how sex bias in job evaluation can arise.
d) Regular progress reports should be given to all employees so they can raise concerns about any possible sex bias.
e) Minutes and records should be kept in case there is a subsequent complaint of discrimination.
f) Guidance and training should be given to those writing job descriptions with a comprehensive list of elements to be included; both the job-holder and his/her manager should be involved in the process.
g) The long tradition of using different titles for the jobs of men and women who are doing essentially the same work has frequently denoted a status difference. Thus, women are more likely to be called supervisor rather than manager, secretary rather than administrator or personal assistant, operator rather than technician. Job titles which are applied predominantly to one sex where there is a different job title for similar work done by the other sex should be examined, eg, 'chef' and 'cook'.
h) 'Male' jobs that have become deskilled through technological change may still be regarded as skilled, even though the work is similar to 'female' jobs which are unskilled.

23 *Bromley v H & J Quick Ltd* [1988] IRLR 249, CA.
24 See *Scott v Beam* (1985) 8860/84.

i) The identification of factors and sub-factors is crucial. Factors associated with work done by women, such as manual dexterity and concentration, must not be left out; length of service should be included only to the extent that it is necessary for the job.
j) Factors are often weighted according to how important they are to the work of the organisation; one factor may be given 10%, another 1%. Care should be taken to ensure that the factors on which the male jobs scored highly are not given unjustifiably high weights. Extreme weights should not be given to factors which are exclusively found in jobs performed predominantly by one sex.
k) Schemes often use benchmark jobs which are seen as typical of a grade or group of jobs. A representative sample of female jobs should be included to ensure that the JES takes account of job elements which are peculiar to predominantly female jobs.

19.2.6 Full results of JES relevant

In *Springboard Sunderland Trust v Robson*[25] the EAT held that in order to decide whether two jobs were rated as equivalent, it is necessary to look at the JES in its entirety. In a scheme where grade/pay bands had been set in advance, this included the allocation to grade or scale at the end of the process. Although in *Robson* the applicant and her comparator had been awarded different points (he had 428; she had 410) the work was to be regarded as rated as equivalent because the scheme provided that all employees who had between 410 and 449 points should be placed in the same salary grade. She was therefore entitled to equal pay.

19.2.7 Implementation of a JES

Once the JES has been carried out and has resulted in the same evaluation for the man's and woman's job, the woman should receive the same pay and terms and conditions of employment as the man, provided that there is no difference which is a material factor between the two employees. In *O'Brien and Others v Sim-Chem Ltd*,[26] at the time that the study was completed, the government had just announced a pay policy and the employer feared that the study would infringe the policy and government contracts would be lost. The HL said that, once the job evaluation had been completed, the EqPA bit immedi-

25 [1992] IRLR 261, EAT.
26 [1980] IRLR 373, HL.

ately – not when it was put into operation through a new grading structure.[27]

19.2.8 *Where JES initiated after a claim for equal value*

If an employer starts a JES after a claim is made for equal value, the JES will not be taken into account unless it has been completed (ie, implemented by employer and employees) before the final hearing takes place. The IT may adjourn a claim pending its completion.

If the JES does not lead to equal pay for the woman she can still argue that the JES was non-analytical and/or was discriminatory and that she should be paid the same under the equal value provisions (see 20.4 to 20.6).

LIKE AND EQUIVALENT WORK: KEY POINTS

- The applicant must first consider if she is doing the same or broadly similar work to a man. There is a two-stage test:
  - whether the work is the same or of a broadly similar nature; and
  - whether there are any significant and important differences in the tasks actually performed.

  The following broad principles should be applied:
  - trivial differences should be ignored;
  - frequency of tasks is important;
  - the time at which work is done is not generally relevant;
  - work done in practice cannot be ignored;
  - extra responsibilities cannot lead to less pay.

  Few cases now proceed on the basis of like work.
- The applicant should consider next whether her work has been rated as equivalent under a JES. There are five main ways of carrying out job evaluation – job ranking, paired comparison, job classification, points rating and factor comparison. Some of these methods are likely to be discriminatory.
- Once a JES has resulted in the same evaluation for the man's and woman's job the woman should receive the same pay and terms and conditions of employment.

27 See *Arnold v Beecham* [1982] IRLR 307, where the EAT said that there must have been a completed JES accepted as valid by all parties.

- Where a JES is started after a claim is made it will not be taken into account unless completed by the final hearing.
- If the JES has not rated the woman's work as equivalent and is not analytical, the applicant can then proceed with an equal value claim.
- If the JES has not rated the woman' work as equivalent and is analytical, the applicant can still proceed with an equal value claim if the JES is discriminatory. It is for the employer to show that the scheme is not discriminatory.

CHAPTER 20

Work of equal value

This chapter covers equal value claims and the detailed procedure for bringing a claim. It applies only to cases under the EqPA, not race discrimination claims.

20.1 Preliminary points

The equal value provisions allow women to claim the same pay as a man in the same employment if they are doing work of at least the same value. This is defined as work which is, in terms of the demands made on the woman (for instance, under such headings as effort, skill and decision), of equal value to that of a man.[1] Women can compare themselves with men doing completely different jobs, and can now question – with some hope of success – whether a man further up the scale really has more skill and responsibility or whether his job title just sounds more important.[2] For example, a part-time domestic compared her job with a full-time porter and ground staff; clerical workers compared their jobs with warehouse workers; clerks with storepersons and caretakers; clerical workers with shopfloor workers. An independent expert (IE) may be appointed by the IT to assess whether the work is of equal value.

20.2 The burden of proof

Under UK law, the burden of proof is clearly on the applicant to show that the work is of equal value.

1 Equal Pay (Amendment) Regulations 1983 SI No 1794 reg 2; EqPA s1(2)(c).

2 *Equal Opportunities Review* does a periodic equal value update which summarises the types of jobs which have been compared; see (1994) 58 EOR and (1996) 70 EOR.

20.3 Is there a like work claim?

If there is any possibility of arguing that the woman's work is the same as or broadly similar to a man's then a claim should be made under the 'like work' provisions (see **19.1**) as well as under the 'equal value' regulations. This is because the procedure in like work claims will usually be quicker, cheaper and easier.

The EqPA also makes it clear that a claim for equal value cannot be made where the comparator is employed on like or rated as equivalent work.[3] However, the fact that a woman is employed on like or work rated as equivalent with one man does not prevent her claiming she is employed on work of equal value to that of another man.[4] In *Pickstone and Others v Freemans plc*,[5] the HL said that ITs must first decide whether the complainant and the man with whom she seeks parity are doing like work. If so, there is no need to go to the time and expense of appointing an IE. In *Pickstone*, the women claimants were warehouse operatives and were claiming equal value with a Mr Phillips who was a checker warehouse operative. There were also male warehouse operatives who were paid the same as the women. The employers argued that a claim for equal pay for equal value could only be made if there were no men doing like work or work rated as equivalent. The HL held that it was irrelevant that *another man* was employed on like work to the applicant. As the HL pointed out, the opposite result would enable an employer to evade the equal work provisions by employing one token man on the same work as a group of potential women claimants who were deliberately paid less than a group of men employed on work of equal value with that of the women.

20.4 Has a JES been carried out?

If there has been a JES and the woman's work has been rated as equivalent in value to the man's, she is entitled to be paid the same (provided that there is no 'material factor' to justify the differential). If the JES rated the woman's work as lower than the man's and if it

3 EqPA s1(2)(c) states that 'where a woman is employed on work which, not being work in relation to which paragraph (a) or (b) applies . . . ' Para (a) refers to like work; (b) to equivalent work.

4 Though if her job has been compared to this man under an analytical, non-discriminatory JES, her claim is likely to be struck out at the preliminary stage (see **20.12.1**).

5 [1988] IRLR 357, HL.

was analytical and non-discriminatory she will be precluded from making an equal value claim.[6]

In *Leverton v Clywd CC*,[7] Lord Bridge said:

> An employer's most effective safeguard against oppressive equal value claims is to initiate his own comprehensive JES under s1(5) which, if properly carried out, will afford him complete protection.

Such a JES can be carried out at any time and will provide a defence if completed before the final hearing (see **19.2.8**). If instituted after the issue of proceedings, the JES will have this effect only where the jobs compared under the JES are those being carried out at the date of issue. If the comparison is not with the same job it will be more difficult for the employer to use the JES as a defence.[8]

In *McAuley and Others v Eastern Health and Social Services Board*,[9] the NICA said that a JES can only be used as a defence to an equal value complaint if it was carried out in respect of the undertaking or groups of undertakings for which the complainant works. Thus, a JES carried out for health boards in Great Britain could not block a claim by women working in similar jobs for health boards in Northern Ireland. The JES was never applied in Northern Ireland so was not relevant.

20.5 JES relevant only if analytical

If the JES did not rate the woman's job as equivalent, but the study was not 'analytical' (see **19.2.3**) she will still be able to make a claim under the equal value provisions. If the method of evaluation was job ranking, paired comparisons or job classification, the JES can be left out of account when considering whether the jobs are of equal value. In *Bromley v H & J Quick*,[10] the CA said that an employer seeking to have an equal value complaint dismissed because there has been a JES must show that the JES satisfied the requirements of EqPA s1(5). This requires that the study evaluate jobs in terms of the demand made on the worker under various headings such as effort, skill, decision, etc. In *Bromley* there were slightly differing views taken by the judges in relation to what constituted a valid JES. Woolf LJ suggested that it

6 EqPA s2A(2).
7 [1989] IRLR 28, HL.
8 See *Dibro Ltd v Hore and Others* [1990] IRLR 129, EAT.
9 [1991] IRLR 467, NICA.
10 [1988] IRLR 249, CA.

was sufficient to identify a group of jobs which, when evaluated under the headings, have no material difference. One of that group of jobs could then be evaluated under headings and slotted into the rank in the appropriate position, having taken into account the factor value; that job can then represent the other jobs within the group. However, in relation to a job which had not been evaluated under headings, it would be open to an employee to argue that her job was materially different from the 'representative' job. Neill LJ did not specify whether *all* jobs had to be evaluated analytically.

It is arguable that the prohibition on bringing an equal pay claim if there is an existing, valid JES is in breach of EC law, where the test is simply whether the applicant and her comparator are doing work of equal value. The existence of a JES may prevent an applicant from having this question determined by the 'judicial process'.

20.6 Discriminatory job evaluation not relevant

Until the equal value regulations were introduced it was very difficult to challenge a JES on the ground that it was carried out in a discriminatory way.

The equal value regulations state that a JES will be discriminatory if it is made under a system which discriminates on the ground of sex 'where a difference, or coincidence, between values set by that system on different demands under the same or different headings is not justifiable irrespective of the sex of the person on whom those demands are made'.[11] Thus, if different values are set for men and women on the same demand this is discriminatory.[12] If higher value is given to a demand (such as physical effort) which is more common in jobs held by men than to a demand (such as mental concentration)

11 EqPA s2A(3) as amended by Equal Pay (Amendment) Regulations 1983 SI No 1794 para 3(3). This does not apparently cover the situation where factors or demands, which are particularly relevant to women's jobs, are omitted. Examples may include factors such as concentration, responsibility for patients, etc. However, such an omission may result in a JES being discriminatory and should at least be challengeable under art 119 and the EPD.

12 In *Rummler v Dato-Druck* [1987] IRLR 32, ECJ, the applicant argued that she should have been placed in a higher pay grade because the work was, for her as a woman, heavy physical work. The same work did not require so much effort from a man. The ECJ held that it would be discriminatory to use values which represent the average capabilities of employees of one sex. This would discriminate against men and would be unlawful. Thus, women cannot be awarded more points because physical work is more effort for women than men.

which is found traditionally in women's jobs and this cannot be justified, it is discriminatory. In *Rummler v Dato-Druck GmbH*[13] where account was taken of heavy work, which favoured men, the ECJ said that, if the job classification scheme were not to be discriminatory, account should be taken of other criteria for which female employees may show particular aptitude. There are a number of factors likely to discriminate against women which have already been mentioned (see **19.2.4** and Equal Pay Code in Appendix 3).

It is for the employer to show that the JES is not discriminatory. It must explain how the JES worked and the factors taken into account.[14] EPD art 1(2) provides that a job classification system 'must be based on the same criterion for men and women and so drawn up as to exclude any discrimination on the grounds of sex'.

Dillon LJ pointed out (obiter) in *Bromley v H & J Quick*:[15]

> as there are no universally accepted external criteria available for measuring how much of a factor or quality is involved in a particular job or for measuring what relative weights ought to be attached to different factors or qualities involved, to differing extent, in various jobs, every attempt at job evaluation will inevitably at some stages involve value judgments, which are inherently to some extent subjective ... Where there are such subjective elements, care has to be taken to see that sex discrimination is not, inadvertently, let in.

20.7 Procedure for equal value cases

The initial stages, such as completion of the IT1 and IT3, referral to ACAS, requests for further and better particulars, discovery, written answers, are the same as for other equal pay and discrimination claims (see Chapter 25). There are additional steps and procedural rules for equal value cases.[16] Although the procedure and order may vary in different cases, the following sets out a relatively common format.

20.8 Directions hearing

A directions hearing is generally held in equal value cases and the IT may consider:

13 Ibid.
14 *Bromley and Others v H & J Quick Ltd* [1988] IRLR 249, CA.
15 Ibid.
16 Industrial Tribunal (Constitution and Rules of Procedure) Regulations 1993 SI No 2687 (hereafter referred to as the IT Rules) Sch 2.

a) whether there is really a 'like' or 'equivalent' work claim, in which case this will be considered first;[17]
b) whether to consider a number of cases together. Such an order may be made if:
   - there is a common question of law or fact in some or all the originating applications; or
   - the relief claimed arises out of or is in respect of the same facts; or
   - for any other reason it is desirable to make an order.[18]

   If there is a separate claim under the SDA by the same applicant against the same employer, it is quite common for the tribunal to consider linking the cases;
c) the identification of comparators;
d) particulars of a like work claim;
e) when and how to deal with any proposed defence under s1(3) (see Chapter 21).

As with other cases an order may also be made for discovery, further and better particulars and/or written answers.

20.9 Invitation to adjourn[19]

Before hearing an equal value claim, the IT must invite the parties to apply for an adjournment in order to try to seek a settlement. If the parties agree, an adjournment must be granted. This may prompt further consideration of settlement but is now usually just a formality because the case would not be before the IT if the parties could agree.

20.10 Preliminary hearing[20]

A preliminary hearing may be held in any IT case in order to decide any issue relating to the entitlement of any party to bring or contest the proceedings. This procedure can be used to decide, for example, whether the applicant has brought her claim in time or what is the appropriate pool for determining whether the employers' pay practice has disproportionate adverse impact on women (relevant to proof of the material factor defence).

17 Though this may also be considered at the initial hearing (see below).
18 IT Rules Sch 2 r18. This is the same as for all tribunal cases.
19 Ibid, Sch 2 r13(6A).
20 Ibid, Sch 1 r6 (see **25.9**).

20.11 Pre-hearing review[21]

This is unusual in equal value cases because of the specific provisions which allow the tribunal to strike out the case if it is 'hopeless'.

20.12 Initial hearing

It is usually at this hearing that the IT decides, where the issues are raised by the employer, whether:

a) there are no reasonable grounds for determining that the work is of equal value, ie, hopeless cases; and/or
b) there is a material factor defence (see **20.12.2** and Chapter 21).

20.12.1 No reasonable grounds

The tribunal may either:

a) decide that it will determine the question of whether the work is of equal value; or
b) appoint an IE,

unless it decides there are no reasonable grounds for determining that the work is of equal value, in which case the tribunal can dismiss the case.[22]

When the regulations were introduced in the HL, the government explained that only 'hopeless' cases would be dismissed on the basis that there were no reasonable grounds for saying the work was of equal value.[23] The tribunal must consider whether a case is 'hopeless' before considering whether to refer it to an IE.[24]

In one case,[25] a fish-packer compared the value of her work to that of a labourer. The tribunal found that the labourer had more training, carried out a wider range of jobs, had a more extensive knowledge of different fish and worked in poorer conditions. There were, therefore, no reasonable grounds for saying that the value of the two jobs was equal. However, tribunals should be very careful before reaching such conclusions. In a similar case,[26] the expert found that fishpackers' and labourers' jobs did merit equal pay.

21 Sch 2 rr7 and 13(2)(d).
22 EqPA s2A(1).
23 *Hansard* HL Debs, col 924, 5 December 1983.
24 *Sheffield MDC v Siberry* [1989] ICR 208.
25 *Kirby v Cawoods (Fish Curers) Ltd* (1984) COIT 1554/159.
26 *Wells and Others v F Smales & Son (Fish Merchants) Ltd* (1985) COIT 1643/113; 6 EOR 12.

Where it is unclear whether there are reasonable grounds for saying that work is of equal value, the applicant should be given the benefit of the doubt.[27]

In *Dennehy v Sealink Ltd*,[28] Ms Dennehy claimed that her responsibilities were equal to those of male clerical officers on a higher grade. She did not, however, name a particular comparator and this is an essential part of any equal pay claim. At a preliminary hearing, evidence was given on her behalf by the applicant and an expert witness. The IT heard the evidence but decided that it could not form part of the basis of its decision; it considered that the EAT's ruling in *Leverton* (see **18.9.6**) required it to decide whether the applicant had established a prima facie case and that she had not. The EAT overturned the IT's decision, saying that the tribunal should have taken into account the applicant's and expert's evidence and then asked 'looking at the matter in the round do we find that there was no reasonable basis for a claim?'

20.12.1.1 Discriminatory JES

One ground for holding that a claim is hopeless is that there has been an analytical and non-discriminatory JES where the relevant jobs have been given different values (see **20.5** and **20.6**).

20.12.2 'Material factor' defence

The rules provide that the tribunal may at this stage, if it considers it appropriate, hear evidence on and determine the 'material factor' defence.[29] If it is heard the IT will assume, when considering the genuine material factor, that the jobs compared are of equal value. If the employer is successful the case will go no further.[30] If unsuccessful, the employer cannot raise the defence again unless there are exceptional circumstances.[31]

27 *Langley and Others v Beecham Proprietaries Ltd* (1985) COIT 1683/206.

28 [1987] IRLR 120; 6 EOR 7, EAT.

29 In *Reed Packaging Ltd v Boozer and Everhurst* [1988] IRLR 333 the EAT held that although the IT was not bound to consider the material factor defence at this stage, if it did, it must either reach a decision on the evidence or refer the case to an IE.

30 In *Leverton v Clwyd* CC [1988] IRLR 239, CA; [1989] IRLR 28, HL, the tribunal said that 'common sense dictates that if a genuine material factor defence is firmly and unequivocally established at the initial hearing stage, it would be ludicrous to go to the expense of appointing an expert when the success of that defence would have been the rejection of any equal value claim in any event'. This was upheld by the HL.

31 IT Rules Sch 1 r9(2E) was amended in April 1994 in order to preclude the IT from considering the defence again if it has been raised at the preliminary hearing.

If the defence is not heard at this stage it can be raised at a later stage after the determination of equal value. This matter is considered in greater detail in Chapter 21.

20.13 Is the work of equal value?

If there is no application to dismiss the claim on the grounds set out above or if the woman succeeds at the initial hearing, the IT must decide whether to refer the case to an IE.[32] Reference to an IE used to be mandatory but since 31 July 1996 the IT has had a discretion to decide the question of equal value itself.[33] The tribunal must first give the parties an opportunity to make representations to the tribunal on whether an expert should be required.[34] Most equal value claims will require an expert evaluation of the relevant jobs. It is difficult to envisage situations where the tribunal will have the expertise to carry out a non-discriminatory, analytical evaluation of the two (or more) jobs being compared. However, there will be cases where both parties want to use their own job evaluation experts and it may then appear redundant to have a third expert from the ACAS panel.

Even where the tribunal decides not to appoint an IE at this stage, it may later require an IE's report but the IT must first give the parties the chance to make further representations.[35]

20.14 The independent expert (IE)

IEs are chosen from an ACAS panel. There are about 16 IEs, all of whom work part-time. They are appointed for a period of two years but their appointment is renewable.

The IE decides how to evaluate the jobs and will always proceed analytically, ie, by looking at the demands made on the employee under headings such as effort, skill, decision-making and responsibility.[36] This must be done on a qualitative, not a quantitative, basis.

32 The IE is a member of an ACAS panel.

33 EqPA s2A(1)(a) as amended by the Sex Discrimination and Equal Pay (Miscellaneous Amendments) Regulations 1996 SI No 438 and IT Rules Sch 2 r8A(1).

34 IT Rules Sch 2 r8A as amended by SI 1996 No 1757.

35 Ibid, Sch 2 r8A(3).

36 Ibid Sch 2 r8A(1). See *Equal pay for Work of Equal Value: A guide to good practice for independent experts* (ACAS, June 1990). The process is similar to carrying out an analytical JES. For examples of what jobs have been compared see EOR November/December 1994 and November/December 1996.

Differences in hours of work and holidays are not matters for the expert. Thus the IE must carry out an *ad hoc* job evaluation study as between the applicant and her comparators.[37]

The IE must compare only what the employees do in practice and qualifications and experience actually required by the job, not hypothetical duties or unnecessary qualifications. The IE will normally draw up a job description based on interviewing the job-holders and their supervisors and observing the jobs being done. Alternatively, the IE may accept as accurate the content of one or more job descriptions provided by the parties or their experts. The IE will then identify factors (and sub-factors), such as:

- basic knowledge;
- experience;
- skills;
- effort (mental and physical);
- responsibility (eg, for people, equipment, training);
- working conditions.[38]

Each factor (and sub-factor) should be separately defined and various levels of demand will usually be identified within each factor (and sub-factor). Points or some other marking system will be devised. In some cases the factor scores will be weighted to show the relative importance of the factor, although it is not usual for IEs to do this expressly. 'Weighting' is often a contentious issue and one which can be used by an employer to preserve the existing hierarchy. It happens less obviously when one factor has more sub-factors (eg, three for working conditions and two for mental effort).[39]

An alternative method, which is simpler and more transparent, is for the IE to compare the information gathered under each factor (or sub-factor) with a view to determining whether the demands on the applicant are greater than/equal to/less than those on the comparator. The jobs performed by the applicant and comparator (or comparators) will then be evaluated under each factor (or sub-factor) head so as to produce a total or final result which can be compared.

37 *Leverton v Clwyd* CC [1989] IRLR 28, HL.
38 See **19.2.3.2.**
39 For examples of how IEs have carried out evaluations see (1996) 70 EOR Nov/Dec 25.

20.15 Procedure for IE

The following procedure applies.

20.15.1 IE's instructions

Any requirement to prepare a report must be in writing and shall set out:

- the name and address of each party;
- the address of the place where the employee works;
- the question of whether the work of the woman and the man is of equal value;
- the name of the man (or men) with whom the woman is comparing herself;
- the date by which the IE is required to send his/her report to the tribunal;
- the date by which the IE must send progress reports to the tribunal.[40]

This information must be sent to the parties with a notice informing them that if a party unreasonably delays the preparation of the IE's report they may have an award of costs made against them[41] and may be struck out.

In addition, the requirements must stipulate that the IE shall:

a) take account of all relevant information and representations;
b) before drawing up his/her report, produce and send to the parties a written summary of the information and representations and invite comment; *then*
c) prepare a report which shall reproduce the summary and contain an account of any representations, and any conclusion (with reasons) as to whether the work is of equal value;
d) take no account of the difference of sex and act fairly.[42]

The IT will then adjourn the hearing, pending receipt of the report.[43]

There are no guidelines on the method the IE must use; in most cases the method used by the IE is accepted by the tribunal.

40 IT Rules Sch 2 r8A(4). The IE must provide regular progress reports to the tribunal on whether s/he can comply with the timescale; if not, s/he must give reasons for the delay and the date by which the report will be ready. Where there is to be delay the report must be sent to the parties. If delay is caused by a party details must be given (ibid, Sch 2 r8A(10)).

41 Which may include the costs of the IEs.

42 Ibid, Sch 2 r8A(5).

43 Ibid, Sch 2 r8A(6).

20.15.2 Discovery by IE

In addition to the rules regarding discovery, inspection and the calling of witnesses which are available in respect of all tribunal hearings, the tribunal may, on the application of the IE, require anyone with relevant information or documents to provide them.[44] An ACAS officer cannot be required to provide such information; nor will such a requirement be made of any person who would have good grounds for refusing to comply with it if the requirement were made in connection with a tribunal hearing.[45] Application can be made, by the person concerned, to set aside the requirement.[46]

The IT has no specific power to order an employer to allow the IE access to the workplace. In order to obtain the necessary information about the jobs, it may be essential for the IE to see employees at work. It could be argued that inspection of the workplace is an integral part of the information to which the IE is entitled, albeit of a visual kind. It may be easier for the employer to allow access than to have to produce detailed specifications of the work which may involve preparation of plans and photographs of the workplace.[47]

Although there are no procedural regulations under EC law, if a woman is unable, because of an obstructive employer, to show that her work is of equal value to a man's, she may be able to challenge the UK equal value regulations as being inadequate under EC law.

20.15.3 Representations by parties

The parties should send their representations to the IE. A summary of representations made, together with an invitation to the parties to comment on them, must be sent to both parties.[48]

44 Ibid, Sch 2 r4(2A).

45 Ibid, Sch 2 r4(2B).

46 Ibid, Sch 2 r5(5A).

47 In *Whitmore and Others v Frayling Furniture* (1985) COIT 1680/204, the IT ordered that the applicant's expert be allowed access to the employer's premises. The order was granted on the basis that, under IT Rules Sch 2 r8(1), a tribunal 'shall conduct the hearing in such manner as it considers most suitable to the clarification of the issues before it and generally to the just handling of the proceedings'(now r9(1)). This was rather stretching the words of the rule in order to attempt a remedy and perceived defect in the powers of the IT. It may be more appropriate for the tribunal to draw inferences from a refusal of access.

48 IT Rules Sch 2 r8A(5).

20.15.4 Delay by IE

IE reports may take months and the new procedure, whereby the IT monitors the IE's progress (see **20.15.1**), is intended to reduce delay. If the IE states that s/he is unable to keep to the timetable the IT may give written notice either:

- that s/he is required to send the report by the required date; or
- substitute a later date; or
- replace the IE; this may be done only if it would be 'in the interests of justice'. In most cases it is likely to cause further delay.

20.15.5 IE's report

The usual format is as follows:

a) The job details will be set out. This is a list of the tasks performed with factual details about what is involved, such as lifting weights of 20 kilos for about 10 metres. Language which involves value judgments, such as 'lifts light weights and carries them a short distance' does not provide the information that will enable the accuracy and consistency of facts to be checked, nor will it allow the IT to assess the evaluation of the task. Similarly, a description which states 'requires a very high degree of prolonged concentration' should be avoided in favour of 'needs to concentrate to the exclusion of all other matters during patient sessions of 50 minutes for about four sessions a day'.
b) A work analysis section is prepared. Material relevant to, for example, concentration or physical effort is collected and listed under the various factor heads.
c) A section (often with appendices) explains the method used, defines the factors (and any sub-factors and levels within the factors) and sets out the scoring system.
d) There will an assessment or evaluation section where the jobs are compared factor by factor.
e) The conclusions section sets out the IE's opinion in respect of equal value and includes a brief resumé of the reasons.

The IE's report must contain a summary of the representations made by the parties, the IE's conclusion as to whether the work is of equal value and the reasons for the conclusions.[49]

49 Ibid, Sch2 r8A(5)(c).

The report, when completed, is sent to the IT which sends a copy to each party.[50]

The IT may require the IE to provide a written explanation of any matter in the report or to give further consideration to the question of equal value and provide his/her conclusion in writing.[51] If the tribunal does this, notice must be given to both parties. This requirement broadly follows the same procedure as the original report.[52] Thus, the instructions to the IE and the provisions in relation to delay are similar (see **20.15.1**). The IE's reply must then be sent to the parties who can make representations. This can all be done by correspondence.

20.15.6 Resumed hearing

Once the report is received by the tribunal, a hearing date may be fixed – not earlier than 14 days from the time that the report was sent to the parties.[53] At the hearing the tribunal may consider whether to admit the IE's report.

20.15.7 Exclusion of report

Either party may apply to the tribunal to exclude the report (so that it does not become evidence) on the basis that:

- it does not comply with the rules relating to the summary of representations and the report; or
- the report could not reasonably have reached the conclusion it did; or
- for some reason (other than disagreement with the conclusions of the report) the report is unsatisfactory.[54]

The IT must take account of any representations and the parties may give evidence, call and question witnesses, including the IE and the parties' experts.[55]

50 Ibid, Sch 2 r8A(10).
51 Ibid, Sch 2 r8A (15) to (17).
52 The only differences are that the secretary of tribunals is not obliged to send a notice about unreasonable delay, the IT may waive the need for progress reports and the IT may cancel the requirement without requiring another expert to fulfil it (IT Rules r8A(16A)(a) and (b)).
53 Ibid, Sch 2 r8A(11).
54 Ibid, Sch 2 r8A(13).
55 Ibid, Sch 2 r8A(14).

If parties wish to dispute any facts contained in the IE's report they should do so at this stage and can examine the IE. The rules state that, once the IE's report has been admitted, no party to a case may give evidence – or question any witness – on any matter of fact on which a conclusion in the report is based, unless it relates to the genuine material factor defence or where the IE did not reach a conclusion because of failure by the parties to provide relevant information.[56] The IE's oral and written evidence will be taken into account if there is a challenge to the admissibility of the report.[57]

In *Hayward v Cammell Laird*,[58] the employer tried to introduce fresh evidence about working conditions after the report had been admitted. The evidence was held by the tribunal to be inadmissible.

The EAT has held that the power to disallow reports hinges on their validity, not their weight, and in most cases the tribunal should admit the report, as rejection simply causes further delay.[59]

If the tribunal decides that the report is to be excluded, it may start again and instruct a different IE.[60] If this happens no further account shall be taken of the first IE's report.[61]

20.15.8 Parties' experts

Each party may, on giving notice to the tribunal,[62] call their own expert witness to:

- challenge a JES at the initial stage;
- give expert evidence at any stage.

In addition, each party may use an expert to:

- draw up job descriptions;
- make submissions to the IE on the issue of equal value; and
- provide assistance in cross-examining the IE and/or other party's expert.

56 Ibid, Sch 2 r9(2C)-(2D).
57 Ibid.
58 [1987] IRLR 186, CA; [1988] IRLR 257, HL.
59 *Aldridge v British Telecommunications plc* [1990] IRLR 10, EAT.
60 IT Rules Sch 2 r8A(13).
61 Ibid, Sch 2 r8A(18).
62 This is usually dealt with at the directions hearing and expert reports will be exchanged prior to the hearing. Late introduction of such a report may lead to an adjournment and a possible costs order.

There is no power to require the applicant to be interviewed by her employer's expert witness but in practice the applicant should be advised to co-operate.[63]

20.15.9 Attendance of IE

The IE's report will be admitted at the resumed hearing provided it has not been excluded (see 20.15.7).[64] If either party wants the IE to attend, the tribunal must order the IE to attend. The tribunal may also ask the IE to attend.[65]

20.15.10 IE's report at the hearing

The hearing proceeds in the same way as other IT claims. The only difference is that the IE is likely to be called to give evidence. Although factual matters cannot be disputed at this stage, the IE's analysis of the facts can be challenged.

In *Hayward* (above), the tribunal said that it would reject the IE's methodology only if s/he had gone badly wrong. However, the NICA, in *Tennants Textile Colours Ltd v Todd*,[66] said that there was nothing to prevent a party from making submissions to contradict the conclusions of the IE. Although the report 'must obviously carry considerable weight', there was no principle that a tribunal can 'only reject the IE's report if the evidence were such as to show that it was so plainly wrong that it could not be accepted'.

In *Dibro Ltd v Hore*,[67] the EAT said (obiter) that:

> an independent expert appointed under s2A has no greater standing as an expert than an expert called by either side or a member of the ACAS staff who is experienced in this field. Each witness and his assessment must be tested in evidence.[68]

It is important to look very carefully at the method of evaluation used. If discriminatory, it may well infringe art 119 or the EPD. The IE is also under a duty not to discriminate and if s/he does then the report is likely to be invalid (see 20.15.7 for when and how to challenge the IE's report).

63 *Lloyds Bank plc v Fox* [1989] IRLR 103, EAT.
64 IT Rules Sch 2 r8A(12).
65 Ibid, Sch 2 r9(2A).
66 [1989] IRLR 3, NICA.
67 [1990] IRLR 129, EAT.
68 See also *Aldridge* (n59 above).

Provided that notice has been given to the tribunal and other parties, any party can call one expert witness each, and s/he may be cross-examined and re-examined in the normal way.[69]

20.16 Disproportionately lower pay

If the woman's work is deemed to be of less value by, say 10%, yet she is paid much less, say 40%, than the comparable man, it is arguable that to the extent that the work is of equal value she should be paid the same as the man; thus the differential should not be 40% but 10%. There is no provision under the EqPA for reducing differentials in this way; either the work is of equal value or it is not.

The EPD principle of equal pay means equal pay:

> for the same work or for work to which equal value is attributed, the elimination of all discrimination on grounds of sex with regard to all aspects and conditions of remuneration.

Thus, there are no specific provisions for reducing pay inequalities where the work is not similar, rated as equivalent or of equal value. However, if employers could give women jobs which, although not of 'equal value' were nearly of equal value, yet pay the women disproportionately less than their male counterparts, the object of the legislation would be defeated and it might infringe art 119.[70]

20.17 What is equal value?

In *Wells and Others v F Smales & Son*,[71] the tribunal said that if the jobs are very nearly equal, so that the differences between the women and the men were not relevant or did not make any real material difference, then equal pay should be awarded. This accords with usual practice whereby workers within a point score range of between 15% and 20% are in the same grade.[72]

69 IT Rules Sch 2 r9(2B).

70 See *Enderby v Frenchay Health Authority and Secretary of State for Health* [1993] IRLR 591 where the ECJ held that in relation to the material factor defence where some of the difference in pay is attributable to one identified factor, only that part of the difference is justified (see **21.2.4**).

71 (1985) COIT 1643/113.

72 See also *Springboard Sunderland Trust v Robson* [1992] IRLR 261, EAT.

EQUAL VALUE: KEY POINTS

- The equal value provisions allow women to claim the same pay as a man doing a different job but one which has 'equal value'.
- The burden of proof is on the applicant.
- A like work claim should always be considered first if the work is the same or broadly similar.
- A JES will be a bar to an equal value claim only if analytical and non-discriminatory.
- Equal value is determined by evaluating the demands made on the employee and this is usually done by an IE appointed by the IT.
- There is a complex procedure for equal value cases which may involve different hearings in order to:
  - give directions;
  - invite the parties to adjourn in order to seek settlement (this is a mandatory requirement);
  - decide any issue relating to the entitlement of the parties to bring or contest the proceedings;
  - decide if the case has any reasonable chance of success.
- There will be an initial hearing to decide:
  a) if the case is hopeless; and
  b) where requested by the employer, if there is a material factor defence.
- The expert can choose the method of evaluation, provided that it is analytical and non-discriminatory.
- The expert's report is not conclusive but carries considerable weight.
- The expert is entitled to discovery of documents.
- There are new time limits for the expert which are monitored by the IT; where a party causes delay costs may be awarded against them and these may include the cost of the IE.
- The expert's report may be excluded if it does not comply with the rules or is unsatisfactory.
- The parties may also call an expert each.
- The independent expert is likely to attend the hearing.

CHAPTER 21

The material factor defence

This chapter looks at the employer's defence to an equal pay claim under the EqPA, whether made under the like work, work rated as equivalent or equal value provisions.

Even where a woman is doing like work, work rated as equivalent or work of equal value, the employer may still avoid paying her the same as the man (or awarding her the same terms and conditions) if the employer can prove that the variation in pay is genuinely due to a material factor *which is not the difference of sex*. There is no specific material factor or any other defence under art 119. However, the ECJ has interpreted art 119 to mean that market forces or other factors may justify a difference in pay and that it was for the national court to determine this (see, for example, *Enderby v Frenchay Health Authority*[1]).

21.1 Material factor and material difference compared

In the case of like and equivalent work claims the material factor *must* be a material difference and in the case of equal value claims it *may* be a material difference. In practice, the principles to be applied are the same (see below). The burden of proof is on the employer to show that there is a material factor. Neither 'material difference' nor 'material factor' is defined by the EqPA so their meaning has to be gleaned from case-law.

Until the HL decision in *Rainey v Greater Glasgow Health Board*,[2] the material difference defence was limited to characteristics of the worker, such as length of service, superior skill or qualifications, red circling; it did not include extrinsic factors.[3] The equal value regula-

1 [1993] IRLR 593, ECJ.
2 [1987] IRLR 26, HL.
3 *Clay Cross (Quarry Services) Ltd v Fletcher* [1979] ICR 1; [1979] 1 All ER 474, CA.

tions of 1983 deliberately extended the defence in equal value claims so as to include a material 'factor'. This encompasses the material difference defence, but is wider and includes extrinsic factors, such as market forces.[4]

In *Rainey* (a like work case) the HL cast doubt on whether there is now any distinction between the 'material difference' and 'material factor' defence. It said that a difference which is connected with economic factors affecting the efficient carrying on of the employer's business or other activity may well be relevant. Thus, the employer was able to justify paying male prosthetists (limb-fitters) more than an existing female prosthetist doing like work because otherwise it would not have been possible to recruit prosthetists. In effect it was saying that market forces, the very factors envisaged by the government as constituting a material factor in equal value cases, could also be a material difference.

21.2 What does the employer need to show?

The employer must prove:

a) the factual basis (or bases) upon which the employer relies to establish the material factor;
b) that the material factor existed and was known to the employer at the date when the wages were fixed and/or like work, etc, commenced (whichever was later) and thereafter up to the date of the equal pay hearing;[5]
c) that this material factor (or factors) is/are significant and relevant to:
   (i) the woman's rate of pay (or bonus, car allowance or any other contractual term);
   (ii) the man's rate of pay (or other contractual term);
   so as to genuinely explain the variation between the two;
d) that this material factor *caused* the variation about which the complaint is made. If the material factor accounts for only part of the variation in pay, the defence is only partly made out and the

4 The government said: 'What we have in mind are circumstances where the difference in pay is not due to personal factors between the man and the woman, but rather to skill shortages or other market forces. If a man is paid more than a woman for work of equal value because his skills are in short supply, this is not sexually discriminatory, provided the reason is genuine and the employer can show this.' (*Hansard*, HC Debs, 20 July 1983, col 48.)

5 See *Post Office v Page* EAT 554/87.

applicant is entitled to an increase to the extent to which the defence is not made out;

e) that the factual basis on which the employer relies to establish the material factor is not itself founded upon or tainted by sex discrimination.

21.2.1 Decisions on factual bases for material factor

One of the main issues is whether the material factor is flawed by either direct sex discrimination (in which case it will not be a defence) or by indirect sex discrimination (or disproportionate adverse impact) in which case the employer must show that there is objective justification (see **21.4** and **21.5**). An applicant should always consider whether the material factor put forward by the employer is in any way tainted by discrimination. If it is, it will not be a defence.

The following are some examples of material factors raised by employers.

21.2.1.1 Geographical distinction

An employer may pay an employee working in London more than one working elsewhere.[6] This may or may not be unfair, but even if there are mainly men working in one location and women in another, it is unlikely to be unlawful discrimination.

21.2.1.2 Red circling

This is a method by which the pay and benefits of a particular worker are protected if, for some reason, the workforce (or part of it) is re-organised and the individual is downgraded. The reasons for the red circling must not be discriminatory (eg, caused by past discrimination).

In *Trico Folberth v S Groves and E Aiston*,[7] men who had been receiving a night-work supplement and a flexibility payment for doing night shifts and for moving jobs if required, were moved to the day shift after the termination of the night shift. The men's pay was to stay the same until the day shift caught up with them so, although they were doing the same work as the women on the day shift, they were paid more. The IT found that the difference in pay was a genuine material difference as it was only to compensate the men for the loss of the pecuniary benefits of the night shift. If, however, the reason for

6 *NAAFI v Varley* [1977] ICR 11, EAT.

7 [1976] IRLR 327, EAT.

the original difference in pay was discriminatory, the red circling would not be a material factor.

Tribunals should also take into account the length of time since the protection was introduced and whether mere custom rather than 'good industrial practice' had determined its continuance.[8]

21.2.1.3 Flexibility

In *Danfoss*,[9] the employer used the criterion of flexibility in determining grading and therefore pay. The ECJ held that the employer could justify this if it referred to adaptability but, because such criteria might discriminate against women with family commitments, the employer had to show that this adaptability was important for the particular job.

21.2.1.4 Merit

General considerations of merit may be taken into account. These may include co-operativeness, time-keeping, efficiency, reliability.[10] Care should be taken to ensure that 'merit' is measured fairly and objectively and not in a discriminatory way. If bad time-keeping or unreliability is caused by childcare or other family responsibilities, an effort should be made to ensure that women with such difficulties can be accommodated, where possible, by, eg, flexi-time arrangements. Failure to do this may lead to a finding of indirect discrimination (see Chapter 3). Where a pay system ostensibly based on merit systematically provides lower pay to women there will be discrimination (see **21.3**).

21.2.1.5 Higher productivity

This may justify a difference in pay, and productivity schemes are quite common. The employer must, however, prove that the man is more productive. If, for example, it is not clear how productivity is measured and there is evidence that women generally score lower, the scheme is likely to be discriminatory (see **21.3**).[11]

21.2.1.6 Training

The employer may justify the use of the criterion of vocational or other training to determine pay but only where s/he demonstrates that

8 *Outlook Supplies v Parry* [1978] IRLR 12, EAT.

9 *Handels-og Kontorfunktionaerernes Forbund i Danmark v Dansk Arbejdsgiverforening (acting for Danfoss)* [1989 IRLR 532, ECJ.

10 *E Buckland v Dowty Rotol Ltd* [1976] IRLR 162, IT.

11 See *Danfoss* (n9).

such training is of importance for the performance of the specific duties entrusted to the worker.[12] Note that there should also be equal access to training (see **11.4**).

21.2.1.7 Responsibility

In *Edmonds v Computer Services (South-West) Ltd*[13] the EAT held that extra responsibility may be a material factor. This must be wrong as responsibility is relevant to the question of whether there is like work, work rated as equivalent or work of equal value. It should not be taken into account when deciding whether there is a defence.

21.2.1.8 Special understanding of 'quality' measures

In *Tyldesley v TML Plastics Ltd*[14] a man was paid more because it was believed that he understood and was committed to the concept of total quality management. The EAT held that this could be a material factor provided it was not tainted by gender discrimination. This is likely to a very subjective measure which is difficult to measure objectively and is not consistent with the principle that pay systems should be transparent (see **21.3**).

21.2.1.9 Skill and qualifications

Skill and qualifications have been given as examples of what might also constitute a material difference.[15] Skill and experience must be related to the job in order to justify differentials in pay because women are less likely to have skill and experience because of breaks in their career.[16]

21.2.1.10 Experience and length of service

Service increments and long service benefits may discriminate against women who are more likely to have shorter service because of breaks in their working lives caused by childbirth and dependant care responsibilities. Although such criteria may be prima facie discriminatory, the courts have said (obiter) in a number of cases that length of service may justify a difference in pay. The ECJ, in *Danfoss*,[17] said

12 Ibid.

13 [1977] IRLR 359, EAT.

14 [1996] IRLR 395.

15 *Shields v E Coomes (Holdings) Ltd* [1978] ICR 1159, CA; *Clay Cross* (n3); and *McGregor and Others v GMBATU* (1987) 328 IRLIB 12, EAT.

16 See *Danfoss* (n9) and *Brunt v The Northern Ireland Electricity Service* [1979] 1 NIJB.

17 See n9.

that, although seniority may result in less favourable treatment of women, it goes alongside experience which generally places a worker in a better position to carry out his/her duties. Thus, it can be rewarded without the need to establish the importance it has for the performance of the specific duties. However, in *Nimz v Freie und Hansestadt Hamburg*[18] the ECJ held that although seniority goes hand in hand with experience which, in principle, should allow the employee to perform better, the objectivity of such a criterion depends on the circumstances. Thus, where the service of full-time workers is fully taken into account but only one half of such service is taken into account for part-timers (where the majority of whom are women), the employer must show the link between the experience and the duties performed. If part-time workers improve their performance at the same rate as full-time workers, the difference cannot be objectively justified and will be discriminatory. In such circumstances it will not constitute a material factor defence.

21.2.1.11 Working conditions

Working conditions should only be considered in relation to whether there is like work, work rated as equivalent or work of equal value. However, the EAT, in *McGregor and Others v GMBATU*[19] and *Davies v McCartneys*[20] held that they could be a material factor. This must be wrong (see **20.12.2**). In *Loughran and Others v British Road Services Ltd* a Northern Ireland IT held that where the defence is considered at the preliminary stage it must be on the basis that the work is of equal value. That includes consideration of working conditions. The IT very reasonably held that if the respondent concedes (for the purposes of the preliminary hearing) that the work is of equal value, the same respondent cannot argue that the working conditions justify the difference in pay.

21.2.1.12 Market forces

Market forces may be a 'material difference' and 'material factor'. However, this defence is not available where the difference in pay arose because of discrimination; the 'market' is itself often discriminatory[21] (see **21.4**).

The following are some examples of market factors.

18 [1991] IRLR 222, ECJ.
19 (1987) 328 IRLIB 12, EAT.
20 [1989] IRLR 439, EAT.
21 See *Ratcliffe v North Yorkshire* CC [1995] IRLR 439, HL.

Compensation for skill shortages. In *Rainey*[22] (see **21.1**) the HL held that a difference connected with economic factors affecting the efficient carrying on of the employer's business may be relevant. The HL found:

a) as a matter of fact, prosthetists who entered employment from private practice had to be paid a higher salary than an existing female prosthetist or the NHS prosthetists service would never have been set up; it was necessary to pay the comparator more in order to attract him;
b) it was coincidental that all those recruited from private practice were men; there was no evidence of discrimination;
c) there were sound, objectively justified, administrative reasons for placing existing prosthetists, men and women, on the Whitley Council scale. From an administrative point of view it would have been anomalous and inconvenient if prosthetists alone were subject to a different salary scale and negotiating machinery from other NHS employees;
d) there was no evidence of discrimination in the Whitley Council scales.

Paying the 'going rate' for the job. Many employers base pay on comparable rates to those used by other employers, without looking at the value of the individual jobs. If this constitutes a defence it will tend to negate the principle of equal pay for work of equal value because of gender segregation and discrimination in the labour market. Thus, what is perceived as 'women's work (eg, caring, welfare and secretarial tasks) is undervalued and underpaid while 'men's work' (eg, labouring, portering, forestry) is more appropriately rewarded even where the work is of equal value. The fact that most employers underpay 'women's work' is a form of discrimination which ought not to provide a defence. This was implicitly accepted by the HL in *Ratcliffe* (see **21.4**).[23]

22 See n2.

23 See also *Lord and Others v Knowsley BC* (1996) 22 August; DCLD 29; Case no: 59559/95 where the pay of home carers, who were almost exclusively female, was reduced in order to compete with outside contractors. The IT pointed out that the women were paid less than the men because their equivalent work attracts lower pay for the women who do it elsewhere. This was not a good reason to pay the women less than male school caretakers or refuse collectors who were primarily men. There was no evidence of a shortage of skills.

Compulsory competitive tendering. The need to reduce women's wages in order to compete with outside competitors has been firmly rejected as a material factor by the HL (in *Ratcliffe*) and by tribunals where the market rate is discriminatory (see **21.4**).

Paying a higher rate to reduce labour turnover. The employer should have to prove the need to reduce labour turnover and that it was higher in the work group which included the comparator than in the applicant's group. If the employer argues that higher pay has in the past reduced labour turnover, an analysis of both the figures showing the reductions and the reasons given as to why the reductions occurred will be important. In addition, the employer must show that the same treatment is given to women and men.

Paying the lowest rate possible. Paying the lowest rate necessary to attract adequately qualified workers, taking account of supply and demand and the bargaining power of the workers may mean paying women less because they are prepared to work for less. This is discriminatory and should not constitute a defence. For example, in *Gamble and Others v Stockham Valve Ltd*[24] the tribunal said that the fact that female clerical staff could be recruited at a lower rate than the lowest paid semi-skilled shopfloor workers (who were all men) was not a defence. It was 'exactly the type of situation which the Equal Pay Act was introduced to prevent – the perpetuation of unequal pay due to the unrestricted operation of market forces'.[25]

21.2.1.13 Agreement to lower wages

The fact that the women agreed to lower wages, in order to keep their jobs, is not a material factor. As the IT said in *Lord and Others v*

24 2513/92.

25 In *White and Others v Alstons (Colchester) Ltd* (1987) 12 EOR 40, female sewing machinists compared their work with that of male upholsterers. The tribunal rejected the employer's argument that a contingency allowance of 16% paid to the men and not the women was a material factor justifying a difference in pay. In 1974, after two years of bargaining, the men had been given an allowance because of the heavy work they did. It could be argued, said the tribunal, that the women should be given a like allowance, by reason of the complexity of the tasks done by them and their rather less pleasant work environment. It concluded that the substance of the matter was that the men put pressure on the respondent in 1974 to which the respondent acceded and the question of pay relativities was never addressed.

Knowsley BC,[26] the women agreed to the changes because they were told they would be dismissed if they did not. 'They are low-paid women in a market unsympathetic to them.'

21.2.1.14 Separate pay structures and collective bargaining

It is quite common for there to be separate pay structures which cover different types of work within an organisation. This often means that there is a different collective bargaining process. In *Enderby*[27] the ECJ held that the fact that the respective rates of pay of two jobs of equal value, one carried out almost exclusively by women and the other mainly by men, were reached by separate collective bargaining processes, was not sufficient objective justification – even where there was no evidence of discrimination in the collective bargaining. The ECJ said that if the employer could rely on the absence of discrimination in the collective bargaining it would be too easy for an employer to circumvent the principle of equal pay by using separate bargaining processes (see **21.4.2**).

In *British Coal Corporation v Smith*[28] the HL held that the simple existence of separate pay structures is not a defence. The question is whether there are objective criteria justifying the difference in benefits (or pay) received by the applicants and their comparators, which were not tainted by sex discrimination.

21.2.1.15 The need to uphold existing agreements

In *Rainey*,[29] the fact that the terms and conditions were negotiated by a Whitley Council[30] was a reason for not paying existing NHS prosthetists the same as prosthetists who had been recruited from private practice. However, this should only apply if there are also other non-discriminatory reasons for the difference in pay (see **21.2.1.12**).

In *R v Secretary of State for Social Services and Others ex p Clarke and Others*,[31] speech therapists in the NHS claimed that they were doing work of equal value with clinical psychologists and pharmacists. The employers argued that health authorities were required by statute to pay their employees according to the salary scales agreed by the Whitley Council. These scales were approved by the Secretary of

26 See n23.
27 See n1.
28 [1996] IRLR 404, HL.
29 See n2.
30 The Whitley Councils were the national negotiating bodies for the NHS.
31 [1988] IRLR 22, DC.

State for Social Services and enacted by way of statutory instrument. The High Court held that this was not in itself a 'material factor' defence.

21.2.1.16 *Other more favourable contractual terms*

Where a woman receives lower pay than her comparator but is entitled to other more advantageous terms, the employer may argue that the fact that she is compensated for lower pay is a material factor. In *Hayward v Cammell Laird Shipbuilders*,[32] Mackay LJ said that the employer would at least have to show that the less favourable term in the woman's contract was due to other more favourable terms.

In *Leverton v Clwyd CC*,[33] the HL held that the difference in working hours and length of holidays between the applicant's contract and her comparator's did constitute a material factor which justified the pay differential. The HL said that:

> where a woman's and a man's regular annual working hours . . . can be translated into a notional hourly rate which yields no significant difference, it is a legitimate – if not necessary – inference that the difference in their annual salaries is both due to and justified by the difference in the hours they work annually and has nothing to do with the difference in sex.

However, careful calculations should be done to ensure that there really is parity.

However, in *Barber*,[34] the ECJ said that:

> The application of the principle of equal pay must be ensured in respect of each element of remuneration and not only on the basis of a comprehensive assessment of the consideration paid to workers.

The difficulties in assessing the value of such benefits as sick pay, longer holidays and fringe benefits, in order to determine whether they fully compensate for lower pay are enormous. Employees will generally have different views about which are the most valuable terms and if women are denied the choice of having the most favourable 'package' this may, in itself, be discrimination. If this is to be a defence, the employer should have to show that the difference in pay is directly attributable to the other more favourable contractual term (see **21.2.4**).

32 [1987] IRLR 186, CA; [1988] IRLR 257, HL.
33 [1988] IRLR 238, CA; [1989] IRLR 28, HL.
34 *Barber v GRE Assurance* [1990] IRLR 240, ECJ.

21.2.1.17 Increased wages might lead to loss of service

In *Leverton* (above), it was argued that if the cost of providing nursery facilities increased (by the payment of higher wages for women), the service might be lost. The tribunal made no decision on this and left the employer to raise it again once the expert had reported. It should not be a defence.

21.2.1.18 Difference in hourly rates between full-timers and part-timers

In most areas of employment a greater proportion of part-time workers are women (usually about 80% of part-timers are women). Thus, when comparing the pay of part-timers with that of full-timers there will usually be disparate adverse impact on women if part-timers are paid less per hour than full-timers and this may be indirect discrimination (see **22.2.3**). Where a woman working part-time is paid at a lower hourly rate than a man working full-time, this may be direct discrimination. It may also be indirect discrimination.[35]

21.2.2 Material factor must be genuine and still in existence

21.2.2.1 Material factor must be genuine

Any difference between the salaries or terms and conditions of the applicant and her comparator must be '*genuinely due to*' and '*caused by*' the material factor. For example, in *Gamble and Others v Stockham Valve Ltd*[36] the tribunal considered that the employer's argument that the difference in pay was due to market forces was:

> . . . a cloak for the fact that the wages were affected by the industrial muscle of the trade unions which represented and negotiated on their behalf while the women's wages were left to be the subject of individual negotiation in a situation where the female clerical staff were not represented by a trade union when they were recruited.

Where the employer argues that the differences in pay were due to a

35 *Jenkins v Kingsgate* [1981] 2 CMLR 24; [1981] IRLR 228, ECJ, and see also *Bilka* (**3.6.7.1**) and *Botel* (**22.3.2.7**). But see *Montgomery v Lowfield Distribution Ltd* where extra payments were made to full-time shift workers where their shift day fell on a bank holiday. Part-time workers were not entitled to such payments as they had fixed hours. The IT held these payments were necessary because of the potential unfairness arising from the chance application of shiftworking to a bank holiday which, because they were on rotating shifts, only the full-time workers faced (DCLD 28; 11 July 1995, Case no: 54943/94).

36 2513/92 EP.

number of material factors (ie, different hours of work or rotas, flexibility, red circling and collective bargaining) the onus is on the employer to show that each factor is genuine and is the cause of the difference in pay (see *Enderby*[37]). However, it may be difficult for the employee to obtain this information from the employer. In *Byrne and Others v Financial Times*[38] the applicants sought, by way of further and better particulars, a breakdown of the difference between their salaries and an allocation of a specific sum to a particular fact in the work record or history of each comparator. The EAT held that the employer was under no obligation to provide such a breakdown, it being often impossible to attribute a particular amount to a specific part of the variation. This is arguably wrong and inconsistent with the ECJ decision in *Enderby*. It is for the employer to justify the differential in relation to each factor.

21.2.2.2 Material factor must still exist

The employer cannot rely on a material factor which no longer exists. In *Post Office v Page*,[39] the applicant was recruited on the lowest scale. Two years later she brought an equal pay claim with staff of the same grade who had been recruited at the same time as her, but on a higher scale. It was agreed that the comparators were doing like work, but the employer argued that higher pay had justifiably been offered to applicants who were particularly experienced. The IT held that when Ms Page had been recruited there *had* been a material difference but that within a short time this had been eroded as her work soon became at least as good as that of most of her comparators. The difference in experience was not reflected in the quality of the work. The material difference no longer applied and the applicant was entitled to equal pay.[40]

It could be argued that if a shortage of skills no longer exists, there is no justification for a continued pay differential. In *Post Office v Page*, the tribunal relied on *Rainey*,[41] accepting that market forces may justify a pay differential but only so long as they persist. Thus, if there comes a time when there is no shortage of prosthetists, Ms Rainey

37 See n1.

38 [1991] IRLR 417, EAT.

39 EAT 554/87.

40 See also *Benveniste v University of Southampton* [1989] IRLR 123, CA, where it was held that where the material factor no longer exists, the defence cannot apply (see **18.8.2**).

41 See n2.

could return to the tribunal and argue that the market forces defence no longer applied.

21.2.3 Material factor must be significant and relevant

The employer must explain the reason for the difference between the pay (or other contractual term) of the woman and her comparator. The employer must show that the reason for the difference in pay was a sufficient influence to be significant and relevant, whether or not it was objectively justified.[42] However, the EAT, in *Tyldesley*,[43] held that the fact that the employer *believed* that the man had more experience (see **21.2.1.8**) was sufficient to establish the defence, provided the mistake was of sufficient influence to be significant or relevant. This must be wrong and would, if followed, defeat the purpose of the EqPA. It is exactly this view – that men's work is worth more or they are more experienced – which leads to lower pay for women. It is extremely difficult in such circumstances for the woman to prove that the employer had no such belief (see **21.5**) for further discussion about whether employers must show objective justification as well as an absence of discrimination).

21.2.3.1 Error should not be a defence

The fact that an employer made a mistake about a man's qualifications should not be a material factor. In *McPherson v Rathgael Centre for Children and Young People*[44] the NICA held that it was not enough for the employer to say it did not intend to discriminate and that the difference was caused by an error, but see *Tyldesley v TML Plastics Ltd* (above).

21.2.4 Material factor must have caused differential

The material factor must be the cause for the differential in pay or other contractual terms.

For example, in *Siberry and Smith v Sheffield CC*,[45] an IT rejected the employer's argument that a difference in holidays was 'genuinely due to a material factor' as there was no evidence that the difference in pay was caused by the longer holidays and no inference could be drawn that this was the case (see also **21.2.1.16**).

42 *Tyldesley v TML Plastics Ltd* [1996] IRLR 395, EAT.
43 Ibid.
44 [1991] IRLR 206, NICA.
45 23295/85. See also *Sheffield CC v Siberry* EAT 508/88.

21.2.4.1 *Material factor must be substantial and the whole cause of differential*

A difference between the woman's case and the men's must be significant and relevant.[46] It is not sufficient to say that the factor accounts for part of the difference, while still leaving a difference in pay for which there is no justification. In *Enderby*[47] the ECJ held if some of the difference in pay is attributable to one factor (such as the need to attract suitable candidates), only that part of the difference is justified. The ECJ held that market forces could have justified *all* the difference in pay but in fact it did not. Thus, to the extent that there is no objective justification for the pay difference, pay must be equalised. This will involve working out the extent to which the difference in pay is due to the material factor.[48]

21.3 Importance of transparency

Where a pay system is not transparent, the burden of proof may shift to the employer to show that pay practices are not discriminatory where a female worker establishes, by comparison with a relatively large number of employees, that the average pay of female workers is lower than that of male workers in the same grade. In *Danfoss*,[49] according to a collective agreement, the employers paid the same basic minimum pay to workers in the same pay grade. Grading was determined by job classification. However, additional payments were made to individuals within a grade on the basis of the employee's 'flexibility'. This resulted in consistently higher pay for men and there was no way of working out how their pay rates were reached. The ECJ held that where there was a lack of transparency the burden was on the employer to show an absence of discrimination, otherwise the workers would be deprived of any effective means of achieving equal pay.

Where performance-related pay schemes result in consistently higher pay for men, they will be discriminatory. In *Danfoss* the ECJ

46 *Rainey* (n2).

47 See n1.

48 In *MacDougall v Taggarts Motor Group Ltd* (DCLD 27) the IT found that the material factor justified only part of the pay differential. Thus, the woman was awarded the £8,000 pay differential less the amount which was justified as being a material factor (because she could not drive, unlike her comparator). In *NCB v Sherwin and Spruce* [1978] IRLR 122, EAT, the EAT upheld an IT decision which found that the pay differential attributed to shift work was too large and could not therefore be a material factor.

49 See n9 (and also **2.12**).

held that criteria relating to the quality of work which systematically discriminated against women were automatically unfair as, the ECJ pointed out, it was inconceivable that women's work would be of a consistently lower quality than men's.

A good example of the subjectivity of some performance-related pay schemes is the tribunal decision of *Latham v Eastern Counties Newspapers Ltd.*[50] In this case a performance-related pay scheme awarded points on 41 work skills and six aptitudes. No guidance was given, nor benchmarks established and there were no parameters within which to consider aptitudes. The IT held that 'there was confusion, double-counting and an absence of transparency in the system' and managers took slightly different matters into account in awarding marks for different aptitudes. The pay practice put the applicant at the bottom and the employer had failed to establish that there was no sex discrimination.

21.4 There must be no discrimination in the material factor

The fact that it was necessary to pass legislation regulating women's pay recognises the reality of the market which, if left to its own devices, would discriminate freely against women. Account therefore needs to be taken of the type of discrimination suffered by women in the market, in order to ensure that discrimination does not creep back in, via the material factor defence. This includes job segregation, the predominance of women in part-time and temporary jobs (both of which tend to be low-status and low-paid), women's willingness to work for lower wages because of their weaker position in the labour market and status in the household, and women's inability to comply with certain job requirements because of commitment to child care and adult dependants.

It is clear that the material factor must not be tainted by sex discrimination in any way. The more difficult question is whether an employer need only show that the difference in pay is *not* caused by discrimination or whether the employer must, in addition, be able to justify the difference objectively (see **21.5**).

If a woman is paid less than a man doing like work, work rated as equivalent or work of equal value where *but for* the fact that she is a woman she would be paid the same as the man, there is direct sex discrimination in pay and the employer cannot rely on the material factor defence in EqPA s1(3).

50 DCLD 20; Case no: 32453/93; 25 January 1994.

This important point is well illustrated by the HL decision in *Ratcliffe v North Yorkshire CC*[51] where three female catering assistants claimed equal pay with mainly male refuse collectors and leisure attendants. The women's jobs had been rated as equivalent under a JES. However, in order to compete for compulsory competitive tendering the council reduced the wages of the catering assistants (but not the refuse collectors or leisure attendants). The IT and HL accepted that the reduction in pay may have been a material factor, but it was a factor due to the difference of sex, arising 'out of the general perception . . . that a woman should stay at home to look after the children and if she wants to work it must fit in with that domestic duty and a lack of facilities to enable her, easily, to do otherwise'. The HL said this was the 'very kind of discrimination in relation to pay which the Act sought to remove'. This establishes judicial recognition of some of the many historical and social reasons why women are paid less and accepts that these must be taken into account when considering whether a potential defence is unacceptable by reason of sex discrimination.

21.4.1 Past discrimination

Where women are paid less because of past discrimination this will not be a material factor. In *Snoxell and Davies v Vauxhall Motors Ltd*[52] there had been a separate grading structure for men and women under which men were paid more. In 1975 a common grading structure was introduced; however, some men were still paid more because they had received higher wages under the old system. The EAT held that an employer can never establish that a difference between the woman's contract and the man's is due to a material difference when past discrimination has contributed to the variation.[53]

21.4.2 Distinction between direct and indirect discrimination

In *Ratcliffe* the HL considered that the EqPA must be interpreted without bringing in the distinction between direct and indirect discrimination. It was not necessary to decide this as the case was about

51 [1995] IRLR 439, HL.

52 [1977] IRLR 123, EAT.

53 See also *Sun Alliance and London Insurance Ltd v Dudman* [1978] IRLR 169, EAT; *United Biscuits Ltd v Young* [1978] IRLR 15, EAT, and *Thompson v Salts of Saltaire Ltd* (1986) 8 EOR 39.

direct discrimination and the HL said that direct discrimination was not capable of justification. The comment is therefore not binding. The HL said that

> . . . [the] relevant question under the Act of 1970 is whether equal treatment has been accorded for men and women employed on like work or for men and women employed on work rated as equivalent.

In other words, for the purposes of this exercise, the Act does *not* require proof of discrimination; it is assumed from the statutory test.[54] However, if the difference in pay is due to direct discrimination there can be no question of justifying it, and it will not be a material factor.

Although the HL, in *Ratcliffe*, said that in pay claims, tribunals and courts should not be concerned with the distinction between so-called 'direct' and 'indirect' discrimination in the SDA, in *Ratcliffe* there was no element of indirect discrimination because the market forces involved direct discrimination.

The distinction may be relevant where, eg, the complaint is about less favourable treatment of part-timers than full-timers. In such cases (which involve indirect discrimination because the vast majority of part-timers are generally women), the employer will not only have to show that part-timers are paid less because of their shorter hours of work but that the difference in pay can be objectively justified.[55]

The distinction between 'direct' discrimination and 'indirect' discrimination (disproportionate adverse impact) may not always be clear. This is particularly apparent in cases where there is job segregation. Men and women may be segregated because of both direct and indirect discrimination. In *Enderby*[56] (see **21.2.1.14**) it was accepted by both sides that there was no deliberate intention to treat women less favourably, but the applicants argued that the salaries of speech therapists were artificially depressed because of the profession's predominantly female composition. It was found that the fact that a lower paid group, that of speech therapists, was almost exclusively

54 This was recognised by the Advocate-General in *Enderby* (n1) when he commented on the evidential difficulties a woman has in proving the causal connection between her sex and the lower pay.

55 In many cases it is more useful to adopt the parallel European definition (of indirect discrimination) which is better described as 'disproportionate adverse impact'. This avoids the need to go through the convoluted defintion of indirect discrimination which is contained in the SDA. Thus, a practice which has a disproportionately adverse impact on women will be unlawful unless the employer can show objective justification; see *Bilka* (**3.6.7.1**) and *Kowalska* (**22.1.6.2**).

56 See n1.

female was not a 'statistical freak' but was due to the fact that the nature of the work, which allows employees to work part-time, made it particularly attractive to women and the low pay made it especially unattractive to men.

The ECJ held that where significant statistics disclose an appreciable difference in pay between two jobs of equal value, one of which is carried out almost exclusively by women and the other predominantly by men, art 119 requires the employer to show that the difference is based on objectively justified factors unrelated to any discrimination on the ground of sex.

The existence of sex segregated groups of workers (doing work of equal value), where the group of women were paid less than the group of men, could be said *either* to raise a presumption of discrimination (which is rebuttable by evidence to the contrary) *or* have a disproportionate adverse impact on women. In either case, the employer must prove that the difference in pay (in respect of jobs assumed to be of equal value) can be justified on grounds other than sex. This was aptly described by the Advocate General in *Enderby*[57] who said that:

> . . . the structure of the reasoning for both direct discrimination and indirect discrimination is comparable with regard to the evidentiary aspect of the proceedings inasmuch as a rebuttable presumption of discrimination can be raised, in one case by means of a specific comparison and, in the other, by a comparison of groups, which places the onus on the employer to *adduce evidence in rebuttal of that presumption* or to produce a *justification*.

Where there are separate groups of workers, segregated by sex, any comparison must be between all the relevant workers in a similar situation. In the *Royal Copenhagen* case[58] there were two main groups, turners and painters. Both groups were subdivided. The painters were divided into two groups, one consisting mainly of women who were the lowest paid (group B) and the other consisting wholly of women who were the highest paid (group C). The lowest paid women compared their pay to a subgroup of higher paid turners which was predominantly male (group A). Thus, one group of women was paid less than the mainly male group and the other group of women was paid more. The ECJ held that, where a comparison is made between two groups which are segregated by sex, the groups

57 See n1.

58 *Specialarbejderfordundet i Danmark v Dansk Industri, acting for Royal Copenhagen A/S, C-40093* [1995] IRLR 648, ECJ.

compared must encompass all the workers who, taking into account a set of factors such as the nature of the work, the training requirements and the working conditions, can be considered to be in a comparable situation. The groups cannot be formed in an arbitrary manner so that one comprises mainly women and the other mainly men. They must cover a relatively large number of workers to ensure the differences are not due to purely fortuitous or short-term factors or to differences in the individual output of the workers.[59]

In addition the job segregation must be significant. When *Enderby*[60] went back to the IT, the respondents challenged the assertion that clinical psychologists were predominantly male. The statistics showed men predominating in eight out of ten years, ranging from 68% to 54%. The IT was impressed with the persistency and consistency of the figures which showed that, throughout the period, men predominated and there was therefore a prima facie case of sex discrimination.

In *Loughran and Others v British Road Services Ltd*[61] the IT accepted that a prima facie case of discrimination had been shown as the applicants were in a group (of clerical workers) which was 75% female and their comparators were in a group (of warehouse workers) which was 100% male. The NICA said that:

> . . . the relevance of a number of females in the group is an indicator of its being traditionally a less well paid group on account of its being composed mainly of women. Logically, a group comprised of 75% females and 25% males has the capacity to provide such an indication.

Thus, evidence that there is job segregation to any significant extent should be sufficient to raise a presumption of direct discrimination or disproportionate adverse impact. In *Loughran* the defence that there were separate bargaining structures was rejected as it was tainted by discrimination.

The claim in *Ratcliffe*[62] was not affected by the fact that there were two men doing the same work as the women. This only meant that two men were also being underpaid: it did not negate the reality of sex discrimination in pay.

59 This is similar to the test for identifying the pool in indirect discrimination where the CA has said that it cannot be subdivided; see *Jones v University of Manchester* [1993] IRLR 218, CA.

60 See n1.

61 [1997] IRLR 92.

62 See n51.

21.5 Must the material factor be justified objectively where there is no discrimination?

It is clear that the material factor must not be tainted by or attributable to sex discrimination. The question as to whether, if the employer can show there is no discrimination, the material factor must still be objectively justified is to be resolved by the HL. If objective justification must be shown, the employer must provide a substantial (non-discriminatory) business-related reason for the difference in pay. Two decisions[63] suggest that the employer need only:

a) identify the *factor* (which must *not* be a difference of sex);
b) satisfy the tribunal that it is a *material* factor; and
c) satisfy the tribunal that the factor causes the material *difference* between the woman's case and the man's case.

In *Tyldesley v TML Plastics Ltd*[64] (see **21.2.1.8**) the EAT held that it was not necessary to show that, in addition to being non-discriminatory, the material factor was objectively justified.[65]

In *Strathclyde RC v Wallace and Others*[66] a group of female teachers were acting up as principal teachers. They claimed equal pay with male principal teachers. Out of 134 unpromoted teachers doing principal teachers' duties, 81 were men and 53 women. As the variation was not due to sex, it was not a sham and it was 'significant and relevant'. It was sufficient to establish a material factor. The CA held that there was no need for the employer to show objective justification. This decision is on appeal to the HL.

Pending a decision from the HL or ECJ, arguably the correct interpretation of *Ratcliffe*[67] and *Enderby*[68] is that:

a) even where there is no discrimination in the material factor defence, the employer must still show that the material factor is genuine and substantial and not merely caused by a mistake. It must be related to the individual (such as red circling) or the need for particular skills or other market forces (see **21.2.1**);

63 *Tyldesley v TML Plastics Ltd* [1996] IRLR 395 and *Strathclyde RC v Wallace and Others* [1996] IRLR 670.
64 See n63.
65 The EAT accepted that if there was direct discrimination it could not be justified and if there was indirect discrimination the employer must show objective justification.
66 [1996] IRLR 670, CS.
67 See n51.
68 See n1.

b) where the unequal pay is due to *direct* discrimination, the employer cannot ever rely on it, even if it is based on market forces;
c) where there is an appreciable difference in pay between two jobs of equal value, one of which is carried out almost exclusively by women and the other predominantly by men (as in *Enderby*), this either raises a *presumption* of direct sex discrimination which must then be rebutted by the employer, or shows disproportionate adverse impact (which must then be justified). No question of *justification* arises with direct discrimination;
d) where the material factor is due to indirect discrimination (such as treating part-time workers less favourably), the test is whether the difference in pay is objectively justified (as per *Bilka*[69]).

21.6 Equalising pay

For the purposes of EqPA s1(3) the employer has to explain the variation in contractual terms of the man and the woman. A tribunal will be concerned not just with why the man is paid £x but also why the woman is paid £x less £20. Thus, in *Rainey* (see **21.1**) the HL considered that the employer had to show not only that there was a good reason for paying the men above the Whitley Council rate, but also that there were good grounds for not bringing the women up to the men's rate.

THE MATERIAL FACTOR DEFENCE: KEY POINTS

- Under UK law, if the employer can show that there is a material factor which justifies the difference in pay, equal pay will not be awarded. Note:
  - the employer must show the factual basis for the difference;
  - the employer must show that the factor existed at the date the wages were fixed, still exists and is genuinely the reason for the pay differential, not merely a later justification;
  - the material factor must be significant and relevant to woman's and man's rate of pay;
  - the material factor must account for the whole of the differential;

69 See **3.6.7.1**.

  - the material factor must not be tainted by discrimination.
- The following material factors have been argued:
  - geographical distinction;
  - red circling;
  - flexibility;
  - merit or good performance;
  - higher productivity;
  - job-related training;
  - job-related skills, experience or qualifications;
  - length of service;
  - market forces, such as skill shortages;
  - differences in contractual terms.
- The HL is to decide if the material factor must be objectively justified, even if there is no discrimination.

CHAPTER 22

Collective agreements and discriminatory pay systems

This chapter concentrates on sex discrimination in collective agreements and rules of undertakings and how to challenge these, as well as the type of sex discrimination which is often found in pay systems. The law on sex discrimination has been influenced by EC law but this has not affected race discrimination, where there are few statutory provisions and little case-law.

22.1 Sex discrimination in collective agreements and rules of undertakings

22.1.1 EC law

The UK provisions need to be read in the light of the broad prohibition, under EC law, of discrimination in collective agreements and rules of undertakings. The ETD provides that:

> Member States shall take all necessary measures to ensure that . . . any provisions contrary to the principle of equal treatment which are included in collective agreements, individual contracts of employment, internal rules of undertakings or in rules governing the independent occupations and professions shall be, or may be declared, null and void or may be amended.

The European Commission considered that the original provisions of the SDA did not comply with EC law and brought enforcement proceedings against the UK government.[1] The SDA 1975 was then amended by the SDA 1986 but this still provided no mechanism for deciding whether a term or rule was discriminatory nor for amending it. Further amendments were made by Trade Union Reform and

1 *Commission of the European Communities v UK* [1982] IRLR 333.

Employment Rights Act 1993 to enable such terms and rules to be declared void by an IT.

22.1.2 *Collective agreements*

Collective agreements are negotiated between employers and trade unions (which act on behalf of their members). This book is concerned only with those agreements relating to the employee's contract of employment on matters such as pay, hours of work, holidays, and other working conditions. The SDAs 1975 and 1986 now cover binding and non-binding collective agreements (see below).

22.1.3 *Rules of undertakings*

Undertakings include employers, organisations, authorities or bodies who may confer authorisations or qualifications which are needed for, or facilitate, engagement in a particular profession or trade.[2] This would include, for example, the General Medical Council, the Law Society and other similar bodies.

22.1.4 *What agreements and rules are covered?*

The SDA 1986 applies to terms and rules made by a wide range of organisations.[3] It covers the following:

a) any term of a collective agreement, whether or not intended to be a legally enforceable contract;
b) any rule made by an employer relating to employees or potential employees;
c) any rule applied by an undertaking to its members or prospective members or to persons on whom it has conferred authorisations or qualifications (or on those seeking the same). This includes rules made by:
   - any organisation of workers (eg, trade unions);
   - any organisation of employers;
   - any organisation whose members carry on a particular profession or trade for the purposes of which the organisation exists;
   - any authority or body which can confer an authorisation or

2 SDA 1986 s6. Cf, SDA s13; RRA s12 which prohibit discrimination by qualifying bodies.

3 SDA 1986 s6. It was amended by the Trade Union Reform and Employment Rights Act 1993.

qualification which facilitates engagement in a particular profession or trade.

22.1.5 Who is protected?

The provisions protect not only existing employees and members of undertakings but also job applicants and those who are seeking membership of undertakings.[4]

22.1.6 Void terms

The SDA 1986 (as amended) provides that discriminatory contractual terms contained in binding and non-binding collective agreements and rules of employers and other bodies (as set out above) are void.[5] Even though employees (and prospective employees) are not parties to the contract they can challenge them in an IT.

Where a discriminatory term or rule may affect an individual in the future (whether an employee or someone actively seeking to become an employee) the individual can also challenge the term or rule. These provisions are likely to be tested in relation to terms which are indirectly discriminatory or where pregnant women are particularly disadvantaged, for example:

- the exclusion of pregnant women from a sick pay scheme on the ground that their sickness is pregnancy-related (see **15.5.3**) could be challenged by a woman who either is, or may in the future become, pregnant;
- a redundancy scheme which was based on last-in-first-out may be indirectly discriminatory and challengeable even before a redundancy situation arises.

The tribunal only has power to declare a term void (see below). A woman may also have other remedies, such as a claim under the EqPA or EC law and these should all be considered.

4 SDA s6(1).

5 SDA 1986 s6. Prior to the SDA 1986, discriminatory terms in collective agreements could be challenged only if: (a) the agreement was incorporated, expressly or impliedly, into the employee's contract of employment; (b) there were terms which related to men only or women only; or (c) the agreement was legally binding. The change was forced on the government after the ECJ held that failure to deal with discriminatory terms in non-binding collective agreements infringed the ETD (*Commission of the European Communities v UK* [1982] IRLR 333, ECJ). The position relating to agreements which are part of the employee's contract remains the same (see below).

22.1.6.1 The effect of a term being declared void

A discriminatory term is void as against a third party (eg, the employee) but is unenforceable against a party to the contract[6] (the employer and union. The Act preserves any rights which the woman may have under the contract, despite the voiding of the discriminatory term. It also preserves the rights of the men to the extent that they are no more favourable than the women's rights.[7]

If, for example, an employer provides training for men but not women, and the agreement is part of the employee's contract, she can claim the benefit of the training. If only men are given training and the agreement is not part of the employee's contract, the term is void so that neither the man nor the woman can claim the right to the training – at least under UK law.

A different situation would arise if there were training available for both men and women but, for example, part-time workers had to pay a contribution to the cost. If this provision were part of the part-timers' contracts and were found to be discriminatory, the employer would not be able to recover the money from the women because the term would be unenforceable. The women could also rely on the EqPA (see **22.1.7**). If the term were not part of the employees' contracts it would be void. However, as the Act protects any rights the employee might otherwise have under the contract, women as well as men would be entitled to the training but not subject to the penalty.[8]

If, as in the above example, the provision discriminated indirectly, eg, because some of the women could comply with the requirement to work full-time or did not suffer a detriment, the term would be unenforceable only against those who had suffered indirect discrimination.[9] The Act allows terms which, for example, indirectly discriminate against some women, but not others, to be valid in respect of the women who have not suffered discrimination.[10]

If the collective agreement is incorporated into the woman's contract of employment, she can, as a party to the agreement, apply to the county court for an order that the unenforceable term be removed or modified. Such order may include provisions relating to a period before the making of the order.[11]

6 SDA s77(2).
7 SDA 1986 s6(5).
8 Ibid.
9 SDA 1986 s6(4).
10 Ibid.
11 SDA s77(5) and (6).

22.1.6.2 The remedy

Individuals will have a right to bring a complaint to an IT. If the IT upholds the complaint it can only make an order that the term or rule is void.[12] There is no mechanism, as there is under the EqPA, for incorporating the more favourable term into the woman's contract.

However, the situation is different under EC law. In *Nimz v Freie und Hansestadt Hamburg*[13] the ECJ held that where a provision in a collective agreement is indirectly discriminatory and contrary to art 119, those disadvantaged by the provision should be treated no less favourably than their comparators.

In *Kowalska v Freie und Hansestadt Hamburg*,[14] the ECJ held that a term in a collective agreement which provided for the payment of a 'severance grant' (comparable to redundancy pay) to full-time workers only was indirectly discriminatory where 'a considerably smaller percentage of men than of women work part time, unless the employer shows that the provision is justified by objective factors unrelated to any discrimination on grounds of sex'. The ECJ said that an individual can rely on art 119 to challenge a discriminatory provision in a collective agreement, as art 119 is sufficiently precise.

The ECJ, in *Kowalska*, approved the ECJ decision in *Ruzius-Wilbrink*[15] holding that:

> . . . where there is discrimination in a provision of a collective agreement, the members of the group which is disadvantaged because of that discrimination must be treated in the same way and have the same system applied to them as applied to other workers, in proportion to their working hours.

This decision has important implications for UK law as it means that in all collective agreements (and the ECJ does not distinguish between binding and non-binding agreements) where there are provisions which are more favourable to men, then they must be extended to women. It would not, therefore, be lawful to treat the discriminatory provisions as simply void as is the present position. Applicants may, therefore, also need to rely on art 119.

12 SDA 1986 s64D.

13 *C-184/89* [1991] IRLR 222, ECJ.

14 [1990] IRLR 447, ECJ.

15 *Ruzius-Wilbrink v Bestur van de Bedrijfsvereniging voor Overheids Diensten (Case no 102/88)* (1989) unreported, 13 December, ECJ.

22.1.7 Situations where EqPA applies

If the collective agreement is part of the employee's contract of employment, the EqPA prohibits any discriminatory provisions.[16] There are three ways in which the terms of a collective agreement may become part of employees' contracts of employment:

a) if the union acts as an agent for employees; in most cases agency is implicit, although it will depend on the union rule book and the circumstances of the case;
b) if the employees' contracts of employment state that the terms of the collective agreement are to be treated as part of their employment contracts;
c) if the employees' contracts impliedly incorporate the terms of the collective agreement. If it has been the practice of the employer and union to reach agreements which bind employees, then the terms of these agreements will form part of individual contracts of employment.

In most cases where unions negotiate pay, hours of work and other matters affecting individual workers, the collective agreement is incorporated into the employee's contract of employment. The EqPA gives employees the right not to be paid less or receive other less favourable terms than others doing like work, similar work or work of equal value (see **18.4**). These rights can be enforced by making a complaint to an IT in the same way as if there were no collective agreement.

Collective agreements which are not part of the contract of employment do not give employees the same right to challenge provisions contained in them under the EqPA as the employees are not parties to the agreement. A claim may be made under these provisions relating to collective agreements or, possibly, the SDA (see Chapter 5).

22.2 Race discrimination in collective agreements

If a contract, including a collective agreement, contains a term which discriminates against a third party, that term is void. Under the RRA,[17] unlike the SDA, this applies only to legally enforceable agreements. Where the unlawful discrimination is against a party to the contract

16 EqPA s1.
17 s72.

the term is unenforceable against that person. Thus, the victim of discrimination can rely on the term to the extent that it provides a benefit but the employer cannot enforce any part which is less favourable to him/her.

A person who has an interest in a contract which contains an unenforceable term can apply to a designated county court for an order to remove or modify the unenforceable term. There is an exception for compromise agreements.

22.3 Discrimination in pay systems

The EOC Code of Practice on Equal Pay states:

> Sex discrimination in pay now occurs primarily because women and men tend to do different jobs or to have different work patterns. As a result it is easy to undervalue the demands of work performed by one sex compared with the demands associated with jobs typically done by the other.

This section looks at how pay systems tend to discriminate against women and ways of challenging the discrimination. The EOC Code also recommends that employers carry out a pay systems review (see Appendix 3 pp596 and 597).

22.3.1 Job segregation

Both the European Commission and the EOC confirm that though the difference between women's and men's incomes is due to a number of factors the main cause is segregation of men's and women's jobs. The main features are:

- horizontal segregation; this is often historical and based on traditional values ascribed to 'male' and 'female' work. Past discriminatory assumptions about the value of what has been regarded as men's or women's work may be reflected in current grading schemes;
- vertical segregation; it is common for men to be in the majority at managerial level and women to occupy lower graded jobs;
- jobs done mainly by men have a higher status and are more highly rewarded than those done by women;
- there are numerous sectors of the economy, where mainly men work, which offer extra pay, working-time bonuses, overtime, on-call allowances, productivity incentives, etc. One local authority

found 21 possible additional payments all of which had been paid only to men!;
- separate collective agreements, which allow salary structures to reflect the negotiating power of different groups of employees;
- different job titles for men and women may disguise the fact that the jobs are similar or of equal value.

Certain occupations are even more segregated as there is a greater concentration of ethnic minority women in lower status, lower paid jobs.[18]

The courts are increasingly recognising the fact that job segregation is both a result of and a cause of discrimination.[19]

22.3.2 Discrimination in the allocation of overtime, shift payments, bonuses, etc

Even when women are paid the same basic hourly rate of pay as men, men's basic wages are often topped up by other payments, such as overtime, shift pay, service increments, bonuses and productivity pay, attendance payments, flexibility and mobility payments. Each element of the contract should be analysed to see if there is any sex or race discrimination. In addition, part-time workers should receive the same pro rata payments as full-time workers.

22.3.2.1 Overtime

Many women cannot work overtime because of family responsibilities. Those that do may not receive overtime payments unless they exceed the standard weekly hours, even though, on any one day, they may work longer than their contractual hours or the standard daily hours. In *Stadt Lengerich v Helmig*[20] the ECJ held that there was no breach of EC law where overtime supplements were only paid for hours worked in excess of the normal full-time working hours. Thus, part-time workers were not entitled to overtime supplements when they exceeded *their* normal working hours. The ECJ said that there was no unequal treatment because the overall pay of full-timers and part-timers was the same for the same number of hours worked.

18 EOC code of practice.
19 See *Enderby* (**21.4**) and *Loughran* (**21.4**).
20 [1995] IRLR 216, ECJ.

Arguably, the correct analysis is that there was no disparate impact, because fewer women work part-time and the real issue related to whether the difference was justified.

22.3.2.2 Shift pay

The fact that a man and woman work at different times should not defeat an equal pay claim, though a premium may be payable for anti-social hours. In *NCB v Sherwin and Spruce*,[21] the EAT held that if the man and woman do the same work, the mere fact that they do it at different times is not relevant. The EAT disaggregated the anti-social element of the men's pay and compared the basic rates.

Premia are commonly paid for working anti-social hours – generally before 6am and after 10pm. Even though shift work may not be available to women (this itself may be discriminatory) it would be hard to argue that workers should not be paid extra for working anti-social hours. However, women frequently do split duty, working from 6am to 10am and then from 7pm to midnight. This is particularly common in the health service and in hotels where there are many women workers.[22] Shift payments should be paid on an equal basis to men and women.

22.3.2.3 Seniority and service-related payments

The aim of length-of-service payments is to reduce job turnover. Recruiting new employees involves a lengthy and costly advertising and interviewing process and necessitates more training. Service payments and benefits are also made in recognition of the employee's increased experience. In *Danfoss*[23] the ECJ said that employers did not need to justify such benefits because of the obvious advantages of retaining trained staff.

Arguably, if service payments are made, then:

- part-time workers should be eligible after the same period as full-timers;
- any period of employment should count as part of the qualifying period so, if women leave to have children and then return, the earlier period should be included; maternity leave and absence should be included, provided in the case of absence the contract continues (see **16.2** and **16.3**);

21 [1978] IRLR 122, EAT.

22 Ibid.

23 *Handels-og Kontorfunktionaerernes Forbund i Danmark v Dansk Arbejdsgiverforening (acting for Danfoss)* [1988] IRLR 532, ECJ.

- service payments should start as early as possible, preferably after one year's service and not ten years, as is sometimes the case. If the justification for increments is an increase in efficiency this is a cumulative process and starts shortly after the beginning of service and not suddenly at the end of ten years;
- it is important that incremental scales are similar for all employees, irrespective of grade.

Sometimes employees in lower grades have to wait much longer to reach the top of their scale. Some employers impose bars so that progression depends on management discretion. There is evidence that more women are adversely affected by such bars. These bars need to be closely monitored to ensure that they do not discriminate against women and black workers.

In *Nimz v Freie und Hansestadt Hamburg*[24] full-time workers were automatically entitled to be upgraded after six years, while part-time employees had to wait for 12 years. The ECJ held that this requirement was in breach of art 119 unless it could be objectively justified. Justification would involve looking at the relationship between the nature of the duties performed and the experience gained by working the number of hours in question. Thus, if there were no difference in experience between full-time workers who had worked six years and part-time workers who had worked for six years, it is likely that the requirement would not be justifiable.

22.3.2.4 Bonus schemes and productivity pay

There are many different types of productivity-related pay. The main ones are as follows:

a) each worker is paid according to the work s/he has done (this is piece-work);
b) a bonus is awarded if more than the allocated work is carried out in the time allowed;
c) a flat-rate payment may be made to certain workers. This is often in exchange for the workers agreeing a new system of working;
d) a bonus may be given to a group of workers to be shared between them. Nearly half of male manual workers receive 25% of their pay in bonuses. Far fewer women receive bonuses;
e) tips, such as at restaurants.

Many women's jobs are suitable for payment of a bonus (because it is

24 [1991] IRLR 222.

possible to assess their productivity) yet have never attracted one. For other jobs, such as nursing or teaching, it may not be appropriate to pay a bonus. If the work of the man and woman is of equal value then the total payments received by each of them should be the same, unless there is a real difference in productivity which would fall under the 'material factor' defence (see **21.2.1.5**). Bonus schemes should not be a way of maintaining the differential between men's and women's wages.[25] If it can be established that bonus payments disadvantage women on average, the employer must show how and on what basis the payments are made and that the criteria are objectively justified and not discriminatory.[26]

22.3.2.5 Flexibility and mobility payments

Employers sometimes pay an extra sum to employees whose job requires them to be flexible in what work they do, at what times and where. Women tend to be more tied to set hours which revolve round dependant care responsibilities. In *Danfoss*,[27] the ECJ said that where the flexibility of the worker is used as a criterion for pay increments and this works systematically to the disadvantage of female workers, the employer may justify the use of the criterion only by demonstrating that such adaptability is important and relevant for the performance of the specific duties of the worker.

Note that a mobility requirement in a contract may be indirect sex discrimination (see **10.12**).[28]

22.3.2.6 Attendance payments

Payments are sometimes made for good attendance. Women may have to take time off to look after sick children and dependants and may consequently not be eligible for these payments. Men often have other people (ie, women) to perform these tasks for them and so are more likely to receive attendance payments. Again, such payments must be justified.

22.3.2.7 Paid leave for training

Where a part-time woman attends a work-related training course which exceeds her normal working hours, she should be paid for the

25 See *Fleming and Others v Short Bros plc* 16–25/84 EB and *Anderson v British Olivetti* [1976] IRLR 287, IT.

26 *Danfoss* (see **21.3** above).

27 See n23.

28 See *Meade-Hill v British Council* [1995] IRLR 478, CA.

full hours. In *Botel*[29] the applicant attended a training course as a member of the staff committee.[30] National legislation provided that members of the staff committee must be released from work without a reduction in salary if necessary to perform their duties. The ECJ held that although full-time and part-time staff committee members devoted the same number of hours to the training, the part-time employees were treated differently since they were not paid as the training course took place outside *their* normal working hours (although within the normal working hours of full-time workers). As the members of the staff committees who were part-time were generally women, the legislative provisions would give rise to indirect discrimination unless there were objective justification unrelated to discrimination. The ECJ pointed out that if part-time workers were not paid equally, it would dissuade them (of whom an undoubtedly larger proportion are women) from acting as members of a staff committee, making the true representation of part-timers all the more difficult.[31]

A different decision was reached by the EAT in *Manor Bakeries Ltd v Nazir*,[32] where the EAT held that the employer did not discriminate against a part-time employee when it only paid her for her normal working hours in respect of her attendance at a trade union annual conference. This was not, in the view of the EAT, 'work'. This decision is inconsistent with *Botel*.[33] The payment was provided for in the collective agreement and was made as a result of the employment relationship.

22.3.3 *Part-time workers*

An EOC report[34] found that many part-time jobs are junior and low paid, and that flexible workers, including part-timers, face significant barriers in obtaining training and promotion. Women account for 86% of part-time workers and 40% of all women workers are part-timers compared with just 4% of all men.

Discrimination against part-time workers is common: part-timers are often denied pro rata rights to many benefits, such as sick pay,

29 *Arbeiterwohlfahrt der Stadt Berlin eV v Botel* 38 EOR 45, ECJ.

30 A staff committee is comparable to a trade union.

31 A similar decision was reached in *Kuratorium Fur Dialyse und Neirentransplantation eV v Lewark* [1996] IRLR 637.

32 [1996] IRLR 604.

33 It is also inconsistent with *Lewark* (n31).

34 'Flexible Employment in Britain: A Statistical Analysis' (1995).

housing loans, occupational pensions, overtime, bonuses, service increments, etc. See also **14.5.1.3** for discrimination in severance payments.

Where pressure for a shorter working week leads to a reduction in hours for full-time workers but not for part-timers, often the hourly rate for such full-time workers is increased so that their pay remains the same, but the pay of part-time workers is unaffected. Such discrimination may well be indirectly discriminatory (see *Bilka*,[35] *Kowalska*[36] and *Rinner-Kuhn*[37]).

The broad principle should be that part-time workers should receive pro rata benefits to full-timers. This may, however, be difficult to achieve if a claim is brought under the EqPA. First, the woman must find a comparator. Second, she must show that she is doing like work, work rated as equivalent or work of equal value with the comparator. Many female part-timers work only with other women.

If a claim is not contractual, and so may only be made under the SDA (see **5.7.1** for differences between SDA and EqPA), there is no need for an actual comparator, nor to show like work, etc. The parallel provisions of the SDA are that the circumstances of the woman and the actual or hypothetical man must be the same – like must be compared to like (see **3.6.5**). This may be easier to show than the EqPA test.

While there is generally no choice about whether to bring a claim under the EqPA or SDA (as they are mutually exclusive), the test under art 119 may be broader. Thus, in *Bilka* (where part-time women claimed that refusal to allow them to join the occupational pension scheme was indirectly discriminatory), there was no comparator. The ECJ held that art 119 is infringed by a company which excludes part-time employees from its occupational pension scheme, where that exclusion affects a far greater number of women than men, unless the undertaking shows that the exclusion is based on objectively justified factors. A similar decision was reached in *Vroege*.[38] Arguably, therefore, where there is a case of indirect discrimination (such as less favourable treatment of part-timers) the test under art 119 will be whether there is disproportionate impact on women and an absence of justification.

35 *Bilka-Kaufhaus GmbH v Weber von Hartz* [1986] IRLR 317, ECJ.
36 *Kowalska v Freie und Hansestadt Hamburg* [1990] IRLR 447, ECJ.
37 *Rinner-Kuhn v FWW Spezial-Gebaudereinigung GmbH* [1989] IRLR 493, ECJ.
38 *Vroege v NCIV Instituut voor Volkshuisvesting BV* [1994] IRLR 651, ECJ.

The European framework agreement on part-time work (agreed on 6 June 1997) provides that in respect of employment conditions, part-time workers shall not be treated in a less favourable manner than comparable full-time workers solely because they work part-time. However, different treatment may be justified on objective grounds. Even if there are no full-time comparators in the organisation, a comparison may be made with a person outside the organisation, by reference to a collective agreement or in accordance with national law or practice. Part-time workers are defined as those doing less than the hours of a comparable full-time worker. It is not clear when these provisions will come into force. It is unlikely to be before the end of 1999 (see also **17.5.8**).

Workers who are below the national insurance lower earnings limit (currently £62 per week) are not entitled to statutory sick pay or statutory maternity pay. This may also be indirectly discriminatory (see *Nolte* and *Megner* at **3.6.7.7**).

22.3.4 Equal pay in Europe

The Equal Value Regulations[39] were introduced because of the ECJ's decision that English law did not comply with EC law. In many respects UK law still does not provide women with the right to claim equal pay as laid down by art 119.

22.3.5 Complexity of law hinders equal pay

The EPD art 6 provides that member states must see that effective means are available to ensure that the principle of equal pay is applied. They have an obligation to introduce into their national legal systems such measures as are necessary to enable all employees who consider themselves wronged by a failure to apply the principle of equal pay to pursue their claims by judicial process.

In the ECJ decision against the UK government,[40] a number of broad principles were laid down by both the European Commission and the Advocate General. It was stated that 'in the final count, individuals should have the possibility of succeeding in the argument that the two jobs in question are of equal value'. Yet because there is no legal aid for industrial tribunals, the regulations are so complex

39 Equal Pay (Amendment) Regulations 1983 SI No 1794.
40 *Commission of the European Communities v UK* [1982] IRLR 333, ECJ.

and women are generally not able to afford independent expert witnesses, many, unless supported by trade unions or the EOC, are deprived of their rights. In *Aldridge v British Telecommunications plc*[41] the EAT said that the procedural restrictions were scandalous and 'amount to a denial of justice to women seeking remedy through the judicial process'. *Enderby*[42] is now in its thirteenth year and the question of equal value has now been conceded. The EOC has referred the failure to provide proper procedure to the European Commission, but the complaint has not been upheld.

In *Emmott v Minister for Social Welfare*,[43] the ECJ said that member states are required to ensure the full application of directives in a sufficiently clear and precise manner so that where directives are intended to create rights for individuals, the latter can ascertain the full extent of those rights and, where necessary, rely on them before the national courts. This is not the case for discrimination in pay.

DISCRIMINATORY PAY SYSTEMS: KEY POINTS

- Terms of a collective agreement which is part of the employee's contract of employment must be free from discrimination under the EqPA.
- Different provisions apply where the collective agreement is not part of the employee's contract. Any discriminatory term is void insofar as it affects a third party (ie, the employee) and is unenforceable as between the parties to the agreement (ie, the employer and union). These provisions apply to the rules of:
  - employers;
  - any organisation of workers;
  - any organisation of employers;
  - any professional or trade organisation;
  - any body which can confer an authorisation or qualification which is needed for a profession or trade.
- EC law may provide greater protection; the ECJ has held that an indirectly discriminatory term in a collective agreement is in breach of art 119. Note:

41 *Aldridge v British Telecommunications plc* [1990] IRLR 19, EAT. See also *British Coal Corporation v Smith* [1996] IRLR 404 where Lord Slynn said that the time taken defeated an essential purpose of the legislation.

42 *Enderby v Frenchay Health Authority* [1993] IRLR 593, ECJ.

43 [1991] IRLR 387, ECJ.

- under EC law there is no distinction between agreements which are part of the employee's contract and those which are not;
- the more favourable term must be extended to women; it is not sufficient to say that the term is unenforceable or void.

- There are many elements of discrimination in pay systems and the following should be carefully examined for discrimination:
  - overtime provisions;
  - shift pay;
  - service payments;
  - bonus schemes and productivity pay;
  - flexibility and mobility payments;
  - attendance payments;
  - different treatment of part-time workers.

CHAPTER 23

Discrimination in occupational pension schemes

23.1 Introduction

Traditionally, men and women have retired at different ages; 65 for men and 60 for women. Occupational pension schemes were generally based on the different retirement age and some excluded married women. The SDA and EqPA had exceptions which allowed these differences. However the development of European law (since *Defrenne*[1]) has dramatically changed UK law. Age differences in retirement and occupational pension schemes are now unlawful and married women must be treated the same as married men (and vice versa). Apart from a few exceptions, there must now be no discrimination on the ground of sex in occupational pension schemes, either in access to schemes or in benefits provided. Note that the pension cases have been brought under the EqPA or art 119 where the crucial question is whether the pension is 'pay'.

The development of the case-law has also led to the passage of the Pensions Act 1995 and the Occupational Pension Schemes (Equal Treatment) Regulations 1995.[2] The statutory provisions largely enact the principles set out by the ECJ in the equal pay cases. However, there is still a different retirement age for the purpose of the state pension. The Sex Discrimination (Social Security) Directive (SSD)[3] allows different treatment for men and women in relation to access to a state pension, contributions periods and the consequences for other benefits.[4] The state pension provisions are to be gradually equalised by 2020.

There is also the Sex Discrimination (Occupational Social Security)

1 *Defrenne v Sabena (No 2)* (Case no 43/75) [1976] ICR 547, ECJ.
2 SI No 3183.
3 Directive 79/7 art 7(1)(a).
4 See *R v Secretary of State for Social Security ex p EOC* [1992] IRLR 376, ECJ.

Directive, which implements existing ECJ case-law on equal treatment of men and women in occupational social security schemes.[5] This was amended with effect from 1 July 1997 by Directive 96/97/EEC. The aim of the Directive is to ensure consistency with art 119 and ECJ decisions, such as *Barber*, *Moroni*, *Bilka-Kaufhaus* and *Fisscher*.

There are no special provisions dealing with pensions under the RRA. Any race discrimination in pensions, whether direct or indirect, will be unlawful (see **6.4**).[6] For disability discrimination in pensions, see Chapter 24 and, in particular, **24.6**.

This chapter looks first at the equal pay cases and how they affect occupational pensions (including access, contributions and benefits), secondly, at the statutory provisions in the Pensions Act 1995 and the regulations and, thirdly, summarises the provisions of the Occupational Social Security Directive.

23.2 Terminology

It is important to understand the difference between the various types of pension provision in order to know whether they come within the scope of the equality legislation.

23.2.1 Statutory social security pension scheme

The state pension scheme is determined by the social security legislation, which has been consolidated in the Social Security Contributions and Benefits Act 1992. Entitlement depends on having paid the relevant national insurance contributions on earnings above the lower earnings limit and having retired. It is quite separate from the relationship between the employer and employee and is not covered by art 119 but by the Sex Discrimination (Social Security) Directive.[7] The state scheme is outside the scope of this book.

5 86/378/EEC as amended by Directive 96/97/EEC. The Pensions Act and regulations have already implemented this in the UK.

6 RRA s4(2)(a) prohibits discrimination in benefits, facilities or services; s4(2)(b) covers any other detriment. See *Barclays Bank plc v Kapur and Others* [1991] ICR 208.

7 Council Directive No 79/7/EEC covers certain social security benefits (non-means-tested benefits) but there are a number of exclusions relating to the equalisation of state pensions.

23.2.2 *State earnings-related pension scheme (SERPS)*

SERPS is an earnings-related pension based on the average earnings of the employee.

An occupational pension scheme which provides benefits which are at least equivalent (or can be deemed to be equivalent) to those provided by SERPS can contract out of SERPS. The employer and employee pay a lower social security contribution and the employee's rights to a SERPS pension are rebated or, for employment after 5 April 1997, completely extinguished.

23.2.3 *Personal pension schemes*

These schemes are not connected to the employment relationship. Historically they were taken out by the self-employed but have also been taken out by employees. They are outside the scope of this book.

23.2.4 *Occupational pension schemes*

These schemes may be determined by the contract of employment, legislative provision and trust law. The important factor is that the pension is paid as a result of the employment relationship. Only employees or office-holders (eg, directors) are eligible to join occupational pension schemes. There are different types of occupational scheme:

a) *final salary scheme or defined-benefit scheme*: this is based on the salary of the employee around the time of retirement or the average salary over the previous few years; a fraction of the salary (usually 1/60th of final salary for each year of pensionable service) is payable to the member on retirement. The employer pays contributions which the actuary considers necessary to meet the cost of providing the pension, taking into account the employee's contributions; or
b) *money purchase scheme or defined contributions scheme*: this is based on contributions made by the employer and employee and income produced from investment as a result of the contributions. The capital sum is often used to buy an annuity from which a pension is paid.

A combination of final salary and money purchase is sometimes adopted. The scheme may be either:

- *contributory*, with the employee paying a percentage of his/her salary (usually about 5%); or
- *non-contributory*, in which case only the employer contributes.

23.2.5 *Retirement lump sums*

At retirement, the individual may normally be able to choose to 'commute' pension rights so that a reduced pension is payable plus a one-off tax-free lump sum.

23.2.6 *Actuarial factors*

These are factors linked to demographic assumptions, such as life expectancy of men and women. As women live on average seven years longer than men, their pensions are more expensive than those of men and may require the employer to pay higher contributions. If the same contributions are made, the man is likely to receive a larger regular pension because he will not live as long.

23.2.7 *Contracted-in and contracted-out schemes*

A scheme may be contracted in to the statutory scheme or contracted out. With a contracted-in scheme members are part of the statutory state scheme and build up rights to the basic state pension and to SERPS. A contracted-out scheme is a substitute for SERPS and reduced contributions are paid to the national scheme.

23.2.8 *Additional voluntary contributions*

These are voluntary payments made by employees in order to secure additional benefits. They are separately identified from the main pension fund .

23.2.9 *Bridging pensions*

These bridge the gap between the occupational pension and state pension that arises because women can receive their state pension at 60 while men must wait until 65. Thus, an extra payment may be made to a man to compensate him for the fact he (unlike a woman) is not yet entitled to a state pension.

23.3 European law and its impact: an overview

Payments under occupational pension schemes constitute pay for the purposes of art 119 and the EqPA. If a pension scheme trust deed contains provisions which are contrary to the principle of equal treatment under art 119 the trustees and employers must take all steps to amend the provisions.

23.3.1 The scope of art 119

As with many areas of discrimination, European law has had a major influence. Article 119 applies to public and private sector employees, to contracts between private individuals and to all collective agreements which regulate paid employment. It applies to all types of scheme which arise out of the employer/employee relationship (see **9.6.4**).

In *Barber*,[8–9] the Advocate General (in distinguishing *Burton*[10]) said that art 119 covered working conditions (including conditions governing dismissal or other forms of redundancy) which directly govern access to remuneration (including a payment or pension benefit in connection with redundancy).

The definition of 'pay' is set out at **18.8.4**

Thus, if there are national provisions which conflict with art 119, art 119 will override them (see Chapter 9). There is a huge body of case-law on the requirement under art 119 for there to be equality in access to pension schemes and their benefits. One of the limitations to this principle is that a claim under art 119 is made through the provisions of the EqPA or Pensions Act (see below) (though subject to any more favourable rights under art 119) and the remedies are limited by national provisions relating to time limits and the backdating of claims (see **23.4.5** and **23.4.6**). The law is complex and the following is a summary of the provisions.

23.3.1.1 Art 119 applies to the following

a) Schemes which are part of the employment relationship, whether they are contracted in or contracted out of the statutory scheme.[11]
b) Schemes which are made compulsory by law, whether or not the reason for their compulsory nature is due to social policy or considerations relating to competition in a particular economic sector, provided they are part of the employment relationship.[12]

8–9 *Barber v GRE Assurance* [1990] IRLR 240.
10 *Burton v British Railways Board* [1982] QB 1080, ECJ.
11 *Barber* (n9).
12 *Dietz v Stichting Thuiszorg Rotterdam* [1996] IRLR 693. In the UK schemes cannot be compulsory.

c) Schemes which supplement or complement the state scheme.[13]
d) Access to an occupational pension scheme.[14]
e) Pensionable ages.[15]
f) Contributions made by the employer.[16]
g) Benefits paid under the scheme including those paid to survivors.[17]
h) Contributory and non-contributory schemes.[18]
i) Final salary[19] and money purchase schemes.
j) Transitional provisions aimed at reducing discrimination over a period.[20]
k) Indirect discrimination, such as less favourable treatment of part-time workers where this is not objectively justified.[21]

Note that art 119 applies to each element of remuneration. Thus, it is no defence to say that an employee who is not entitled to an immediate pension will receive a higher terminal payment. Each benefit must be equal (see **18.8.3**).

23.3.1.2 Where there are no comparators

Article 119 does not generally apply to schemes which have at all times had members of only one sex as there will be no comparator.[22]

13 *Moroni v Firma Collo GmbH* [1994] IRLR 130, ECJ. Under German law if a worker claimed a state pension before normal retirement age s/he could claim early payment of the company pension. The ECJ held that the direct and close interdependence of the statutory and occupational schemes could not have the consequence of excluding the occupational pension scheme from art 119. The ECJ also held that the provisions of the SSD could not limit art 119.

14 *Vroege v NCIV Instituut voor Volkshuisvesting BV* [1994] IRLR 651, ECJ, and *Fisscher v Voorhuis Hengelo BV* [1994] IRLR 662, ECJ. Note that for the purposes of access to a scheme the retrospective provisions in *Barber* (n9) do not apply. Thus, an employee who has been denied access to a scheme could claim to join from the time s/he could first have joined, though will have to make up the contributions (see **23.3.2**).

15 *Barber* (n9), except in respect of the state pension.

16 *Worringham and Humphreys v Lloyds Bank* [1981] IRLR 178, ECJ.

17 *Ten Oever v Stichting Bedrijfspensioenfonds voor het Glazenwassers-en Schoonmaakbedrijf* [1993] IRLR 601, ECJ.

18 *Coloroll Pension Trustees Ltd v Russell and Others* [1994] IRLR 586, ECJ.

19 Ibid.

20 *Van Den Akker and Others v Stichting Shell Pensioenfonds* [1994] IRLR 616, ECJ, and *Smith and Others v Avdel Systems Ltd* [1994] IRLR 602, ECJ.

21 *Bilka-Kaufhaus GmbH v Weber von Hartz* [1986] IRLR 317, ECJ.

22 *Coloroll* (n18); but note that comparisons may sometimes be made between workers at different workplaces, particularly in the public sector where the employment is controlled by one government body (see **18.9.2**).

However, if there are different pension schemes for different groups of workers (doing work of equal value) and the groups are mainly segregated by sex, a presumption of discrimination may arise if benefits available to women are less favourable (see **23.4.1.9**).

A man may be able to bring a claim on the basis that if a provision is indirectly discriminatory to women, then if they succeed in their claim, he would have a direct discrimination claim. Thus, there would be no actual comparator at the time he commenced proceedings, but there would be at a later stage. In *Preston and Others v Wolverhampton Healthcare NHS Trust*[23] the CA refused to strike out a claim by a male part-timer where there was no comparator as there were no female part-timers in the scheme. The applicant argued that the exclusion of temporary and part-time workers was indirectly discriminatory against women; if women then became entitled to benefits so should he – otherwise the provisions would be *directly* discriminatory. The CA held that if a man were not able to institute proceedings unless and until a female employee is admitted to a scheme in the future, he would be prejudiced in his claims for equal pay. A female part-time employee might not be admitted until the conclusion of all the proceedings. The woman would be able to get backdated benefits, but the man, if not allowed to institute proceedings, would have no remedy for the same period.[24]

*23.3.1.3 Schemes to which art 119 does **not** apply*

a) The statutory social security scheme which is governed by legislation and does not involve any agreement within the trade or undertaking (see **23.2.1**). The EAT has held that a local authority statutory scheme is outside art 119 but this is arguably wrong (see **23.4.2.3**).
b) The use of actuarial factors in final salary schemes;[25] inequalities in the amounts of lump sums, transfer values and reduced pensions on taking early retirement, which depend on arrangements chosen for funding the scheme are not covered by art 119[26] (see **23.4.2.1**).

23 [1997] IRLR 233.
24 The decision in *Preston* (ibid) may be distinguished because the man was bringing a claim in parallel to similar claims by women. It is unlikely the result would have been the same if he had brought a claim on his own when there was no potential comparator.
25 *Coloroll* (n18).
26 *Neath v Hugh Steeper Ltd* [1994] IRLR 91, ECJ, and see *Coloroll* (n18).

c) Additional voluntary contributions;[27] thus, where a member has the option to make additional contributions and these are administered by the scheme, the additional benefits are not pay (see **23.4.2.2**).
d) bridging pensions (see **24.3.2.4**).

23.3.2 Retroactivity

The obligations to ensure equal treatment, in relation to benefits for members and for survivors, do not apply to benefits in respect of service before 17 May 1990.[28] In *Barber*[29] the ECJ held that member states and the parties were entitled to consider that art 119 did not apply to occupational pensions paid because of the exception contained in the Social Security Directives.[30] A crucial factor was that if the judgment in *Barber* did apply retrospectively it would cause serious difficulties for pension schemes and their financial balance. The ECJ was very aware of the enormous financial implications of its decision. This was clarified further in *Ten Oever*[31] where the ECJ held that all new pensions paid after 17 May 1990 must not be based on discriminatory provisions after that date. The limitation on the effect of the judgment was incorporated in the Maastricht Treaty *Barber Protocol*[32] and so forms part of art 119.

Where the benefits are not linked to length of actual service, such as a lump-sum payment made if the member dies during his/her employment, art 119 applies where the death occurs on or *after* 17 May 1990.

The limit on retroactive effect does not apply to the right to *join* the scheme (see *Fisscher*[33]). Nor does it apply to the right to payment of a

27 *Coloroll* (n18).

28 Unless the employee had already issued proceedings or made an equivalent claim (see *Howard v Ministry of Defence* [1995] ICR 1074, EAT, where asserting a claim by correspondence was held to be insufficient).

29 See n9.

30 Directive 79/7 art 7(1) and Directive 86/378 art 9(a).

31 See n17.

32 Protocol No 2, which came into force on 1 November 1993, provides that: 'For the purposes of Article 119 of this Treaty, benefits under occupational social security schemes shall not be considered as remuneration if and in so far as they are attributable to periods of employment prior to 17 May 1990, except in the case of workers or those claiming under them who have before that date initiated legal proceedings or introduced an equivalent claim under the applicable national law.' See *Bestuur van het Algemeen Burgerlijk Pensioenfonds v Beune* [1995] IRLR 103, ECJ.

33 *Fisscher* (n14) and *Vroege* (n14).

retirement pension where there has been a denial of access, ie, the worker was excluded from membership of the scheme in breach of art 119. In *Dietz v Stichting Thuiszorg Rotterdam*[34] the applicant was employed for seven hours a week until she reached the age of 61 when she took voluntary early retirement. She was excluded from the compulsory occupational pension scheme which only applied to workers who worked more hours than she did. Ms Dietz claimed she was entitled under art 119 to a pension based on her periods of employment after 8 April 1976. The ECJ held that she was entitled to join the scheme (as from 1976) and was also entitled to payment of a retirement pension. As the ECJ pointed out, membership of a pension scheme would be of no interest to employees if it did not confer entitlement to the benefits provided.

Where a worker is able to claim retroactively the right to join an occupational pension scheme and to claim the benefits, s/he must still pay the contributions relating to the period of membership concerned.[35] However, enforcing such claims (to join and to receive the benefits) may be difficult because of national time limits and the limitation on claiming arrears (see **23.4.5** and **23.4.6**).

23.3.3 Equalling up or down

Retroactive reduction of advantages is not allowed.[36] Thus, employees who have been disadvantaged must be given the same rights as other employees in relation to service before the discrimination was removed, but under *Barber* only in relation to pensionable service after 17 May 1990. The treatment must be equalised upwards for the period where there was discrimination. Once the discrimination has been removed the employer can reduce the advantages previously enjoyed by employees, provided male and female employees are treated equally.[37] This is subject, however, to the provisions in the trust deed and trust law which may prevent trustees altering a scheme if it would reduce women's future benefits. If this is the case, no levelling down would be permitted.[38] In addition, if pension entitlement is part of the contract of employment it is doubtful whether the employer can make a unilateral variation.

34 [1996] IRLR 692.

35 *Fisscher* (n14) and *Dietz* (n12).

36 *Coloroll* (n18). See also Pensions Act 1995 (**23.5.7**).

37 *Smith v Avdel Systems Ltd: C-408* [1994] IRLR 602.

38 See *Lloyds Bank Pension Trust Corporation v Lloyds Bank plc* [1996] PLR 263, Ch D.

23.4 Impact of art 119 in practice

23.4.1 What is covered by art 119?

23.4.1.1 Access to occupational pension schemes

There must be no discrimination, direct or indirect, in access to a pension scheme. The exclusion of women or categories of women, such as married women, will be a breach of art 119.[39] Any less favourable treatment of part-time workers, where this is indirectly discriminatory and cannot be objectively justified, will be unlawful.[40]

In *Fisscher*[41] the applicant was employed from January 1978 to April 1992. Prior to January 1991 she was excluded from the pension scheme because she was a married woman. When she was allowed into the scheme on 1 January 1991 she was allowed retroactive membership for a period of three years. She claimed that she should be granted membership with effect from 8 April 1976, the date of the *Defrenne* (*No 2*) decision,[42] in which the ECJ held for the first time that art 119 had direct effect.

Similarly, in *Vroege*[43] the applicant was excluded from the pension scheme because the rules allowed only men and unmarried women working at least 80% of the normal full working day to be members and Mrs Vroege never worked more than 80% of the working day. The rules were changed in 1991 but she was not allowed to purchase years of membership in respect of her service prior to 1991.

In both cases the ECJ held that the limitation on claiming retroactive benefits in *Barber*[44] did not apply to the right to join an occupational pension scheme. Unlike *Barber* (where employers acted in good faith and there would be a risk of serious difficulties if a limitation were not applied) it had been clear since the decision in *Bilka*[45] that there should be equal access to pension schemes. As *Bilka* did not limit its effect in time, the applicants could backdate their membership to 8 April 1976 (the date of the *Defrenne* (*No 2*) decision that art 119 has direct effect) and receive benefits relating to this period (see *Dietz*[46]). This again is subject to national rules on time limits and the limitation on claiming back pay (see **23.4.5** and **23.4.6**).

39 *Fisscher* (n14).
40 See *Bilka* (n21) and *Vroege* (n14).
41 See n14.
42 See **9.6.4**.
43 See n14.
44 See n9.
45 See n21.
46 See n12.

Where an employee wants to backdate his/her membership of a scheme, having previously been excluded because of discrimination, s/he will have to make up the employee's contributions.[47]

23.4.1.2 *Differential pension ages*

Equal pension benefits under occupational pension schemes must be paid to men and women at the same age. In *Barber*[48] the ECJ held that benefits under a private, contracted-out, occupational pension scheme constitute 'pay' under art 119. Mr Barber was a member of a non-contributory, contracted-out scheme where the normal pensionable age was three years earlier than the statutory scheme, ie, 62 for men and 57 for women. In the event of redundancy, members who had reached age 55 for men or 50 for women were entitled to an immediate pension as well as a payment equal to the statutory redundancy payment. Mr Barber was made redundant when he was 52, so he was not granted an immediate pension. He complained that if he had been a woman he would have received an immediate pension. The ECJ said that benefits paid by an employer to a worker in connection with the latter's compulsory redundancy fall within art 119 whether they are paid under a contract of employment, by virtue of legislative provisions or on a voluntary basis. Thus, held the ECJ, it was contrary to art 119 to impose an age condition which differs according to sex in respect of pensions paid under a contracted-out scheme, even if the difference between the pensionable age for men and that for women is based (as it was in *Barber*) on the national statutory state pension scheme.[49] Note that the same principles will apply to contracted-in occupational pension schemes (see *Moroni*).

23.4.1.3 *Each element of payment must be equal*

The ECJ also held in *Barber*[50] that the principle of equal pay applied to each element of remuneration, not to the total consideration paid to workers (see **18.8.3**).

23.4.1.4 *Different contributions by employers for men and women*

In *Worringham and Humphreys v Lloyds Bank*,[51] male and female clerical staff joined different occupational pension schemes. Women

47 *Fisscher* (n14) and *Dietz* (n12).

48 See n9.

49 See also *Moroni* (n13) (concerning a supplementary pension) where the ECJ held it was a breach of art 119 where a male employee could claim a pension only at a later age than a female employee because of the different pensionable ages.

50 See n9.

51 [1981] IRLR 178, ECJ.

under 25 did not have to contribute, and they received nothing if they left the bank before they were 25. Men under 25 were obliged to pay a contribution but the employer made up the difference so that the net pay of men and women was the same. Men leaving the bank before they were 25 received their contributions back. The employer's contributions for the men meant that their *gross* pay was higher than women's and this determined other salary-related benefits. The ECJ held that the employer's contributions should be treated as pay and should be equal for men and women.

23.4.1.5 *Survivors' pensions*

A survivor's pension provided for by an occupational pension scheme is within art 119.[52] As the ECJ pointed out, in *Coloroll*,[53] the benefit derives from the survivor's spouse's membership of the scheme and the pension is vested in the survivor by reason of the employment relationship between the employee and member.

In *Razzouk and Beydoun v Commission of the European Communities*[54] the ECJ held that restricting the payment of contractual survivors' pensions to widows was discriminatory. Mr Razzouk's wife had worked for the EC but when she died Mr Razzouk was refused a pension as pensions were automatically given only to widows; widowers could receive a pension but only if permanently incapacitated and unable to work. The court awarded Mr Razzouk a pension with interest. The ECJ did not rely on art 119, though the Advocate General considered that art 119 excluded only statutory social security schemes and not pension schemes entered into outside a national system of social security.[55]

23.4.1.6 *Transfer of rights from one scheme to another*

Where there is a transfer to a second scheme, eg, on a change of job, that second scheme must increase benefits to eliminate the effect of previous discrimination.[56] If there is insufficient funding, the second scheme should do everything possible to ensure that there is equality. They may need to make a claim under national law for the necessary additional sums from the first scheme which made the inadequate

52 *Ten Oever* (n17).
53 See n18.
54 *Case nos 75/82* and *117/82* [1984] 3 CMLR 470, ECJ.
55 The claim was brought under the Staff Regulations for Community Officials. The ECJ held that the staff regulations were contrary to 'a fundamental right', as they treated surviving spouses unequally according to their sex.
56 *Van den Akker* (n20).

contributions and transfer. The members of the scheme should receive a pension calculated in accordance with the principle of equal treatment. This is also limited to service subsequent to 17 May 1990.

23.4.1.7 Transitional provisions

Where the employer raises the pension age for women it cannot take steps to limit the consequences for women as this would mean treating men less favourably.[57] In *Van den Akker and Others v Stickting Shell Pensioenfonds*[58] the pension scheme had a normal pensionable age of 60 for men and 55 for women. The age was equalised at 60 in 1985 but, under transitional arrangements, existing women members were given the option of maintaining the pensionable age of 55. After *Barber*[59] the pension fund abolished, with effect from 1 June 1991, the option for women to maintain a pensionable age of 55. The applicants, who had elected to maintain the pensionable age of 55, challenged the pension fund's argument that this was necessary as a result of the *Barber* decision. The ECJ held that equality could be achieved by equalising at the age of 60 even though this reduces the advantage previously enjoyed by women. Once equalisation has happened, the employer cannot treat women more favourably in respect of service after the new rule, even if the more favourable treatment arose from an election made by women before the *Barber* judgment. However, between 17 May 1990 and 1 June 1991 (when equalisation was implemented) pension rights for men and women had to be calculated on the basis of the lower retirement age of 55 (see **23.3.3**).

23.4.1.8 Less favourable treatment of part-time workers/members

Direct and indirect discrimination is unlawful. In *Bilka*[60] and *Vroege*[61] the ECJ held that part-time workers should be treated in the same way (on a pro-rata basis) as full-time workers unless the employer can show objectively justified reasons (see **23.3.3**).

23.4.1.9 Exclusion of low-grade workers from pension schemes

Low paid, part-time workers are protected in the same way as any other employees. Under German social security law, individuals working fewer than 15 hours per week and whose income does not exceed one-seventh of the average monthly salary are called 'minor'

57 *Smith v Avdel Systems Ltd* (n37).
58 See n20.
59 See n9.
60 See n21.
61 See n14.

workers. They are not covered by the statutory old-age insurance scheme and do not pay contributions. In *Nolte*[62] and *Megner*[63] the applicants were cleaners working a maximum of ten hours per week. They claimed that their exclusion from the statutory state insurance schemes was indirect discrimination. The ECJ held that persons in minor employment are part of the 'working population' within the meaning of the SSD. On the same basis, such workers would be protected by art 119. The ECJ, however, held that the exclusion of such workers from the statutory state scheme was justified (see **3.6.7.7**).

A more difficult question is whether it is a breach of EC law to exclude lower-grade workers from pension schemes where many more women than men work in the lower grades. The principle is not so different from that laid down in *Bilka*[64] and *Kowalska*,[65] where the exclusion of part-time workers was challenged. In the same way that part-time workers should receive the same pro-rata benefits as full-timers, so should lower-paid workers receive access to the same benefits, albeit at a reduced rate tied to the salary level. However, under the EqPA and Pensions Act at least, the applicant can only bring a claim by comparing herself with a man doing like work, equivalent work or work of equal value and such a comparison would clearly be very difficult as the work is not likely to be equal. It is possible that a claim could be made under art 119. In *Bilka* the ECJ did not consider that there was a need for a comparator. The adverse effect on women was sufficient to move the onus onto the employer to justify the exclusion. In addition, the amended Occupational Social Security Directive provides that the exclusion of workers on the ground of the nature of their work contracts from a scheme may be indirect discrimination against women.

23.4.1.10 Length of service requirements

Similarly, length of service requirements may discriminate indirectly against women (see **22.3.2.3**). An employer may be able to justify such a requirement if the setting-up costs are high and where it would be impractical to provide a pension for an employee who was not going to stay for very long. One solution, which is sometimes adopted, is to allow access after a year of service and to backdate entitlement.

62 *Nolte v Landesversicherungsanstalt Hannover* [1996] IRLR 225.
63 *Megner and Scheffel v Innungskrankenkasse Vorderpfalz* [1996] IRLR 236.
64 See n21.
65 *Kowalska v Freie und Hansestadt Hamburg* [1990] IRLR 447, ECJ.

23.4.2 Exceptions to the equal treatment principle

23.4.2.1 Actuarial factors outside art 119

The use of actuarial factors in final salary (or defined benefit) occupational pension schemes which take account of the fact that women live longer than men does not come within article 119. In *Neath v Hugh Steaper Ltd*[66] the ECJ has held that in respect of final salary occupational pension schemes, the employer's commitment to its employees concerns the payment of a periodic pension. As this is based on final salary the employer must make sufficient contributions to meet this commitment. Although the *periodic pension* is pay under art 119, the *funding arrangements* chosen to secure the pension are outside art 119. Thus, where an employer pays higher contributions for women because of their longer life expectancy, these contributions are outside art 119. This may mean, as it did in *Neath*, that the sums to which male employees are entitled, in particular where part of the pension is converted into a capital sum or where acquired rights are transferred, are lower than those to which female employees are entitled. This is not a breach of art 119 because the difference is based on actuarial factors taken into account in funding arrangements.

The same principles apply where a reversionary pension is payable to a dependant in return for the surrender of part of the annual pension and where a reduced pension is paid when the employee opts for early retirement. Funding arrangements based on actuarial factors are outside art 119 (at least for defined benefit schemes) and so is any inequality of the amounts of those benefits arising from the use of actuarial factors in the funding of the scheme.

It is not clear whether the amount of contributions paid by employers and employees in money purchase schemes must be the same for men and women.[67] Arguably, it is only the use of actuarial factors in final salary occupational pension schemes which fall outside art 119 and capital benefits or substitute benefits arising out of such funding arrangements (which are based on actuarial factors).[68] In money purchase schemes, equal contribution will, in the absence of unisex annuity rates, result in lower pensions for women. Where the pension is based on the sum of the employer's and employee's contributions, arguably both the employer's and employee's contributions constitute pay so must be equal for men and women.

66 [1994] IRLR 91, ECJ.
67 *Neath* (n26) and *Coloroll* (n18).
68 *Coloroll* (n18).

23.4.2.2 Additional voluntary contributions

In *Coloroll*[69] AVCs were calculated separately, solely on the basis of the value of the contributions paid, which were credited to a distinct fund. The additional benefits payable as a result of purely voluntary contributions are not covered by art 119.[70]

23.4.2.3 Statutory public sector pension schemes

In *Griffin*[71] the EAT held that a local government pension scheme which was determined exclusively by statutory provisions was outside art 119. This was because the scheme was governed entirely by statute as opposed to by the employer and employee. However, there is a strong argument that this is a breach of EC law as the pension is only payable *as a result of* the employment relationship. In *Beune*[72] the ECJ held that legislation whereby the calculation of a pension was different for male married civil servants to that for female married civil servants was covered by art 119. The ECJ said that the only possible decisive criterion is whether the pension is paid to the worker as a result of the employment relationship between the employee and his/her former employer. If the pension paid by the public employer concerns only a particular category of workers, if it is directly related to the period of service and if its amount is calculated by reference to the employee's salary it is comparable to a private occupational pension scheme. In *Beune* the ECJ held that married men were entitled to the benefit of the same rules as married women.

23.4.2.4 Bridging pensions

Where a man is paid a higher pension to compensate him for not receiving the state retirement pension which would be paid to a woman, that is not in breach of art 119 (see **23.5.3.1**).

23.4.3 Enforcement

23.4.3.1 By employees

Employee members of pension schemes can enforce the EqPA or art 119 against their employers or the trustees of the scheme, whether they work for the private or public sector.

69 See n18.
70 Ibid.
71 *Griffin v London Pension Fund Authority* [1993] IRLR 248, EAT.
72 See n32.

23.4.3.2 By survivors

Where a member has died, leaving a spouse or other person entitled to the benefit of the pension, the survivor can enforce the provisions of art 119. Since the pension scheme is a trust the survivor does not have to be a party to the employment contract to enforce his/her rights – as a beneficiary s/he can bring an action for breach of trust. As the ECJ pointed out in *Coloroll*,[73] if the survivor were to be denied the possibility of enforcing art 119, this would deprive art 119 of all its effectiveness as far as survivors' pensions are concerned.

23.4.3.3 Against employers and trustees

In *Coloroll* the ECJ said that the direct effect of art 119 can be relied on against the employer *and* trustees or administrators of an occupational scheme. Thus, the trustees are bound by the principle of equal treatment when carrying out their duties. If there is a conflicting provision in the trust deed, the trustees must do all they can to eliminate the discrimination, including seeking a declaration from the court.[74]

23.4.4 Remedies

If women (or men) have been treated less favourably, the employer and trustee is obliged to remedy this by, for example, paying additional sums into the scheme or paying out of surplus funds or the fund's assets. This applies even if no claim has been made against the employer. The national court is under an obligation to order such measures. If funds are insufficient the ECJ has held that the problem must be resolved on the basis of national law in the light of the principle of equal pay. Presumably, the resolution will depend on the facts of the case but the end result should be that men and women receive equal benefits.

In *Preston*[75] the applicants argued that they should be able to receive compensation for the loss of benefits under the pension scheme. The CA held that the only remedy was a declaration as to their rights of access to the scheme – limited to a period of two years (see below). The CA said that the majority of applicants were not yet entitled to benefits under the scheme. The benefits flowed from the rights of access and contributions.

73 See n18.
74 Ibid.
75 [1997] IRLR 233, CA.

23.4.5 *Time limits*

The ECJ has held that in the absence of EC rules, national rules relating to time limits for bringing actions are also applicable to actions based on EC law *provided* that they are 'no less favourable' for such actions than for similar actions of a domestic nature and they do not render the exercise of rights conferred by EC law 'impossible in practice'.[76] Under UK law (the EqPA) the time limit for bringing a claim is within six months from the date on which the contract of employment containing the equality clause ended.[77] Where there has been a series of fixed-term contracts the six months runs from the end of each particular contract in force, not the end of the employment.[78]

23.4.6 *Two-year limitation on back-pay*

Under the EqPA an employee can recover back-pay for only two years prior to the issue of proceedings. Thus, even though women and men may, in theory, have a right to backdated pension rights, these can be enforced only for the previous two years.[79] The question as to whether this is in breach of EC law has been referred to the ECJ in *Magorrian v Eastern Health and Social Services Board*.[80] The Advocate General's view is that the two-year limitation does render it impossible in practice for an individual's rights under art 119 to be exercised. Thus, this provision is a breach of EC law. Where the claim relates to being denied access to a scheme (see **23.3.2**) there would be little benefit in backdating access if the employer was not obliged to make up the contributions. Thus, both employer and employee should have to make up the contribution for the relevant period.

A parallel case to *Preston* (*Levez v T H Jennings (Harlow Pools)*

76 *Rewe-Zentralfinanz eG v Landwirtschaftskammer fur das Saarland 33/76* [1976] ECR 1989, ECJ, and *Fisscher* (n14).

77 EqPA s2(4).

78 *Preston* (n23). There may be an exception to this rule where a succession of contracts is governed by an 'umbrella' contract.

79 Ibid. A similar conclusion was reached by the ECJ in relation to the one-year limit on backdating incapacity benefit in *Steenhorst-Neerings v Bestuur* [1994] IRLR 244, ECJ. The ECJ held that the rule did not affect the right of individuals to rely on the Directive but merely limited the retroactive effect of claims made for the purpose of obtaining the relevant benefits. This was a social security case and the ECJ stressed the need to preserve financial balance in the scheme.

80 Northern Ireland Industrial Tribunal; Case nos 2632–37/92; 12 September 1995.

Ltd[81]) has been referred by the EAT to the ECJ for a decision about whether the limitation period is the same as 'the nearest similar domestic action'.[82] In *Magorrian*, the Advocate General considered that benefits for part-timers should be calculated as from 8 April 1976. The comparison should at least be with contract claims where a claimant would be able to claim up to six years' back-pay loss, or under the RRA where there is no limitation for discrimination in pay. Unfortunately, no reference to the ECJ was made in *Preston*.[83]

23.5 Statutory provisions for equal treatment in pension schemes

Barber[84] forced the government to introduce legislation to bring UK law in line with EC law. The relevant parts of the Pensions Act 1995, which came into force on 1 January 1996, broadly follow the decisions of the ECJ's rulings.[85]

23.5.1 Pensions Act 1995 and regulations

The equal treatment provisions of the Pensions Act are supplemented by the Occupational Pension Schemes (Equal Treatment) Regulations 1995[86] which also came into force on 1 January 1996. The regulations mainly cover amendments to the EqPA, exceptions and remedies. In general the provisions only apply to pensionable service on or after 17 May 1990 (but see **23.3.2**).[87]

81 EAT 812/94 (1996) 549 IRLIB 16, EAT.

82 Required by *Rewe* (n76); see also the Advocate General in *Marshall v Southampton and South West Hampshire Area Health Authority (No 2)* [1990] IRLR 481, CA.

83 See n75.

84 See n9.

85 Some of the provisions were previously in force. The Occupational Pension Schemes (Equal Access to Membership) Regulations 1976 SI No 142, as amended by the Occupational Pension Schemes (Equal Access to Membership) Amendment Regulations 1995 SI No 1215, made direct and indirect sex discrimination in access to occupational pension schemes unlawful. The new Act also covers benefits, thus implementing the *Barber* decision (n9). It effectively replaces Social Security Act 1989 Sch 5 most of which was not brought into force (but see **16.2.5** for provisions in relation to maternity leave and absence).

86 SI No 3183; referred to as the Equal Treatment Regs.

87 For an excellent article on the provisions of the Act and its compatibility with European law, see Christopher McCrudden, 'Third Time Lucky? The Pensions Act 1995 and Equal Treatment in Occupational Pensions' (1996) March ILJ 28.

23.5.2 The equal treatment rule

An occupational pension scheme is to be treated as containing an 'equal treatment rule'. This is a rule which relates to:

- access to membership of the pension scheme; and
- how members of the scheme are treated, eg, in relation to benefits and contributions.[88]

Thus, it means that there must be equal access to a pension scheme and equal treatment of existing members. Direct and indirect discrimination are prohibited.

Where occupational pension terms differ according to the person's family or marital status, the comparison is between a man and a woman with the same family or marital status; thus a married woman should be treated in the same way as a married man.[89]

Terms which have effect for the benefit of dependants of members are also covered.[90]

The Act operates in a very similar way to the EqPA and it is specifically provided that the 'equal treatment rule' is to be construed as one with EqPA s1[91] (see Chapters 18 to 21).

23.5.3 When does the equal treatment rule apply?

The rule applies when:

a) a woman is employed on like work with a man in the same employment (see **19.1**);
b) a woman is employed on work rated as equivalent with that of a man in the same employment (see **19.2**); or
c) a woman is employed on work which does not come under (a) or (b) but which is work of equal value in terms of the demands made upon her (see Chapter 20).

If, in these circumstances, access to the scheme or treatment of a member is less favourable the term must be modified so as to be no less favourable.[92] The Act applies equally to men and women.

As with the EqPA, where a woman establishes she is doing like work, work rated as equivalent or work of equal value, but is being paid less,

88 Pensions Act 1995 s62.
89 Ibid, s63(2).
90 Ibid, s63(1).
91 Ibid, s63(4).
92 Ibid, s62(3).

there is an assumption that there is discrimination.[93] The respondent then needs to prove that the reason for the unequal pay is not tainted by discrimination – through the material factor defence (see **21.4**).

The Act also applies where trustees or managers have discretionary powers. These must not be exercised in a discriminatory way.[94] The effect of the equal treatment rule is that the term is treated as modified so as not to allow the discretion to be exercised in a way which is less favourable to a woman (or man).

23.5.3.1 Exceptions

Material factor defence. This is similar to the defence under the EqPA (see Chapter 21). The equal treatment rule does not apply if there is a difference in treatment which is genuinely due to a material factor which:

a) is not the difference of sex; but
b) is a material difference between the woman's case and the man's case.[95]

It is for the trustees or managers of the occupational pension scheme to prove the material factor defence.

Pensionable service prior to 17 May 1990. In relation to the *terms* on which members are treated, no claim can be made in relation to pensionable service prior to 17 May 1990.[96] This does not apply to *access* to schemes (see **23.4.1.1**).

Bridging pensions. Where a man and woman receive different amounts of occupational pension, and this is due to the differences between men and women in what they receive under the state retirement pension, the equal treatment rule does not apply.[97] Thus, in certain circumstances, occupational pension schemes can, by means of a bridging pension, compensate for the current inequalities in the state scheme. This exception would cover the situation which arose in *Birds Eye Walls Ltd v Roberts*.[98] In that case the ECJ held that an

93 Compare this with the approach under the SDA where discrimination must be proved.
94 Pensions Act 1995 s62(5).
95 Ibid, s62(4).
96 Ibid, s63(6).
97 Ibid, s64(2).
98 [1991] IRLR 29, ECJ. Note that in *Beune* (see n32) the ECJ did not accept that a difference in the state pension justified inequality in an occupational pension.

employer could reduce the amount of a bridging pension to take account of the state pension which the employee will receive even if it meant that female ex-employees received smaller bridging pensions than men in a similar situation.

This exception applies in two situations:

a) Where a man:
   - has not reached pensionable age but would have done so if he were a woman;
   - is in receipt of an occupational pension;
   - receives an additional amount of pension (not exceeding the amount of Category A retirement pension) which is no more than a woman with the same earnings would receive.

   This means that a man may be paid an additional amount so that he is receiving the same total amount as a woman who is entitled, in addition to her occupational pension, to a state retirement pension.[99]
b) Where the scheme is a contracted-out final salary scheme under which the member receives more than s/he would have done if s/he had been of the other sex and the extra amount does not exceed the SERPS top-up. Thus, the occupational pension may differ between a man and woman to take account of the difference between the top-up from SERPS s/he actually receives and the amount s/he would receive if s/he were of the opposite sex.[100] This is intended to cover the situation where there are differences in the rate of occupational pensions on account of part of the inflation-proofing of the guaranteed minimum pension element which is paid as part of SERPS.[101]

Actuarial factors. If there is a variation in pay due to actuarial factors which fall within a prescribed class or description and differ for men and women in relation to:

- the calculation of employers' contributions; or
- the determination of benefits (ie, payment or other benefit made to or in respect of a member);

the equal treatment rule does not apply.

99 Equal Treatment Regs reg 13.
100 Ibid, reg 14.
101 See the Memorandum by the Department of Social Security to the Select Committee on the Scrutiny of Delegated Powers; HL Paper 25 (Session 1994–95) (HMSO, January 1995), para 65.

Different actuarial factors cover differences in the average life expectancy of men where the aim is to provide equal periodical pension benefits for men and women. The exception covers the following:[102]

a) a lump sum payment which consists of a commuted periodical pension or part of such a pension;
b) a periodical pension granted in exchange for a lump sum payment;
c) money purchase benefits within Pension Schemes Act 1993 s181(1);
d) transfer credits and any rights allowed to a member by reference to a transfer from a personal pension scheme;
e) a transfer payment including a cash equivalent under Pension Schemes Act 1993 s94;
f) a periodical pension payable in respect of a member who opts to take such benefits before normal pension age or in respect of a member who defers taking such benefits until after normal pension age;
g) benefits payable to another person in exchange for part of a member's benefits and the part of the member's benefits given up for that purpose;
h) benefits provided in respect of a member's voluntary contributions under Pension Schemes Act 1993 s111.

It is arguable that the exceptions in the regulations are much wider than permitted by European law and could therefore be challenged under art 119. Thus, if, the decision in *Neath*[103] is limited to final salary schemes where the funding arrangements are unequal (because of the different life expectancy of men and women) so arguably should these exceptions (see **23.4.2.1**).

The Act enables further regulations to be made which may permit further variables or amend or repeal the exceptions relating to bridging pensions and actuarial factors or permit further variations.[104]

23.5.4 Indirect discrimination in pensions

If a woman is denied access to a pension scheme because she is working part-time, she will have to show that there is a man doing like work, work rated as equivalent or work of equal value. The onus will then shift to the employer to show that there is a material factor

102 Pensions Act 1995 s64(3) and Equal Treatment Regs reg 15.
103 See n26.
104 Pensions Act 1995 s64(4).

which is *not* discriminatory. Thus, the test is that adopted by the EqPA and not the SDA. It is arguable that the SDA model, which does not require an actual comparator, is more consistent with the approach taken by the ECJ in *Bilka*,[105] *Vroege*[106] and *Royal Copenhagen*.[107] In *Bilka* there was no comparator (see **23.4.1.8**). The test is whether the exclusion affects a disproportionate number of members of one sex. Thus, if all part-timers are excluded and the great majority are women, the exclusion would disproportionately affect women. In *Vroege* the ECJ held that where a practice had a significant adverse impact on a particular gender, a prima facie case was made out under art 119 (see also **23.4.1.1**). However, any such claim would have to be brought under art 119 as the SDA is unlikely to apply (see **5.7.1**).

23.5.5 *Transfer of undertakings*

Occupational pension schemes are specifically excluded from the general rule that all the transferor's liabilities shall be transferred to the transferee. Thus, there is no obligation for the transferee to maintain a previous pension, but rights which have accrued at the time of transfer are protected.[108] There is a parallel exception in the European Acquired Rights Directive.[109] However, the EAT has held that a subsisting allegation of sex discrimination will be transferred[110] and it must be assumed that this would also apply to an existing equal pay claim, including one made under the Pensions Act 1995.

23.5.6 *Enforcement*

Trustees or managers are given power to make appropriate alterations to a scheme by way of resolution in order to comply with the equal treatment rule. This applies if they do not otherwise have the power or if the procedure is unduly complex or protracted or involves the obtaining of consents which cannot be obtained (or cannot be obtained without delay).[111]

105 See n21.
106 See n14.
107 *Specialarbejderforbundet i Danmark v Dansk Industri (acting for Royal Copenhagen A/S* [1996] IRLR 648.
108 Transfer of Undertakings (Protection of Employment) Regulations 1981 SI No 1794 reg 6.
109 Directive 77/187/EEC art 3(3).
110 *DJM International Ltd v Nicholas* [1996] IRLR 76, EAT.
111 Pensions Act 1995 s65. The alterations may be backdated (s65(2)).

The same provisions apply to disputes and enforcement as apply under the EqPA (see Chapter 26).[112] The applicant will be the member (or prospective member) of the scheme. The respondents will be the trustees or managers of the scheme.[113] However, in tribunal proceedings, the employer shall, for the purposes of the rules governing procedure, be treated as a party and be entitled to appear and be heard.[114]

Claims must be made within six months of the woman being employed in relevant employment to which the scheme relates.[115] Arrears of pay can be awarded only in respect of the two years prior to the issue of proceedings (but see **23.4.6**).

There are different remedies for members and pensioners. The aim is to put the disadvantaged member or pensioner in the position s/he would have been in had there been equal treatment. Thus, no compensation will be awarded to members (as they would not be entitled to a pension), only to pensioners.

The same principles apply whether:

- the claim is for a breach of the equal treatment rule;[116] or
- where the claim is for breach of an equality clause (in a contract of employment) which relates to membership of or rights under a scheme.[117]

23.5.6.1 *Equal treatment in the terms on which persons become members*[118]

Where there has been a breach of an equality clause or a breach of the 'equal treatment' rule in relation to the terms on which a person becomes a member, the court or tribunal may declare that an employee is entitled to be admitted to the scheme as from a specified date. The date may not be more than two years earlier than the date the proceedings were instituted but see *Magorrian* (**23.4.6**).[119] If the deemed date is earlier than the date of the tribunal's decision, the IT may require the employer to provide such resources as are necessary

112 EqPA ss2 and 2A apply; Pensions Act 1995 s63(4).
113 Pensions Act 1995 s64(3)(b). The references in the EqPA to employers and employees are to be treated as references to trustees or managers (on the one hand) and members or prospective members (on the other).
114 Equal Treatment Regs reg 4 (EqPA s2(5A)).
115 Pensions Act 1995 s63(4)(c).
116 Equal Treatment Regs regs 2 to 7.
117 Ibid, regs 8 to 12.
118 Ibid, regs 5 and 10.
119 Ibid, reg 5 (EqPA s2(6A)).

to make up for the loss in respect of the employee's accrued rights.[120] It is the employer who must pay, not the applicant, nor other members of the pension scheme.

23.5.6.2 Equal treatment for existing members[121]

Where there has been a breach of the equality clause or of the equal treatment rule in respect of the terms on which members of a scheme are treated, the court or tribunal may declare that a member has a right to equal treatment in respect of a specified period, provided it is not before 17 May 1990. The employer must provide the resources to ensure that the member has the same accrued rights for the period as other members, subject to the two-year limit (but see *Magorrian* above). Again, it is the employer who must pay, not the member, nor other members.

In relation to **23.5.7.1** and **23.5.7.2** above, a member is not entitled to any payment by way of arrears of benefits or damages.[122]

23.5.6.3 Claim by pensioner member[123]

Where there has been a breach of the equality clause or the equal treatment rule relating to the terms of a scheme, a pensioner member can claim damages or any other financial award. The employer must again provide the resources. Compensation can be recovered only for the two years immediately prior to the complaint (but see *Magorrian* above).[124]

23.5.6.4 Other beneficiaries under the scheme.

There are no provisions in the Act for other beneficiaries, such as survivors, to make a claim, though the Regulations define a pensioner member as a person entitled to the present payment of pension or other benefits derived through a member.[125] The Act should be interpreted to allow a beneficiary to make a claim. It may be wise, however, also to make a claim under the ordinary provisions of EqPA and art 119.

120 Where the breach relates to terms concerning the age or length of service needed for becoming a member the resources must secure the accrued benefits in respect of the period to which the declaration relates. In other cases it cannot be back-dated beyond 31 May 1995: Equal Treatment Regs reg 5 (EqPA s2(7A)).
121 Equal Treatment Regs regs 6 and 11.
122 Ibid, regs 3 and 9 (EqPA s2(5)).
123 Ibid, regs 7 and 12.
124 EqPA ss2(6C) and 7(C).
125 Equal Treatment Regs reg 1.

23.5.6.5 *The Pensions Ombudsman*

The Pensions Ombudsman has power to investigate and determine complaints made by a member (or his/her survivor) about maladministration by the trustees or managers of an occupational or personal pension scheme.[126]

23.6 EC Occupational Social Security Directive

Council Directive 96/97/EC amends the 1986 Directive[127] and member states have to comply with it by 1 July 1997. The aim of the Directive is to bring the 1986 Directive in line with art 119 as interpreted by the ECJ in the various pension cases.

The Directive applies to employees, those whose employment is interrupted by illness, maternity, accident or involuntary unemployment and persons seeking employment, to retired and disabled workers and to those claiming under them.

The amended Directive provides that provisions contrary to the principle of equal treatment shall include those based on sex, either directly or indirectly, in particular by reference to marital or family status, for:

a) deciding who can join an occupational pension scheme;
b) fixing the compulsory or optional nature of participation in an occupational scheme;
c) laying down different rules as regards:
   - the age of entry into the scheme; or
   - the minimum period of employment; or
   - membership of the scheme;

   required to obtain the benefits;
d) laying down different rules for the reimbursement of contributions when a worker leaves a scheme without having fulfilled the conditions guaranteeing a deferred right to long-term benefits; there is an exception where (h) or (i) below apply;
e) setting different conditions for the granting of benefits or restricting such benefits to workers of one or other of the sexes;
f) fixing different retirement ages;

126 Pension Schemes Act 1993 ss145 to 152.
127 Directive 86/378/EEC.

g) suspending the retention or acquisition of rights during periods of maternity leave or leave for family reasons which are granted by law or agreement and are paid by the employer;
h) setting different levels of benefit, except in so far as may be necessary to take account of actuarial calculation factors which differ according to sex in the case of money purchase schemes. In the case of final salary schemes, certain elements may be unequal where the inequality is due to actuarial factors differing according to sex at the time when the scheme's funding is implemented;
i) setting different levels for workers' contributions;
j) setting different levels for employers' contributions, except:
   - in the case of money purchase schemes if the aim is to equalise the amount of the final benefits or to make them more equal for both sexes;
   - in the case of final salary schemes where the employer's contributions are intended to ensure the adequacy of the funds necessary to cover the cost of the benefits defined;
k) laying down different standards as regards the guarantee or retention of entitlement to deferred benefits when a worker leaves a scheme, except where (h) or (i) apply.

23.7 Conclusion

It is important to consider the Pensions Act 1995, the equal treatment provisions of both art 119 and the EqPA and the Occupational Social Security Directive. There may be areas where the provisions of the Pensions Act may not comply with the requirements of art 119 and the Directive.

OCCUPATIONAL PENSION SCHEMES: KEY POINTS

Article 119 and the EqPA

- Payments under occupational pension schemes constitute pay under art 119 and the EqPA.
- Article 119 applies to:
  - contracted-in or contracted-out schemes;
  - schemes which supplement or complement the state scheme;
  - access to an occupational pension scheme;
  - pensionable ages;
  - contributions made by the employer and employee;

- contributory and non-contributory schemes;
- final salary and money purchase schemes;
- transitional provisions;
- indirect discrimination in pension schemes.

- Article 119 does not apply to:
  - the statutory social security scheme;
  - the use of actuarial factors in funded defined-benefit schemes;
  - additional voluntary contributions.
- The obligations to ensure equal treatment for members and survivors do not apply to benefits in respect of service before 17 May 1990.
- The rule on retroactivity does *not* apply to:
  - the right to join a scheme (which may go back to 1976); or
  - where there is a right to join back to 1976, the benefits which accrued during the intervening period;

  provided in both cases the worker pays his/her contributions for that period.
- Benefits must be equalled upwards until the scheme equalises but then may equalise downwards.
- There must be no direct or indirect discrimination in access to occupational pension schemes.
- Equal pension benefits under occupational pension schemes must be paid to men and women at the same age.
- Contributions to schemes must be the same for men and women, unless the exception for actuarial factors applies.
- There must be no discrimination in survivors' benefits.
- Less favourable treatment of part-time workers is likely to be unlawful indirect discrimination unless objectively justified.
- Employees or survivors may enforce these provisions against employers and trustees of schemes.
- The remedy is the same as under the EqPA.
- Time limits under EC law are the same as under national law, which, with the two-year limitation on back-pay, means that there is likely to be a limit on backdating benefits; this may be a breach of EC law.

The statutory scheme under the Pensions Act

- The Pensions Act 1995 came into force on 1 January 1996. It applies to pensionable service on or after 17 May 1990.
- An occupational pension scheme is to be treated as containing an 'equal treatment rule' which relates to:

- membership of the pension scheme; and
- how members are treated.

- The equal treatment rule applies in the same situation as the EqPA, ie, when a woman is doing like work, work rated as equivalent or work of equal value. The material factor defence applies.
- There are three exceptions:
  - where a bridging pension varies according to what the person receives under the state pension to allow the *total* amount from both to be the same; and
  - where, in a contracted-out final salary scheme, the variation in pension pay is due to different indexation factors between men and women which are attributable to SERPS; and
  - where, in specified circumstances, there is a variation in pay due to actuarial factors.
- The same provisions apply to disputes and enforcement as apply under the EqPA.

Part V

Disability discrimination

CHAPTER 24

Disability discrimination

24.1 Introduction

This chapter explains how the law prohibits discrimination against disabled people in the area of employment. Because the Disability Discrimination Act 1995 (DDA) has only recently come into force,[1] there is as yet no appellate case-law interpreting its provisions. There are, however, many similarities between the employment provisions in the DDA and those in the RRA and SDA. So it can safely be assumed that much of the existing case-law on the general principles of liability for discrimination will be applied by ITs when interpreting the DDA. This chapter also refers to the government's comments on the DDA when it was passing through Parliament, where these shed some light on the meaning of the Act.

While the DDA resembles the earlier discrimination legislation in some ways, there are several, more significant ways in which it differs from the earlier Acts. In particular, the DDA's definition of discrimination allows for the possibility that direct discrimination against a disabled person may be lawful. The DDA does not prohibit indirect discrimination, but it does place an obligation on employers to take positive steps to adjust their work environment to accommodate disabled people.

There are as yet no legally enforceable EC provisions on disability discrimination in employment.

24.1.1 The quota scheme

When the employment provisions of the DDA came into force on 2 December 1996, the quota and designated employment schemes

1 Almost all of the employment-related provisions came into force on 2 December 1996 – see the Disability Discrimination Act 1995 (Commencement No 3 and Saving and Transitional Provisions) Order 1996 SI No 1474.

established by the Disabled Persons (Employment) Act 1944 were abolished. The 1944 Act enabled people with disabilities to register as disabled, and required employers to employ a 3% quota of registered disabled people. It also reserved certain jobs, namely passenger lift attendant and car park attendant, for registered disabled people. In practice, the 1944 Act was largely unenforced. There were only ten prosecutions, the last being in 1975.[2]

24.1.2 Who is covered?

One of the most significant shortcomings of the DDA is that it does not cover employers with fewer than 20 employees (s7). According to government figures, 17% of employees work in firms employing less than 20 people.[3] The government must review this exemption for small employers by December 2000 at the latest, and it may then be more narrowly drawn.

The DDA *does* cover:

a) contract workers (see **24.8.6.1**);
b) self-employed people, provided that they are working for the employer under a contract personally to do any work (s68(1)) (see **5.2**); this type of worker is also included when calculating whether an employer has 20 or more 'employees';
c) apprentices (s68(1));
d) most people working in or applying for Crown employment (s64); and
e) work as a member of the staff of both Houses of Parliament (s65).

The DDA *does not* cover:

a) holders of an office set up by or under any legislation (s64(2)(a) – but, in making an appointment to such a statutory office, the relevant minister must nevertheless act in accordance with the principles of the DDA, unless regulations stipulate otherwise: s66);
b) the armed forces (s64(7));
c) prison officers (s64(5));
d) fire-fighters (s64(6));
e) police officers;[4]

2 HL Debs, 27 June 1995, vol 565, col 697.
3 HC Debs, 24 January 1995, vol 253, cols 147 and 231.
4 According to the government, police officers clearly fall outside the DDA's provisions, being neither employees nor Crown servants, and an express exemption for them in the DDA would therefore 'simply cause confusion' (HC Debs, 28 March 1995, vol 257, col 895).

f) members of the Ministry of Defence Police, the British Transport Police, the Royal Parks Constabulary, or the UK Atomic Energy Authority Constabulary (s64(5));
g) employment on board a ship, aircraft or hovercraft, except in cases which may be prescribed (s68(3) – no exceptions have yet been prescribed);
h) admission as a partner to partnerships (although applicants for employment by a partnership and employees of a partnership are covered).

Unusually for legislation on employment rights, the DDA applies to employment at establishments in both Great Britain and Northern Ireland (s70(6)). In this context, if work is not done at an establishment, it is treated as done at the establishment from which it is done. If the work is not done from any establishment, then it is treated as done at the establishment with which it has the closest connection (s68(5)). Jobs which are done wholly or mainly outside the UK are not covered (s68(2)).

24.2 The meaning of disability

In order to be protected from discrimination, a person has to have a disability which falls within the definition set out in DDA s1 and Sch 1. These provisions have been supplemented by regulations (the Definition Regulations[5]) which effectively prevent certain conditions from being treated as a disability. In addition, the government has issued Guidance on the definition.[6] This Guidance has considerable legal significance, since it must be taken into account by an IT when it is considering whether a person has the right to bring a complaint under the DDA (s3(3)). Advisers seeking to ascertain whether their client falls within the protection of the DDA will therefore need to bear in mind the Guidance as well as the statutory framework.

In order to analyse the definition of disability, which is complex, it is helpful to break it down into its constituent parts. According to the DDA, a person has a disability if s/he has:

– a physical or mental impairment; and

5 Disability Discrimination (Meaning of Disability) Regulations 1996 SI No 1455.

6 *Guidance on matters to be taken into account in determining questions relating to the definition of disability*, Department for Education and Employment and Social Security, (HMSO, 1996).

- that impairment has an adverse effect on his or her ability to carry out normal day-to-day activities; and
- that effect is substantial; and
- that effect is long-term.

24.2.1 Impairments

The DDA says that a disability may arise from a physical or mental impairment, and the Guidance confirms that sensory impairments, such as those affecting sight or hearing, are included in this (para 12).

A mental impairment can include learning, psychiatric and psychological impairments.[7] A mental impairment consisting of a mental illness is covered, however, only if it is, as the DDA puts it, 'a clinically well-recognised illness'.[8] This, says the Guidance, means that the illness must be recognised by 'a respected body of medical opinion', and any illness which is specifically mentioned in publications 'such as' the *World Health Organisation's International Classification of Diseases* is 'very likely' to be included (para 14). According to the government, schizophrenia, manic depression, and severe and extended depressive psychoses are intended to be covered,[9] but moods and 'mild eccentricities' are not.[10]

Under the Definition Regulations, addiction to alcohol, nicotine or 'any other substance', including dependency on such a substance, does not amount to an impairment under the DDA, unless it originally resulted from taking drugs which were medically prescribed, or from other medical treatment (reg 3). As the Guidance points out, however, a person may develop an impairment as a result of drug addiction which may amount to a disability under the DDA, even if the addiction itself does not qualify. It cites the example of liver disease as a result of alcohol dependency (para 11).

Under the Definition Regulations, certain personality disorders do not amount to impairments under the DDA. These are: a tendency to set fires; a tendency to steal; a tendency to physical or sexual abuse of other persons; exhibitionism; and voyeurism (reg 4(1)).

7 HC Debs, 2 February 1995, Standing Committee E, col 74.
8 Sch 1 para 1(1).
9 HC Debs, 7 February 1995, Standing Committee E, cols 100 and 104.
10 HC Debs, 7 February 1995, Standing Committee E, col 104.

24.2.2 Normal day-to-day activities

According to the DDA,[11] a person's impairment amounts to a disability only if it affects his/her ability to carry out one of these normal day-to-day activities:

- mobility;
- manual dexterity;
- physical co-ordination;
- continence;
- ability to lift, carry or otherwise move everyday objects;
- speech, hearing or eyesight;
- memory or ability to concentrate, learn or understand; or
- perception of the risk of physical danger.

Some of these activities are broader than they may at first appear. According to the Guidance, for example, 'mobility' covers moving or changing position in its widest sense, and so includes a person's ability to get around unaided or using public transport, to sit, stand, bend, or reach, or to get around in an unfamiliar place (para C14).

24.2.3 Substantial adverse effect

As a general rule, the effect of a person's impairment has to be assessed without taking into account any medical treatment, or any prosthesis or other aid, which s/he may be using to treat or correct it.[12] There is, however, an exception to this rule. An assessment of the effect of a person's visual impairment can take into account the extent to which the impairment can be corrected by glasses or contact lenses (whether or not the person uses these aids).[13]

During debate on the DDA during its passage through Parliament, the government pointed out that substantial and long-term effects can result from conditions which are not severe. The focus is on the effect, not on the impairment itself. So, eg, a moderate degree of dyslexia can amount to a disability, because it has a substantial adverse effect on a day-to-day activity such as the ability to learn.[14]

The Guidance confirms that the requirement for the effect to be

11 Sch 1 para 4(1).
12 Sch 1 para 6(1) and (2).
13 Sch 1 para 6(3)(a).
14 HL Debs, 13 June 1995, vol 564, col 1650.

'substantial' means that it must be more than minor or trivial, the intention being to reflect 'the general understanding of "disability" as a limitation going beyond the normal differences in ability which may exist among people' (para A1). Several examples of what would, and what would not, be reasonable to regard as substantial adverse effects are set out in the Guidance (para C14–21).

For example, the Guidance says that it would be reasonable to regard an impairment as having a substantial adverse effect on mobility if it results in an inability to walk other than at a slow pace or with unsteady or jerky movements; but it would not be reasonable to regard an impairment as having a substantial adverse effect if it results in difficulty walking unaided a distance of about a mile without discomfort or having to stop (the appropriate distance varying according to the age of the person and the type of terrain).

When assessing the effect of a person's impairment, says the Guidance, both the time taken to carry out the activity and the way in which it is carried out should be taken into account (paras A2 and A3). Furthermore, both direct and indirect effects of an impairment should be assessed. For example, a person may have been given medical advice to limit his/her activity, or may be limited in carrying out an activity by the pain or fatigue associated with doing so (para C6).

24.2.3.1 Cumulative effects

The Guidance emphasises that it is an impairment's overall effect that is determinative (para A4). Even if a person's impairment has only a minor effect on his/her ability to carry out each of the day-to-day activities taken separately, the cumulative effect on his/her ability to carry out those activities overall may be substantial.

It may also, the Guidance confirms, be necessary to take into account the cumulative effect of more than one impairment. So, for example, a person's ability may be substantially affected by the combined effect of a minor impairment which affects his/her physical co-ordination and a minor leg injury which affects his/her mobility (para A6).

24.2.3.2 Surrounding circumstances

The effect of a person's impairment may differ according to the surrounding circumstances, such as the time of day or night, and whether or not the person is tired or under stress. When assessing whether the effects of the impairment are substantial, says the Guidance, the extent to which these factors are likely to have an impact should be taken into account (para A10).

24.2.3.3 *Managing an impairment*

According to the Guidance, account should also be taken of the extent to which a person can reasonably be expected to modify his/her behaviour in order to reduce the effects of an impairment (para A7). If the person can manage the impairment to ensure that its effect is only minor, then s/he no longer meets the definition of disability, whether or not s/he actually takes those steps. The Guidance accepts that it may be necessary, however, to take into account the possibility that a person's ability to manage his/her impairment may be affected by the surrounding circumstances, such as, eg, where someone with a stutter is placed under stress (para A8).

Since the DDA stipulates that the effect of a person's impairment has to be assessed without taking into account the effect of any 'measures' being taken to treat or correct it, the Guidance acknowledges that any action that a person takes to manage his/her impairment on the advice of a medical practitioner might need to be disregarded in deciding whether the person has a disability (para A9).

24.2.3.4 *Severe disfigurements*

As a general rule, an impairment which consists of a severe disfigurement is treated as having a substantial adverse effect on a person's ability to carry out normal day-to-day activities, whether or not it actually does so.[15] The examples of disfigurements given in the Guidance are scars, birthmarks, limb or postural deformations and diseases of the skin. The Guidance says that an assessment of the severity of a disfigurement may need to take account of where on the person's body it is (para A17).

According to the Definition Regulations, however, a disfigurement is not to be treated as having a substantial adverse effect if it consists of a tattoo which has not been removed, or 'a piercing of the body for decorative or other non-medical purposes, including any object attached through the piercing for such purposes' (reg 5).

24.2.3.5 *Progressive conditions*

The DDA acknowledges that difficulties might arise in defining the point at which someone with a progressive condition – such as cancer, multiple sclerosis, muscular dystrophy, or infection by human immunodeficiency virus (HIV) – becomes disabled. The Act therefore states that where such a condition has resulted in an impairment which has affected the person's day-to-day activities, but that effect is

15 Sch 1 para 3(1).

not yet substantial, it is nevertheless to be treated as having a substantial effect if that is the likely outcome.[16]

24.2.4 Long-term effect

An impairment has a long-term effect, and so amounts to a disability under the DDA, only if it has lasted at least 12 months, or is likely to do so[17] – that is, according to the Guidance, it is 'more probable than not' that it will do so (para B7). In order to cover the case of a person who is terminally ill, a person's impairment is also viewed as long-term if it is likely to last for the rest of his/her life.[18] When assessing the likelihood of an effect lasting for a particular period, the Guidance says that account should be taken of how long the effect has in fact lasted, the typical length of such an effect, and the individual characteristics of the individual, such as his/her state of health and age (para B8).

According to the Guidance, the effect of an impairment need not be the same throughout the 12-month period in order to meet the 'long-term' criterion. Its original adverse effects might diminish or even disappear, but other adverse effects might continue or develop. Provided the impairment has, or is likely to have, a substantial effect throughout a 12-month period, its effect is to be viewed as long-term (para B2).

24.2.4.1 Recurrent conditions

The DDA makes special provision for conditions which are subject to remission and periods of good health, such as arthritis and multiple sclerosis.[19] If an impairment stops having a substantial adverse effect on a person's ability to carry out normal day-to-day activities, it is nevertheless treated as continuing to have that effect if it is likely to recur – that is, according to the Guidance, if it is 'more probable than not' that it will recur (para B3). In other words, it is treated as continuing during the period of remission or good health. Nevertheless, the effect of the impairment still has to be long term, so that for a recurring condition to be a disability within the definition in the DDA, one recurrence has to be, or be likely to be, at least 12 months after the first.

When assessing the likelihood of a recurrence, says the Guidance, it is necessary to take into account anything which a person might

16 Sch 1 para 8.
17 Sch 1 para 2(1)(a) and (b).
18 Sch 1 para 2(1)(c).
19 Sch 1 para 2(2).

reasonably be expected to do to prevent the recurrence, such as avoiding substances to which s/he is allergic (para B5). If medical or other treatment is likely to cure an impairment, so that its effects would be unlikely to recur even if there were no further treatment, then that can be taken into account. If, however, the treatment simply delays or prevents a recurrence, and a recurrence would be likely if the treatment stopped, then the normal rule that the treatment must be disregarded applies (see **24.2.3**), and the effect must be regarded as likely to recur (para B6).

24.2.4.2 Hay fever

One condition that is likely to recur in this way is seasonal allergic rhinitis, more commonly known as hay fever. Reflecting the government's view that hay fever is not generally viewed as a disability, the Definition Regulations state that this condition is not to be treated as an impairment in itself (reg 4(2)). It can be taken into account, however, where it aggravates the effect of another condition (reg 4(3)).

So if, for example, a person has a respiratory disorder which is aggravated by hay fever, the overall effect of the two conditions can be taken into account. Even if the effect of a person's respiratory disorder is usually only minor, if it becomes substantial at the times when it is aggravated by the hay fever, the person may satisfy the definition of disability.

24.2.5 Past disability

During the Act's passage through Parliament, the government was persuaded to extend its scope to cover discrimination against people who have in the past had a disability as defined in the DDA, but no longer do so (s2). When determining whether a person has had a disability in the past, his/her impairment is taken to have had a long-term effect if it lasted for at least 12 months. If his/her impairment ceased to have a substantial adverse effect, it is treated as continuing to have that effect if it actually recurred. So, provided that one occurrence was 12 months or more after the other, the person is treated as having had a disability throughout the period.[20]

24.2.6 Registered disabled people

Anyone who was registered as a disabled person under the Disabled Persons (Employment) Act 1944 both on 12 January 1995 and on 2

20 Sch 2 para 5.

December 1996 is deemed to be a disabled person until 2 December 1999, and is therefore automatically covered by the DDA during that period even if s/he does not meet the DDA definition. Even after that date, the person is to be treated as having had a disability from 2 December 1996 until 2 December 1999.[21]

24.3 Discrimination in employment

Like the SDA and RRA, the DDA outlaws discrimination in every aspect of employment, from recruitment through to dismissal (s4). It is unlawful for an employer to discriminate unjustifiably against any person who is currently disabled, or has been disabled:

- in the arrangements it makes for the purpose of deciding to whom employment should be offered;
- in the terms on which employment is offered; or
- by refusing to offer, or deliberately not offering, the person employment.

In relation to existing staff, it is unlawful for an employer to discriminate against an employee who is currently disabled, or has been disabled:

- in the terms on which it employs the employee;
- in the opportunities which it gives the employee for promotion, transfer, training or receiving any other benefit, facility or service;
- by refusing to give the employee any such opportunity, or deliberately not offering it;
- by dismissing the employee; or
- by subjecting the employee to 'any other detriment' (which would include, for example, harassment relating to the employee's disability – see Chapter 13).

According to the government, the DDA is intended to cover 'the use of standards, criteria, administrative methods, work practices or procedures that adversely affect a disabled person'.[22]

By virtue of DDA s4(3), it is not unlawful for an employer to discriminate in the provision of any benefit (including any facility or service) to a disabled employee, if the employer provides the benefit in question to the public, or to a section of the public which includes the

21 Sch 1 para 7(1) and (2).
22 HC Debs, 7 February 1995, Standing Committee E, col 142.

employee (although the employer is also under an obligation as a service provider not to discriminate against disabled people in the way it provides those services – see DDA Part III).

Discrimination in the provision of a benefit remains unlawful, however, if:

- the employer's provision of the benefit to the public differs in a material respect from its provision of the benefit to its employees; or
- the benefit in question is governed by the employee's contract of employment; or
- the benefit relates to training.

24.3.1 The Code of Practice

The government has issued a Code of Practice[23] on the legislation which provides advice to employers on how to avoid discrimination. Although it is not unlawful in itself for an employer not to observe the Code, ITs hearing complaints of disability discrimination must take it into account where it appears to them to be relevant (s53(4) and (6)). The Code is fuller than those issued under the SDA and the RRA, and contains many illustrative examples of the way in which the DDA operates. Anyone involved in advising on, or enforcing their rights under, the DDA will need to read the Code carefully.

24.4 Definition of discrimination

The definition of discrimination, set out in DDA s5, is complicated. An employer discriminates against a disabled person (or a person who has had a disability) if:

- for a reason relating to the person's disability;
- it treats him/her less favourably than it treats, or would treat, others to whom that reason does not or would not apply; and
- it cannot show that that treatment is justified.

In order to illustrate how this definition works, let us take the example of a man with arthritis who applies for a job as a clerical assistant. Let us assume that, because of his arthritis, he cannot use a keyboard. If the employer refuses to recruit him because he cannot

23 *Code of Practice for the elimination of discrimination in the field of employment against disabled persons or persons who have had a disability*, Department for Education and Employment, (HMSO, 1996).

type, it is treating him less favourably than it would treat a person to whom that reason does not apply, namely a person who can type, and it is doing so for a reason relating to his disability. For the purposes of the definition, it is immaterial that the reason for the employer's action could also apply to non-disabled people who would also be rejected, such as applicants who cannot use a keyboard because they have never learnt. Whether the employer's rejection of the disabled applicant amounts to unlawful discrimination then turns on whether the employer can establish that it is justified in treating him less favourably than the employer treats or would treat applicants who can type.

It is important to note that this definition of discrimination parts company with the definitions in the SDA and the RRA in three significant ways.

- Unlike the SDA and RDA, the DDA provides for the possibility that direct discrimination against its protected group may be justified. The rationale for this is that, save in exceptional circumstances, a person's sex or race has no bearing on his/her ability to do a job, whereas a person's physical or mental impairment may have.
- Unlike the SDA and RRA, the DDA does not prohibit positive discrimination, so that it remains lawful for most employers to discriminate in favour of disabled people, if they wish to do so. (Local authorities are, however, more restricted. Under Local Government and Housing Act 1989 s7, local authorities are legally obliged to appoint staff on the basis of merit alone.)
- The DDA contains no prohibition on indirect discrimination, which, under the SDA and RRA, makes it unlawful for an employer to impose a requirement or condition which has a disproportionate impact on a particular sex or racial group, unless it can objectively justify doing so (see Chapter 3). In the government's view, the DDA 'addresses the overall problems of indirect discrimination' by imposing a requirement on employers to accommodate the disabilities of job applicants and employees by making reasonable adjustments to their practices and premises, as explained below.[24]

24.4.1 Justification

The DDA says that less favourable treatment of a disabled person for a reason relating to his/her disability is justified only if the reason for it is both 'material' to the circumstances of the particular case and

24 HC Debs, 7 February 1995, Standing Committee E, col 143.

'substantial'. According to the House of Lords in *Rainey v Greater Glasgow Health Board*,[25] where it interpreted the employer's 'genuine material factor' defence to an equal pay claim, 'material' means 'significant and relevant'. The Code says that the reason must 'relate to the individual circumstances in question and not just be trivial or minor' (para 4.6).

So, going back to the example used above to illustrate the definition of discrimination, the employer could justify its refusal to recruit the job applicant with arthritis if it could show that his disability meant that he could not perform the duties of the job for which he was applying, or was able to perform them less well than the person who was appointed. Before it assessed the applicant's suitability, however, the employer would need to comply with its important duty to consider making reasonable adjustments, discussed further below (see 24.5), which could, eg, include amending the job content, adapting the keyboard or providing other equipment.

In para 4.6, the Code gives examples of when discrimination will and will not be justified, emphasising that less favourable treatment of a disabled person will be justified only if the reason for it is both material to the circumstances of the particular case and substantial. For example, turning down a disabled person for employment solely because other employees would be uncomfortable working alongside him/her would be unlawful: 'such a reaction by other employees will not in itself justify less favourable treatment of this sort – it is not substantial. The same would apply if it were thought that a customer would feel uncomfortable.' Likewise, the Code says that discrimination will not be justified if it stems from an employer's generalised assumptions about a disabled person's abilities, or is based on the disabled person's productivity or attendance record and this record is only slightly worse than that of non-disabled employees or job applicants.

24.4.1.1 Performance-related pay

Pay practices linking reward to performance could result in lower pay for any disabled person whose work performance is affected by his/her disability. In order to ensure that such pay practices are not unlawful, regulations have been made (the Employment Regulations[26]) which provide that discriminatory treatment is justified if it results from applying to a disabled person a term or practice under which an

25 [1987] IRLR 26.

26 Disability Discrimination (Employment) Regulations 1996 SI No 1456.

employee's pay is wholly or partly dependent on his/her performance (reg 3(1)(a)). There is a proviso to this, which is that the term or practice must be applied to all of the employer's workforce, or to all of a class of its workforce which includes the disabled person but is not defined by reference to any disability (reg 3(1)(b)).

For these purposes, 'pay' is not limited to salary, but includes remuneration of any kind, including any benefit. 'Performance' includes performance assessed by reference to any measure, whether relative or absolute, of output, efficiency or effectiveness (reg 2).

These provisions do not detract, however, from an employer's duty to consider reasonable adjustments to any of its arrangements or premises which, by placing a disabled employee at a substantial disadvantage, cause his/her performance to be reduced (reg 3(3) – see 24.5).

24.4.1.2 Agricultural Wages Board

The Employment Regulations also make special provision for workers covered by the Agricultural Wages Boards (reg 6). These Boards set minimum rates of pay and other terms and conditions in the agricultural sector, but also provide for permits to be issued to workers with disabilities who are 'incapacitated', allowing them to be employed at a lower minimum rate of pay or on specified revised terms. The effect of the Regulations is to make it lawful for employers to continue to employ workers on the terms provided for in these permits.

24.4.1.3 Assumptions from advertisements

If a disabled person brings an industrial complaint that s/he has been discriminated against in recruitment, and the job was advertised in a way which indicated that the employer intended to discriminate, then the tribunal must assume, unless the contrary is shown, that the employer's reason for not offering the applicant the job was related to his/her disability (s11).

This assumption applies where the advertisement indicated, or might reasonably be understood to have indicated, that the success of any application for the job would or might rest on the candidate not having any disability or the applicant's particular category of disability, or on the employer's reluctance to make reasonable adjustments (see below). The assumption of discrimination applies whether the job was advertised before or after the applicant applied for it, and includes any advertisement or notice, whether made to the general public or not (s11(3)).

24.5 Duty to make adjustments

Standing on its own, the definition of discrimination as outlined so far would be largely ineffective. Many would argue that people with physical and mental impairments are disabled not so much by those impairments as by society's failure to accommodate them. The DDA therefore imposes an obligation on employers to make certain adjustments to their premises and the ways in which they operate, in order to accommodate disabled employees and job applicants (s6).

It is important to note that a failure to comply with the duty to consider reasonable adjustments is, in itself, an act of unlawful discrimination, unless it can be justified for a reason which is both material to the circumstances of the particular case and substantial (s5(2) and (4)). Furthermore, if an employer treats a disabled person less favourably for a reason relating to his/her disability and has unjustifiably failed to comply with its duty to make adjustments, the less favourable treatment of the disabled person cannot be justified, unless it would have been justified even if the employer had complied with its duty (s5(5)). So, eg, it would be lawful for an employer not to make an adjustment to accommodate a disabled job applicant if the employer could show that s/he would not meet the basic requirements for the job even if that adjustment were made.

24.5.1 To whom is the duty owed?

An employer's duty to make adjustments is not triggered until it employs a disabled person, or a disabled person applies to it, or considers applying to it, for a job.

In relation to recruitment arrangements, the duty applies only in relation to any disabled person who is, or has notified the employer that s/he may be, an applicant for the job (s6(5)(a)). More generally, the employer has a duty to make adjustments only in relation to an actual or potential job applicant or employee whom it knows, or could reasonably be expected to know, has a disability (or has had a disability) and is likely to be put at a substantial disadvantage by the employer's existing arrangements or premises (s6(6)(b)).

It may not be immediately apparent to an employer that a job applicant or employee is, or has been, disabled. The Code of Practice points out that, since an employer is released from its obligation to make a reasonable adjustment only if it does not know, *and could not reasonably be expected to know*, that a person has a disability, 'an employer must ... do all he could reasonably be expected to do to find out whether this is the case' (para 4.57). On the other hand, the Code stresses, once an employer has information about a person's disability, it may need to maintain the confidentiality of that information, and the Code gives guidance on how the employer can reconcile this duty of confidentiality with its duty to make reasonable adjustments (see paras 4.58–4.62). A disabled job applicant or employee may, therefore, consider it advisable to let his/her prospective or current employer know about his/her impairment, so that the possibility of adjustment can be discussed.

24.5.2 Substantial disadvantage

The duty to make adjustments arises if 'arrangements' made by or on behalf of the employer or any physical feature of the employer's premises puts a disabled person at a 'substantial' disadvantage in comparison with people who are not disabled (or puts a person who has had a disability at a substantial disadvantage in comparison with people who are not disabled and have not had a disability[27]). According to the government, the word 'substantial' here simply means 'of some substance', and is intended to exclude only the most minor disadvantage.[28]

The term 'arrangements' means arrangements for determining who should be offered employment (s6(2)(a)), so it would cover, eg, the way in which interviews are conducted. It also means any term, condition or other arrangements on which employment, promotion, a transfer, training or any other benefit is offered or provided (s6(2)(b)). The government has made clear that 'the broad term "arrangements" has deliberately been used . . . to cover anything done by or for an employer as part of his recruitment process or in making available opportunities in employment. It would not only include work practices and procedures, so far as such practices and procedures have any bearing on determining who is offered employment or to whom such opportunities are made available: it would go wider than that.'[29]

24.5.3 What steps should be considered?

Where arrangements or features do put a disabled person at a substantial disadvantage, it is the employer's duty 'to take such steps as it is reasonable, in all the circumstances of the case, for him to have to take' in order to remove that disadvantage (s6(1)).

27 Sch 2 paras 2 and 3.
28 HC Debs, 14 February 1995, Standing Committee E, col 196.
29 HC Debs, 7 February 1995, Standing Committee E, col 142.

The DDA gives a non-exhaustive list of steps that an employer might have to take in order to comply with its duty (s6(3)):

- making adjustments to premises;
- allocating some of the disabled person's duties to another person;
- transferring the disabled person to fill an existing vacancy;
- altering the disabled person's working hours;
- assigning him/her to a different place of work;
- allowing the disabled person to be absent during working hours for rehabilitation, assessment or treatment;
- training the disabled person, or arranging for him/her to be given training;
- acquiring or modifying equipment;
- modifying instructions or reference manuals;
- modifying procedures for testing or assessment;
- providing a reader or interpreter; and
- providing supervision.

Some examples of reasonable adjustments given by the Code include: reallocating minor or subsidiary duties of a job that a disabled person cannot fulfil for a reason relating to his/her disability; transferring a wheelchair user's work station from an inaccessible third-floor office to an accessible one on the ground floor; enabling a disabled person to work flexible hours so that s/he can take additional breaks to overcome fatigue arising from his/her disability; and providing an adapted telephone for someone with a hearing impairment (para 4.20).

The Code also suggests the possibility of changing a disabled person's working hours to fit in with the availability of a personal assistant. During the passage of the DDA through Parliament, the government accepted that 'the needs of carers might need to be taken into account as a reasonable adjustment for a disabled person. If the needs were such that a disabled person had to fit in with the position of a carer, the carer's needs could be taken in as part of the reasonable adjustment.'[30]

24.5.4 Reasonableness

In determining whether it is reasonable for an employer to take a particular step in order to comply with its duty, the following factors must be taken into account (s6(4)):

- the extent to which the adjustment would prevent the disabled person being put at a disadvantage (it would be more reasonable, the

30 HL Debs, 18 July 1995, vol 566, col 184.

Code suggests, to expect an employer to make an adjustment that would significantly improve a disabled employee's entitlement to performance-related pay than to make one which would effect only a relatively small improvement (see para 4.22));

- the extent to which it is practicable for the employer to make the adjustment (the Code suggests that, while it might be impracticable for an employer needing urgently to recruit an employee to have to wait for an adjustment to a building entrance to be made to allow a disabled person to be employed, it might still be practicable for the employer to make a temporary adjustment until the permanent work is completed (see para 4.23));
- the financial and other costs which would be incurred by the employer in taking the step (including, says the Code, not only the cost of the adjustment but also the cost of staff time and other resources, and taking into account the value of the disabled persons's experience and expertise to the employer. In particular, the Code suggests, it would be reasonable for an employer to have to spend at least as much on an adjustment to enable the retention of a disabled person – including any retraining – as might be spent on recruiting and training a replacement (see paras 4.24–4.26));
- the extent to which making the adjustment would disrupt the employer's activities;
- the size of the employer's financial and 'other resources' (which, says the Code, includes the size of its workforce. The Code suggests that the fact that an employer's resources are split between different business units or profit centres should not detract from an assessment of its overall ability to make adjustments (see para 4.29));
- the availability to the employer of financial or other assistance in making the adjustment (whether from the disabled person him/herself, from an outside organisation, or from some other source such as the government-funded Access to Work scheme – see Appendix 4).

24.5.5 Adjusting premises

The Employment Regulations specify that, for the purposes of an employer's duty to make reasonable adjustments, the following are to be treated as physical features of its premises, whether they are permanent or temporary (reg 9):

- any feature arising from the design or construction of a building on the premises;

- any feature on the premises of any approach to, exit from or access to such a building;
- any fixtures, fittings, furnishings, furniture, equipment or materials in or on the premises; and
- any other physical element or quality of any land included in the premises.

For these purposes, a 'building' includes an erection or structure of any kind (reg 2).

Employers' duties to make adjustments to physical features of premises extends only to their own premises. It seems, therefore, that it does not extend to making adjustments to a disabled employee's own home, even if s/he is working from there, nor does it extend to other employers' premises which an employee may visit if, eg, s/he works as a travelling salesperson. Likewise, an employer which leases part of a building is under no obligation to make alterations to, eg, parts of the building not covered by its lease.

24.5.5.1 Impact of Building Regulations

According to the Employment Regulations, it is never reasonable for an employer to take steps which would involve altering any physical characteristic of its premises which was adapted with a view to meeting the requirements of Part M of the Building Regulations[31] or, in Scotland, Part T of the Technical Standards,[32] which deal with minimum standards of access and facilities for disabled people (reg 8).

There is a proviso to this, which is that the physical feature in question must actually have met the requirements in force at the time the building works were carried out, and must continue substantially to meet those requirements (reg 8(1)(b)). Further, as the Code of Practice points out, the fact that, eg, a door meets the width requirements in the Building Regulations does not preclude a reasonable adjustment being needed to another feature of the door, such as its handle (para 4.35).

24.5.5.2 Restrictions in mortgages and covenants

An employer may be under a binding obligation, such as a condition in a mortgage or a restrictive covenant, to obtain the consent of another person before it makes any alteration to its premises. (Such

31 Building Regulations 1991 SI No 2768 Sch 1 Pt M.

32 The technical standards for compliance with the Building Standards (Scotland) Regulations 1990.

restrictions in leases are dealt with separately – see **24.5.5.4.**) In these circumstances, the Employment Regulations state that it is always reasonable for the employer to have to take steps to obtain that consent (reg 10(1)). The only exception to this is where obtaining consent involves applying to a court or tribunal (reg 10(2)). Whether it is reasonable for an employer to take this step will depend on the circumstances of the individual case. The Regulations also state that it is never reasonable for the employer to have to make the alteration before the required consent is obtained.

24.5.5.3 Statutory consents

Some adjustments to premises may require statutory consents, such as planning permission, listed building consent or fire regulations approval.

Since any act done to comply with a statutory requirement does not breach the DDA (s59 – see **24.8.5**), an employer does not need to make an adjustment which requires a statutory consent which it has not been able to obtain. However, as the Code of Practice points out, an employer might still need to consider whether it can make a temporary adjustment until the statutory consent can be obtained, or to identify an adjustment which does not need consent at all, perhaps in consultation with its planning authority (paras 4.38 and 4.39).

24.5.5.4 Leased premises

If an employer's premises are leased, it may encounter problems in meeting its duty to make reasonable adjustments: the lease may prohibit alterations, or provide for alterations to be made only with the landlord's consent, which may be subject to conditions.

In these circumstances, the DDA overrides the terms of the lease. The lease must be read as entitling the employer to make alterations to the premises with its landlord's written consent. The employer's application for consent must be made in writing, and the landlord must not unreasonably withhold it, but can make it subject to reasonable conditions (s16). An employer will not be able to argue that it is prevented from making reasonable adjustments by the terms of its lease, unless it has applied for consent to make the relevant alterations.[33] On the other hand, Employment Regulations reg 15 states that it is not reasonable for an employer to have to take a step which is contrary to the terms of its lease if:

33 Sch 4 para 1.

- it has applied to the landlord in writing asking for its consent, indicating that it proposes to take the step in order to comply with its duty under the DDA to make reasonable adjustments;
- the landlord has withheld its consent; and
- the employer has informed the disabled person that it has applied for the consent of the landlord and the landlord has withheld it.

If the employer has taken these steps, therefore, it will not be liable for its failure to make the adjustment, but its landlord may be.

On any subsequent discrimination complaint, either the complainant or the employer can ask the IT to join the landlord as a party to the proceedings.[34] The IT will then decide whether the landlord has unreasonably refused its consent to the alterations, or imposed unreasonable conditions.

Usually, the reasonableness of the landlord's actions will be assessed according to the circumstances of the particular case. The Code of Practice suggests, eg, that where the employer's premises adjoin other leased units, and an adjustment would cause significant disruption or inconvenience to the other tenants, the landlord would be likely to be acting reasonably in withholding consent (para 4.45). However, the Employment Regulations stipulate some circumstances in which the landlord must be taken to have acted reasonably or unreasonably for these purposes, as summarised in the box on pp491–3.

REASONABLE ADJUSTMENTS TO LEASEHOLD PREMISES

The Employment Regulations[1] have laid down that in certain circumstances a landlord must be taken to have acted reasonably or unreasonably in withholding its consent to an employer making alterations to premises, or in imposing conditions when it gives consent to the alterations.

Deemed refusal through inaction

The landlord will be taken to have unreasonably refused the employer's application for consent unless, within a period of 21 days beginning with the day on which it receives the application, or such longer period as is reasonable, it takes one of two courses of action (reg 11(1) and (2)).

1 The landlord replies to the application, either granting or withholding consent. (If the decision is to withhold consent, the reasonableness of that decision will be assessed on its merits.)
2 The landlord consents to the application, subject to obtaining the consent of another person, which may be required under a superior lease or pursuant to some other binding legal obligation.

34 Sch 4 para 2.

Within the same 21-day period, the landlord must then seek that consent in writing, indicating that it has been asked for its consent to the alteration in order to comply with a duty to make reasonable adjustments under the DDA, and that it has given its consent conditionally on obtaining the other person's consent (reg 11(4)).

If the landlord takes one of these steps but outside the time limit, it is taken to have unreasonably withheld its consent from the date the time limit expired until the time it took the step (reg 11(3)).

Other unreasonable refusals

A landlord that withholds its consent will always be taken to have acted unreasonably in two sets of circumstances. One is where the lease states that consent will be given to an alteration of the kind in question (reg 12(a)). The other is where the lease provides that consent will be given to an alteration of the kind in question if consent is sought in a particular way, and the employer has sought consent in that way (reg 12(b)).

Reasonable refusals

On the other hand, a landlord will be taken to have acted reasonably in withholding its consent if it is under a binding obligation to obtain another person's consent to the alteration, and it has sought that consent, but consent has either been refused, or it has been given subject to a condition which makes it reasonable for the landlord to withhold its consent (reg 13(1)). (This does not cover obligations to obtain consent contained in a lease. There are separate rules to cover landlords who are themselves tenants under a superior lease – see below.)

It is also always reasonable for the landlord to withhold consent where the landlord is bound by an agreement which allows it to consent to the alteration in question subject to a condition that it makes a payment, but that condition does not allow it to make its own consent subject to a condition that the employer must reimburse that payment (reg 13(2)).

Reasonable conditions

Where the landlord gives its consent subject to a condition, it must be taken to be a reasonable condition if the condition is that:

- the employer must obtain any necessary statutory consents, such as planning permission (reg 14(1)(a)); or
- the employer must submit any plans or specifications for the alterations to the landlord for approval, which will not be unreasonably refused, and the work must be carried out in accordance with those plans or specifications (reg 14(1)(b)); or
- the landlord must be given a reasonable opportunity to inspect the work when completed (reg 14(1)(c)); or
- the employer must reimburse the landlord's costs reasonably incurred in connection with the giving of its consent (reg 14(1)(d)).

If it would have been reasonable for the landlord to withhold consent, then it is also reasonable for the landlord to give consent on condition that at the end of the lease the employer, or any person to whom the lease has been assigned, must reinstate the premises into its pre-alteration state (reg 14(2)).

[1] The Disability Discrimination (Employment) Regulations 1996 SI No 1456

If the tribunal decides that the landlord has unreasonably refused its consent to the alterations, or imposed unreasonable conditions, then it can take one or more of these steps: make a declaration; authorise the employer to make a specified alteration, which may be subject to conditions; and order the landlord to pay compensation to the complainant.[35] Any order that the tribunal makes against the landlord can be instead of or in addition to any order it makes against the employer, save that, if it orders the landlord to pay compensation, it cannot order the employer to do so.[36]

Regulations[37] have also been made which confirm that, where an employer's premises are held under a sub-lease or sub-tenancy, its application for consent to an alteration should be made to its immediate landlord. If the immediate landlord is itself subject to restrictions on alterations in its lease, then that lease is also to be read as if it provided for the tenant to make a written application to the landlord for consent to the alteration, which it cannot unreasonably withhold, but can make subject to reasonable conditions. The provisions in the DDA on a landlord's liability, and the Regulations on when refusals and conditions will be viewed as reasonable, then apply to the superior landlord.

24.6 Pensions

In principle, the DDA applies to discrimination against disabled people in occupational pension benefits. However, as a result of the Employment Regulations, discrimination is lawful where a person's disability and prognosis mean that the cost of providing benefits for him/her in relation to termination of service, retirement, old age, death, accident, injury, sickness or invalidity is likely to be substantially greater than it would be for a comparable person without that disability. In these circumstances, the Regulations state that the

35 Sch 4 para 4(6).
36 Sch 4 para 4(8) and (9).
37 Disability Discrimination (Sub-leases and Sub-tenancies) Regulations 1996 SI No 1333.

employer is justified in treating the disabled person less favourably in relation to eligibility conditions for, or the amount of, those benefits (reg 4).

The Code of Practice points out, however, that less favourable treatment may only be possible when a disabled person is first considered for admission to the scheme – once a member, a disabled person can be treated less favourably for a reason relating to his/her disability only if the terms on which s/he was admitted allow for this (para 6.12). The Code of Practice also stresses the need for employers to satisfy themselves, if necessary with actuarial advice and/or medical evidence, of the likelihood that a particular individual's admission to the scheme is likely to result in a substantially greater cost (para 6.11). An assumption that disabled people generally, or people with particular impairments or illnesses, will necessarily involve greater cost is not enough.

The Employment Regulations go on to provide that, even if a disabled person is not eligible to receive the same type or amount of benefit as other employees, the employer is justified in requiring him/her to pay the same rate of contribution as it requires from other employees, whether generally or in relation to the class of employees to which the disabled person belongs (reg 5).

Furthermore, an employer's usual duty to make reasonable adjustments does not apply in relation to any benefit under an occupational pension scheme, or any other benefit payable in money or money's worth under a scheme or arrangement for the benefit of employees in respect of termination of service; retirement, old age or death; accident, injury, sickness or invalidity; or any other matter that may be prescribed (s6(11)). This means, eg, that where an employee works fewer hours for a reason relating to his/her disability, and so is paid less, his/her pension may reflect that pay difference.

Trustees and managers of occupational pension schemes are bound by the same principles of non-discrimination as employers, in relation to the terms on which people become members, and the way in which members are treated (s17). Any unjustified discrimination by them will be deemed to be contrary to the scheme rules, and any disabled person who is affected can seek redress through the scheme's dispute resolution mechanisms,[38] or complain to the Occupational Pensions Advisory Service or the Pensions Ombudsman.

38 From 6 April 1997, it is compulsory for all schemes to have an internal disputes resolution procedure – see Pensions Act 1995 s50.

24.7 Insurance benefits

The DDA makes special provision to cover discrimination by providers of insurance-based employment benefits (s18). Where an insurance provider makes arrangements with an employer to provide its employees, or a class of its employees, with insurance services, or to give them the opportunities to receive them, then it has the same obligation not to discriminate as it would have if it were supplying the service direct to the employees as members of the public. The phrase 'insurance services' includes the provision of benefits for: termination of service; retirement, old age or death; accident, injury, sickness or invalidity; and any other matter that may be laid down in future regulations. It therefore covers permanent health insurance and life insurance provided by an insurance company.

However, it is lawful for an insurance provider to treat a disabled person less favourably in certain circumstances.[39] These are where the treatment is based on information, such as actuarial or statistical data or a medical report, which is relevant to the assessment of the risk to be insured, and is from a source on which it is reasonable to rely, and it is reasonable to treat the disabled person less favourably in the light of that information and 'any other relevant factors'.[40]

A disabled person who considers that s/he has been the subject of unjustified discrimination in relation to insurance-based benefits can make a tribunal complaint jointly against the insurance company and the employer (s8).

39 Disability Discrimination (Services and Premises) Regulations 1996 SI No 1836.

40 See Disability Discrimination (Services and Premises) Regulations 1996 SI No 1836 reg 2. The Regulations make special provision for insurance policies which came into effect before 2 December 1996. In effect, discrimination in such a policy is not unlawful until it is renewed or its terms are reviewed. A review which is part of, or incidental to, a general reassessment of the pricing structure for a group of policies does not amount to a review for these purposes (reg 3). Where an insurance provider issues insurance cover under a master policy, it is not unlawful for it to discriminate against a disabled person by refusing to issue a cover document, or in the terms on which cover is issued, if this occurs before 2 December 1997, unless the master policy was itself entered into, renewed or reviewed on or after 2 December 1996. However, any unjustified discrimination in relation to a cover document which is renewed or reviewed on or after 2 December 1997 will be unlawful (reg 4).

24.8 Liability for discrimination

When deciding issues of liability for discrimination under the DDA, tribunals are likely to be guided by the principles established by case-law under the SDA and RRA, as outlined in Chapter 7.

24.8.1 Vicarious liability and agents

For the purposes of the DDA, anything which is done by an employee in the course of his/her employment is treated as done by the employer, whether or not it was done with the employer's approval (s58(1)). The employer can escape liability, however, if it can prove to the tribunal that it took such steps as were reasonably practicable to prevent the employee from doing the unlawful act, or doing acts of that description in the course of his/her employment. One of the most important parts of the Code of Practice in relation to establishing liability for discrimination is therefore the section dealing with the role of management systems in avoiding discrimination. This section of the Code emphasises the need for employers to communicate policies on the employment of disabled people to all employees, and to provide training and guidance on how the policies are to be implemented (para 4.56).

Anything done by a person as an agent for the employer with the employer's express or implied authority, given before or after the act was done, is treated as done by the employer (s58(2) and (3)).

24.8.2 Employee liability

Anyone who knowingly aids another person to do an act which is unlawful under the DDA is treated as having committed the same unlawful act (s57). This means that employees who commit acts of discrimination in the course of their employment are liable for that discrimination, as well as their employers.

However, a person is not viewed as aiding another to do an unlawful act if s/he acts in reliance on the other person's assurance that, because of some provision of the legislation, the act would not be unlawful, provided that it was reasonable to rely on that assurance (s57(3)). Anyone who knowingly or recklessly gives such an assurance which is false or misleading in a material respect is guilty of a criminal offence, and is liable to a fine of up to level 5 on the standard scale.[41]

41 Currently £5,000.

24.8.3 Contracting out

Any term of a contract of employment or other agreement is void if it requires a person to contravene the DDA, or attempts to exclude or limit the Act's operation (s9(1)). This principle also applies to any agreement which attempts to prevent a person from presenting a complaint to an IT, unless it results from conciliation by ACAS or the agreement complies with the usual conditions relating to compromise agreements and contracts (s9(2) and (3)).

24.8.4 Disability charities and supported employment

The DDA provides a specific exemption for charities acting in pursuance of their charitable purposes to enable them to provide benefits for particular categories of people defined by physical or mental capacity (s10(1)). The idea behind this exemption is to enable organisations which work for particular groups of disabled people to employ people with those particular disabilities, in order to take advantage of the experience of those people or the techniques they have learned to cope with their specific impairment.[42–43]

There is also an exemption for providers of supported employment who treat members of a particular group of disabled people more favourably than other people (s10(2)). The supported employment programme provides job opportunities for people who, because of the severity of their impairment, find it very difficult to obtain or retain work in open employment.

24.8.5 Statutory authority and national security

The DDA does not apply to any act which is done in pursuance of a statutory provision, or to comply with any condition or requirement imposed by a minister by virtue of any statutory provision (s59(1)). Nor does the DDA apply to any act done for the purpose of safeguarding national security (s59(3)).

Any action an employer takes to meet its obligations under health and safety legislation cannot, therefore, amount to a breach of the DDA. The Code states, however, that this does not detract from an employer's obligation to consider reasonable adjustments. It gives the example of an employer considering not shortlisting a blind job applicant because of its belief that she would be a safety risk, and

42–43 HL Debs, 15 June 1995, vol 564, cols 1932 and 1933.

suggests that it might be reasonable for the employer to provide the applicant with mobility training to familiarise her with the work area, thus removing any risk (para 4.65).

24.8.6 Discrimination by those other than employers

24.8.6.1 By users of contract workers

In line with the other discrimination legislation (see 8.6), the DDA outlaws discrimination not only by employers but also by those who use contract workers. Contract workers are supplied by their employer under a contract between their employer (usually a temporary employment agency) and a third party, referred to in the DDA as the 'principal' (s12).

It is unlawful for the principal to discriminate against a disabled worker:

- in the terms on which it allows the worker to do the work;
- by not allowing the worker to do the work or continue to do it;
- in the way it gives the worker access to any benefits, or by refusing to or deliberately not giving access to any benefits; or
- by subjecting the worker to any other detriment.

As in the case of discrimination by employers, this does not apply to discrimination in relation to benefits of any description if the principal provides the benefits to the public, or a section of the public which includes the contract worker, unless the provision to the public differs in a material respect from the provision to the contract worker.

Since the same definition of discrimination applies to the principal as applies to an employer, the principal is under an obligation to justify any less favourable treatment of a disabled worker, and to make reasonable adjustments. The Employment Regulations indicate how the responsibility to make reasonable adjustments should be divided between the principal and the contract worker's own employer (that is, the employment agency – see reg 7).

If a contract worker is likely to be placed at a similar substantial disadvantage by the arrangements or premises of all or most of the principals to whom s/he is or might be supplied, then the worker's employer must take whatever steps it would be reasonable for it to take if the arrangements or premises were its own, to the extent that this is within its power (reg 7(1) and (2)). The principal is not under an obligation to take any step which it is reasonable for the worker's employer to take (reg 7(3)).

On the other hand, the principal may have to make adjustments that are necessary because of any aspects of its arrangements or premises which are not common to most or all of the worker's other principals, or which are under its control and not the employer's. Whether it is reasonable for the principal to make such an adjustment will depend on all the circumstances, including, as the Code of Practice suggests, the amount of time for which the disabled person is working for it (para 7.5).

24.8.6.2 By trade unions and other trade organisations

The DDA also outlaws discrimination by 'trade organisations' (s13). This phrase covers organisations of workers (such as trade unions), organisations of employers, and any other organisation whose members carry on a particular profession or trade for the purposes of which the organisation exists. A profession includes any vocation or occupation, and a trade includes any business (s68).

It is unlawful for a trade organisation to discriminate against a disabled person in the terms on which it is prepared to admit him/her to membership, or by refusing to accept, or deliberately not accepting, his/her application for membership. In relation to existing members, the organisation must not discriminate in the way it affords access to benefits, or by refusing or deliberately omitting to provide access to them; by depriving disabled people of membership or by varying the terms on which they are members; or by subjecting them to any other detriment. The definition of discrimination by trade organisations in DDA s14 closely follows that which applies to employers, so that, eg, they may be able to justify less favourable treatment of a disabled person.

Although this provision of the DDA had not yet been brought into force at the time of publication, trade organisations will in due course also be under an obligation to make reasonable adjustments to their arrangements and premises so that disabled members or applicants for membership are not at a substantial disadvantage in comparison with people who are not disabled (s15). The government gave the example of a union providing, where reasonable, its literature in Braille, and providing signers at union meetings.[44] If they lease their premises, trade organisations are also covered by the provisions which enable them to obtain their landlord's consent to alterations.

44 HL Debs, 18 July 1995, vol 566, col 225. Consultation on the implementation of s15 is scheduled to begin in mid-1997, with the possibility of a commencement date falling before the end of the year.

24.9 Enforcement of the DDA

Complaints of unlawful discrimination under the DDA are dealt with by ITs, in the same way as all other complaints of discrimination in employment.[45] So, for example, the three-month time limit for bringing a complaint is the same (see **25.2.1**), the questionnaire procedure is available (see **25.8**),[46] and, where a complaint is upheld, the tribunal has power to make a declaration, award unlimited compensation, including compensation for injury to feelings, and to make recommendations (s8(2) (see **26.1**)). Significantly, however, there is no equivalent of the Commission for Racial Equality or the Equal Opportunities Commission (see Chapter 27) to provide assistance to complainants under the DDA.

A tribunal hearing a complaint under the DDA has power to make a restricted reporting order (see **25.9.12**) where 'evidence of a personal nature' is likely to be heard by the tribunal (ie, evidence of a medical, or other intimate nature, which might reasonably be assumed to be likely to cause significant embarrassment to the complainant if reported[47]). If the DDA complaint is being dealt with together with any other proceedings, then the tribunal may direct that the order should apply in relation to all or any part of those other proceedings. The Employment Appeal Tribunal has similar powers when hearing an appeal from an interlocutory decision of an IT where the IT has made a restricted reporting order, and when hearing an appeal against an IT decision to make, or not to make, a restricted reporting order.[48]

24.9.1 Victimisation

In common with the order discrimination legislation, the DDA makes it unlawful for an employer to victimise any person, whether or not s/he is disabled, who has alleged that discrimination has occurred. According to DDA s55, it is unlawful for one person (A) to treat another person (B) less favourably than it treats or would treat other people in the same circumstances as B (disregarding any disability that B may have), for the following reasons:

45 For full details of procedure and remedies in discrimination complaints see Chapters 25 and 26.

46 See DDA s56 and the Disability Discrimination (Questions and Replies) Order 1996 SI No 2793.

47 See Industrial Tribunals Act 1996 s12. For further details on restricted reporting orders see **25.9.12**.

48 See Industrial Tribunals Act 1996 s32.

- B has brought proceedings under the DDA against A or any other person;
- B has given evidence or information in connection with any proceedings under the DDA;
- B has done any other thing under the DDA in relation to any person;
- B has alleged that A or any other person has acted in a way which breaches the DDA.

The same protection applies if A believes or suspects that B has done or intends to do any of these things. B is not protected, however, in respect of any allegation if the allegation was both false and not made in good faith (s55(4)).

Chapter 4 sets out the case-law on victimisation under the SDA and the RRA, and ITs are likely to apply similar principles when interpreting the DDA.

DISABILITY DISCRIMINATION: KEY POINTS

- The DDA does not apply to employers of fewer than 20 people.
- In order to qualify for the DDA's protection, a person must have, or have had, a physical or mental impairment causing a substantial and long-term adverse effect on his/her ability to carry out normal day-to-day activites.
- The DDA makes it unlawful for an employer to treat a person less favourably, for a reason related to the person's present or past disability, than it treats or would treat a person to whom that reason does not or would not apply.
- It is not, however, unlawful for an employer to treat a disabled person less favourably if it can show that that treatment is justified for a reason which is both material to the circumstances of the particular case and substantial.
- Where any arrangement made by an employer, or any physical feature of its premises, puts a disabled job applicant or employee at a substantial disadvantage, then the employer is under an obligation to make a reasonable adjustment in order to prevent that disadvantage arising. An unjustified failure to meet this duty amounts to unlawful discrimination, and means that any act of discrimination by the employer cannot be justified, unless it would have been justified even if the duty had been met.

- Discrimination by an employee in the course of his/her employment results in legal liability for the employer, unless it can show that it took all such steps as were reasonably practicable to prevent the discrimination occurring.
- The DDA also outlaws discrimination by trade organisations, including trade unions and employers' organisations.
- It is unlawful for an employer to victimise anybody for bringing or supporting proceedings under the DDA or making an allegation that the DDA has been breached, unless the allegation was false and not made in good faith.

Part VI

Enforcement

CHAPTER 25

Procedure

25.1 Overview

Complaints under the SDA, RRA, EqPA, DDA and ERA are made to an IT. Appeals are made to the EAT, then the CA and finally the HL. Any tribunal or court can refer a point of sex discrimination law to the ECJ which will decide the point of law and refer the case back to the originating tribunal or court.

25.1.1 Industrial tribunal

An applicant *must* apply to an IT within three months of the discriminatory act[1] (under the SDA, RRA, ERA or DDA). Under the EqPA an application can be made at any time during employment or within six months of the employee's contract ending (see **25.2.2**).[2] Compensation in equal pay cases can only be awarded for the two years immediately prior to the claim (see **23.4.6**).

There is no legal aid for the hearing, though 'green form' advice is available for the preparation provided that the solicitor only advises and does not hold him/herself out as a representative (see below). The CRE or EOC may provide help (see below). IT decisions are not binding on subsequent tribunals so are of only limited importance.

25.1.2 Employment Appeal Tribunal

There is a right of appeal from an IT to the EAT on a point of law. The appeal must be made within 42 days of the date that the written decision was entered on the register; time will be extended only in exceptional circumstances.[3] Legal aid may be available for the

1 SDA s76(1); RRA s68(1); DDA Sch 3 para 3.
2 *Etherson v Strathclyde RC* [1992] IRLR 392.
3 Employment Appeal Tribunal Rules 1993 SI No 2854 r3(2).

hearing. EAT decisions are binding on all ITs, but not on subsequent EATs, although they will be persuasive.

25.1.3 Court of Appeal

There is a further appeal to the CA on a point of law provided that the EAT gives leave to appeal; if the EAT does not grant leave, then it can be requested from the CA. There is a four-week period within which an appeal must be lodged and this runs from the date of judgment.[4] If no leave to appeal is sought at the hearing, an appellant may risk being out of time as it may take the EAT time to re-assemble to consider the leave application. The CA has said that a party wishing to appeal, where leave was not sought at the time of judgment, should apply to the EAT for an extension of time when the application for leave is made. Legal aid may be available.

Decisions of the NICA are persuasive authority for the CA and EAT.

25.1.4 House of Lords

Appeal on a point of law can be made from the CA to the HL within three months of the CA's judgment.[5] Leave must first be obtained from the CA or HL. Legal aid may be available. The HL must make a reference to the ECJ on a question of European law unless the answer to the European point is so clear as to make it unnecessary (see **9.3.1**).

25.1.5 European Court of Justice

Any English court or tribunal can refer a question about the interpretation of European law to the ECJ (see **9.3.1**). Pre-existing legal aid certificates can be extended to cover proceedings in the ECJ,[6] alternatively the ECJ may make limited legal aid available (see **9.3.1.2**).

25.1.6 Jurisdiction of ITs over equal pay claims

An IT can hear an equal pay case in the following circumstances:

4 RSC Ord 59 r4(1).

5 *House of Lords: Practice Directions and Standing Orders applicable to Civil Appeals* (July 1994) r8.1.

6 Civil Legal Aid (General) Regulations 1989 SI No 339 reg 51.

- on the application of an employee;[7]
- on the application of an employer for a declaration relating to its employees' rights in relation to an equality clause;[8]
- on a reference by the Secretary of State on behalf of an aggrieved employee where it is not reasonable to expect the parties to have the question determined themselves;[9]
- on a direction by the court where it is considered more appropriate for an IT to determine the operation of an equality clause.[10]

A discriminatory collective agreement can be referred to a county court by an interested person. The court may remove or modify any unenforceable term.[11]

Any discriminatory term in an Agricultural Wages Order may be referred by the Secretary of State (either at the request of a worker or at his/her own volition) to the Central Arbitration Committee for amendment.

25.1.7 Access to information

There are five ways of getting further information from the employer: use of the questionnaire both prior to and after the issue of proceedings (see **25.8**), disclosure in collective bargaining, an application for further and better particulars (see **25.9.2**), written answers (see **25.9.4**) and discovery (see **25.9.3**).

25.1.7.1 From employers

Obtaining information from an employer on the breakdown of the workforce by sex and race and the qualifications of job applicants and employees is a very important and difficult task. Often applicants will be told that other applicants were better qualified but that information about their qualifications is confidential and cannot be divulged. In requests for further and better particulars on discovery ITs commonly attempt to maintain a degree of confidentiality by making the information anonymous, other applicants may be identified by a number or letter (see **25.9.3.1**).

Indirect discrimination is largely about statistics: evidence is required of the number of men and women or the number of black

7 EqPA s2(1).
8 EqPA s2(1A).
9 EqPA s2(2). In practice this never happens.
10 EqPA s2(3).
11 SDA s77; SDA 1986 s6.

and white employees or job applicants in the relevant pool who can comply with job requirements (see **3.6.5** for definition of pool). The difficulties in obtaining such information is well illustrated by the *Orphanos*[12] case (see **3.6.1.1**). If the pool is to be the workforce or job applicants then the statistics can be obtained only from the employer.

25.1.7.2 From other sources

In indirect discrimination cases the pool may comprise those living in a particular neighbourhood from which workers are likely to be recruited or the whole of the UK. This information may be obtained from:

- censuses and surveys (population census; Labour Force Survey; New Earnings Survey; annual census of employment; local authority surveys);
- publications (*Labour Market Trends* (Department of Employment), DE/OPCS survey, *Ethnic minorities in Britain* (CRE), *Equal Opportunities Review, Social Trends*));
- organisations (see Appendix 1) (EOC and CRE, Labour Research Department, Runnymede Trust, Central Office of Information, TUC, universities' research departments, etc).

25.2 Procedure in discrimination cases

Applications to ITs are governed by the Industrial Tribunals (Constitution and Rules of Procedure) Regulations 1993.[13] For the rules covering general tribunal procedure the reader is referred to J McMullen and J Eady, *Employment Tribunal Procedure.*[14] In this chapter only such procedures as are specific or particularly relevant to discrimination applications are covered.

25.2.1 Time limits under the SDA, RRA and DDA

Under the SDA, RRA and DDA an application must be made within three months of the discrimination taking place. If the last act of discrimination was on the 25 March the last day for commencing proceedings will be 24 (*not* 25) June (for how this applies in different situations see below). However, if the discrimination is continuing,

12 [1985] 2 All ER 233.
13 SI No 2687.
14 LAG, 1996.

then the time limit runs only from the time the discrimination ceased.[15] Note that acts outside the time limit may be adduced in evidence as further proof of the discrimination.

25.2.1.1 When is discrimination continuing?

The Acts provide that 'any act extending over a period shall be treated as done at the end of that period'. There is a distinction between:

a) a specific act which has continuing consequences; and
b) an act or course of conduct which extends over a period of time because it takes the form of a 'policy rule or practice in accordance with which decisions are taken from time to time'.[16]

It is often difficult to distinguish between (a) and (b) above, so it is advisable to lodge an application within three months of the earliest date the discrimination took place. If this has not been done it may still be possible to argue that there has been continuing discrimination. This will depend on the circumstances in each case.

Where an employee is denied a benefit because of a practice or policy, the discrimination is likely to be continuing. Thus, in *Calder v James Finlay Corporation Ltd*[17] the refusal to give the applicant a mortgage subsidy because she was a woman was held to be continuing discrimination. The EAT held that even though the refusal took place more than three months before her claim, it was a discriminatory act extending throughout her employment until she left and her claim which was brought within three months of her leaving was in time. Similarly, in *Barclays Bank plc v Kapur*, the HL held that less favourable treatment of the applicants in relation to their pension rights was a policy which continued throughout the period of their employment.[18]

An act extends over a period of time, so is continuing, if it takes the form of some policy, rule or practice, in accordance with which decisions are taken from time to time. A succession of specific instances can indicate the existence of a practice, which, in turn, can constitute a continuing act extending over a period. This will be a question of fact to be determined in every case. In *Owusu v London Fire and Civil Defence Authority*[19] the applicant complained that he

15 SDA s76(6)(b); RRA s68(7)(b); DDA Sch 3 para 3(3)(b).
16 See, eg, *Owusu v London and Civil Defence Authority* [1995] IRLR 574 at para 21.
17 [1989] IRLR 55.
18 [1991] ICR 208; [1991] IRLR 136.
19 [1995] IRLR 574.

had not been regraded or been given the opportunity to act up to a higher grade job. The EAT held that if there was a practice which, when followed or applied, excluded the applicant from re-grading or opportunities to act up, this would constitute continuing discrimination. The important point is that there must be some linking practice, as opposed to one-off decisions, with different explanations.

In *Sougrin v Haringey Health Authority*[20] the CA held that a decision of a grading appeal hearing is a one-off act with continuing consequences rather than a course of conduct. If the grading criteria themselves had been inherently discriminatory and thereby excluded the applicant from regrading or there had been a policy the decision may have been different.

Where there is a series of acts of discrimination the time limit may run from the last act. In *GMC v Rovenska*[21] the applicant, a Czechoslovakian doctor, applied to the General Medical Council (GMC) for registration as a doctor in the UK. The GMC required her to pass a test although doctors qualifying at certain specified overseas universities were exempt from sitting the test. She argued that the exemptions scheme discriminated against her as she had unsuccessfully applied for an exemption on a number of occasions. The CA did not decide if there was a continuing act but held that each time there was a refusal this was a further act of discrimination (but see *Cast* at **3.6.3**).[22]

25.2.1.2 Harassment

In cases of harassment there is often, though not necessarily, a course of conduct. Each individual act of harassment is an act of discrimination, but may also be part of a continuing course of conduct. The safest course is to put in a claim within three months of the first act of harassment. However, if the harassment continues over a period it may amount to a practice or policy of continuing discrimination, in which case the time limit will run from the last act. In *Wade v West Yorkshire Police*[23] the EAT assumed that it was appropriate to treat a course of harassment as a continuing act. The EAT said that it would

20 [1992] IRLR 416.

21 [1997] IRLR 367.

22 It is unclear whether there needs to be a change in circumstances or fresh material in relation to each new application. See also *Akhter v Family Service Unit* (1996) 30 EOR DCLD; 18 June 1996; EAT no 1285/95, where the EAT held that each refusal of an employee's request to use a contractual grievance procedure was a separate act for time limit purposes when a different person took the decision.

23 EAT/899/96 and EAT/900/96.

have expected an IT to look at the allegations of harassment jointly and deal with the contention that the conduct complained of was all part of a piece. Importantly, they said that some apparently trivial incidents may appear in a different light if they are seen as a pattern of behaviour. It may be, therefore, that one minor act of harassment will not be sufficient to show discrimination, but a series of acts will show a course of conduct.

If there is evidence that the aim of the harassment is to force the victim to leave or transfer, it will be easier to show a continuing act. In addition, a failure by the employer to deal properly with complaints of harassment may constitute a continuing act (see **13.3.3.4**).

25.2.1.3 Omissions

A deliberate omission is treated as done when the person decided on it.[24] This means at a time and in circumstances when the person is in a position to implement that decision.[25] In the absence of evidence to the contrary, such decision is presumed to have been taken either when someone does something inconsistent with the omitted act or at the end of the time when s/he might reasonably have been expected to do the omitted act.[26] So, for example, if all male employees (but no female employees) are given special training during their first year, the three months would begin to run at the end of the year.

Where there has been a failure to appoint a person to a job vacancy and the position is then filled, the time will run from the decision not to appoint or the appointment of a successful candidate. However, if no-one is appointed, the time limit will run from the date the applicant found out that the decision not to appoint him/her had been made.

In *Clarke v Hampshire Electro-Plating Co Ltd*,[27] the EAT held that where there is a failure to select or promote the question is when the cause of action crystallised, or was completed, rather than when the applicant felt s/he had been discriminated against. Thus, it could be argued that time runs from the date that the vacancy was filled. However, where possible, applications should be lodged within three months from the date of the rejection.

25.2.1.4 Grievance procedures

As a general rule, an applicant should not wait until the result of a grievance or appeal before submitting a claim. If the act of discrimi-

24 SDA s76; RRA s68(7); DDA Sch 3 para 3(3)(c).
25 *Swithland Motors plc v Clarke* [1994] IRLR 275.
26 SDA s76(6)(c); RRA s68(7)(c); DDA Sch 3 para 3(4).
27 [1991] IRLR 490.

nation occurred more than three months previously the claim may be out of time. However, in some circumstances time may not run if no final decision has been made pending an appeal or grievance, or the grievance procedure is itself discriminatory provided the person is still an employee.[28] In *Ford Motor Company Ltd v Shah*[29] the applicants were refused transfers. They used the internal grievance procedure after which the the application for transfer was finally refused. They alleged that the internal procedure was discriminatory as it failed to recognise that the earlier decision was itself racially discriminatory. The EAT held that while there was an extant grievance procedure there was an act extending over a period. In addition, the failure fully to implement agreed remedial measures meant that the discrimination continued. A similar decision was reached in *Littlewoods v Traynor*[30] where the EAT held that where promised remedial action is awaited, the discrimination continues until the action is complete.

25.2.1.5 Requests to work part-time

In cases where an employee asks to work part-time the EAT has held that even if she repeats her request in different circumstances time will run from the date of the first refusal. This is arguably wrong and inconsistent with *Rovenska*[31] where time ran from the date of the last refusal. In addition, if there is a policy not to allow part-time working this will be continuing discrimination. It is arguable that if the refusal leads the employee to resign time may run from the date of resignation.[32]

25.2.1.6 Unfair dismissals

A claim for unfair dismissal under the ERA must also be made within three months of the effective date of termination as defined by ERA s97(1).[33]

If the claim relates to a discriminatory unfair dismissal or a constructive discriminatory unfair dismissal,[34] the time limit runs from

28 See *Adekeye v Post Office (No 2)* [1997] IRLR 105, CA.
29 EAT 530/95.
30 *Littlewoods v Traynor* [1993] IRLR 154.
31 See n21.
32 See *Cast v Croydon College* [1997] IRLR 14; this is currently being appealed to the CA.
33 ERA s111.
34 The SDA expressly provides that a constructive dismissal is to be treated as a dismissal (see s82(1A)(b)). The same result is probably achieved by applying the common law in respect of repudiation of contracts to the RRA and DDA.

the date when the contract of employment was terminated. In *Yaseen v Strathclyde RC and General Teaching Council for Scotland*,[35] the complaint related to discriminatory reports which had been written more than three months before the complaint was filed, as the applicant complained only after he had been dismissed. The EAT held that the complaint was not out of time as the time ran from the date of dismissal. However, it is advisable to apply to the IT within three months of the discriminatory act.

Note that an originating application is 'presented' when the application arrives at the Office of the Industrial Tribunals, whether it is sent by post, hand delivery or fax. It is always advisable to ring the tribunal to check that it has been received before the time limit runs out. It does not need to be registered.[36]

25.2.2 Time limits under the EqPA

Claims for breach of an equality clause should be brought during the existence of the contract or within six months of the employee leaving.[37] However, backpay can be ordered for a period of only two years prior to the application (this may be contrary to EC law and a question on this has been referred to the ECJ; see **23.4.6**).

25.2.3 Time limits under EC law

The ECJ has said that time limits are a matter for the member state's domestic law. In *Emmott v Minister for Social Welfare and Attorney General*,[38] the ECJ held:

> in the absence of community rules on the subject, it is for the domestic legal system of each member state to determine the procedural conditions governing actions at law intended to ensure the protection of the rights which individuals derive from the direct effect of Community law, provided that such conditions are not less favourable than those relating to similar actions of a domestic nature nor framed so as to render virtually impossible the exercise of rights conferred by community law.

A member state is entitled to apply reasonable time limits. Where the applicant is relying on rights under art 119 s/he is bound by the domestic time limits set out above. In *Biggs v Somerset CC*[39] a

35 EAT Case no 6/90; see also *Lupette v Wrens Old House* [1984] ICR 348, EAT.
36 *Dodd v British Telecom* [1988] IRLR 16.
37 EqPA s2(4). See also *Etherson v Strathclyde RC* [1992] ICR 579; [1992] IRLR 392.
38 [1991] IRLR 387.
39 [1996] IRLR 203.

part-time teacher put in an unfair dismissal claim 18 years after she was dismissed. She claimed that she did not realise that she had any rights to claim unfair dismissal until after the case of *R v Secretary of State for Employment ex p EOC*[40] had decided that part-time workers were eligible for the same rights as full-timers. The CA decided that Ms Biggs' complaint should be dismissed as it was out of time and it was 'reasonably practicable' for her to present her claim in time. This appears to give no weight to the fact that at the time of her dismissal few people had realised that EC law could affect the interpretation of UK law and this must 'render virtually impossible the exercise of rights conferred by community law'. The CA did not refer the time limit point to the ECJ.

In *BCC v Keeble* the EAT distinguished *Biggs* and allowed a sex discrimination claim out of time. It held that it was 'just and equitable' to allow the claim saying that, if the only reason for the delay is a wholly understandable misapprehension of the law, that must be a matter which Parliament intended the IT to take into account. Thus emphasising the different tests for unfair dismissal and sex discrimination claims. See **9.6.8**.

However, where a directive has not been fully implemented into national law, the member state may not rely on an individual's delay in initiating proceedings against it. Thus, where an individual is relying on a directive, as opposed to UK law, time does not run until the directive has been implemented and no national time limits bite.[41]

25.2.4 *What happens if the time limit has expired?*

A court or tribunal can consider a *discrimination* application which is out of time if, in all the circumstances, it considers that it is 'just and equitable' to do so.[42] The tribunal can take into account anything which is relevant, including the merits of the case.[43] Ignorance of the time limit is not generally sufficient, though ignorance of rights may be.[44] In *Singh v Allmey and Layfield Ltd*,[45] an IT allowed an out-of-time claim because the delay had been caused by the union's attempt

40 [1994] IRLR 176.
41 See *Emmott v Minister for Social Welfare* [1991] IRLR 387.
42 SDA s76(5); RRA s68(6).
43 *Hutchinson v Westward Television Ltd* [1977] IRLR 69.
44 *MacMillan Bloedel Containers Ltd v Morris* (1984) 267 IRLIB 13, EAT. See also *Dimtsu v Westminster* CC [1991] IRLR 451.
45 Case no 10884/89.

to resolve the issue under the equal opportunity procedures. In *Hawkins v Ball and Barclays Bank plc*[46] the EAT held that ITs have a broad discretion and confirmed a decision of the IT that it was 'just and equitable' to extend the time limit where the applicant had received erroneous legal advice.

If the employee also complains of *unfair dismissal* time may be extended if it was 'not reasonably practicable' to present the complaint in time and that it was brought within such time as was reasonable.[47] This is a different and more restrictive test. It is seldom sufficient for an applicant to say that s/he has put the matter into the hands of a competent adviser,[48] but if a government official has wrongly advised on the time limit this may be a sufficient reason.[49]

Although some late claims are barred, there is nothing to lose by making the claim. A detailed letter setting out reaons for the delay should be sent to the IT as soon as possible.

25.3 How to apply

The first step in making a claim is to submit a letter or a form known as an IT1, available from the local job centre, employment office or advice agency. The letter or IT1 should give:

- the name and address of the applicant;
- the name and address of the respondent;
- the grounds for the claim.

In *Dodd v British Telecom plc*,[50] the EAT said that these requirements were directory, not mandatory. It said that the written application need contain only sufficient information to identify who is making it, against whom it is made, and what sort of complaint it is; the failure to specify whether the complaint was of sex discrimination or race discrimination or both was not fatal, as any deficiency could be remedied subsequently.

The application should then be sent, delivered or faxed to the local office of industrial tribunals within the relevant time limit.

46 [1996] IRLR 258.
47 ERA s111; see also *Walls Meat Co v Khan* [1979] ICR 52; [1978] IRLR 499.
48 *Dedman v British Building & Engineering Appliances Ltd* [1974] ICR 53; [1973] IRLR 379.
49 *Jean Sorell Ltd v Rybak* [1991] ICR 127; [1991] IRLR 153, where an employee of an IT office gave the wrong information about time limits.
50 [1988] IRLR 16.

25.3.1 *Amendment of IT1*

Provided that the claim is in writing, failure to provide the required information is not necessarily fatal as the tribunal can allow amendments.[51] There are no time limits for making amendments. A claim for discrimination will include both direct and indirect discrimination, and victimisation.[52] If the amendment changes the basis of the claim, from say unfair dismissal to discrimination, the amendment may be allowed only if the facts set out in the claim would also give rise to a claim of discrimination.[53] It is often better to submit another claim and ask for them to be heard together, provided that the time limit has not expired. Where it is necessary only to explain better the nature of the complaint it may be more sensible to serve voluntary further and better particulars (see **25.9.2**) rather than to apply to the IT for leave to amend the IT1.

A discrimination questionnaire can be sent to the employer within 21 days of lodging the IT1 (see below).

25.3.2 *Whom to sue*

The first respondent will usually be the employer. If it is not clear whether the employer is an individual, a partnership or a limited company it is advisable to make every possible person or organisation a respondent. Once the IT3s have been sent out and replies received it will be easier to identify the correct respondent. At that stage the IT1 can be amended to show only the correct respondent/s. Substitution of a respondent may be allowed if the employee was mistaken as to the real identity of his/her employer.[54] Employees can also sue individual discriminators (see **7.3**).

Particular examples where it may be advisable to sue more than one person are:

- *Sexual or racial harassment*: the employee can sue *both* the employer and the perpetrator/s of the harassment (see **13.5**).
- *Transfer of undertakings*: if the employee has been transferred to the new employer s/he should sue the new employer even if the discrimination occurred during his/her employment under the

51 See *Dodd v British Telecom* [1988] IRLR 16; *British Newspaper Printing Corp v Kelly* [1989] IRLR 222 and *Quarcoopome v Sock Shop* [1995] IRLR 353.

52 See *Quarcoopome v Sock Shop* (n51).

53 *Home Office v Bose* [1979] ICR 481.

54 *Cocking v Sandhurst (Stationers) Ltd* and *Jackson v Gardner Security Ltd* [1974] ICR 650.

previous employer. Since it is not always clear if and when there has been a transfer it is sensible to include the old employer as well. It can be withdrawn subsequently if necessary.

25.3.3 Representative actions

Although there is no procedure in English law for class actions, in *Ashmore v British Coal Corporation*,[55] where there were 1,500 like work claims by canteen workers, the IT had ordered that representative sample cases should be chosen for trial. The sample cases were dismissed on the basis that the claimants were not employed on like work and that there was a material factor defence. Ms Ashmore attempted to have her case listed for hearing and the IT struck it out on the ground that it was an abuse of process and vexatious. The IT said that her claim had been stayed pending the determination of sample cases raising similar factual issues; these had been resolved in the employer's favour. Upholding the IT decision, the CA said that it was contrary to the interests of justice and public policy to allow the same issues to be litigated again, unless there were fresh evidence.

Ashmore is an important case in demonstrating that women claiming discrimination/equal pay can effectively bring class actions, thus saving each individual fighting on her own. If, in *Ashmore*, the IT had found in favour of the employees, then the employer would similarly have been barred from defending the other claims. Ms Ashmore claimed that her case was different from the others; this should have been raised before the cases were submitted as 'representative actions' and not after the decision had been made. The CA also pointed out that the applicant could have applied to be one of the sample cases but she had not done so.

If a person who subsequently brings a similar claim was not a party to the original action then the initial decision will not necessarily bind him/her. In *DES v Taylor*[56] two college lecturers took action when they were made redundant and won compensation. Later a further 23 lecturers who had not been concerned with the first case were made redundant. It was agreed that the issues of law and fact were the same as in the earlier cases, however, the same facts could be re-litigated because different parties were involved and the action could not be struck out as an abuse of process.

55 [1990] IRLR 283.
56 [1992] IRLR 308.

In *Kowalska*,[57] the ECJ said that 'the prohibition of discrimination between men and women . . . extends to all agreements which seek to regulate wage-earning work collectively, as well as to contracts between individuals'. It has been argued that this may permit a representative action under EC law so that all those affected by the collective agreement's discriminatory term could claim as a group.[58]

25.4 Duty to mitigate

In cases of dismissal and refusal of a job, an applicant should take steps to find alternative employment in order to minimise the loss resulting from the dismissal. Evidence of such steps will be required, so it is important to keep a record of job applications, interviews, visits to the job centre and any other measures taken to find work. The costs of taking such steps are recoverable (provided that evidence is available).

In an unfair dismissal claim, if re-employment or reinstatement is sought, the employer should be informed as soon as posssible to try to avoid the respondent's employing a replacement.

25.5 The employer's reply

The secretary of tribunals will send a copy of the IT1 to the respondent. The employer has 21 days in which to reply, though the time limit can be extended. Failure to reply may debar the employer from resisting the claim. The form on which the employer replies is known as an IT3.

25.6 ACAS

Where a complaint is presented to an IT under the SDA, EqPA, ERA, RRA or DDA, a copy is sent to an ACAS conciliation officer who has a duty, if requested to do so by both complainant and respondent or if s/he thinks that there is a reasonable chance of achieving a settlement, to try to promote such a settlement.[59] This also applies, prior to a complaint being submitted, if there is a request by a potential complainant or respondent.[60]

57 *Kowalska v Freie und Hansestadt Hamburg* [1990] IRLR 447, ECJ.
58 See (1990) 34 EOR 38.
59 SDA s64(1); RRA s55(1); DDA Sch 3 para 1(1).
60 SDA s64(2); RRA s55(2); DDA Sch 3 para 1(2).

Any settlement reached through ACAS not to pursue a claim to the IT is binding on the parties so as to exclude any complaint to a tribunal, even if the agreement has not been put in writing.[61] In 1994/95 24% of race cases and 25% of sex discrimination cases were settled by conciliation, compared with 39% of unfair dismissal cases.[62]

Any communications to the ACAS officer for these purposes is not admissible in evidence before the tribunal unless the person who made them consents. This does not necessarily apply to documents sent to ACAS.[63]

25.7 Settlement through 'a qualified lawyer'

A binding settlement can also be made if, before signing an agreement the employee has received legal advice from a 'qualified lawyer'.[64] A qualified lawyer is either a barrister or a solicitor. The legal advice must cover the terms and effect of the agreement and in particular its effect on the employee's rights to pursue his/her claim in the IT. The qualified lawyer must be covered by professional negligence insurance at the time of the agreement.

In order for the agreement to be binding on both parties it must be:

- in writing;
- relate to the particular complaint;
- identify the qualified lawyer who has advised the employee; and
- state that the conditions relating to compromise agreements under the relevant Act/s are satisfied.

Any other settlement that is stated to be in full and final settlement of a claim will not prevent an employee applying to the IT, however, the IT may take it into account in deciding any award for compensation.[65]

25.8 The questionnaire

Standard forms are set out in the Sex Discrimination (Questions and Replies) Order 1975,[66] Race Relations (Questions and Replies) Order

61 *Gilbert v Kembridge Fibres Ltd* [1984] ICR 188; [1984] IRLR 52.
62 Labour Market Trends (July 1996).
63 See *M & W Grazebrook v Wallens* [1973] 2 All ER 868.
64 ERA s203; SDA s77; RRA s72; DDA s9.
65 *Courage Take Home Trade Ltd v Keys* [1986] ICR 874.
66 SI No 2048.

1977[67] and the Disability Discrimination (Questions and Replies) Order 1996.[68] The questionnaire applies to claims made under the RRA, SDA and DDA. Its aim is to help a complainant decide if s/he should start proceedings and, if so, to aid him/her to present them in the most effective way. A complainant can question the discriminator about his or her reasons for doing a particular act or on any relevant matter. The forms do not have to be used, but they do give useful guidance on their purpose and provide a good basis for cross-examination. There is no restriction on the questions that can be asked; however, if the questions are wider than is appropriate to the proposed action this could provide a reasonable excuse for an employer to fail to answer them. Forms are also available for the respondent's reply. As the EqPA is technically a schedule to the SDA the questionnaire procedure should also be available in equal pay cases (see **18.9.6**).[69]

25.8.1 *Time limits for serving a questionnaire*

The questionnaire must be served on the employer within three months of the act of discrimination. If a complaint has been presented to an IT, it must be served within 21 days of presentation (or if the complaint is out of time within a period specified by the tribunal). However, it may be possible to serve a second or later questionnaire with the consent of the IT and in some cases it may be very sensible to do so (see **25.9.1**).

25.8.2 *Admissibility in evidence*

The questions and replies are admissible in evidence.[70] If the employer deliberately or without reasonable excuse fails to reply or is evasive or equivocal the tribunal can draw any inference it thinks appropriate, including that the employer has discriminated unlawfully.[71]

The questionnaire procedure is in addition to, and separate from, the rules relating to further and better particulars, written answers and discovery.[72] Thus if the employer refuses to reply to a question it can be asked again in a request for further and better particulars or as a written question (see **25.9**).

67 SI No 842.
68 SI No 2793.
69 SDA s8 and Sch 1 included the EqPA, as amended, as part of the SDA.
70 SDA s74(2)(a); RRA s65(2)(a); DDA s56(3)(a).
71 SDA s74(2)(b); RRA s65(2)(b); DDA s56(3)(b).
72 SDA s74(5); RRA s65(5); DDA s56(5).

25.8.3 What questions?

Useful questions, in the case of a discriminatory job refusal, include:

- How and where was the job advertised?
- What qualifications and requirements were wanted of applicants?
- What was the job description?
- Why was the successful applicant chosen and what qualifications did s/he have?
- Breakdown by sex or race of applicants for similar jobs over a period of, say, two years.

The questions depend on the type of discrimination and the facts of the case. In indirect discrimination cases, using the questionnaire before submitting a claim may be a useful way of eliciting a 'requirement' or 'condition' which would not otherwise be expressed as such.

In *Oxford v DHSS,*[73] the applicant, who had been refused a job as a clerical officer, asked for the name, address, sex and age of all the successful candidates. Later he asked for their qualifications. The DHSS gave the sex and age only and this was upheld by the EAT because all candidates were qualified. Normally, it said, qualifications should be given.

25.9 Interlocutory matters

There are special procedures for equal value cases; see **20.7**.

25.9.1 Further questionnaire

In *Carrington v Helix Lighting Ltd,*[74] the EAT, recognising that applicants may face considerable difficulties in proving a case of discrimination, said that 'it is a sensible and necessary part of the procedure that after an initial questionnaire an applicant should be able to seek leave, on notice, to administer a further questionnaire'. The EAT pointed out that the respondent could argue that any question was unnecessary, too wide or oppressive. The EAT suggested that this step might be taken after discovery. In practice, further questions are increasingly common. They help to identify the issues, extract the relevant facts and generally clarify the differences between the parties. An application to serve a further questionnaire (if not agreed) can be made in writing to the IT or at a directions hearing.

73 [1977] ICR 884; [1977] IRLR 225.
74 [1990] IRLR 6.

25.9.2 *Further and better particulars*

Either party to IT proceedings can ask the other for further details of the grounds on which that party relies and any relevant facts. The purpose of this is to ensure that each party can prepare to meet the other's case at the hearing. This can be done by sending a letter to the other side requesting particulars. If they are not forthcoming, the tribunal, on application, may order the provision of the particulars.[75] The tribunal may also, of its own accord, ask for further details of either party's case (see below for consequences of failure to provide particulars).

25.9.3 *Discovery of documents*

Similarly, either party (or the tribunal of its own motion) can ask for discovery of the other side's documents. The IT can order discovery as might be granted by a county court and this should be requested. Disclosure should be ordered of documents which are or have been in either party's 'possession, custody or control relating to any matter in question in the proceedings' unless disclosure 'is not necessary for disposing fairly of the action or saving costs'.[76] Documents can be obtained from third parties by taking out a witness summons (see **26.9.9**). It is important to ask for full discovery of all relevant documents rather than to accept discovery of only those documents on which the other side intends to rely as documents helpful to the applicant may not otherwise be disclosed.

25.9.3.1 *What information can the employer refuse to give?*

It has been judicially recognised that it is the employer who is likely to have the information necessary to make out a case of discrimination and that the 'fullest information should be before the tribunals'. In *Nasse v Science Research Council* and *Vyas v Leyland Cars*,[77] the HL laid down the following principles:

- employers usually have the information necessary to prove discrimination cases;
- confidentiality alone is not a reason for refusing discovery but it is a relevant factor; the tribunal should examine the documents to see if disclosure really is necessary and, if so, consider whether

75 For guidelines on the ordering of further and better particulars see *Byrne and Others v Financial Times* [1991] IRLR 417.

76 CCR Ord 14 rr1(1) and 8(1).

77 [1980] AC 1028; [1979] ICR 921; [1979] IRLR 465.

confidentiality could be preserved by covering up irrelevant parts (such as the names);
- the test is whether discovery is necessary for the fair disposal of the proceedings or for saving costs.

In *West Midlands Passenger Transport Executive v Singh*,[78] the CA allowed discovery of the number of applicants, broken down according to race, over a period of two years (see **2.13.1**). The CA said that the statistical material was relevant in that it might assist the complainant in establishing positively that treatment of ethnic minority employees was on racial grounds, which was an effective cause of his failure to obtain promotion. It might also assist the complainant to rebut the employer's contention that it operated an equal opportunities policy which was applied in his case. However, the IT will not order discovery of material which is not readily to hand and which can be made available only with difficulty and at great expense.

In *Munglani v MSC*,[79] the EAT ordered disclosure of internal memoranda between the discriminator and others on 'ethnic minority problems', as it said that these might reveal his attitude and were relevant in deciding whether his behaviour was racially motivated.

Discovery will not be ordered if it is considered by the tribunal to be oppressive.[80]

25.9.4 Written questions and answers

The Industrial Tribunal (Constitution and Rules of Procedure) Regulations 1993[81] Sch 1 r4(3) introduced a new provision for either party to ask formal questions of the other which would help clarify any issue in the proceedings or which would assist the progress of the proceedings. If these are not provided on request the IT can be asked to order their production.

25.9.5 Striking out

A tribunal can strike out an IT1 or IT3 in whole or part if it is scandalous, frivolous or vexatious, or can strike out an IT1 for want of prosecution.[82] An application to strike out may be made by either

78 [1988] IRLR 186.
79 EAT Case no 108/88.
80 *Nasse v Science Research Council* (n77 above) and *Forex Neptune (Overseas) Ltd v Miller and Others* (1987) 322 IRLIB 5.
81 SI No 2687 (hereafter the IT Regs).
82 IT Regs Sch 1 r13.

party or the tribunal may raise the possibility itself. Notice must be given to the parties to give them an opportunity to be heard).

25.9.6 Preliminary hearing

A preliminary hearing will take place if there is a dispute over whether the tribunal has jurisdiction. Thus, if, for example, the employer argues that the applicant is working overseas so is outside the Act, then this can be raised at a preliminary hearing. Frequently, issues of jurisdiction are so closely linked to the facts of the case that they cannot be dealt with adequately unless all the facts of the case are heard. In such cases it is better, and more economical, to have the preliminary issue dealt with at a full hearing of the case.

25.9.7 Combined cases

A tribunal can order that several cases be heard at the same time where:

- there is some common question of law or fact;
- the relief claimed arises out of the same set of facts; or
- it is otherwise desirable to do so.[83]

The parties must be given notice before such an order is made, to allow them to object. The decision is at the tribunal's discretion.[84]

An order for cases to be heard together may be appropriate in equal value cases where different applicants may compare themselves with a number of comparators. One expert may then be required to look at all the different jobs to determine whether they are of equal value. If there are separate claims under the SDA and EqPA, they may be combined.

25.9.8 Adjournment pending other proceedings

If other proceedings have been issued which relate to the same facts (eg, in the High Court for, say, assault in sexual harassment cases), it is quite common for one party to apply for an adjournment pending the other hearing. When an applicant lodges a claim to comply with time limits, the applicant should state that a stay of that claim will be sought.[85]

83 Ibid, Sch 1 r18.
84 See *Dietman and Wahlstrom v LB Brent* [1987] IRLR 146.
85 *Warnock v Scarborough Football Club* [1989] ICR 489.

25.9.9 Witnesses

Both parties can call witnesses and the tribunal can order a witness to attend and to produce relevant documents.[86] Application for a witness order is made by letter to the secretary of the tribunals, summarising, in brief, the nature of the evidence to be given by the witness, explaining why it is relevant and giving reasons why the witness may not otherwise attend. Failure to attend is punishable by a fine of up to £200.

25.9.10 Interlocutory hearings and directions hearings

An interlocutory hearing may take place, on the application of either party or on the initiative of the tribunal, on procedural matters. Any application for an interlocutory hearing should be made to the secretary of the tribunals setting out the grounds for the application.

Such hearings are increasingly common in discrimination cases and the IT will deal with particulars, discovery, further questionnaires, listing of the case, whether witness statements are to be served in advance and any other matters that may need to be resolved.

Failure to comply with an interlocutory order for further and better particulars or discovery may lead to part or all of the IT1 or IT3 being struck out. Appeal against interlocutory orders lies to the EAT, though such appeals will succeed only if the IT made an error of law or no reasonable tribunal could have made the decision.

25.9.11 Pre-hearing review

A tribunal has a discretion, either on the application of a party or of its own motion, to hold a pre-hearing review to determine whether the application or arguments of either party have any chance of success. Notice must be given to the parties. Both parties can make written and oral representations to summarise their case. If the tribunal considers that the arguments of either party have no reasonable prospect of success it may require a deposit of up to £150 from that party as a condition of proceeding further or it may issue a costs warning.[87] The deposit will be used as security against costs being awarded to the other party.

86 IT Regs Sch 1 r4(2)(b).
87 Industrial Tribunals Act 1996 s9.

25.9.12 Restricted reporting orders

Where a case involves allegations of sexual misconduct such as sexual harassment the IT can make a 'restricted reporting order'.[88] A similar order can be made in DDA cases involving evidence of a personal nature.[89] The order will name those who cannot be identified. An application must be made by one or both parties; the tribunal must give the parties an opportunity to advance oral arguments and must consider whether such an order is in the public interest.[90] Unfortunately, the order remains in force only until the decision is delivered, then the media can publish.

However, if there are allegations of a sexual offence having been committed the IT must omit or delete from the register any material which might 'lead members of the public to identify any person affected by or making such an allegation'.[91]

The EAT does not have similar powers. It can only make a restricted reporting order in cases where the granting or refusal of a restricted reporting order is the subject of the appeal or where there is an appeal on an interlocutory matter in proceedings which are already subject to such an order.[92]

25.10 After the hearing – all claims

Full written reasons must be given in all cases arising out of the discrimination legislation.[93] In *Hampson v DES*[94] the CA said that the IT must 'give reasons sufficient to explain to the parties why they have won or lost'.

25.10.1 Review of decisions

There is a right of review if:

- the decision was wrongly made because of an error on the part of the tribunal staff;

88 Ibid, s11; IT Regs Sch 1 r14(1).
89 DDA s62; IT Regs Sch 1 r14(1A).
90 *X v Z Ltd* (1997) *Times* 18 April.
91 IT Regs Sch 1 r13(6).
92 Industrial Tribunals Act 1996 ss31 and 32; see also *In re A v B ex p News Group Newspapers* (1997) *Times* 27 June, EAT.
93 Ibid, Sch 1 r10(4).
94 [1989] IRLR 69.

- a party did not receive notice of the proceedings leading to the decision;
- the decision was made in the absence of a party or person entitled to be heard;
- new evidence has become available since the conclusion of the hearing and its existence could not have been reasonably known or foreseen at the time of the original hearing;
- the interests of justice require such a review.[95]

In *Wileman v Minilec Engineering Ltd*,[96] the EAT said that the test for admitting fresh evidence was that first, the evidence could not have been obtained with reasonable diligence for use at the hearing; second, the evidence would probably have an important influence on the result of the case; third, the evidence must be apparently credible.

If an application is made to review a decision, the tribunal must first consider if there are grounds for a review. If there are grounds, then there must be a new hearing.

Application must be made within 14 days of the date on which the decision was sent to the parties.

25.10.2 Right of appeal

There is a right of appeal, within 42 days of receiving the IT decision, to the EAT. The EAT cannot interfere with a finding of fact, unless it is perverse.

25.11 Judicial review against public bodies

Where a local authority or other public body adopts a policy which is in breach of the SDA, RRA, DDA, EqPA or European law it may, in some circumstances, be possible for the applicant to bring proceedings for judicial review seeking an order that the policy is unlawful (a declaration), quashing the decision (certiorari) or an order forcing the authority to take specified action (mandamus). Such proceedings must be brought as soon as possible or within at most three months of the act or decision complained of. The action can be brought by any 'person with sufficient interest', which can be any individual affected by the decision,[97] a union or a public body with an interest in

95 IT Regs Sch 1 r10.

96 [1988] IRLR 144.

97 See *R v Secretary of State for Employment ex p Seymour Smith and Another*; judgment 13 March 1997.

the subject matter of the complaint.[98] Proceedings are commenced by issuing a Form 86A with an accompanying affidavit in the High Court.

In *R v LB Hammersmith ex p NALGO*,[99] the High Court held that if a public authority proposes to embark on an employment or redeployment policy which is in breach of the SDA or RRA or is otherwise unlawful, the public law remedies should be available to the unions and employees affected. In this case, the union argued that various redundancy criteria adopted by the council, such as attendance records, work performance indicators, 'last in first out', were discriminatory. The High Court held that the most that could be said on the available evidence was that the implementation of the policy might offend the law in individual cases, depending on how the implementation were carried out. Thus, the allegations of discrimination could be tested only on a case-by-case basis in an IT. However, if the policy had, for example, been to make part-timers redundant first, there would have been a much stronger case for arguing that the policy was unlawful *per se*.[100]

TRIBUNAL PROCEDURE FOR DISCRIMINATION CASES: KEY POINTS

- Complaints under the SDA, RRA and DDA are made to an IT, with appeals to the EAT, then the CA and, finally, the HL. Any of the above can refer a point of EC sex discrimination law to the ECJ. There are time limits for applying and appealing. Legal aid or advice and assistance may be available. The EOC and CRE can give advice or assistance.
- Access to information is crucial and may be obtained:
  - from censuses, publications and organisations (statistics);
  - through the questionnaire process under the SDA, RRA and DDA;
  - by requesting further and better particulars;
  - through discovery.
- Under the SDA, RRA and DDA the application must be made within three months of the discrimination taking place. Note:

98 *R v Secretary of State for Employment ex p EOC* [1994] ICR 317; [1994] IRLR 176.

99 [1991] IRLR 249.

100 See *R v Secretary of State for Employment ex p EOC* (n98).

  - if the discrimination is continuing, the limit runs from when the discrimination stopped;
  - if the discrimination relates to a term in a contract, the act is treated as extending throughout the duration of the contract;
  - a deliberate omission is treated as done when the person decided upon it.
- Other points on time limits:
  - under EC law the national time limits apply;
  - a court or tribunal can consider a case which is out of time if it is just and equitable (SDA, RRA and DDA only).
- Procedure for cases under SDA, RRA and DDA:
  - application is on form IT1 (or letter) setting out specified information;
  - the IT1 can be amended subsequently with the leave of the IT;
  - the employer must reply within 21 days – on form IT3;
  - a copy of the complaint will be sent to an ACAS conciliation officer;
  - either party can ask for further and better particulars;
  - either party (or the IT) can ask for discovery of the other side's documents where relevant;
  - a further questionnaire may be submitted by the applicant with the leave of the IT;
  - an IT can strike out an IT1 or IT3 if it is scandalous, frivolous or vexatious;
  - a preliminary hearing will take place if there is a dispute over the IT's jurisdiction;
  - cases can be consolidated where there is a common question of law or fact or it is desirable;
  - interlocutory hearings may take place on procedural matters;
  - the IT has a discretion to hold a pre-hearing review to determine whether the arguments of either party have any chance of success and a deposit may be required;
  - both parties can call witnesses who may be ordered to attend by the IT.
- After the hearing (all claims):
  - full written reasons must be given for the decision;
  - there is a right to a review in specified circumstances, such as the availability of new evidence;

  - there is a right of appeal (on a question of law only) to the EAT within 42 days of the decision.
- Judicial review against public bodies for adopting a policy in breach of the SDA, RRA, DDA, EqPA or EC law is an alternative approach which may be effective in some circumstances.

CHAPTER 26

Remedies

Remedies under the discrimination legislation are different from those under the ERA. However, the aim of any order under either provision is to make good the loss suffered by the complainant and as far as possible put him/her in the same position that s/he would have been in had the discrimination not occurred.

ITs can consider the question of remedies at the end of the liability hearing. Alternatively, they can make a decision on liability and then leave the applicant to apply for a remedies hearing if it is needed (ie, if the parties have been unable to agree a settlement). A separate liability hearing can mean further delays before the applicant gets his/her money. On the other hand it can provide an opportunity to call expert evidence on loss (eg, from an actuary in relation to pension loss or a doctor). Applicants should be ready to provide evidence about their loss at the liability hearing.

26.1 Tribunal orders in discrimination cases

Winning a case under the SDA, RRA, DDA or EqPA does not necessarily mean that the applicant gets precisely what s/he wants – a job, promotion or training. It does, however, generally mean that in indirect discrimination cases the discriminatory practice will be declared unlawful and this can have enormous implications for others who have suffered as a result of the practice. There are three remedies, a declaration, a recommendation and/or compensation. The tribunal shall make such order as 'it considers just and equitable'.

26.1.1 A declaration of rights

This is a statement declaring the rights of the complainant and respondent.[1] Its purpose is to acknowledge that the applicant has

1 SDA s65(1)(a); RRA s56(1)(a); DDA s8(2)(a).

suffered unlawful discrimination. If the respondent ignores the declaration it may lead to the EOC or CRE deciding to carry out an investigation or bringing proceedings to stop persistent discrimination (see **27.1**). A declaration can be made as well as a recommendation and order for compensation.

26.1.2 A recommendation

This is a recommendation that the employer take certain action to obviate or reduce the adverse effect of the discrimination on the applicant.[2] The focus of the recommendation must be the applicant although it may have implications for other employees. The tribunal cannot recommend changes in practices unless they affect the applicant him/herself.[3] The recommendation must give a time limit within which the relevant action must be taken.[4]

Tribunals have made various recommendations:

- In *Price v CSC (No 2)*[5] (see **10.7**), the tribunal recommended that the employer and the union try to agree an appropriate upper age limit within a specified time limit.
- In *Steel v The Post Office (No 2)*[6] (see **11.5.3.2**), the tribunal recommended that the Post Office backdate the applicant's seniority to the time when, if she had not been a woman, she would have been entitled to become a permanent postwoman.
- In *Bayoomi v British Railways Board*[7] (see **11.4.5**), the tribunal recommended that if a reference were required, it should be noted that, 'Mr Bayoomi left the Board's employment in circumstances which reflected no discredit on him, and which were later held by an Industrial Tribunal to amount to discrimination'. No other recommendation was appropriate because Mr Bayoomi had found another job by the time the decision was made.
- In *Hicks v North Yorkshire CC*,[8] the IT recommended that a full-time teacher be allowed to return on a part-time basis after maternity leave and with a pro-rata salary.

2 SDA s65(1)(c); RRA s56(1)(c); DDA s 8(2)(c).
3 *Ministry of Defence v Jeremiah* [1979] IRLR 436; *Bayoomi v British Railways Board* [1981] IRLR 431.
4 *Prestcold v Irvine* [1980] IRLR 267.
5 [1978] IRLR 3.
6 [1978] IRLR 198.
7 [1981] IRLR 431.
8 COIT 1643/117.

- In *Campbell v Datum Engineering Co Ltd*[9] the IT recommended that the company obtain the CRE's Code of Practice and give the appropriate training to all managers and employees, introduce a formal racial harassment procedure and review the pay system to eradicate small anomalies and differentials.

In a case of harassment the IT might recommend that action is taken to move or discipline the harasser provided it was intended to protect the applicant and prevent repetition (see **13.6.1** and **13.6.2**).

26.1.2.1 Can a recommendation include re-instatement or re-engagement?

In *Noone v North West Thames Regional Health Authority (No 2)*,[10] the CA refused to uphold a tribunal recommendation that a woman who had suffered race discrimination with respect to an appointment as consultant microbiologist, should be offered the next available post. The respondent health authority would have had to seek the Secretary of State's authorisation to dispense with its statutory obligations to advertise its next vacancy, and this, said the CA, would 'set at nought the statutory procedure set out for the benefit of the National Health Service ... for making that particular consultant appointment'. The court substituted the more limited recommendation offered by the authority to the effect that the appointment committee would have drawn to its attention the fact that the candidate's previous application failed because of racial discrimination. It is not clear to what extent the statutory provisions influenced the CA and whether, without them, the court would have upheld a recommendation that a victim of discrimination be offered the next available post.

In *British Gas v Sharma*[11] the EAT held that an IT cannot recommend that employers promote a successful complainant to the next available vacancy as this would involve not considering other applicants who might have superior qualifications. Arguably, this is wrong as the purpose of the recommendation is to put the applicant, as far as possible, in the same position that s/he would have been in had s/he not been subjected to discrimination. If the tribunal takes the view that, but for the discrimination, the job applicant would have got the job then it should follow that the appropriate remedy is to award him/her the next suitable job. However, there is a distinction between getting the job that was applied for and getting another later job.

9 (1995) 24 EOR DCLD.
10 [1988] IRLR 530.
11 [1991] IRLR 101.

26.1.2.2 Failure to comply with the recommendation.

If the employer does not comply with the recommendation, the tribunal can either make an order for compensation (if one was not originally made)[12] or increase the compensation.[13] No compensation can be awarded if there was no power to make such an award in the first place; so that failure to comply with a recommendation arising out of unintentional indirect race discrimination where no compensation is awarded attracts no financial penalty (see **26.1.7**). It may however, lead to intervention by the CRE (see **27.1**).

Some delay in complying with the recommendation may be allowed where there are practical difficulties in carrying it out immediately.[14]

The CA have held that a tribunal cannot recommend that the applicant's pay be increased (unless this is the effect of an equality clause); this is a matter for compensation.[15]

26.1.3 Compensation for loss of earnings and benefits

Compensation is intended to reimburse the applicant for the loss that s/he has suffered; for injury to feelings see **26.1.4**. Under the SDA, RRA and DDA, an order can be made requiring the respondent to pay the complainant damages which could have been awarded in the county court.[16] The amount is unlimited.[17] Compensation can be awarded in cases of indirect race discrimination unless the employer can show that it was unintentional (see **26.1.7**). Both the EOC and CRE publish lists of recent awards in discrimination cases which are useful to refer to in an IT remedies hearing.

Compensation can be awarded for:

a) loss of earnings up to the date of the hearing;
b) loss of future earnings (if, for example, the applicant was unlawfully refused a job or promotion or was dismissed); where an applicant had a one-third chance of getting promoted, one-third the salary differential projected over the period it is likely to take to achieve promotion;[18] where an applicant had half a chance of

12 SDA s65(3)(b); RRA s56(4)(b); DDA s8(5)(b).
13 SDA s65(3)(a); RRA s56(4)(a); DDA s8(5)(a).
14 *Nelson and Another v Tyne & Wear Passenger Transport Executive* [1978] ICR 1183.
15 *Prestcold v Irvine* [1981] ICR 777; [1980] IRLR 267.
16 SDA s65(1)(b); RRA s56(1)(b); DDA s8(2)(b) and s8(3).
17 Sex Discrimination and Equal Pay (Remedies) Regulations 1993 SI No 2798 and the Race Relations (Remedies) Act 1994.
18 *Woodcock v Boots the Chemist* Case no 29586/76.

getting a job, had there been no discrimination, the loss was estimated over a two-year period and halved;[19]

c) lost wages in new job if the wages are lower than in his/her previous job; this can be continued for a 'reasonable' period until the wages of the new job are likely to reach the same level as they were in the previous job;
d) value of pension benefits lost (it may be worth getting an actuary to give evidence of this);[20]
e) loss of the value of any benefit, such as a bonus, company car or insurance; and
f) any other quantifiable loss arising out of the unlawful act, such as out-of-pocket expenses in looking for alternative work.

Compensation for loss of earnings may be assessed as continuing for a considerable period of time but they will not be indefinite. The IT will assess how long it is likely to take the applicant to get a job. Evidence can be called on the state of the relevant job market. In some of the Ministry of Defence cases sums in excess of £100,000 were awarded. In *Chan v LB Hackney*[21] Mr Chan was awarded £45,874 loss of earnings together with £23,890 in respect of future loss of earnings and £19,200 in respect of loss of pension rights.

Where discrimination has been proved, but the applicant would not have been given the job or promotion in any event for other non-discriminatory reasons, the damages are likely to be restricted to compensation for injury to feelings and expenses. However, if the IT finds that there was a chance of success rather than a certainty, the compensation for lost wages will be assessed to reflect that chance.

The CA has said that compensation should be awarded for foreseeable damage arising directly from an unlawful act of discrimination.[22] A claim will therefore cover any pecuniary loss attributable to an unlawful act of discrimination.[23] If the employer has already made a payment in respect of the damages s/he has suffered the IT will take this into account.[24] In calculating a mother's loss of earnings (or

19 *Bentham v North East Regional Airport* COIT 903/132.

20 *Ministry of Defence v Mutton* [1996] ICR 590. Note that since the limit on compensation in discrimination cases has been removed, the guidance given to IT chairs on assessment of loss on pension rights may no longer be valid. ITs should assess the *actual* loss.

21 (1997) 31 EOR DCLD.

22 *Coleman v Skyrail Oceanic Ltd* [1981] ICR 864; [1981] IRLR 398.

23 See also *Stone v Hills of London Ltd* (1984) EAT 12/83.

24 This excludes any redundancy payment which can be offset only against a basic award.

father's if he has had primary care of the children) the child care costs that she would have had to incur should be set off against her loss of earnings.[25]

It is often useful to produce for the IT a schedule, or list, of damages setting out the losses incurred as a result of the discrimination.

For special considerations in pregnancy dismissal cases, see Palmer *Maternity Rights* (LAG, 1996).

26.1.3.1 Duty to mitigate

The applicant is under a duty to mitigate his/her loss and although the burden is on the respondents to show failure to mitigate all records of attempts to find another job should be kept. Applicants should keep a diary in which to record jobs applied for, interviews attended and the costs incurred in looking for work.

26.1.4 Compensation for injury to feelings

In cases of direct sex and race discrimination, disability discrimination, indirect sex discrimination and indirect race discrimination which is intentional, awards for 'injury to feelings' may also be awarded (see **26.1.7**).[26]

An award of injury to feelings is not made automatically in a discrimination case,[27] however, the EAT has said 'in our view, it is almost inevitable in sex discrimination cases that a claim for hurt feelings be made'.[28] The same would apply to race discrimination or disability discrimination cases.

In *Alexander v Home Office*[29] the applicant alleged that he had not been permitted to work in the prison kitchens on grounds of his race. The CA said that his injury to feelings must have resulted from knowledge of the discrimination. The CA distinguished defamation cases, saying that in such cases the principal injury is to the plaintiff's reputation and it is doubtful whether this will play a large part in discrimination cases. On the other hand, the court continued, if the plaintiff knew of the racial discrimination and so had been held up to 'hatred, ridicule or contempt', then the injury to his/her feelings

25 *Ministry of Defence v Cannock* [1994] ICR 918; [1994] IRLR 509.
26 SDA s66(4); RRA s57(4); DDA s8(4).
27 See *MOD v Sullivan* EAT/159/93 and *MOD v Cannock* [1994] IRLR 509.
28 *Murray v Powertech (Scotland) Ltd* [1992] IRLR 257.
29 [1988] IRLR 190.

will be an important element in the damages. The court said that awards should not be minimal nor should they be excessive.

In *Hurley v Mustoe (No 2)*,[30] an IT awarded Ms Hurley 50p for injury to feelings after she had been refused employment because she had children. The IT took into account the fact that she had taken part in demonstrations outside the respondent's restaurants. The EAT, on appeal, overruled this decision and held that the existence of demonstrations and the complainant's presence at them had no relevance to the issue of compensation except insofar as they showed the degree of her hurt feelings. The choice of order to be made should be what was just and equitable. The amount of damages should then be awarded on the basis of what damages would be recoverable in a county court. This should include all reasonably foreseeable loss arising from the discrimination.

In the case of *Chan v LB Hackney*[31] the IT awarded a council officer £25,000 injury to feelings after he was forced to take medical retirement after months of being put under pressure because his 'face did not fit'.

Higher awards for injury to feelings are often made in sexual and/or racial harassment cases. In *ARG Armitage, Marsden and H M Prison Service v Johnson*[32] the IT awarded £21,000 for injury to feelings to an Afro-Caribbean prison officer who had suffered serious racial harassment over a long period. The EAT held that although the award was high it was not out of line with Elton John's Court of Appeal award of £25,000 in a defamation action for injury to reputation. It held that the relevant principles to be considered in assessing awards for injury to feelings were:

a) awards for injury to feelings are compensatory, they should compensate fully without punishing the wrongdoer;
b) awards should not be too low as this would diminish respect for the anti-discrimination laws. Nor should they be too high so that they are seen as untaxed riches;
c) awards should bear some similarity to the range of awards in personal injury cases;
d) tribunals should bear in mind the value in everyday life of the sums they are awarding;
e) tribunals should bear in mind the need for public respect for the level of awards made.

30 [1983] ICR 422.
31 (1997) 31 EOR DCLD; COIT case no 40002/92.
32 [1997] IRLR 162.

The IT takes account of the degree of upset suffered by the applicant, so that if the harassment is seen only as a 'minor irritation', compensation will be nominal.[33] If the applicant has lost his/her job, an award for injury to feelings may include a sum for loss of congenial employment.[34] In cases of harassment involving loss of liberty a comparison might be made with cases of false imprisonment.[35]

The appeal courts are reluctant to interfere with awards for injury to feelings, and the CA has said that the EAT should interfere with an award for damages only if the award 'is so out of the normal run that it can properly be described as a wholly erroneous estimate of the damage'.[36]

In California[37] awards for injury to feelings are considered under the following headings:-

- feelings and emotions,
- personal integrity and dignity;
- mental well-being;
- capacity to work, earn and live a free life;
- good name;
- privacy;
- relationship with family including status as a parent or spouse;
- access to job and ability to associate with co-workers and peers;
- professional future; and
- standing in the community.

Advisers may find it useful to collect evidence under these headings when applying for awards for injury to feelings.

Applicants wanting to claim for injury to feelings *must* produce evidence of the injury to their feelings if they are to get an award. It can be helpful to get evidence of this, ie doctors or other health professionals could write a report and in serious cases a psychiatrist's report can be very helpful.[38] Friends and colleagues at work could also give evidence of an applicant's reaction to discrimination.

33 *Wileman v Minilec Engineering Ltd* [1988] IRLR 144.

34 *Ministry of Defence v Cannock* [1994] ICR 918; [1994] IRLR 509.

35 See, eg, *Thompson and Hsu v Commissioner for Police* (1997) *Times* 20 February.

36 See *North West Thames Regional Health Authority v Noone* [1988] ICR 813; [1988] IRLR 530.

37 See A Thomas, *Minimum Justice: resolving claims of racial discrimination in Great Britain and the United States of America* (Wellingborough District Racial Equality Council, 1991).

38 Organisations such as the EOC, CRE and WASH may be able to provide names of psychiatrists willing to prepare such report.

26.1.5 Aggravated damages

Aggravated damages may, and in some cases should, be awarded where the defendant has behaved in a high-handed, malicious, insulting or oppressive manner in committing the act of discrimination.[39] These damages are in effect for injury to feelings which are 'justifiably heightened by the manner in which or motive for which the defendant did it'.[40] In *Bradford City MC v Arora*,[41] the EAT said that, in considering an award of aggravated damages, an IT is entitled to take into account unsatisfactory answers to a questionnaire. The applicant was awarded £2,000 including aggravated damages. In *ARG Armitage, Marsden and the H M Prison Service v Johnson* (above) the applicant was awarded £7,500 aggravated damages because the employer's investigation of his grievances only served to inflame the injury to his feelings as the employer said that the complainant thought that all white people were racists and blamed his problems on non-existent discrimination. The EAT went on to say that awards of aggravated damages can be mitigated by an apology.

In *Bamber v Fuji International Finance plc*[42] the IT awarded £20,000 in aggravated damages to reflect the way in which the employers had conducted the case and their attack on the honesty and integrity of the applicant. In the *Chan* case (above) the IT awarded £5,000 aggravated damages to reflect the council's failure to investigate the serious complaints made to it and its insistence that he drop his grievance proceedings and take medical retirement.

These cases highlight the importance of employers operating a proper grievance procedure that undertakes a full and unbiased investigation into employees' complaints and, if appropriate, offers a full and complete apology when wrongdoing has been found.

26.1.6 Exemplary damages

Exemplary damages are no longer available in ordinary discrimination cases.[43] However, since exemplary damages are intended to be punitive and the ECJ in *Marshall (No 2)*[44] held that damages must

39 *Alexander v Home Office* (n29 above).

40 Lord Reid in *Cassell v Broome* [1972] 1 All ER 801.

41 [1991] ICR 226.

42 COIT Case no 28081/94/LS.

43 See *Deane v LB Ealing* [1993] IRLR 209, following *AB v South West Water Services Ltd* [1993] QB 507.

44 *Marshall v Southampton and South-West Hampshire Area Health Authority (No 2)* [1993] IRLR 445, ECJ.

have a 'real deterrent effect' on the employer, it is open to argument that in sex discrimination cases this may be contrary to EC law. Moreover, the ECJ ruled in *Factortame* that, if a public authority acts oppressively, arbitrarily or unconstitutionally in respect of EC law rights, exemplary damages may be payable.[45]

26.1.7 Unintentional indirect race discrimination

Compensation is payable in cases of indirect race discrimination unless the employer can show that the discrimination was unintentional.[46] This bar on compensation should be restricted to those cases where the respondent did not intend to discriminate *and* did not appreciate the discriminatory effect of the requirement or condition.

In *J H Walker Ltd v Hussain*[47] the employer introduced a rule that holidays could not be taken at certain times, which included the period when the Muslim festival of Eid fell. Many of the workforce were Muslims and in previous years had been allowed to take holiday on Eid. The workers asked to have the day's holiday and offered to make up the work at other times. The employer refused. Some workers took holiday anyway and consequently were given final warnings. They complained of indirect race discrimination and were awarded £1,000 each for injury to feelings. The EAT held that intentional indirect discrimination occurs when the employer does the relevant act knowing that it will adversely affect a particular minority. The company knew that Eid was important to its employees who were of Asian origin, and were the only group of employees adversely affected by the requirement not to take holiday at that time.

26.1.8 Interest payable on discrimination awards

Interest is payable on injury to feelings awards from the date of the discriminatory act to the date of the decision and on other compensatory awards from a date midway between the date of the discrimination and the date of the decision.[48] Where there are 'exceptional circumstances' relating to the case or the award which mean that a

45 See *R v Secretary of State ex p Factortame Ltd* [1996] IRLR 267 at paras 89–90.

46 RRA s57(3).

47 [1996] IRLR 11.

48 Industrial Tribunal (Interest on Awards in Discrimination Cases) Regulations 1996 SI No 2803.

serious injustice would be caused then interest may be awarded for a different period.

Interest is payable on discrimination awards from the day after the decision until it is paid, although no interest is payable if the award is paid in full within 14 days of the decision.[49] No interest is payable on future losses.

26.1.9 Recoupment

The state will recoup certain social security benefits paid to unfairly dismissed employees who are awarded compensation,[50] however, these provisions do not apply to discrimination awards. It may therefore be beneficial to ensure that awards are made under the discrimination provisions rather than under the ERA where possible.

26.1.10 Compensation under EC law

The ECJ has ruled[51] that member states are required to adopt measures which are sufficiently effective to achieve the objective of directives and that:

> . . . while the Equal Treatment Directive did not require a specific form of sanction for breach of the prohibition on discrimination, it nonetheless implied that the sanction had to be of such a nature as to ensure real and effective protection. It also had to have actual dissuasive effect on the employer . . . National legislation which limited the rights of persons discriminated against in access to employment to a purely symbolic sum, such as reimbursement of the costs incurred in applying, was incompatible with the requirement to implement the Directive effectively in national law.

As UK law has to be interpreted in such a way as to give effect to EC provisions it may be worth referring to this in sex discrimination cases.

26.2 Tribunal orders in dismissal cases

In the case of an unfair dismissal, the tribunal can award compensation consisting of:

- a basic award;
- a compensatory award;

49 Industrial Tribunals (Interest) Order 1991 SI No 479 reg 10(a).
50 See Kibling & Lewis *Employment Law* (LAG, 3rd edn, 1996), p220.
51 *Von Colson v Land Nordrhein-Westfalen* [1984] ECR 1891.

- a special award where the dismissal is related to trade union membership;
- an additional award if the employer does not comply with an order for reinstatement or re-engagement (see below).

A basic award consists of:

- half a week's gross pay for the each of the years worked while under the age of 22;
- one week's gross pay for the years in which the worker was between the ages of 22 and 40;
- one-and-a-half weeks' gross pay for each year of employment when the employee was 41 years old or more, until s/he reaches 65 years.

The week's pay is subject to a maximum limit of £210 gross per week (as at 1 April 1997) and 20 years' calculable continuous service. The award may be reduced on the ground of the worker's conduct, or if the worker unreasonably refuses an offer of reinstatement or receives a redundancy or *ex gratia* payment. The award will also be reduced by each month of service over the age of 64 years.

The compensatory award is an amount which the tribunal considers just and equitable having regard to the loss suffered, including any expenses reasonably incurred and loss of any benefit. This will include immediate loss of wages (up to the hearing date), future loss of wages, loss of statutory protection in respect of unfair dismissal (about £200) and loss of pension rights. The applicant must provide evidence of the loss. The award may be reduced if the employee has contributed to the dismissal, or has failed to take steps to mitigate the loss (by, for example, seeking another job). State benefits (income support and jobseekers' allowance) actually received by the employee are deducted from the award under the recoupment regulations (see **26.1.9**) unless a settlement is made out of court. Under the ERA there is no power to make an award for injury to feelings.

The maximum amount that can be awarded for the unfair dismissal compensatory award is £11,300 (as at 1 April 1997).

26.2.1 Reinstatement and re-engagement

These remedies are available only in cases of unfair dismissal under ERA s94. Reinstatement is where the complainant is given his/her job back and re-engagement where s/he is re-employed but not in the same job.[52] When deciding whether to make such an order the IT must

52 ERA ss113 to 115.

consider whether it would be practicable for the employer to comply with it and, where the employee has contributed to his/her dismissal, whether it would be just. If the employer refuses to reinstate or re-engage a complainant after an order to do so, an additional award of compensation can be made. This is in addition to the maximum award of £11,300 and is between 13 and 26 weeks' pay. This additional award is higher in sex and race discrimination cases when it can be between 26 and 52 weeks' pay.[53]

26.2.2 Interest on compensation

If compensation for unfair dismissal is not paid within 42 days of the order, interest is payable.[54]

If there is a finding that a dismissal is unlawful discrimination on the ground of race or sex or related to disability the overall compensation will not be limited. It is always advisable to claim under both the ERA and the relevant discrimination Act/s. Of course, compensation will not be awarded twice for the same loss, just because it is found to be a result of both an unfair dismissal and a discriminatory dismissal.

26.2.3 Costs

Costs are not normally awarded in the IT unless one of the parties has acted frivolously, vexatiously, abusively, disruptively or otherwise unreasonably in bringing or conducting the proceedings.[55] Thus, costs may be awarded if a party either knew or should have known that s/he was bound to fail or if the case was pursued out of malice.[56]

A costs order is not punitive, it is intended to compensate for the extra costs incurred as a result of the way in which one of the parties brought or conducted the proceedings.[57]

In *Bamber v Fuji International Finance plc*[58] costs were ordered against the respondent on an indemnity basis. The IT described the case as 'exceptional' and found that there was an intention 'to embarrass, intimidate and deter the Applicant from pursuing the case'.

53 ERA s117(5).
54 Industrial Tribunals (Interest) Order 1991 SI No 479.
55 IT Regs Sch 1 r12.
56 *E T Marler Ltd v Robertson* [1974] ICR 72.
57 *Davidson v John Calder (Publishers) Ltd and Calder Education Trust Ltd* [1985] ICR 143; [1985] IRLR 97.
58 COIT Case no 28081/94/LS.

Comparison of major differences between the remedies for unfair dismissal and discrimination	
DISCRIMINATION	*UNFAIR DISMISSAL*
No basic award	Basic award
Compensation unlimited and not subject to recoupment.	Compensatory award limited and subject to recoupment of state benefits received.
Extra compensation award for injury to feelings.	No compensation for injury to feelings.
Recommendation which may include re-employment. Extra award may be made in default.	Order for reinstatement or re-engagement enforceable by extra compensation.
Interest assessed as part of decision.	If award not paid within 42 days interest becomes due.
Declaration.	

The threat of an application for costs is far too frequently made in the course of preparing for a hearing. Advisers should bear in mind that such orders are rarely made in practice.

26.3 Orders under the EqPA

Once the tribunal has found that a woman is doing like work, work rated as equivalent or work of equal value with a man, then an 'equality clause' is automatically inserted into her contract giving her the same pay and other contractual terms as the man. A maximum of two years' back-pay can be awarded under the EqPA. Under EC law the member state's rules as to remedies apply providing they are not less favourable than those that apply to similar claims. The clearest parallel to an equal pay case would be a claim for damages for breach of contract; such claims can be backdated for six years. Hence the two-year limitation for back-pay in equal pay claims appears to be in breach of art 119. A reference has been made to the ECJ to determine this point.[59]

Costs may also be awarded on the same basis as above.

59 *Levez v T H Jennings* [1996] IRLR 499.

26.4 Taxation on awards and settlements

The way in which tribunal awards or settlements are taxed will depend on the nature of the payment.

26.4.1 Industrial tribunal awards

- Basic award or redundancy payment: this is tax-free.
- Compensatory awards: tax is taken into account in assessing the amount of the award and so it is received tax-free.[60]
- In discrimination cases, awards of injury to feelings: arguably, these are akin to personal injury awards of damages and should not be taxable.[61]

26.4.2 Settlements

Money received as a settlement for loss of, or change in, office or employment, including any statutory redundancy payment or basic award, up to the value of £30,000 is not taxable.[62] Sums in excess of this are taxable.

Payments made in respect of a contractual obligation, eg, notice payments, unpaid wages, loss of earnings or commission, holiday pay are taxable as income received from the job. Payments in respect of injury to feelings are, arguably, akin to personal injury awards of damages and should not be taxable.

It may be important in drawing up a settlement to specify how much of the money being paid is attributable to which heading, so that it is easy to ascertain how much is taxable.

REMEDIES: KEY POINTS

- An IT can make the following orders under the SDA, RRA and DDA:
  - a declaration of the parties' rights (not enforceable);
  - an action recommendation;
  - unlimited compensation in the case of direct and indirect discrimination (but not unintentional indirect race discrimination) for loss of earnings, loss of the value of any

60 See *MOD v Mutton* [1996] ICR 590 at p605G.
61 See also *Mutton* (ibid).
62 Income and Corporation Taxes Act 1988 s148.

benefit, any other quantifiable loss arising out of the discrimination and injury to feelings.

- Compensation may include:
  - aggravated damages where the respondent has behaved in a high-handed, malicious, insulting or oppressive manner;
  - interest on compensation.
- Exemplary damages are not available.
- Under the ERA an IT can, for an unfair dismissal, order:
  - reinstatement;
  - re-engagement;
  - compensation consisting of a basic and a compensatory award (subject to a maximum);
  - an additional award for failure to comply with a re-employment order;
  - interest on compensation.
- Under the EqPA, an equality clause is automatically inserted into the applicant's contract once the IT has found that she is doing like or similar work, work rated as equivalent or work of equal value.
- Costs can be awarded in exceptional cases but this is rare.

CHAPTER 27

The Commissions

The RRA and the SDA set up two publicly funded bodies to enforce the law on discrimination. The CRE replaced the Race Relations Board which had been in existence since 1965, and the EOC was a new body. They have broadly the same statutory duties:

- to work towards the elimination of discrimination;
- to promote equality of opportunity (and, in the case of the CRE, good relations between persons of different racial groups);
- to keep under review the working of the Acts and, where necessary, submit proposals for amending them.[1]

The National Disability Council set up by the DDA does not have parallel powers to the EOC and CRE; its functions are limited to:

- providing advice to the Secretary of State on issues relating to disability discrimination and measures that could be taken to tackle it, and the operation of the DDA; and
- preparing Codes of Practice when requested to do so by the Secretary of State.[2]

The CRE and EOC are empowered by the legislation to carry out the same kinds of activities within their own fields. These are as follows:

a) to assist individuals making complaints[3] (see **28.4**);
b) to undertake or assist (financially or otherwise) others to carry out research or educational activities;[4]
c) in the case of the EOC, to review the discriminatory provisions in health and safety legislation and, where appropriate, propose amendments;[5]

1 SDA s53; RRA s43.
2 DDA ss50 to 52.
3 SDA s75; RRA s66.
4 SDA s54; RRA s45.
5 SDA s55.

d) to prepare annual reports about their activities;[6]
e) to issue codes of practice containing practical guidance to eliminate discrimination in employment and promote equality of opportunity;
f) in the case of the CRE, to give financial or other assistance to organisations concerned with the promotion of equality of opportunity and good relations between persons of different racial groups;[7]
g) to conduct formal investigations.[8] The purpose of investigations is to identify and root out widespread discrimination. This is an important strategic role of the Commissions (see **27.1**);
h) to take proceedings in respect of discriminatory practices.[9] This covers indirectly discriminatory practices. The Commissions can issue non-discrimination notices or apply for injunctions (see below). This allows action to be taken in respect of practices which are discriminatory but where there is no known victim, because, for example, the practice deters certain applicants from applying for a job;
i) to take proceedings in respect of discriminatory advertisements.[10] The provisions under the two Acts are slightly different: under the SDA it is not unlawful to publish an advertisement if the discrimination would not be unlawful, whereas under the RRA some, but not all, advertisements are unlawful even though the act itself is not unlawful (see **10.3**);
j) to take proceedings in cases where a person who has authority over another person instructs, procures or attempts to procure that other to do an unlawful act (see **27.2.2**).[11] This applies to acts which are unlawful under Part II of either Act (the employment provisions);
k) to take proceedings where one person induces or attempts to induce another to commit an unlawful act by providing or offering a benefit or subjecting or threatening to subject him/her to a detriment (see **27.2**). The offer or threat may be made

6 SDA s56; RRA s46.
7 RRA s44.
8 SDA ss57–61; RRA ss48–52.
9 SDA s37; RRA s28.
10 SDA s38; RRA s29. A discriminatory advertisement may be used as evidence in an individual IT case but if there is no 'victim' only the EOC or CRE can take proceedings.
11 SDA s39; RRA s30.

indirectly.[12] This applies to acts which are unlawful under Part II of either Act (the employment provisions).

In the last three cases (discriminatory advertisements, instructions to discriminate and pressure to discriminate) the Commissions have the power to enforce the provisions by making an application to an IT for an order that the act was unlawful or they can carry out a formal investigation. The tribunal may also, in certain circumstances, make a declaration or recommendation.[13] If a Commission believes that a person has done an unlawful act and, unless restrained, is likely to do further unlawful acts, the Commission may apply to a county court for an injunction restraining the person from doing such acts.[14]

27.1 Formal investigations

27.1.1 When can the CRE and EOC carry out an investigation?

In the UK it is not possible for an applicant to bring class actions whereby one person represents a group of people in the same situation (but see **25.3.3**). Thus enforcement of the SDA and RRA relies mainly on individuals bringing claims in tribunals. The only other way of dealing with discrimination is for the Commissions to use their investigatory powers. The CRE and EOC can carry out formal investigations for any of the purposes connected with its duties (see above).[15] They must carry out such an investigation if required to do so by the Secretary of State.

In *CRE v Home Office*,[16] the CRE's powers were discussed by the CA when the CRE wanted to investigate the Home Office's administration of the Immigration Act. The court said that this could not be done to eliminate discrimination as the CRE could investigate only discrimination outlawed by the RRA and discrimination in immigration laws was not prohibited. The court did, however, allow the investigation to continue, on the basis that it came within the CRE's duty to promote good relations between persons of different racial groups.

12 SDA s40; RRA s31.
13 SDA s73; RRA s62.
14 SDA s72; RRA s63.
15 SDA s57(1); RRA s48(1).
16 [1982] QB 385.

27.1.2 *What type of investigation can be carried out?*

The CRE and EOC can carry out two types of investigation:[17]

- a 'named-person' investigation: where the activities of a named individual or organisation are investigated; or
- a general investigation: where there are no allegations of discrimination against any particular individual.

27.1.3 *The procedure for carrying out an investigation*

27.1.3.1 Terms of reference

The Commission must draw up terms of reference for the investigation (unless the Secretary of State has required the investigation, in which case s/he shall do so).[18] Once the terms have been drawn up, the investigation must be confined to the terms unless they are subsequently revised.[19]

The Commissions must believe that discrimination has taken place if they are to investigate a named individual. They cannot conduct 'fishing expeditions'. In *LB Hillingdon v CRE,*[20] the CRE's powers were challenged when it wanted to investigate the allegations that the Hillingdon housing policy was racist. A white Rhodesian family which arrived at Heathrow was given accommodation by the council whereas an Asian family had been refused accommodation and had been deposited on the steps of the Foreign Office. The HL said that as the CRE believed only that there may have been discrimination against homeless families arriving at Heathrow it could not extend the investigation to all homeless families who applied to the council for rehousing; only those who had recently arrived in the UK would be covered. The Lords said that the CRE should not embark on a formal investigation unless it has reasonable grounds for believing that a named person might have done an unlawful act and those grounds are strong enough to warrant a probing investigation. The terms of reference should not be in wide, general words such as to enable an extensive search to be made over all the books and papers of the named person. In addition, the Commission should consider both sides of the story before deciding whether it has reasonable grounds for suspicion.

17 SDA s57; RRA s48.
18 SDA s58(2); RRA s49(2).
19 SDA s58(4); RRA s49(5). See also *CRE v Prestige plc* [1984] 1 WLR 335; [1984] ICR 473.
20 [1982] 3 WLR 159; [1982] IRLR 424.

27.1.3.2 Notice

The Commissions must give notice of the impending investigation.[21] In the case of a general investigation, general notice must be given to the public so that persons likely to be affected will see the notice. If, for example, the EOC intended to investigate redundancy practices in a particular industry, notice should be given to employers and employees in that industry.

In the case of a named-person investigation, if the Commission believes that a person may have carried out an unlawful act, it must inform that person of its belief and its proposal to investigate the act, and give the person an opportunity of making oral or written representations.[22] The Commission must hold a preliminary hearing if requested to do so at which the parties can be represented. This provision allows the individual to challenge any part of the investigation and may result in long delays. If at the end of the hearing the Commission decides that there are reasonable grounds for believing the named person has discriminated on the alleged grounds, the formal investigation will proceed (see *LB Hillingdon v CRE* above; there is, however, no right to be heard after the preliminary hearing, once the formal investigation has started).

27.1.3.3 Changing from a general to a named-person investigation

During a general investigation into the Prestige Group the CRE came across information which led it to suspect unlawful discrimination by named persons. The HL said that the CRE had to start the investigation again as it was not possible to switch from one type to another.[23]

27.1.3.4 Power to obtain information

Where the Commissions suspect that a person has unlawfully discriminated under the SDA or RRA or contravened EqPA ss37–40 or if the Secretary of State so authorises or if the purpose of the investigation is to monitor compliance with the requirements of a non-discrimination notice, the Commissions can require, by notice, any person to provide relevant information. The information may be written or oral and they may be required to produce documents relating to any matter contained in the notice.[24] The Commission can enforce

21 SDA s58(3); RRA s49(3).

22 SDA s58(3A); RRA s49(4).

23 See *CRE v Prestige plc* (n19 above).

24 SDA s59; RRA s50. The notice cannot require a person to produce information which s/he would not be required to produce in the High Court and attendance cannot be required unless travelling expenses are paid.

the notice by application to the county court. It is an offence not to comply with an order or to alter, suppress or conceal information or make false statements.

27.1.4 *Recommendations*

If the Commissions consider it necessary or expedient, they may make recommendations to any person that certain action be taken to promote equality of opportunity. They may also make recommendations to the Secretary of State.[25]

27.1.5 *Report*

In all cases the Commissions must prepare a report which must be available for inspection;[26] this need not be done as soon as the investigation is concluded,[27] but should be within a reasonable time.

27.1.6 *Restriction on disclosure of information*

The Commission must not disclose any information provided by any person for the purposes of an investigation unless that person consents, or in other limited circumstances.[28]

27.1.7 *Non-discrimination notices*

If the CRE or EOC finds that there has been discrimination in either a general or named-person investigation it can issue a non-discrimination notice.[29] The non-discrimination notice may:

- require the discriminator not to commit the specified unlawful acts; and
- if the above involves changes in his/her practices or other arrangements, require the employer to inform the Commissions of the changes that have been made and to take reasonable steps to inform persons affected by the changes;
- require the discriminator to provide the Commissions with other information necessary to verify that the notice has been complied with.

25 SDA s60(1); RRA s51(1).
26 SDA s60(2); RRA s51(2).
27 *CRE v Amari Plastics Ltd* [1982] All ER 499; [1982] IRLR 252.
28 SDA s61; RRA s52.
29 SDA s67; RRA s58.

The Commissions may enforce the above provisions by application to the county court for an order that the relevant information be provided[30] (see above).

27.1.7.1 Procedure

Before serving a non-discrimination notice the Commission must first:

- notify the person that it may serve the notice, giving the grounds for serving it; and
- give the person an opportunity to make oral or written representations within a period of not less than 28 days; and
- take account of such representations.

Any person served with a non-discrimination notice may, within six weeks, appeal to an IT against any requirement of the notice and the tribunal can vary or quash the requirement.[31] In some cases respondents have issued proceedings for judicial review.

In *CRE v Amari Plastics Ltd*,[32] the CA said that an appeal against the requirements of a non-discrimination notice is not limited to appealing against the terms of the requirements. All the findings of fact which led to the issuing of the notice are open for consideration. This effectively means that the investigation will be reopened from the beginning.

27.1.7.2 Enforcement of a non-discrimination notice

This may be done in three ways:

a) carrying out a further investigation to monitor compliance with a notice (which must be done within five years of the notice) the Commissions may require information in respect of the notice;[33]
b) obtaining a county court order to enforce the notice;
c) obtaining an injunction from the county court.

27.1.8 Injunctions

If, within the previous five years, a person has been served with a non-discrimination notice or has been found by a tribunal to have discriminated and the EOC or CRE believes that s/he will continue

30 SDA ss59 and 67(7); RRA ss50 and 57(7).
31 SDA s68; RRA s59.
32 See n27.
33 SDA s69; RRA s60.

to discriminate unless restrained, the Commission may apply to the county court for an injunction restraining that person from discriminating.[34] With a view to applying for an injunction, the EOC or CRE may itself make a complaint to an IT that a person has discriminated. If the complaint is upheld, the IT may make a declaration and/or recommendation, but not award compensation.

27.1.9 Conclusion

The powers of investigation given to the Commissions have not been very widely used and when they have been invoked have been subjected to close scrutiny by the courts. Lord Denning, in *CRE v Amari Plastics Ltd* (above) said he was sorry for the CRE because it had been caught up in a spider's web spun by Parliament from which there was little hope of escape, and that the machinery established by Parliament for formal investigations was so elaborate and cumbersome that it was in danger of grinding to a halt.

27.2 Pressure or instructions to discriminate

27.2.1 Pressure to discriminate

To apply pressure so as to induce a person to discriminate is unlawful. Under SDA s40(1) it is unlawful to persuade, or attempt to induce, a person to do any act which contravenes SDA Parts II or III (ie, to discriminate unlawfully) by 'providing or offering to provide him with a benefit or subjecting or threatening to subject him to any detriment'. Under the RRA, any inducement or attempted inducement is unlawful; there is no need to prove the offer of a benefit or threat of a detriment – a mere request to discriminate is sufficient (see *CRE v Imperial Society of Teachers of Dancing* (below)). These sections apply even if any threats or offers to induce the person to discriminate are made indirectly if they are 'made in such a way that he is likely to hear of it'.[35] Only the CRE and EOC can bring proceedings under these sections of the Acts.[36]

In *CRE v Powell and City of Birmingham DC*,[37] the EAT distinguished between the giving of information and inducing discrimination. A YTS development officer asked Mr Powell for

34 SDA s71; RRA s62.
35 RRA s30(1) and (2); SDA s40(1) and (2).
36 SDA s72; RRA s63.
37 7 EOR 31, EAT.

addresses of garages where a trainee mechanic could be placed. Mr Powell asked if the trainee was white and said that he knew of a garage but it had said that it would not take a black. The CRE brought a complaint alleging that Mr Powell had attempted to induce the development officer to discriminate by persuading him not to send a black trainee. The EAT said that 'induce' meant 'to persuade or to prevail upon or to bring about' and that whether the giving of information is an attempt to persuade is purely a question of fact, taking into account the intention of the parties. As Mr Powell had not attempted to persuade the development officer to do anything, but was only stating a fact, there was no pressure to discriminate.

Powell must be compared with *CRE v Imperial Society of Teachers of Dancing*,[38] where the EAT held that the respondents had induced discrimination when they told a school careers officer that they would rather she did not send any coloured person for a job vacancy because that person would feel out of place as there were no other coloured employees. In *Powell*, there was no evidence that Mr Powell had any desire to ensure that only white applicants were sent to the garage, nor was he the person with the power to make a decision about which trainee should be taken on by the garage. In the dancing school case, it was the potential employers who said that the school should not send a coloured person, making it quite clear that they wanted the careers officer to discriminate.

In *R v CRE ex p Westminster CC*,[39] the council wanted to employ a black man as a refuse collector, but it appeared that they had withdrawn the appointment after pressure from other members of the (all white) workforce, expressed through representatives of the union. The CRE initiated a formal investigation and as a result served non-discrimination notices on the council and the union branch chairman. The council challenged the notice through judicial review. The CA held that the decision not to employ the black man was made on racial grounds, even though management was motivated not by racial prejudice but by fear of industrial unrest.

The CRE code of practice restates the law and makes the following recommendations to avoid unlawful instructions and pressure to discriminate:

a) guidance should be given to all employees, particularly those in positions of authority or influence on the relevant provisions of the law;

38 [1983] ICR 491; [1983] IRLR 315.
39 [1985] ICR 827; [1985] IRLR 426.

b) decision-makers should be instructed not to give way to pressure to discriminate;
c) giving instructions or bringing pressure to discriminate should be treated as a disciplinary offence.

27.2.2 *Instructions to discriminate*

It is unlawful for a person who has authority over another person to instruct, procure or attempt to procure that person to discriminate unlawfully. There must be an existing relationship between the persons concerned and the person being instructed must be used to acting in accordance with the wishes of the person in authority (see *CRE v Imperial Society of Teachers of Dancing* above).

In *EOC v Bull t/a Arkwright's Night Club*[40] the nightclub asked the job centre to send only women applicants for a job as a receptionist. The job centre pointed out that this was unlawful. The respondent replied that he had neither the time nor the inclination to get involved 'in these ridiculous rules and regulations of the equal opportunities garbage'. The IT found that he had acted unlawfully.

If there is no victim, only the CRE or EOC can enforce these provisions.

27.3 Judicial review by the EOC and the CRE

Any person or body with a sufficient interest may apply for a judicial review and seek orders of certiorari, prohibition or mandamus.[41] In *R v Secretary of State for Employment ex p EOC and Another*,[42] the HL held that the EOC could seek a declaration also. The EOC challenged the Secretary of State, claiming that the statutory thresholds under the EPCA (now the ERA) were indirectly discriminatory and in breach of EC law. The House of Lords held:

- the actions of the Secretary of State were susceptible to judicial review;
- the EOC had sufficient interest, having regard to its statutory duties, to give it locus standi;
- since the main issue was whether the EPCA was lawful in requiring part-time employees to complete five years' continuous employ-

40 (1995) 24 EOR DCLD.
41 SDA s62; RRA s53.
42 [1994] ICR 317; [1994] IRLR 176.

ment to qualify for redundancy pay and not whether the treatment of the individual applicant had been discriminatory, and since the issues affected every part-time employee made redundant after less than five years' employment, it was appropriate that proceedings should be brought by judicial review;
- the directly enforceable EC rights which the EOC sought to enforce were rights under UK law as well as community law and the EOC was entitled to have them determined by the UK courts; and
- the court had power to make a declaration that these provisions of the EPCA were incompatible with EC law.

The CRE also has standing to bring judicial review proceedings.[43]

Judicial review is only available against public sector bodies, such as government departments, local authorities and health bodies, etc.

THE COMMISSIONS: KEY POINTS

- The CRE and EOC may:
  - assist individuals making a complaint;
  - undertake research;
  - take proceedings in respect of discriminatory practices;
  - take proceedings in respect of discriminatory advertisements;
  - take proceedings in respect of instructions or pressure to discriminate;
  - conduct formal investigations.
- Formal investigations can result in the Commission:
  - making a recommendation;
  - issuing a report;
  - issuing a non-discrimination notice.
- The National Disability Council does not have similar powers in respect of the interests of disabled people.
- Under the SDA it is unlawful to induce, or attempt to induce (directly or indirectly) a person to do an unlawful act by:
  - providing or offering to provide him/her with a benefit; or
  - subjecting or threatening to subject him/her to any detriment.
- Under the RRA any inducement or attempted inducement (made directly or indirectly) to carry out an unlawful act is unlawful, without further evidence.

43 See, eg, *R v Cleveland CC ex p CRE* (1992) 91 LGR 139.

- A distinction must be made between giving information (which is not unlawful) and inducing discrimination (which is unlawful).
- It is unlawful for a person who has authority over another person to instruct, procure or attempt to procure that person to discriminate unlawfully.
- If there is no victim, only the CRE or EOC can enforce these provisions.
- The Commissions do have locus standi to challenge the Secretary of State by way of judicial review.

CHAPTER 28

Financial help and legal advice

28.1 Legal aid

Legal aid does not cover representation at the IT. However, advice and assistance with the preparation of the case may be covered by the 'green form' scheme for those on a low income and with little capital. The equivalent of two hours' advice is available in the first instance but extensions may be obtained. There is no limit to the number of extensions. The test is whether it is reasonable to grant an extension, however, the Legal Aid Board has stated that it considers that the average IT discrimination case should take no longer than four hours to prepare and where there are complex legal issues or substantial documentation this could be extended by a further three to six hours. However, once the solicitor 'represents' an applicant this form of legal aid ceases to be available. This is activated once the solicitor puts his/her name as representative on the application form to the IT or in correspondence with the employer.

Legal aid is available (for those who come within the income and capital limits) for appeal to the EAT or to the higher courts, provided that the case has sufficient merit.

Generally, any money recovered as a result of the case goes to repay the Legal Aid Board up to the amount spent on legal costs. However, this will not apply to awards from the EAT nor to half of a redundancy payment.[1] This is known as the statutory charge and applies to both the green form scheme and full legal aid.

28.2 Unions

Unions sometimes provide legal help for complainants. Even if local branch officers or stewards are not familiar with discrimination law, their national officers, particularly the equalities officers, and legal

1 Legal Advice and Assistance Regulations 1989 SI No 340 Sch 4(c).

departments should be able to help. If the local officer is unwilling to help, the full-time officer or the national equalities officer may advise.

28.3 Other agencies

If there is a law centre, citizens advice bureau (CAB) or other advice agency in the area they may offer legal advice and/or representation.

There are also two organisations that provide help with representation. The first is an organisation of trainee and junior barristers who represent claimants, called the Free Representation Unit (FRU). It takes referrals from CABx, law centres and some solicitors who are members. The Bar Pro Bono Unit is an organisation of practising barristers which will also take referrals from solicitors and law centres and occasionally individuals. Both organisations provide free representation in employment cases. There are a number of organisations providing assistance in specific areas of discrimination law. For names and addresses of these see Appendix 1.

28.4 The EOC and CRE

The EOC can give advice or financial assistance under the SDA or EqPA or the CRE under the RRA. Assistance may include:

- giving advice;
- negotiating a settlement;
- arranging for assistance by a solicitor or barrister;
- arranging for representation by any person (eg, a trade union officer);
- any other form of assistance the Commissions consider appropriate.[2]

The CRE must consider and decide on any written application within two months of receiving it (unless it gives notice that it intends to extend the period to three months.[3] There is no parallel requirement for the EOC.

The EOC, in deciding which cases to assist, will take into consideration whether the case is likely to:

- clarify important points of law or principle;
- affect large numbers of people;
- bring about change;

2 SDA s75(2); RRA s66(2).
3 RRA s66(3) and (4).

- succeed;
- provide Commission follow-up work.

It will also consider whether the case falls within one of their current priorities. The CRE has similar criteria.

Both the EOC and CRE will usually advise about the drafting of questionnaires and IT1s until a decision is made by their legal Committee about whether they will give assistance. They also advise on agencies and solicitors who do discrimination cases.

Any costs or expenses recovered by the applicant must be repaid to the Commissions.[4] There is no equivalent to the legal aid statutory charge so that costs are not paid out of compensation.

28.5 Legal costs insurance

Many people are not aware that they have legal costs insurance and all applicants should check their:

- mortgage;
- house insurance;
- contents insurance;
- other policies;

to find out if they provide such cover. Some policies include legal costs insurance free of charge. Others require a small additional premium of about £20 per year. Usually the insurance cover is limited to a maximum (eg, £25,000). There is also often a waiting period which means that the insurance policy must have been taken out well before any claim occurs.

Many policies cover employment matters, including discrimination. However, some exclude claims under the EqPA.

It is also worth checking if a credit card gives any cover. Barclaycard, for example, provides unlimited free access to a legal helpline which is staffed by experienced employment lawyers.

It is important to note that applicants have a right to choose their solicitor, subject to a limit on their charges. Such a right should be expressly recognised in the policy.[5]

4 SDA s75(3); RRA s66(5).

5 Insurance Companies (Legal Expenses Insurance) Regulations 1990 SI No 1159 reg 6 provides that 'where, under a legal expenses insurance contract, recourse is had to a lawyer . . . to defend represent or serve the interests of the insured in any enquiry or proceedings, the insured shall be free to choose that lawyer'. Infringement amounts to an offence under the Insurance Companies Act 1982.

With discrimination as common as it is, a cynic might consider that any woman or black worker should take out such insurance!

There is also a company which provides legal insurance after a claim has arisen.[6] It costs about £362 for cover of up to £6,000. However, there is a big catch. Solicitors' costs will only be paid if the case is *wholly unsuccessful*. Where, for example, the applicant gets a declaration that there has been discrimination but no compensation is awarded, then the company will not pay anything. If the proceedings are settled, no claim can be made. Such 'after the event' insurance may be appropriate in very substantial cases where costs may be very high but it is difficult to envisage it being relevant in the majority of discrimination cases.

28.6 Contingency fees – no win, no fee

Contingency fees mean that if the applicant does not win his/her case s/he will not have to pay the solicitor's legal fees. If s/he does win, her/his solicitor's legal fees will come out of the compensation. However, there is likely to be a significant uplift on normal fees charged in order to compensate the lawyer for the risk that no fees will be recovered in unsuccessful cases. The solicitor may also take a percentage of the compensation.

In general, solicitors are not allowed to do work on a contingency fee basis, though there are some exceptions (such as personal injury work). However, the rules prohibiting contingency fees apply only to contentious matters.[7] Proceedings in the IT (not the EAT) are non-contentious and therefore, the restrictions on contingency fees do not apply. Solicitors must, however, ensure that fees are fair and reasonable.[8]

There are different types of agreement for contingency fees and these are beyond the scope of this book. The Law Society may be able to give advice to solicitors prepared to do work on this basis. Generally, solicitors are likely to do cases on a contingency fee basis if it is a good case with a strong chance of recovering substantial compensation. However, applicants should make sure that they are not liable to pay a substantial amount of compensation to a solicitor who has done very little work.

6 Greystoke Legal Services.
7 Solicitors Practice Rules r8.
8 See 'Question of Ethics' (1996) 9 October *Law Society Gazette* 28.

FINANCIAL HELP AND LEGAL ADVICE: KEY POINTS

- Legal aid is not available for representation in ITs.
- 'Green form' legal aid is available on a means-tested basis for advice and assistance on bringing an IT claim.
- Legal aid is available for hearings in the EAT, CA, HL and ECJ if financial and merits tests are satisfied. The ECJ can itself award limited legal aid if no other form of legal aid is available.
- Unions often provide legal help for their members.
- Law centres, CABx or other advice agencies may provide legal help and/or representation.
- The EOC and CRE give help and assistance with sex and race discrimination cases and provide representation in cases that fall within their current priorities.
- Legal costs insurance can provide cover for the legal costs of taking a discrimination case.
- Contingency fees comprise an agreement that a fee is paid only if the case is won. Such an arrangement could apply only to IT cases.

Appendices

APPENDIX 1

Useful addresses and agencies

Advice Services Alliance,
2nd Floor,
Universal House,
88–94, Wentworth Street,
London E1 7SA
0171 247 2441
– Can give addresses of local advice agencies.

AIRE (Advice on Individual Rights in Europe),
49, Effra Road,
London SW2 1BZ
0171 924 0927

Bar Pro Bono Unit,
7, Grays Inn Square,
Grays Inn,
London WC1R 5AZ
0171 831 9711
– Can provide free representation in discrimination cases.

Campaign for Homosexual Equality,
38, Mount Pleasant,
London WC1X 0AP
0171 833 3912

Central Office of Information,
Hercules Road,
London SE1 7DU
0171 928 2345

Citizens Advice Bureaux (National Association of),
Myddleton House,
115–123, Pentonville Road,
London N1 9LZ
0171 833 2181
– Can give addresses of local citizens advice bureaux.

Commission for Racial Equality,
Elliot House,
10–12, Allington Street,
London SW1
0171 828 7022
– Can advise and/or assist in cases of race discrimination.

Department of Employment,
Caxton House,
Tothill Street,
London SW1
0171 213 3000

Disability Alliance,
Universal House,
88–94, Wentworth Street,
London E1 7SA
0171 247 8776

Disability Discrimination Act Representation and Advice Project,
11, Broadway House,
Jackman Street,
London E8 4QY
– Can provide free representation in cases of general, legal or practical importance.

Disability Law Service,
Room 241,
49–51, Bedford Row,
London WC1R 4LR
0171 831 8031
– Can advise and/or assist in cases of disability discrimination.

Discrimination Law Association,
c/o Victoria Centre,
Palk Road,
Wellingborough NN8 1HT
01933 278000
– Organisation of people involved in discrimination law; can give names of local agencies or solicitors.

Employment Appeals Tribunal,
58, Victoria Embankment,
London EC4Y 0DS
0171 273 1027

Equal Opportunities Commission,
Overseas House,
Quay Street,
Manchester M3 3HN
0161 883 9244
– Can advise and/or assist in cases of sex discrimination.

Federation of Independent Advice Centres (FIAC),
13, Stockwell Road,
London SW9 9AU
0171 274 1839
– Can give addresses of local independent advice agencies.

Free Representation Unit,
Room 140,
49–51, Bedford Row,
London WC1R 4LR
0171 831 0692
– Can provide free representation in employment cases if referred by an advice agency, law centre or some solicitors.

Help the Aged,
St James Walk,
London EC1R 0BE
0171 253 0253

Immunity Law Centre,
1st Floor,
32–38, Osnaburgh Street,
London NW1 3ND
0171 388 6776
– Can advise and/or assist those who are HIV-positive.

Industrial Tribunals Service,
General enquiry line: 0345 959775.
– Can give the address of the relevant industrial tribunal.

Labour Market Enquiry Helpline
0171 533 6176
– Source of information on the labour market.

Labour Research Department,
78, Blackfriars Road,
London SE1 8HF
0171 928 3649
– Publishes information on employment law and statistics.

LAGER,
Lesbian & Gay Rights,
St Margarets House,
Oldford Street,
London E2 9PL
0181 983 0696

Law Centres Federation,
Duchess House,
18–19, Warren Street,
London W1P 5DB
0171 387 8570
– Can give addresses of local law centres.

Lesbian and Gay Switchboard,
PO Box 7324,
London N1 9QS
0171 837 7324

Maternity Alliance,
45, Beech Street,
London EC2P 2LX
0171 588 8583
Information line: 0171 588 8582
– Can give advice on maternity rights.

National Disability Council,
Room 403,
Caxton House,
Tothill Street,
London SW1H 9NF
0171 273 5628

New Ways to Work,
309, Upper Street,
London N1 2TU
0171 226 4026
– Organisation which supports alternative ways of working, eg, job-shares and part-time work, and can provide information on this.

Office for National Statistics,
1, Drummond Gate,
London SW1
0171 233 9233

Rights of Women,
52, Featherstone Street,
London EC1Y 8RT
0171 251 6577
– Organisation of women lawyers.

Runnymede Trust,
11, Princelet Street,
London E1 6QU
0171 375 1496
– Organisation which researches race issues.

Trades Union Congress,
Congress House,
Great Russell Street,
London WC1B 3LS
0171 636 4030

Women against Sexual Harassment (WASH),
The Wheel,
4, Wild Court,
London WC2B 4AU
0171 405 0430
– Can advise on sexual harassment.

APPENDIX 2

Precedents

Industrial tribunal application

Although it is usual to submit an application to the industrial tribunal on an IT1 form, it is not essential. It is only necessary to give your name and address, that of your employer or former employer and the nature of your complaint. However, if application is made by letter, it should cover the following points, which are the questions listed on the IT1.

1. The type of complaint/s you want the tribunal to decide.
2. Your name, address, telephone number and date of birth.
3. Name, address and telephone number of representative (if any).
4. Date employment began and ended.
5. Name and address of respondent you are complaining about (ie, employer) and the place where you worked or applied for work, if different from above.
6. Job you did for the employer (or what job you applied for). If not applicable give your connection with the employer.
7. Give number of normal basic hours you worked per week.
8. a) Basic wages/salary.
   b) Average take-home pay.
   c) Other bonuses/benefits.
9. If the complaint is not about dismissal, give the date when the action you are complaining about took place (or the date when you first knew about it).
10. Unfair dismissal claimants only (indicate what you would want if you win your case):
    - Reinstatement.
    - Re-engagement.
    - Compensation.
11. Give the full details of your complaint.

Signature:

 Date:

INDUSTRIAL TRIBUNALS
ENGLAND and WALES

Received by Industrial Tribunals	FOR OFFICE USE
	Case Number
	Code
	Initials / ROIT

Application to an Industrial Tribunal

- This form has to be photocopied. If possible please use BLACK INK and CAPITAL letters.
- Where there are tick boxes, please tick the one that applies.

1 Please give the type of complaint you want the tribunal to decide (for example: unfair dismissal, equal pay). A full list is given in booklet ITL1. If you have more than one complaint list them all.

Race discrimination

2 Please give your details.

Mr ☑ Mrs ☐ Miss ☐ Ms ☐

Surname: SMITH

First names: BENJAMIN

Date of birth: 29.7.70

Address: 3 GREEN ST
LONDON
Postcode: NW5

Telephone: 0171-267-2000

Daytime Telephone:

Please give an address to which we should send documents if different from above:

Postcode:

3 If a representative is acting for you please give details.

Name: ANYTOWN LAW CENTRE

Address: RANDOM ROAD
ANYTOWN
Postcode: AN1

Telephone: 0101 111 2222

Reference:

4 Please give the dates of your employment.

From: N/A To: N/A

5 Please give the name and address of the employer, other organisation or person against whom this complaint is being brought.

Name of employer, organisation or person: QUICK SALES & CO

Address: 71 HIGH ST
LONDON
Postcode: NW1

Telephone: 0171 485 2000

Please give the place where you worked or applied to work, if different from above.

Address:

Postcode:

6 Please say what job you did for the employer (or what job you applied for). If this does not apply, please say what your connection was with the employer.

REGIONAL SALESMAN

7 Please give the number of normal basic hours worked each week.

Hours per week: 40

8 Please give your earning details.

Basic wage/salary	£ 15,000 :	p, per ANNUM
Average take home pay	£ :	p, per
Other bonuses /benefits	£ :	p, per

9 If your complaint is *not* about dismissal, please give the date when the action you are complaining about took place

1.7.97

10 Unfair dismissal applicants only.
Please indicate what you are seeking at this stage, if you win your case.

- [ ] **Reinstatement:** to carry on working in your old job as before. (An order for reinstatement normally includes an award of compensation for loss of earnings.)
- [ ] **Re-engagement:** to start another job or new contract with your old employer: (An order for re-engagement normally includes an award of compensation for loss of earnings.)
- [x] **Compensation only:** to get an award of money

11 Please give details of your complaint.
If there is not enough space for your answer, please continue on a separate sheet and attach it to this form.

Please see attached details

12 Please sign and date this form , then send it to the address given on page 2

Signed ____________ Date ____________

A Race discrimination – direct discrimination

Industrial tribunal application (IT1)

Question 1: Race discrimination.

Question 11:

1. The Applicant was born in Nigeria and is of African ethnic origin. He has lived and worked in the UK since 1993.
2. On the 4 June 1997 the Applicant was interviewed by the Respondents' manager for a position as a 'regional salesman'. He was unsuccessful.
3. In the course of the interview the Respondents' manager asked the Applicant whether he thought that the Respondents' customers would be able to understand him.
4. Further the manager suggested that the Applicant would soon return to Nigeria to live or that he would go for a long holiday and not return on the due date at the end of the holiday.
5. The Applicant assured the manager that he had encountered no difficulties in being understood and that he had successfully held a sales position at an instore shop in the West End of London for one year. He produced good references from his former employers.
6. Further the Applicant assured the Respondents that:
   a) he was reliable;
   b) although he would wish to visit his family in Nigeria in due course he had been granted indefinite leave to remain in the UK; and
   c) he intended to make his home here and to apply for citizenship in due course.
7. The Applicant was informed by letter dated 7 June 1997 that he would not be appointed to the position.
8. By reason of the matters set out above the Applicant has suffered unlawful direct or indirect race discrimination contrary to the Race Relations Act 1975.[1]

Questionnaire

Question 2: Set out points 1–7 above.

Question 3: Delete 'because' and leave blank.

Question 6:

1. Please explain the duties, responsibilities, grading and pay of the post of 'regional salesman'.
2. Please give the ethnic origin of the persons who held line management responsibility for the post.

---

1 At this stage it is not clear whether the discrimination is direct or indirect and, if it is indirect, what the condition or requirement may be. Applicants should then apply to amend the IT1 as soon as it becomes clear that there is a condition or requirement.

3. Please supply a copy of the job description, person specification, and contract of employment applicable to the post.
4. Please give the criteria for selection and by whom it was devised.
5. Please identify the ethnic origin and qualifications and experience of all of the persons who applied for the job; also of all of the persons who were shortlisted for interview. If necessary to preserve confidentiality, the candidates' names may be omitted and each person may be identified by letter.
6. Please identify by letter who was the successful candidate.
7. Please identify the ethnic origin and qualifications of each member of the salesforce, and also of the whole of the firm. Again their names may be omitted and they may be identified by letter.
8. Please explain fully why the following matters were raised at the interview:
   a) Whether the complainant thought that the Respondents' customers would not be able to understand him.
   b) Whether the complainant would soon return to Nigeria to live,
   c) Whether the complainant would go for a long holiday and not return on the due date at the end of the holiday.
9. What relevance did the above matters have to the interview?
10. Did the manager ask similar questions of any of the other persons interviewed; if so, please identify the ethnic origin of each of the persons who were asked the same or similar questions?
11. What consideration was given to the complainant's and the successful candidate's references? Did this affect the decision not to give the job to the complainant in any way; if so, please explain how?
12. What consideration was given to the complainant's and the successful candidate's right to work in the UK? Did this affect the decision not to give the job to the complainant in any way; if so, please explain how? Please explain and supply a copy of any policy that the Respondents follow in relation to the work status of employees.
13. Why was the complainant unsuccessful?
14. Please supply a copy of the firm's equal opportunity policy. When was the policy adopted?
15. How many complaints of racial discrimination has the firm had in the last five years, either within the firm through the grievance procedure or to the industrial tribunal?

Notice of appearance by Respondents (IT3)

1. The Respondents admit that their manager interviewed the Applicant for the post of Regional Sales Person on 4 June 1997 and that he was unsuccessful. They deny any discrimination.
2. He was unsuccessful at interview because he did not interview as well as the successful candidate who had superior experience as a sales executive.

3. Moreover he was rude at the interview and refused to discuss his future career plans.
4. Because the Applicant appeared to have arrived recently from Nigeria the Respondents felt that they should check his immigration status. However the Applicant refused to produce his passport.
5. The Respondents did ask the Applicant how committed he was to life in the UK but they did not suggest that he would not stay here. It appeared that the Applicant was himself unsure as to how long he would wish to stay in the UK.
6. Because the Respondents' business is highly technical they asked the Applicant to demonstrate that he could clearly explain technical matters. They did not ask whether the Applicant thought that their customers would be able to understand him.
7. The Respondents have an active equal opportunities policy and are very proud of their achievements in the field of equal opportunities.

Request for further and better particulars of the IT3

1. Of 'Paragraph 2 . . . interview as well as the successful candidate who had superior experience as a sales executive.'

State each respect in which it is said that he did not interview as well as the successful candidate and each respect in which it is said that the successful candidate had superior experience.

State what qualifications did the successful interviewee have and in what respect it is alleged that the Applicant's experience was not as good.

2. Of 'Paragraph 3 . . . he was rude at interview and refused to discuss his future career plans.'

State exactly what was said by the Applicant and the gist of the conversation in which it was said.

3. Of 'Paragraph 4 . . . the Applicant refused to produce his passport.'

State when, where, by whom, and why the Respondents asked the Applicant to produce his passport.

State which other candidates were asked to produce their passports stating which candidates complied with this request.[2]

4. Of 'Paragraph 7 . . . the Respondents have an active equal opportunities policy.'

---

2 See **6.4.1.6.**

State what steps the Respondents have taken to train their managers in equal opportunities interviewing.

Request for discovery

Please provide full discovery, as it may be ordered in the county court, and in particular the following documents:

1. All documents used by the Respondents to prepare for the interviews for the job, including job description, and person specification.
2. All score sheets used to rank the interviewees.
3. Any notes taken by the interviewer(s) before, during or after the interview of each of the interviewees. These may be kept confidential by masking the name of any candidate and replacing it with a letter.
4. Contract of employment for the successful candidate.

[5. *Any other document that had already been sought in the questionnaire but had not yet been supplied.*]

B Letter before action – constructive dismissal – change of hours – indirect sex discrimination

Dear . . . .

I have worked for the Workman's Cafe as a cook for the last five years during which time I have always worked the 8 am to 3 pm shift. As you know I took this job so that I could collect my children from school.

Last Thursday you informed me that with effect from next week I would have to work from 11 am until 6 pm. I told you that this would not be possible for me. I cannot agree to the change because I have no childcare arrangement to cover this period. I believe that this amounts to a unilateral change to an important term of my contract of employment and discrimination.

I would be grateful if you could reconsider your decision and confirm by the end of the week that you will not be imposing this change. If, however, you refuse to re-consider your decision I shall be forced to consider myself constructively dismissed and to apply to the industrial tribunal for compensation.

Yours sincerely,

Application to industrial tribunal (IT1)

Question 1: Constructive unfair dismissal/indirect sex discrimination.

Question 11:

1. The Applicant has been employed as a cook by the Respondent from January 1992 until 4 April 1997. The Applicant worked the 8 am to 3 pm shift. The Respondent knew that she chose to work this shift because of her childcare responsibilities. The applicant has never been given a written contract of employment.
2. In January 1997 the Respondent brought his nephew to work as the second cook doing the second shift, from 11 am to 6 pm. In February the Respondent's nephew asked the Applicant to exchange shifts with him as he wished to attend an evening course. The Applicant refused and explained the reason.
3. On or about 27 March the Respondent informed the Applicant that with effect from 7 April she would have to work from 11 am to 6 pm. The Applicant told the Respondent that she could not work these hours because of her childcare arrangements and that she was not prepared to agree to these changes to her contract of employment.
4. On 1 April the Applicant wrote to the Respondent confirming this and saying that she would consider herself to have been constructively dismissed if the Respondent did not reconsider his decision.
5. On Friday 4 April the Respondent informed the Applicant that he was not prepared to change his mind.
6. The requirement to work from 11 am to 6 pm was indirectly discriminatory on the ground of sex as:
   a) the Respondent applied to the Applicant a requirement or condition which applied equally to men; but
   b) the proportion of women who can comply with this requirement is considerably smaller than the number of men who can comply with it;
   c) the condition or requirement is to the Applicant's detriment because she could not comply with it; and
   d) the condition or requirement is not justifiable.
7. The Applicant believes that she has been constructively unfairly dismissed and has suffered discrimination.

Questionnaire

Question 2: Set out points 1–7 above.

Question 3: Delete 'because' and leave blank.

Question 6:

1. Please provide a list of all your staff, showing job title, sex, hours of work and length of service of each of them.
2. Please state the age, sex, marital status, employment experience and length of service of anyone now carrying out the work previously undertaken by the Applicant and of anyone else employed by you as a cook.

3. Please provide a copy of your equal opportunities policy and describe what steps you have taken to implement the EOC's Code of Practice.
4. Please state why the Applicant's hours of work were changed.

C Letter before action – constructive dismissal – return from maternity leave – indirect sex discrimination

Dear . . . .

I have worked for the Blankshire Council as a planning officer for 15 years. During this time there have never been any complaints about my work and I have been promoted twice.

On 20 November 1995 I gave written notice of the commencement of my maternity leave and that I intended to return to work after the birth of my baby. After the birth of my baby on 4 February 1996 I was unable to find satisfactory full-time child care. I therefore wrote to you on 9 August asking to be allowed to return to work part-time or on a job-share arrangement in accordance with the Council's guidelines.

I was dismayed to receive your letter of 10 August refusing even to consider my request, though job-sharing has been tried successfully in both the legal and the enviromental health departments.

The requirement to work full-time is indirectly discriminatory.

During the time that I have worked for the Council I have acquired considerable experience and expertise which the Council would lose if I am not permitted to return to work.

If I do not hear from you with an appropriate offer of a part-time job or a job-share I will be forced to resign and claim that I have been unfairly constructively dismissed and that your actions are contrary to the Sex Discrimination Act 1975.

Yours sincerely,

Industrial tribunal application (IT1)

Question 1: Unfair dismissal/indirect sex discrimination.

Question 11:

1. The applicant was employed by the Respondents as a Planning Officer from December 1980.
2. On or about 10 November 1995 the Applicant gave her Maternity Certificate (MAT B1) to the Respondents which showed that her expected week of childbirth was the week beginning 11 February 1996.
3. On 20 November 1995 the Applicant gave written notice that her last working day before the commencement of her maternity leave was 5

January 1996. She stated that she intended to return to work after the birth of her baby.

4. The Applicant commenced her maternity leave on 6 January 1996 and her baby was born on 4 February 1996.
5. The Applicant was entitled to return to work in the job in which she was employed before she went on maternity leave.
6. On 9 August 1996 the Applicant wrote to the Respondents requesting that she return to work on a part-time or job-share arrangement within the Planning Department.
7. On 10 August 1996 the Respondents wrote to the Applicant stating that they were not prepared to offer a part-time position or a job-share arrangement within the Planning Department.
8. The Applicant was not able to return to work full-time because she was unable to make satisfactory childcare arrangements. Further or alternatively, the Applicant wanted to spend more time with her child.
9. There were implied into the contract of employment between the Applicant and the Respondent terms of trust and mutual confidence and/or that the employer would not discriminate. Further, the Respondents' maternity guidelines state that requests for part-time work should be considered sympathetically on an individual basis.
10. The requirement to work full-time is indirectly discriminatory on the ground of sex, as:
    a) the Respondents applied to the Applicant a condition or requirement (namely – if you want to continue in our employment, you must work full-time) which they applied equally to men; but
    b) the proportion of women who can comply with this requirement or condition is considerably smaller than the proportion of men who can comply with it;
    c) the condition or requirement is to the Applicant's detriment because she could not comply with it; and
    d) the condition or requirement is not justifiable.
11. The Applicant was unable to work full-time and felt that she had no alternative but to resign, which she did.
12. The Respondents' conduct towards her entitled her to terminate her contract of employment. In the circumstances the Applicant considers that she has been constructively unfairly dismissed and has suffered discrimination.
13. Further and in the alternative, the Respondents failed to follow their job-sharing policy.
14. The Applicant claims:
    a) a declaration that she has suffered discrimination;
    b) a recommendation that she be re-engaged or reinstated on a job-share or part-time basis;
    c) compensation for unfair dismissal and discrimination, including injury to feelings;
    d) interest.

D Sexual and racial harassment

Industrial tribunal application (IT1)

Question 1: Sex and race discrimination/unfair constructive dismissal.

Question 5: Name of harasser/s and/or name of organisation.

Question 11:

1. The Applicant, who is of African origin, started work as a secretary to the Managing Director, Mr Male, on 18 November 1996.
2. Mr Male frequently sexually and racially harassed the Applicant. He often referred to her as 'the tart', 'my black gem' and 'the wog' in front of the other members of staff. The Applicant found this upsetting and demeaning and asked him to stop.
3. During December Mr Male regularly asked the Applicant to stay late to do overtime and would suggest going out for a drink afterwards. The Applicant refused.
4. At the Christmas party Mr Male put his arm round the Applicant, tried to feel her breast and then asked her to go home with him. When she refused to go he said that she would suffer for it.
5. Thereafter Mr Male gave the Applicant increasing amounts of work and criticised her for being slow. He complained about her work to other employees in such a way that the Applicant would overhear.
6. On the 23 January 1997 Mr Male called the Applicant into the main office and told her that she would no longer be working as his secretary but would have to work partly in the stores and partly as the cleaner. The Applicant was reduced to tears and went home early.
7. The next day when the Applicant returned to work Mr Male criticised her for not coming in early and complained about the state of the office which he said was very dirty.
8. The Applicant was again reduced to tears and gave in her notice whereupon Mr Male said, 'Good riddance'.
9. The Applicant suffered the above treatment on grounds of her race and/or sex.
10. The Applicant claims that she has suffered unlawful direct racial and/or sexual discrimination/unlawful constructive dismissal and seeks a declaration, compensation including injury to feelings, and interest unlawful constructive dismissal.

Questionnaire

Question 2: Set out points 1–8 above.

Question 3: Delete 'because' and leave blank.

Question 6:

1. Please supply a copy of my terms and conditions of employment and provide full details of my duties and responsibilities prior to the termination of my employment.
2. Please confirm that I was employed as a secretary.
3. Please explain why I was required to work in the stores and as a cleaner and when and by whom this decision was taken.
4. Please state the name, age, sex, job title and length of service of any staff now carrying out the work previously undertaken by me.
5. What instructions are issued to staff about the avoidance of sexual or racial harassment at work?
6. Please provide a copy of the equal opportunities policy stating when it was adopted and detailing the steps taken to implement it effectively.
7. What steps have been taken to comply with the European Commission's Code of Practice on the Dignity of Men and Women at Work?
8. Please provide a list of your staff showing the job title, sex, race and length of service of all job-holders. Please state what is the size of your total workforce.
9. Do you accept that Mr Male called me 'the tart', and/or 'my black gem' and/or 'the wog'? Please explain why he used such language.
10. Has Mr Male ever subjected other employees to treatment similar to that described in part 2 of this form?
11. Please give details of any harassment complaints made in the last three years, stating against whom they were made, and what action was taken as a result.

E Disability discrimination

Industrial tribunal application (IT1)

Question 1: Disability discrimination and/or unfair dismissal.

Question 11:

1. The applicant has worked for the Respondent, Good Read Publishing Ltd, as a marketing executive since February 1990. The Respondent publishes magazines and has recently launched two new titles. It employs around 500 people.
2. No criticism has ever been made of the Applicant's performance during his employment by the Respondent. The Applicant's formal appraisals have confirmed that his performance meets or exceeds the Respondent's expectations in all respects.
3. At the beginning of 1995, the Applicant was diagnosed as having multiple sclerosis, and he informed the Respondent of that fact. At the end of

1996, the Applicant's condition began to have a slight effect on his mobility and physical co-ordination, but this has not materially affected his performance at work.

4. At the beginning of May 1997, the Applicant caught a cold which then developed into a mild respiratory infection. The Applicant informed the Respondent of this and sent in a doctor's certificate to cover his absence. This was his second period of sickness absence since he began working for the Respondent. The previous period of absence occurred three years previously and lasted three days.
5. On 14 May 1997, the Applicant received a letter from the Respondent while he was still on sick leave. The letter stated that he was to be made redundant in eight weeks' time as part of a reorganisation exercise affecting the marketing and sales departments, but that he did not need to work out his notice.
6. The Applicant was not warned or consulted about being made redundant and the possibility of alternative employment in the company was not discussed with him.
7. The Applicant believes that he was either dismissed unjustifiably for a reason relating to the fact that he has multiple sclerosis rather than for redundancy, or selected unjustifiably for redundancy for a reason relating to his condition. He also believes that the Respondent unjustifiably failed to take reasonable steps to prevent its employment arrangements putting him at a substantial disadvantage compared with non-disabled people.
8. The Applicant believes that he has been the subject of unlawful discrimination contrary to the Disability Discrimination Act 1995 and/or has been unfairly dismissed.

Questionnaire

Question 2: Set out points 1–7 above.

Question 3: Delete 'because' and leave blank.

Question 6:

1. Please specify when and why the company decided to implement redundancies.
2. Please describe the procedure the company followed in implementing the redundancies.
3. Please specify:
   a) how many redundancies have been made; and
   b) the job titles of those who have been dismissed.
4. Please specify the pool of employees from which the redundancies were made.
5. Please:
   a) specify the selection criteria used to select employees for redundancy; and

   b) show how those criteria were applied in relation to each employee within the redundancy selection pool, including myself. (If necessary to preserve confidentiality, letters may be substituted for the names of employees other than myself.)
6. Please give details of your attendance records for all your employees for the past two years indicating which employees were within the redundancy selection pool. (If necessary to preserve confidentiality, letters may be substituted for the names of employees other than myself.)
7. Please give details of all vacancies existing within the three months prior to the date of this questionnaire, specifying salary, job title and the date the vacancy arose.
8. Does the company have an equal opportunities policy? If it does:
   a) when was the policy adopted?
   b) what does it say?
   c) has it been amended to incorporate the requirements of the Disability Discrimination Act 1995, and, if it has, when and how was it amended?
9. Please describe what steps the company has taken to implement the Code of Practice issued under the Disability Discrimination Act 1995, specifying in particular what changes have been made to company personnel policies.
10. Please specify:
   a) the number and job titles of the company's disabled employees and
   b) the size of the company's workforce.
11 Please provide copies of the company's accounts for the past three financial years.

F Equal pay

Industrial tribunal application (IT1)

Question 1: Equal pay under the Equal Pay Act 1970 and/or Article 119 and/ or the Equal Pay Directive 75/117.

Question 11:
1. The Applicant is a woman employed by the Respondents as a filing clerk. The Respondents are a local authority.
2. In carrying out her duties the Applicant is carrying out work of equal value to that of Mr Speed the postal clerk.
3. The Applicant's rate of pay is determined by her contract of employment at a rate of £xx per week. That clause is less favourable than the comparable clause in Mr Speed's contract of employment which provides for his rate of pay to be £2xx per week.

4. The Applicant therefore claims:
   a) A declaration that the term of her contract relating to pay be treated as modified so as not to be less favourable than the clause relating to pay in the contract of Mr Speed.
   b) Damages, being the arrears of pay from .... to the date of the determination of the case at the rate of £2xx-xx per week.
   c) Interest.

Questionnaire

Question 2: Set out points 1–3 above.

Question 3: Delete 'because' and leave blank.

Question 6:

1. Please provide full details, including job description, contract of employment and person specification for the Complainant's post and that of Mr Speed.
2. Please provide details of basic pay and any additional contractual benefits for the both the Complainant and Mr Speed as at 1 January 1997 and as at 31 May 1997.
3. Do you accept that the Complainant was paid less than Mr Speed?
4. On what objective basis is there a differential in pay between the Complainant and Mr Speed?
5. Please provide full details of the pay and/or grading system operating within the authority.
6. Do you accept that the Complainant was employed to do similar work or work of equal value to that of Mr Speed?
7. Do you consider that there are material differences between the Complainant's post and that of Mr Speed? If so please state clearly what you consider these differences to be and why you say that they are material.

G Settlement agreement

This agreement is made between .... (the Applicant) and .... (the Respondent).

It is agreed between the parties that:

1. The Respondent will pay to the applicant the sum of £xxxx within 14 days.
2. The Respondent will provide a reference in the terms attached, or in no worse terms, to anyone seeking a reference in respect of the Applicant's employment with the Respondent.
3. The Applicant accepts the sum of £xxxx for loss of office. For the avoidance of doubt this sum is in full and final settlement of all and any claims

arising out of her contract of employment with the Respondent[3] (save any claim for damages for personal injury and/or arising out of loss of pension rights). The Applicant will apply to withdraw his/her case without further order from the industrial tribunal immediately on receipt of full payment referred to in clause 1.

4. The Applicant confirms that, before signing the agreement, s/he received independent legal advice from .... [*name of adviser*] ... , a qualified lawyer of .... [*address*] .... as to the terms and effect of this agreement and, in particular, its effect on his/her ability to pursue his/her rights before an industrial tribunal.
5. The regulations relating to compromise agreements under the ERA and/ or SDA and/or RRA and/or DDA are satisfied under this agreement.

Signed................... Dated.............. ...

Signed................... Dated.............. ...

---

3 If the settlement is for a sum in excess of £30,000 it may be worth specifying for tax purposes how much is attributable to injury to feelings, how much to a termination payment and how much to loss of earnings (see **26.4.2**).

APPENDIX 3

Reference materials

Commission Recommendation No 92/131/EEC on measures to combat sexual harassment

Protecting the dignity of women and men at work: A code of practice on measures to combat sexual harassment

ANNEX

1. Introduction

1.1 This Code of Practice is issued in accordance with the Resolution of the Council of Ministers on the protection of the dignity of women and men at work,[1] and to accompany the Commission's Recommendation on this issue.

1.2 Its purpose is to give practical guidance to employers, trade unions, and employees on the protection of the dignity of women and men at work. The Code is intended to be applicable in both the public and the private sector and employers are encouraged to follow the recommendations contained in the Code in a way which is appropriate to the size and structure of their organisation. It may be particularly relevant for small and medium-sized enterprises to adapt some of the practical steps to their specific needs.

1.3 The aim is to ensure that sexual harassment does not occur and, if it does occur, to ensure that adequate procedures are readily available to deal with the problem and prevent its recurrence. The Code thus seeks to encourage the development and implementation of policies and practices which establish working environments free of sexual harassment and in which women and men respect one another's human integrity.

1.4 The expert report carried out on behalf of the Commission found that sexual harassment is a serious problem for many working women in the European Community[2] and research in Member States has proven beyond doubt that sexual harassment at work is not an isolated phenomenon. On the contrary, it is clear that for millions of women in the European Community, sexual harassment is an unpleasant and unavoidable part of their working lives. Men too may suffer sexual harassment and should, of course, have the same rights as women to the protection of their dignity.

1.5 Some specific groups are particularly vulnerable to sexual harassment. Research in several Member States, which documents the link between the risk of sexual harassment and the recipient's perceived vulnerability, suggests that divorced and separated women, young women and new entrants to the labour market and those with irregular or precarious employment contracts, women in non-traditional jobs, women with disabilities, lesbians and women from racial minorities are disproportionately at risk. Gay men and young men are also vulnerable to harassment. It is undeniable that harassment on grounds of sexual orientation undermines the dignity at work of those affected and it is impossible to regard such harassment as appropriate workplace behaviour.

1.6 Sexual harassment pollutes the working environment and can have a devastating effect upon the health, confidence, morale and performance of those affected by it. The anxiety and stress produced by sexual harassment commonly leads to those subjected to it taking time off work due to sickness, being less efficient at work, or leaving their job to seek work elsewhere. Employees often suffer both the adverse consequences of the harassment itself and short- and long-term damage to their employment prospects if they are forced to change jobs. Sexual harassment may also have a damaging impact on employees not themselves the object of unwanted behaviour but who are witnesses to it or have a knowledge of the unwanted behaviour.

1.7 There are also adverse consequences arising from sexual harassment for employers. It has a direct impact on the profitability of the enterprise where staff take sick leave or resign their posts because of sexual harassment, and on the economic efficiency of the enterprise where employees' productivity is reduced by having to work in a climate in which individuals' integrity is not respected.

1.8 In general terms, sexual harassment is an obstacle to the proper integration of women into the labour market and the Commission is committed to encouraging the development of comprehensive measures to improve such integration.[3]

2. Definition

2.1 Sexual harassment means "unwanted conduct of a sexual nature, or other conduct based on sex affecting the dignity of women and men at work."[4] This can include unwelcome physical, verbal or non-verbal conduct.

2.2 Thus, a range of behaviour may be considered to constitute sexual harassment. It is unacceptable if such conduct is unwanted, unreasonable and offensive to the recipient; a person's rejection of or submission to such conduct on the part of employers or workers (including superiors or colleagues) is used explicitly or implicitly as a basis for a decision which affects that person's access to vocational training or to employment, continued employment, promotion, salary or any other employment decisions; and/or such conduct creates an intimidating, hostile or humiliating working environment for the recipient.[5]

2.3 The essential characteristic of sexual harassment is that it is *unwanted* by the recipient, that it is for each individual to determine what behaviour is acceptable to them and what they regard as offensive. Sexual attention becomes sexual harassment if it is persisted in once it has been made clear that it is regarded by the recipient as offensive, although one incident of harassment may constitute sexual harassment if sufficiently serious. It is the unwanted nature of the conduct that distinguishes sexual harassment from friendly behaviour which is welcome and mutual.

3. The law and employers' responsibilities

3.1 Conduct of a sexual nature or other conduct based on sex affecting the dignity of women and men at work may be contrary to the principle of equal treatment within the meaning of Articles 3, 4 and 5 of Council Directive 76/207/EEC of 9 February 1976 on the implementation of the principle of equal treatment for women and men as regards access to employment, vocational training and promotion and working conditions. This principle means that there shall be no discrimination whatsoever on grounds of sex either directly or indirectly by reference in particular to marital or family status.[6]

3.2 In certain circumstances, and depending upon national law, sexual harassment may also be a criminal offence or may contravene other obligations imposed by the law, such as health and safety duties, or a duty, contractual or otherwise, to be a good employer. Since sexual harassment is a form of employee misconduct, employers have a responsibility to deal with it as they do with any other form of employee misconduct as well as to refrain from harassing employees themselves. Since sexual harassment is a risk to health and safety, employers have a responsibility to take steps to minimise the risk as they do with other hazards. Since sexual harassment often entails an abuse of power, employers may have a responsibility for the misuse of the authority they delegate.

3.3 This Code, however, focuses on sexual harassment as a problem of sex discrimination. Sexual harassment is sex discrimination because the gender of the recipient is the determining factor in who is harassed. Conduct of a sexual nature or other conduct based on sex affecting the dignity of women and men at work in some Member States already has been found to contravene national equal treatment laws and employers have a responsibility to seek to ensure that the work environment is free from such conduct.[7]

3.4 As sexual harassment is often a function of women's status in the employment hierarchy, policies to deal with sexual harassment will be most effective where they are linked to a broader policy to promote equal opportunities and to improve the position of women. Advice on steps which can be taken generally to implement an equal opportunities policy is set out in the Commission's Guide to Positive Action.[8]

3.5 Similarly, a procedure to deal with complaints of sexual harassment should be regarded as only one component of a strategy to deal with the problem. The prime objective should be to change behaviour and attitudes, to seek to ensure the prevention of sexual harassment.

4. Collective bargaining

4.1 The majority of the recommendations contained in this Code are for action by employers, since employers have clear responsibilities to ensure the protection of the dignity of women and men at work.

4.2 Trade unions also have responsibilities to their members and they can and should play an important tole in the prevention of sexual harassment in the workplace. It is recommended that the question of including appropriate clauses in agreements is examined in the context of the collective bargaining process, with the aim of achieving a work environment free from unwanted conduct of a sexual nature or other conduct based on sex affecting the dignity of women and men at work and free from victimisation of a complainant or of a person wishing to give, or giving, evidence in the event of a complaint.

5. Recommendations to employers

5.1 The policies and procedures recommended below should be adopted, where appropriate, after consultation or negotiation with trade unions or employee representatives. Experience suggests that strategies to create and maintain a working environment in which the dignity of employees is respected are most likely to be effective where they are jointly agreed.

5.2 It should be emphasised that a distinguishing characteristic of sexual harassment is that employees subjected to it often will be reluctant to complain. An absence of complaints about sexual harassment in a particular organisation, therefore, does not necessarily mean an absence of sexual harassment. It may mean that the recipients of sexual harassment think that there is no point in complaining because nothing will be done about it, or because it will be trivialised or the complainant subjected to ridicule, or because they fear reprisals. Implementing the preventative and procedural recommendations outlined below should facilitate the creation of a climate at work in which such concerns have no place.

A. Prevention

Policy statements

5.A.1 As a first step in showing senior management's concern and their commitment to dealing with the problem of sexual harassment, employers should issue a policy statement which expressly states that all employees have a right to be treated with dignity, that sexual harassment at work will not be permitted or condoned and that employees have a right to complain about it should it occur.

5.A.2 It is recommended that the policy statement makes clear what is considered inappropriate behaviour at work, and explains that such behaviour, in certain circumstances, may be unlawful. It is advisable for the statement to set out a positive duty on managers and supervisors to implement the policy and to take corrective action to ensure compliance with it. It should also specify that appropriate disciplinary measures will be taken against employees found guilty of sexual harassment.

5.A.3 In addition, it is recommended that the statement explains the procedure which should be followed by employees subjected to sexual harassment at work in order to obtain assistance and to whom they should complain; that it contains an undertaking that allegations of sexual harassment will be dealt with seriously, expeditiously and confidentially; and that employees will be protected against victimisation or retaliation for bringing a complaint of sexual harassment. It should also specify that appropriate disciplinary measures will be taken against employees found guilty of sexual harassment.

Communicating the policy

5.A.4 Once the policy has been developed, it is important to ensure that it is communicated effectively to all employees, so that they are aware that they have a right to complain and to whom they should complain; that their complaint will be dealt with promptly and fairly; and so that employees are made aware of the likely consequences of engaging in sexual harassment. Such communication will highlight management's commitment to eliminating sexual harassment, thus enhancing a climate in which it will not occur.

Responsibility

5.A.5 All employees have a responsibility to help to ensure a working environment in which the dignity of employees is respected and managers (including supervisors) have a particular duty to ensure that sexual harassment does not occur in work areas for which they are responsible. It is recommended that managers should explain the organisation's policy to their staff and take steps to positively promote the policy. Managers should also be responsive and supportive to any member of staff who complains about sexual harassment; provide full and clear advice on the procedure to be adopted; maintain confidentiality in any cases of sexual harassment; and ensure that that is no further problem of sexual harassment or any victimisation after a complaint has been resolved.

Training

5.A.6 An important means of ensuring that sexual harassment does not occur, and that if it does occur the problem is resolved efficiently, is through the provision of training for managers and supervisors. Such training should aim to identify the factors which contribute to a working environment free of sexual harassment and to familiarise participants with their responsibilities under the employer's policy and any problems they are likely to encounter.

5.A.7 In addition, those playing an official role in any formal complaints procedure in respect of sexual harassment should receive specialist training, such as that outlined above.

5.A.8 It is also good practice to include information as to the organisation's policy on sexual harassment and procedures for dealing with it as part of appropriate induction and training programmes.

B. Procedures

5.B.1 The development of clear and precise procedures to deal with sexual harassment once it has occurred is of great importance. The procedures should ensure the resolution of problems in an efficient and effective manner. Practical guidance for employees on how to deal with sexual harassment when it occurs and with its aftermath will make it more likely that it will be dealt with at an early stage. Such guidance should of course draw attention to an employee's legal rights and to any time limits within which they must be exercised.

Resolving problems informally

5.B.2 Most recipients of harassment simply want the harassment to stop. Both informal and formal methods of resolving problems should be available.

5.B.3 Employees should be advised that, if possible, they should attempt to resolve the problem informally in the first instance. In some cases, it may be possible and sufficient for the employee to explain clearly to the person engaging in the unwanted conduct that the behaviour in question is not welcome, that it offends them or makes them uncomfortable, and that it interferes with their work.

5.B.4 In circumstances where it is too difficult or embarassing for an individual to do this on their own behalf, an alternative approach would be to seek support from, or for an initial approach to be made by, a sympathetic friend or confidential counsellor.

5.B.5 If the conduct continues or if it is not appropriate to resolve the problem informally, it should be raised through the formal complaints procedure.

Advice and assistance

5.B.6 It is recommended that employers should designate someone to provide advice and assistance to employees subjected to sexual harassment, where possible, with responsibilities to assist in the resolution of any problems, whether through informal or formal means. It may be helpful if the officer is designated with the agreement of the trade unions or employees, as this is likely to enhance their acceptabililty. Such officers could be selected from personnel departments or equal opportunities departments, for example. In some organisations they are designated as "confidential counsellors" or "sympathetic friends". Often such a role may be provided by someone from the employee's trade union or by women's support groups.

5.B.7 Whatever the location of this responsibility in the organisation, it is recommended that the designated officer receives appropriate training in the best means of resolving problems and in the detail of the organisation's policy and procedures, so that they can perform their role effectively. It is also important that they are given adequate resources to carry out their function, and protection against victimisation for assisting any recipient of sexual harassment.

Complaints procedure

5.B.8 It is recommended that, where the complainant regards attempts at informal resolution as inappropriate, where informal attempts at resolution have been refused, or where the outcome has been unsatisfactory, a formal procedure for resolving the complaint should be provided. The procedure should give employees confidence that the organisation will take allegations of sexual harassment seriously.

5.B.9 By its nature sexual harassment may make the normal channels of complaint difficult to use because of embarrassment, fears of not being taken seriously, fears of damage to reputation, fears of reprisal or the prospect of damaging the working environment. Therefore, a formal procedure should specify to whom the employee should bring a complaint, and it should also provide an alternative if in the particular circumstances the normal grievance procedure may not be suitable, for example because the accused harasser is the employee's line manager. It is also advisable to make provision for employees to bring a complaint in the first instance to someone of their own sex, should they so choose.

5.B.10 It is good practice for employers to monitor and review complaints of sexual harassment and how they have been resolved, in order to ensure that their procedures are working effectively.

Investigations

5.B.11 It is important to ensure that internal investigations of any complaints are handled with sensitivity and with due respect for the rights of both the complainant and the alleged harasser. The investigation should be seen to be independent and objective. Those carrying out the investigation should not be connected with the allegation in any way, and every effort should be made to resolve complaints speedily – grievances should be handled promptly and the procedure should set a time limit within which complaints will be processed, with due regard for any time limits set by national legislation for initiating a complaint through the legal system.

5.B.12 It is recommended as good practice that both the complainant and the alleged harasser should have the right to be accompanied and/or represented, perhaps by a representative of their trade union or a friend or colleague; that the alleged harasser must be given full details of the nature of the complaint and the opportunity to respond; and that strict confidentiality should be maintained throughout any investigation into an allegation. Where it is necessary to interview witnesses, the importance of confidentiality should be emphasised.

5.B.13 It must be recognised that recounting the experience of sexual harassment is difficult and can damage the employee's dignity. Therefore, a complainant should not be required to repeatedly recount the events complained of where this is unnecessary.

5.B.14 The investigation should focus on the facts of the complaint and it is advisable for the employer to keep a complete record of all meetings and investigations.

Disciplinary offence

5.B.15 It is recommended that violations of the organisation's policy protecting the dignity of employees at work should be treated as a disciplinary offence; and the disciplinary rules should make clear what is regarded as inappropriate behaviour at work. It is also good practice to ensure that the range of penalties to which offenders will be liable for violating the rule is clearly stated and also to make it clear that it will be considered a disciplinary offence to victimise or retaliate against an employee for bringing a complaint of sexual harassment in good faith.

5.B.16 Where a complaint is upheld and it is determined that it is necessary to relocate or transfer one party, consideration should be given, wherever practicable, to allowing the complainant to choose whether he or she wishes to remain in their post or be transferred to another location. No element of penalty should be seen to attach to a complainant whose complaint is upheld and in addition, where a complaint is upheld, the employer should monitor the situation to ensure that the harassment has stopped.

5.B.17 Even where a complaint is not upheld, for example because the evidence is regarded as inconclusive, consideration should be given to transferring or rescheduling the work of one of the employees concerned rather than requiring them to continue to work together against the wishes of either party.

6. Recommendations to trade unions

6.1 Sexual harassment is a trade union issue as well as an issue for employers. It is recommended as good practice that trade unions should formulate and issue clear policy statements on sexual harassment and take steps to raise awareness of the problem of sexual harassment in the workplace, in order to help create a climate in which it is neither condoned nor ignored. For example, trade unions could aim to give all officers and representatives training on equality issues, including dealing with sexual harassment and include such information in union-sponsored or approved training courses, as well as information on the union's policy. Trade unions should consider declaring that sexual harassment is inappropriate behaviour and educating members and officials about its consequences is recommended as good practice.

6.2 Trade unions should also raise the issue of sexual harassment with employers and encourage the adoption of adequate policies and procedures to protect the dignity of women and men at work in the organisation. It is advisable for trade unions to inform members of their right not to be sexually harassed at work and provide members with clear guidance as to what to do if they are sexually harassed, including guidance on any relevant legal rights.

6.3 Where complaints arise, it is important for trade unions to treat them seriously and sympathetically and ensure that the complainant has the opportunity of representation if a complaint is to be pursued. It is important to create an environment in which members feel able to raise such complaints knowing they will receive a sympathetic and supportive response from local union representatives. Trade unions could consider designating specially-trained officials to advise and counsel members with complaints of sexual harassment and act on their behalf if required. This will provide a focal point for support. It is also a good idea to ensure that there are sufficient female representatives to support women subjected to sexual harassment.

6.4 It is recommended too, where the trade union is representing both the complainant and the alleged harasser for the purpose of the complaints procedure, that it is made clear that the union is not condoning offensive behaviour by providing representation. In any event, the same official should not represent both parties.

6.5 It is good practice to advise members that keeping a record of incidents by the harassed worker will assist in bringing any formal or informal action to a more effective conclusion; and that the union wishes to be informed of any incident of sexual harassment and that such information will be kept confidential. It is also good practice for the union to monitor and review the union's record in responding to complaints and in representing alleged harassers and the harassed, in order to ensure its responses are effective.

7. *Employees' responsibilities*

7.1 Employees have a clear role to play in helping to create a climate at work in which sexual harassment is unacceptable. They can contribute to preventing sexual harassment through an awareness and sensitivity towards the issue and by ensuring that standards of conduct for themselves and for colleagues do not cause offence.

7.2 Employees can do much to discourage sexual harassment by making it clear that they find such behaviour unacceptable and by supporting colleagues who suffer such treatment and are considering making a complaint.

7.3 Employees who are themselves recipients of harassment should, where practicable, tell the harasser that the behaviour is unwanted and unacceptable. Once the offender understands clearly that the behaviour is unwelcome, this may be enough to put an end to it. If the behaviour is persisted in, employees should inform management and/or their employee representative through the appropriate channels and request assistance in stopping the harassment, whether through informal or formal means.

NOTES

1. 99/C 157/02, 27.6.1990 s.3.2.
2. "The dignity of women at work: a report on the problem of sexual harassment in the Member States of the European Communities", October 1987, by Michael Rubenstein (ISBN 92 825 8764 9).
3. Third Action Programme on Equal Opportnnities for Women and Men, 1991-1995, COM (90) 449, 6 November 1990.
4. Council Resolution on the protection of the dignity of women and men at work 90/C 157/02, 27.6.1990, s.1.

5. Ibid.
6. OJ No. L39, 14.2.1976, p.40, Article 2 (Appendix II).
7. Council Resolution on the protection of the dignity of women and men at work 90/C 157/02, 27.6.1990, s.2.3(a).
8. "Positive action: equal opportunities for women in employment – a guide", OPCE, 1988.

Extracts from the EOC Code of Practice on Equal Pay

Sex discrimination in pay systems

21. Sex discrimination in pay now occurs primarily because women and men tend to do different jobs or to have different work patterns. As a result it is easy to undervalue the demands of work performed by one sex compared with the demands associated with jobs typically done by the other. Such differences can be reinforced by discriminatory recruitment, training, selection and promotion procedures which may restrict the range of work each sex performs; for example, by allocating the full-time, higher paid, bonus-earning jobs mainly to men.

Different jobs

22. a) There is some degree of job segregation in most employing organisations. Frequently the jobs done mainly by men have a higher status and are more highly rewarded than those done by women. Commonly men and women do different types of work within an organisation. It is also common for men to be in the majority at managerial level and women to occupy lower graded jobs. In certain occupations there is further segregation to the extent that there is an even greater concentration of ethnic minority women in lower status, lower paid jobs.

b) Gender segregation in employment is often historical. Consequently it may be difficult to recognise the discriminatory effects of past pay and grading decisions based on traditional values ascribed to 'male' and 'female' work. In addition, the pay and conditions of 'male' and 'female' jobs within a firm might have been bargained separately by different unions. It is not sufficient to explain how the difference in pay came about. Arguments based on 'tradition' or separate bargaining would not justify paying women less than men when their work is of equal value.

c) The fact that certain jobs are associated with one sex can affect the level of wages for those jobs which in turn can result in discrimination.

d) Past discriminatory assumptions about the value of what has been regarded as men's or women's work may be reflected in current grading schemes. For example, men and women may be doing the same or very similar work but have different job titles and consequently be in separate grades, with the women's jobs being graded lower. They may, on the other hand, be doing quite different jobs which are actually of equal value though the women are in lower grades. In both examples the grading scheme could result in discrimination and fail to value the actual work done.

Different Work Patterns

23. a) Many women take time out of work for pregnancy and maternity. Women also tend to carry the main responsibility for family care. As a result women in general have shorter periods of service than men and more women than men work part-time. This difference in work patterns has contributed to the gender segregation of jobs.

b) There has been a tendency for payment systems to be designed to reward work patterns traditionally associated with men's employment and fail to recognise the different pattern of 'female' work. For example, a performance pay scheme which relies on an annual appraisal could mean that a woman who begins maternity leave before the appraisal, but has performed well for part of the year, will be denied a performance pay increase altogether. Another example is where pay benefits, such as occupational pensions or sick pay, are available only to full-time employees. This rule may mean that a group of female employees, ie. those who work part-time, are denied access to important benefits.

24. Most of the discrimination in pay systems takes the form of indirect or hidden discrimination. This occurs where pay rules and agreements appear to be neutral between men and women but the effect of their application is to disadvantage substantially more of one sex than the other. Whatever the cause of the discrimination and regardless of whether it was intentional or not, once an applicant has established that someone of the opposite sex is paid more for equal work, the employer will be required to show that the difference is not based on sex, using the criteria set out [*not reproduced here*] under 'Material Factor Defence' and 'Objective Justification'.

Review of pay systems for sex bias

25. a) Pay arrangements are frequently complicated and the features which can give rise to sex discrimination are not always obvious. Although pay systems reviews are not required by law, they are recommended as the most appropriate method of ensuring that a pay system delivers equal pay free from sex bias.

b) A pay systems review also provides an opportunity to investigate the amount of information employees receive about their pay. Pay systems should be clear and easy to understand. Where they are not and where pay differentials exist, these may be inferred to be due to sex discrimination. It is therefore in an employer's interest to have transparent pay systems to prevent unnecessary equal pay claims.

c) The Equal Opportunities Commission recommends that a pay systems review should involve the following stages:

Stage One

Undertake a thorough analysis of the pay system to produce a breakdown of all employees, which covers for example, sex, job title, grade, whether part-time or full-time, with basic pay, performance ratings and all other elements of remuneration.

Stage Two

Examine each element of the pay system against the data obtained in stage one (see paragraph 27).

Stage Three

Identify any elements of the pay system which the review indicates may be the source of any discrimination.

Stage Four

Change any rules or practices, including those in collective agreements, which stages 1 to 3 have identified as likely to give rise to discrimination in pay. It is recommended that this should be done in consultation with employees, trade unions or staff representatives where appropriate. Stages 1 to 3 may reveal that practices and procedures in relation to recruitment, selection and access to training have contributed to discrimination in pay; in that event, these matters should also be addressed.

Stage Five

Analyse the likely effects of any proposed changes in practice to the pay system before implementation, to identify and rectify any discrimination which could be caused.

Stage Six

Give equal pay to current employees. Where the review shows that some employees are not receiving equal pay for equal work and the reasons cannot be shown to be free of sex bias, then a plan must be developed for dealing with this.

Stage Seven

Set up a system of regular monitoring to allow checks to be made to pay practices.

Stage Eight

Draw up and publish an equal pay policy with provision for assessing the new pay system or modification to a system in terms of sex discrimination. Also, in the interests of transparency, provide pay information as described on [*not reproduced here*] where this is not already usual practice.

The pay review process

The following section provides guidance on carrying out stages 1 to 3 of the review process.

Initial Analysis

26. Undertake a thorough analysis of pay systems. This will require a breakdown of all employees to include for example, sex, job title and grade, whether part-time or full-time, with performance ratings and the distribution of basic pay and all other elements of the remuneration package, to identify potential vulnerability to claims of pay discrimination. This will reveal whether there are any vulnerabilities, and what their extent is, and enable a plan to be developed to correct any problems.

Identification of discriminatory elements

27. a) Pay systems vary in complexity. Some have more elements than others. In the process of a review, each element will require examination against the statistical data generated at the initial analysis stage. Investigation may show discrimination in written rules and agreements, for example, limiting profit-related pay to employees who work above a minimum number of hours; or in the way processes are interpreted and applied, for example, failure to obtain adequate job descriptions during a job evaluation exercise.

b) Some of the more common pay elements are set out below, with examples of facts which could indicate problems of discrimination in pay and suggestions of further questions to be asked to reveal the cause of the pay difference and whether it can be shown to be free of sex bias in the terms explained under 'Material Factor Defence' and 'Objective Justification' on [*not reproduced here*].

Basic Pay

28. a) **Problem:**

Women are consistently appointed at lower points on the pay scale than men.

Recommended Action:

Check the criteria which determine promotion or recruitment starting pay. Are these spelt out clearly?

Examine recruitment and promotion records for evidence of criteria which appear to be disadvantaging women. Can these criteria, eg. qualification requirements, be justified objectively in terms of the demands of the job?

Check the records for evidence of sex bias in the application of managerial discretion.

b) **Problem:**

Women are paid less per hour than men for doing virtually the same job, but with different job and grade titles.

Recommended Action:

Check whether there are any reasons other than custom and practice for the difference; if so, are these reasons justified objectively?

c) **Problem:**
Women progress more slowly through incremental salary scales and seldom reach higher points.
Recommended Action:
Investigate the criteria applied for progression through the scale. Are these clearly understood? Does any particular criterion, eg. length of service, work to the detriment of women more than men? If so, can the use of that criterion, or the extent to which it is relied on, be justified objectively?
Review the length of the incremental scale. Is the scale longer than it need be? Are there good practical reasons for a scale of that length?

d) **Problem:**
Women progress more slowly through non-incremental salary ranges and seldom reach higher points.
Recommended Action:
Check the criteria that applied when the structure was introduced and the current criteria for new recruits/promotees to each salary.
Check whether there is a clear, well-understood mechanism for progressing through the salary range.
Investigate the criteria for progression through the salary range and whether there are performance, qualification or other bars to upward movement. Can these be justified?
Review the length of the salary range. Can this be justified by real need?

Bonus/Premium Rates/Plus Elements

29. a) **Problem:**
Female and male manual workers receive the same basic pay but only jobs mainly done by men have access to bonus earnings and those mainly done by women do not.
Recommended Action:
Check the reason why. Does this reflect real differences, for example, in the value of the work or in productivity? Can it be justified objectively on grounds unrelated to sex?

b) **Problem:**
Where shift and overtime work is available and paid at a premium rate, fewer full-time women employees have access to this higher rated work.
Recommended Action:
Check that women and men employees have equal access to this work and, if not, that the reasons can be justified objectively.

c) **Problem:**
A smaller percentage of women employees receive enhanced rates for weekend and unsocial hours work.

Recommended Action:
Check the eligibility requirements for this work. Do any of these, for example, requiring that employees must be working full-time, work to the disadvantage of women? Can these requirements be objectively justified?

d) **Problem:**
Average female earnings under a variable payment system are lower than average male earnings (even where some women may have higher earnings than most men).
Recommended Action:
Review the design and operation of the variable payment system. Do these genuinely reflect the demands of the jobs and the productivity needs of the organisation?
In particular, check how factors such as down-time and personal needs breaks are dealt with in a variable payment system covering men and women.

Performance Pay

30. a) **Problem:**
The performance pay system is applied largely to employees of one sex only and results in a pay discrepancy to the advantage of that group.
Recommended Action:
Investigate the reasons why employees of the other sex are largely excluded from performance pay awards. Are these justified objectively for reasons unrelated to sex?

b) **Problem:**
Women receive lower performance ratings on average than men.
Recommended Action:
Investigate the performance rating system. Is it really likely that women would on average perform less well than men? What are the possible reasons for this?
Review the criteria for performance rating. Do employees and managers know what these are? Do any of these disadvantage women? Do any of these disadvantage ethnic minority women in particular? If so, are these criteria justified objectively?
Monitor the ratings of individual managers. Do the results of the monitoring suggest a stereotypical interpretation of criteria? Are there appropriate controls on managerial discretion?

c) **Problem:**
Although women and men receive similar ratings, men achieve higher performance pay awards.
Recommended Action:
Investigate the reasons for this. Is it linked to managerial discretion? Are potentially discriminatory criteria being applied in the linking of ratings to pay? Can these be justified objectively?

Pay Based on Additional Skills or Training

31. **Problem:**
In practice only or mainly male employees receive this supplement.
Recommended Action:
Investigate the reasons for this. Are 'female' skills not recognised? Do women have the same access to any skills or training modules offered? Review the training/skills/qualifications criteria. Do they genuinely reflect enhanced ability to carry out the job duties?
Review the procedures for implementing the supplement. Are managers and employees aware of the procedure? Are they operated fairly between men and women?

Pay Based on an Assessment of Individual Competencies

32. **Problem:**
There is a pay gap between the male and female employees who are assessed in this way.
Recommended Action:
Review the competencies assessed. Are women and men assessed for the same set of competencies? Are the competencies being interpreted in a consistent way?
Are potentially discriminatory criteria being applied? If so, are these justified objectively?
Monitor the assessment of individual managers.

Pay Benefits

33. a) **Problem:**
A smaller percentage of women employees than men are covered by the organisation's sick pay, pensions, low interest loans, share option schemes.
Recommended Action:
Check eligibility requirements. Are there restrictions which impact negatively on women? For example, are any of these limited to employees working over a minimum number of hours?
Can these requirements be justified objectively?

b) **Problem:**
Proportionately fewer women than men are in receipt of contractual benefits, for example, cars, telephone rentals and bills, rent and rates on tied accommodation, reimbursement of council tax in residential occupations.
Recommended Action:
Review the criteria for such benefits and any differences in treatment between male and female dominated groups. Can these differences be justified in terms of the needs of the work?
Review policies for the payment of such benefits between departments within the organisation. Are they consistent and can any differences be justified?

Grading

34. a) **Problem:**
Jobs predominantly occupied by women are graded lower than jobs predominantly occupied by men.
Recommended Action:
Review the method of grading. Was it devised for the current jobs? Is it adapted from a scheme used in a different organisation? What was the method used to determine job size? Some methods, eg. felt-fair or whole job comparison, are potentially more discriminatory than others, eg. analytical job evaluation. Are separate grading schemes used for jobs predominantly done by women and those predominantly done by men? If so, why, and is this difference objectively justified?

b) **Problem:**
Some jobs held mainly by men are in higher grades because of 'recruitment and retention' problems.
Recommended Action:
Check that there is genuine evidence of a current 'recruitment and retention' problem.
Check that the whole of the difference in pay is attributable to market pressure. If not, investigate the reasons for the rest of the difference.
Consider amending the grading/pay structure so that the 'labour market' element of pay is 'transparent'.

c) **Problem:**
Red-circling, for example, where salary is protected when a job has been downgraded, is mainly applied to male employees.
Recommended Action:
Check the criteria for red-circling. Why do they favour male jobs? Can this be justified objectively?
Investigate whether other criteria which are more equitable could be used.
Ensure the difference in pay is phased out as soon as possible so that unequal pay is not unnecessarily perpetuated.

Job Evaluation Method of Grading

35. a) **Problem:**
An analytical job evaluation scheme has resulted in jobs predominantly done by women being graded lower than those predominantly done by men.
Recommended Action:
Check that all features of the scheme's design and implementation took full account of the need to avoid sex bias. Was the job information collected consistently and accurately? Do the factors and weighting favour characteristics typical of jobs dominated by one sex? If so, is this justified objectively? Was training in the avoidance of sex bias given to those responsible for implementing the scheme?

b) **Problem:**
Jobs which have been evaluated as the same have widely differing salaries to the detriment of jobs largely held by women.
Recommended Action:
Investigate the possible causes, for example, how were the jobs assimilated to the evaluated structure?
Are different pay scales in use?
Could elements like additional skills payments or performance pay awards be responsible? What part do market rate or productivity considerations play? Can the cause of the difference be justified objectively?

Monitoring
36. Once the current pay systems have been reviewed it is important that periodic checks are made to ensure that discrimination does not creep in. This is best done by incorporating statistics on pay broken down by sex into the existing management information package, so that the necessary information can be checked regularly.

Council Directive No 76/207/EEC
of February 1976
on the implementation of the principle of equal treatment for men and women as regards access to employment, vocational training and promotion, and working conditions

Article 1
1 The purpose of this Directive is to put into effect in the Member States the principle of equal treatment for men and women as regards access to employment, including promotion, and to vocational training and as regards working conditions and, on the conditions referred to in paragraph 2, social security. This principle is hereinafter referred to as 'the principle of equal treatment'.
2 With a view to ensuring the progressive implementation of the principle of equal treatment in matters of social security, the Council, acting on a proposal from the Commission, will adopt provisions defining its substance, its scope and the arrangements for its application.

Article 2
1 For the purposes of the following provisions, the principle of equal treatment shall mean that there shall be no discrimination whatsoever on grounds of sex either directly or indirectly by reference in particular to marital or family status.
2 This Directive shall be without prejudice to the right of Member States to exclude from its field of application those occupational activities and, where appropriate, the training leading thereto, for which, by reason of their nature or the context in which they are carried out, the sex of the worker constitutes a determining factor.

3 This Directive shall be without prejudice to provisions concerning the protection of women, particularly as regards pregnancy and maternity.
4 This Directive shall be without prejudice to measures to promote equal opportunity for men and women, in particular by removing existing inequalities which affect women's opportunities in the areas referred to in Article 1(1).

Article 3

1 Application of the principle of equal treatment means that there shall be no discrimination whatsoever on grounds of sex in the conditions, including selection criteria, for access to all jobs or posts, whatever the sector or branch of activity, and to all levels of the occupational hierarchy.
2 To this end, Member States shall take the measures necessary to ensure that:

(*a*) any laws, regulations and administrative provisions contrary to the principle of equal treatment shall be abolished;
(*b*) any provisions contrary to the principle of equal treatment which are included in collective agreements, individual contracts of employment, internal rules of undertakings, or in rules governing the independent occupations and professions shall be, or may be declared, null and void or may be amended;
(*c*) those laws, regulations and administrative provisions contrary to the principle of equal treatment when the concern for protection which originally inspired them is no longer well founded shall be revised; and that where similar provisions are included in collective agreements labour and management shall be requested to undertake the desired revision.

Article 4

Application of the principle of equal treatment with regard to access to all types and to all levels, of vocational guidance, vocational training, advanced vocational training and retraining, means that Member States shall take all necessary measures to ensure that:

(*a*) any laws, regulations and administrative provisions contrary to the principle of equal treatment shall be abolished;
(*b*) any provisions contrary to the principle of equal treatment which are included in collective agreements, individual contracts of employment, internal rules of undertakings or in rules governing the independent occupations and professions shall be, or may be declared, null and void or may be amended;
(*c*) without prejudice to the freedom granted in certain Member States to certain private training establishments, vocational guidance, vocational training, advanced training and retraining shall be accessible on the basis of the same criteria and at the same levels without any discrimination on grounds of sex.

Article 5
1 Application of the principle of equal treatment with regard to working conditions, including the conditions governing dismissal, means that men and women shall be guaranteed the same conditions without discrimination on grounds of sex.
2 To this end, Member States shall take the measures necessary to ensure that:
(*a*) any laws, regulations and administrative provisions contrary to the principle of equal treatment shall be abolished;
(*b*) any provisions contrary to the principle of equal treatment which are included in collective agreements, individual contracts of employment, internal rules of undertakings or in rules governing the independent occupations and professions shall be, or may be declared, null and void or may be amended;
(*c*) those laws, regulations and administrative provisions contrary to the principle of equal treatment when the concern for protection which originally inspired them is no longer well founded shall be revised; and that where similar provisions are included in collective agreements labour and management shall be requested to undertake the desired revision.

Article 6
Member States shall introduce into their national legal systems such measures as are necessary to enable all persons who consider themselves wronged by failure to apply to them the principle of equal treatment within the meaning of Articles 3, 4 and 5 to pursue their claims by judicial process after possible recourse to other competent authorities.

Article 7
Member States shall take the necessary measures to protect employees against dismissal by the employer as a reaction to a complaint within the undertaking or to any legal proceedings aimed at enforcing compliance with the principle of equal treatment.

Article 8
Member States shall take care that the provisions adopted pursuant to this Directive, together with the relevant provisions already in force, are brought to the attention of employees by all appropriate means, for example at their place of employment.

Article 9
1 Member States shall put into force the laws, regulations and administrative provisions necessary in order to comply with this Directive within 30 months of its notification and shall immediately inform the Commission thereof.

However, as regards the first part of Article 3(2)(*c*) and the first part of Article 5(2)(*c*), Member States shall carry out a first examination and if necessary a first revision of the laws, regulations and administrative provisions referred to therein within four years of notification of this Directive.
2 Member States shall periodically assess the occupational activities referred to in Article 2(2) in order to decide, in the light of social developments, whether there is justification for maintaining the exclusions concerned. They shall notify the Commission of the results of this assessment.
3 Member States shall also communicate to the Commission the texts of laws, regulations and administrative provisions which they adopt in the field covered by this Directive.

Article 10
Within two years following expiry of the 30-month period laid down in the first subparagraph of Article 9(1), Member States shall forward all necessary information to the Commission to enable it to draw up a report on the application of this Directive for submission to the Council.

Article 11
This Directive is addressed to the Member States.

APPENDIX 4

The Access to Work scheme

The Access to Work scheme had a budget of £19m in 1997–98 to provide disabled people with practical assistance in obtaining and retaining employment. The scheme can help, for example, with the cost of modifications to equipment or premises, the cost of a taxi to work if a person's disability makes it difficult or impossible for him/her to use public transport, and the cost of a communicator for a person with a hearing impairment.

Until 1995–96, all approved costs of a disabled person up to a total value of £21,000 over five years were met by the scheme. After a review of the scheme's operation completed in 1996, the rules have been amended. The upper limit on approved costs has been retained, but an element of cost-sharing has been introduced. For disabled people who are unemployed or changing jobs, the scheme will continue to meet 100% of the approved costs. All approved costs relating to travel to work and communicator support at interviews will also be met for everyone. For disabled people in employment, however, the scheme will now meet a maximum of 80% of approved costs, and only to the extent that they exceed a lower threshold of £300. In order to take account of the needs of the most severely disabled people, the scheme will provide 100% of approved costs, to the extent that they exceed £10,000 over a three-year period. Applications for continuing costs are now approved for a maximum of three years rather than five, but will then be reconsidered.

Since the Disability Discrimination Act 1995 also prohibits discrimination against self-employed workers working under contracts personally to execute any work or labour, it is significant to note that the scheme will meet up to 90% of approved costs over a lower threshold of £100 for all new applications from self-employed people. Costs in excess of £10,000 over three years are met in full.

Any disabled person who wants to apply for assistance from the Access to Work scheme should get in touch with his/her disability employment advisor, contactable through the local jobcentre. The Employment Service has placement, assessment and counselling teams, which are available to give help and advice to people with disabilities and employers on adjustments that might be made to enable a disabled person to obtain or retain employment.

APPENDIX 5

Access to tribunals for disabled people

Industrial tribunals need to provide a service which is accessible to disabled people, not only because they are the bodies that will deal with complaints of disability discrimination under the Disability Discrimination Act 1995 (DDA), but also because they are themselves under an obligation under the DDA not to discriminate, as suppliers of services to the public.

The covering notes on the standard tribunal forms of originating application and notice of appearance (Forms IT1 and IT3) already invite disabled people who need any special arrangements when visiting an industrial tribunal to contact tribunal staff, 'who will do all they can to help'. The administrators of the industrial tribunals in all parts of the UK have been reviewing what further steps might be needed to ensure that tribunals are accessible to disabled people who may be involved in complaints under the DDA or other employment legislation, whether as applicants, respondents, witnesses, representatives or tribunal members.

The review included an assessment of the physical accessibility of tribunal offices. Some steps have already been taken to improve access and more are planned, although hearings can be held at a location other than the tribunal office where this proves necessary. Consideration is being given to providing financial help with the cost of communicators at hearings for people with hearing, speech or sight impairments, and for people with mental illnesses and learning disabilities. It is also possible that the guidance booklet on tribunal procedure, which is supplied to the parties to proceedings, will be made available in other formats, such as in large print, in braille or on audio tape.

APPENDIX 6

List of specified documents pursuant to the Asylum and Immigration Act 1996 s8

(see **6.4.1.6**)

- A document containing the employee's NI number, such as P45, pay slip, P60, NINO card or letter from a government body.[1]
- A passport describing the holder as a British citizen or as having a right of abode in – or an entitlement to re-admission to – the UK.
- A passport containing a certificate of entitlement certifying that the holder has the right of abode in the UK.
- A certificate of registration or naturalisation as a British citizen.
- A birth certificate (including a certified copy issued after birth) issued in the UK or Repulic of Ireland, if it appears to relate to the applicant; it includes a short and standard certificate.
- A passport or national identity card issued by a EEAA[2] state which describes the holder as a national of that state.
- A passport or other travel document endorsed to show that the person is exempt from immigration control, has indefinite leave to enter, or remain in, the UK or has no time limit on his/her stay; or a letter issued by the Home Office confirming that the person has such status.
- A passport or other travel document endorsed to show that the person named has current leave to enter or remain in the UK and is not precluded from taking employment; or a letter by the Home Office confirming this.
- A UK residence permit issued to a national of a state which is a party to the EEAA.
- A passport or other travel document endorsed to show that the holder has a current right of residence in the UK as the family member of a named national of a state which is a party to the EEAA and who is resident in the UK.
- A letter issued by the Immigration and Nationality Directorate of the Home Office indicating that the person named in the letter is a British citizen or has permission to take employment.

1 A document showing a temporary NI number would not be satisfactory. A temporary number is made up of the letters TN, the employee's date of birth and the letter F or M to indicate the employee's sex.

2 European Economic Area Agreement.

- A work permit or other approval to take employment issued by the Department for Education and Employment.
- A passport describing the holder as a British Dependent Territories citizen and which indicates that the status derives from a connection with Gibraltar.

Index